A Companion to
New Media Dynamics

A Companion to
New Media Dynamics

Edited by

John Hartley, Jean Burgess, and Axel Bruns

WILEY Blackwell

This paperback edition first published 2015
© 2013 John Wiley & Sons, Ltd.

Edition History: Blackwell Publishing Ltd. (hardback, 2013)

Registered Office
John Wiley & Sons Ltd, The Atrium, Southern Gate, Chichester, West Sussex, PO19 8SQ, UK

Editorial Offices
350 Main Street, Malden, MA 02148-5020, USA
9600 Garsington Road, Oxford, OX4 2DQ, UK
The Atrium, Southern Gate, Chichester, West Sussex, PO19 8SQ, UK

For details of our global editorial offices, for customer services, and for information about how to apply for permission to reuse the copyright material in this book please see our website at www.wiley.com/wiley-blackwell.

The right of John Hartley, Jean Burgess, and Axel Bruns to be identified as the authors of the editorial material in this work has been asserted in accordance with the UK Copyright, Designs and Patents Act 1988.

Library of Congress Cataloging-in-Publication Data

A companion to new media dynamics / edited by John Hartley, Jean Burgess and
Axel Bruns.
      p. cm.
   Includes bibliographical references and index.
    ISBN 978-1-4443-3224-7 (hbk. : alk. paper) ISBN 978-1-1190-0086-0 (pbk) 1. Mass media –
Technological innovations. 2. Digital media. 3. Social media. I. Hartley, John, 1948- II. Burgess,
Jean (Jean Elizabeth) III. Bruns, Axel, 1970-
   P96.T42C626 2013
   302.23′1 – dc23   2012023047

A catalogue record for this book is available from the British Library.

Cover image: © altrendo images / Getty

Set in 10.5/13pt Minion by Laserwords Private Limited, Chennai, India
Printed and bound in Malaysia by Vivar Printing Sdn Bhd

2 2015

Contents

Notes on Contributors

Anders Albrechtslund is Associate Professor at the Department of Aesthetics and Communication, Aarhus University, Denmark. His main research is within surveillance studies, philosophy of technology, new media, and ethics. He is a member of the Management Committee of "Living in Surveillance Societies" (EU COST Action, 1099–13: see www.liss-cost.eu/about-liss/description) and is taking part in the research project "Surveillance in Denmark," funded by the Danish Research Council. His publications include "Empowering Residents: A Theoretical Framework for Negotiating Surveillance Technologies" (with Louise Nørgaard Glud, *Surveillance & Society*, 2010); *Internet and Surveillance* (ed. with Christian Fuchs, Kees Boersma, and Marisol Sandoval, 2011); and "Participatory Surveillance in Intelligent Living and Working Environments" (with Thomas Ryberg, *Design Issues*, 2011).

Ben Aslinger is Assistant Professor of Media and Culture in the Department of English and Media Studies at Bentley University, USA. His research focuses on popular music licensing in television and video game texts and the globalization of video game consoles. His publications include articles in the collections *Teen Television: Essays on Programming and Fandom* (2008), *LGBT Identity and Online New Media* (2010), and *Down to Earth: Satellite Technologies, Industries, and Cultures* (2012).

Feona Attwood is a Professor in the Media Department at Middlesex University, UK. Her research is in the areas of sex in contemporary culture, with particular interests in "onscenity," sexualization, new technologies, identity and the body, and controversial media. She is the editor of *Mainstreaming Sex: The Sexualization of Western Culture* (2009) and *porn.com: Making Sense of Online Pornography* (2010), and coeditor (with Vincent Campbell, I.Q. Hunter, and Sharon Lockyer) of *Controversial Images and Sex, Media and Technology*. She is also coeditor of journal special issues on "Controversial Images" (with Sharon Lockyer, *Popular Communication*, 2009), "Researching and Teaching Sexually Explicit Media" (with I.Q. Hunter, *Sexualities*, 2009), and "Investigating Young People's Sexual Cultures" (with Clarissa Smith, *Sex Education*, 2011). She is a founding member of the Onscenity Research Network.

Christoph Bieber is Professor of Political Science at the NRW School of Governance, University of Duisburg-Essen, Germany. The position is funded by the Johann-Wilhelm-Welker-Stiftung, where the main area of research is ethics in political management and society. Previously he was an Assistant Professor of Political Science at the Justus-Liebig-University of Giessen. His dissertation thesis on *Political Projects on the Internet: Computer-Mediated Communication and the Political Public Sphere* was published in 1999. He has published widely on the effects of online communication for political actors. His books include *Politik digital. Online zum Wähler* (2010) and *Unter Piraten: Erkundungen einer neuen politischen Arena* (ed. with Claus Leggewie, 2012). He blogs at http://internetundpolitik.wordpress.com and on Twitter he is known as @drbieber.

Grant Blank is the Survey Research Fellow at the Oxford Internet Institute, University of Oxford, UK. His special interests are statistical and qualitative methods, the political and social impact of computers and the Internet, and cultural sociology. He previously taught at American University in Washington, DC.

Erik Borra is a PhD candidate at the University of Amsterdam, The Netherlands, as well as Digital Methods Initiative's lead developer. He holds an MSc in artificial intelligence. His research focuses on rethinking the web as a source of data for social and cultural science.

Danielle Brady is a Lecturer in Media, Culture and Mass Communications and Coordinator of Higher Degrees by Research in the School of Communications and Arts at Edith Cowan University, Perth, Australia. Following a previous career in research science and further postgraduate study in the arts, she has specialized in advising on research methods across a range of disciplines and in facilitating multidisciplinary research. Her research interests lie in the social study of science and technology.

Axel Bruns is Associate Professor in the Creative Industries Faculty at Queensland University of Technology in Brisbane, Australia, and a Chief Investigator in the ARC Centre of Excellence for Creative Industries and Innovation (CCI). He is the author of *Gatewatching: Collaborative Online News Production* (2005) and *Blogs, Wikipedia, Second Life and Beyond: From Production to Produsage* (2008), and editor of *Uses of Blogs* (with Joanne Jacobs, 2006). His research website is at http://snurb.info. His work focuses on the development of new research methodologies for the study of public communication in social media spaces; see http://mappingonlinepublics.net for more information.

Jean Burgess is Deputy Director of the ARC Centre of Excellence for Creative Industries and Innovation (CCI), Queensland University of Technology in Brisbane, Australia. She is a coauthor of the first research monograph on YouTube – *YouTube: Online Video and Participatory Culture* (2009, also translated into Polish, Portuguese, and Italian) and coeditor of *Studying Mobile Media: Cultural Technologies, Mobile Communication, and the iPhone* (2012). Her research focuses on methodological innovation in the context of the changing media ecology, especially the "computational turn" in media and communication studies.

Stephen Coleman is Professor of Political Communication at the Institute of Communications Studies, University of Leeds, UK. His three most recently published books are *The Internet and Democratic Citizenship: Theory, Practice, and Policy* (with Jay G. Blumler, 2009), *The Media and the Public: "Them" and "Us" in Media Discourse* (with Karen Ross, 2010), and *Connecting Democracy: Online Consultation and the Flow of Political Communication* (coedited with Peter Shane, 2011). His next book, *How Voters Feel*, is forthcoming from Cambridge University Press and is based on research conducted for his AHRC-funded project "The Road to Voting," which explores the affective and aesthetic dimensions of democratic engagement.

Kate Crawford a Principal Researcher at Microsoft Research in Cambridge, USA, and an Associate Professor in Media at the University of New South Wales, Sydney. For 10 years, she has published widely on the social, political, and cultural practices that surround and inform media technologies. She has conducted large-scale studies of mobile and social media use at sites around the world, including in India and Australia. Her book on technology, culture, and generational critique, *Adult Themes* (2006), won the Manning Clark Cultural Award. Her current projects include the long-term implications of Big Data, social news, young people's use of mobiles, and media use during disasters and other acute events.

Sean Cubitt is Professor of Film and Television at Goldsmiths, University of London, UK; Professorial Fellow of the University of Melbourne, Australia; and Honorary Professor of the University of Dundee, UK. His publications include *Timeshift: On Video Culture* (1991), *Videography: Video Media as Art and Culture* (1993), *Digital Aesthetics* (1998), *Simulation and Social Theory* (2001), *The Cinema Effect* (2004), and *EcoMedia* (2005). He is the series editor for Leonardo Books at MIT Press. His current research is on the history and philosophy of visual technologies, on media art history, and on ecocriticism and mediation.

Ranjana Das is a Lecturer in Media and Communications at the University of Leicester, UK. From 2011 to 2012 she was a Post-Doctoral Fellow at the University of Lüneburg, Germany. She completed a PhD (2008–2011) in the Department of Media and Communications at London School of Economics and Political Science, UK, where she researched media audiences and media literacies. She is Grad Student Rep for the International Communication Association (2011–2013), and was Young Scholars' (YECREA) Representative (2010–2012) on the Audience and Reception

Studies Thematic Section of the European Communication Research and Education Association. Her interests lie in media audiences across a range of different genres. She has been involved with cross-national projects in Europe to do with the media and families, transforming audiences, and children and the Internet.

William H. Dutton is Professor of Internet Studies at the Oxford Internet Institute (OII), University of Oxford, and Fellow of Balliol College, UK. Before coming to Oxford in 2002, he was Professor in the Annenberg School for Communication at the University of Southern California, USA, where he is an Emeritus Professor. In the UK, he was a Fulbright Scholar, National Director of the UK's Programme on Information and Communication Technologies (PICT), and founding director of the OII during its first decade. He is editing a handbook of Internet Studies and writing a book on the network society's Fifth Estate.

Emily Easton is a PhD student in Communication at the University of Illinois at Chicago, USA. She holds an MA in Social Sciences from the University of Chicago and has taught in the Cultural Studies Department at Columbia College Chicago. Her research interests lie at the intersections of cultural capital, cultural consumption, and technology. She has coauthored *Harnessing Social Technology in Students' Transition to College: Facebook's Role in Student Adjustment and Persistence* (with R. Gray, J. Vitak, and N. Ellison, 2012).

Cherian George is Associate Professor at Nanyang Technological University's Wee Kim Wee School of Communication and Information, Singapore. His research focuses on journalism and politics, including online alternative media. He is the author of *Contentious Journalism: Towards Democratic Discourse in Malaysia and Singapore* (2006). A former journalist with *The Straits Times*, Singapore, he blogs at Journalism.sg and Airconditionednation.com. He has a PhD in communication from Stanford University and a Masters from Columbia University's graduate school of journalism.

Tarleton Gillespie is Associate Professor in the Communication Department of Cornell University, USA, with affiliations in the Department of Information Science and the Department of Science and Technology Studies. His research examines the ways in which public discourse is structured by legal, political, and economic arrangements. His first book, *Wired Shut: Copyright and the Shape of Digital Culture* (2007), on the debates about digital copyright and the implications of technological regulation, was chosen as Outstanding Book by the International Communication Association. His second book will examine how the content guidelines imposed by online media platforms, social networking sites, and smartphone app stores set the terms for what counts as "appropriate" user contributions, and will ask how this private governance of cultural values has broader implications for freedom of expression and the character of public discourse.

Gerard Goggin is Professor of Media and Communications in the Department of Media and Communications, University of Sydney, Australia. He is widely published on the cultural and social dynamics of new media, with books including *Digital Disability* (2003), *Virtual Nation: The Internet in Australia* (2005), *Cell Phone Culture* (2006), *Internationalizing Internet Studies* (2009), *Mobile Technologies: From Telecommunications to Media* (2009), *Global Mobile Media* (2011), *New Technologies and the Media* (2012), and *Mobile Technology and Place* (2012).

Lelia Green is Professor of Communications at Edith Cowan University, Perth, Australia, and Co-Chief Investigator of the ARC Centre of Excellence for Creative Industries and Innovation (CCI). She is the author of *The Internet: An Introduction to New Media* (2010), which includes work arising from two projects funded by the Australian Research Council to investigate schoolchildren's use of the Internet in the context of their family life and that of their peers. She is a collaborating researcher with the EU Kids Online project in Europe. In 2010 the CCI funded its "Risk and Representation" program, comprising Lelia Green, Catharine Lumby (UNSW), and John Hartley (QUT), and conducted research in Australia to parallel that carried out in Europe by the EU Kids Online network.

Alexander Halavais is Associate Professor of Sociology at Arizona State University, USA, where he teaches in a graduate program in Interactive Communications. He also serves as the Technical Director of the Digital Media and Learning Hub, and as President of the Association of Internet Researchers. His research addresses questions of social change and social media, and particularly questions of attention, metrics, and learning. His book *Search Engine Society* (2008) discussed the ways in which search is changing us individually and socially. His work explores the role of formal metrics in guiding attention and social change. He blogs at alex.halavais.net and tweets as @halavais.

John Hartley, AM, is Professor of Cultural Science and Director of the Centre for Culture & Technology, Curtin University; Researcher at the ARC Centre of Excellence for Creative Industries and Innovation (Australia); and Professor in the School of Journalism, Media & Cultural Studies (JOMEC), Cardiff University (Wales). He is former Dean of the Creative Industries Faculty, and ARC Federation Fellow at Queensland University of Technology, Brisbane, Australia. His research interests include cultural, media, and communication studies; creative industries; and cultural science. He has published 24 books and over 200 papers, including *Creative Industries* (ed. 2005), *Television Truths* (2008), *Story Circle* (ed. 2009), *The Uses of Digital Literacy* (2009/10), and *Digital Futures for Cultural and Media Studies* (2012). He is founding editor of the *International Journal of Cultural Studies* (Sage), and a member of the ARC College of Experts.

Bernie Hogan is Research Fellow at the Oxford Internet Institute, University of Oxford, UK. His research focuses on the relationship between technologically mediated social cues (such as friend lists, real names, address books, etc.), social identity, and network structure. Hogan has also focused on novel techniques for the capture and analysis of online social networks. His work has been featured in *Information, Communication & Society*, *City & Community*, *Field Methods*, *Bulletin* *of Science, Technology & Society*, and several edited collections. He is working on identity and social conflict on Wikipedia and crossnational perceptions of social norms in online dating.

Indrek Ibrus is a researcher at Tallinn University's Estonian Institute of Humanities. He received his PhD from the London School of Economics and Political Science with a thesis on the evolutionary dynamics of mobile web-media forms. He received his MPhil from the University of Oslo, Norway. His research interests include the practices of crossmedia content production, the evolution of transmedia narratives, and the forms of the ubiquitous and device-agnostic web. He is also investigating the possibility of dialogue between disciplinarily distant evolutionary approaches to media change (evolutionary economics, cultural semiotics, complexity theory, political economies of media) with the purpose of working toward a transdisciplinary approach to "media innovation."

Jeffrey P. Jones is Director of the Institute of Humanities at Old Dominion University in Norfolk, Virginia, USA. He is the author of *Entertaining Politics: Satirical Television and Political Engagement* (2nd edn., 2010) and coeditor of *The Essential HBO Reader* (2008) and *Satire TV: Politics and Comedy in the Post-Network Era* (2009). With Geoffrey Baym, he is also coeditor of *News Parody and Political Satire Across the Globe* (2012).

Charles Leadbeater is an independent author based in London, UK. He is the author of several books about the rise of the web and cultural industries, from *Living on Thin Air* (1998) to *We-Think: Mass Innovation Not Mass Production* (2008). *The Independents: The Rise of Cultural Entrepreneurs*, was published by Demos, the London think-tank. His most recent book is *Innovation in Education: Lessons from Pioneers Around the World* (2011). His website is charlesleadbeater.net.

Andrew Lih is a new media researcher and technology journalist, and Associate Professor at the Annenberg School for Communication and Journalism, University of Southern California, USA, where he directs the new media program. He is the author of *The Wikipedia Revolution: How a Bunch of Nobodies Created the World's Greatest Encyclopedia* (2009) and is a noted expert on online collaboration and participatory journalism. In his previous life as a software engineer, he worked for AT&T Bell Laboratories and was a principal/founder of Mediabridge Infosystems, creator of the first online city guide for New York City (ny.com).

Sonia Livingstone is Professor of Social Psychology, Department of Media and Communications at the London School of Economics and Political Science, UK. Her research examines children, young people, and the Internet; media and digital literacies; the mediated public sphere; audience reception for diverse television genres; Internet use and policy; public understanding of communications regulation; and research methods in media and communications. She is the author or editor of sixteen books and many academic articles and chapters, including *Audiences and Publics* (ed., 2005), *The Handbook of New Media* (ed. with Leah Lievrouw, 2006), *The*

International Handbook of Children, Media and Culture (ed. with Kirsten Drotner, 2008), *Children and the Internet* (2009), *Media Consumption and Public Engagement* (with Nick Couldry and Tim Markham, 2010), *Children, Risk and Safety Online* (ed. with Leslie Haddon and Anke Goerzig, 2012), and *Media Regulation: Governance and the Interests of Citizens and Consumers* (with Peter Lunt, 2012).

Alice E. Marwick is an Assistant Professor at Fordham University, USA, in the department of Communication and Media Studies and a research affiliate at the Berkman Center for Internet and Society. Her work looks at online identity and consumer culture through lenses of privacy, consumption, and celebrity. She is currently working on two ethnographic projects, one examining youth technology use and the other looking at femininity and domesticity in social media such as fashion blogs, Tumblr, and Pinterest. Her book, *Status Update: Celebrity, Publicity and Self-Branding in Web 2.0*, is forthcoming from Yale University Press. She has a PhD from New York University's Department of Media, Culture and Communication, and was previously a postdoctoral researcher in social media at Microsoft Research New England.

Willard McCarty is Professor of Humanities Computing, King's College London, UK, and Professor in the School of Computing, Engineering and Mathematics, University of Western Sydney, Australia. He is the editor of the British journal *Interdisciplinary Science Reviews* (2008–), founding editor of the online seminar *Humanist* (1987–), and founding convenor of the London Seminar in Digital Text and Scholarship (2006–). He was the 2005 recipient of the Canadian Award for Outstanding Achievement (Computing in the Arts and Humanities), the 2006 Richard W. Lyman Award (Rockefeller Foundation), and the 2013 Roberto Busa Award (Alliance of Digital Humanities Organizations). He is the editor of *Text and Genre in Reconstruction* (2010) and author of the first comprehensive theoretical treatment of his field, *Humanities Computing* (2005). He lectures widely in Europe, North America, and Australia. See mccarty.org.uk.

Sabine Niederer is the Director of CREATE-IT, the applied research center of the School for Design and Communication at the Amsterdam University of Applied Sciences. She is also coordinator of the Digital Methods Initiative, the new media PhD program at the Department of Media Studies, University of Amsterdam. In her PhD project she studied the technicity of online content, such as the nonhuman content agents that coauthor online content (e.g., Twitter bots, Wikipedia bots), in an analysis of climate change skepticism on the web. From 2004 until 2012, Sabine worked at the Institute of Network Cultures, with Director Geert Lovink.

Zizi Papacharissi is Professor and Head of the Communication Department at the University of Illinois-Chicago, USA. Her work focuses on the social and political consequences of online media. Her book, *A Private Sphere: Democracy in a Digital Age* (2010) discusses how online media redefine our understanding of public and private in late-modern democracies. She has also edited a volume on online social networks, *A Networked Self: Identity, Community, and Culture on Social Network*

Sites (2010). She is the author of three books and over 40 journal articles, book chapters, and reviews, and editor of the *Journal of Broadcasting and Electronic Media* (from 2012).

Jussi Parikka is Reader in Media & Design at Winchester School of Art, University of Southampton, UK, and Adjunct Professor of Digital Culture Theory at University of Turku, Finland. He is the author of *Digital Contagions: A Media Archaeology of Computer Viruses* (2007), *Insect Media: An Archaeology of Animals and Technology* (2010), and *What is Media Archaeology?* (2012). His coedited books include *The Spam Book: On Viruses, Porn and Other Anomalous Objects from the Dark Side of Digital Culture* (2009) and *Media Archaeology* (2011). Homepage and blog can be found at jussiparikka.net.

Mark Pesce has been exploring the frontiers of media and technology for 30 years, fusing virtual reality with the World Wide Web to coinvent VRML in 1994. He is Honorary Associate in Digital Culture at the University of Sydney, Australia, and chaired the Emerging Media and Interactive Design programs at both the University of Southern California School of Cinema (USA) and the Australian Film Television and Radio School (Sydney, Australia). Pesce was for seven years a panelist and judge on the hit ABC series *The New Inventors*. He regularly contributes to ABC websites and has a monthly column in *NETT* magazine. He is working on his sixth book, *The Next Billion Seconds*.

Thomas Pettitt is Associate Professor in Medieval and Renaissance Studies at the Institute for the Study of Culture, University of Southern Denmark, Odense, Denmark. He teaches courses on early English literature and theater, Shakespeare, and Folklore in the undergraduate and graduate programs in English Studies and Comparative Literature. His research seeks to integrate popular vernacular traditions (tales and legends, songs and ballads, customs and entertainments) into a more embracing history of English and European verbal and performance cultures. He has published extensively in these fields, including two contributions (on customs and fairytales respectively) to the *Blackwell Companion to English Renaissance Literature and Culture* (2010). The encounter with the notion of a Gutenberg Parenthesis has prompted the disconcerting perception that much of this can be construed as media history, and may have contemporary relevance.

John Quiggin is ARC Federation Fellow in Economics and Political Science at the University of Queensland, Australia. He is prominent both as a research economist and as a commentator on Australian economic policy. He has produced over a thousand publications, including five books and over 300 journal articles and book chapters, in many fields of economics and other social sciences. He has been an active contributor to Australian public debate in a wide range of media. He is a regular columnist for the *Australian Financial Review*, to which he also contributes review and feature articles. He frequently comments on policy issues for radio and TV. He was one of the first Australian academics to present publications on a website (now at www.uq.edu.au/economics/johnquiggin). In 2002, he commenced publication of a blog (now at http://johnquiggin.com) that provides daily comments on a wide range of topics.

Penelope Robinson is Research Officer at the University of Sydney, Australia, with a PhD in sociology from the University of Western Sydney, Australia, and a BA (Hons) in gender studies. Her doctoral thesis examined the role of popular culture in marking a generation and in shaping young women's relationship with feminism. Her research interests include social and generational change, new media cultures, feminist cultural studies, and theories of postfeminism.

Richard Rogers is University Professor and holds the Chair in New Media & Digital Culture at the University of Amsterdam, The Netherlands. He is Director of Govcom.org, the group responsible for the Issue Crawler and other info-political tools, and the Digital Methods Initiative, which reworks methods for Internet research.

Tony D. Sampson is a London-based academic and writer. He lectures on new technology, affective experience, and interactive design at the University of East London. He received his PhD from the Department of Sociology at the University of Essex. He is a coeditor of *The Spam Book: On Viruses, Porn, and Other Anomalies From the Dark Side of Digital Culture* (with Jussi Parikka, 2009) and the author of *Virality: Contagion Theory in the Age of Networks* (2012) (his virality blog is at http://viralcontagion.wordpress.com).

Jan-Hinrik Schmidt is Senior Researcher for digital interactive media and political communication at the Hans-Bredow-Institute, an independent media research institute based in Hamburg, Germany. After studying sociology at Bamberg University, Germany, and West Virginia University, USA, he gained his PhD in 2004. His research interests focus on the characteristics, practices, and social consequences of online-based communication and the social web. Additionally, he is researching uses of digital games. He is the author of several monographs, journal papers, book chapters, and research reports; a reviewer for various conferences and journals; and a member of the editorial board of the open-access online journal *kommunikation@gesellschaft* as well as the print journal *Medien & Kommunikationswissenschaft*. Further information is available on his weblog at schmidtmitdete.de.

Theresa M. Senft is the author of *Camgirls: Celebrity and Community in the Age of Social Networks* (2008) and a coauthor of *History of the Internet: A Chronology, 1843 to the Present* (1999). She is a coeditor of the *Routledge Handbook of Social Media* and coedited a special issue of *Women & Performance* devoted to the theme "sexuality & cyberspace." Her thoughts have appeared in media venues such as *The New York Times* and in a recent talk at TED London. Formerly a Senior Lecturer at the University of East London, UK, she is currently on faculty at the Global Liberal Studies Program at New York University, USA.

Pelle Snickars works as Head of Research at the Swedish National Library. He has published numerous edited books on media history as well as on digital media.

Recent anthologies include *After the Pirate Bay* (2010, in Swedish), *The YouTube Reader* (2009), *Moving Data: The iPhone and the Future of Media* (2012), and *The Myth of the Net* (2012, in Swedish). He is currently completing a web book manuscript, with the working title *Heritage as Data*. For more information, see http://pellesnickars.se.

Peter Swirski is Professor of American Literature and Culture at the University of Missouri-St. Louis, USA and Honorary Professor in American Studies at Jinan University, China. His research ranges from American Literature and American Studies to interdisciplinary studies in literature, philosophy, and science, and the work of the late writer and philosopher Stanislaw Lem. He has been featured on European, Russian, and Chinese TV and on the BBC World Service Radio, and is the author of twelve books including the bestselling *From Lowbrow to Nobrow* (2005) and the National Book Award-nominated *Ars Americana, Ars Politica* (2010).

Esther Weltevrede is a PhD candidate with the Digital Methods Initiative, the New Media PhD program at the Department of Media Studies, University of Amsterdam, The Netherlands, where she also teaches. Her research interests include national web studies as well as platform and engine politics.

Patrik Wikström is Associate Professor at Northeastern University, USA, where he teaches in a graduate program in Music Industry Leadership. His work primarily focuses on innovation and learning in music and media organizations. He is the author of *The Music Industry: Music in the Cloud* (2009) and has published his research in journals such as *Technovation, International Journal of Media Management, Journal of Media Business Studies, Journal of Music Business Studies,* and *Popular Music and Society*. He has previously served as a faculty member at Karlstad University, Jönköping International Business School, and the University of Gothenburg in Sweden.

Basile Zimmermann is Assistant Professor in Chinese Studies at the University of Geneva, Switzerland, where he teaches contemporary China studies and conducts research in the fields of Chinese Studies, Science and Technology Studies, and Sociology of Art. His research projects are on electronic music in Beijing, Chinese social networking site design, online advertisement in China, and methodology in Chinese Studies.

Acknowledgments

This project could not have been attempted or completed without the combined efforts of many people.

Jayne Fargnoli – and her team – at Wiley-Blackwell commissioned the book and then trusted us to produce a slightly different one, thereby proving the importance of dynamics in the *publishing* of new media studies.

Nicki Hall project-managed us, our authors, and the manuscript with a competence and commitment that always went well beyond the call of duty and a cheerful optimism that frequently went well beyond the empirical evidence. However, with her help and professionalism we came in "on time and on budget," as they say. Nicki has been a longstanding colleague at QUT, and as always she has made working on a complex project with many personalities a simple pleasure.

The Australian Research Council, whose financial support provided us with time, research assistance, and institutional support, through several schemes: Discovery Project DP0879596: "Australian Television and Popular Memory: New Approaches to the Cultural History of the Media in the Project of Nation-Building" (Hartley); Discovery Project DP1094281: "New Media and Public Communication: Mapping Australian User-Created Content in Online Social Networks" (Bruns and Burgess); and The ARC Centre of Excellence for Creative Industries and Innovation SR0590002 (the CCI) (Hartley, Burgess, Bruns).

We are especially indebted to the 43 brilliant, argumentative, and scarily knowledgeable globally dispersed colleagues who we are now able to claim as coauthors. Thanks so much to you all. What an interesting book you have written!

Introducing Dynamics
A New Approach to "New Media"

John Hartley, Jean Burgess, and Axel Bruns

What's New . . . ?

The term "new media" has been in play for decades now, and one might be forgiven for wondering how much longer digital forms and platforms can really be called "new," or even what the scholarship of new media contributes to knowledge. Is it possible to say new things about new media? We think so. This *Companion* not only demonstrates the variety, salience, and importance of new media studies but also proposes a distinctive approach to the topic: an approach we call "new media dynamics." In this view, what's interesting about "new media" is not novelty as such but *dynamism*. Capitalism, technology, social networks, and media all evolve and change, sometimes to our delight, sometimes our dismay. This incessant process of disruption, renewal, and eventual (if often partial) replacement is now one of humanity's central experiences.

This cutting-edge collection brings together a stellar array of the world's top researchers, cultural entrepreneurs, and emerging scholars to give the *dynamics* of new media their first full-length, multidisciplinary, historical, and critical treatment. Across 34 chapters, an international line-up of the very best authors reflects on the historical, technical, cultural, and political changes that underlie the emergence of new media, as existing patterns and assumptions are challenged by the forces of "creative destruction" and innovation, both economic and cultural. At the same time they show that familiar themes and problems carry through from "old" media – questions of identity, sexuality, politics, relationships, and meaning.

. . . about New Media?

Everyone thinks they know what they mean by the term "new media," but in practice it will always be a shifting, contingent term. "New" describes something real, since inventions continually appear, but it always remains incomplete and contestable, with different media included and excluded in any given usage and over time.

However, the term persists in both ordinary language and scholarly work, not least because new forms and platforms emerged in the 1990s and 2000s that seriously disrupted the established and mainstream media of the day, and thus put into crisis an existing field of research and teaching as well. Broadcast media (radio, television, film) and popular publishing (newspapers, magazines, books) had been reasonably coherent industries, and stable objects of study, for a generation and more. The emergence of the Internet and the World Wide Web, with their attendant digital, networked, and online platforms, and transmedia forms that took "the media" out of the household and into mobile devices, *changed* what people thought they were talking about when they used the word "media." What counts as "new" in this context are those media that depart most radically from the broadcast or mass-media model.

Here it becomes clear that the term "media" is as troublesome as the term "new," because some of the most disruptive innovations do not resemble "media" at all, compared with their predecessors. Further, even though their position has stabilized, it is not always clear whether a given form, platform, or application can be termed a medium. This is not only a definitional problem; it is also a feature of the commercial and regulatory environment, where some unwisely disregarded upstart venture suddenly (it seems) achieves global scale and threatens the viability of existing players, including international firms and whole media sectors. In other words, "new media" cannot be seen as part of a gradualist process of incremental development or competitive advantage among established organizations and forms. Instead, they demonstrate the Schumpeterian process of "creative destruction" of individual firms and tried-and-trusted business plans (Schumpeter 1942) that have continued to operate on the inherited "industrial" model of broadcast media, mass communication, and popular culture.

It follows that examples of "new media" will always reflect the date on which the list is generated, so attention must be paid to historical changes – not only in the succession of origination, adoption, retention, and eventual decay of new media as such but also in the scholarly field, which needs to be as dynamic and nimble as its analytical quarry. "New media studies," then, requires a reconfiguration of disciplinary approaches and new interdisciplinary collaborations. It is also just as important to study the process of disruptive renewal as it is to identify the distinctive features of each new media form – to make dynamics part of the object of study. Hence the inclusion of that term in our title.

"Dynamics" are both *endogenous*, referring to rapid change over time within a given new medium, and *exogenous*, referring to the turbulent relations across a range of different media – say, between broadcast TV or printed newspapers on the one hand and online video such as YouTube or the blogosphere on the other. Given the often fraught relations across different platforms, the single-platform structural analysis familiar in media studies is not sufficient to explain what's happening in new media. A heightened focus on the *dynamics* of new media enables us also to draw more explicitly on the growing contribution to new media studies that is being made by fields that have a rich history of studying dynamic processes and systems from both empirical and theoretical perspectives. An undercurrent of ideas gleaned from areas as diverse as evolutionary science, economics, network analytics, physics, and mathematics informs many of the contributions to this volume and – as a dynamic field in its own right – new media studies itself is currently undergoing a process of rapid adoption and adaptation of these outside influences. What results from this process of change are revised and – we believe – more powerful and more flexible conceptual tools for the continuing investigation of "new media" and their place in the world.

The Dynamics of the Book

A Companion to New Media Dynamics takes a pragmatic stance toward definitional matters; therefore

- counting as "new" those media that are associated with the postbroadcast era of interactive or participatory communication using networked, digital, online affordances;
- counting as "media" those applications that have achieved sufficient ubiquity across populations and territories to be usable by ordinary consumers (as opposed to specialist experts), especially where such popular scale is itself productive of "new" or unanticipated possibilities;
- including the dynamics of change as part of the object of study, and developing theoretical and conceptual frameworks that not only account for but also anticipate further change; and
- reflexively understanding the disruptive renewal of intellectual paradigms as an inevitable component of the field of study.

The guiding principle is thus to assist in the process of adjusting to the "creative destruction" of inherited media and cultural studies while explaining emergent media forms and formats. This is especially important in the context of formal education, where there is an inevitable tension between the need for a stable curriculum (achieved by establishing a "canon" of selected forms, approaches, and methods) and teaching the latest developments, which while absolutely essential can seem to be uncoordinated or ad hoc unless these novelties are introduced as part of a graspable sequence.

Similarly, while not tied to the needs of replicable courseware (including choosing appropriate forms of pedagogy, syllabus, and assessment), research also requires an explicit conceptual framework and a theorized perspective if it is to make a meaningful contribution to scholarship more generally. The challenge therefore is to see the field and the object of study alike as open, dynamic, and unpredictable, but to have a coherent and explicit approach to both. This *Companion* provides such an approach to its account of "new media." While open and pragmatic about what particular phenomena might count as new media for the time being, it presents a coherent overall approach that amounts to a new way of doing media and cultural studies – one that enables the emergence of new explanatory frameworks more suited to the realities under scrutiny.

In order to do justice to both openness and coherence, the *Companion* includes interdisciplinary contributions encompassing the sciences, social sciences, humanities, and creative arts; it addresses a wide range of issues, from the ownership and regulation of new media (including questions of intellectual property and digital rights management) to their form and cultural uses (including questions of access, agency, and consumer co-creation).

Further, we have sought authors where we have found expertise. Our authors represent a wide range of disciplinary backgrounds – and most work across disciplinary boundaries within their own contributions. We have also sought authors who are active in the development of new media, whether from a business, technical, or activist perspective, so not all of the chapters are academic "business as usual." Some are written by practitioners. As well, there is a refreshing mix of senior and emergent scholars, often collaborating with one another, so that a full sense of the dynamics of renewal in the field itself can be glimpsed in the differences and connections between the contributors. We believe that this mix of disciplines, institutional positions, and professional perspectives is itself an essential component of "new media studies."

Cumulatively, within and between the individual contributions, the *Companion* advances a new approach to new media that explains their generative potential, marketized adoption, and corporate retention; their multifarious and often mashed-up forms; and their value, both economic and cultural, as widely available means by which knowledge and entertainment may mingle and grow in volatile times.

The book is suitable for different levels of use and for different types of pedagogical approaches. Its own structure provides a coherent syllabus for use as courseware. The range of topics, authors, and debates provides an overview of the best new writing in the field for graduate education. The interdisciplinary mix offers new methodological skills for research training. The book promotes multivalent "graduate attributes" among those who understand the dynamics of cultural change, including critical, research, interdisciplinary, practical, and conceptual skills.

The chapters are organized into three Parts, moving from the consideration of large-scale conceptual and disciplinary issues to more detailed, localized, or specialist concerns in later sections. As a result, the chapters in Part 1 tend to be longer essays while those in Parts 2 and 3 are shorter treatments across a wider field of topics. We hope this mix of styles will successfully encompass the significance as well as the variety of new media dynamics, while showing how the problems that arise in specific circumstances can also be seen as part of a larger fabric of explanation. Overall, then, we hope to give readers a glimpse of new media dynamics at three levels of scale: the "macro" or system level; the "meso" or institutional level; and the "micro" or agency (personal or enterprise) level.

Part 1: Approaches and Antecedents

This section gives the scholarly context and lays out the approaches and terminology that have shaped the field and will continue to do so. The eight chapters, written by leading authors from different disciplinary perspectives, establish how "new media" have thus far been approached in each case.

These chapters address the history of *new media*, contextualizing contemporary new media studies with preceding periods of rapid and significant technological and cultural change. They also attend to the history of new media *studies*. In doing so, the authors reflect on their own disciplines' contributions to the development of new media studies, and how interdisciplinary collaboration might be needed to do justice to the field as a whole.

While recognizing certain very long-term continuities, this Part also establishes how contemporary "new media" differ from "old" – in particular, how user-created content, social network markets, and enterprising agency (both individual and organizational) have challenged and reconfigured longstanding distinctions between producer and consumer, expert and amateur, culture and market, knowledge and entertainment.

In Chapter 1, **Sean Cubitt** provides a magisterial overview of the historical coevolution of the textual, technological, and political dynamics of media systems, and media *studies* – which, as he points out, has always been in itself a dynamic site of disciplinary collision and crossfertilization. In the contemporary era, he argues, the network is "no longer emergent" but rather has become the terrain upon which high-stakes struggles over the governance and the future of new media and politics writ large are being waged, leaving new media studies with plenty more to do.

In Chapter 2, **Willard McCarty**, a pioneer in the field of digital humanities, notes that projecting the future by extrapolating from current technologies – even new ones – is "a mug's game." Instead, he recommends a historical approach in order to identify what is shaping the cultural forms of the digital era. He traces "clues of a profound disquiet" about digital technologies going back to the beginning of the computing era. Seeking to learn how change actually works, specifically in the field of digital humanities, he recommends that "we look to the sciences of our times for an analogy that preserves otherness and forceful change but substitutes interaction for impact and assertive self-identity for passive victimhood," in order to get beyond the current phase of "knowledge jukeboxes" and reach for an understanding of digital media that is fully immersive: not a "gauntlet to be run" but a true medium – "as water is to the swimmer, gravity to the dancer, or wood to the carver."

In Chapter 3, **Thomas Pettitt** considers the dynamics of emergent media from a long-run historical perspective, leading him to consider a rather different model of historical sequence (and thus of the dynamics of newness) to the linear succession of progressive phases or stages. Instead, he suggests that certain "new media" may be seen as "an interlude, an interruption" (like a parenthetical insertion into a sentence) that is followed by what he calls a "restoration" of "earlier features of cultural mediation, only now at a more advanced level of technology." Pettitt considers different traditions of conceptualization that see the era of print – the "Gutenberg parenthesis" – as one such interruption; a line of argument or "topos" that he proceeds to critique and deconstruct.

Peter Swirski continues the theme of comparing book culture with new media culture in Chapter 4, showing that, despite dire predictions, book publishing is growing, not collapsing, around the world, as part of what he calls the "age of infoglut." Swirski considers the implications for literary or "highbrow" publishing and for scholarly and scientific publishing, and the impact of various forms of Internet publishing, not least on the "theory of mind," the human ability to infer "what other people feel, think, and know." Swirski finds that our ability to "think in stories" is unimpaired, citing "the power of the word over the number, of the narrative over the database." He moves on to an optimistic conclusion about the "literary system" in the light of these developments.

In Chapter 5, **John Quiggin** examines the economics of new media, as well as the impact of new media on the economy as such. Indeed, he concludes that a more thorough theorization of new media economics "would lead to a radical transformation of the way in which we understand the economy" – but that this is a project yet to be attempted in any seriousness.

In Chapter 6, **Sonia Livingstone** and **Ranjana Das** approach the question of new media dynamics from the perspective of one of the media's core constituencies – the audience. They build on the intertwined histories of both audiences and audience research to argue for the vital and ongoing importance of reception-oriented audience practices such as meaning-making and interpretive work even in contemporary new media environments.

Grant Blank and **William Dutton** focus on the dynamics of Internet access in Chapter 7, using the results of representative survey data collected for the Oxford Internet Institute and its international partners. They analyze the very agents of dynamic change – the "next-generation" users of the Internet, who are not simply children and teenagers but those who use "next-generation" equipment (such as the mobile phone or tablet) to access the Internet from "multiple locations and devices" – this amounts to 44 percent of Internet users in the UK in 2011. The implications of these changes are not just technical: "next-generation" users are much more likely to be producers as well as consumers than previously; they "listen to music online, play games online, download music, watch videos online, and download, as well as upload, videos or music files." Not surprisingly, compared with previous users they see the Internet as "essential."

In Chapter 8, **Richard Rogers**, **Esther Weltevrede**, **Erik Borra**, and **Sabine Niederer** translate into practice Rogers' own call for the development of "natively digital" methods for the study of the societal role and impact of new media. They propose "an approach to conceptualizing, demarcating and analyzing a national web," using Iran as a case study; a move that usefully – and revealingly – territorializes the study of new media dynamics.

Part 2: Issues and Identities

This Part contains 12 chapters subdivided into six sections: Agency, Mobility, Enterprise, Search, Network, and Surveillance. The subsections reflect the proposed conceptual shift away from linear models of communication (from producer to consumer) and structural models of power toward complex and dynamic systems of culture, knowledge, and control. For instance, where studies of broadcast media tend to subdivide the field into "producer, text, and audience," we offer "agency, network, and enterprise" – and these categories are themselves complicated by "mobility, search, and surveillance." We have used this arrangement to organize issues into a coherence based on *social network markets* (Potts et al. 2008), in order to give shape to the discussion. Critical, feminist, and other approaches associated with new social movements inform this section without signposting or isolating each point of difference. Concerns with cultural diversity are integrated into the substance of the collection, and at the same time do not assume a uniform antimarket stance among authors (or any other agent).

Agency

In Chapter 9, **Zizi Papacharissi** and **Emily Easton** apply Bourdieu's concept of habitus to understand how the permanent novelty of "new" media, and the social architectures associated with such media, generate a specific set of dispositions among their users. Ultimately, they point to the importance of digital fluency, and to the persistence of class distinctions between digital haves and have-nots: "those without fluency lose agency, and fluency is a product of class." In Chapter 10, **Andrew Lih** points to the crossroads at which *Wikipedia* now finds itself: at a point where the task of capturing the low-hanging fruit (the well-documented fields of human knowledge) is nearly complete, and where it is time to tackle the more difficult challenge of capturing oral history and folk knowledge. But he remains optimistic that the right groundwork is in place: "a coming golden age of discovery and feature storytelling... will be facilitated by an Internet-connected, multimedia-capable crowd distributed around the globe."

Mobility

In Chapter 11, **Gerard Goggin** weaves together the scholarship around mobility, as a broadly pervasive dynamic of modernity, with a detailed reading of the interdependent role played by the new technologies of mobility – mobile phones and other cellular devices. In doing so he traces the shift (in which smartphones such as the iPhone are playing a central role) toward an era not only of mobile technologies but of mobile *media*. **Ben Aslinger** focuses in Chapter 12 on a different kind of mobility: the migration of computer or video games (and the devices upon which they are played) into all manner of new domestic and public spaces via a proliferation of devices and (mobile) platforms, discussing how locations for play "might add to or challenge definitions of domestic space that place television at the center."

Enterprise

In Chapter 13, **Charles Leadbeater** distinguishes three main strands of cultural entrepreneurs in the twentieth century – dubbed the "improvers, entertainers, and shockers" – and adds a fourth archetype, emerging with the digital age: the "makers." Makers, he suggests, return us to an older, preindustrial approach to culture: culture as connected, part of life, rather than separate from it; something we do with one another rather than having done for and to us. In Chapter 14, **Patrik Wikström** shows how media organizations forced to adapt to a rapidly changing market environment are able to draw on the experience of other industries (chiefly, information technology) to understand these challenges. The key problem for these industries, he suggests, is that "increasingly active media audiences infuse a similar multisided logic into these markets": old producer/consumer logics no longer hold.

Search

Alexander Halavais suggests in Chapter 15 that search engines and their impact on society "deserve our undivided attention." He points to the tension between the push toward ever greater personalization of access to content and the role of these "global, mechanized gatekeepers" of information. In Chapter 16, **Pelle Snickars** addresses the problem of archives and access given the contemporary data deluge and the proliferation of navigation methods (browsing, recommendation engines, and folksonomies) that extend well beyond the "search" paradigm. He discusses the new "computational logics" required "in order to facilitate access to deep data" both on the web and in more traditional institutional libraries and archives.

Network

In Chapter 17, **Indrek Ibrus** considers the evolutionary dynamics of media by examining the historical trajectory of the mobile web. Highlighting divergences, path dependencies, and convergences in this sociotechnological developmental history, he points to the key complexities in establishing an evolutionary perspective on such multifaceted processes. In Chapter 18, **Bernie Hogan** tackles one of the most pressing issues for contemporary Internet governance – the nature of identity in the context of the growing dominance of social networking sites such as Facebook.

In particular, he critiques from the perspective of communication rights the rise of the "real-name web" and the uncertain futures of anonymity and pseudonymity.

Surveillance

In Chapter 19, in responding to contemporary concerns about online privacy, data-mining, and surveillance in social network sites, **Anders Albrechtslund** proposes a new conceptual model of surveillance: "participatory surveillance." Albrechtslund uses this model to describe the complexity of power relations in an environment where, via the architectures and practices associated with platforms such as Facebook, we are always simultaneously both watcher and watched, listened-to and listening in. In Chapter 20, **Christoph Bieber** uses WikiLeaks as a case that points to the growing political power of code and coding: beyond the media furor around the site and its enigmatic founder, Julian Assange, WikiLeaks shows how new media platforms can "shift regime behavior," as Assange himself has put it.

Part 3: Forms, Platforms, and Practices

This Part builds on the guiding concepts and issues identified in the previous two Parts, exploring them through a range of exemplary domains. It covers established and emerging media forms and technologies, with a focus on the ways in which, as "new media," they represent multiple forms of remediation as well as technological, cultural, and social convergence. Again, this Part is subdivided into sections: Culture and Identity; Politics, Participation, and Citizenship; and Knowledge and New Generations. These three sections take up some of the traditional concerns of cultural, communication, and media studies – concerns about identity, relationships, meaning, and knowledge – and situate these questions in different "new media" contexts. The book ends with a nod in the direction of the "new" generations who, even as we speak, are busily inventing *new* "new media," even as they play with, copy, explore, and disrupt the ones currently passing as "new."

Culture and Identity

In Chapter 21, **Feona Attwood** charts some recent and ongoing shifts in the cultural economy of the web through the lens of sex and porn cultures, arguing from a range of examples that "while it has become accepted wisdom that [professional] pornographers are lead users" of ICTs, more recent developments indicate that, like the mainstream media industries, sex media are seeing the effect of "the broader trend toward user-generated media content and the creation of online community." In Chapter 22, drawing on her well-known work on "cam girls," which prefigures the current ascendancy of videobloggers on YouTube, **Theresa Senft** considers a relatively new modality of mediated identity: the "branded self" as "microcelebrity" and the ways in which this notion recasts identity as a product of the *audience*, not the subject. In Chapter 23, drawing on sociology, feminism, and queer theory, **Alice Marwick** provides a cogent overview of some of the key issues in and dominant contemporary approaches to the problem of social identity in relation to the Internet – as a product of interaction, discourse, and performance. She concludes that the "back and forth between concepts of singularity and multiplicity" that currently characterizes ideas and practices of identity is likely to continue for quite some time. In Chapter 24, **Jan Schmidt** tackles the complex concept of *networked* identity: a fluid, changeable identity that is highly context-dependent and expressed across a series of what he describes as "personal public spheres" that "are formed when and where users make available information that is personally relevant to them."

Politics, Participation, and Citizenship

In Chapter 25, **Stephen Coleman** suggests that politics is being redefined by new media: he sees "an opening up of politics taking place online." Through this, the established vocabulary and institutional logic of politics is rejected, and new, playful forms of expression and participation are injected into the political process, even in spite of sustained attempts to frustrate these changes. In Chapter 26, **Cherian George** presents Singapore as exhibit A for how new media are used to effect political change. He points to a "dynamic, dialectical relationship between state power and Internet-assisted insurgency," evident in how Singaporean activists are using the Internet to turn the instruments of state power against the state itself. **Jeffrey P. Jones** discusses "the impact satire is having on democratic citizenship and political participation" in Chapter 27. He notes the emergence of political satire TV shows in reaction to staleness and stagnation in the news media, and positions them as examples of the use of performativity and play as tools of citizenship. In Chapter 28, **Tarleton Gillespie** focuses on the pervasiveness of the term "platform" and the distinctive moment in the evolution of the cultural economy of new media that it represents. He artfully reveals the slipperiness of the term as used by (and to refer to) web-based services such as YouTube, Facebook, and Twitter, showing how the multivalence of the term allows platform providers and other actors to maintain an address to multiple constituencies whose interests do not always coincide. In Chapter 29, **Axel Bruns** traces the evolution of personal homepages, from the first hand-coded HTML pages to social network profiles. He notes the tensions between individualism and standardization, between personal identity and social embeddedness, and shows how individual personal presence now exists in the interweavings between these different models and platforms.

Knowledge and New Generations

In Chapter 30, **Mark Pesce** outlines the new media toolkit now available to humanity, as we enter an age of "hyperconnectivity, hyperdistribution, hyperintelligence, and hyperempowerment." The new environment currently emerging, he suggests, is redefining us, our relationships, our social structures – and that process of reconfiguration has only just begun. Drawing on his own materialist analyses of instances of the Chinese web, in Chapter 31 **Basile Zimmermann** demonstrates how, even in the age of "big data," close, descriptive accounts of discrete phenomena can produce points of comparison that are useful in understanding how cultural difference plays out in new media – not only via language but also via the design and architecture of new media platforms. In Chapter 32, **Tony Sampson** and **Jussi Parikka** point to the lessons we might learn from network dysfunctionality: from viruses, malware, astroturfing, and other "bad" new media practices. The network, they suggest, is "the perfect environment for both the sharing of information and the dysfunctionality of viral spreading" – and the same processes that drive viral dysfunctionality can also drive beneficial sharing activities. Framed against a backdrop of constant social worry about young people and the Internet – and taking forward some of the themes raised by Blank and Dutton in Part 1 – in Chapter 33 **Lelia Green** and **Danielle Brady** draw on the findings of the EU and AU Kids Online projects to explore the ideas surrounding "risk" and young people online, and young people's own perceptions and experiences of Internet use, including risk. In Chapter 34, **Kate Crawford** and **Penelope Robinson** critique the very idea of "youth" as a highly significant category in such debates. They demonstrate how, throughout history, "generationalism" persistently recurs in discourses around new media technologies, becoming particularly marked in contemporary ideas such as "digital natives" and the "us-and-them" rhetoric that often accompanies such notions. They call for a more holistic and multifaceted approach to understanding the relations between identities and technologies.

*

Overall, the book can be used as a "good companion," to whose company the reader may return to explore new media forms and devices bit by bit – from Wii to Wikipedia; Wi-Fi to WikiLeaks. Or it can be read more intensively, as a syncopated interweaving of voices and themes, each with their own rhythm and leitmotif. Like all orchestrations, the whole is more than the sum of the parts. And, true to the conversational, collaborative, and co-creative spirit of many chapters, the *Companion* invites readers – researchers, policymakers, entrepreneurs, students, and users – to add their own voices to the chorus.

References

Potts, J., Cunningham, S., Hartley, J., and Ormerod, P. (2008) "Social Network Markets: A New Definition of the Creative Industries." *Journal of Cultural Economics*, 32(3), 167–185.

Schumpeter, J. (1942) *Capitalism, Socialism and Democracy*. New York: Harper & Bros.

Part 1
Approaches and Antecedents

1

Media Studies and New Media Studies

Sean Cubitt

History and Geography

Media studies lies at a crossroads between several disciplines, as reflected in the multiple names of academic departments dealing in media. This typically undisciplined discipline arose in a concatenation, still unresolved, of scholars from several traditions in the humanities and social sciences – ethnographers of everyday life, US and European communications scholars, interpersonal and commercial communications specialists, literary scholars, sociologists of subcultures – and today includes a range of activities whose approaches include economics and political economy, regulation, technology, textual analysis, aesthetics, and audience studies. There is no single canon of defining theoretical works, and only a loose assumption as to which media are to be studied, often defined by institutional matters: which media are studied may be circumscribed by the existence of journalism, pubishing, photography, or music schools claiming title to those media forms, as more frequently art history, literary, and linguistic studies bracket off their specific media formations. By media studies we presume the study of the technical media as they have arisen since the nineteenth century, in four broad categories: print, recording, broadcasting, and telecommunications. Given the typical shapes of neighboring disciplines studying specific media such as literature and music, a common concentration has been on industry, governance, and audience, with a specific address to aesthetics only in the case of the technical media. A specific change then for *new* media studies has been that the genres and business models once regarded as proper to each of these categories have, with the rise of digital media, converged aesthetically and economically. This has not posed a significant challenge to most of the schools of enquiry that have grown up over the past century that have taken technical media as their focus. In fact, the hybrid origins of the field of study have tended to produce a surprisingly holistic sense of mission: to understand media we need to understand their materiality as objects and systems,

A Companion to New Media Dynamics, First Edition. Edited by John Hartley, Jean Burgess, and Axel Bruns.
© 2013 John Wiley & Sons, Ltd. Published 2015 by John Wiley & Sons, Ltd.

as economies and polities, in their operations in the social, cultural, economic, and political lives of the people whose thoughts and passions they mediate. Though we are constrained to use the phrase, few media studies researchers care for the expression "the impact of media on ... ": mediation *is* the material form in which we exchange wealth, exercise power, and reproduce our species. The convergence of previously somewhat discrete media and corporations might be understood as creating the possibility of thinking this way about media; or we might believe that the idea of universal mediation is common to both phenomena, and perhaps an aspect of our stage of social evolution. Either way, the holistic approach is by now integral to media studies' confrontation with and assimilation into new media.

Discussions of new media must include some definition of the new. In media studies, that newness can be given a practical date: October 13, 1993, the date of the release of the Mosaic web browser, which opened up network computing for the mass participation of the later 1990s and the new century. Other dates might work as cleanly – the personal computer revolution of the 1980s, perhaps – but do not entail the common-sense awareness that emerged in the ensuing months that something massive and life-changing had begun. Prior phases, as far as mainstream media studies is concerned, constitute a prehistory of the popular or mass uptake (depending on the school of thought involved) that turned laboratory or experimental formats into technical media of the scale and significance of the press or television. 1993 can, then, serve as the watershed of the new in media studies.

Statements of this kind are controversial, not only because other competing dates might serve but also because media historiography is a central and hotly debated aspect of media studies. Among the most cited texts in the field, Walter Benjamin's "Work of Art" essay (1969, 2003) and Marshall McLuhan's *Understanding Media* (1964) both established periodization as a major feature of media studies, the former distinguishing handcraft from mechanical; the latter distinguishing oral, alphabetic, print, and electronic media as distinct epochs of human history. While McLuhan's ostensible technological determinism has been warmly debated ever since, the fundamental notion that the history of media is important to understanding contemporary media formations has become doctrinal. Political historians intersect with communications specialists in key works in the British tradition of Thompson (1963), Williams (1958, 1961), and Anderson (1983), and rather differently in key works the European tradition such as Mattelart (1994, 1996, 2000) and Debray (1996, 2000, 2004). A significant reorientation of these analytical studies has come in the wake of digitization (though not specifically because of it) in the form of media archeology, an approach to historiography that takes as its problem the origins of the contemporary. Leading figures Lisa Gitelman (1999, 2006), Oliver Grau (2003), Erkki Huhtamo (2005, 2006), Jussi Parikka (2007, 2012), Jonathan Sterne (2003), Siegfried Zielinski (1999, 2006), and perhaps the best-known exponent, Friedrich Kittler (1997, 1999, 2010), differ in many respects but share a passion for meticulous scholarship, a readiness to understand technical detail, an openness to long durations, and a sense of the contingency of media evolution that learns from but cuts across the orientation to progress that characterized McLuhan's work. The arrival of new media brought about a serious reconsideration of the mathematical as well as engineering bases of computing, and a fascination with ostensibly marginal media that, however, have had important reverberations in contemporary media: technologies as varied as spirographs (Huhtamo 2007) and filing systems (Vismann, 2008).

In many instances, media archeology points toward continuities between earlier and contemporary forms of media, based on specific discoveries in visual perception (e.g., the phi-effect, previously thought of as persistence of vision) or the physics of light (lens design from Galileo to Zeiss Ikon). Relatively few media archeologists also attend to the structure of the industries involved in developing, standardizing, and disseminating media innovations (although film historians provide a counter example: see Crafton 1997; Gomery 2005). But, while individual, often national, industries have received significant attention, the lack of archeological enquiry into the histories of regulatory instruments and institutions has been a significant lacuna, one that has begun to weigh on more recent attempts to theorize the interplay of influences in the formation of emergent media forms among engineers, corporations, governments, and international agencies such as the International Telecommunications Union. As a result, important critical insights into the evolution and changing capabilities and orientations of such bodies have received less attention than have the technologies they serve to constrain and regulate (see MacLean 2003 for an example of how such historical research can inform present policy). Since one of the most imposing results of new media dynamics has been the increasingly rapid globalization of communications infrastructures, and increasing dependence on them for economic, political, social, and cultural globalizations, the lack of work historicizing the new terrain of global media governance is a specific weakness in contemporary media studies, albeit one that is being addressed, if tangentially, in the context of significant new work on Internet and telecommunications governance in the international field (Chakravartty and Sarikakis 2006; Goldsmith and Wu 2008; deNardis 2009; Collins 2010).

The relative poverty of institutional histories can perhaps be explained by a double phenomenon coinciding with the emergence of new media networks in the 1990s. Under the influence of postmodern critique, the thesis that history was becoming a cipher encouraged a new spatial emphasis in media analysis. Meanwhile, the acceleration of both global flows and everyday life tended to reduce the felt importance of time, and to replace it with (often troubled) new orientations to space and place. The most influential study of these phenomena remains the three-volume *The Information Age* by Manuel Castells (2000 [1996], 2004 [1997], 2000 [1998]). Building on foundations of substantial empirical research, Castells conceptualized the network as the central form of globalization in the late twentieth century. Drawing on world systems theory but challenging theorists for whom the decline of the nation state as a political force and the fixed relation of core to periphery were doctrine, Castells – along with other leaders in the geographical turn such as

David Harvey (1989) and Saskia Sassen (1991, 1994) – emphasized the space–time compression of the new media landscape, the rise of flexible accumulation in post-Fordist, informationalized industries, and the cosmopolitanism of corporate elites, in a world in which access to the speed of networks connected such elites from city to city, bypassing both rural and industrial hinterlands and the urban poor. While the point had been made theoretically before (e.g., by Virilio 1986), the mass of data supporting the hypothesis deepened the theory by opening up new insights into the different modes in which place (e.g., Augé 1995) and time (e.g., Hassan 2003) are experienced in the global network. The geographical turn also coincided with the rise of postcolonial challenges to entrenched cultural studies analyses, which knocked on into media studies. De-Westernizing media studies (Curran and Park 2000) became a significant project in its own right, not least as new media began to shift from their early US/European biases toward, among other factors, a stage at which English was no longer the dominant or even the majority language of the Internet. Older theories of media imperialism continued to be voiced, especially by North American activists such as Chomsky (2003) and McChesney (2008), but more sophisticated accounts of media experience, informed by research into migration and diaspora, began to offer less paranoid, but in certain senses even more uncomfortable, accounts (e.g., Thussu 1998, 2000). David Morley's work (2000, 2007) and his collaboration with Kevin Robins (1995; see also Robins 2007) are exemplary of these enriched dialogues with, for example, the complex constructions of home that aggregate around not only technological devices (the mobile phone, the home page) but also the imagination of "home" among migrants and nationals afraid of their arrival. As a number of researchers have established, migration no longer means being severed from the life of the home culture: live news, music and film downloads, and VOIP (voice over Internet protocol) calls can keep migrants as close to their cultures of origin as they wish, even as migration offers economic options and sometimes cultural freedoms that may not be available where they grew up.

In the 1980s, in a first inkling that such issues might become major political arenas, the European Union published the green paper "Television Without Frontiers" (Commission of the European Communities 1984), whose title played on a popular Eurovision coproduction. The document was based on the arrival of satellite television, one of the first electronic technologies to entirely ignore the nature of state boundaries. Early radio treaties had allowed small nations such as Luxembourg to broadcast to their neighbors; there was always at least an implicit if not explicit agreement to permit some infringement of what was regarded as a domain of territorial sovereignty. The role of the International Telecommunication Union (ITU) here explains some of the subsequent anomalies: broadcast wavebands were a scarce resource, needed for emergency services and defense as well as news and entertainment. They were legitimate matters for intergovernmental address. However, with the vastly increased spectrum availability brought about by satellite and digital technologies, the ostensibly natural monopolies of governments over spectrum ceased to hold water. The ITU's state-based structure, however, did not allow it to evolve into the kind of global instrument of governance that would be required by the organically growing and exponentially expanding Internet of the early 1990s (O'Siochrú et al. 2002). A number of ad hoc groups took over critical areas such as the domain name system (Mueller 2004), effectively laying claim to a functioning Habermasian public sphere of enlightened engineers devoted to "rough consensus and running code" (Froomkin 2003). By the time of the UN-organized World Summit on the Information Society in 2005, at the lowest count 15 bodies claimed jurisdiction over different, often overlapping, aspects of Internet governance, and many more laid claim to a stake in particular aspects from indigenous rights to censorship. The central concern – whether nations could still stake a claim to sovereignty over "their" media – remains one of the most contentious in media policy circles. As we will see below, recent developments in media studies point toward a dialectical solution to the apparent impasse, suggesting that we are beyond the period of emergence and are now already reorienting political struggle and economic competition toward the new terrain, neither state nor market, of the network.

Political Aesthetics

Immediately prior to the launch of the World Wide Web and overlapping with its early years, the dominant discourse was interactivity, and the characteristic media CD-ROM and – discursively if not in actuality – immersive virtual reality. During the 1990s, the new buzzword was connectivity, a term whose meaning was to change in connotation in the 2000s, when it was increasingly allied to discourses of creativity, user-generated content, and crowd-sourcing. The rise of apps toward the end of the 2000s signaled a major return to interactivity, which had never gone away but had been pretty much corralled in the games arena during the previous decade. The new e-readers of the 2009–2010 season already featured interaction-rich content, especially for younger users, signaling a return to the style of the CD-ROM, which had been gradually sidelined during the heady rush toward the Internet as the primum mobile of contemporary media. The period also saw the rise of an increasingly digital cinema. Disney Studios' *Tron* (1982) had for the most part used analog devices to depict a digital virtual world; 1992's *Lawnmower Man* featured several minutes of rather lurid computer-generated imagery (CGI) and a script that centered on the network capability of computing. One decade on, with *Harry Potter and the Chamber of Secrets*, *The Lord of the Rings: The Two Towers*, *Men in Black II*, *Spiderman*, and *Star Wars: Episode II – Attack of the Clones* slugging it out for the top box-office slot, scarcely a frame of any event movie was free of digital attention, from special effects to nonlinear video editing to digital grading. Meanwhile, the typical media for recording and playing back content had moved from analog magnetic tape to digital optical systems, and in the music business to MP3 files.

The move from physical objects to screen displays and speakers directly driven by software has lead in two directions: toward a comparative analog–digital aesthetics, especially in specialist discourse on recorded media, and toward a political economy of "immateriality." The discourse on digital aesthetics began early in photography, where commentators were quick to point out the malleability of digital images and the severance of an older belief in the veracity and verisimilitude of the photographic image (Ritchin 1990; Wombell 1991; Mitchell 1992). The realist paradigm, which focused on the privileged relation between the photographic image and the situation it depicted, was perhaps stronger among photography critics than in film studies, where decades of semiotics had placed the relation between image and scene deeply in doubt. All the more curious, then, that in the 2000s very similar concerns began to be voiced among cinema scholars, in their most sophisticated expression in D.N. Rodowick's *The Virtual Life of Film* (2007). The discussion is marred by a lack of understanding concerning the operation of light-reactive chipsets in comparison with the older photo-mechanical processes. Here photographers have a stronger background, the technical aspects of photography being integral to its analysis in ways that are rarely the case in film studies. The equivalent complaint in musicology is, however, rare: popular discourse concerns fidelity and response of different formats, and their currency rather than their distinctive forms. Jonathan Sterne's work on music file formats (2006, 2012) is a welcome innovation in its articulation of the importance of compression–decompression algorithms (codecs), an issue scarcely raised in audiovisual media (but see Mackenzie 2008).

The issue of immateriality has been voiced most assertively in the political economy of Italian postautonomist thought (Lazzarato 1996) but has received specific attention in relation to labor in the media and software industries, in particular from scholars such as Terranova (2006). The concept derives once again from a binary opposition between analog and digital, this time, however, in terms of products and production. Where the economics of Fordism concentrated on the production of physical goods, the move to brands and intangibles such as TV shows or celebrities in the post-Fordist economy produced artifacts that have no physical form. Instead, the "mere" physical goods – sneakers, or indeed computers and mobile phones – are manufactured in sweatshop conditions because there is no longer major profit to derive from manufacture: the source of wealth is the immaterial good represented by the Nike swoosh or Apple's logo and characteristic Jonathan Ives designs. The immaterialization of labor does lead to a characteristic legal form that has become a major topic in new media studies: intellectual property. Unlike material goods, where the legal definition of privation applies (private property is distinguished by conferring the right to deny use to another; theft as depriving the owner), intellectual or immaterial goods are not privative; that is, I can have an idea, give it to you, and still have it myself. Creating a new property regime (ostensibly by extending and toughening historic provisions for copyright and patent law) is a constitutive aspect of the business models that have developed to exploit new media since 1993. We will return to them below.

Closely aligned with the immaterial labor thesis is the thesis of affective labor, which proposes that much of the highly geared production of the creative industries is designed not to meet needs but to articulate with flows of desire and sensual or emotional connectivity (Massumi 2002). Between Marx on one side and Deleuze and Guattari on the other, the affective turn points beyond the digital toward what Patricia Ticineto Clough (2008) calls "biomediated" subjectivity. The emphasis on affect distinguishes instinctual and preindividual formations from the subjectively experienced, socialized emotions, seeing in them the promise of a new form of sociality and subjectivity while at the same time, again in Clough's analysis, seeing them as prone to being recruited to biopolitical management in the form, for example, of the racist expression of cultural anxieties. On the one hand, this has led to celebrations of user-generated content as a new democratization of culture in the figure of the "produser" (Bruns 2008). On the other, observations of the clustering of like-minded communities and their capacity for withdrawing from public debate (Sunstein 2007) and critiques of the exploitation of freely given labor have opened the field of affective labor to new forms of political debate (Scholz and Liu 2011).

The phrase "biopolitical" points to the third major influence on the new media studies of the last decade: a return to the work of Michel Foucault, but this time to the late work on governmentality and specifically on the transitions from disciplinary to biopolitical rule. The former, it will be recalled, had as its icon Bentham's panopticon, the prison run from a central tower through whose windows all inmates could be surveyed at any time while the guard remained invisible, thus promulgating a habit of acting as if under constant surveillance, internalizing the disciplinary codes of the institution. Such a vision of surveillant government informed important early studies of the surveillance society (Gandy 1993; Lyon 1994) and remained important in the increasingly sophisticated turn to analysis of the imbrication of commerce in contemporary surveillance (Elmer 2004; Lyon 2007). This characterization fit a particular dystopian account of cyberspace in the 1990s and early 2000s, countering the heady boosterism characteristic of *Wired* magazine. In some respects, it can be read as a remnant of the distrust, even hatred, of the "military-industrial complex" that fired the late 1960s counter-culture, that same counter-culture that, as Fred Turner (2006) argues, was also responsible for the development of the free-wheeling but ultimately military-industrial culture of Silicon Valley.

This binary of surveillant disciplinary rule and the metaphor of cyberspace as postnational frontier and libertarian sanctuary (Barlow 1996) gave out, however, in the first great crisis to affect the new medium: the dot-com crash of 2001. After a bubble of overinvestment in vaporware, fostered by the belief that business models imported from pre-Internet media would build fortunes, the NASDAQ's plunge from its March 2000 peak of 5132.52 points seemed to provide a fitting conclusion to the first wild period of homesteading the open prairies of the Internet. But entrepreneurs were swift to learn lessons from the handful of companies that survived the crash. While AOL Time Warner, which had used a combination of retail mall and magazine business models, took substantial losses, three firms came through smelling of roses: Amazon, eBay, and Google. All three were net-native, all three had built their businesses and their customer bases in the online arena using online techniques, and all three were pioneers of social media. The dot-com crash was instrumental in focusing business attention on social media – Web 2.0 – as the way to monetize what the web was best at: connectivity. While some early start-ups such as FriendFinder and MySpace have subsequently lost their major market position, other portals such as Facebook, Flickr, Twitter, and YouTube have thrived. Meanwhile, retailers such as Amazon and more recently iTunes have embraced the potential of social networks to tailor word-of-mouth recommendations to customers in the guise of communities of taste and interest, and Google has perfected the art of inviting users to participate in improving their services in hundreds of ways, from donating features to Google apps to folksonomies, which provide metatags for material that eludes standard word searches, such as music, images, and video.

This leads us to one of the key media studies problematics of the 2000s. In 1977, Dallas Smythe (1994) opined that the economics of advertising depended on the unpaid work of paying attention that audiences provided to TV stations, who on-sold to advertisers. In the case of the Internet, not only do users pay attention and not only do they (like TV audiences) pay for the devices required to do so, but they also often, indeed increasingly, produce the content that attracts the attention and so the advertising revenue. Even if the theses of immaterial and affective labor are incorrect, the accusation remains that the Internet presents itself as a playground but is in effect a factory for the production of playful activities that then become intellectual property of portal owners, or provide unpaid content on which advertisers batten, or both.

The extent to which this constitutes a market is disputed. While Marxist scholars (informed by systems theory and other contemporary intellectual trends) such as Christian Fuchs (2008) maintain that this is the most recent form of capitalist exploitation, others see it as the precursor of a new kind of economy. In an early version of the theory, Richard Barbrook (1998) suggested that the Internet economy was a hybrid affair, one side still tied to the old capitalist economy, the other an emergent gift economy. This premise became a highly practical platform for software developers in the free-libre open-source software (FLOSS) movement, as canonized in the work of Richard Stallman (2002), and has been more broadly promulgated by the peer-to-peer (P2P) movement, especially through the instigator of the P2P Foundation, Michel Bauwens (see e.g. Bauwens 2005). Bauwens' fundamental thesis is that the gift economy works. In instances such as Linux and Wikipedia, to take the best known, a single user might donate ten hours of work and in return receive the fruits of thousands, even hundreds of thousands, of hours in return. The principle has been adapted for real-world projects such as the design of an environmentally viable car (the open-source or OScar), microloan concepts adapted from Grameen Bank's pioneer development economics, and Kickstarter (a site on which creatives and others post projects and invite visitors to invest small sums with small or purely symbolic returns). Bauwens, an indefatigable conferencier and public advocate, freely admits that bricks-and-mortar businesses still require capital investment but looks forward to the gradual replacement of the banking system with a more personal and networked economics of reciprocity. Bauwens – and others, notably the late green radical André Gorz (2010) and the Oekonux community (www.oekonux.org) – may be regarded as representing the radical end of a spectrum that also includes such luminaries of the liberal tradition as Lessig (2004, 2006), von Hippel (2005), and Benkler (2006). At the most conservative end of the spectrum, von Hippel proposes an extension of the prosumer principle, according to which businesses and consumers both stand to gain when the consumer takes over the final elements of production, such as tailoring kitchen designs for just-in-time manufacture, assembling an automobile design from a menu of options, or installing software and other custom features on a new computer. This principle, von Hippel argues, should be extended to user-generated content online, including software development and other creative conceptual (or "immaterial") labor. Benkler sees this process as vital to the renewal of capital. Together with Lessig, he has been a major voice in campaigns against the increasingly rigidity with which intellectual property laws have been legislated and applied in national and international fora. They have been instrumental in establishing Creative Commons, a more property-oriented license than Stallman's General Public License (GPL) (www.fsf.org), which allows authors to retain some rights over their productions.

The debates over intellectual property have been extremely heated in part because they implicate not only economic benefits but also principles of socialization and polity, especially what has been dubbed the hacker ethic (Levy 1984; Himanen 2001): the principle that access to information should be unlimited and total. The principle clashes not only with principles of private property but also with professional media ethics – notably in the case of WikiLeaks – and with the principles of centralized authority. In the early period of Internet communications, a favored metaphor was the rhizome, a thesis mooted in 1980 by the French philosophers Deleuze and Guattari (1980). The typical form of authority, they argued, was tree-like: a single organism rooted to its own place. Rhizomatic organization linked hundreds of quasi-autonomous organisms into a single interdependent complex assemblage. Allied with the metaphors of the nomad – for whom territory was not about occupying position but trajectories – and of smooth space (permitting flows) versus striated, hierarchized, static spaces, the rhizome offered a vivid image for the fluidity and interconnected network experience of the early web. However, already by the mid-1990s, Critical Art Ensemble (1994) had begun to observe that innovative forms of capitalist corporate culture had already begun to employ exactly these characteristics in the interests of what David Harvey (1989) would describe as "flexible accumulation."

In the same Italian intellectual milieu that brought the ideas of Marx, Deleuze, and Foucault together, the conditions of employment so determined were described in a term that has become critical to new activist politics and to the media analysis of new media formations: precarity. The history of the term is usefully traced by Raunig (2010). In a first iteration, precarity referred to the status of factory workers threatened with the sack, and was extended to include the reserve army of labor for whom Marx had reserved the damning term *Lumpenproletariat*: migrants, the homeless, illegals, and the gray economy. Swiftly, however, the original themes of precarious labor and precarious social conditions were perceived as a victimology, suggesting a passive class without resources to struggle. In a significant revaluation associated with the politics of not working and the exit from capital, precariousness or precarity was seen instead as a productive state of autonomy from capital. The idea was rapidly assimilated into the already-existing hacker culture as well as the bohemian underworld of European and increasingly also American cities, of both North and South. Precarity was seen as the condition that permitted people to hold down a paying job temporarily so that they could invest their real time and energies into code-hacking, creative arts, community-building, and any other autonomous activity designed for pleasure or communion rather than profit (Berardi 2009, n.d.).

The Study of New Media Practice

The critical ethnography that David Morley (1980) launched in relation to television audiences rapidly met older traditions: the subcultural sociology of Becker's *Outsiders* (1966) and the anthropology of institutions (from Alvarado and Buscombe 1978 to Born 2005). Sociology of both online and computer-based subcultures drew on many of the base techniques of earlier sociologists and anthropologists. Pioneering works by Kidder (1981) on software engineers and Turkle (1984) on nascent geek culture paved the way for a determined ethnography of the Internet pioneered by the founders of the Association of Internet Researchers (e.g., Jones 1999). Because fans took to the Internet like ducks to water, early studies of fan literature (e.g., Vermorel and Vermorel 1989, based on letters sent to David Bowie and others) were supplemented by studies based on easy access to vast archives of online interactions, stories, art, and conversations. These openings have powered extensive literature in online ethnography, a new practice based largely on textual (and to a lesser extent visual and auditory) materials shared in fan communities. An unusual quality of this kind of ethnography is that the researcher may never meet the people studied, bringing a host of challenges to the truth-claims of older ethnographic practices where emotional cues, for example, were visibly and audibly integral to the meeting. Much of the analysis of audiences is therefore still based on textual aesthetics and interpretation.

Games studies' accounts of "audience" have especially broken free of the training early researchers gained in film studies, first through the "ludology" debates of the 1990s (Aarseth 1997) and now due to the rich mixture of traditions flourishing today (Wolf and Perron 2003; Perron and Wolf 2009). A number of influential, mainly US, texts address the cultural forms of new media (Bolter and Grusin 1999; Manovich 2001; Jenkins 2008), with Jenkins especially asserting the power of the active audience to create meanings and cultures, more so now that digital tools enable both making and sharing of cultural artifacts. A more innovative line of enquiry is associated with Silverstone and Hirsch's (1992) investigation into the meanings and uses of domestic technologies. In many respects these studies, which also drew on design history and the then-emergent field of science and technology studies, opened the way for some of the most important sociological investigations, including both games and software studies. An important aspect of Silverstone and Hirsch's work, and of Morley's continuing research, is the articulation of these cultural aspects of consumption with the reorganization of labor in the digital economy. This is a significant advance on an older formation in media studies that, like cultural studies, eschewed analysis of the workplace as a communicative and cultural environment. Early analysts noted, on the one hand, the transformation of the workplace and the proletarianization of office work (Braverman 1974), and, on the other, the failure of new media to provide, alone, the efficiencies they were expected to, as workers learned to subvert workplace computers for entertainment and other personal purposes (Sproull and Kiesler 1991). Analyses of the media (e.g., Tufte 2006) and cultures of the digital workplace such as Knorr-Cetina and Brügger's (2002) study of the finance industry indicate a continuing growth in concern with workplace media as well as entertainment and news functions.

The mediation of work in the twenty-first century is difficult to separate from changes in the mediation of power. The reduction of political life to biopolitical population management is not necessarily efficient, as suggested by hung parliaments in Britain and Australia, gridlocked Presidential–Congressional relations in the USA, and the suspension of the Canadian parliament. The political event – in the sense of a history-changing action – seems increasingly rare in political life (Badiou 2006); and, as the authors of a recent activist text argue, the problem with Badiou's events is that they all seem to be in the past (Papadopoulos et al. 2008). As Jodi Dean (2009) has argued, all that we appear to have gained from Web 2.0 is the obligation to Twitter. We feel no similar duty to listen and respond. That attitude is magnified and refined in the case of politicians, she argues: the phrase "I hear you" uttered by a President or Prime Minister is code for "I must allow you your right to free speech but I have no intention whatever of paying attention to your point of view." It is for this reason that activist networks have become so important to new media studies: unlike finance workers, activists constantly debate why and how they operate, including the nature of the software they operate in (Kelty 2008).

This extends to the most recently emerging trend in new media studies: ecocritical accounts of the materials, production, energy use, and recycling of digital hardware. Such studies address, for example, the notorious dependency of the mobile phone industries on coltan extracted by child labor from war-ravaged Eastern Congo, with consequent habitat destruction and the threatened species loss of the iconic mountain gorilla (Hayes and Burge 2003). Others look at the environmental and health impacts of semiconductor manufacture (Holden and Kelty 2005) and at the energy signature of cloud computing (Cubitt et al. 2010), while a great deal of work has followed the Basel Action Network (2002, 2005) in engaging with both consumer generation of e-waste (Grossman 2007) and the specifics of labor in the processing of toxic residues (Maxwell and Miller 2008; Feilhauer and Zehle 2009). Indications are that strategic minerals are already in too short supply for current rates of growth to continue; and debates over whether technical solutions or austerity measures are the better response will be vivid.

The ethical, political, economic, and environmental futures of network communications and new media more generally are, then, in flux. Struggle for governance will be exacerbated by the accelerating "Internet of things" and ubiquitous computing; the digital divide will continue to grow, even though access to low-level equipment and skills is increasing in the developing world and among the homeless in the wealthy regions. Environmentalism is unlikely to have a purchase in the normative politics of gridlock: not when the top ten companies in the Fortune 500 are exclusively in the petroleum and automobile sectors, only in 2010 joined by finance companies who benefit from consumer debt associated with homes, cars, and of course computers. Demands to integrate "emergent markets" into the global economy will keep human labor cheaper than cleaner automated recycling and ensure that technical standardization will be increasingly important. In this area, the success of the QWERTY keyboard layout is instructive: responsible for the epidemic of forearm injuries among computer users, the standard was developed to slow typists by placing letters in a less efficient order, yet 140 years later it still dominates. Efficiency and elegance do not secure standardization, which rests on the interplay between economics, politics, and cultural inertia. At the same time, while monopolies such as those of IBM, Microsoft, and now Google and Facebook will continue to mark the rapidly evolving media scene, the mass participation of users in the new media indicates that not all battles are lost. A history of user-generated innovation also points toward the opposite conclusion: that corporations and governments have constantly to keep up with grassroots network communications innovation, and that the political economy of intellectual property rights and exclusion no longer fit the new conditions. We can expect to see amplified in the near future two major fields of dispute: open-source and universal service. The first is already under attack in debates over the implementation of HTML5 and IP version 6, while the second is most clearly exposed in the use of industrial and political espionage in major cyber-attacks on US defense contractors and military personnel apparently originating in China. The network is no longer emergent – it is the terrain on which a grand battle is being fought between three forces: the nation state, re-emergent in the form of the new economies of the BRICK countries (Brazil, Russia, India, China, Korea); the market, now firmly dominated by intellectual property rights; and the net-native forces of both profit-based corporations such as Google and nonprofit communities such as Linux. The shape of the new net-natives will evolve through a period of intense pressure to ensure that the claims of both older formations are heard. Thus, we may stand on the brink of extraordinary proliferations of creative interaction (Gauntlett 2011) or we may be faced with increasing monopolization (as in key software markets) and political control (as in China's Golden Shield policy). It is unlikely that new media studies will be lacking in matters to discuss, or a public purpose for its deliberations.

References

Aarseth, E. (1997) *Cybertext: Perspectives on Ergodic Literature.* Baltimore, MD: Johns Hopkins University Press.

Alvarado, M. and Buscombe, E. (1978) *Hazell: The Making of a Television Series.* London: BFI.

Anderson, B. (1983) *Imagined Communities: Reflections on the Origin and Spread of Nationalism.* London: Verso.

Augé, M. (1995) *Non-Places: Introduction to an Anthropology of Supermodernity*, trans. J. Howe. London: Verso.

Badiou, A. (2006) *Being and Event*, trans. O. Feltham. New York: Continuum.

Barbrook, R. (1998) "The Internet Gift Economy." *First Monday.* http://firstmonday.org /htbin/cgiwrap/bin/ojs/index.php/fm/article/view/1517/1432.

Barlow, J.P. (1996) "A Declaration of the Independence of Cyberspace." https://projects .eff.org/~barlow/Declaration-Final.html.

Basel Action Network (2002) *Exporting Harm: The High-Tech Trashing of Asia.* www.ban .org/E-waste/technotrashfinalcomp.pdf.

Basel Action Network (2005) *The Digital Dump: Exporting High-Tech Re-use and Abuse to Africa.* www.ban.org/BANreports/10-24-05/index.htm.

Bauwens, M. (2005) "The Political Economy of Peer Production." *C-Theory.* www.ctheory .net/articles.aspx?id=499.

Becker, H. S (1966) *Outsiders: Studies in the Sociology of Deviance.* New York: Macmillan.

Benjamin, W. (1969) "The Work of Art in the Age of Mechanical Reproduction" in H. Arendt, ed., *Illuminations*, trans. H. Zohn. New York: Schocken, pp. 217–251.

Benjamin, W. (2003) "The Work of Art in the Age of its Technological Reproducibility: Third Version" in H. Eiland and M.W. Jennings, eds., *Selected Writings*, vol. 4: *1938–1940.* Cambridge, MA: Bellknap Press/Harvard University Press, pp. 251–283.

Benkler, Y. (2006) *The Wealth of Networks: How Social Production Transforms Markets and Freedom.* New Haven, CT: Yale University Press.

Berardi, F. ("Bifo") (2009) *Precarious Rhapsody: Semiocapitalism and the Pathologies of the Post-Alpha Generation*, trans. A. Bove, E. Empson, M. Goddard, et al. London: Minor Compositions.

Berardi, F. ("Bifo") (n.d.) "Info-Labour and Precarisation," trans. E. Empson. www .generation-online.org/t/tinfolabour.htm.

Bolter, J.D. and Grusin, R. (1999) *Remediation: Understanding New Media.* Cambridge, MA: MIT Press.

Born, G. (2005) *Uncertain Vision: Birt, Dyke and the Reinvention of the BBC.* London: Vintage.

Braverman, H. (1974) *Labour and Monopoly Capital: The Degradation of Work in the Twentieth Century.* New York: Monthly Review Press.

Bruns, A. (2008) *Blogs, Wikipedia, Second Life, and Beyond: From Production to Produsage.* New York: Peter Lang.

Castells, M. (2000 [1996]) *The Rise of the Network Society, The Information Age: Economy, Society and Culture Vol. I*. Cambridge, MA; Oxford, UK: Blackwell.

Castells, M. (2004 [1997]) *The Power of Identity, The Information Age: Economy, Society and Culture Vol. II*. Cambridge, MA; Oxford, UK: Blackwell.

Castells, M. (2000 [1998]) *End of Millennium, The Information Age: Economy, Society and Culture Vol. III*. Cambridge, MA; Oxford, UK: Blackwell.

Castells, M. (1998) *The Information Age: Economy, Society and Culture volume 3: End of Millenium*. Oxford: Blackwell.

Chakravartty, P. and Sarikakis, K. (2006) *Media Policy and Globalization*. Edinburgh: Edinburgh University Press.

Chomsky, N. (2003) *Media Control: The Spectacular Achievements of Propaganda*, 2nd edn, New York: Open Media.

Clough, P.T. (2008) "The Affective Turn: Political Economy, Biomedia and Bodies". *Theory Culture Society* 1(25), 1–22.

Collins, R. (2010) *Three Myths of Internet Governance*. Bristol: Intellect.

Commission of the European Communities (1984) *Television Without Frontiers, COM (84) 300 Final*. Brussels: CEC.

Crafton, D. (1997) *The Talkies: American Cinema's Transition to Sound*. Berkeley, CA: University of California Press.

Critical Art Ensemble (1994) *The Electronic Disturbance*. Brooklyn, NY: Autonomedia.

Cubitt, S., Hassan, R., and Volkmer, I. (2010) "Does Cloud Computing Have a Silver Lining?" *Media Culture & Society*, 32(2), 149–158.

Curran, J. and Park, M.-J., eds. (2000) *De-Westernizing Media Studies*. London: Routledge.

Dean, J. (2009) *Democracy and Other Neoliberal Fantasies: Communicative Capitalism and Left Politics*. Durham, NC: Duke University Press.

Debray, R. (1996) *Media Manifestos: On the Technological Transmission of Cultural Forms*, trans. E. Rauth. London: Verso.

Debray, R. (2000) *Transmitting Culture*, trans. E. Rauth. New York: Columbia University Press.

Debray, R. (2004) *God: An Itinerary*, trans. J. Mehlmann. London: Verso.

Deleuze, G. and Guattari, F. (1980) *Mille plateaux (Capitalisme et Schizophrénie II) [A Thousand Plateaus]*. Paris: Editions de Minuit.

deNardis, L. (2009) *Protocol Politics: The Globalization of Internet Governance*. Cambridge, MA: MIT Press.

Elmer, G. (2004) *Profiling Machines: Mapping the Personal Information Economy*. Cambridge, MA: MIT Press.

Feilhauer, M. and Zehle, S., eds. (2009) "Ethics of Waste in the Information Society", special issue of *International Review of Information Ethics*, 11.

Froomkin, A.M. (2003) "Habermas@Discourse.net: Toward a Critical Theory of Cyberspace." *Harvard Law Review*, 116, 751–873.

Fuchs, C. (2008) *Internet and Society: Social Theory and the Information Age*. London: Routledge.

Gandy, O.H. Jnr. (1993) *The Panoptic Sort: The Political Economy of Personal Information*. Boulder, CO: Westview Press.

Gauntlett, D. (2011) *Making Is Connecting: The Social Meaning of Creativity, from DIY and Knitting to YouTube and Web 2.0*. Cambridge: Polity.

Gitelman, L. (1999) *Scripts, Grooves, and Writing Machines: Representing Technology in the Edison Era*. Stanford, CA: Stanford University Press.

Gitelman, L. (2006) *Always Already New: Media, History, and the Data of Culture*. Cambridge, MA: MIT Press.

Goldsmith, J. and Wu, T. (2008) *Who Controls the Internet: Illusions of a Borderless World*. Oxford: Oxford University Press.

Gomery, D. (2005) *The Coming of Sound: A History*. London: Routledge.

Gorz, A. (2010) *Ecologica*, trans. C. Turner. London: Seagull.

Grau, O. (2003) *Virtual Art: From Illusion to Immersion*. Cambridge, MA: MIT Press.

Grossman, E. (2007) *High Tech Trash: Digital Devices, Hidden Toxics, and Human Health*. Washington, DC: Shearwater.

Harvey, D. (1989) *The Condition of Postmodernity: An Enquiry into the Origins of Cultural Change*. Oxford: Blackwell.

Hassan, R. (2003) *The Chronoscopic Society: Globalization, Time and Knowledge in the Networked Economy*. New York: Lang.

Hayes, K. and Burge, R. (2003) *Coltan Mining in the Democratic Republic of Congo: How Tantalum-Using Industries Can Commit to the Reconstruction of the DRC*. Cambridge: Fauna & Flora International.

Himanen, P. (2001) *The Hacker Ethic and the Spirit of the Information Age*. New York: Random House.

Holden, J. and Kelty, C. (2005) "The Environmental Impact of the Manufacturing of Seminconductors". *Connections*. http://cnx.org/content/m14503/latest.

Huhtamo, E. (2005) "Slots of Fun, Slots of Trouble. Toward an Archaeology of Electronic Gaming" in J. Raessens and J. Goldstein, eds., *Handbook of Computer Games Studies*. Cambridge, MA: MIT Press, pp. 1–21.

Huhtamo, E. (2006) "Twin-Touch-Test-Redux: Media Archaeological Approach to Art, Interactivity, and Tactility" in O. Grau, ed., *MediaArtHistories*. Cambridge, MA: MIT Press, pp. 71–101.

Huhtamo, E. (2007) "The Urban Spirograph, or an Archaeology of a Loser". Paper presented at the FIAF Congress 2007, Tokyo, Japan (April 7–12).

Jenkins, H. (2008) *Convergence Culture: Where Old and New Media Collide*, rev. edn. New York: New York University Press.

Jones, S.G., ed. (1999) *Doing Internet Research: Critical Issues and Methods for Examining the Net*. London: Sage.

Kelty, C.M. (2008) *Two Bits: The Cultural Significance of Free Software*. Durham, NC: Duke University Press.

Kidder, T. (1981) *The Soul of a New Machine*. Harmondsworth: Penguin.

Kittler, F.A. (1997) *Literature, Media, Information Systems: Essays*, ed. J. Johnston. Amsterdam: G+B Arts International.

Kittler, F.A. (1999) *Gramophone, Film, Typewriter*, trans. G. Winthrop-Young and M. Wutz. Stanford, CA: Stanford University Press.

Kittler, F.A. (2010) *Optical Media: Berlin Lectures 1999*, trans. A. Enns. Cambridge: Polity.

Knorr-Cetina, K. and Brügger, U. (2002) "Traders' Engagement with Markets: A Postsocial Relationship." *Theory Culture & Society* 19(5/6), 161–185.

Lazzarato, M. (1996) "Immaterial Labour", trans. P. Colilli and E. Emery, in M. Hardt and P. Virno, eds., *Radical Thought in Italy: A Potential Politics*. Minneapolis, MN: University of Minnesota Press, pp. 133–147.

Lessig, L. (2004) *Free Culture: How Big Media Uses Technology and the Law to Lock Down Culture and Control Creativity*. New York: Penguin.

Lessig, L. (2006) *Code v.2: Code and Other Laws of Cyberspace*, rev. edn. New York: Basic Books.

Levy, S. (1984) *Hackers: Heroes of the Computer Revolution*. New York: Anchor Press/Doubleday.

Lyon, D. (1994) *The Electronic Eye: The Rise of Surveillance Society*. Cambridge: Polity.

Lyon, D. (2007) *Surveillance Studies: An Overview*. Cambridge: Polity.

Mackenzie, A. (2008) "Codecs" in M. Fuller, ed., *Software Studies: A Lexicon*. Cambridge, MA: MIT Press, pp. 48–55.

MacLean, D. (2003) "The Quest for Inclusive Governance of Global ICTs: Lessons from the ITU in the Limits of National Sovereignty." *Information Technologies and International Development*, 1(1), 1–18.

Manovich, L. (2001) *The Language of New Media*. Cambridge, MA: MIT Press.

Massumi, B. (2002) *Parables for the Virtual: Movement, Affect, Sensation*. Durham, NC: Duke University Press.

Mattelart, A. (1994) *Mapping World Communication: War, Progress, Culture*, trans. S. Emmanuel and J.A. Cohen. Minneapolis, MN: University of Minnesota Press.

Mattelart, A. (1996) *The Invention of Communication*, trans. S. Emanuel. Minneapolis, MN: University of Minnesota Press.

Mattelart, A. (2000) *Networking the World 1794–2000*, trans. L. Carey-Liebrecht and J. Cohen. Minneapolis, MN: University of Minnesota Press.

Maxwell R. and Miller, T. (2008) "Creative Industries or Wasteful Ones?" *Urban China* 33, 122.

McChesney, R.W. (2008) *The Political Economy of Media: Enduring Issues, Emerging Dilemmas*. New York: Monthly Review Press.

McLuhan, M. (1964) *Understanding Media: The Extensions of Man*. London: Sphere.

Mitchell, W.J. (1992) *The Reconfigured Eye: Visual Truth in the Post-Photographic Era*. Cambridge, MA: MIT Press.

Morley, D. (1980) *The "Nationwide" Audience*. London: BFI.

Morley, D. (2000) *Home Territories: Media, Mobility and Identity*. London: Routledge.

Morley, D. (2007) *Media, Modernity and Technology: The Geography of the New*. London: Routledge.

Morley, D. and Robins, K. (1995) *Spaces of Identity: Global Media, Electronic Landscapes and Cultural Boundaries*. London: Routledge.

Mueller, M.L. (2004) *Ruling the Root: Internet Governance and the Taming of Cyberspace*. Cambridge, MA: MIT Press.

O'Siochrú, S. and Girard, B. with Mahan, A. (2002) *Global Media Governance: A Beginner's Guide*. New York: Rowan and Littlefield.

Papadopoulos, D., Stephenson N., and Tsianos, V. (2008) *Escape Routes: Control and Subversion in the Twenty-first Century*. London: Pluto.

Parikka, J. (2007) *Digital Contagions: A Media Archaeology of Computer Viruses*. New York: Peter Lang.

Parikka, J. (2012) *What is Media Archaeology?* Cambridge: Polity.

Perron, B. and Wolf, M.J.P., eds. (2009) *The Video Games Theory Reader 2*, 2nd edn. New York: Routledge.

Raunig, G. (2010) *A Thousand Machines*, trans. A. Derieg. New York: Semiotext(e).

Ritchin, F. (1990) *In Our Own Image: The Coming Revolution in Photography*. New York: Aperture Foundation.

Robins, K. (2007) "Transnational Cultural Policy and European Cosmopolitanism." *Cultural Politics* 3(2), 147–174.

Rodowick, D.N. (2007) *The Virtual Life of Film*. Cambridge, MA: Harvard University Press.

Sassen, S. (1991) *The Global City: New York, London, Tokyo*. Princeton, NJ: Princeton University Press.

Sassen, S. (1994) *Cities in a Global Economy*. Thousand Oaks, CA: Pine Forge.

Scholz, T. and Liu, L.Y. (2011) *From Mobile Playgrounds to Sweatshop City*, Situated Technologies Pamphlets 7. New York: Architectural League of New York.

Silverstone, R. and Hirsch, E., eds. (1992) *Consuming Technologies: Media and Information in Domestic Spaces*. London: Routledge.

Smythe, D. (1994) [1977] "Communications: Blindspot of Western Marxism" in T. Guback, ed., *Counterclockwise: Perspectives on Communication*. Boulder, CO: Westview Press, 266–291.

Sproull, L. and Kiesler, S. (1991) *Connections: New Ways of Working in the Networked Organisation*. Cambridge, MA: MIT Press.

Stallman, R.M. (2002) *Free Software, Free Society: Selected Essays*, ed. J. Gay. Boston, MA: GNU Press/Free Software Foundation.

Sterne, J. (2003) *The Audible Past: Cultural Origins of Sound Reproduction*. Durham, NC: Duke University Press.

Sterne, J. (2006) "The MP3 as Cultural Artifact." *New Media & Society* 8(5), 825–842.

Sterne, J. (2012) *MP3: The Meaning of a Format*. Durham, NC: Duke University Press.

Sunstein, C. (2007) *Republic.com 2.0*. Princeton, NJ: Princeton University Press.

Terranova, T. (2006) "Of Sense and Sensibility: Immaterial Labour in Open Systems." *Data Browser 03*. www.kurator.org/media/uploads/publications/DB03/Terranova.pdf.

Thompson, E.P. (1963) *The Making of the English Working Class*. Harmondsworth: Pelican.

Thussu, D.K., ed. (1998) *Electronic Empires: Global Media and Local Resistance*. London: Arnold.

Thussu, D.K. (2000) *International Communication: Continuity and Change*. London: Arnold.

Tufte, E.R. (2006) *The Cognitive Style of PowerPoint*, 2nd edn. Cheshire, CT: Graphics Press.

Turkle, S. (1984) *The Second Self: Computers and the Human Spirit*. London: Granada.

Turner, F. (2006) *From Counterculture to Cyberculture: Stewart Brand, the Whole Earth Network, and the Rise of Digital Utopianism*. Chicago, IL: University of Chicago Press.

Vermorel, J. and Vermorel, F. (1989) *Fandemonium*. London: Omnibus.

Virilio, P. (1986) *Speed and Politics: An Essay in Dromology*, trans. M. Polizotti. New York: Semotext(e).

Vismann, C. (2008) *Files: Law and Media Technology*, trans. G. Winthrop-Young. Stanford, CA: Stanford University Press.

von Hippel, E. (2005) *Democratising Innovation*. Cambridge, MA: MIT Press.

Williams, R. (1958) *Culture and Society 1780–1950*. Harmondsworth: Penguin.

Williams, R. (1961) *The Long Revolution*. Harmondsworth: Penguin.

Wolf, M.J.P and Perron, B., eds. (2003) *The Video Games Theory Reader*. New York: Routledge.

Wombell, P., ed. (1991) *Photovideo: Photography in the Age of the Computer*. London: Rivers Oram Press.

Zielinski, S. (1999) *Audiovisions: Cinema and Television as Entr'actes in History*. Amsterdam: Amsterdam University Press.

Zielinski, S. (2006) *Deep Time of the Media: Toward an Archaeology of Hearing and Seeing by Technical Means*, trans. G. Custance. Cambridge, MA: MIT Press.

2

The Future of Digital Humanities Is a Matter of Words

Willard McCarty

ἔνθα καὶ ἠματίη μὲν ὑφαίνεσκον μέγαν ἱστόν,
Then by day I would weave at the great web,
νύκτας δ᾽ἀλλύεσκον, ἐπεὶ δαῖδας παραθείμην.
but by night under torchlight I would unravel it.
Homer, Odyssey 19.149–150.

Prologue

The job I have been given is to take up the whole question of digital humanities and the digital mediation of knowledge among the various humanities disciplines with a view to what's driving the change, where it is heading, and what the humanities might look like as a result – and what "new media" might mean in this context. I am tempted to ask ironically in return "Is that all?" The question is fascinating and needs to be asked, but where does one begin on such a vast and uncertain project?

First, however, allow me to anticipate what I think an adequate response might be. For reasons I will explain, it could not be what we almost always get: a projection of current technical know-how into an imagined future. Rather, it would have to be a history written to address current predicaments in order to open up the complexity of the present as staging post for the future. Its historiography would have to look like a perpetual weaving and unweaving of many threads, or like a bird's-eye view of a complex drainage system: strands of quite separate development or channels of diverse influence coming together and intermingling for a time before dispersing to

A Companion to New Media Dynamics, First Edition. Edited by John Hartley, Jean Burgess, and Axel Bruns.

mingle again elsewhere (cf. Mahoney 2011: 13, 57). Speaking of the future, Terry
Winograd and Fernando Flores have argued that

> all new technologies develop within the background of a tacit understanding of human
> nature and human work. The use of technology in turn leads to fundamental changes
> in what we do, and ultimately in what it is to be human. We encounter the deep
> questions of design when we recognize that *in designing tools we are designing ways of
> being*. By confronting these questions directly, we can develop a new background for
> understanding computer technology – one that can lead to important advances in the
> design and use of computer systems. (1986: xi, emphasis added)

These authors suggest that confronting these questions also means bringing as
much as possible of that unspoken understanding into the light so that it may be
implemented or used to guide the design of things to come. This is no simple
matter: such understanding is *tacit* and, its behaviors show, so highly variable that
only by virtue of subtle argument can we even get close to speaking of "human
nature and human work" meaningfully. At the local level of the digital humanities,
we have more than a half-century of work to draw upon. With this resource we can
reasonably suppose that if we could only figure out how to be properly historical the
discipline's past could tell us enough about what this discipline is that we might then
articulate its intellectual trajectory. Then, not only would we have a better purchase
on its most promising futures but we would also know how to look for the help this
emerging discipline needs and have reason on our side when we adapt promising
theories and practices to its requirements.

That gets us to the historical record, without which a forward-looking vision is
likely to be a waste of time. But forming it into a genuine history is also a challenge:
no one has yet done it, as holds true for computing generally (see Mahoney 2011).
I won't do it here because I don't know how, but I will suggest some indications of
its difficulty and its fascinations.

Projecting the Future

I began by saying that projecting the future from known technological possibilities
is a mug's game. However difficult the technical challenges and obviously desirable
their solution would be, thinking in terms of inevitable outcomes is undesirable
because it obscures choice and injects an enervating determinism into the discussion.
We are in effect told "behold and prepare for what will be!" – or, more cautiously,
"behold what might be!" But giving ourselves one *might be*, or two or three, or any
number we can hold in our heads, is still too heavily deterministic (a topic I will
return to later). What we need as builders of this future is to be ready in the moment
to reimagine the outcomes of our previous efforts as these have been unpredictably
realized in a world we can explore but not control.

The problem for the prognosticator is that the social world in which technologies
are embedded does not stand still, stay uninvolved, or simply acquiesce. An example

of the error is computer scientist Ian Foster's "How Computation Changes Research" (2011), in which he places us in the year 2030, when, he imagines, developments will have been realized as seems probable from observations of current technology. His futurology runs aground on "the sheer number and scale of . . . problems not touched upon," as Alan Liu comments in a response accompanying Foster's essay (2011: 94). "Ultimately, perhaps we will not just work at knowledge," Liu rhetorically allows, "We will really *know* (i.e. make sense of it all)" (89). But who actually is this "we"? Liu asks. All of us know from science fiction what happens when one straightforwardly projects ordinary life into a technologically advanced future. The movie *Just Imagine* (1930) is a good example: New York depicted as if in 1980 but inevitably populated by 1930s people behaving and thinking in 1930s ways amid technologies that may not have been commonplace then but have a distinctly 1930s look.

Liu notes that such predictive speculations conveniently ignore the messy "social, economic, political, psychological, cultural, and ethical" dimensions of human existence. Like him I am cautious and critical, but I hang back from prognostication for a simpler reason: its vulnerability to the unpredictable or even merely the overlooked. Perhaps not just fortuitously, Liu's summary formulation, "We will really *know*" echoes the emphatic declaration inscribed on mathematician David Hilbert's tombstone, *WIR MÜSSEN WISSEN / WIR WERDEN WISSEN* (We must know / We will know), which Hilbert spoke in September 1930 (Figure 2.1) (cf. Vinnikov 1999).

Figure 2.1   Declaration inscribed on mathematician David Hilbert's tombstone: WIR MÜSSEN WISSEN / WIR WERDEN WISSEN – "We must know, we will know!"

Within six years, before Hilbert death in 1943, hope for knowing in the mathematical sense he intended had been destroyed, first by Kurt Gödel's incompleteness
theorem (1931) and then by Alan Turing's negative proof of the "decision problem" (1936) – in a paper in which, as by-product, we got Turing's sketch of the
abstract machine from which the changes I am asked to survey, and all that brings
us together here, have in part come (McCarty 2005: 167–170). As so often happens, out of a passion for an absolute – in Hilbert's case, an axiomatic bedrock to
mathematics – erupted numerous fructifying questions and a host of unforeseen,
and I think unforeseeable, consequences.

If even within the rigorous world of mathematics world-altering surprises are
possible, how much more so for technological invention and its complex outcomes?[1]

Writing the History

As I suggested, the historian's response is that we prepare ourselves for what is to
come by understanding where we have been. For the digital humanities, in the first
instance this means looking to the last 60 years of professional literature on the
subject. The writings of the early period, from the first work in 1949 (Busa 1980)
to the public release of the web in 1991, yield the most helpful results because
computing was new then, and the need to justify and explain its relevance to the
humanities was commonly felt. Further, as I will explain later, we have reason to
think that the first decades of this period gave a kind of stamp to the field that has
had great shaping influence on what has followed.

Historian of computing Michael Mahoney argues that, typically, an innovative
field constructs its legitimacy by identifying precedents (2011: 56). To recall my
recent metaphor, the field weaves its interrelations with the past from available
strands and so creates a history in order that its innovations may fit into a
recognizable tradition and be understood. But the fit is seldom or never perfect.
Between computing on the one hand and the humanities on the other – at that
time as two-cultured as we might imagine – the fit was very rough. Thus, in the
early years we find anxiety occasionally overcoming professional decorum when
the massively publicized, enormously hyped, culturally prestigious, and successful
machine from the techno-sciences came into contact with literary texts, artistic
images, sculptures, and music. Technical difficulties were painful in ways we can
now hardly imagine, but of more enduring historical value are the struggles for
recognition within the disciplines of application. Matters came to a head in the
mid-1960s, when the honeymoon period seems to have ended for humanities
computing (see Milic 1966) and almost simultaneously for machine translation
(see Automatic Language Processing Advisory Committee, ALPAC, 1966; Wilks
1972: 3–4) and artificial intelligence (see Dreyfus 1965). A genre of complaint and
blame-fixing lasting almost to the present day then began, inaugurated by the first
article of the first issue of the first professional journal of the field, *Computers and*

the Humanities. In "The Next Step" (1966), literary critic Louis Milic expressed his impatience with the unimaginative though useful work published to that point. His view from within must have been widely shared in related disciplines, though perhaps for different reasons, since it soon became evident that mainstream critics were not even bothering to notice work that should at least have upset them. By 1989 it was clear, as Rosanne Potter wrote, that literary computing had "not been rejected, but rather neglected" (1989: xvi). When she reviewed the subject two years later for *Computers and the Humanities,* Potter identified nine articles reflecting on the state of the art. All of these, she noted, pointed to theoretical poverty, the most incisive of them indicating as the core problem the dominant and highly positivistic "idea of text" taken from ageing New Criticism (Wittig 1978). This diagnosis seems not to have had much of an effect on the inertial course of the field, however. Jerome McGann observed it still to be the case for the interpretative core of the humanities at the beginning of the twenty-first century (McGann 2004), despite the popularity of the digital humanities in the forecourts of interpretation.

The stalemate becomes historically significant when we ask Anthony Kenny's question: why "computers came just at the wrong time . . . when scholars' interests were moving from textual studies to critical theory" (1992: 9–10). Was the move to the theoretical high ground in the 1950s and 1960s in some sense a reaction to the juggernaut of quantification fuelled by the spectacular early successes of computing, as Kenny speculates? This juggernaut arose in the Anglophone world with the triumphalism of victory in the Second World War, in which superior technology played a spectacular role and the utopian promise of computing seemed limitless. But, as the immediately subsequent Cold War progressed, the computer began to take on sinister baggage through the uses to which it was put, for example in workplace automation (see Zuboff 1984), military defense systems, and the "electronic battlefield" of Vietnam.[2] These remained culturally dominant until, in 1991, the end of the Cold War and the beginning of the World Wide Web inaugurated a great change.[3]

I am radically simplifying the historical situation here (also omitting the role of personal computing hardware) in order vividly to raise a crucial series of questions: why did these events happen when they did? How are they connected? More generally, what *is* the scope of a historical enquiry into the digital humanities? How far afield must we go to contextualize it properly? Strands of development come together, but why? By what kinds of circumstances or forces are they nudged or triggered into relation? My specific purpose in asking is to begin to tease out a way of understanding technological history that can then be used to ask what beyond specific digital phenomena is shaping the cultural forms of the digital for the future, and how this shaping is to be grasped so that we might be shapers as well as shaped. Was there a process at work then that we can see now?

The occasional clues within the professional literature of those initial decades – mostly anomalous remarks and odd emphases – may seem quite minor and thoroughly dated, but they are worth following up to get to the desires and fears of the time. (Again, we are schooled to ask the same of the present for the future: what are our shaping desires and fears?) These prove significant beyond their bulk and time. Two examples follow.

First is the repeated linking of the computer with "drudgery," especially during the early period. It is true that the burden of calculation prior to machinery was a very real problem: it required mathematical abilities but made their exercise unworthy of those caught up in the activity (Goldstine 1993: 8ff; Pratt 1987: 20–44). Drudgery in the humanities is much rarer but it can be found, more in some kinds of work than others.

Milic zeroed in exactly here. He noted that, while good things were being made as a result of offloading drudgery onto computers, scholars' discovery of relief from "the brute labor of scholarship" had already led to their shift of interest from exploration to the type of work that "puts a premium on labor-saving" and so holds them "to projects which do not begin to take account of the real complexity and the potential beauty of the instrument." They were, he thought, "in danger of becoming [the machine's] victims" or mere attendants (1966: 3–4). He noted "the odium likely to greet" (which in fact did greet) some of the more imaginative ideas on offer – such as the automatic poetry-generation that linguist Margaret Masterman promoted as research into poetics.[4]

Now as then, assigning the role of drudge to computing tends severely to militate against imaginative play, participatory exploration, or experiment. It also, as Milic and others noted, invokes the language applicable to those devoted to a life of drudgery, namely servants and slaves – my second example. Once the language of servitude and slavery becomes the language of computing, the machine is thereby anthropomorphized as an underling; the technicians who tend it fit all too easily into the all-too-familiar position of rude mechanicals.[5] Caught up in the master–servant dialectic, high-status users, such as senior academics, tend to be affected analogously as masters are by their servants – that is, put into a relationship often imagined as that of parent to child. As Ruth Gladys Garcia has shown, this relationship is, however, potentially quite ambiguous, readily flipping polarity so as to infantilize the master (2009: 11). But, whichever polarity is active, separation is ensured, inequality is reinforced, and (by our lights, certainly) the potentialities of both master and servant are attenuated. Projection of the ancient social model onto the machine and into the culture of its use thus works powerfully against design for conversational interaction – against the computer as interlocutor and for it as passive respondent – and so shapes the future of the discipline and all it touches.

The problem we have had and still have – and will continue to have if we do nothing about it – is illustrated by the striking similarly of two near-term predictions for computing, one made in 1965, the other in 2001.

The first, written nearly 50 years ago by a correspondent for the Toronto *Globe and Mail*, imagines a typical domestic quandary soon to be solved, the journalist thinks, by a massive mainframe:

"There are six of us.

"The youngest is Bobby, who's 8.

"We've brought our own lunch.

"We've $20 to spend.

"Granny can't do much walking.

"And we have to be out by 7 o'clock.

"What is our best itinerary?"

One minute later, the Browns have their answer and are on their way through the streets of Montreal to enjoy a day at Expo 67.

(Webster 1965)

The other, a decade old but still current, carries the name of the inventor of the World Wide Web, Tim Berners-Lee, in a prominent *Scientific American* feature on the so-called but yet to be realized Semantic Web:

The entertainment system was belting out the Beatles' "We Can Work It Out" when the phone rang. When Pete answered, his phone turned the sound down by sending a message to all the other local devices that had a volume control. His sister, Lucy, was on the line from the doctor's office: "Mom needs to see a specialist and then has to have a series of physical therapy sessions"... At the doctor's office Lucy instructed her Semantic Web agent through her handheld Web browser. The agent promptly....
(Berners-Lee et al. 2001: 36)

Since 1965, progress has clearly been made in all but the imaginative form of computing: nearly 40 years on, computing is still in the popular imagination an obedient servant assigned to drudgery.

Identifying the computer thus and so reconfiguring the user as liberated for another purpose also invokes the curiously vacuous ideal of leisure, with the nagging question of what the liberated person is to do, hence what he or she is then *for*. It points also to the disturbing social effects of automation rippling through the society from long before Taylorian principles and Fordist practices codified industrial relations (Zuboff 1984); indeed, it identifies industrial automation as the future. While the release of Charlie Chaplin's *Modern Times* and the publication of Alan Turing's crucial paper in the same year, 1936, is a coincidence (though both perhaps respond in their very different ways to the same thing), nevertheless the circumstances of work depicted in both have repeatedly been dominant in applications of computing.

Nor has the "knowledge worker" been spared. Effects on intellectual work have not simply been a matter of making it more convenient, for, although artificial intelligence has progressed more slowly than expected, the distinction between knowledge known and information processed has been steadily eroded. This erosion began very early in the scientific work given specific form by Turing;[6] it entered the public sphere through popularizations in newspapers, magazines, and books,

such as Edmund Callis Berkeley's *Giant Brains, or Machines that Think* (1949),
and was reinforced by highly respected experts. The possibility of the computer
transgressing one of the few remaining areas of human uniqueness, the ability to
reason, could thus have seemed imminent to scholars from the beginning of the
digital humanities. Traces in the professional literature tell us that the threat seemed
real enough, opening up the question of what there remained for the scholar to do,
and thus to be for.[7]

Despite the technologists' many disappointments by problems that have proven
far more difficult than initially suspected, this threat lives on, though the level of hype
has declined. It is given real bite, however, by a tradition that goes far beyond the
immediate historical circumstances of computing's entry into the broader culture.
I am referring to the general assault of the sciences on human identity. Sigmund
Freud's often-repeated catalog of the "great outrages against [humankind's] self-
love" is the best-known account: he lists Copernicus in the sixteenth century,
Darwin in the nineteenth, and then himself for "the third and most irritating
insult... flung at the human mania of greatness": the psychoanalytic discovery
that we are not masters of our own house (1920: 246–247). But, as the molecular
biologist Jacques Monod explains (1972: 47–48), the moral imperative to defeat
human self-deception that Galileo championed is by its very nature set against
humankind's anthropocentric illusion. Hence, with the progress of the sciences,
Freud's list can only be the beginning of an indefinitely extensible catalog that has
in recent years seemed to grow by the day. From its very beginning, computing has
inspired and powered the assault as well as joined it.

Hence – so my argument goes – the clues of a profound disquiet about digital
machinery we find in both high- and lowbrow journalism, advertising, and other
forms of popular literature, including cartoons and comics, especially but not
exclusively during the early period. Such publications are an obvious first port of
call not only because they were so quick to react but also because scholars when
at home could not have avoided coming into contact with at least some of them.
These sources of scientific information, gossip, speculation, and hype demonstrate
among other things that beyond doubt scholars were exposed not only to the claims
and fantasies about computing but also to the genuine excitement surrounding the
new machine. The question then becomes why they were not more curious than
they seem to have been – why, as Milic said, they were satisfied "with such limited
objectives" as we find in the professional literature. "We are still not thinking of
the computer as anything but a myriad of clerks or assistants in one convenient
console," he concluded (1966: 4). And here, again, is the question to whose
various forms I keep returning: what about now? To what degree do we think any
differently today?

Unsurprisingly, by far the most imaginative and enthusiastic responses to computing outside of its immediate developers came from architects, artists, actors,
filmmakers, novelists, poets, and makers of other cultural artifacts. Catalogs of
exhibitions, such as "Cybernetic Serendipity" (Reichardt 1968), numerous articles

in the journal *Leonardo* (1968–), the historical retrospective essays in *White Heat Cold Logic* (Brown et al. 2010), and cultural histories such as Katherine Hayles' *How We Became Posthuman* (1999) and Hugh Kenner's *The Counterfeiters: An Historical Comedy* (2005) document the wealth. To choose but one example: the career of Gordon Pask, creator of "maverick machines" (Bird and Di Paolo 2008), suggests how surprisingly, wonderfully adventurous the early experimenters were – we might say, so far ahead of their time as still in essential ways to be ahead of ours. And again I ask, why is that? What is holding us back? What went wrong?

Looking back at that early period in the digital humanities, we must ask why such dull choices were being made. Practitioners were not forced by the technology, however primitive it may seem to us, to choose as they did. We know by looking to those wild artistic productions the great degree to which they were not forced. And yet again, looking from the present into the future, considering what seems an imaginative pathology, we must ask how we might treat the disease so as to do better.

Destinations Evolve

So far I have argued that predicting the future by projecting it from current technical know-how misleads: it ignores the multiple contingencies of history and human nature and so cannot prepare us to become knowing actors in making the future where it is made, in the present moment. I have argued that the history of the digital humanities, which we neither have nor know how to write but can begin to glimpse, is essential to that preparation. I have indicated how, once we allow ourselves to look outward into popular as well as scientific and scholarly contexts, the facts we do have begin to suggest the questions out of which history could be written. I have indicated a few of these. In the remainder of this chapter I want to turn first (in this section) to question our freedom in doing anything about the future and then (in the next) to consider what we might do.

Better *techné* should mean greater freedom to change the material conditions of life for better or worse, but discussions involving it so often imply an inevitable outcome, therefore a narrowing rather than expanding of possibilities. The deterministic language we find ourselves using – "impact" is currently the worst but not the only offender – implicitly places us in a space populated by objects like billiard balls, acted on by forces beyond our control, acting on others by impacting them.[8] I myself have verged on such language by suggesting we think about a *trajectory* for the digital humanities, though I was implying a piloted vehicle of exploration rather than an unmanned projectile. But now I want to be more cautious than before, not just to avoid suggesting that scholarship is a helpless creature of Fate but also to question our whole way of speaking about these matters. For, if we cannot get around this deterministic way of speaking, we cannot begin usefully to imagine the possible futures of the digital humanities, or anything else involved with technology.

When television was still relatively new, Raymond Williams began his study of its effects by noting the technological determinism in ordinary discourse:

> People often speak of a new world, a new society, a new phase of history, being created – "brought about" – by this or that new technology. Most of us know what is generally implied when such things are said. But this may be the central difficulty: that we have got so used to statements of this general kind, in our most ordinary discussions, that we can fail to realise their specific meanings .... For behind all such statements lie some of the most difficult and most unresolved historical and philosophical questions. Yet the questions are not posed by the statements; indeed they are ordinarily masked by them. (2004: 1)

The curious fact is that, although this determinism is trivially easy to dismiss as simply "wrong-headed superstition or ... a form of false consciousness" (Wyatt 2008: 172; on determinism see also the essays collected in Smith and Marx 1994), brushing it aside is evidently no cure: the majority of people, inside the academy and beyond, keep on talking as if machines made history. What is worse, by suggesting that nothing but perversity or stupidity is causing us to be so wrong-headed, dismissal only remasks the important questions to which Williams has pointed.

Writing specifically about the metaphor of "impact," John Law and John Whittaker argued some years ago that

> our problem ... does not lie in the fact that consequences, sometimes good and sometimes bad, have followed from the introduction of new technologies .... It lies, rather, *in the vocabulary that is used to describe these consequences.* This vocabulary is Newtonian in character. [Computers] are treated as being like projectiles which arrive from [wherever] and subsequently have an "impact" on social arrangements. It is as if the social world were best seen as a set of craters, the passive target of bits and pieces that are lobbed at it. This is surely wrong. (1986: 21)

Surely it is. But, as they say, the important matter here is the vocabulary – the words that bear the implicit perspectives – not the truth or falsity of any proposition these words are used to articulate.[9] In his essay on television, Williams seems to me exactly right when he argues that "the reality of determination is the setting of limits and the exertion of pressures, within which variable social practices are profoundly affected but never necessarily controlled" (2004: 133). But beneath the level of argument and beyond the specialized fields where it happens – hence in all the other academic disciplines and in the popular media – the billiard-ball/projectile analogy of impact, borne into use by its vocabulary, keeps uncritical belief in circulation. What can be done?

My suggestion is first to examine the remarkably successful analogy of impact close up so that we may figure out where its weaknesses lie, then to look for a stronger one, providing a better way of thinking and speaking. Some analogy is required because that is how we reason, by inferring conjecturally from the known to the unknown, or from simpler systems that we understand to more complex ones that we don't. Unlike a proposition, the correctness or incorrectness of an analogy is beside the point – all analogies are false by definition. Rather, they are useful in proportion to their strength. Thus, the projectile analogy is not so much wrong in itself as it is weak. The question we need to ask is how it fails: how is the computer *not* like a projectile, the disciplines *not* necessarily like a defenseless and passive target?

The projectile's otherness with respect to its target holds true: the digital computer *did* originate elsewhere, in the techno-sciences of warfare and commerce, and remains a techno-scientific instrument. So also the machine's autonomy, since by definition and design it *is* an automaton. The radical change in our working practices likewise confirms the aptness of a projectile's forceful impact. But the analogy breaks down fatally when we consider the necessarily instantaneous and irreversible linearity of this impact. Truth to computing in any discipline or other human culture requires cybernetic feedback between incoming technology and recipient practices, in an interaction that continues for as long as we wish to imagine, in ways that are not predictable and in which the technology is continually modified by its recipients. To put the matter another way, the analogy fails because no projectile's target has the remarkably robust self-identity of human social institutions, which change much more selectively than promotional hype would lead us to believe. Change in them is negotiated and very often rejected. How else could the library, for example, have endured in recognizable form for the past five thousand years?

As an alternative, I suggest that we look to the sciences of our times for an analogy that preserves otherness and forceful change but substitutes interaction for impact and assertive self-identity for passive victimhood. Rather than think in terms shaped by linear causality – which, again, is not simply wrong but rather inadequate to our more complex problem – I suggest drawing an analogy from biological evolution. A very strong candidate is molecular biologist Jacques Monod's formulation of evolutionary struggle, not for a Spencerian "survival of the fittest" in contest among individuals but between an organism's genetically programmed "reproductive invariance" and the randomness of the environment in which the organism lives. In *Chance and Necessity: An Essay on the Natural Philosophy of Modern Biology* (1972), Monod makes a persuasive case for the origins of the entire biosphere, in all its rich complexity, in this evolutionary struggle.

By invoking Monod I am suggesting that we think of the relationship between computing technology and the disciplines of the humanities as a moment-by-moment becoming of their futures, to some degree unpredictably, through an ongoing contest between the disciplines' strong sense of themselves on the one hand and all that contingently affects them, including the relentless development of digital technologies, on the other. If the analogy holds, then it offers a way not only of avoiding both disciplinary essentialism and technological determinism (again the two extremes in Raymond Williams' argument) but also of interrelating the academy and society much more helpfully than the old monastic or the new commercial models have to offer us now.

"Analogy is an identity of relationships," not of things, Simone Weil once pointed out (1978: 85). But to invoke an analogy is to assume that the two parties involved operate under the same laws, or exist in the same world: otherwise the relationships would be incommensurable. That social systems are made by biological entities as extensions of their evolutionary development would thus seem to make analogies between the two inherently promising. Perhaps this likelihood, the rising cultural importance of biology, and the apparent fitness of Monod's model are enough to recommend further exploration. Limited space stops me from doing that here.

Destination is Resonance

What might we look forward to?

Writing in the mid-1970s for the journal *Leonardo*,[10] operations researcher Michael Thompson observed that "when the user directly 'converses' with the machine . . . the almost instantaneous replies immediately suggest the possibility of improvisations, as if on a musical instrument" (1974: 227). His analogy – researcher is to computer as musician is to instrument – points back to the cybernetics of human–machine systems.[11] Among many other things, cybernetics inspired an exuberant flowering of experimental art (to which I referred earlier) at least in part because, as Roy Ascott said, it represented "a development in science which [held] out the promise of taking art seriously" (1968: 257) and so giving it new scope for action. The action it inspired was specifically interactive and participatory, constituting in the words of cinematographer and haptic digital artist Jeffrey Shaw "a new relationship between the producer and the consumer of artefacts, one where the builder of the interactive system and its users participate in a situation of cocreative formulation, discovery and experience" (Shaw et al. 2011: 223).

It seems to me that the central question for research in the digital humanities most promisingly begins here, with the artists. The question is how – with help from several other fields – we might design and engineer digital means for enabling a corresponding relationship between interpreter and artifact – or, in simpler terms, how we might put into the interpreter's cognitive hand a tool as powerfully co-creative as a chisel or a paintbrush. For the humanities I am thinking, for example, of nothing more exotic than the phenomenology of reading, in which according to the best theorizing we have reader and text co-create each other. (Or, say that something else happens when we read, or look at a painting, or listen to music critically. The challenge is to model that digitally.) But when we consider the current products of the digital humanities, fine and helpful as they are, we see very little if anything at all that gets beyond the forecourts of interpretation to that inner core of scholarly experience, to where scholarship actually happens. What we see mostly are "knowledge jukeboxes," as I call them: resources that are clever to be sure, filled with important data whose manipulation and vending do real service to the humanities, but still built for research that in large measure happens elsewhere by other means. What's stopping us from going further?

There are *very* difficult technical challenges. But more formidable because less visible than these is a notion that, like technological determinism, remains powerful despite persuasive argument from the specialists. It comes to us with the popular term *mediation* – which I have been studiously avoiding throughout this essay. Now is time to say why.

Mediation is a highly complex word entangled within several different systems of thought. The difficulty it causes us in the present context stems from a failure to distinguish two senses of its root term, *medium*: (a) a neutral conduit or instrument and (b) something like an ecological niche or cybernetic system.[12] Referring to (a), Williams remarks that "In most modern science and philosophy, and especially in thinking about language, this idea of a medium has been dispensed with" (2004: 203). Nevertheless it remains, instantiated for us in the form of human–machine communication thought to be and so constructed as a linear point-A-to-point-B process across an interface.

There are at least two historical sources for this idea of human–machine communication: the mathematical model proposed by Claude Shannon and Warren Weaver in 1948–1949 and the actual experience of using digital machinery in the 30-year period from the first installations in businesses and universities until the widespread adoption of the "microcomputer" in the 1980s. Let me explain briefly. In his *Scientific American* popularization of the model (1949), Weaver begins by asking "How do men communicate, one with another?" He lists several means familiar to his readers, then in effect reduces the human situation to the diagram given in Figure 2.2, which passes into mathematical form, picks up both the world-changing potential for widespread application *and the authority of the science it invokes*, and then returns to ordinary discourse as an answer to his initial question: this is how men communicate, one with another. The clarity of the argument and demonstrable success in application made this "transmission model of communication" hugely influential well beyond engineering. Despite opposition from the relevant social sciences and from system designers, it continues; "its endurance in popular discussion is a real liability," as David Chandler has written (2008; OTA [Office of Technology Assessment, Congress of the United States], 1995: 77; see also McLuhan et al. 1978: 93–94, which reports on work eventually published in McLuhan and McLuhan 1980).

That much of the story is well known. In addition, however, the viral idea of a neutral conduit drew strength from users' formative encounters with computing

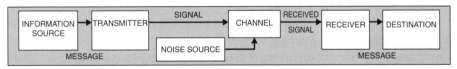

Figure 2.2 The mathematical model proposed by Claude Shannon and Warren Weaver in 1948-49. *Source:* Warren Weaver (1949) "The Mathematics of Communication." *Scientific American*, 181(1), 11–15. Reproduced with permission. Copyright © 1949 Scientific American, Inc. All rights reserved.

machinery during the mainframe era, *when the transmission model diagrammed experience*. Like a signal in Weaver's diagram, the typical user had to traverse physical distance from office to computing center to deliver his or her program, back and forth as many times as it took to get it to work properly. The "turn-around time," measured in hours or days, compelled very careful planning, proofreading, and checking; the casual experimentalism we now practice was then unknown. The formidably rebarbative nature of the whole process (its "noise") gave purchase and staying power to the linear metaphor. So also the public's vicarious experience of the machine, copiously imagined in the popular press, which mythologized it, in one telling instance as "The Oracle on 57th Street" – IBM's World Headquarters, where from 1948 to 1954 the huge, glittering Selective Sequence Automatic Calculator was on public display (*Saturday Evening Post*, December 16, 1950; see IBM Archives n.d.).

Once computers became "personal" one might think that immediate presence, familiarity, and interactivity would have worked to defeat the transmission model, the more so as machines became faster and friendlier. But we know from various sources that social phenomena are marked, often indelibly, by the historically specific contexts of their origins (Stinchcombe 1965; cf. Tillyard 1958: 11–12; Lounsbury and Ventresca 2002). They are, as we say, *imprinted*. I suggest, then, that this is what happened during the cultural assimilation of computing in the early years, and that we need a new figure of thought, such as Thompson's, to replace that imprint.

Watchfulness

My argument for the future as we might build it, then, is that it lies most hopefully in the exploration of an analogy of resonance, conversation, or the like. If computing is to be useful for more than putting stuff out there and getting it back again then we'll have to confront the predicament toward which (to borrow words from Wittgenstein) "the crystalline purity of [algorithmic] logic" drives us: "slippery ice where there is no friction," rendering us "unable to walk" (1958: 46 (item 107)). Projecting current know-how into the future gives us no traction. It gives us only a better-engineered "myriad of clerks or assistants in one convenient console," not the sighting of "the real complexity and the potential beauty of the instrument" that Milic longed for. And ultimately, as Winograd and Flores said, the question is what "ways of being" we want to make possible.

But the world does not stand still, as I said earlier. Joseph Weizenbaum argued in 1972 that "much more subtle and ultimately much more important side effects" of computing are at play than our immediate research projects conceive (1972: 609). For the humanities, the proverbial thief in the night seems to me the accumulation of primary and secondary resources – all those knowledge jukeboxes bulging with their texts, images, and sounds. What does it mean to have these as the regular furniture of research?

My best guess is that there are at minimum four threshold effects:

1. spreading of the researcher's attention over a widening field of possibilities under constraints of time, with growing emphasis on interdisciplinary research, a concomitant imperative for us to understand how to do it well, and a shift from an essentialist epistemology, which seeks knowledge by going deep, to one that proceeds by assembling and correlating a multitude of voices, and so going wide (cf. Rorty 2004);
2. rising importance for many fields of argument in the face of ever greater masses of easily available evidence for any conceivable proposition;
3. growing realization that along with everything else in the living and nonliving world our cultural artifacts are fundamentally probabilistic and theorizing about them susceptible to computational modeling and simulation (McCarty 2010: 5–6); hence
4. bridging of the sciences and humanities by making explicit the conjectural space in which digital models of these artifacts allow them to be treated as if they were natural objects and so fit subjects for scientific reasoning (McCarty 2007).

So here, I think, is the digital medium in that other, better sense: not a Shannon–Weaver gauntlet to be run but as water is to the swimmer, gravity to the dancer, or wood to the carver. William Wulf once remarked that engineering practice is "design against constraint" (2000). Here, perhaps, are our constraints.

"What's driving the change, where is it heading and what might the humanities look like as a result?" Frighteningly, thrillingly, it's up to us.

Notes

1. Consider, for example, IBM's announcement (at the time of writing) of "cognitive computing" circuitry in a working prototype that, if equal to the promise, would change what we mean by "computer" (IBM 2011).
2. On computing in the Cold War, see Edwards (1996); on the Cold War more generally, see Whitfield (1996).
3. The events in question are these: Tim Berners-Lee's initial proposal for an information management system, March 1989; the fall of the Berlin Wall, November 1989; Berners-Lee's formal proposal for a "World Wide Web," November 1990; public release of the web, August 1991; dissolution of the Soviet Union, December 1991.
4. On computerized poetry see Masterman and McKinnon Wood (1970) and Masterman (1971); cf. Leavis (1970) for a severe reaction; note Milic (1966).
5. The term is Shakespeare's , referring to Bottom and his fellows in *A Midsummer Night's Dream*, III.ii.9.
6. The influence of machine on brain and brain on machine forms a cybernetic loop: from Turing's imagined mathematician to his abstract machine (1936); from that machine to McCulloch's and Pitts' model of the brain (1943); from their brain to von Neumann's design for digital machinery (1945, as we know from its neurophysiological vocabulary

and McCulloch 1961: 9); from that design to models of cognition; and so on. Cf. Otis (2001) for the reciprocal relationship between ideas of the body and designs for machines.

7. See, for example, Pegues' curious reassurance that "The purpose of the machine is . . . to free the humanist for the important work of literary criticism by providing him with large and accurate masses of data that may be used by him in the work *which only he can accomplish*" (Pegues 1965: 107, emphasis added). See also Nold (1975).

8. On "impact" see Law and Whittaker (1986, quoted below), Pannabecker (1991), Petrina (1993), and Edwards (1994).

9. Here I use the terms "metaphor" and "analogy" more or less interchangeably; both are highly polysemous terms. For the literature on analogy see the summary in McCarty (2005: 28–29). The work on metaphor since the 1980s has shown that figures of speech are figures of thought with profound consequences for everything we do; see especially Ortony (1993) and Gibbs (2008). Note also Morgan and Morrison (1999), whose collected essays show that scientific models do not merely stimulate research but also shape and direct it; see also McCarty (2005: 20–72).

10. *Leonardo* was founded in 1968 in Paris to emphasize "the writings of artists who use science and developing technologies in their work"; see www.leonardo.info.

11. On the cybernetics movement and its legacy, see Heims (1993), Dupuy (2000), and Husbands and Holland (2008).

12. In Raymond Williams' more philosophical terms, (a) "the neutral process of the interaction of separate forms" and (b) "an active process in which the form of the mediation alters the things mediated, or by its nature indicates their nature" (1983: 204–207).

References

Ascott, R. (1968) "The Cybernetic Stance: My Process and Purpose." *Leonardo*, 1(2), 105–112.

Automatic Language Processing Advisory Committee (ALPAC) (1966) *Language and Machines: Computers in Translation and Linguistics*. Publication 1416. Washington, DC: National Academy of Sciences, National Research Council.

Berkeley, E.C. (1949) *Giant Brains or Machines that Think*. New York: John Wiley & Sons.

Berners-Lee, T., Hendler, J., and Lassila, O. (2001) "The Semantic Web: A New Form of Web Content that is Meaningful to Computers Will Unleash a Revolution of New Possibilities." *Scientific American* (May), 35–43.

Bird, J. and Di Paolo, E. (2008) "Gordon Pask and His Maverick Machines" in P. Husbands, O. Holland, and M. Wheeler, eds., *The Mechanical Mind in History*. Cambridge, MA: MIT Press, pp. 185–211.

Brown, P., Gere, C., Lambert, N., and Mason, C. (2010) *White Heat Cold Logic: British Computer Art 1960–1980*. Cambridge, MA: MIT Press.

Busa, R. (1980) "The Annals of Humanities Computing: The *Index Thomisticus*." *Computers and the Humanities*, 14, 83–90.

Chandler, D. (2008) "The Transmission Model of Communication." www.aber.ac.uk/media /Documents/short/trans.html.

Dreyfus, H.L. (1965) "Alchemy and Artificial Intelligence." *Rand Papers*, P-3244. Santa Monica, CA: RAND Corporation.

Dupuy, J.-P. (2000 [1994]) *The Mechanization of the Mind: On the Origins of Cognitive Science*, trans. M.B. DeBevoise. Princeton, NJ: Princeton University Press.

Edwards, P.N. (1994) "From 'Impact' to Social Process: Computers in Society and Culture" in S. Jasanoff, G.E. Markle, J.C. Petersen, and T. Pinch, eds., *Handbook of Science and Technology Studies*. Berkeley, CA: Sage, pp. 257–285.

Edwards, P.N. (1996) *The Closed World: Computers and the Politics of Discourse in Cold War America*. Cambridge, MA: MIT Press.

Foster, I. (2011) "How Computation Changes Research" in T. Bartscherer and R. Coover, eds., *Switching Codes: Thinking Through Digital Technology in the Humanities and the Arts*. Chicago, IL: University of Chicago Press, pp. 15–37.

Freud, S. (1920) *A General Introduction to Psychoanalysis*, trans. G. Stanley Hall. New York: Boni & Liveright.

Garcia, R.G. (2009) *"I Will Not Call Her Servant": Ambiguity and Power in Master–Servant Relationships in the Eighteenth-Century Novel*. Doctoral dissertation. City University of New York.

Gibbs, R.W., ed. (2008) *The Cambridge Handbook of Metaphor and Thought*. Cambridge: Cambridge University Press.

Gödel, K. (2004 [1931]) "On Formally Undecidable Propositions of *Principia Mathematica* and Related Systems" in M. David, ed., *The Undecidable: Basic Papers on Undecidable Propositions, Unsolvable Problems and Computable Functions*. Mineola, NY: Dover Publications, pp. 4–38.

Goldstine, H.H. (1993 [1972]) *The Computer from Pascal to von Neumann*, 2nd edn. Princeton, NJ: Princeton University Press.

Hayles, N.K. (1999) *How We Became Posthuman: Virtual Bodies in Cybernetics, Literature, and Informatics*. Chicago, IL: University of Chicago Press.

Heims, S.J. (1993 [1991]) *Constructing a Social Science for Postwar America: The Cybernetics Group, 1946–1953*. Cambridge, MA: MIT Press.

Husbands, P. and Holland, O. (2008) "The Ratio Club: A Hub of British Cybernetics," in P. Husbands, O. Holland, and M. Wheeler, eds., *The Mechanical Mind in History*. Cambridge, MA: MIT Press, pp. 91–148.

IBM (2011) "IBM Unveils Cognitive Computing Chips" (August 18). www-03.ibm.com /press/us/en/pressrelease/35251.wss.

IBM Archives (n.d.) "John Backus." www-03.ibm.com/ibm/history/exhibits/builders /builders_backus.html.

Kenner, H. (2005 [1968]) *The Counterfeiters: An Historical Comedy*. Norman, OK: Dalkey Archive Press.

Kenny, A. (1992) *Computers and the Humanities*. Ninth British Library Research Lecture. London: The British Library.

Law, J. and Whittaker, J. (1986) "On the Malleability of People and Computers: Why the PC is not a Projectile" in *Proceedings of the Third ACM-SOGOIS Conference on Office Automation Systems*. New York: Association of Computing Machinery, pp. 21–32.

Leavis, F.R. (1970) "'Literarism' versus 'Scientism': The Misconception and the Menace." *Times Literary Supplement* (April 23), 441–444.

Liu, A. (2011) "'We Will Really Know'" in T. Bartscherer and R. Coover, eds., *Switching Codes: Thinking Through Digital Technology in the Humanities and the Arts*. Chicago, IL: University of Chicago Press, pp. 89–94.

Lounsbury, M. and Ventresca, M.J. (2002) "Social Structure and Organizations Revisited." *Research in the Sociology of Organizations*, 19, 3–36.

Mahoney, M.S. (2011) *Histories of Computing*, ed. T. Haigh. Cambridge, MA: Harvard University Press.

Masterman, M. (1971) "Computerized Haiku" in J. Reichardt, ed., *Cybernetics, Art and Ideas*. London: Studio Vista, pp. 175–183.

Masterman, M. and McKinnon Wood, R. (1970) "The Poet and the Computer." *Times Literary Supplement* (June 18), 667–668.

McCarty, W. (2005) *Humanities Computing*. Basingstoke: Palgrave.

McCarty, W. (2007) "Being Reborn: The Humanities, Computing and Styles of Scientific Reasoning." *New Technology in Medieval and Renaissance Studies* 1, 1–23.

McCarty, W., ed. (2010) *Text and Genre in Reconstruction: Effects of Digitization on Ideas, Behaviours, Products and Institutions*. Cambridge: Open Book.

McCulloch, W. (1965 [1961]) "What Is a Number, that a Man May Know It, and a Man, that He May Know a Number?" in W. McCulloch, ed., *Embodiments of Mind*. Cambridge, MA: MIT Press, pp. 1–18.

McCulloch, W. and Pitts, W. (1965 [1943]) "A Logical Calculus of Ideas Immanent in Nervous Activity" in W. McCulloch, ed., *Embodiments of Mind*. Cambridge, MA: MIT Press, pp. 19–39.

McGann, J. (2004) "Marking Texts of Many Dimensions" in S. Schreibman, R. Siemens, and J. Unsworth, eds., *A Companion to Digital Humanities*. Oxford: Blackwell, pp. 198–217.

McLuhan, M. and McLuhan, E. (1980) *The Laws of Media: The New Science*. Toronto, ON: University of Toronto Press.

McLuhan, M., Hutchon, K., and McLuhan, E. (1978) "Multi-Media: The Laws of Media." *English Journal*, 67(8), 92–94.

Milic, L. (1966) "The Next Step." *Computers and the Humanities*, 1(1), 3–6.

Monod, J. (1972 [1970]) *Chance and Necessity: An Essay on the Natural Philosophy of Modern Biology*, trans. A. Wainhouse. London: Collins.

Morgan, M.S. and Morrison, M., eds. (1999) *Models as Mediators: Perspectives on Natural and Social Science*. Cambridge: Cambridge University Press.

Nold, E.W. (1975) "Fear and Trembling: The Humanist Approaches the Computer." *College Composition and Communication*, 26(3), 269–273.

Ortony, A., ed. (1993 [1979]) *Metaphor and Thought*, 2nd edn. Cambridge: Cambridge University Press.

OTA [Office of Technology Assessment, Congress of the United States] (1995) *Global Communications: Opportunities for Trade and Aid*. OTA-ITC-642. Washington, DC: US Government Printing Office.

Otis, L. (2001) *Networking: Communicating with Bodies and Machines in the Nineteenth Century*. Ann Arbor, MI: University of Michigan Press.

Pannabecker, J.R. (1991) "Technological Impacts and Determinism in Technology Education: Alternate Metaphors from Social Constructivism." *Journal of Technology Education*, 3(1). http://scholar.lib.vt.edu/ejournals/JTE/v3n1/pannabecker.pdf.

Pegues, Fr. J. (1965) "Editorial: Computer Research in the Humanities." *Journal of Higher Education*, 36(2), 105–108.

Petrina, S. (1993) "Questioning the Language that We Use: A Reaction to Pannabecker's Critique of the Technological Impact Metaphor." *Journal of Technology Education*, 4(1), 51–57.

Potter, R., ed. (1989) *Literary Computing and Literary Criticism: Theoretical and Practical Essays on Theme and Rhetoric*. Philadelphia, PA: University of Pennsylvania Press.

Potter, R. (1991) "Statistical Analysis of Literature: A Retrospective on *Computers and the Humanities, 1966–1990.*" *Computers and the Humanities*, 25, 401–429.

Pratt, V. (1987) *Thinking Machines: The Evolution of Artificial Intelligence.* Oxford: Blackwell.

Reichardt, J., ed. (1968) "Cybernetic Serendipity," *special issue of Studio International* (August).

Rorty, R. (2004 [2000]) "Being that can be Understood is Language." *London Review of Books*, 22(6), 23–25.

Shaw, J., Kenderdine, S., and Coover, R. (2011) "Re-place: The Embodiment of Virtual Space" in T. Bartscherer and R. Coover, eds., *Switching Codes: Thinking Through Digital Technology in the Humanities and the Arts*. Chicago, IL: University of Chicago Press, pp. 218–237.

Smith, M.R. and Marx, L., eds. (1994) *Does Technology Drive History? The Dilemma of Technological Determinism*. Cambridge MA: MIT Press.

Stinchcombe, A.L. (1965) "Social Structure and Organizations" in J.G. March, ed., *Handbook of Organizations*. Chicago, IL: Rand McNally, pp. 142–193.

Thompson, M. (1974) "Intelligent Computers and Visual Artists." *Leonardo*, 7(3), 227–234.

Tillyard, E.M.W. (1958) *The Muse Unchained: An Intimate Account of the Revolution in English Studies at Cambridge*. London: Bowes & Bowes.

Turing, A. (2004 [1936]) "On Computable Numbers, with an Application to the Entscheidungsproblem" in *The Undecidable: Basic Papers on Undecidable Propositions, Unsolvable Problems and Computable Functions*. Mineola, NY: Dover Publications, pp. 115–154.

Vinnikov, V. (1999) "We Shall Know: Hilbert's Apology." *Mathematical Intelligencer*, 21(1), 42–46.

von Neumann, J. (1993 [1945]) "First Draft of a Report on the EDVAC." *IEEE Annals of the History of Computing*, 15(4), 27–75.

Weaver, W. (1949) "The Mathematics of Communication." *Scientific American*, 181(1), 11–15.

Webster, A. (1965) "Computers: The New Age of Miracles. Hundreds of Brains in a Thimble." *Globe and Mail* (Toronto, Canada) (November 16).

Weil, S. (1978 [1959]) *Lectures on Philosophy*, trans. H. Price. Cambridge: Cambridge University Press.

Weizenbaum, J. (1972) "On the Impact of the Computer on Society." *Science*, NS 176(4035), 609–614.

Whitfield, S.J. (1996 [1991]) *The Culture of the Cold War*, 2nd edn. Baltimore, MD: Johns Hopkins University Press.

Wilks, Y.A. (1972) *Grammar, Meaning and the Machine Analysis of Language*. London: Routledge & Kegan Paul.

Williams, R. (1983 [1976]) *Keywords: A Vocabulary of Culture and Society*, rev edn. New York: Oxford University Press.

Williams, R. (2004 [1974]) *Television: Technology and Cultural Form*, 2nd edn, ed. E. Williams. London: Routledge.

Winograd, T. and Flores, F. (1986) *Understanding Computers and Cognition: A New Foundation for Design*. New York: Addison-Wesley.

Wittgenstein, L. (1958 [1953]) *Philosophical Investigations*, trans. G.E.M. Anscombe, 2nd edn. Oxford: Blackwell.

Wittig, S. (1978) "The Computer and the Concept of Text." *Computers and the Humanities*, 11, 211–215.

Wulf, W.A. (2000) "The Nature of Engineering, the Science of the Humanities, and Gödel's Theorem (Interview)." *Ubiquity*, 1(28). http://ubiquity.acm.org/article.cfm?id=351308.

Wyatt, S. (2008) "Technological Determinism is Dead; Long Live Technological Determinism" in E.J. Hackett, O. Amsterdamska, M. Lynch, and J. Wajcman, eds., *The Handbook of Science and Technology Studies*, 3rd edn. Cambridge, MA: MIT Press, pp. 165–180.

Zuboff, S. (1984) *In the Age of the Smart Machine: The Future of Work and Power*. New York: Basic Books.

3

Media Dynamics and the Lessons of History

The "Gutenberg Parenthesis" as Restoration Topos

Thomas Pettitt

At a time when change in media technology is accelerating to the degree that a handbook on media studies prefers to deal not with the media but with media dynamics, a glance at the historical dimension may be a salutary exercise. We are not the first to cope with a media revolution by expatiating on its real or anticipated impact (see Baron 2009 for a lively survey), but, perhaps precisely because of this acceleration, commentators over the past half-century or so have been particularly given to comparing recent or ongoing developments with earlier changes reckoned to be of a similar magnitude.

Renaissance commentary responding to the impact of printing generated a disputed historiography of when, where, and by whom it was discovered; a disputed mythology of its origins (a gift from God for the propagation of the true faith or one of the diabolical arts for which Dr. Faustus sold his soul); and a disputed diagnosis of its results (a blessing that would spread texts or a curse that would corrupt them). And, thanks precisely to the medium whose arrival was the issue of disagreement, contributions to these disputes have survived in ample quantities for media historians to work on (Eisenstein 2011).

Responses to the arrival of the Internet (likewise as recorded in the new medium itself) can match most of this. There are legends that it was invented by the American military; that it was invented by Al Gore; that Al Gore claimed he invented it. The digital social media are being deployed by popular freedom movements around the globe, but Google is making us stupid (Carr 2008). The thousands of sites claiming the Internet was created by God happily outnumber the hundreds claiming it was invented by the Devil (unless we include the two million claiming that the Internet *is* the Devil). But, whereas Renaissance observers do not seem to have invoked parallels between the printing revolution and the arrival of writing, juxtaposing our digital, Internet revolution with both the printing and writing revolutions is routine in current commentary, academic and otherwise.

A Companion to New Media Dynamics, First Edition. Edited by John Hartley, Jean Burgess, and Axel Bruns.
© 2013 John Wiley & Sons, Ltd. Published 2015 by John Wiley & Sons, Ltd.

A historical perspective predictably discovers that an emergent media technology can achieve dominance for a while and, when its day is over, decline to residual status as something newer takes it place: "In the long history of the book, the mass-produced volumes of our time constitute only a single chapter" (Wright 2009: 59). But it has also prompted paradoxical suggestions to the effect that one or other of the media technologies to emerge in recent times, despite the advances that qualify it as revolutionary, can in other respects be seen as restoring media conditions obtaining prior to some earlier revolution. What came in between, rather than a phase (day; chapter) in an ongoing sequence, is perceived as an interlude, an interruption of something else that resumes when it is over.

A "restoration" of this kind is distinct from an actual technological set-back like the reversion to predominantly illiterate conditions that may have occurred in Western Europe following the fall of the Roman Empire, or our imminent recourse to pen and paper when the Internet succumbs to the final, incurable, virus. A restoration is the resumption of prior conditions qualified by whatever has happened in the meantime – here the return to prominence, after a hiatus, of earlier features of cultural mediation, only now at a more advanced level of technology. And it is of course other and more than the ephemeral "retro" fashions that assign a cultural cachet to the media technologies of the day before yesterday, be it the current fads for gramophone records, typewriters, and fountain pens or the preference in refined Renaissance circles for manuscript copies even though printed texts were available.

Recognizable despite variations in the revolutions that are identified as the interruption and the resumption, and beneath the various images and metaphors deployed to formulate it, the restoration pattern has been advocated over the past several decades with an incidence qualifying it as a currently active topos in the discourse of media history.[1] That is to say, it belongs among those commonplace but powerful concepts, images or lines of argument ("the book is dead"; "agent of change"; "the medium is the message"; "the walled garden") which prove viable and useful in discussion within a particular field of study, in this case the deep history of media technology which includes not only the "new" (digital) and the "old" (analog) media, but print, writing and speech. In the nature of things it is unlikely that all applications of a given topos are right: once established it can shape perceptions as well as reflect realities. But it should not be assumed, conversely, that a given application, just because it *is* a topos, must be wrong.

This one comes in various guises, not infrequently with negative connotations: witness novelist John Updike's exclamation at the prospect of having to make a living in a postcopyright, digital age not from publication royalties but from the interviews and personal appearances for which his works provided the stimulus:

> Does this not throw us back to the pre-literate societies, where only the present, live person can make an impression and offer, as it were, value? Have not writers, since the onset of the Gutenberg revolution, imagined that they already were, in their written and printed texts, giving an "access to the creator" . . . ? (Updike 2006)

In an equally appalled response to current media developments that emphasizes the perspective of a completed interlude, Nicholas Carr fears that with the decline of the "deep reading" enabled and encouraged by printed books we will "revert to the historical norm" – for widespread book reading "was a brief 'anomaly' in our intellectual history" (Carr 2010: 108).

One of the latest variants of the restoration topos is the suggestion that we are in the process of closing a "Gutenberg Parenthesis" in the history of media technology: a period of four to five centuries in which the mediation of verbal culture has been dominated by print technology in general and the printed book in particular. Developed in the mid-1990s by Professors Lars Ole Sauerberg (the originator of the term itself) and Marianne Børch of the University of Southern Denmark, this is a highly appropriate formulation of the restoration trajectory, given the way a sentence resumes a line of thought when an interjected parenthesis closes while the ultimate import of the sentence is nonetheless affected by its presence. The extent and vigor of responses to its more recent international propagation (Pettitt 2007; Sauerberg 2009) may be an acknowledgment of the effectiveness of the parenthesis image in conveying exactly what is at stake in asserting an interruption–restoration pattern in media history (for a review see Sauerberg et al. 2011).

Present and Past: Juxtapositions

Comparisons between modern media conditions and those of other eras in both scholarly and journalistic discussion take various forms. The most straightforward approach is a one-to-one equation between a medium or device currently in the public eye and something ancient or at least quaintly outdated, suggesting an analogy in their natures or an equivalence in their functions – occasionally for effect, mainly as a means of better understanding one or both of them.

So the printed almanac has been explained both as "the iPhone of early America" (McCarthy 2010) and as "the information superhighway (or cobbled lane, at any rate) of the later sixteenth century" (Rhodes 2000: 185). The iPod fills the same cultural niche as the Aldine Press pocket editions of classics in the early sixteenth century (Perrault and Crummett 2009), while blogging was anticipated by paragraph-length snippets of news and information in early newspapers (Darnton 2010) and the pencil might be seen as "the first laptop" (Baron 2009: 40). If the telegraph was "the Victorian Internet" (Standage 1998) or the information highway of Thoreau's day (Baron 2009: 33), the wax "tables" on which Shakespeare's tragic hero noted down the import of the ghost's message qualified as "Hamlet's Blackberry" (Powers 2010) and the social function of medieval bards has its modern analogue in popular television and digital storytelling (Hartley 2009).

Other historical comparisons rather juxtapose major upheavals in the development of media technology, and invoking the printing revolution has become something of a formula in introducing studies of the digital media, which are causing "a textual revolution comparable to the one initiated by the invention of printing from moveable type in the fifteenth century" (Shillingsburg 2006: 4; cf. Darnton 2009: xiv). The implication is often that, since the two revolutions produced challenges and confusions of similar complexity and magnitude, comparisons will be conducive to insight, and in both directions.

Introducing a collection of studies on early modern media that will "explore the complex interactions between a technologically advanced culture of the printed book and a still powerful traditional culture based on the spoken word, spectacle, and the manuscript," Michael Bristol and Arthur Marotti emphasize that their contributors do so from the privileged vantage point of "our own transitional moment as we attempt to negotiate the shift from typographic to electronic and visual media" (Bristol and Marotti 2000: 6–7). This is also the main thrust of an exciting collection of papers on early-modern literature and culture based on the perception that aspects of the period's print technology amount to a "Renaissance Computer": "The experience of our own new technology has enabled us to re-imagine the impact of new technologies in the past" (Rhodes and Sawday 2000: 1–2).

Conversely, we will be better able to understand and so cope with the rapid advances in media technology in our own times by seeking insights into the equally powerful typographical revolution in late-medieval and early-modern media (Finnegan 1988: 5; Landow 2006: 49–52). The point was made explicitly in the title of James Dewar's position paper for the Rand Corporation: "The Information Age and the Printing Press: Looking Backward to See Ahead" (1998). Nor has it escaped attention that this perspective offers a persuasive argument for the modern relevance of academic research into media history: "Understanding print and its history is thus more than simply a quest to understand a past communications revolution; it is also a means of better understanding our world as we negotiate the current communications revolution and anticipate its future" (Baron et al. 2007: 313). Such juxtapositions of revolutions approximate to the restoration topos when acknowledging that the later one encompasses the demise of the media technology that emerged with the earlier, invariably print and the book. As early as 1894 this was the startling message of a European commentator after visiting the workshop of Thomas Edison: "printing, which since 1436 has reigned despotically over the mind of man, is ... threatened with death by the various devices for registering sound which have been lately invented" (in Eisenstein 2011: 224), and the digital revolution has in turn prompted the many current predictions that "the book is dead" (Young 2007), "print is dead" (Gomez 2009), and "print is dying" (Mod 2010), and heralding of "the end of the reign of the book" (Chartier 1997) – the metaphors implying there was an earlier beginning to what is now terminating, sometimes with the explicit suggestion that we are returning to conditions "that preceded the triumph of print" (Birkerts 2006: 160).

The same sense of a beginning and ending also applies to attitudes or practices associated with the book: "Where books created the need for protecting intellectual property rights, the Internet is destroying those protections" (Dewar and Ang 2007: 370). Parenthetical imagery is affectively achieved when Gutenberg and digital technology are said to be "historical bookends" that "bracket" the period of printed mass media (Kluth 2006).

Restorations: Media Technology

Fully fledged formulations of the restoration topos, including the Gutenberg Parenthesis, specify not merely the rise and fall of the intermediate technology but also the medium that was deposed and is now restored, and variants can be classified in terms of their identification, among the options available, of the interrupting and restoring revolutions: the arrival of writing and printing for the first; of analog and digital media for the second.

Analog Mass Media

The latter choice was not available to the two best-known exponents of the restoration topos, Marshall McLuhan and Walter Ong, as they wrote (respectively) before the digital revolution got under way and before it was clear how important it would be and what direction it was taking. But, while agreeing that the restoration was achieved by analog media, they differ on the nature and timing of the interruption.

As its title announces, Marshall McLuhan's *The Gutenberg Galaxy* points to the arrival of the printing press as definitive of the first, disruptive, revolution. What it disrupts is nonetheless "preliterate" or "nonliterate" mediation, the apparent contradiction resolved by McLuhan's insistence that scribal transmission had very limited significance in the overall media picture, so that the cultural impact of literacy had to await the arrival of print (McLuhan 1962: 54). In his time, the ascendancy of print was being threatened by the growth of analog media technologies, notably radio, television, records, and film, leading to a restoration of earlier conditions, a "reversal which makes our age 'connatural'... with non-literate cultures." We no longer have difficulty in understanding "the native or non-literate experience, ... because we have recreated it electronically within our own culture" (McLuhan 1962: 45–46).

More specifically, what was being "recreated... electronically" was the dominance of sound in the mediation of verbal material, as in preliterate conditions, when verbal communication was transmitted orally by the voice and received aurally by the ear. During the hiatus constituted by the printing era, words had been communicated as letters on paper and so processed visually.[2] These apparently simple shifts in the relative significance of the senses engaged in verbal communication were claimed to have far-reaching repercussions for the societies in which they occurred.

Walter Ong, who had been a student of McLuhan, pursued similar ideas in somewhat different directions in a series of studies, culminating in 1982 with his acclaimed *Orality and Literacy. The Technologizing of the Word*. His main interest was "differences between the ways of managing knowledge and verbalization in primary oral cultures (cultures with no knowledge at all of writing) and in cultures deeply affected by the use of writing" (Ong 1982: 1). He therefore saw the decisive break as the arrival of the alphabet, "the most momentous of all human technological inventions" (Ong 1982: 85), and his point of departure was therefore preliterate culture as represented for instance by ancient Greece. As we shall see, however, he did attribute greater significance to print in discussing the wider cultural impact of developments in media technology.

Ong devoted much less time to the restoration phase, which he agreed is the result of the resumption of spoken communication in the analog mass media, but managed nonetheless to make a significant contribution to the field's terminology. While McLuhan's "Gutenberg Galaxy" designated the intermediate period, Ong provided terms for the phases before the interruption and after the restoration. The former was characterized by a "primary orality," which is restored, at a higher level of technology, in the latter's "secondary orality" (Ong 1982: 136–138).

Together the terms usefully signal both resumption and change, but for Ong the orality of analog technology was "secondary" in the rather vague sense of being dependent on literacy in the ambient culture, without which the technology could neither have been developed nor successfully operated. It might be a more useful perspective that, while in "primary" orality communication proceeds directly from the mouth of a speaker to the ear of a listener, "secondary" orality is at second hand, the voice heard indirectly via recording and/or broadcasting technology.

Digital and Internet Technologies

The theories of both McLuhan and Ong are technically outdated, as the analog technology that prompted them has been absorbed in and superseded by our digital technologies, which are not merely more of the same. By 1982 they had just attracted attention as what Ong called "composition on computer terminals," but he saw them as continuing and reinforcing the notion, characteristic of print, that verbal communication was something to be seen (Ong 1982: 136) – effectively a step backward in relation to the secondary orality of sound media. This would ultimately prove unsustainable, and Ong's less-well-known responses to subsequent developments will be touched on in later discussion.

In the case of McLuhan, such updating has necessarily involved the reassessment of his views by others in the light of the new media, often hailed as a "McLuhan Renaissance" (Cooper 2006) that combats a long-standing skeptical trend that dismissed both his and Ong's views as "social science fictions" (Price 2006: 9). However, much of this rehabilitation relates to McLuhan's contributions other than the restoration topos (Levinson 1999; Meyrowitz 2001), and when it does encompass *The Gutenberg Galaxy* is more relevant for matters beyond media technology strictly speaking; this too will be explored later.

The intervening years have seen the development of a number of new formulations of the topos in which the restoration is seen as having been achieved by digital and Internet technologies rather than the analog mass media. Most of them are focused on quite specific applications or platforms, and are fairly equally divided between those who, like McLuhan, see the first revolution as the arrival of the printing press and those who, like Ong, opt for writing as the interruption in media history.

For the former, our latest media technologies are restoring aspects of the scribal mediation that preceded the advent of print: "electronic reproduction has more in common with the fourteenth-century scriptorium than with the print capitalism that replaced it" (Nunberg 1993: 22; cf. Baron et al. 2007: 306). Observing recent publication trends, Mark and Catherine West predict "a future for the book much closer to the medieval model, where individuals will collect fragments of texts, culled from the Internet, in a medieval-style commonplace book" (2009: 71). The digital social media may, suggests Margaret Ezell (2003), facilitate the return of "social authorship," a system predating the dominance of print, by which provincial authors circulated their works in manuscript copies among what we would now call their social network – only now the medium is Internet-based and the network comprises "friends" who can be given immediate access. Harold Love similarly observes that the early London presses were in competition with a system of manuscript circulation that "even as we read, *is reconstituting itself* in the world around us to the clicking of keyboards and the hum of computer fans" (Love 2002: 112; emphasis added).

Leah S. Marcus' "Cyberspace Renaissance" (1995) heralds the emergence of a new generation of Renaissance specialists who will not merely recognize the shared characteristics of digital and scribal technologies but also be qualified to exploit that compatibility by deploying the one in the study of the other. For, as scholarly tools, the resources of cyberspace and digital technology are better adapted than print as a context for analyzing scribally mediated texts, precisely because they reproduce – at a higher level of technology – some of their more salient features, not least textual fluidity.

The alternative (Ong's) permutation of revolutions sees digital technology and the Internet as restoring aspects not of scribal but of preliterate oral mediation. John December suggests that the "emotive, expressive, participatory" features in Internet textual discourse (much of it, appropriately, labeled "chat") are a throwback to oral communication (December 1993). Clay Shirky's *Cognitive Surplus* similarly sees in our new social media a restoration of premodern conditions when "a significant chunk of culture was participatory – local gatherings, events, and performances" (Shirky 2010: 18–19). Jill Walker Rettberg considers one of those social media, blogging, to be a restoration of pre-Gutenberg, oral culture in its social, conversational, colloquial characteristics and in its constant updating, after an intervening phase of very different "print writing" – for which she invokes the Gutenberg Parenthesis (Rettberg 2008: 33). In an early but prescient contribution, Stevan Harnad perceived that the speed of verbal communication facilitated by digital technology, while still textual, was bringing us back to the immediacy of speech, following a period of slower, cumbersome communication via publication (Harnad 1991).

One of the celebrated responses to the increasing deployment of writing was the criticism of the Greek philosopher Socrates, as reported by Plato, of its many unfortunate effects. Socrates would manifestly have been more comfortable, Matthew Kent (2007) suggests, with the Internet than with books. The implication here that digital technology has something in common with the voice-and-memory-based mediation favored by Socrates and Plato, and that the change we are going through now reverses their experience then, is spelled out by Eric McLuhan: "Plato stood on the dividing-line, surrounded by *pre-* and proto-Literates. We too stand on a dividing line, actually the same one, though *facing the other way*, and surrounded by proto-Literates and *post*-Literates" (McLuhan 2009, emphasis added). Richard A. Lanham's *The Electronic Word* delays the transition, arguing that the Greek culture of oral mediation persisted in a European educational tradition based on rhetoric that not until the Renaissance was usurped by educational practices based on the acquisition of knowledge and wisdom contained in "great books" – and then, in 1993, was being restored at a higher level of technology in the form of digital word-processing (1993: 101–111).

This pattern of alternative interruption–restoration permutations repeats itself in historical discussions of a digital technology that has been particularly influential in new verbal media: the hypertext system, which facilitates immediate shifting between different passages in a given document, between different documents, or, when the device is deployed on the Internet, between different websites. David Burnley (1995), for example, takes a closer look at what hypertext means for authors in the broader context of similarities between digital and scribal text-processing, and their shared differences from the printed books that came in between. Tatjana Chorney (2005) sees analogies between hypertext and more practical aspects of medieval and Renaissance manuscript culture: the use of a reading wheel to access multiple texts simultaneously and the copying of poems, fragments, and citations followed by their reuse in new compilations. As another scholar put it, "the hypertext reader is more at home in the age of the manuscript than in the age of print" (Littau 2006: 34).

Conversely, Jay David Bolter, another classicist who senses there is something reminiscent of ancient Greek culture in modern developments, sees hypertext rather as related to oral tradition, for it "more closely resembles oral discourse than it does conventional printing or handwriting" (1991: 58–59). George P. Landow's *Hypertext*, more intent on pursuing the connections between hypertext technology and postmodern literary theory, nonetheless discerns in passing a reversion to preliterate conditions (2006: 116).

In contrast to McLuhan and Ong, the work of the third major exponent of the restoration topos, John Miles Foley, emerged directly out of engagement with the digital media, and, while standing very much on its own merits as in many ways the most significant engagement with the topos to date, it is also something of a culmination of the applications just surveyed, both specific and general.

Foley was an authority on the Homeric epics (the question of whose orality was the context and inspiration for the work of McLuhan and Ong), on the oral aspects of medieval vernacular literatures, and on living oral traditions of our times, not least the South Slavic epic singers whose performances, to complete the circle, galvanized Homeric and medieval studies in the second half of the twentieth century (Lord 2003). In addition to effectively bearing the mantle of the next generation of this distinguished research tradition – as founder and director of the University of Missouri's Center for Studies in Oral Tradition and as founder and editor of its Internet journal *Oral Tradition* – he also presided over significant projects (fulfilling the trend noted earlier) that deployed digital technology in the analysis, and in the mediation of the results of this analysis, of oral traditions. This eminently qualified Foley for the extension of this focus to encompass those digital technologies as media themselves in the *Pathways Project*, which looks set to achieve a comprehensive identification and understanding of the analogies between oral tradition ("OT," what Foley also called the oral marketplace, or *o-agora*) and electronic, Internet technology ("IT"; *e-agora*), and of their shared contrasts with the intervening world of artifactual texts (*t-agora*): "The major purpose of the Pathways Project is to illustrate and explain the fundamental similarities and correspondences between humankind's oldest and newest thought-technologies: oral tradition and the Internet" (Foley 2011a).

The period intervening between "OT" and the restoration of many of its salient characteristics in "IT" Foley conceptualized as the book (he largely ignored the analog mass media), but evidently in a broad definition that does not privilege print, including as it does writing on clay tablets, papyrus, and parchment. It also includes static electronic files, reflecting Foley's view that the text on a computer screen might just as well be in a book until the platform enables or even invites intervention on the part of the user to reshape the verbal material to their own wishes or requirements.

The Gutenberg Parenthesis

As an image for the restoration topos, a *parenthesis* carries the obligation to specify and justify the placing of those uncompromisingly sharp brackets with which it opens and closes – a built-in disadvantage in dealing with a complex media history that manifestly involves multiple developments, each of which at a given moment is at a different stage of fulfillment. Rather than compromising the image by speaking of multiple, laminated, broad, or fuzzy brackets, it might be feasible to identify relatively significant moments of cumulative culmination in the changes constituting the interruption and restoration processes.

Postulating a "Gutenberg" Parenthesis announces that in each case print technology is the most decisive of those developments, agreeing with McLuhan that, even though the alphabet was in itself a greater revolution, in practice its significance was limited. It was qualitatively limited because scribal culture retained what Walter

Ong called a "residual orality," not least in the way most manuscripts were read aloud, even by a solitary reader. Script usurped only the storage phase in a so-called "oral" tradition in which the link between performances was the memory of the performer. To this can be added the qualities in which digital mediation resembles the scribal and differs from the typographical (some noted in studies surveyed earlier), including the way the copying of texts, like retrieval from memory, could involve a good deal of conscious and unconscious change: "Print spread texts in a different way from manuscripts" (Walsham and Crick 2004: 20; cf. Ong 1982: 117).

Meanwhile, in quantitative terms, the printed book far outscored the manuscript in the number of units produced, the number of people reading them, and the range of cultural domains in which they were deployed. This is also the response to the plausible claims that the development of the codex (the book of bound sheets) in late antiquity was more revolutionary than print (Chartier 2007: 407), and that it is therefore this codex revolution that digital technology is reversing (Stallybrass 2002: 42): at some point in the sixteenth century, the copies of printed books produced on the European presses outnumbered all the manuscripts written in the millennium or more since the codex's introduction. The process is cumulative: the print medium inherited the impact of the codex, as it inherited the impacts of paper, ink, and the alphabet, but made more out of each of them and added features of its own.

The culmination of these cumulative changes is manifestly not the year of the first printed book or even the first portable formats: in media history "technologies actually become significant only after they have reached the point of 'lock-in', the point at which the propagation of a particular technique or device through the population reaches a critical number" (Bristol and Marotti 2000: 3). The publication of the first edition of Shakespeare's complete plays in 1623 is both a potent symbol and a significant reality: originally perceived (preparenthetically) as merely scripts for performances, only half of his plays had been published in his lifetime, and only half of those with his name on the title page. Others might prefer to delay the point of no return until the period of the industrial revolution: "the age of the modern book began in 1810, when a German inventor . . . patented a steam-powered press that for the first time could create a printed page through mechanical means" (Wright 2009: 60). This would make the parenthesis shorter but not disqualify it as a formulation of the restoration topos: modern technology can still be seen as restoring the media landscape before the conventional book as we know it (Knight 2009: 340).

Situating the closing of the parenthesis is also a matter of identifying the culminating moment in a cumulative process, and in retrospect it does seem that hailing analog technology as a restoration was premature: as much a threat to professional entertainment and domestic pastimes, radio and television may have achieved a role alongside books, but "the Internet has greater potential to supplant, rather than supplement, the primacy of print on paper" (Pearson 2008: 12). The Gutenberg Parenthesis should accordingly not be seen as the hiatus between Ong's primary and secondary oralities.

While they may take further whatever radio, television, film, and records achieved by way of emphasizing heard speech at the expense of seen texts, the digital media have a strong and indeed growing textual element: mobile "phones" are now used more for texting and reading than for speaking and listening. But, as some of the studies surveyed point out, and as Walter Ong acknowledges in later observations, this is a quite new textuality, not least in its immediacy and informality: although in visible letters, it feels like speech (Walter 2006; see also Wright 2007: 231–232). Ong toyed with designating this a "secondary literacy," but it is more plausibly a lettered quasi-orality – speech in a textual mode but not a simple transcript of speech: a speaking through the fingers, which is digital in more than one sense.

Restorations: Beyond Technology

A characteristic of the more comprehensive expressions of the restoration topos, including the Gutenberg Parenthesis, is the extension of their focus beyond media technology itself to synchronous and presumably related changes in the host culture.

Cultural Production

These include, not surprisingly, cultural production, from oral narrative and Renaissance poetry to TV soaps and YouTube videos, mediated by technology. In David Bolter's terms, each technology constitutes a "writing space" and "each fosters a particular understanding both of the act of writing and of the product, the written text, and this understanding expresses itself in writing styles, genres, and literary theories" (2001: 12). Added to which, the mediating technology can impose significant change on the material confided to it before it reaches its recipients.

Marshall McLuhan shows little interest in cultural production in its own right; his extensive appeals to Renaissance literature and the plays of Shakespeare are designed rather to illustrate the quite distinct thesis that "the medium is the message": that changes in media technology determine changes in ways of thinking (to be touched on later). Both Walter Ong and John Foley in contrast explore in considerable depth the way the restoration pattern manifests itself in cultural production as well as media technology, and both emphatically consider that the two are related. The Gutenberg Parenthesis offers a welcoming context for a compound of their insights on the exact nature of the changes involved in the restoration trajectory – with a few new ingredients.

The compatibility is signaled, happily but coincidentally, by the etymology of "parenthesis," including the notion of a putting ("thesis") inside ("en") – containment within boundaries being characteristic of both media technology and cultural production in the era of print. Ong's major concession to McLuhan's view that print, as well as writing, represents a major revolution takes the form of a chapter (five) entitled, precisely, "Printing as Containing Medium." It includes a characterization of how, quite physically, print "situates words in space more relentlessly than writing ever did" (Ong 1982: 121, here somewhat elaborated).

The central, defining moment in print technology brings together metal letter types that have been created in a mold, stored in upper and lower cases, and set in a forme, and paper sheets made of fibers compressed and dried in a frame and stored in bundles (reams) or rolls. The artifact emerging from the appropriately named "press" comprises letters confined within a text block, itself contained within margins on a page, part of a sheet that has been folded into a gathering and stitched and glued with others to make a book (codex), which is bound and perhaps enclosed in a dust jacket or inserted into a slip-case. This "volume" with its "contents" is stored in a book case, and to be read has to be taken out and opened: not that the words hereby escape; the pages may equally invite an "immersive" reading during which the reader is "lost in" the book.

For Ong there is an organic relationship between this containment of the print medium and the containment that in various ways characterizes the material it mediates:

> Print is curiously intolerant of physical incompleteness. It can convey the impression, unintentionally and subtly, but very really, that the material the text deals with is similarly complete or self-consistent. Print makes for more tightly closed verbal art forms.... Print culture ... tends to feel a work as "closed," set off from other works, a unit in itself. (Ong 1982: 133)

Accordingly, the verbal culture produced for and mediated in books and pages tends to take the form of works whose containment is manifested in multiple ways: their completeness (clear boundary at beginning and ending), their independence (boundary between work and source), their autonomy (boundary between this work and other works), and their integrity (resistance to addition or subtraction involving textual transgression, in the one way or the other, across those boundaries) (Ong 1982: 132–135).

This also covers many of the items on Foley's list of the essential qualities of material in the t-agora – "fixity, exact replicability, resistance to morphing, free-standing status" (Foley 2011b) – and is also applicable to his remaining items "single authorship" and "proprietary nature": a given work being contained within the canon of a named author, and the right to copy being the property of a specific owner, metaphorically analogous to the book kept in a case.

Outside the Gutenberg Parenthesis, both technology and production display distinctly less emphatic boundaries. Materially, digital technology is achieving "Libraries without Walls" (Chartier 1993) and texts are no longer bound within covers. An oral performance, like an Internet session, has no fixed duration, and the effective endlessness of oral narrative unconfined by the limits of a page or a book is restored in the "liberation of space" of computer games (e.g., Babic 2007). Pierre Lévy and Roxanne Lapidus describe "hypertextual operations and digital networks" that have "brought about the emergence of a text without clear boundaries, without a definable interiority. Now there is *text*, as one might speak of water, or sand. The text is put in motion, taken in a flux, vectorized, metamorphic" (Lévy and Lapidus 1997: 14).

And, while the vocabulary may differ, preparenthetical cultural traditions (epics, romances, ballads, folktales) are as familiar as postparenthetical with the processes of mix and remix, in which a new work is achieved respectively by combining existing works or revising a given work, often deploying "samples" extracted from others – all these processes involving breaching the boundaries of all the works concerned, their vulnerability to transgression also caught in Foley's term "public access," applied to the reduced sense of individual ownership.

The last feature in Foley's characterization of media and production in the t-agora is "absence of pathways," an effective formulation of a positive aspect of the purely negative absence of boundaries outside the Gutenberg Parenthesis. The bard, minstrel, or folk singer embarking on a performance – like the reader at the start of a hypertext novel, the player at the start of a computer game, or the Internet surfer at the beginning of a session – is entering an experience that, at one level or another, involves repeatedly coming to a crossroads and making a decision about which way to go. It is striking that leading developers of computer games and interactive e-literature are aware that their real antecedents and inspiration are to be found not in novels but in the Greek oral epics: "whatever the technological progress achieved, these authors constantly seek to restore [*revivre*] the original experience of the teller of tales, at the roots of civilization" (Sussan 2010, my translation).

As the Gutenberg Parenthesis closes, words are restored to the liberty they had before they were bound in books, or confined to authorial canons and the ownership of the copyright holder. When contextualized in longer-term media history, such perceptions can take on imagery analogous to the parenthesis, Paul Eggert anticipating (without condoning) assertions that, with hypertext breaking down the integrity of verbal products, the whole notion of the individual work has been a "historical blip, yoked to the period of the printed book" (Eggert 2004: 172). Roger Chartier, on the eve of a debate on copyright in the French parliament, wondered, "could the right of the author, born with the printing press, die with the Internet?": it might indeed be "a historical parenthesis" (Chartier 2005, my translation).

Ways of Thinking

At their most ambitious, extended versions of the restoration topos also encompass changes in the general ways of thinking within the host society; for example, a chapter in Ong's *Orality and Literacy* is uncompromisingly entitled "Writing Restructures Consciousness." This formulation also reflects the notion of "technological determinism," shared with McLuhan, which saw media change as having cognitive effects. In approaching this cognitive dimension, the Gutenberg Parenthesis acknowledges that the reverse is equally plausible, as is the possibility that correlated changes reflect mutual subjection to contextual, sociocultural influences.

Of the major exponents, John Foley's interest is limited to this topic's direct relevance to mediation and cultural production, not least the workings of the memory of people in preliterate cultures engaged in the composition and transmission of verbal material. It leads to the speculation that from this perspective, too, postparenthetical digital media are in some ways a restoration: "Could it be that with the internet we're returning to a way of representing and communicating more fundamental than the default medium of the book and page? ... the kind of medium that ... mimes the way we think?" (Foley 2011a: "Online with OT").

For McLuhan in *The Gutenberg Galaxy*, the central thesis is precisely that print's modulation of verbal communication from the aural to the visual had a massive, and vitally civilizing, impact on the minds of the listeners who became readers: "Civilization gives the barbarian or tribal man an eye for an ear" (McLuhan 1962: 26). The restoration of the dominant role of listening in the twentieth-century mass media he therefore regretted as "the return of the Africa within" (McLuhan 1962: 45). McLuhan explained that the "galaxy" of the book's title was a synonym for "environment" (McLuhan 1962: vi), which by implication impinged on the creatures (ways of thinking) living in it, and the implications of the image have been sustained in the school of media ecology, which, Neil Postman notes, "looks into the matter of how media of communication affect human perception, understanding, feeling, and value" (2000).

It is in this aspect of the restoration topos that a "McLuhan Renaissance" may be most plausible, as the new, digital media have sparked renewed interest in the cognitive impact of changes in media technology: "The most potent yet elusive consequences of a new media are arguably its cognitive effects" (Baron et al. 2007: 312). And the interest is shared by those who study the acquisition of reading abilities and those who electronically scan brains to see how they work. One of the former is confident that learning to read involves a substantial "rewiring" of the brain, and that "The historical moment that best approximates the present transition from a literate to a digital culture is found in the ancient Greeks' transition from an oral culture to a literacy-based culture" (Wolf 2010). One of the latter, the Director of the Center for Cognitive Brain Imaging at Carnegie Mellon University, confirms that

> processing print isn't something the human brain was built for. The printed word is a human artifact. ... Even the spoken language is much more a given biologically than reading written language

and responds affirmatively to an interviewer's query (complicated by equating "digital" with "visual") as to whether current developments in media technology amount to a restoration process:

> Does this mean that as we move out of the era of print and paper and into the digital era with more visual media, it's going to be a more natural environment for humans to take in information than when it was the printed words? (Ludke 2010).

In seeking to encompass this cognitive dimension, the Gutenberg Parenthesis could plausibly appeal to a striking correlation between the nature of the cognitive changes synchronous with the media revolutions demarcating the restoration trajectory, and the "en-thetical" qualities of both mediating technology and cultural production in the parenthetical phase just reviewed. For an emphasis on boundaries and containment is evident under all headings (see Pettitt 2009b for a more elaborate survey).

It has at least been asserted in quite different research traditions that, at the time print was passing its lock-in point in England (around the generation of Shakespeare), there began a massively increased emphasis on the environment as comprised of enclosures, and on the body as an envelope, in the way they were perceived, in the way they were represented, and in the way they were actually treated. The right order of things in each instance required the integrity of the boundary that demarcated inside from outside and prevented inappropriate ingress or egress (Stallybrass 1986; Burt and Archer 1994; Hillman 2007). It might accordingly be a subsidiary postulate of the Gutenberg Parenthesis that our digital revolution is or soon will be accompanied by a decline in the emphasis on boundaries and containment in perceptions, representations, and treatment of space and bodies. This will simultaneously involve the restoration of preparenthetical perceptions, which for both bodies and spaces evidently put less stress on boundaries and containment and more on the kind of network structures implied by Foley's "pathways": space as avenues and junctions; bodies as limbs and joints (Bolens 2000; Pettitt 2009a).

There may be support for this postulate in the analogous restoration pattern discerned by Robert Deibert in the changing realities and perceptions of "world order." Indeed, his evidence suggests his perception is relevant for social and political relationships more generally, and these in turn have a spatial dimension connecting them to this matter of boundaries. The print era has been dominated by contained, "territorially distinct, mutually exclusive sovereign nation-states," in contrast to medieval structures "based on nonterritorial logics of organization" (Deibert 1997: 13). But, in correlation with our current media revolution, a reverse shift is discernible "*away* from single mass identities, linear political boundaries, and exclusive jurisdictions centered on territorial spaces" and back "*toward* multiple identities and non-territorial communities, overlapping boundaries and nonexclusive jurisdictions" (Deibert 1997: 15).

The parallel incidence at these many levels – media technology, cultural production, and cognition (perceptions of bodies, spaces, and social relationships) – of the restoration of freedom from boundaries after a period of containment strongly suggests that all are part of a comprehensive, parenthetically structured, trajectory in Western media history. In which case it is disturbing to contemplate that the notion of a "Gutenberg Parenthesis" as a discrete period in media history with clear (bracketed) boundaries may itself be one of those modes of perception that see the world in terms of containment, and whose natural habitat is in rounded cultural productions (such as academic essays) within integrated works (such as a companion) mediated on pages in printed and bound books by publishers who insist on the copyright of their contents and acknowledgment of the copyright of others in material quoted. All of which suggests that the Gutenberg Parenthesis will not be over until "book people" stop perceiving parentheses in media history (a *mise en abîme* is also a form of containment).

Notes

1. I developed this perspective from the suggestion of colleague, Simon Frost, that the Gutenberg Parenthesis might best be seen as a "trope."
2. This introduces a potential confusion into the terminology. In media studies generally, it is film and television, in contradistinction to records and radio, that are the "visual" media; not so for McLuhan with his focus on verbal communication: in none of these can you *see* the words.

References

Babic, E. (2007) "On the Liberation of Space in Computer Games." *Eludamos. Journal for Computer Game Culture*, 1(1), 1–9.

Baron, D. (2009) *A Better Pencil: Readers, Writers, and the Digital Revolution*. Oxford: Oxford University Press.

Baron, S.A., Lindquist, E.N., and Shevlin, S. (2007) "Agency, Technology, and the New Global Media Revolution," in S.A. Baron, E.N. Lindquist, and S. Shevlin, eds., *Agent of Change: Print Culture Studies after Elizabeth L. Eisenstein*. Amherst, MA: University of Massachusetts Press, pp. 301–314.

Birkerts, S. (2006) *The Gutenberg Elegies: The Fate of Reading in an Electronic Age*, 2nd edn. New York: Faber & Faber.

Bolens, G. (2000) *La logique du corps articulaire: Les articulations du corps humain dans la littérature occidentale* [The Logic of the Articulated Body: The Articulations of the Human Body in Western Literature]. Rennes: Presses Universitaires de Rennes.

Bolter, J.D. (1991) *Writing Space: The Computer, Hypertext, and the History of Writing*. Hillsdale, NJ: Lawrence Erlbaum Associates.

Bolter, J.D. (2001) *Writing Space: Computers, Hypertext, and the Remediation of Print*, 2nd edn. Mahwah, NJ: Lawrence Erlbaum Associates.

Bristol, M.D. and Marotti, A.F. (2000) "Introduction," in A.F. Marotti and M.D. Bristol, eds., *Print, Manuscript and Performance*. Columbia, OH: Ohio State University Press, pp. 1–29.

Burnley, D. (1995) "Scribes and Hypertext." *The Yearbook of English Studies*, 25, 41–62.

Burt, R. and Archer, J.M., eds. (1994) *Enclosure Acts: Sexuality, Property, and Culture in Early Modern England*. Ithaca, NY: Cornell University Press.

Carr, N. (2008) "Is Google Making Us Stupid?" *The Atlantic* (July). www.theatlantic.com /magazine/archive/2008/07/is-google-making-us-stupid/6868.

Carr, N. (2010) *The Shallows: How the Internet is Changing the Way We Think, Read and Remember*. London: Atlantic Books.

Chartier, R. (1993) "Libraries without Walls." *Representations*, 42(1), 38–52.

Chartier, R. (1997) "The End of the Reign of the Book." *Sub-Stance*, 26(1), 9–11.

Chartier, R. (2005) "Le droit d'auteur est-il une parenthèse dans l'histoire? [Are Authors' Rights a Historical Parenthesis?]." *Le Monde* (December 17).

Chartier, R. (2007) "The Printing Revolution: A Reappraisal" in S.A. Baron, E.N. Lindquist, and S. Shevlin, eds., *Agent of Change: Print Culture Studies after Elizabeth L. Eisenstein*. Amherst, MA: University of Massachusetts Press, pp. 397–408.

Chorney, T. (2005) "Interactive Reading, Early Modern Texts and Hypertext: A Lesson from the Past'." *Academic Commons* (December 12). www.academiccommons.org/commons/essay/early-modern-texts-and-hypertext.

Cooper, T. (2006) Review of L. Strate and E. Wachtel, eds. (2005) *The Legacy of McLuhan*. Cresskill, NJ: Hampton Press. *Journal of Communication*, 56(2), 433–6.

Darnton, R. (2009) *The Case for Books: Past, Present and Future*. New York: Public Affairs.

Darnton, R. (2010) "Blogging, Now and Then." *New York Review of Books* (March 18). www.nybooks.com/blogs/nyrblog/2010/mar/18/blogging-now-and-then.

December, J. (1993) "Characteristics of Oral Culture in Discourse on the Net." Paper presented at the 12th annual Penn State Conference on Rhetoric and Composition, University Park, PA (July 8). www.december.com/john/papers/pscrc93.txt.

Deibert, R.J. (1997) *Parchment, Printing, and Hypermedia: Communication in World Order Transformation*. New York: Columbia University Press.

Dewar, J.A. (1998) "The Information Age and the Printing Press: Looking Backward to See Ahead." Rand Papers, P-8014. www.rand.org/pubs/papers/P8014.html.

Dewar, J.A. and Ang, P.H. (2007) "The Cultural Consequences of Printing and the Internet" in S.A. Baron, E.N. Lindquist, and S. Shevlin, eds., *Agent of Change: Print Culture Studies after Elizabeth L. Eisenstein*. Amherst, MA: University of Massachusetts Press, pp. 365–377.

Eggert, P. (2004) "The Way of All Text: The Materialist Shakespeare" in R. Modiano, L.F. Searle, and P.L. Shillingsburg, eds., *Voice, Text, Hypertext: Emerging Practices in Textual Studies*. Seattle, WA: University of Washington Press, pp. 162–176.

Eisenstein, E.L. (2011) *Divine Art, Infernal Machine: The Reception of Printing in the West from First Impressions to the Sense of an Ending*. Philadelphia, PA: University of Pennsylvania Press.

Ezell, M.J.M. (2003) *Social Authorship and the Advent of Print*, 2nd edn. Baltimore, MD: Johns Hopkins University Press.

Finnegan, R. (1988) *Literacy and Orality: Studies in the Technology of Communication*. Oxford: Blackwell.

Foley, J. (2011a) *Pathways Project*. www.pathwaysproject.org/pathways/show/HomePage.

Foley, J. (2011b) "The tAgora: Exchanging Tangible Goods." *Pathways Project*. http://pathwaysproject.org/pathways/show/tAgora#.

Gomez, J. (2009) *Print Is Dead: Books in Our Digital Age*. New York: Palgrave Macmillan.

Harnad, S. (1991) "Post-Gutenberg Galaxy: The Fourth Revolution in the Means of Production of Knowledge." *Public-Access Computer Systems Review*, 2(1), 39–53.

Hartley, J. (2009) "TV Stories: From Representation to Productivity" in J. Hartley and K. McWilliam, eds., *Story Circle: Digital Storytelling Around the World*. Oxford: Wiley-Blackwell, pp. 16–36.

Hillman, D. (2007) *Shakespeare's Entrails: Belief, Scepticism and the Interior of the Body*. New York: Palgrave/St. Martin's Press.

Kent, M.A. (2007) "Is the Internet too Platonic? Books, Electronic Media, and the Purpose of Communication." *International Journal of the Book*, 4(4), 95–100.

Kluth, A. (2006) "Among the Audience: Survey of New Media." *The Economist* (April 20). www.economist.com/node/6794156.

Knight, J.T. (2009) "Making Shakespeare's Book: Assembly and Intertextuality in the Archives." *Shakespeare Quarterly*, 60(3), 304–340.

Landow, G.P. (2006) *Hypertext 3.0: Critical Theory and New Media in an Era of Globalization*, 3rd edn. Baltimore, MD: Johns Hopkins University Press.

Lanham, R.A. (1993) *The Electronic Word: Democracy, Technology, and the Arts*. Chicago, IL: University of Chicago Press.

Levinson, P. (1999) *Digital McLuhan: A Guide to the Information Millenium*. London and New York: Routledge.

Lévy, P. and Lapidus, R. (1997) "Artificial Reading." *Sub-Stance*, 26(1), 12–15.

Littau, K. (2006) *Theories of Reading: Books, Bodies and Bibliomania*. Cambridge: Polity.

Lord, A.B. (2003) *The Singer of Tales*, 2nd edn, ed. S. Mitchell and G. Nagy. Cambridge, MA: Harvard University Press.

Love, H. (2002) "Oral and Scribal Texts in Early Modern England" in J. Barnard and D.F. McKenzie, eds., *The Cambridge History of the Book in Britain*, vol. IV: *1557–1695*. Cambridge: Cambridge University Press, pp. 97–121.

Ludke, M. (2010) "Watching the Human Brain Process Information: Conversation with Marcel Just." *Nieman Reports*. www.nieman.harvard.edu/reportsitem.aspx?id=102399.

Marcus, L.S. (1995) "Cyberspace Renaissance." *English Literary Renaissance*, 25(3), 388–401.

McCarthy, M. (2010) "Redeeming the Almanac: Learning to Appreciate the iPhone of Early America." *Common-Place*, 11(1). www.common-place.org/vol-11/no-01/reading.

McLuhan, E. (2009) "Literacy in a New Key." *Proceedings of the Media Ecology Association*, 10, 9–18.

McLuhan, M. (1962) *The Gutenberg Galaxy. The Making of Typographic Man*. Toronto, ON: University of Toronto Press.

Meyrowitz, J. (2001) "Morphing McLuhan: Medium Theory for a New Millenium." *Proceedings of the Media Ecology Association*, 2, 8–22.

Mod, C. (2010) "Books in the Age of the iPad." *@Craigmod* (March 2010). http://craigmod.com/journal/ipad_and_books.

Nunberg, G. (1993) "The Places of Books in the Age of Electronic Reproduction." *Representations*, 42(1), 13–37.

Ong, W.J. (1982) *Orality and Literacy. The Technologizing of the Word*. London: Methuen.

Pearson, D. (2008) *Books as History: The Importance of Books Beyond their Texts*. London: British Library.

Perrault, A.H. and Crummett, C. (2009) "From Aldus to iPod: Books and Personal Media Devices as Extensions of the Self." *The International Journal of the Book*, 7(1), 1–8.

Pettitt, T. (2007) "Opening the Gutenberg Parenthesis: Media in Transition in Shakespeare's England." Paper presented at the Creativity, Ownership and Collaboration in the Digital Age Conference, Massachusetts Institute of Technology, Cambridge, MA (April 27–29). http://web.mit.edu/comm-forum/mit5/papers/Pettitt.Gutenberg%20Parenthesis.Paper.pdf.

Pettitt, T. (2009a) "Books and Bodies, Bound and Unbound." *Orbis Litterarum*, 64(2), 104–126.

Pettitt, T. (2009b) "Containment and Articulation: Media Technology, Cultural Production and the Perception of the Material World." Paper presented at the Stone and Papyrus: Storage and Transmission Conference, Massachusetts Institute of Technology, Cambridge, MA (April 24–26). http://web.mit.edu/comm-forum/mit6/papers/Pettitt.pdf.

Postman, N. (2000) "What is Media Ecology." *Media Ecology Association.* www.media
-ecology.org/media_ecology/index.html.

Powers, W. (2010) *Hamlet's Blackberry: A Practical Philosophy for Building a Good Life in the
Digital Age.* New York: Harper.

Price, L. (2006) "Introduction: Reading Matter." *Publications of the Modern Language
Association,* 121(1), 9–16.

Rettberg, J.W. (2008) *Blogging.* Cambridge: Polity.

Rhodes, N. (2000) "Articulate Networks: The Self, the Book and the World" in N. Rhodes
and J. Sawday, eds., *The Renaissance Computer: Knowledge Technology in the First Age of
Print.* London and New York: Routledge, pp. 184–196.

Rhodes, N. and Sawday, J., ed. (2000) *The Renaissance Computer: Knowledge Technology in
the First Age of Print.* London and New York: Routledge.

Sauerberg, L.O. (2009) "The Encyclopedia and the Gutenberg Parenthesis." Paper presented at the Stone and Papyrus: Storage and Transmission Conference, Massachusetts
Institute of Technology, Cambridge, MA (April 24–26). http://web.mit.edu/comm
-forum/mit6/papers/sauerberg.pdf.

Sauerberg, L.O. et al. (2011) *The Gutenberg Parenthesis – Print, Book and Cognition.* www.sdu.dk/Om_SDU/Institutter_centre/Ilkm/Forskning/Forskningsprojekter
/Gutenberg_projekt.

Shillingsburg, P.L. (2006) *From Gutenberg to Google.* Cambridge: Cambridge University
Press.

Shirky, C. (2010) *Cognitive Surplus: Creativity and Generosity in a Connected Age.* New York:
Penguin.

Stallybrass, P. (1986) "Patriarchal Territories: The Body Enclosed" in M.W. Ferguson, ed.,
Rewriting the Renaissance: Discourses of Difference in Early Modern Europe. Chicago, IL:
Chicago University Press, pp. 123–142.

Stallybrass, P. (2002) "Books and Scrolls: Navigating the Bible," in J. Andersen and E. Sauer,
eds., *Books and Readers in Early Modern England: Material Studies.* Philadelphia, PA:
University of Pennsylvania Press, pp. 42–47.

Standage, T. (1998) *The Victorian Internet: The Remarkable Story of the Telegraph and the
Nineteenth Century's On-line Pioneers.* New York: Walker.

Sussan, R. (2010) "Ecrits numériques: Vers une fiction interactive et collaborative [Digital
Texts: Towards an Interactive and Collaborative Fiction]." *Le Monde* (July 23).
www.lemonde.fr/technologies/article/2010/07/23/vers-une-fiction-interactive-et-
collaborative_1391694_651865.html.

Updike, J. (2006) "The End of Authorship." *New York Times* (June 25). www.nytimes
.com/2006/06/25/books/review/25updike.html?pagewanted=all.

Walsham, A. and Crick, J., ed. (2004) *The Uses of Script and Print, 1300–1700.* Cambridge:
Cambridge University Press.

Walter, J. (2006) "Ong on Secondary Orality and Secondary Literacy." *Notes from the
Walter Ong Collection.* http://johnwalter.blogspot.dk/2006/07/ong-on-secondary-orality
-and-secondary.html.

West, M.D. and West, C.J. (2009) "Reading in the Internet Era: Toward a Medieval Mode of
Understanding." *International Journal of the Book,* 6(4), 71–88.

Wolf, M. (2010) "Our 'Deep Reading' Brain: Its Digital Evolution Poses Questions." *Nieman
Reports.* www.nieman.harvard.edu/reportsitem.aspx?id=102396.

Wright, A. (2007) *Glut: Mastering Information Through the Ages.* Washington, DC: Joseph
Henry Press.

Wright, A. (2009) "The Battle of the Books." *Wilson Quarterly*, 33(4), 59–64.
Young, S. (2007) *The Book is Dead (Long Live the Book)*. Sydney, NSW: University of New
    South Wales Press.

Further Reading

Eisenstein, E.L. (1979) *The Printing Press as Agent of Change: Communications and Cultural
    Transformations in Early Modern Europe*, 2 vols. Cambridge: Cambridge University Press.
Foley, J. (1988) *The Theory of Oral Composition*. Bloomington, IN: Indiana University Press.
Foley, J. (2012) *Pathways of the Mind: Oral Tradition and the Internet*. Champaign, IL:
    University of Illinois Press.
Logan, R.K. (2010) *Understanding New Media: Extending Marshall McLuhan*. New York:
    Peter Lang.
Ong, W.J. (1977) *Interfaces of the Word*. Ithaca, NY: Cornell University Press.

4

Literature and Culture in the Age of the New Media
Dynamics of Evolution and Change

Peter Swirski

In the age of blogs, tweets, and webinars; in the age of Wi-Fi, u-streams, and podcasts; in the age of cable, satellite, and pay-per-view HDTV; in the age of fiction factories, direct mail-order publishing, and multimedia-packaging, is old-time literary culture a thing of the past? Is the book itself, the paperbound, dog-eared, old-fashioned medium of artertainment, destined to go the way of the LP, the floppy disk, and Betamax? Or are there reasons to believe that the death of the old media in the age of the new is at least to some extent a self-serving myth cooked up by public-relations departments of multinational communication conglomerates?

The Book Culture

In 2001 the old (print) media reported on a Gallup poll that diagnosed what appeared to be a new trend: *aliteracy*. "I didn't finish one book," reported an archetypal undergraduate who had, nonetheless, aced her English course: "I skimmed every second page" (Babiak 2001: A9; for background and analysis, see Swirski 2005). This willing suspension of belief in book reading was also diagnosed among educated professionals, including American teachers who in the same poll confessed to the same aliteracy rate as their students: 50 percent.

"The book is dead," we have been hearing for decades, slain by the twin assassins of TV and Tinseltown flicks. Yet, as *Publishers Weekly* pointedly reported in 1974, a full one-third of all motion pictures produced annually in the USA are based on previously published novels. Nor is this umbilical connection between books and films anything new. Even during the silent film era, Penguin's Reader's Library raked in massive profits from film novelizations that appeared on bookstands even as the marquees hit the town. Von Harbou's *Metropolis*, *The Sea Beast* (with Douglas Fairbanks), *My Best Girl* (with Mary Pickford), and *Cobra* (Rudolf Valentino) were

A Companion to New Media Dynamics, First Edition. Edited by John Hartley, Jean Burgess, and Axel Bruns.
© 2013 John Wiley & Sons, Ltd. Published 2015 by John Wiley & Sons, Ltd.

all readily available to those who preferred the allure of the printed page to the moving pictures.

As for the alleged death of book culture in the postwar decades – the period that saw the rise of a raft of new media such as broadcast television, cable, VHS video, CD-ROM, and now the Internet – the facts tell a different story. The television era ushered in such a runaway boom in book publishing that the industry has long been sending red flares for some form of reduction in numbers. Apparently less *is* more sometimes, even in the highly competitive world of mass-market fiction.

These days some hi-tech futurologists point to broadband technology with its interactive, on-demand, socially networked content as the reason why book culture is supposedly working under a death sentence. Books are going the way of the dodo, they claim, even as they tote next to the obligatory iPod and iPhone the *nouveau chic*, the iPad. Like its many market rivals, this tablet touch-screen computer can hold – or access – the contents of whole digitized libraries, newspapers, and other communication platforms and even provide the illusion of page turning. Some protective covers are even designed to look like . . . a hardback book.

The medium may indeed be the message but, among the hype about the former, few care to remember Mighty Words Inc., a digital provider and Internet publisher of Stephen King's e-novella, *Riding the Bullet*. In 2002, this ambitious startup joined the ranks of innumerable other Internet publishers by going out of business. "I thought electronic publishing was going to be big," rued its founder and CEO. "What a rude awakening I got" (Associated Press 2001b: E1).

Succumbing to the futuristic hype, in which books were mere roadkill on the information autobahn, in the 1990s academic and public libraries even began to scale down purchases of new volumes, expecting e-ducation to go entirely digital by Y2K. Yet, despite the relentless pressure from the electronic media and their increasingly portable and powerful G4 gizmos, the old-time, page-rustling, cover-creased book refuses to throw in the towel. After all, quipped the director of Princeton University Press in the days before e-books and instant downloads, "Who wants to go to bed with a floppy disk – or with a microfilm projector?" (cited in Tebbel 1995: 155).

Indeed, book publishing has not only flourished during the broadcast era – the very same era that many feared was going to bury Gutenberg's galaxy – but continues to flourish in the era of broadband. Worldwide book production, as indexed by the number of titles published annually, grew more than threefold between 1950 and 1980, when a whole new generation grew up glued to the monochrome vacuum tube and then the monochrome-compatible solid-state color screen. From global estimates of under a quarter-million new titles in 1950, the total climbed to almost three-quarter million in 1980. This rate of growth was much higher than that of the world's population, which during the same 30-year period rose from 2.5 billion to 4.5 billion.

There are, of course, well-known methodological issues that surround such global tallies, beginning with the basic collection problem: how detailed and/or reliable are a country's output surveys? One also wonders about persistent collection lags (how come nations don't report their surveys more often?), missing data (why do some fail to report in certain years?), discrepancies (why do national estimates sometimes depart from UNESCO tallies or show illogical spikes and troughs from year to year?), and even the absence of reports from certain countries altogether.

In spite of these and related difficulties, crosschecks reveal a high degree of consistency across various reporting agencies. And the picture they paint is unrelenting. The total number of book copies printed around the world, estimated at 2.5 billion in 1950, was close to 9 billion in 1980 and more than 13 billion in 1996, and is close to 15 billion today. In other words, from there being one paper volume per person worldwide in 1950, 30 years later there were already two – a 100 percent increase in little more than the lifespan of just one generation (during the same period, global literacy only rose from 1.2 billion to 2.5 billion, a rate far below that of book production).

That same generation passed the baton to ours, which continues to produce books at the same supercharged rate – so much so that, despite demographic expansion, the ratio of books to people in the third millennium is edging close to two and a quarter. But even these astronomical figures do not amount to much until understood in their *cumulative* context. Difficult as it is to believe, more than half of all the books ever published appeared after the first season of *Dragnet*. More than half of all wordsmiths who ever put pen to paper did so after the original broadcast of *I Love Lucy*.

In the second decade of the third millennium, the number of new book titles published worldwide in any given year exceeds two million. Some 400 new paperback titles are released *monthly* in the USA. The number of *Heftromans*, inexpensive 64-page pulp fiction novelettes that flood the German market, exceeds 200 million copies a year. Despite the nostalgic idealization of the Renaissance as the time when one could allegedly keep up with the flow of information, those days (if they ever existed) are gone forever, never to come back.

More than ever before in the history of our civilization, the production and consumption of books has reached unsustainable proportions. An upside-down pyramid or a giant time cone, its apex in the past and its cavernous maw in our face, is how Salvador Dali might paint the book world as we know it. Take all these books and add to them the output from the myriad literary journals, magazines, newsletters, fugitive publishing, underground presses, Internet posts, and the like, and you can begin to comprehend the number of words deposited year in, year out on library bookshelves and in mainframe memory banks.

The volume of the printed word in circulation is difficult to comprehend. Google has by now digitized close to 15 million of the (lowball) estimate of 150 million *titles* released since the invention of the Gutenberg press in 1450. In 2011 the British Library teamed up with Google to bring another quarter million of out-of-copyright books – some 40 million pages in all – online. With the Internet giant willingly footing the bill, other libraries are only waiting to jump on the broadbandwaggon. All this, of course, is but a fraction of the total of several *exabytes* of cultural information produced in the history of our civilization coming at us from all around (gigabyte × 1000 = terabyte; terabyte × 1000 = petabyte;

petabyte × 1000 = exabyte). YouTube alone has 24 hours of video uploaded on it every *minute* of every hour of every day of the year.

Put all these numbers together and they add up to a trend that is as dramatic as inevitable: the end of cultural history. Every statistical index of every area of cultural production attests to the fact that the volume of infobits per unit of time is soaring. This means that the dateline that divides the total amount of cultural production into two halves is creeping closer and closer to the present – and will continue to do so. Currently this halfline is still a few decades or at least a few years behind (in 2011 *The Economist* estimated that "the amount of data stored worldwide doubles every 18 months"). But the function that describes this process is asymptotic, meaning that we are edging ever closer to the day when all of our cultural past becomes but a negligible fraction of the cultural present in which we are apparently destined to be trapped forever.

So much for serving citizens and consumers by bringing more and more information to their fingertips. We live in the age of infoglut that willy-nilly turned all of us into infogluttons. The proportion of what is original to the totality of cultural output may not have changed, but multiplying both a millionfold has the effect of burying the former as if it wasn't there at all. Though it may take a long time, you can be sure to find 10 good books in a thousand. But you will never find 10 million good books in a billion – or wrap your head around the cultural tsunamis beating daily at our door.

As far as reading culture goes, the figures are equally unequivocal in establishing that the book is not going anywhere. Quite the contrary. The number of new titles released in the USA alone more than quadrupled between 1950 and 1991, and more than quadrupled again in the 20 years hence (Steinberg 1996: 243). Even as Amazon.com – whose online retail model facilitates offering a much wider selection of titles than was feasible for old-time neighborhood walk-in bookstores – is putting bricks-and-mortar rivals out of business, its rise as the world's prime book retailer is another proof of the power of the printed and/or pixelated word.

Naturally, it is possible to question the correlation between publishing and readership; so, to honor the skeptic, let us follow the link between book publishing and the intermediate stage: book purchasing. Here the numbers are even more eloquent. Book sales in 1991 were 35 times greater than in 1950. The mushroom cloud of money to be made in publishing books in the age of the new media just keeps getting bigger and bigger. In 2000, net sales in the USA crept close to 25 billion dollars, due to expand by another 3 percent in 2001 (Associated Press 2001a).

Even though the twin Anglo-American markets are the giants of publishing, they make up just a fraction of the global trends all moving in the same direction. The numbers speak for themselves. Rounded up, the growth in the selected international book title output during the six years between 1990 and 1996 alone was as follows: China up from 74 000 to 110 000; Germany up from 61 000 to 71 000; Spain up from 36 000 to 46 000; and Italy up from 25 000 to 35 000. Even as France reported a wee drop and Russia held steady, in the early 1990s Japan chalked up a Godzilla-size upswing from 35 000 to 56 000 while Holland zoomed from 14 000 to 34 000. Even minor-league players such as Canada found a seat on this runaway train, going from 8000 in 1990 to an estimated 20 000 in 1996 (*Bowker's Annual* 2000: 530–534).

Of course, bigger does not necessarily amount to better, and one must be careful about greeting these colossal numbers with uncritical hurrahs. There is no straightforward correlation between quantity and quality in the world of publishing – at least none has ever been established – and even less so in the world of art. Averaging statistical data, moreover, frequently conceals an uneven distribution of readership. Back in 1951, for instance, a mere 10 percent of the adult population accounted for 70 percent of book reading, while 10 percent of buyers accounted for 80 percent of sales (Berelson 1951: 8; see also Dutscher 1954). Notwithstanding ensuing demographic changes and gains in general education, it is at least conceivable that the percentages may be similarly skewed today.

Likewise, the fact that these days there are many more outlets for buying novels cannot hide that the lion's share belongs to a handful of hot-off-the-press-bestseller-list-and-moccacino-latte-hold-the-sugar-please chains whose priorities are often at odds with those of book lovers and book buyers. Worse, bottom-line balance-sheet considerations mean that most booksellers refuse to buy first novels altogether and balk at storing titles that do not promise better-than-average sales. Howard Kaminsky, president of Warner Books, rued a generation back: "Six years ago, we were publishing perhaps twenty books a month. Now we publish fourteen, including reissues. And our sales are about six times what they were six years ago. We publish more books by publishing fewer books" (in Whiteside 1980: part 3, 132; a similar point is made in Dessauer 1974).

Be that as it may, a sure sign of the publishing industry's vitality is the keen interest that Wall Street has evinced in its operations over the past half-century. The key players thrived by becoming public stock companies and funding a wave of expansion (Random House, Houghton Mifflin), diversifying into other fields (Macmillan, Harcourt), swallowing their smaller brethren (Harper and Row buying out J.B. Lippincott; the Hearst syndicate adding the hardcover Arbor House to their softcover Avon Books), or succumbing to the widely publicized "urge to merge" (Doubleday and Dell, Viking and Penguin).

Others ended up grafted onto multimedia corporate giants. Matsushita Electric, for one, acquired not only the Music Corporation of America but also, riding coattails, the Putnam-Berkeley Publishing Group. By the early 1980s, Doubleday remained the only family-owned business in the book business before it too became absorbed by Bertelsmann, the German communications conglomerate that served as the template for the menacing dot-com empire fought by 007 in *Tomorrow Never Dies*. The clearest index, however, of how profitable book publishing is today is the speed with which the movie industry got into the act.

MCA, Filmway Pictures, Gulf and Western, and others all now own reputable publishing houses. Gulf and Western, for instance, boasts Paramount, Simon & Schuster, and Pocket Books in its entertainment division, while Warner Communications has gone as far as to found its own Warner Books. Oprah Winfrey, the recently "retired" queen of daytime TV and a media titan in her own right, has her own book club and a literary magazine. In a 2003 ceremony, she received not only accolades but a standing ovation from the Association of American Publishers for her contributions to publishing.

The Highbrow Margins

Besides proving beyond reasonable doubt that old-time book culture is not in decline, what else do the relevant data document? First and foremost is the increasing marginalization of the literature traditionally accorded the bulk of attention by academic and highbrow institutions, namely the classics, poetry, and new "literary" fiction. The numbers from book distribution by US general retailers are emphatic in this regard. For the relevant categories of fiction, their respective shares of the American market in 1999 were 44 percent for popular fiction and bestsellers versus a little over 1 percent for the classics, new literary fiction, and poetry (Dessauer 1999: 133).

Comparatively speaking, the classics, literary fiction, and poetry amount to a little over 2.5 percent of the volume of popular fiction sold in America. Needless to say, the picture is equally lopsided elsewhere on the planet. An astounding 45 percent of all books and periodicals sold in Japan are, for example, the popular manga cartoons. Some of them are, of course, little more than the soft porn and hardcore violence that social critics accuse them of being. Others, however, exhibit high degrees of graphic, narrative, and psychological sophistication, targeting every demographic and cultural niche, from young girls' bildungsroman to company men's escapist fantasies to stories that tap into golden agers' yen for historical nostalgia.

Two quick rejoinders. First, book distribution numbers can sometimes be misleading due to the common practice of remaindering unsold copies, which can add up to a jaw-dropping 40 percent of total run. Second, a counterpoint: the above is at least partly offset by the presence of other fiction categories (e.g., juvenile), which, when brought into the picture, take us right back to where Harry Potter left it in the last paragraph. A crosscheck with recent data compiled for the American Booksellers Association proves, in fact, that the above figures are highly accurate.

Not only does popular fiction's share of consumer purchases of adult books not change but it also closely matches the distribution figures. Take 1991, for example. Fiction (comprising categories such as adult, espionage/thriller, fantasy, general, historical, male adventure, mystery/detective, occult, religious, romance, science fiction, suspense/psychology, TV movies, and western) commanded almost 55 percent of the buyers' market as opposed to highbrow's less than 3 percent. The 1998 figures once again gave the lion's share of 52 percent to popular literature, with less than 4 percent going to art/literature/poetry (the latter beefed up by categories such as art/architecture, literature-classics/contemporary, performing arts, poetry/plays, and somewhat ironically pop arts).

It is true that, in terms of titles released annually, highbrow fiction commands a greater share of the market than distribution figures document. But there yawns a gulf the size of Sophie Kinsella's bank account between the public and the custodians of letters with regard to what they buy and read and what they peg their cultural literacy on. The knee-jerk riposte that the highbrow margin constitutes the cream of the literary crop must contend with several caveats. Quite apart from the patent inaccuracy of such protestations, documented in the bestselling *From Lowbrow to Nobrow* (Swirski 2005), such elitism is simply misplaced when considering any media, old or new, in their sociocultural contexts.

Outside of (qualitative) allegations of inferiority, there are familiar quantitative reasons for this educational and curricular inattention to popular fiction. More books have seen the light of day since 1950 than in the whole literary tradition stretching as far back as *Gilgamesh*. "The point has long since passed," concede the editors of *Five Hundred Years of Printing*, "when any library or bookseller can stock more than a fraction of the books in print, or when every book which merits reviews receives any" (Steinberg 1996: 243). Doubleday, to take only one example, estimates that each year it receives 10 000 manuscripts "over the transom" (the industry's term for unsolicited) alone, of which a few may be signed on (Balkin 1977: 6).

An instructive microcosm of this state of affairs is the world of scholarly and scientific publishing. At the formation of the Association of American University Presses in 1932, only eight presses were reported at an informal meeting of directors. Fifty years on there were already more than 70, and at the beginning of our millennium no less than 125. Similarly, where there were "only" 100 000 science journals in the world in the mid-1960s, there are more than a million today. Between 1960 and 2010, the number of journals in economics alone went from 80 to 800.

The flood of academic publications is so urgent that, beginning in the 1980s, it became necessary to publish indices to indices of publication titles. One only wonders how much time such meta-indices can buy, and how many years we are from publishing indices of indices of indices. No wonder that, even as today's libraries still spend most of their effort on digitizing and compressing data, tomorrow they will have to focus exclusively on selecting and searching. Paradoxically, it may become easier to generate new information than identify where existing data might be found.

Computers that facilitate search and access do not, after all, attack the information glut but merely alleviate its symptoms. Google may put millions of web pages at your fingertips in milliseconds, creating a potent illusion of better and faster access to the treasury of information out yonder in cyberspace; however, you will never be able to check even a tiny fraction of this embarrassment of riches or monitor the algorithm's search priorities. The blind search-engine demands blind faith from its end users, a quaint notion in view of the docketful of lawsuits against Google for fixing their results.

One of the paradoxes generated by this state of affairs is the leveling effect in the case of literary reviews by the taste-makers. In the case of well-known authors, the system still works – more or less. Raves in the *New York Times Book Review* or *Los Angeles Book Review* still pump up sales, whereas pans bring them down. But, as research shows, this correlation obtains only for already established literary names. For everybody else, the rules in the age of the new media are pure Alice in Wonderland. Two thumbs up or two thumbs down have exactly the same upshot in the contemporary marketplace. *Both* will give your sales a boost.

Once again, there is little new in this new-media twist on the old adage that any publicity is supposed to be good publicity. Except that we are no longer speaking of media fads and stunts contrived to bring their authors their 15 minutes of fame but of the incipient collapse of the entire critical superstructure. Tasked by society to sieve out art from chaff in the name of values that far transcend the merely aesthetic, cultural institutions are fighting a rearguard and losing battle. When branding – in this case the brand name of the source of the review – trumps the actual content of the review, encounters between art and critical taste-makers are best modeled in terms of random Brownian motion.

These days, as long as they issue forth from the critical pantheon, a critical pan and a critical rave will have the same effect: plucking a book out of the obscurity of being but one of a million titles published each year. The memory of the review fades, whereas the memory of its source lingers. As advertisers, marketers, spin gurus, and prospect theorists know all too well, brands simplify choices. And, in a world that inundates us with too many choices, ballpark guesstimates have to satisfice. What was that? Oh yeah, the name's familiar, saw it in the *NYT* (see Sorensen et al., 2010).

The New Old Media

The above is not meant to suggest that the emergence of the new media has had no perceptible effect on the old. Early in 2011, Eric Schmidt, the executive chairman of Google, made waves by declaring that, in the world of com-tech, "old" companies such as Microsoft (founded in 1975) have fallen terminally behind the "gang of four" of new consumer-oriented businesses: Amazon, Apple, Facebook, and Google. The marketplace and share-buyers concurred in this upbeat assessment. In mid-2011, LinkedIn, a social network for professionals, floated shares on the New York Stock Exchange only to see them balloon to almost nine billion dollars – more than 500 times the company's profits from only a year before.

Even though the hype about Renren (Chinese Facebook), Groupon (where customers sign up for offers from local firms), LinkedIn, Twitter, and other Internet colossi obscures the fact that frequently they serve old wine in new-media wineskins, in some respects the changes have been as real as dramatic. For one, at least in the developed countries, the word of mouth has by and large morphed into the word of mouse. Crowd-sourcing, harnessed prominently and dominantly by Wikipedia, has taken over what used to be the domain of paid professionals. Cloudsourcing – removing software from the desktop to banks of web-based computers so that consumers need only log in to find all manner of word-processing, image-editing, music-mixing, data-crunching, social-networking capabilities at their fingertips – is the next grail.

Online programs streamed live in broadband are perhaps the clearest reminder of how much the role position of the broadcast and print media has changed since the coming of age of the Internet and its multiplex image-and-text sharing platforms. Even as the established media – television, radio, newspapers – lose ground in the struggle for the attention of younger audiences, the popularity of real-time streaming has grown as an inexpensive and democratic alternative to the news delivered by major broadcasting conglomerates that routinely edit content for length, format, and political slant.

Uploaded in real time, raw unedited footage has a proven record of drawing viewers who are increasingly skeptical, not to say suspicious, of the manner in which news is reported (or not) by mainstream broadcasters and newspapers. Interested segments of the public can verify what appears in the national or local media or, even more often, get hold of information that does not make it there at all. Nor has this new delivery platform escaped the attention of marginalized political parties, public figures, or even regular citizens discontent with six o'clock news coverage.

All are taking advantage of the opportunities offered by the new media technologies by uploading unedited footage by the truckload, bypassing not just the censors but also the need for buying prohibitively expensive airtime. Unlike private broadcasters, who are crucially dependent on advertising revenue, online services are frequently supported by paying users. This allows streaming services to run programs that mainstream and even local TV stations will not run for fear of backlash from their sponsors.

The mainstream media defend themselves with this or that version of the cub-reporter's truism that you cannot report everything. The key questions are, of course, who does the selecting and who selects the selectors? Time and again, evidence proves that mainstream news providers – broadcast *and* broadband – snap to their corporate owners' heel. What passes for selectivity is, in reality, consistent media bias: consistent over an apparent diversity of programs, news crews, and networks. The bias favors laissez-faire economics over social planning, well-to-do WASPs over low-income ethnics, officialdom over reformers, management over labor, and corporations over community critics. Given who owns the media, such distortions are not innocent errors of omission but errors of commission perpetrated in the name of vested and suited interests (for background and analysis, see Swirski 2010a: Chapter 4).

Such partisan bias was recently dragged into the sunlight by a muckraking documentary, *Outfoxed* (Greenwald 2004). Subtitled *Rupert Murdoch's War on Journalism*, the picture paraded a roster of former Fox News producers, bookers, writers, consultants, and reporters, all grimly testifying as to how they were pressured as a matter of course "to push a 'right-wing' point of view or risk their jobs" (Greenwald 2004: back cover). After months of monitoring Fox News programming, *Outfoxed* exposed what lies behind the network's "fair and balanced" self-promotions. Selective reporting, biased consulting, event doctoring, and inter-view bullying are almost routine and corroborated by all echelons of the network's former staff.

Although the media like to shroud themselves in bromides about being a private profit-making enterprise that serves the public, they serve one public only. Media companies and the staff in their employ work first of all for the corporate owners who pay their salaries, second for the financial interests who sponsor the programming, and finally for the higher-income-bracket audiences targeted by the advertising. The consequences are plain to see. Fearful of losing the ratings battle to the upstarts, broadcasters rewrite the standards on tolerance and excitement. Mundane reporting is out, extreme journalism is in. The demands of the marketplace dictate that consumers must never be bored – or educated.

Internet companies, with individual bloggers and podcasters snapping at their heels, vie with television, newspapers, and magazines for the public's scant time and attention, shrugging off such old-fangled notions as objective stenography of events. Forget assiduous reportage of the ins and outs of the political process or of the complexities of multicultural eclecticism. Today the media's role is to provoke and titillate with hyperbolic headlines, exclusive covers, and flash-news story breaks, more often than not juiced up by blood-spattered visual aids. To sell copy, infotainment thrives on exaggeration and embellishment, and even occasional out-and-out lies.

In 1998 Stephen Glass, the *New Republic* point-man for sociopolitical analysis and commentary, was caught making up quotations, websites, faxes, and even organizations for his highly sought-after reports. Evoking the changes in the media business, he pleaded the pressures of extreme journalism as extenuating circumstance. So did Jayson Blair of *The New York Times*, after being caught plagiarizing quotes and fabricating outright fictions in dozens of articles. So did Janet Cooke, formerly of the *Washington Post*, Patricia Smith of the *Boston Globe*, and Jay Forman of *Slate*. In 2011 an entire "newspaper" – Murdoch's British Sunday tabloid *News of the World* – went out of existence following the scandal ignited by its phone hacking, all in the name of scooping the competition in the cutthroat struggle for a dwindling market share.

The advent of the Internet media has unwittingly created a paradise for plagiarists. Copy pasting is facilitated not only by the electronic technology but also – perhaps especially – by the information glut. Blogging, whether in its news-reporting, narcis-sistic, or flaming incarnations, is inundating the web, with each new post rendering each new post that much less likely to be ever read. The opportunity to steal content from this ever-expanding infosphere is ubiquitous, tacitly or overtly sanctioned by new media such as Facebook, which works hard to obliterate traditional notions of privacy and property (except when it comes to its own brand name and bottom line).

The results are predictable. Plagiarism is on the rise, documented among jour-nalists and bloggers who sometimes do not even bother to change the font and formatting of the source text. Others resort to handy algorithms, developed origi-nally by news services to parse and summarize items for syndication. These shield the word thieves from detection by dint of a handful of crude but effective techniques: paraphrasing critical passages, substituting synonyms for adjectives and verbs, changing passive into active voice or vice versa – the entire text remixed and repackaged at a keystroke.

You would have to live under a rock or in Utopia to believe that academia or education in general is immune. More and more institutions block students from bringing cell phones to exams lest they take advantage of Wi-Fi environments by searching for and downloading information. The educational arms race continues as some schools and teachers avail themselves of software that scours billions of online pages to check for cut-and-paste plagiarism or even uses advanced frequency analysis algorithms to identify copy-cat free-riders.

The new media – exemplified by new social media – are indeed flexing their muscles in the contest to be the next new thing. Ironically, despite the New Age corporate mottos (starting with Google's "Don't be evil") in their market practice, they are hardly distinguishable from the old media. In 2011 a minor scandal erupted when Facebook was revealed to have hired Burston-Marsteller, a leading PR company, to commission bloggers and newspaper reporters to smear Google, its closest business rival. Mudslinging, story spinning by freely distributing ready-made copy, news doctoring by soliciting favorable experts, lawsuits designed to stall research or even launch of a rival product – any trick to secure the edge over competition in the race for continued expansion.

Hype and hyperbole thrive in this environment. Facebook is held as a textbook example of how to get from corporate zero to hero, with 400 million users and growing fast (its own sources claim the number is already 500 million). No one cares to take note that, like Groupon, the company does not track users but accounts, many of which are dormant, used only once or only once in a while, or multiple accounts belonging to a single user (personal interview with Ufuk Kirtis, Project Manager and Media Analyst for T2 Teknoloji, October 2011). Groupon itself is a case in point. It boasts more than 80 million users of whom a mere 15 million have actually used its services.

Standard statistical distribution and saturation models make it very likely, indeed, that there are only about 100 million active Facebook users among seven billion people on the planet. While the raw number is not insignificant, it adds up to 1.4 percent of the world's population, a quarter of which, as the World Bank estimates, does not even have access to a fixed-line or mobile telephone. Put differently, 98.6 percent of the world live in the world of real faces and real books without being the worse for it.

The Evolutionary Story

It is time to pause and reflect on the data at hand and on what it says about literature and culture in the age of the new media. First and foremost, it is clear that rumors of book culture's demise in the era of television and now in the era of the Internet have been greatly exaggerated. The art and the mass culture of telling stories are doing fine, thank you very much. Moreover, the secret of their success is not so secret at all. As the growing number of studies in the bio-sciences, the social sciences, and even the humanities document, our propensity for telling stories is an inalienable part of our human nature and thus an inalienable part of our lives (see Black and Bower 1980; Swirski 2007; Boyd 2009).

Even though our modern urban lives are orders of magnitude more complex than in prehistorical times, we approach our social and physical environment pretty much in the same terms as we did when we roamed the plains, ate bark and scavenged carrion, and interacted only with a handful of other hunter-foragers in our group. To be more precise, our psychological and social life – which includes our extraordinary propensity for inventing stories and sharing them with others – capitalizes on our evolved ability to attribute motives, intentions, and beliefs to individuals with whom we daily interact. Without this adaptive faculty, human life and human society as we know them could not exist.

To put it differently, what lies at the heart of human society and human sociability is our mentally mediated capacity for cooperative interaction. This capacity hinges, in turn, on sharing a common mental world and, no less crucially, on the awareness of other participants in this joint mental construct. Within this worldwide web of minds, we recognize each other's intentions and express them in ways meant to be reflexively recognized as having been meant to be recognized (unless, of course, we decide to engage in deception). This Gricean picture, still overlooked by literary criticism at large but informing every field of study of human sociality, underlies our inferences about each other's behaviors, beliefs, and motivations. It underlies, in other words, what is commonly known as Theory of Mind (ToM): a set of cognitive abilities for modeling and making inferences about one another's mental states (see Grice 1957, 1968, 1969, 1971, 1982; on ToM see Sober and Wilson 1999; Tomasello 1999, 2009, 2010; Baron-Cohen 2005; Tomasello et al. 2005).

Theory of Mind is not some obscurantist academic theory. It is something that all normal human beings do effortlessly, developing this uncanny psychological faculty in infancy, as early as around one year old. We make reliable inferences about what other people feel, think, and know on the basis of behavioral clues gathered and frequently provided for this very purpose during the process of communication – clues ranging from language and gestures to facial mimicry and other aspects of behavior.

We all do it and, equally importantly, we all do it well. As communicators, literary or otherwise, we do not just respond to actions as viewed from the outside but rather to interpreted actions as viewed "from the inside." Think of a blink of an eye, which can be an involuntary reflex or a signaling wink. The difference could not be greater and more significant, insofar as human interaction, and thus human psychology, is characterized by responses to intentions and not behaviors. In short, interpretation, including literary interpretation, entails inferring motives or goals from actions.

Why is this important? Because this uniquely human, cooperative, mentally mediated interaction forms the adaptive basis of social organization with everything it entails, from the emergence of a dazzling variety of cultures to the cumulative evolution of social and cultural assets. We are equipped with cognitive adaptations that are the mental equivalent of bodily organs, in that they have evolved to perform specific tasks and perform them well and fast, for the most part without any reflective awareness in the mind's "I."

This has demonstrable consequences for the way we process information and emotions. As I showed at length in *Of Literature and Knowledge* (2007), we think in stories and, when we think in stories, we think better. In the rationalist tradition, logic and formal analysis have long been extolled as class achievers with storytelling playing the role of an enlightening but remedial diversion. No longer. Research into cognitive processing upturns the received wisdom on the subject. It turns out that inferences derived from constructing and manipulating mental models have often less to do with formal analysis than with narrative framing. Not only do we remember stories better than theorems but we tend to think *in* stories, not theorems, and when we do we memorize and retrieve data with more accuracy.

The ramifications of all this are enormous – and still largely overlooked by many literary and cultural scholars, not to mention literary and cultural educators. Not surprisingly, therefore, it takes philosophers of science such as Nancy Nersessian to spell out the essence of the emergent paradigm. People typically process contextual information by falling back on narrative patterns, she writes, "rather than by applying rules of inference to a system of propositions representing the content of the text" (Nersessian 1993: 293; see also Bruner 1973; Lakoff and Turner 1989; Turner 1996; Swirski 2007). In *The Literary Mind*, Mark Turner pulls, if anything, even fewer punches. In terms of language development, story-like thinking and metaphorical projections precede the advent of grammar. "Parable is the root of human thinking" (Turner 1996: 168).

The power of the word over the number, of the narrative over the database, is borne out by every aspect of our daily lives. As we all know, people's recollection of natural language is far superior than of strings of digits. Bitwise, 237874992 on the telephone keypad is equivalent to BESTPIZZA, yet canny spammers and advertisers exploit the fact that the slogan will be retained long after the number has vanished from memory. Evidence from neuroscience and psychology documents that human beings are disposed toward human-interest information, not abstractions and numbers. In the cognitive science, fledgling research in a new subfield, narrative intelligence, marks the recognition of this hitherto neglected component of cognitive processing.

Anthropologists corroborate that, on top of being efficient information conveyers, stories outclass rivals in facilitating information storage. In foraging tribes, practical information about consumable resources is routinely conveyed in the form of stories. Strung into a narrative, useful knowledge about plants and animals is stored and retrieved more vividly than an informationally equivalent series of discrete data points. Contextualizing information, the narrative form fosters good memory and good recollection – first steps toward good thinking. Most preliterate societies employed professional memorizers charged with storing prodigious amounts of data – historical, social, legal, cultural, religious – in mind. Oftentimes such sensitive data were organized into verse narrative, as in the case of Mohammed's *Qur'an*.

Medieval troubadours were apt to recite chansons of credulity-defying length thanks to the latter's high mnemonic quotient. Human-indexed relations between narrative agents and events helped them to memorize and then reproduce massive amounts of information. Evolutionary predisposition to symmetry further aids in grouping and organizing diffuse facts. Repetition – whether in the form of a rhyme scheme, alliteration, refrain, chorus, allusion, periphrasis, or any other – is none other than a form of translational symmetry. Its mnemonic quotient, detectable in the propensity to recollect, is even higher for verse than for narrative prose, while both are vastly superior to digits or nonsense syllables (see the classic experimental results by Lyon 1941a, 1941b, 1941c).

This is not to say that abstraction does not play a significant role in the cultural world of the old and the new media. Consider the Flynn effect – the startling rise in average intelligence test scores over time. In the USA, scores in Wechsler's Intelligence Scale for Children have risen on average by 3 percent per decade, but the effect has been observed and confirmed worldwide. James R. Flynn (2010) himself has argued persuasively that it this is owing to our embeddedness in a civilization that, saturated with science and culture that demand higher-level integration and problem-solving skills, drives general cognition forward.

Significantly, from the standpoint of literature, the same effect has been observed for semantic (concept-based) and episodic (contextual) memory – two fundamental components of storytelling. This is, again, why old-time literary culture has little to fear from the advent of the new media. The recent fad of serializing novels by streaming them via podcasts may be new in terms of a delivery platform but it is nothing but Dickens remixed for the twenty-first-century new-media technology. Indeed, Flynn himself has notoriously contended that people can learn more from reading great works of literature than from going to university.

Nobrow, Evolist, and Beyond

In the age of the new media, the literary system may look like it is belching smoke, losing parts, and shuddering when negotiating cultural and technological corners. Even so, it shows no signs of slowing down. Two of the trends to consolidate over the last decades that give renewed hope for its future are the emergence of the nobrow taste culture in literature and evolutionary literary studies (evolist) in literary criticism and theory. Even as the study of popular literature has made strides in legitimacy since the days of T.S. Eliot, it has spawned an increasingly visible nobrow culture, indifferent to rhetorical tugs of war between aesthetic highs and genre lows, liberally borrowing from both while relishing the attendant intellectual cachet *and* popular (not to say commercial) appeal.

At the same time, aiming to revitalize the sterile canons of postmodernist free-for-all, literary scholarship is in the process of trying to reinvigorate (not to say reinvent) the discipline by promoting more responsible, aesthetically nuanced, and methodologically consilient forms of discussing art (see Wilson 1998; Carroll 2001; Swirski 2007, 2010b). One such comes through the realization that literature, like any other aspect of human culture, is a manifestation of our species' adaptation to the conditions imposed by the physical, biological, and cultural environments we have inhabited in the struggle for existence. This evolutionary perspective, which endeavors to account as much for the invariant nature of thought and art as for its subjectively aesthetic aspects, is a milestone on the road into the literary-critical twenty-second century and beyond.

In the end, the twenty-first century will end up looking very different from the one we are familiar with when it comes to literary culture. The game changer will most likely be electronic publishing. In the four years since Amazon introduced its first e-reader, the volume of e-books sold has grown so rapidly that it now accounts for a staggering half of the company's sales. The number of self-published books in America alone has already passed the three-quarter million mark *a year*. Put these two trends together and they could not make it clearer that book culture is thriving, having jumped from printed to electronic formats – at least for those who prefer their Lem, McBain, and Dostoyevsky in pixels rather than inkblots.

References

Associated Press, Chicago (2001a) "Book Sales Edge Up in US Market." *Edmonton Journal* (June 3), C6.

Associated Press, Chicago. (2001b) "Stephen King's E-Novella Not Enough to Keep Mighty Words Solvent." *Edmonton Journal* (December 14), E1.

Babiak, T. (2001) "A Nation of 'Aliterates': Are We Too Busy to Really Read?" *Edmonton Journal* (June 3), A1, A9.

Balkin, R. (1977) *A Writer's Guide to Book Publishing*. New York: Hawthorn Books.

Baron-Cohen, S. (2005) "The Empathizing System: A Revision of the 1994 Model of the Mindreading System" in B.J. Ellis and D.F. Bjorklund, eds., *Origins of the Social Mind: Evolutionary Psychology and Child Development*. New York: Guilford, pp. 468–492.

Berelson, B. (1951) "Who Reads What Books and Why?" *Saturday Review of Literature* (May 12), 7–8, 30–31.

Black, J. B and Bower, G.H. (1980) "Story Understanding as Problem Solving." *Poetics* 9, 223–250.

Bowker's Annual, 45th edn. (2000). London: Bowker.

Boyd, B. (2009) *On the Origin of Stories: Evolution, Cognition, and Fiction*. Cambridge, MA: Belknap.

Bruner, J.S. (1973) *Beyond the Information Given: Studies in the Psychology of Knowing*. New York: Norton.

Carroll, J. (2001) *Reading Human Nature: Literary Darwinism in Theory and Practice.* New York: SUNY Press.

Dessauer, J.P. (1974) "Some Hard Facts about the Economics of Publishing." *Publishers Weekly* (August 5), 22–25.

Dessauer, J.P. (1999) *Book Publishing: The Basic Introduction. New Expanded Edition.* New York: Continuum.

Dutscher, A. (1954) "The Book Business in America." *Contemporary Issues*, 5, 38–58.

The Economist (2011) "Schumpeter: Too Much Information." (July 2), 59.

Flynn, J.R. (2010) *The Torchlight List: Around the World in 200 Books.* New Zealand: Awa Press.

Greenwald, R., dir. (2004) *Outfoxed: Rupert Murdoch's War on Journalism.* Carolina Productions; MoveOn.Org.

Grice, H.P. (1957) "Meaning." *Philosophical Review*, 66, 377–388.

Grice, H.P. (1968) "Utterer's Meaning, Sentence Meaning and Word Meaning." *Foundations of Language*, 4, 225–242.

Grice, H.P. (1969) "Utterer's Meaning and Intentions." *Philosophical Review*, 78, 147–177.

Grice, H.P. (1971) "Intention and Uncertainty." *Proceedings of the British Academy*, 57, 263–279.

Grice, H.P. (1982) "Meaning Revisited" in N.V. Smith, ed., *Mutual Knowledge*. New York: Academic, pp. 223–243.

Lakoff, G. and Turner, M. (1989) *More than Cool Reason: A Field Guide to Poetic Metaphor.* Chicago, IL: University of Chicago Press.

Lyon, D.O. (1914a) "The Relative of Length of Material to Time Taken for Learning, and the Optimum Distribution of Time. Part I." *Journal of Educational Psychology*, 5(1), 1–9.

Lyon, D.O. (1914b) "The Relative of Length of Material to Time Taken for Learning, and the Optimum Distribution of Time. Part II." *Journal of Educational Psychology*, 5(2), 85–91.

Lyon, D.O. (1914c) "The Relative of Length of Material to Time Taken for Learning, and the Optimum Distribution of Time. Part III." *Journal of Educational Psychology*, 5(3), 155–163.

Nersessian, N. (1993) "In the Theoretician's Laboratory: Thought Experimenting as Mental Modelling" in D. Hull, ed., *Proceedings of the Biennial Meeting of the Philosophy of Science Association*. East Lansing, MI: Philosophy of Science Association.

Sober, E. and Wilson, D.S. (1999) *Unto Others: The Evolution and Psychology of Unselfish Behavior.* New York: Dutton.

Sorensen, A. Berger, J., and Rasmussen, S. (2010) "Positive Effects of Negative Publicity: Can Negative Reviews Increase Sales?" *Marketing Science*, 29(5). http://mktsci.journal.informs.org/content/29/5/815.abstract.

Steinberg, S.H. (1996) *Five Hundred Years of Printing. Revised edition*, ed. J. Trevitt. London: British Library and Oak Knoll Press.

Swirski, P. (2005) *From Lowbrow to Nobrow.* Montreal, QC: McGill-Queen's University Press.

Swirski, P. (2007) *Of Literature and Knowledge: Explorations in Narrative Thought Experiments, Evolution, and Game Theory.* London and New York: Routledge.

Swirski, P. (2010a) *Ars Americana, Ars Politica: Partisan Expression and Nobrow American Culture.* Montreal, QC: McGill-Queen's University Press.

Swirski, P. (2010b) *Literature, Analytically Speaking: Explorations in the Theory of Interpretation, Analytic Aesthetics, and Evolution.* Austin, TX: University of Texas Press.

Tebbel, J. (1995) "The History of Book Publishing in the United States" in P.G. Altbach and E.S. Hoshino, eds., *International Book Publishing: An Encyclopedia*. New York and London: Garland, 147–155.

Tomasello, M. (1999) "The Human Adaptation for Culture." *Annual Review of Anthropology* 28, 509–529.

Tomasello, M. (2009) *Why We Cooperate*. Boston, MA: MIT Press.

Tomasello, M. (2010) *Origins of Human Communication*. Boston, MA: MIT Press.

Tomasello, M., Carpenter, M., Call, J. et al. (2005) "Understanding and Sharing Intentions: The Origins of Cultural Cognition." *Behavioral and Brain Sciences*, 28, 675–735.

Turner, M. (1996) *The Literary Mind*. New York: Oxford University Press.

Whiteside, T. (1980) "Onward and Upward with the Arts: The Blockbuster Complex." *New Yorker* (September 29), 48–101; (October 6), 63–146; (October 13), 52–143.

Wilson, E.O. (1998) *Consilience: The Unity of Knowledge*. New York: Knopf.

5

The Economics of New Media

John Quiggin

The rise of new media associated with the Internet has radically changed many aspects of daily life, and enabled us to do things that would have seemed unimaginable even a few decades ago. The speed and volume of communications have increased by a factor of a million or more since the Internet first emerged in the 1990s, and there has been a corresponding proliferation of information.

Yet the economic implications of new media are hard to discern. The famous observation of Robert Solow (1987) that "you can see the computer age everywhere but in the productivity statistics" is just as valid today as it was when he first made it more than 20 years ago.

The age of new media has produced only a handful of profitable new companies (Amazon and Google are the most notable examples). At the same time, while old media (newspapers, TV, radio) have proved more resilient than many observers expected, their business models have been severely undermined.

This chapter will discuss what economics can tell us about new media. More interestingly, perhaps, at least to those concerned with the long-term impact of new media, it will examine the implications of new media for economics and economic organization, and offer some policy recommendations.

What Can Economics Tell Us about New Media?

All media convey information. However, it is worth considering McLuhan's (1964) gnomic observation that "the medium is the message." For old media, and particularly broadcast mass media, information content is subordinate to the media product as a whole. As a result, economic analysis of old media can treat its outputs in much the same way as consumer goods, except for the fact, discussed below, that the provision of old media is typically financed by advertising rather than direct sale.

A Companion to New Media Dynamics, First Edition. Edited by John Hartley, Jean Burgess, and Axel Bruns.
© 2013 John Wiley & Sons, Ltd. Published 2015 by John Wiley & Sons, Ltd.

By contrast, with new media the flow of information is overwhelmingly dominant. Considered as media products, the output of new media is commonly of lower quality than that of old media (compare YouTube to broadcast TV, or blogs to glossy magazines). What makes them so appealing is the vast profusion of information of every possible kind.

So, an economic analysis of new media must begin with the economics of information and, in particular, with the idea of information as a public good.

Information as a Public Good

The idea of a public good, according to Samuelson (1954), is central to modern economics. In the absence of public goods (broadly defined to include public bads, such as pollution, and related concepts such as "natural monopoly"), a competitive economy will produce the best possible outcome consistent with any given distribution of income. In this situation, the only role of government is to allocate, and then to enforce, property rights. Further, there is no need for non-market institutions such as clubs or nongovernmental organizations. When public goods are present, everything changes. Market prices can no longer be relied upon to give a reliable guide to the allocation of resources.

Nonrivalry

A public good is defined by two characteristics: nonrivalry and nonexcludability. The more important of the two is nonrivalry, which means that consumption of the good by one person does not affect its availability for others. Once a nonrival good has been produced, it is socially undesirable to prevent anyone who wants to from consuming it – their consumption benefits them and does not harm anyone else. A "pure" public good has the happy property that it is nonexcludable, so that it is impossible to prevent anyone from consuming it once it has been produced. It is also logically possible to consider goods that are rival in consumption but not excludable. But, unless the population of consumers is small, such "open-access" goods are typically exhausted or degraded very rapidly, and therefore tend not to be observed.

Information is an almost perfect example of a pure public good. It is completely nonrival and largely nonexcludable. Nonrivalry means that, once produced, information can be used by as many people as can gain access to it, without reducing its availability to others. The crucial development of the information revolution has been to reduce the cost of distributing information, in many cases effectively to zero. Nonexcludability means that it is hard (though not impossible) to make information available to some users while excluding others. The crucial development here is the ease with which information can be reproduced.

Most public goods are local in some sense. The usual textbook examples of pure public goods include national defense and protection against floods, both of which apply only to the nation or river basin being protected. Public goods are also, in most cases, time-specific. Services (e.g., fireworks displays) are commonly consumed simultaneously with their production, while physical goods depreciate.

By contrast, information is naturally global and timeless in its nonrivalry. Once information has been discovered, it is available for all time and in all places. The words of Homer are still available to us, despite the thousands of years and (for Australians) thousands of kilometers that separate us from the courts of ancient Greece. Our inheritance from the past consists, ultimately, of information (technology and culture) rather than physical goods.

Not only is information nonrival but it also constitutes positive externalities arising from sharing information. As information is used or transmitted, it is refined and modified in various ways. Both conscious elaboration and the quasi-evolutionary processes that produce what Dawkins calls "memes" (others might prefer terms such as "folk tradition") allow information to be transformed into more useful or memorable forms through the very process of use.

Nonexcludability

The second crucial characteristic of a pure public good is nonexcludability. That is, if the good is provided at all, it is available to everyone. The classic example is defense against foreign invasion. If some particular region is protected from invasion, all the inhabitants of that region are protected.

Information is potentially excludable. The simplest exclusion procedure is secrecy. If I discover something and tell no-one else, the information remains a private good. The same is true if information is passed on to a selected group (paying customers, for example) under the condition that they keep it secret. But, the more people that are in on a secret, the harder it is to keep. And, even if I tell no-one, I may reveal my information by acting on it. For example, if I know that a company is going to announce an increased profit, I will naturally wish to keep the information to myself. But if I act on it, by buying shares, the price will go up, and others may guess what I have discovered.

More interesting in the present context are legal and technical devices to keep information private. The main legal devices are institutions such as copyright and patent laws, which allow the owner of information (the original creator or someone who has acquired their rights) to take action against anyone who uses it without their permission.

The critical factor, in the end, is technology. Where information is hard to reproduce, it is relatively easy to protect. When manuscripts had to be handwritten, it was easy enough to control what was written. Similarly, in the early days of film, it was sufficient to keep control of a small number of copies distributed to cinemas. Over time, however, the general tendency has been to make both reproduction and dissemination of information easier. In the case of music and video, copying technology first became available to households with audio and video tape machines. Attempts by copyright holders to suppress or tax home copying proved unsuccessful.

Copying on a much larger scale became feasible with the Internet. While many consumers, from a variety of motives, continued to purchase CDs and DVDs, unlicensed copies were distributed on a large scale. Ferocious attempts at enforcement of copyright law proved largely unavailing. Moreover, these attempts created substantial political problems for the main industry associations (the Recording Industry Association of American and the Motion Picture Association of America) in cases such as the prosecution of a poor single parent for downloads apparently made by her children.

For a time it seemed that the whole industry model of sales of music and video might be in jeopardy. However, by reducing the transaction cost of online purchases, and the price of the product, Apple's iTunes was able to create a viable market in downloadable MP3s, which attracted competitive entry from Amazon and others. Nevertheless, total music industry revenue has continued a downward trend. Many musicians have now moved to a model in which music is distributed freely with the aim of building paying audiences for live performances.

Property Rights And Pricing

The system of property rights in market societies is based on private property in private goods; that is, goods that are rival and excludable in consumption. There is a natural fit between these concepts that sometimes obscures the fact that private property is a right created and ultimately enforced by law while the economic concept of private goods relates to the properties of the good in question. So, not all goods that are rival and excludable are subject to property rights.

Conversely, public goods such as information may be the subject of property rights, most notably in the form of "intellectual property" rights such as copyrights and patents. Enforcement of such rights typically involves the imposition, after the fact, of penalties for reproducing information without the consent of the owner of the rights. Their feasibility depends, to a large extent, on the existence of limits on the technology of reproduction.

Even where the enforcement of strong intellectual property rights is feasible, it is commonly not socially desirable. The creation of intellectual property rights provides an incentive to generate new ideas, or at least ideas that are sufficiently distinctive in their formulation to attract intellectual property protection. But the enforcement of these rights means that use of the ideas in question is restricted, even though, since ideas are nonrival, there is a social benefit to unrestricted use.

Economists have examined the trade-off between the costs and benefits of intellectual property protection and have concluded, in general, that the costs of strong forms of intellectual property protection outweigh the benefits.

Another view of the trade-off is reflected in the famous observation of Stewart Brand that

> on the one hand information wants to be expensive, because it's so valuable. The right information in the right place just changes your life. On the other hand, information wants to be free, because the cost of getting it out is getting lower and lower all the time. (in Brockman 2011)

This quote frames the debate on the pricing of public-sector information. Much of the time, only the point that "information wants to be free" is quoted. In some ways, this is appropriate – all economic goods and services are costly to produce, and therefore "want to be expensive." By contrast, only nonrival goods, of which information is the paradigm example, "want to be free."

But the term "free" is itself ambiguous in English. Information can be "free as in speech" (i.e., available for access, downloading, and modification) without being "free as in beer" (i.e., given away for no charge, as is implied in the phrase "free beer").[1] The terms "libre" and "gratis" are often used to refer to this distinction.

Advertising

In the absence of explicit charges, the primary way of funding the "free" provision of information through public media has been advertising. Mass media typically offer a package in which advertising is interspersed with information content in such a way that it is difficult to consume the content without being exposed to the advertisements. So, it is not necessary to exclude consumers who are unwilling to pay.

Economists are divided both on how best to represent advertising in economic models and on how to evaluate its effects. A traditional approach distinguished between advertising that is informative (product X has property Y and sells for price P) and advertising that is persuasive, aiming at changing tastes ("Things go better with Coke"). This is problematic, since even pure statements of information can be (and usually will be) selected to promote the case for buying the product in question. On the other side of the distinction, the fact that consumers are willing to pay a premium for high-status brands, even when they are fully aware that a cheaper alternative may have the same objective properties, suggests that messages of the form "this product has high status for the group to which you (wish to) belong" are in fact informative.

A more modern approach (Becker and Murphy 1993) avoids the question. Advertising for a good or service is treated simply as a secondary service complementary in consumption with the good or service in question. Here "complementary" means that consuming one encourages you to consume the other, in the way that free salted peanuts in a bar might encourage patrons to drink more beer.

In the Becker–Murphy approach, the value or otherwise of advertising may be evaluated in terms of whether consumers choose to consume it. In this respect, advertising runs a spectrum. At one extreme are advertisements that consumers are willing to pay, or at least make a positive choice, to consume, such as "trading post"-style magazines and their online equivalents. At the other are those consumed involuntarily such as billboards, direct marketing, and so on. According to a Becker–Murphy analysis, advertising of the first class is socially beneficial while that of the second class is not. This distinction coincides in broad terms, but not exactly, with the older distinction between informative and persuasive advertising.

Media advertising falls between these extremes and is characterized by a spectrum of its own. Special-interest media (such as magazines) are commonly concerned with marketed activities, goods, and services associated with the interest in question, and may be purchased as much for the advertising as for the editorial content. By contrast, television programs are aimed at a mass audience with disparate interests, with the result that consumers of the program would typically prefer not to consume the associated advertising. A variety of techniques, from careful timing to product placement within the program, are used to overcome this reluctance.

New media shifts activity along the spectrum in several ways. First, because of the unbounded profusion of the Internet, special-interest media have expanded at the expense of, though not to the exclusion of, mass media. This encourages more narrowly targeted advertising that is more likely to be informative and desired by consumers. Second, the development of new media has made it easier for consumers to avoid advertising they don't wish to see. The early years of the commercial Internet were marked by increasingly intrusive attempts to force ads on consumers' attention (spam, popups, popunders, and so on), but technological blocks and adverse consumer reaction have killed most of these. So, advertisements must be at least reasonably desirable. The third, and perhaps the most important, development has been the central role of search engines, and Google in particular.

Network Economics

In recent decades economists have devoted a lot of attention to the economics of networks. Some of this literature has explored territory already familiar to sociologists, dealing with networks that involve relatively small numbers of individuals and focusing on the topological structure of the pairwise links between them. These ideas have been applied to questions such as the extent to which links between blogs reinforce or undermine ideological divisions between the left and the right.

More significant in relation to the dynamics of new media is the notion of network externalities. The central point is that the value of a communications network to its existing users increases as new users are added – there is no point in owning the only telephone in town. We can give this benefit a simple mathematical formulation. In a network with n members, there are $n \times (n-1)$ possible one-way connections, since each member can in principle connect with all the others. A new user gets the benefit of potential connections with all the existing members of the network, but also creates an additional connection available to each other user. It is this latter effect that creates the externality.

Network externalities aren't always positive. Connections may be unwanted (spammers) or the number of possible connections may make it impossible to find those that are actually desired. The first problem is real but generally seems manageable through constraints of various kinds imposed on network abusers. The second creates room for a substantial industry of intermediates including directories, search engines, and so forth. Often, though not always, these have proved sufficient to overcome the negative effects of network size, leaving the positive effects dominant.

If the problems associated with increased network size can be overcome, network externalities create incentives for rapid growth, as we have seen in the case of the Internet as a whole and in specific networks such as the blogosphere and Facebook.

The "walled garden" concept was inherent in early private-sector online services, the most prominent of which was CompuServe. These companies offered dialup access to a proprietary network, with its own interface, offering a range of services such as email, discussion forums, and access to online applications.

Although highly successful in the 1980s, commercial online providers found it impossible to compete with the appeal of the Internet, and particularly the World Wide Web, which emerged in 1991. By the late 1990s, most had disappeared. The only successful response was that of AOL (formerly America OnLine), which, rather than competing with the Internet, sought to join it.

AOL attempted, with some success, to transfer the "walled garden" concept to the Internet. The central idea was to allow its customers full access to the Internet but to encourage them to remain, as much as possible, within the AOL online community. This strategy was designed to produce a group of "locked-in" consumers who would be unwilling to switch to cheaper Internet service providers and to increase the appeal of AOL to advertisers. A weaker version of the "walled garden" concept was that of the "web portal," a website designed as the first point of access to the Internet for users, exemplified by Yahoo.com. In the end, neither AOL nor Yahoo succeeded in convincing users to remain within their walled gardens, though both are still in business, unlike the vast majority of their would-be competitors.

Although the opening up of walled gardens has sometimes been seen as inevitable, Lessig (1999, 2001) argues that the emergence of open or closed systems is the result of political, legal, and commercial choices, and that there will always exist substantial pressure toward closed systems because of the potential for profitability.

The walled garden concept appeared, by 2005, to be dead. However, in confirmation of Lessig's view, it has reappeared with the rise of Facebook (opened to the general public in 2006) and Twitter. Apple's iOS for the iPhone (launched in 2007) and iPad (2010) represent a different version of the walled garden.

What does an Information Economy Mean for Economics?

In principle, mainstream economic theory has the tools needed to describe information as a particularly pure public good, characterized by network externalities. In practice, however, most economic analysis is undertaken on the assumption that public goods are peripheral features of an economy in which most economic activity is based on the production, processing, distribution, and sale of physical goods (excludable and rival almost by definition) and, to a lesser extent, of marketed services. An analysis based on information as the primary driver of economic activity, as is needed in an information economy, will be radically different.

Information, Scale Economies, and Endogenous Growth

Analysis of economic growth has traditionally focused on the accumulation of the physical factors of production – land, labor, and capital (machinery and buildings). By the mid-twentieth century, however, it became apparent that an analysis of this kind could explain only a relatively small part of the growth in economic output and ultimately in living standards. Moreover, ever since the nineteenth century, economists had struggled with a paradox. For a given population and supply of land, the well-established law of diminishing marginal returns implied that additional investments in capital would produce smaller and smaller increases in output until the economy ultimately reached a stationary state. However, experience showed (or seemed to show) that growth could continue indefinitely, with no obvious tendency to slow down. Something was missing.

It was soon recognized that the "missing factor" was technological progress, and models of economic growth were adjusted to include technological progress. This change allowed economic models to fit the observed data, but it did not really add any explanatory power. Technological change appeared as an exogenous deus ex machina, not affected by economic outcomes. But, as Arrow (1962) observed, technological progress and the inventions and discoveries on which it rests are products of economic activity.

Although various attempts were made to capture this insight in models of economic growth, the crucial advances were made in the 1980s with the development of "endogenous growth theory" ("endogenous," as opposed to "exogenous," means that technological progress is explained within the model rather than being imposed from outside). The most important observation was that, unlike labor and capital, information is a public good. That is, the use of information by one person does not reduce its availability for others. On the contrary, the more information is used, the more it is refined and extended.

This observation points the way to resolution of the great paradox that had bedeviled growth theory. The law of diminishing returns applies on the assumption that the economy as a whole is characterized by constant returns to scale; that is, if the inputs of land, labor, and capital are all doubled, so is total output. The idea is simple. With a doubling of all inputs, each worker has access to the same amount of land and capital and so can produce exactly the same amount as before. Since there are twice as many workers, total output is doubled. More generally, if all inputs increase proportionally, output increases in the same proportion. The law of diminishing marginal returns now follows. If only one input, such as capital, increases, output must decrease less than proportionally.

By contrast, since information is a public good, production based on information displays increasing returns to scale. If there are twice as many workers, and twice as much information, each worker has twice as much information to work with. So each worker will produce more and, with twice as many workers, output will more than double.

This insight is of fundamental importance in understanding technological progress in an information economy. Unfortunately, economists did not spend a lot of time thinking about it. Instead, they were concerned to show that the increasing returns to scale were consistent with steady economic growth, rather than an explosive acceleration producing what Kurzweil (2005) and others refer to as "the singularity." Romer (1994) and others showed that, as long as new knowledge had to be produced by a commercial R&D sector, endogenous growth models could produce steady rather than explosive growth. Attention in the literature then turned to issues of industry structure that need not concern us here.

The shift of attention in endogenous growth theory left unexplored many crucial questions about the production of information and its implications for the economy.

Household Production and Monetary Incentives

One of the striking features of Web 2.0 and the associated technological developments is the extent to which crucial contributions have been made without any direct, or, in many cases, indirect, financial reward. The most striking example is surely the Wikipedia project, where an almost entirely voluntary effort has generated, in many different languages, the most comprehensive encyclopedia ever produced. But there are many more examples, such as the Gracenote music database, a commercial enterprise that provides automatic identification of music tracks on CDs, a service valuable to anyone using software such as iTunes. All the information is uploaded by users cataloging their own collections.

Many different motives explain contributions to amateur collaboration (Raymond 1998; Quiggin 2006; Hunter and Quiggin 2008). In general, these motives are complementary or at least mutually consistent. For example, an altruistic desire to improve open-source software will be complemented by enjoyment of a technically challenging task, and by a desire for the admiration of a peer group.

However, motives like these do not coexist well with a profit motive. Benkler (2004) notes the absence of monetary side payments in the case of car-pooling and this is typical of cooperative endeavors of various kinds. There is a strong desire to keep money out of this kind of activity, except where there is necessary interaction with the monetary economy (e.g., car-poolers contributing to tolls, bloggers sharing the costs of hosting services, and so on).

The observation that financial motives may conflict with other motives has been discussed at length in the literature on motivational crowding out. However, this literature has focused on the conflict between monetary payment and altruism, where the incompatibility between motives is seen as being more or less self-evident. In view of the variety of motives associated with contributions to amateur collaborative content and innovation, it is necessary to consider when and why motives are going to be complements (mutually reinforcing) or substitutes (leading to crowding out).

One possible approach to this question is to consider the extent to which particular combinations of motives, such as altruism and self-expression, are psychologically consistent or inconsistent. As we have observed, the evidence seems to suggest that a wide variety of motivations are potentially compatible. The problematic nature of monetary motives seems hard to analyze in purely psychological terms. Rather, it is necessary to consider the social context of monetary interactions.

Monetary interactions naturally give rise to rational calculus of action that is a set of rules, based on a fundamental principle (such as profit maximization), that potentially govern all behavior in the relevant domain. Rational systems of action may be contrasted with heuristic guides to action that apply under particular (not necessarily well-defined) circumstances. In general, a range of heuristics, associated with different kinds of motivation, can coexist. By contrast, a rational calculus naturally tends to crowd out both heuristics and alternative rational systems.

At a superficial level, it is apparent that people act differently, and are expected to act differently, in the context of relationships mediated by money than in other contexts. Behavior that would be regarded favorably in a nonmonetary context is regarded as foolish or even reprehensible in a monetary context.

One of the most important general differences relates to rationality and calculated reciprocity. In a nonmarket context, careful calculation of costs and benefits and an insistence on exact reciprocity is generally deprecated. By contrast, in market contexts, the first rule is never to give more than you get.

Why is it more important to observe this rule in market contexts? One reason is that markets create opportunities for systematic arbitrage that do not apply in other contexts. In an environment where trust is taken for granted, a trader who consistently gives slightly short weight can amass substantial profits. If trading partners assume honorable behavior, none will suffer enough to notice. This is much more difficult to do in ordinary social contexts.

Similar points can be made about other motives. There is a whole range of sales tricks designed to exploit altruism, friendship, desire for self-expression, and so on. Hence, to prosper in a market context, it is necessary to adopt a view that "business is business" and to (consciously or otherwise) adopt a role as a participant in the market economy that is quite distinct from what might be conceived as one's "real self."

Policy Implications

Undersupply

Market processes are unlikely to generate adequate support for innovation, or to promote valuable innovations over trivial or even destructive innovations. It has long been clear that market models based on payment for content, including text, audiovisual material, data, and net-based software services, have only a marginal role to play in a networked economy. Apple's iTunes service is a notable success among a sea of failures, but attempts to replicate it have proved almost entirely unavailing.

The vast majority of market returns from Internet services are tied to advertising. The most successful model is that of Google. Unfortunately, the sale of advertising provides a prime illustration of the point that the capacity to capture returns from the Internet bears only an indirect and unreliable relationship to beneficial innovation or to the provision of useful services.

In summary, there is no reason to expect that market forces will provide appropriate incentives for innovation. Neither the resources devoted to innovation nor the way in which those resources are allocated is likely to be socially optimal. Hence, there are potential benefits from a well-designed innovation policy.

Intellectual Property

The first problem in innovation policy is to stop doing things that are clearly counterproductive. Throughout the period of collaborative innovation, the main thrust of reform in innovation policy has been actively counterproductive though, fortunately, largely ineffectual.

The key idea of this policy thrust has been "strong intellectual property" – the idea that all kinds of ideas, modes of expression, and technical processes should be subject to unfettered private ownership, through devices such as copyright, patents, and licensing. Limits on the duration of such rights have been attacked through extensions in the term of copyright.

In the absence of strong economic arguments, advocates of strong intellectual property have relied heavily on legal and ethical claims, essentially based on the assumption that since patents and copyrights are called "intellectual property" they have the same status as ordinary property rights over goods. The familiar advertisements in which copying a video clip is compared to stealing a car are an illustration of a simile that can be extended to almost any intellectual activity over which someone seeks to exert a property claim.

Strong intellectual property regimes represent an obstacle to network innovation. The problem is most obvious in relation to amateur and open-source innovation, which has played a central role in the development of the networked economy. Amateurs have little or nothing to gain from intellectual property rights and are correspondingly unwilling, and often unable, to pay others for the right to use patented or copyright items that derive much of their value from the collective contributions that make up the network.

Even in for-profit enterprises, intellectual property rights such as patents are widely seen as a barrier to innovation. The ease of filing patents on ideas that are, at most, minor variants on existing techniques means that even simple steps to improve software run the risk of infringing on intellectual property. Conversely, the actual revenue that can be obtained by licensing intellectual property is typically modest at best.

Formal and informal systems of patent pooling overcome many of the problems. Innovative firms can make use of the ideas of others while sharing their own ideas. However, this system has been undermined by the recent emergence of "patent trolls," firms that specialize in accumulating patents and suing actual innovators for (often highly dubious) infringements in the hope that their victims will prefer to pay to settle cases rather than put up with long-running disruption and legal costs.

Fortunately, it appears that the push to strengthen intellectual property is failing. The most prominent instance of patent trolling, the SCO Group's attempt to assert ownership over Unix and Linux code, an action financed by Linux rival Microsoft, ended in failure on all points and bankruptcy for SCO.[2] Courts have become less willing to sustain patent claims.

Social attitudes have similarly changed. The majority of people routinely violate copyright and licensing prohibitions, such as prohibitions on "ripping" CDs to digital media. Recent attempts to strengthen copyright law in Canada have provoked strong opposition, particularly among younger and more highly educated voters (Angus Reid Strategies 2008).

Finally, and most importantly, the emergence of alternatives to strong intellectual property such as open-source software and the Creative Commons license has changed the default assumptions under which innovation takes place. The volume of material available under explicit Creative Commons conditions has grown massively. More generally, despite the legal presumption (introduced in the USA in the 1970s) that published material is automatically subject to copyright, the norm of free sharing has emerged as the default presumption for items published on the Internet. Attempts to restrict access to paying subscribers or to prevent republication have largely been abandoned as counterproductive. Such restrictions discourage the inward links that are crucial to high rankings from search engines such as Google.

If strong intellectual property, often presented as the market model for innovation, is undesirable, the polar opposite, central planning, is no more appealing. Attempts to predict and control the path of network innovation have proved ineffective at best and counterproductive at worst.

Creativity and Public Cultural Institutions

It is difficult, at this stage, to formulate a detailed policy program for networked innovation. However, some general principles and policy directions can be indicated. First, it is necessary to encourage creativity in all its forms. Since the outcomes of creativity cannot be prescribed in advance, policies to encourage creativity must rely on providing space for creativity (including access to the necessary resources), free time for creative workers to pursue their own projects, and the communications networks necessary to facilitate creative collaborations.

The coalescence of technical and cultural innovation suggests the need for a hybrid between, on the one hand, models of support for scientific research and technical innovation and, on the other, models that have been used to promote cultural innovation, particularly in the creative arts.

Another important direction of support for network innovation is that of public contributions to the (creative) commons. Moves to extend claims for intellectual property over publicly funded creative works should be abandoned and replaced by a commitment to make all such work available either as part of the public domain or on free-sharing conditions such as those of the Creative Commons license.

Public cultural institutions such as the Australian Broadcasting Corporation (ABC) have long played a major role in supporting the public good model of creative production. This model needs to be extended. Gruen (2008) provides a number of useful suggestions, beginning with the development of a freely accessible archive on the World Wide Web and continuing with suggestions of ways in which the ABC could help to develop the resources of Web 2.0 and community broadcasting.

The opportunities and challenges created by the Internet-based information economy are both complex and potentially radically transformative as they relate to cultural institutions such as galleries, libraries, archives, and museums (acronymically, the GLAM sector), not to mention botanical and zoological gardens and performing arts bodies.

Concluding Comments

To paraphrase Solow (1987), we can see the impact of new media everywhere but in the market economy. The transformations under way as a result of the development of new media have had relatively little impact on standard measures of economic activity. Whereas previous waves of technological innovation saw new companies rise to the forefront of economic activity, the age of new media has been more notable for spectacular collapses than for durable successes.

Economic theory provides many of the tools needed to understand new media. However, consistent application of these tools would lead to a radical transformation of the way in which we understand the economy, which would in turn call forth substantial changes in economic policy. This process of change has barely begun.

Notes

1. The juxtaposition of free beer and free speech is attributed to Richard Stallings, quoted in Gay (2002).
2. The case is documented in detail at www.groklaw.net.

References

Angus Reid Strategies (2008) "Angus Reid Poll: Canadians Evenly Split on Proposed Amendments to Copyright Act." www.angusreidstrategies.com/index.cfm?fuseaction=news&newsid=245.

Arrow, K. (1962) "Economic Welfare and the Allocation of Resources for Invention" in *The Rate and Direction of Inventive Activity*. Princeton, NJ: Princeton University Press, pp. 409–425.

Becker, G.S. and Murphy, K.M. (1993) "A Simple Theory of Advertising as a Good or Bad." *Quarterly Journal of Economics*, 108(4), 941–964.

Benkler, Y. (2004) "Sharing Nicely: On Shareable Goods and the Emergence of Sharing as a Modality of Economic Production." *Yale Law Journal*, 114, 273–358.

Brand, S. (1987) *The Media Lab: Inventing the Future At MIT*. New York: Viking.

Brockman, J. (2011) "Conversation in Munich." *Edge*, 338. http://www.edge.org/documents/archive/edge338.html.

Gay, J., ed. (2002) *Free Software, Free Society: Selected Essays of Richard M. Stallman*. Boston, MA: GNU Press.

Gruen, N. (2008) "Two Economic Paradoxes of Our Time: Part Two – What to Do with a Sketch of an Example Using the ABC." http://clubtroppo.com.au/2008/04/01/two-economic-paradoxes-of-our-time-part-two-what-to-do-with-a-sketch-of-an-example-using-the-abc.

Hunter, D. and Quiggin, J. (2008) "Money Ruins Everything." *Hastings Communications & Entertainment Law Journal*, 30, 203–255.

Kurzweil, R. (2005) *The Singularity is Near*. New York: Viking.

Lessig, L. (1999) *Code and Other Laws of Cyberspace*. New York: Basic Books.

Lessig, L. (2001) *The Future of Ideas: The Fate of the Commons in a Connected World*. New York: Random House.

McLuhan, M. (1964) *Understanding Media; The Extensions of Man*. New York: McGraw-Hill.

Quiggin, J. (2006) "Blogs, Wikis and Creative Innovation." *International Journal of Cultural Studies*, 9(4), 481–496.

Raymond, E. (1998) "The Cathedral and the Bazaar." *First Monday*, 3(3). http://firstmonday.org/htbin/cgiwrap/bin/ojs/index.php/fm/article/view/578/499.

Romer, P.M. (1994) "The Origins of Endogenous Growth." *Journal of Economic Perspectives*, 8(1), 3.

Samuelson, P.A. (1954) "The Pure Theory of Public Expenditure." *Review of Economics and Statistics*, 36, 387–389.

Solow, R. (1987) "We'd Better Watch Out." *New York Times Book Review* (July 12), 36.

6

The End of Audiences?
Theoretical Echoes of Reception Amid the Uncertainties of Use

Sonia Livingstone and Ranjana Das

The Death of the Audience?

> *The report of my death was an exaggeration.*
> *(Mark Twain, 1897)*

Once, ordinary people occupied much of their leisure time sitting on the sofa, often together with others, watching prescheduled hours of mass broadcast television or reading a national newspaper, whether in a concentrated or distracted manner and, later, talking about it over supper or the next day. Today, people gaze at their computer or mobile phone screen, often alone, while multitasking social networking, music downloading, peer-to-peer (P2P) chat, information searching, or playing games and, simultaneously, discussing their experiences with others elsewhere. Just a couple of decades divide these two time periods, hardly time for people to change in their fundamental interests and concerns. Yet their everyday habits – and their communicative possibilities – are considerably altered, reflecting the historic shift from mass to networked society, from push to pull media, from one-way to multiway communication. So, are they still audiences? In this chapter, we argue that this question matters: conceptualizing people as audiences (not instead of but as well as publics, masses, consumers, or users) builds insightfully on the history of audiences and audience research to reveal continuities and changes in the mediation of identity, sociality, and power.

We ask this question about audiences at a time of change, aware that the nature of this change is widely contested. Is society dramatically different or just a little different from a decade or several decades ago? Or, are the continuities across decades or even centuries far more telling? Our argument is that, in relation to people's engagement with media and, more importantly, in relation to people's engagement with each other through media, the changes are indeed noteworthy;

A Companion to New Media Dynamics, First Edition. Edited by John Hartley, Jean Burgess, and Axel Bruns.
© 2013 John Wiley & Sons, Ltd. Published 2015 by John Wiley & Sons, Ltd.

but this does not mean that the conceptual repertoire best able to analyze them must be entirely new. On the contrary, we pursue the possibility that the critical repertoire of ideas and insights developed to rethink the mass television audience in the 1980s and 1990s – a repertoire that challenged the often presumed passivity and mindlessness of our opening image – is only now coming into its own, only now finding sufficient scope, in the multimodal, converged digital environment, to reveal its full analytic power and potential.

Audience studies asked how people converge and diverge in making sense of media texts, how people respond critically to dominant messages, and how audiences participate in civil society. Today, in a networked moment of multimodal and user-generated media, similar questions arise about practices of reading, writing, and interpretation, and about the consequences of such practices for inclusion or exclusion, acceptance or critique. Though some may be surprised to see audience researchers defending the text, we assert that these questions are, crucially, tied to the continued importance of texts. As we explore in what follows, only through recognition of the mutuality of texts and readers can we analyze the age of digital networks, as we did that of mass broadcasting.

Today we are witnessing an explosion of texts and technologies – everything is digital, everything is mediated. Urban spaces especially are covered in physical messages – commercial, political, persuasive, or merely graffitied. More and more, they are experienced also through digital messages – increasingly annotated by geo-located systems of representation, while co-located face-to-face interactions have been remediated by the constant flicking of one's eye to a mobile screen, by our permanent availability to absent others, and by the imagined ear of the digital bystander. Whether we are working or at leisure, studying or playing, being sociable or private, or contributing to community life, we are surrounded by a cacophony of messages, voices, signs, and images – many of which we are simultaneously responding to or circulating onwards to others. Meanwhile, the politics of representation has reached the top of public and policy agendas worldwide (Orgad 2012), unsurprising given late modernity's fascination with life political movements, the fraught struggles over religious and cultural politics, and the widespread marke-tization of party politics. Just as we are surrounded by texts that hail us on all sides, so too are we embedded in an explosion of technological artifacts for information and communication, with ever larger screens on our buildings and public spaces, ever newer gadgets in our living rooms and bedrooms, and ever smaller ones in our pockets, under our pillows, beneath our thumbs, and plugged into our ears.

This doubly articulated nature of media and communications – as both text and as object, or as medium and as message (Silverstone 1994; Livingstone 2007) – doubly articulates the audience also. On the one hand, audiences produce meanings by negotiating the mutual interface of text and reader. On the other, audiences produce social relations by negotiating the material/social determinations that structure their everyday contexts of action. The former articulation foregrounds questions of interpretation. These have long been theorized via semiotics and reception aesthetics, sometimes framed in terms of literacy; and, in today's complex media and communications environment, further questions of interpretation arise – about navigation and search, about trust and reliability, about knowledge and creativity. Additionally, the latter articulation raises questions of social relations. These have long been theorized via macro/micro relations of political economy versus cultural ethnography, sometimes framed in terms of system and lifeworld; and, in today's complex and globalizing society, further questions about social roles and relations arise – audiences and publics, producers and produsers, citizens and consumers are converging and diverging in parallel with the media texts and technologies with which they engage.

To be sure, in practice, the texts and technologies of today's media environment are interacting, further complicating matters, as the one can no longer be mapped neatly onto the other (programs on television, films at the cinema, books in print form, etc.). Content spans diverse media, platforms connect and converge (see Jenkins 2006), and brands transcend even the bounds of media – as in *Harry Potter* or *Lord of the Rings* the book (original and spoof), film, game (computer and board), website (official and fan), duvet cover, and Lego toy. However, these empirical interconnections need not undermine the value of the analytic distinction between semiotic and material articulations of audiencehood. Further, the vitality of recent decades of research on audiences, which for a while electrified the wider field of media and communication, lies, we suggest, precisely in the creative bridging of these very different approaches. Whether scholars root their work primarily in the social semiotic, reception-aesthetic, encoding/decoding, critical, anthropological, feminist, or any of a range of other trajectories, most recognize that both approaches are needed, even when (or because) their articulation generates friction. Audiences are always situated, and situate themselves, between text and context; and, although much is indeed changing in the mediated environment, people's relation to and through media remains doubly articulated. Thus, they have always required and will continue to require a dual lens from those who seek to understand them.

But, for some, the concept of the audience is no longer useful. Indeed, the phenomenon itself is claimed to be obsolete, or at least disappearing (Jermyn and Holmes 2006), most famously by Gillmore (2006), who states in *We the Media* that "the former audience" is making the crucial shift, enabled by networked technologies, from consumer to citizen, and also in Jay Rosen's (2006) celebration that "the people formerly known as the audience" are at last claiming the producer power that (technologically) enhanced opportunities for speech surely afford – as well in the work of a host of academic scholars. Whether such activity equates to the high standards society holds for its citizens and publics (Butsch 2000; Dayan 2005) or whether it indeed brings the power to match or challenge that of the major media owners remains rightly disputed (Jenkins 2003), generating many empirical projects recently and currently underway. Setting aside the wealth of evidence that reports of the audience's death are exaggerated (for television viewing figures are holding up, cinema audiences are growing, few could live without their TV set, and radio remains the world's most enjoyed medium), we are more interested here in the validity (or otherwise) of the theoretical claim.

In "Not Dead Yet?," Elizabeth Bird (2009) observes that digital media enable the externalization of much audience activity – from silent responses to visible practices of interpretation. And, as one of this chapter's authors has previously noted, now that people make visible their role in the production of meaning by searching, clicking, typing, moving, and merging text, the activity of the audience can surely no longer be in doubt (Livingstone 2004). Yet such new activities have, contrarily, precisely been used to confirm the comparative passivity of earlier times. According to some new media enthusiasts, the more the Internet user is seen to do, the more passive the television viewer appears with the benefit of hindsight. So, not only is the audience now dead, say some, but by comparison with the vivid life of the digerati it was never very much alive – a new twist to the much-recounted critiques of the (supposedly) overcelebrated active audience (e.g., Morris 1988; Seaman 1992; although see Hartley 2006).

While for both theoretical and empirical reasons (as hinted in the foregoing) we are convinced of the continued importance of audiences, our present focus is different. For our question is not really whether audiences still exist (it seems evident to us that they do) but, rather, whether it is illuminating to analyze the activities of people engaging with today's simultaneously converging and diverging media and communication environment by using the conceptual repertoire developed to analyze the mass audience (for an empirical approach to this, see Das 2011, 2012). In other words, even if audiences are alive and well, it may not follow that users of digital and online technologies have anything in common with them. Indeed, for those who have arrived at the study of new media users from a completely different direction – from science and technology studies, human–computer interaction, sociology of consumption, history of literacy, library and information studies, or any of the other disciplinary trajectories now productively informing the multi-disciplinary analysis of digital media (for instance, see Rosen, 2006; Barjak et al., 2010; Kim et al., 2010; Kimmerle et al., 2010; Paul and Morris 2011) – the putative continuities between people watching television from the sofa and people using a computer via a mouse or keypad may seem tangential. However, for those of us asking what the audience researcher is to do in the age of the Internet (Livingstone 2004), this is a challenge worth taking up.

A Crossgenerational Dialogue

"You are old, Father William," the young man said, "And your hair has become very white; And yet you incessantly stand on your head – Do you think, at your age, it is right?"

(Lewis Carroll, Alice's Adventures in Wonderland, *1865)*

As Lewis Carroll nicely observed, the older generation gains its white hair after a lifetime of argumentation and experience, but it may still surprise the younger generation. Yet, despite its association with power, white hair does not always generate respect; the younger generation may instead treat its elders with perplexity, critique, or disregard. Any teacher must, therefore, ask themselves: what do I have that is worth handing on to the next generation, and for how long will it hold its value before becoming irrelevant? Meanwhile, their students must ask themselves: what knowledge is on offer and how far can it take me in addressing new problematics, or must I start over? Thus, there is nothing new in this mutual questioning about the transfer or evolution of knowledge across generations and, for the six or seven decades of media studies' existence, several generations of communication scholars have lived through overlapping technological, societal, and intellectual histories, contributing empirically and theoretically to the multistranded narrative of media studies in general and audience studies in particular. As Katz et al. put it:

> It is in the workaday world of reading and writing and researching – inspired by predecessors and contemporaries – that we look over our own shoulders, sensing the presence of an ancestor, dimly discerned at first, who is cheering us on in the direction that we ourselves (so we think) have chosen. That is how we give birth to those whom we recognize as intellectual parents. And often, we find it worthwhile to get to know these parents better. (2003: 2)

We write this chapter from the perspective of two contrasting yet perhaps parallel generations of media scholars, each finding herself at the start of something new. For the one of us who "came of age" at the birth of active audience theory, the theoretical, empirical, and critical challenges directed to structuralist, literary, and semiotic accounts of texts as well as to political-economic accounts of media power by the new theorists of audience reception, cultural studies, ethnographic methods, and the feminist revalorization of the everyday – especially of women's, working class, and marginalized voices – were decisive. For the one of us who is now "coming of age" at the birth of Web 2.0, decisive factors shaping the research agenda instead center on crossmedia convergence and hybridity, multidisciplinary debates over globalization and the network society, a fascination with the experiences of youthful "digital natives," and a shift from critically working to undermine to critically engaging with the normative agenda of policy-making.

To be sure, the older generation does not stand still, and in researching this chapter we have found it noteworthy that a number of scholars grounded in the field of television audience reception have taken on the analysis also of how people engage with new and digital media. Knowing that some of their (our) peers from earlier times have not made this same move (instead, for example, extending their path further into cultural and media anthropology or staying with television studies), and now finding ourselves also in new company (with technologists, educators, historians, and political scientists, among others), it seems that many audience researchers may be asking themselves what they can usefully bring from the former to illuminate the new research agenda. Every time we conduct a literature review, build a theoretical framework, design a course curriculum, or critique the work of others, these questions become pressing: how far back should one reach into the history of the field, to what effect, when is it time to let go, and what new analytic tools might instead be needed?

One starting point lies in the meta-narratives that retell the contribution of audience reception studies. Without rehearsing, or taking time to contest, the stereotypical narrative (the trouncing of the "hypodermic needle" of effects research; the canonical trio of Radway, Ang, and Morley; the discovery of unfettered polysemy and the uprising of the actively resistant audience), it is worth pausing to reflect on what did emerge from that "new and exciting phase in so-called audience research" (Hall 1980: 131). The contribution of audience reception studies, after several decades of theoretical work and empirical study, might be distilled into three key insights – each an argument against what went before (Livingstone 2008).

First, audience reception studies revealed that audiences' readings could not be predicted from knowledge of the text alone, which undermined the analyst's authority in presuming a singular, underlying meaning of any media text by demonstrating that empirical readers often do not mirror the expectations of model or implied readers – far from it, they can be playful, critical, creative, or plain contrary (Liebes and Katz 1993). Second, this enabled cultural and ethnographic explorations of empirical audiences (plural) that – far from opening the door to unfettered polysemy or radical resistance – emphasized that interpretation is situated in specific, structuring, social contexts that, however, may undermine totalizing claims of media imperialism and dominant ideologies with evidence of counterflows and "glocalization" (Tomlinson 1999). As Morley comments acerbically, "these models of audience activity were not . . . designed . . . to make us forget the question of media power, but rather to be able to conceptualize it in more complex and adequate ways" (2006: 106). Third, close attention to the contextualization of media reception in everyday life identified not only the reproductive power of social stratification and forms of structured inequality but also the ways in which microtactics of appropriation reshape and remediate media texts and technologies, it being through such contingent processes of mediation that universalizing accounts of passive audiences and powerful media effects are contested.

These three insights concern, in essence, the audience's role in meaning-making, the structuring importance of context, and the potential of agency. Together, they find their mutual connections within what Richard Johnson (1986) called the "circuit of culture" or what others, more recently, frame in terms of theories of mediation or, looked at historically, mediatization (see Krotz 2007). In this way, audience reception studies contribute to understanding the wider significance of everyday processes of interpretation, thereby also bringing audience researchers into dialogue with a wider array of disciplines – for example, the civic potential of audiences (as citizens or publics) engaging with the mediated public sphere (see Butsch 2000; Dahlgren 2003; Livingstone et al., 2007); the contested balance between creative and commodified conceptions of audiences (as consumers or markets or producers or produsers (Bruns 2008)); and the contribution of people's daily, local media practices to processes of globalization and transnational flows (here audiences are conceived as communities, whether cosmopolitan, local or diasporic (Aksoy and Robins 2000; Georgiou 2001; Dayan 2005)).

These debates are, surely, still current, so that the insights of audience reception studies need not be tied to a now-obsolete social/mediated context. At the same time, new questions are also pressing. People's relation with media is shifting from the predominance of one medium, television, to embrace the simultaneously diversifying and converging technologies that define the new media environment, extending the Abercrombie and Longhurst (1998) dispersed audience to the point where it is no longer sensible to ask whether or when people are part of an audience, only when and why it is useful to focus on their audiencehood (or, as Fiske (1992) proposed, on their "audiencing" – thereby substituting a verb for the noun so problematically appropriated by the industry (Ang 1996)). Also important is the transcendence of a once-strong boundary between mass and interpersonal communication to a world of multiple forms of networked communication blurring complex, quasi-, hybrid, and P2P forms of communication in addition to – and therefore now remediating (Bolter and Grusin 1998) – the more familiar one-to-many and one-to-one communication modes that have defined and separated mass and interpersonal communication research. Yet even these are shifts that have taken place over decades, not radical changes introduced by the advent of the mass Internet, encouraging us to pursue the promise of conceptual continuities further, as below.

Conceptual Continuities

As he composes his thoughts in words, a speaker or writer hears these words echoing within himself and thereby follows his own thoughts, as though he were another person. Conversely, a hearer or reader repeats within himself the words he hears and thereby understands them, as though he were himself two individuals.
(Ong 1962, cited in Farrell and Soukup 2002: 29)

The repertoire of concepts developed by audience researchers to understand people's interpretation of television and other media bears striking parallels with that which information theorists work with when analyzing the use of interactive and digital information. The inscribed users discussed by the latter remind us, as audience researchers, of sutured subjects; meanwhile, implied users echo implied audiences and ideal readers; the semiotics of links and nodes parallel the polysemy of televi-sual codes; technological affordances resemble preferred readings; communities of practice expand on interpretive communities; remix cultures extend recognition of playful or resistant readers; and, in both new and old media contexts, notions of genre organize texts and usage/reading practices. For example, when Steve Woolgar (1996), as a sociologist of scientific knowledge, discusses the "textuality of the artefact" along with "preferred" and "implied" users of information technologies, there are many parallels with the analysis of media texts and genres, and the preferred and implied readers, as discussed by literary reception-aesthetics theorist Wolfgang Iser (1974) and, later, the implied and actual viewers of audiovisual media (Livingstone 1998a). Thus, we see researchers reaching back for old concepts, refashioning them for this new digital era. Some hark back to the audiovisual age while others look further back, to the print era or even earlier, to rethink the analysis of face-to-face, oral communication for present times.

In extending the conceptual repertoire of audience reception analysis to the study of new media use, we propose as a core focus the interpretative interface between, and thus mutual definition of, texts and readers, along with a series of parallel pairings (depending on disciplinary origins and focus) as follows. The cultural studies approach to audiences begins with the dual moments in the circuit of culture brought to prominence by Stuart Hall (1980), namely encoding/decoding; this prioritizes the importance of codes and coding as a process embedded in material circumstances, generating a cycle of the production and reproduction of meaning with no linear start or end point. Others in audience reception studies draw on the literary theorists' pairing of text/reader (or, in screen studies and film theory versions, text/spectator), notwithstanding that in practice the analysis more often focused on texts and implied or ideal readers than empirical readers (although see Holland 1975; Staiger 2005). Both the foregoing were strongly influenced by semiotics, the cultural studies approach also encompassing the power dimensions (dominant and resistant) of mediation while the literary approach engaged more with questions of textuality (and inter- or extra-textuality), as well as textual quality (high versus low culture) and type (or genre). The concept of audiences, then, encompasses half of each of these paired terms – encoding, reading, spectating, and so forth. As argued above and elsewhere (Livingstone 1998b), the "thingness" of the audience is misleading (as Ang 1991 elegantly captured in *Desperately Seeking the Audience*) for the noun merely stands in as shorthand for the verbs that account for the textually/technologically mediated communicative processes that connect people.

However, these pairings are paralleled in science and technology studies by the pairing of affordance/user and, relatedly, in material consumption studies by production/appropriation, both approaches now being applied to digital media studies. This circumvents assumptions of technological determinism and passivized consumers just as, in audience studies, conceiving of the interpretative relations between text and reader circumvents assumptions of powerful media effects and vulnerable audiences while, in both cases, refusing a naïve celebration of agency. As Ian Hutchby put it, "affordances are functional and relational aspects which frame, while not determining, the possibilities for agentic action" (2001: 44). Or, as Woolgar says, in a manner reminiscent of Hall's writing on the preferred reading (or the previous, literary notion of the intended address of a message), "certain features of the structure and design of the artefact make certain interpretations and uses more likely than others. By way of textual analysis one can discern, in particular, which sorts of readers are implied by the text" (1996: 580) and, thus, "notions about the ideal user tend to get built into the design of a technical artefact" (581). This is particularly intriguing when now analyzing how people (users) operate in a P2P environment – collaborating to rewrite the texts that they and others experience. And unsurprisingly, given the history of audience reception studies, we would advocate that such analysis includes empirical research.

Last, we note a pairing from the world of information and education studies originating several centuries ago (Luke 1989), that of literacy and, to coin a term, legibility. Although newly salient in the age of hypertextual and online media, the varying literacy demands of different media interfaces – oral, print, audiovisual, networked – have long been debated (Farrell and Soukup 2002), ever since that very first communicative pairing of speaker/hearer, from which much communication theory stems and to which, in an age of the rediscovery of P2P communication, many theorists now return (Goffman 1981; Kress 2003). Spanning all communicative modes, whether mediated by communication technology or the affordances of the human body (Jensen 2010), the concept of literacy makes us ask: what does the reader or user (or hearer) bring to bear on the process of interpretation, and what are the conditions of capability (that resource their literacy) and legibility (as designed into the media environment) that enable literacy?

As with our other pairings, the notion of literacy implies a text to be read, raising questions of legibility – what interpretations are afforded, what knowledge is expected, what possibilities are enabled or impeded? The case may also be made in reverse – the more complex or, especially, the more "illegible" (or hard to read or decode) the text or media environment, the greater the task of media literacy. On this account, many new digital interfaces should be understood as illegible (ill-designed, non-user-friendly, possibly deliberately obscure or deceptive); only as literacy develops and, one hopes, as the text/technology is redesigned responsively, can literacy and legibility achieve a tolerable balance. The focus on legibility, together with the recognition that literacy is culturally and historically conditioned, not simply a matter of individual cognition (Scribner and Cole 1973; Snyder 2001), foregrounds a critical perspective long important to audience research.

Indeed, since the concept of literacy applies across all modes of communication, it is arguably a more securely political concept than audiences or readers or users. Literacy has long been linked to the politics of emancipation (think of the evident inequity in the concept of illiteracy, whereas not being part of an audience generally matters little). Now that knowledge, participation, citizenship, resistance, self-determination, and much more are all mediated (Livingstone 2009), the normativity inherent in the concept of literacy becomes valuable. Researchers are now, rightly, asking not only what people know or understand or do in relation to the digital media environment but also what should they know, understand, and do, and who should take responsibility, or in whose interest is it, if they do not.

All of the foregoing involves a rejection of that traditional pairing in media and communication research, namely stimulus and response. Although this remains prominent in the psychological traditional of media effects research, it eschews any notion of interpretation – the meaning of the stimulus is given, there is no semiosis, and thus the response is contingent only on circumstances, not on meaning (Livingstone 1998a). Instead, we emphasize the remarkable similarities in terms of relationships of co-construction across different fields. Each foregrounds a paired concept in which each element in the pair defines, shapes, resources, and constrains the other in a (generally unequal) struggle over meaning and power. Together, each pair marks out the interpretative "contract" that holds the elements together – text and reader, for instance, are mutually specified in terms of the "expectations" each embodies regarding the other and neither has meaning without the other. Take, for example, the soap opera and the soap opera viewer: the generic conventions of the text are thoroughly understood by their long-standing viewers – consider the cliff-hangers that gratify rather than frustrate (though if found at the end of a detective drama or when seen by a novice viewer they would indeed frustrate) precisely because it is understood that the gap is left for interpretative readers to fill, individually and together, before the next episode moves the narrative onwards. Or, to take a new media example, consider the social networking site and its users: again, the generic conventions of the text are thoroughly understood by their users who do not, contrary to the misunderstandings of nonusers, abandon all norms of privacy but rather reclassify their friends, their images, and their experiences according to the proffered tools of distribution and display, simultaneously providing the feedback by which the site then adapts the tools it offers.

The Short History and Long Past of Audiences

As the pioneering experimental psychologist Hermann Ebbinghaus (1908) said of psychology a century ago, it "has a long past but only a short history." In other words, the formal history of a discipline does not capture the long past of thinking, theorizing, and reflecting on a field. It certainly does not capture the long past of the phenomenon – in our case, audiences – itself. For audiences were not discovered in the 1980s, despite the attention attracted by Stuart Hall's exciting new phase of research. Nor did they originate in the importance of television for the postwar 1950s celebration of the nuclear family in the living room (although, as Stephanie Coontz (1997) eloquently argued, what she calls the 1950s family experiment certainly shaped both popular and academic values regarding domesticity and belonging). Nor, even, were the Payne Fund studies the beginning of audiences, though the history of their analysis is rarely traced back further. Rather, as Richard Butsch's (2000) history of the making of the American audience vividly illustrates, the long past of audiences is likely as long as that of human communication itself, certainly predating the mass media. Their longevity, and the diversity of forms and focus that characterizes their history, gives the lie to their supposed present-day fragility – the

Internet is no more killing off audiences than did television replace reading or cinema destroy the art of conversation. Rather, changing social and technological conditions drive the evolving contexts within which people engage with and through media and, therefore, they also drive the ever-new (yet often strangely familiar) claims about the status and significance of audiences.

At present, the language of users rather than audiences holds sway, however, leading us to observe that one benefit of bringing the legacy of audience reception studies to a new generation of scholarship is to caution against repeating old mistakes. Recall that audience reception theory was originally developed precisely to counter the reduction of audiences to instrumental media users (as in the functionalist theory of uses and gratifications (Blumler and Katz 1974)). Although pragmatically we bow to commonplace adoption of the terms "use" and "user," analytically we insist that this is an unfortunate reductionism that misses two vital dimensions of audiences that are precisely worth preserving in a digital age. First, notwithstanding the explosion of texts and textuality already observed, in the double articulation of media and communication processes, the concept of "use" recognizes no texts, only objects. People use objects to do things, yes, but they interpret texts, simultaneously changing the text and themselves – or, as Iser put it, "As the reader passes through the various perspectives offered by the text, and relates the different views and patterns to one another, he sets the work in motion, and so sets himself in motion too" (1974: 106). Second, users are resolutely singular, and though they can be aggregated they cannot encompass the collectivity captured by "audience" (and by its contrasting alternatives – public, mass, crowd, market). Thus, the properties of collectives, and any (often rather unpredictable) power that thereby accrues, is missed by a reductively individual level of analysis.

Perhaps the very banality of the concept of use permits the easy assumption that users need not be studied empirically. Undoubtedly, there is a plethora of descriptive studies charting the nature of digital media uses. There is also, more interestingly, a host of studies tracing the significance of such use in diverse domains (education, family life, intimate relations, political participation, and so on). But there is surprisingly little on the processes of meaning-making involved: oddly, the more researchers contextualize people's engagement with screens in ever wider social spheres, the less subtle is their appreciation of the complexities of engaging with what is on those screens (Livingstone 2007). In terms of Silverstone's double articulation of media and communications, the material is displacing the semiotic, leaving only a single articulation of power and process to be unpacked and thus a less rich critical analysis. In a manner reminiscent of the Screen theorists, political economists, and anxious policy-makers of old, we are again hearing homogenizing, dismissive, patronizing, or just taken-for-granted claims about what people (audiences, users) do or think or understand about new media. Has it been so quickly forgotten that the analyst's interpretation of the text (the game, the webpage, the social networking site) may not accord with that of the user and that decoding the layers of meaning is always context-dependent? An audience perspective insists on including the phenomenological experience of living in a mediated society, not least because

Table 6.1 Evolving cultures of communication.

Dimension	Oral	Print	Broadcast	Networked
Interpretative pair (communication at the interface)	Speaker/hearer	Text/reader	Encoding/decoding	Affordances/user
Modality (of the text/ technology)	Multi/situated	Mono	Audio/visual	Multi/distanciated
Structure (of the message)	Linear	Linear	Linear	Hypertextual
Social relations (among readers/ users)	Niche/co-located	Niche/dispersed	Mass	Niche and mass
Literacy requirements (of the reader/user)	Low	High	Low	High
Collective nouns (for people engaged in communication)	Community; crowd; public	Citizens; public; readership	Audience; market; mass	Consumers; netizens; users

empirical work with people as audiences readily surprises or contracts established assumptions while revealing other, often marginalized, phenomena. Thus, the mere act of going out to speak to the people one is speaking on behalf of can generate critical knowledge (Hartley 2006).

But these are debates within the short history of media research. What of that longer past? In Table 6.1, we identify four different and yet intriguingly parallel moments of mediation that reveal not only continuities and changes but also, more interestingly, occasional but crucial returns. While the modal change is distinctive and new (notwithstanding the presence of multimodality in many printed texts and the monomodal nature of countless web interfaces), the change in social relations reflects a return in the digital age to that which preceded the age of mass broadcasting. So, networked communication only appears distinctive in addressing niche audiences by comparison with the mass media it follows, but this is far from novel in the longer history of communication. In other words, it is less the present than the preceding 50 years that require a distinctive explanation in this regard (Katz and Scannell 2009).

Networked media, however, are more complex in both modality and legibility than any previous form of communication – in terms of the criteria prioritized in our analysis, they offer the richest array of communicative possibilities in human history. Other parallels are also evident. As for oral communication, broadcast communication's reliance on audiovisual modes of communication renders it immediately accessible. Indeed, the literacy requirements of today's complex and often illegible media environment are more like those of the early days of print than of the broadcast era (radio and television), highly demanding of their reader/viewer/user. This necessitates new efforts to increase and support literacy – from the state, civil society, and the media themselves. While in the eighteenth century the spread of mass literacy was enabled by the birth of the school (Luke 1989), in the twenty-first century, digital literacy is again demanding considerable institutional efforts, this time underpinned by the normative turn in the academy (e.g., Hobbs 2010). The risk – as for print but not so much for oral or audiovisual literacy – is that, without such institutional efforts, illiteracy perpetuates and extends social inequality.

Table 6.1 reveals both continuities and transitions across differently mediated communicative conditions. The continuities are considerable, enabling the comparison of communicative conditions over time and place in terms of their technological affordances, textual conventions, and practices of use. Although each set of conditions is distinctive to its particular context, all can be theorized in terms of complex relationships of mutuality and co-construction of meaning between the interpreter and that which is interpreted. As we have emphasized, this is variously theorized in terms of texts and readers, affordances and appropriation, legibility and literacy, technology and use. Each element in these pairs defines, shapes, resources, and restrains the other. Thus, guided by the continuing relevance of analytic concepts from reception studies in the age of networked media, in this chapter we have proposed that this conceptual repertoire holds much promise for the empirical study of people's engagement with diverse forms of new media. One reason that we have urged the extension of concepts from reception studies is that claims about "users" – made within and, especially, beyond the field of media and communications (e.g., in literacy and education studies, information systems, human–computer interaction, and cybernetics, and across the social sciences) – are often speculative or based on descriptive more than critical or theory-led research.

But it is the transitions that gather most attention during the intellectual, empirical, and public debates surrounding the move from audiences to users, or from mass to converged media. And, to understand these changes, it may well be that the field of media and communications has much to learn from the other fields that border it, especially insofar as they theorize users, in one way or another. For example, literacy studies have a strong focus on questions of textuality, visuality, authorship, learning, and writing; information systems bring perspectives on organizational procedures, software, hardware, and data processing; and human–computer interaction focuses on the exchange between the user and a technical interface, noting problems, errors, and inconsistencies. Interestingly, these fields tend not – unlike the attitude toward audiences within media and communications – to denigrate or marginalize the importance of readers or users. However, we can retain from media and communications research its well-developed analysis of cultures and subcultures, of power (in relation to gender, ethnicity, and other forms of identity), of the political economy of media organizations and networks, and much more. Media and communication more than other fields, it seems, emphasizes the significance of, or unexpected responses and divergent interpretations of, audiences (in all their forms), in turn forcing a careful examination of the particular contexts within which people engage with media.

Conclusion

We look forward, we look back, we decide, we change our decisions, we form
expectations, we are shocked by their nonfulfillment, we question, we muse,
we accept, we reject; this is the dynamic process of recreation. This process is
steered by two main structural components within the text: first a repertoire of
familiar (literary) patterns and recurrent (literary) themes . . . ; second, techniques
or strategies used to set the familiar against the unfamiliar.

(Iser, The Implied Reader, *1974: 289*)

Faced with a sense of radical change in the media environment, this chapter has argued for the continued need for a theory – and the continued validity of the theory developed for audience reception of television – to understand how people engage not only in terms of motivation, choice, or habit but also in semiotic terms, whether accepting, creative, or critical, with media texts old and new. This should help today's generation of researchers of new media avoid the mistakes made by their predecessors when researching older media. For, already, today's researchers are grappling with some familiar problems. Research once again risks celebrating an excessive notion of agency. It still struggles to keep in its sights both users' engagement with texts on the screen and the real-world social contexts that shape that engagement. And we are witnessing the inadvertent return of the singular, closed authoritative text (and text analyst), forgetting the insight that texts (online and offline) are subtly open to multiple interpretations and leave gaps for users to fill, preferring instead readings that shape users' responses (Burbules 1998).

Once again, there is a pressing task: of countering implicit assumptions of the World Wide Web as a window on the world, of websites whose meaning can be straightforwardly stated by the researcher, of an online world that presents the same face to all comers, in which MySpace and Wikipedia and *Second Life* are inviolate objects of singular meaning, however diverse the uses to which they are put. A singular text, of course, makes for an audience that is either homogenous (everyone responds in the same way) or whose heterogeneity is merely idiosyncratic or to be explained solely by social determinants (everyone responds as dictated by their circumstances). But it does not allow for diverse modes of engagement in which the very meaning of the text is realized only in the act of interpretation – in Eco's (1979) terms, of actualization, as today's readers pass through digital texts (Fornas et al., 2002). Hence, few studies reveal multiple *readings* of digital texts, either implied by a polysemic text or as shown among empirical users. Some scholars even appear content, as before audience reception studies, to analyze online spaces with no reference to audiences or users at all, reducing people to subjects and losing sight of both agency and context. At this point, then, we rest our case that there is much to learn from the previous generation of audience reception and interpretation.

Although presented in the traditional mode of linear print, this chapter was born out of the more fluid and interactive exchange that Ong captures in the quotation above. It sought to celebrate the conversations across as well as within generations of scholars who, with Iser, are constantly looking back and looking forward in order to orient themselves to the present, necessarily retelling what has gone before in order to anticipate what might be to come. Thus, we have revisited the conceptual repertoire from audience reception studies in order to explore the continued relevance of these debates in the age of new media. First, we argued for retention of the co-constructionist text–reader relation or interpretative contract, for it has proved illuminating in parallel manifestations across diverse disciplines. The text–reader metaphor, especially when grounded in reception aesthetics (Iser, Eco) brings with it many other concepts of value to the networked age – consider open and closed texts, horizons of expectation, gap-filling, wandering viewpoints, and communities of interpretation. Moreover, while seemingly micro in their ambitions of investigating meaning at the interface of readers and texts, this approach connects also to a macro level of analysis, for it bridges structure and agency in a dialectic relation that considers not only resources but also constraints, and it contextualizes the circuit of culture within wider society in a manner that privileges neither one nor the other of texts and readers in its critical examination of how the relations between people at all levels are increasingly and ceaselessly mediated. Rather, it observes the continued relevance of texts and readers or audiences in today's world, and it thus urges that scholars continue to learn from past insights in recognizing, appreciating, and standing up for the contribution and interests of ordinary people in the digital, networked age.

References

Abercrombie, N. and Longhurst, B. (1998) *Audiences: A Sociological Theory of Performance and Imagination*. London: Sage.

Aksoy, A. and Robins, K. (2000) "Thinking Across Spaces. Transnational Television from Turkey." *European Journal of Cultural Studies*, 3(3), 343–365.

Ang, I. (1991) *Desperately Seeking the Audience*. London and New York: Routledge.

Ang, I. (1996) *Living Room Wars: Rethinking Media Audiences for a Postmodern World*. London: Routledge.

Barjak, F., Lane, J., Poschen, M., et al. (2010) "E-infrastructure Adoption in the Social Sciences and the Humanities – Cross-National Evidence from the AVROSS Survey." *Information, Communication & Society*, 13(5), 635–651.

Bird, E.S. (2009) "Not Dead Yet? Some Thoughts on the Future of Qualitative Audience Studies." Keynote presentation at "Transforming Audiences," University of Westminster, London (September).

Blumler, J.G. and Katz, E., eds. (1974) *The Uses of Mass Communications: Current Perspectives on Gratification Research*. Beverly Hills, CA: Sage.

Bolter, J.D. and Grusin, R. (1998) *Remediation: Understanding New Media*. Cambridge, MA: MIT Press.

Bruns, A. (2008) *Blogs, Wikipedia, Second Life, and Beyond: From Production to Produsage*. New York: Peter Lang.

Burbules, N. (1998) "Rhetorics of the Web: Hyperreading and Critical Literacy" in I. Snyder, ed., *Page to Screen: Taking Literacy into the Electronic Era*. London: Routledge, pp. 102–122.

Butsch, R. (2000) *The Making of American Audiences: From Stage to Television 1750–1990*. Cambridge: Cambridge University Press.

Coontz, S. (1997) *The Way We Really Are: Coming to Terms with America's Changing Families*. New York: Basic Books.

Dahlgren, P. (2003) "Reconfiguring Civic Culture in the New Media Milieu" in J. Corner and D. Pels, eds., *Media and the Restyling of Politics*. London: Sage, pp. 151–170.

Das, R. (2011) "Converging Perspectives in Audience Studies and Digital Literacies: Youthful Interpretations of an Online Genre." *European Journal of Communication*, 26(4), 343–360.

Das, R. (2012) "The Task of Interpretation." *Participations: The International Journal of Audience and Reception Studies*, 9(1), 2–25.

Dayan, D. (2005) "Mothers, Midwives and Abortionists: Genealogy, Obstetrics, Audiences and Publics" in S. Livingstone, ed., *Audiences and Publics: When Cultural Engagement Matters for the Public Sphere*. Bristol: Intellect Press, pp. 43–76.

Ebbinghaus, H. (1908) *Abriss der Psychology*. Vol. 1. Leipzig: Veit.

Eco, U. (1979) *The Role of the Reader: Explorations in the Semiotics of Texts*. Bloomington, IN: Indiana University Press.

Farrell, T.J. and Soukup, P.A., eds. (2002) *An Ong Reader: Challenges for Further Inquiry*. Cresskill, NJ: Hampton Press.

Fiske, J. (1992) "Audiencing: A Cultural Studies Approach to Watching Television." *Poetics*, 21(4), 345–359.

Fornas, J., Klein, K., Ladendorf, M. et al. (2002) *Digital Borderlands: Cultural Studies of Identity and Interactivity on the Internet*. New York: Peter Lang.

Georgiou, M. (2001) "Crossing the Boundaries of the Ethnic Home: Media Consumption and Ethnic Identity Construction in the Public Space: The Case of the Cypriot Community Centre in North London." *Gazette*, 63(4), 311–329.

Gillmor, D. (2006) *We the Media: Grassroots Journalism by the People, for the People*. Sebastopol, CA: O'Reilly Media.

Goffman, E. (1981) *Forms of Talk*. Oxford: Blackwell.

Hall, S. (1980) "Encoding/Decoding" in S. Hall, D. Hobson, A. Lowe, and P. Willis, eds., *Culture, Media, Language*. London: Hutchinson, pp. 128–138.

Hartley, J. (2006) "'Read thy Self': Text, Audience, and Method in Cultural Studies" in M. White and J. Schwoch, eds., *Questions of Method in Cultural Studies*. Oxford: Blackwell, pp. 71–104.

Hobbs, R. (2010) *Digital and Media Literacy: A Plan of Action*. Washington, DC: The Aspen Institute John S. and James L. Knight Foundation.

Holland, N. (1975) *5 Readers Reading*. New Haven, CT: Yale University Press.

Hutchby, I. (2001) "Technologies, Texts and Affordances." *Sociology*, 35(2), 441–456.

Iser, W. (1974) *The Implied Reader*. Baltimore, MD: John Hopkins University Press.

Jenkins, H. (2003) "Quentin Tarantino's Star Wars? Digital Cinema, Media Convergence, and Participatory Culture" in D. Thorburn and H. Jenkins, eds., *Rethinking Media Change: The Aesthetics of Transition*. Cambridge, MA: MIT Press, pp. 281–312.

Jenkins, H. (2006) *Convergence Culture: Where Old and New Media Collide*: New York: New York University Press.

Jensen, K.B. (2010) *Media Convergence: The Three Degrees of Network, Mass, and Interpersonal Communication*. London: Routledge.

Jermyn, D. and Holmes, S. (2006) "The Audience Is Dead; Long Live the Audience! Interactivity, 'Telephilia' and the Contemporary Television Audience." *Critical Studies in Television*, 1(1), 49–57.

Johnson, R. (1986) "What Is Cultural Studies Anyway?" *Social Text*, 16, 38–80.

Katz, E. and Scannell, P. (2009) "The End of Television? Its Impact So Far," special issue of *Annals of the American Academy of Political and Social Science*, 625.

Katz, E., Peters, J.D., Liebes, T., and Orloff, A. (2003) "Editors' Introduction" in E. Katz, J.D. Peters, T. Liebes, and A. Orloff, eds., *Canonic Texts in Media Research*. Cambridge: Polity, pp. 1–8.

Kim, W., Jeong, O.-R., and Lee, S.-W. (2010) "On Social Web Sites." *Information Systems*, 35(2), 215–236.

Kimmerle, J., Moskaliuk, J., Harrer, A., and Cress, U. (2010) "Visualizing Co-Evolution of Individual and Collective Knowledge." *Information, Communication & Society*, 13(8), 1099–1121.

Kress, G. (2003) *Literacy in the New Media Age*. London: Routledge.

Krotz, F. (2007) "The Meta-Process of 'Mediatization' as a Conceptual Frame." *Global Media and Communication*, 3(3), 256–260.

Liebes, T. and Katz, E. (1993) *The Export of Meaning: Cross-Cultural Readings of Dallas*. Cambridge: Polity.

Livingstone, S. (1998a) "Audience Research at the Crossroads: The 'Implied Audience' in Media and Cultural Theory." *European Journal of Cultural Studies*, 1(2), 193–217.

Livingstone, S. (1998b) "Relationships Between Media and Audiences: Prospects for Future Audience Reception Studies" in T. Liebes and J. Curran, eds., *Media, Ritual and Identity: Essays in Honor of Elihu Katz*. London: Routledge, pp. 237–255.

Livingstone, S. (2004) "The Challenge of Changing Audiences: Or, What is the Audience Researcher to Do in the Age of the Internet?" *European Journal of Communication*, 19(1), 75–86.

Livingstone, S. (2007) "On the Material and the Symbolic: Silverstone's Double Articulation of Research Traditions in New Media Studies." *New Media & Society*, 9(1), 16–24.

Livingstone, S. (2008) "Engaging with Media – A Matter of Literacy?" *Communication, Culture & Critique*, 1(1), 51–62.

Livingstone, S. (2009) "On the Mediation of Everything. ICA Presidential address." *Journal of Communication*, 59(1), 1–18.

Livingstone, S., Couldry, N., and Markham, T. (2007) "Youthful Steps Towards Civic Participation: Does the Internet Help?" in B. Loader, ed., *Young Citizens in the Digital Age: Political Engagement, Young People and New Media*. London: Routledge, pp. 21–34.

Luke, C. (1989) *Pedagogy, Printing and Protestantism: The Discourse of Childhood*. Albany, NY: SUNY Press.

Morley, D. (2006) "Unanswered Questions in Audience Research." *Communication Review*, 9(2), 101–121.

Morris, M. (1988) "Banality in Cultural Studies." *Discourse*, 10(2), 3–29.

Orgad, S. (2012) *Media Representation and the Global Imagination*. Cambridge: Polity.

Paul, S. and Morris, M. (2011) "Sensemaking in Collaborative Web Search." *International Journal of Human–Computer Interaction*, 26(1&2), 72–122.

Rosen, J. (2006) "The People Formerly Known as the Audience." *The Huffington Post* (June 30). www.huffingtonpost.com/jay-rosen/the-people-formerly-known_1_b_24113.html.

Scribner, S. and Cole, M. (1973) "Cognitive Consequences of Formal and Informal Education." *Science*, 182(4112), 553–559.

Seaman, W.R. (1992) "Active Audience Theory: Pointless Populism." *Media, Culture & Society*, 14(2), 301–311.

Silverstone, R. (1994) *Television and Everyday Life*. London: Routledge.

Snyder, I. (2001) "A New Communication Order: Researching Literacy Practices in the Network Society." *Language and Education*, 15(2), 117–131.

Staiger, J. (2005) *Media Reception Studies*. New York: New York University Press.

Tomlinson, J. (1999) *Globalization and Culture*. Chicago, IL: University of Chicago Press.

Woolgar, S. (1996) "Technologies as Cultural Artifacts" in W.H. Dutton, ed., *Information and Communication Technologies: Visions and Realities*. Oxford: Oxford University Press, pp. 87–102.

7

The Emergence of Next-Generation Internet Users

Grant Blank and William H. Dutton

Introduction

The Internet is over four decades old. The inception of this "network of networks" is most often tied to ARPANET, built by researchers sponsored by the Advance Research Projects Agency (ARPA) of the US Department of Defense in the late 1960s. It has been the product of new services and applications, such as email, the web, and browsers that have continually reinvented the Internet in new ways – making it truly new among the new media. After the development of the web and browsers that provided a graphical user interface, the personal computer soon became the primary point for accessing the Internet from around the world, whether from a household or an Internet café. In line with this, whether an individual has access to a personal computer linked to the Internet (at home or work) has become a major focus of social research on the Internet. Without access, directly or through intermediaries, many of the potential benefits and risks of the Internet are out of reach. This has led social research on the Internet to focus on issues surrounding the digital divide in access, and the resources, whether financial, geographical, or skill-based, required for individuals or households to bridge the divide.

Several trends emerged in the early years of the twenty-first century that could change patterns of Internet access in significant ways. One is the phenomenal global diffusion of mobile phones and the subsequent development of smartphones that enable access to the Internet while on the move. Another is the development of new appliance-like devices for accessing the Internet that can supplement or replace the personal computer.[1] These devices include what are commonly called tablet computers and readers, which are designed to be more portable and easier to use for a limited number of purposes, such as browsing the web or reading an e-book.

How have these new forms of access changed the way people access the Internet? What differences might they make in relation to how people use the Internet, such as for various entertainment or information services? Who uses these devices? Are they

A Companion to New Media Dynamics, First Edition. Edited by John Hartley, Jean Burgess, and Axel Bruns.
© 2013 John Wiley & Sons, Ltd. Published 2015 by John Wiley & Sons, Ltd.

closing down the Internet, making it less creative, or opening it up to new users and uses? If they are valuable new channels for access, are they more widely accessible, enabling new users, or does access on new devices reinforce existing digital divides?

Approach

This chapter addresses these issues around new patterns of Internet access by focusing on the analysis of survey data gathered in Britain as part of the Oxford Internet Survey (OxIS), which is one component of the World Internet Project (WIP), a consortium of over two dozen national partners. OxIS began in 2003 and is organized around a number of themes that allow us to analyze the dataset for specific trends and topics, including digital and social inclusion and exclusion; shaping, regulating, and governing the Internet; safety, trust, and privacy online; social networking and entertainment; and online transactions and commerce. Based on the demographic and attitudinal questions asked in the survey, it is possible to construct profiles of the survey participants, which include users and nonusers of the Internet. Our analyses relate these profiles to the data about use and nonuse to allow us to draw detailed conclusions about who uses the Internet, in which ways, and to what extent.

Unless otherwise noted, all data cited in this chapter are from OxIS.[2] OxIS data are collected by professionally trained field survey staff via face-to-face interviews in people's homes. OxIS is a biennial sample survey of adult Internet use in Britain, including England, Wales, and Scotland. The first survey was conducted in 2003 and subsequent surveys followed in 2005, 2007, 2009, and 2011. Each survey has followed an identical sampling methodology. The respondents are selected based on a three-stage random sample of the population. The data are then weighted based on gender, age, socioeconomic grade, and region. Response rates using this sampling strategy have been very high: 60 percent in 2003, 66 percent in 2005, 68 percent in 2007, 53 percent in 2009, and 51 percent in 2011.[3] Although questions have been added as new issues emerged, many questions have remained the same to facilitate comparisons between years.

An important strength of OxIS is that it is not a convenience sample. This distinguishes it from many otherwise excellent datasets. This has both methodological and theoretical implications. Methodologically, as a representative sample, OxIS allows us to project to the adult (14 and over) population of Britain. This is not possible for a convenience sample. Theoretically, a random sample of adults allows us to explore a number of interesting variables. The convenience samples are often composed of college students who have limited variations in age, social status, and income compared to the general population of Internet users. We can explore the effects of these demographic variables where convenience samples cannot.

We will use the 2011 survey, which contains the results of interviews with 2057 respondents. Our analyses are based either on the full sample of 2057 or on the subset of current Internet users: 1498 respondents, 72.8 percent of the full sample.[4]

However, while the focus of our analysis is on a snapshot of one nation, as part of the WIP we are able to compare our findings with the results in nations around the world to determine whether our findings are more or less consistent. Our analysis was innovative within the WIP collaboration, meaning that our exact analysis does not replicate that of other countries, but we have found no reports from our partner countries that would suggest the UK findings are unique in the patterns we discuss. The main differences are in levels, such as the level of Internet adoption, but not in the basic patterns of relationships that we report.

The Emergence of Next-Generation Users

In 2011, in line with trends in mobile phone use and the diffusion of appliances, such as tablets, we saw two dramatic and interrelated shifts appearing in our survey results. One was in the portability of devices and the other in the range of available devices that have emerged to change how users access the Internet. Together they define the "next-generation user," who comprises 44 percent of Internet users in Britain. Next-generation users are not just teenagers: as a consequence of long-term trends in patterns of use, they emerged across all age groups. They did not appear overnight: with the benefit of hindsight, we can look back and see that the proportion of next-generation users grew from 20 percent in 2007 to 32 percent in 2009 to 44 percent in 2011 (Figure 7.1).

From the Oxford Internet Institute's (OII) first survey of Internet use in 2003, and in line with most other developed nations, access has been based primarily on the use of a personal computer in one's household, linked to the Internet through a modem or broadband connection. For many, this was complemented by similar access at work or school. The major change in access since 2003 was the

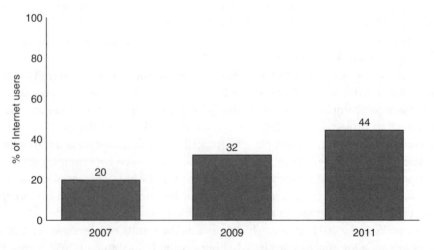

Current users. OxIS 2007: N = 1578; OxIS 2009: N = 1401; OxIS 2011: N = 1498

Figure 7.1   Next-generation Internet users as a percentage of all users.

move from narrowband dial-up to broadband always-on Internet connections. By 2009, nearly all Internet users had a broadband connection, increasingly including wireless connections within the household, such as over a Wi-Fi router. While speeds will continue to increase through initiatives such as "superfast" broadband and wireless connections will expand, this pattern of Internet access characterizes the "first-generation user" in Britain.

We will contrast the characteristics of first-generation and next-generation users in the coming pages. But, first, how can we explain the rise of the next-generation user, and the significance of this rise, in the context of the study of the Internet? There are three general and competing theoretical perspectives on the social role of the Internet that might be useful in understanding this shift and its consequences.

Theoretical Perspectives

There are several theoretical perspectives on the social implications of a shift in patterns of access to the Internet, such as the shift to next-generation users. They are all qualitative explanations of patterns of relationships, rather than operationally defined models, but they capture the major competing perspectives on the role of the Internet in everyday life.

Technical Rationality

One dominant perspective is a technical rationality that draws on major features of new technologies to reason about the likely implications of adoption. While many social scientists view this as a technologically determinist perspective, it characterizes some of the most prominent scholars of the Internet and new technology, such as Lawrence Lessig (1999) and his view that "code is law."[5] The view from this perspective is that the move toward "appliances" is bound up with the adoption of closed applications or "apps" that have a limited set of functions. They restrict the openness and "generativity" of the Internet, compared to general-purpose personal computers, which enable users to program, write code, and not be limited by a secured set of applications and sites (Zittrain 2008). Since those who adopt the new appliance devices, such as tablets, are satisfied with the closed applications, they are likely to be less sophisticated than those who remain anchored to personal computing and less creative in their use and application of the Internet. Will they move users toward a role as passive browsers of information and consumers of entertainment?

Domestication: A Social Rationality

In contrast, there is a more socially deterministic perspective on the social role of the Internet and related information and communication technologies (ICTs) in the household that is best captured by work on the "domestication" of the Internet.

Domestication (Silverstone et al. 1992; Haddon 2006, 2007, 2011) emphasizes the influence of households or work places on shaping, taming, or domesticating technologies as users fit them into the values and interests of their particular social context. People adopt and integrate technologies into their everyday routines in ways that follow and reinforce existing practices, which differ across households.

The concept of domestication was developed as a way to elaborate a conceptual model for exploring the role of ICTs in life within the household (Livingstone 1992; Silverstone et al. 1992; Silverstone 1996). The formulation entails four "nondiscrete elements" that constitute the domestication process: appropriation, objectification, incorporation, and conversion (Silverstone et al. 1992: 20). Appropriation occurs when the technology product is purchased and its entry into a household must be managed. Objectification refers to the location of a technology in the household, both physically and symbolically. Incorporation is when the technology is fitted into the everyday routines of a household. Finally, conversion designates the ways in which technologies are displayed to others for impression management.[6] These elements do not have a strict order. Although appropriation is clearly prior, the other three elements interact and shape each other.

This chapter is particularly interested in the incorporation of the Internet into the daily routines of people as they appropriate the technologies and practices of the next-generation user and incorporate them into their everyday routines. It is characteristic of the Internet that it is not a single new technology. Rather, it gives access to a variety of innovations, including web browsers, location and direction services, email, and social networking. This presents a large menu of items to be incorporated into people's day-to-day lives. It will not be done all at once; for many the Internet is a continuing, multiyear exploration of new possibilities.

This domestication model is in line with earlier conceptions of the social shaping of technology in organizations, such as "reinforcement politics," which argued that organizations adopt and shape information technologies to follow and reinforce the prevailing structures of power and influence within the adopting organizations (Danziger et al. 1982). Since domestication suggests people shape the Internet to their pre-existing interests and values, we would not expect the adoption of new technologies, as represented by the next-generation user, to make much difference in how people use the Internet, nor have a significant, transformative impact on the social role of the Internet in their lives.

Reconfiguring Access

A different theoretical perspective revolves around the concept of "reconfiguring access" (Dutton 1999, 2005). From this perspective, it is impossible to determine the implications of technologies in advance, either by rationally extrapolating from the technical features of the innovations or by assessing the interests and values of users.

This distinguishes this perspective from both a more technologically deterministic view and a socially determinist position. Reconfiguring access takes note of the fact that users often reinvent technologies, employing them in ways not expected by their developers. In addition, the social role of a technology can be influenced by the actions of many actors other than users, and from choices far outside the household, which distinguishes this perspective from the notion of domestication. Control of new technologies, particularly a networked technology such as the Internet, is distributed across a wide array of actors, including users, Internet service providers, hardware manufacturers, search engines, and social networking companies. Rather than expecting the impacts to be determined by features of the technology, or the values and interests of the household, reconfiguring access places a central emphasis on observing the actual use and impact across a diversity of users to discern emergent patterns of use and impact.

However, like a more technologically deterministic model, the concept of reconfiguring access is based on the expectation that technologies do matter – they have social implications – in two major respects. They reconfigure (1) how people do things and (2) the outcome of these activities. People adopt and use technologies, such as the Internet, more or less intentionally to reconfigure access in multiple ways, including their access to people, information, services, and technologies, and access to themselves. From this perspective, the technology does not simply fit into existing practices but changes them. If a person enjoys reading the newspaper, they might decide to use the Internet to get access to the news. However, this changes how they get the news and how much news they can get, as well as what news they obtain and how easily they obtain it. It reconfigures their access to the news, in this case.

The Internet can change the outcome of information and communication activities by virtue of changing cost structures, creating or eliminating gatekeepers, redistributing power between senders and receivers, making a task easier or more difficult, changing the circumstances under which a task can be performed, restructuring the architecture of networks (many to one versus one to many), and changing the geography of access. By changing costs, or eliminating gatekeepers, for example, the Internet can reconfigure access to information, people, services, and technologies, for example by making millions of computers accessible to a user of a smartphone.

The ability of the Internet to reconfigure access can be used to reinforce existing social arrangements, for example by helping friends to stay in touch, or to reconfigure social relations, for example by helping a person to meet new people. It can be used to reinforce a person's interest in the news but also open up new channels and sources for news.

The main methodologies used to study domestication have been qualitative, usually ethnographic (Silverstone 2005). This chapter uses survey data, but in a qualitative manner, which has certain disadvantages because it cannot address questions of meaning in the ways that an ethnographic approach seeks to do.

However, others have used surveys to study domestication (e.g., Punie 1997), and sample surveys have the major advantage that their results can be generalized to a population. In this case, we can generalize to the British population and, by reflecting on other WIP research, speculate on the wider applicability of our findings.

Defining the Next-Generation User

Are next-generation users domesticating recent developments in the Internet, or is their access to the Internet and the wider world being constrained by new appliances, or reconfigured in other ways by these new technical devices? In contrast to the first generation of Internet users, the next-generation user is defined by the emergence of two separate but related trends: portability and access through multiple devices.

First, there has been a continuing increase in the proportion of users who use the Internet over one or another mobile device, such as a smartphone. In 2003 this was a small proportion. At that time, 85 percent of British people had a mobile phone but only 11 percent of mobile phone users said they accessed email or the Internet over their mobile phone. By 2009, 97 percent of British people owned a mobile phone, and the proportion of users accessing email or the Internet over their phone had doubled to 24 percent – albeit still a minority of users. In 2011, this increased to nearly half (49 percent) of all users. By 2011, the mobile phone had become one of a number of portable devices for accessing the Internet within and outside the household.

Second, Internet users often have more devices, such as multiple computers, readers, tablets, and laptop computers, in addition to mobile phones with which to access the Internet. In 2009, only 19 percent had a PDA (personal digital assistant). Since then, the development of readers and tablets has boomed, for example with Apple's successful introduction of the iPad. The very notion of a PDA has become antiquated. In 2011, almost one-third of Internet users had a reader or a tablet, with 6 percent having both devices. Fully 59 percent have access to the Internet via one or more of these multiple devices other than the household personal computer.

Most observers have treated these developments as separate trends. There are even academics who focus only on mobile communication, and others who focus on tablets or the use of smartphones.[7] However, these two trends are not just related but also synergistic. Those who own multiple devices are also more likely to use the Internet on the move and from multiple locations.

We have therefore defined the next-generation user as someone who accesses the Internet from multiple locations and devices. Specifically, we operationally define the next-generation user as someone who uses at least two Internet applications (out of four applications queried)[8] on their mobile or who fits two or more of the following criteria: they own a tablet, own a reader, or own three or more computers. By this definition, in 2011, almost a third of Britons, and 44.4 percent of Internet users in Britain, were next-generation users (Figure 7.1 and Figure 7.2).

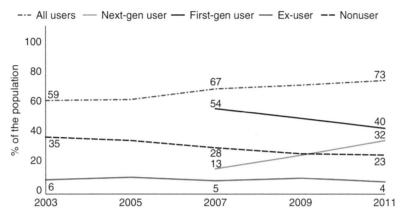

OxIS 2003: N = 2029; OxIS 2005: N = 2185; OxIS 2007: N = 2350; OxIS 2009: N = 2013; OxIS 2011: N = 2057

Figure 7.2   Internet use in Britain.

Why Does this Matter?

The following pages show how this transformation in Internet access is linked to important changes in patterns of use and in the social implications of use. We show that next-generation users are not evenly distributed but have higher incomes, indicating a new digital divide in Britain and almost certainly in other nations.

Figure 7.2 shows that the rapid growth of next-generation users has taken place amid slow growth in overall Internet use. Internet use in Britain grew from just over 60 percent in 2003 to 73 percent in 2011, leaving more than a quarter of the British population without access to the Internet. There has been a steady but slow decline in the proportion of people who have never used the Internet (nonusers) and relative stability in the proportion of those who used the Internet at one time but no longer do (ex-users). Despite multiple government and private initiatives aimed at bringing people online, digital divides remain in access to the Internet.

On the one hand, there is apparent stability, particularly visible in the proportion of British people with access to the Internet. On the other, a dramatic transition is occurring among users. The proportion of first-generation users is declining while the proportion of next-generation users us rising (Figure 7.2). Clearly, the promotion of new technical devices, such as the tablet, has changed the way households access the Internet. It is hard to see this as simply a process of domestication rather than a consequence of new product and service offerings.

How individual users access the Internet shapes the ways in which they use the technology, and how people wish to use the Internet is shaping the technologies they adopt. This is shown by the contrast between first- and next-generation use of the Internet in three areas: content production, entertainment and leisure, and information-seeking. In each case, a technical rationality might see innovations reducing the openness and generativity of users, while from a domestication perspective one would expect to see little change in patterns of use between next- and first-generation users.

Content Production

In contrast to the technical rationality, with its focus on how the limited openness of new devices restricts users, next-generation users are more likely to be producers of content than are first-generation users, who concentrate more on consumption than production. For many types of content, next-generation users are as much as 25 percentage points more likely to be producers (Figure 7.3). Specifically, next-generation users are more likely to update or create a profile on a social networking site. They are also more likely than first-generation users to post pictures and videos, post messages on discussion boards or forums, and post stories, poetry, or other creative work. Concerning more demanding types of content, such as maintaining a personal website or writing a blog, next-generation users are almost twice as likely to be producers than are first-generation users. Innovations are reconfiguring access by enabling greater production of content by next-generation users, but in a direction opposite to that expected on the basis of the more limited features of appliances.

Entertainment and Leisure

Compared with first-generation users, the next-generation users are much more likely to listen to music online, play games online, download music, watch videos online, and download, as well as upload, videos or music files (Figure 7.4). As with content production, these are large differences, often exceeding 20 or 25 percentage points. Also, next-generation users are more likely to watch "adult" sexual content

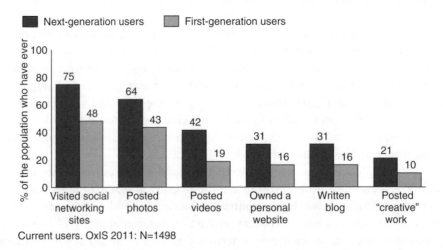

Current users. OxIS 2011: N=1498

Figure 7.3 Next-generation vs. first-generation Internet users by content production.

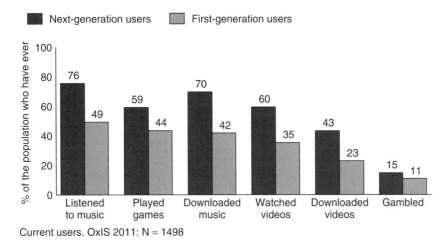

Figure 7.4 Next-generation vs. first-generation users by entertainment and leisure.

and bet or gamble online, but this difference is less pronounced than in the case of content production. Next-generation users seem to have integrated the Internet more extensively into their entertainment and leisure activities. In this respect, an association with listening to more music or watching more video productions is in line with the technical rationality of appliances but still relates to reconfiguring access in significant respects, which would not be anticipated from the perspective of domestication.

The Essential Importance of the Internet

Next-generation users are much more likely to agree that the Internet is "essential." Figure 7.5 reports the percentage that consider various media essential for information, whereas Figure 7.6 gives the same figures for entertainment. Both figures tell a consistent story about next-generation users. For information, they are 16 percentage points more likely to consider the Internet essential; for entertainment, they exceed first-generation users by 10 percentage points. Also notable is that the Internet is the only medium (with the exception of spending time with other people for entertainment) where next-generation and first-generation users differ. These figures underline the disproportionate value that next-generation users place on the Internet.

Information-Seeking

It is as interesting to look at how next-generation users differ from first-generation users as it is to examine how they are similar. One of the major changes over the

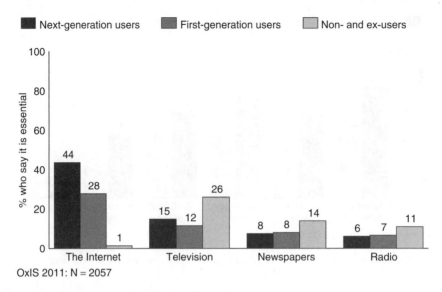

Figure 7.5   Importance of media for information.

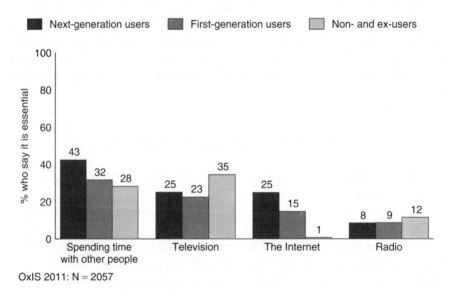

Figure 7.6   Importance of media for entertainment.

past decade has been the growing use of the Internet as a source of information, particularly with the rise of powerful and usable search engines such as Google. All Internet users increasingly go to the Internet for information. It is their first port of call. However, next-generation users are more likely than first-generation users to go to the Internet first for all kinds of information (Figure 7.7).

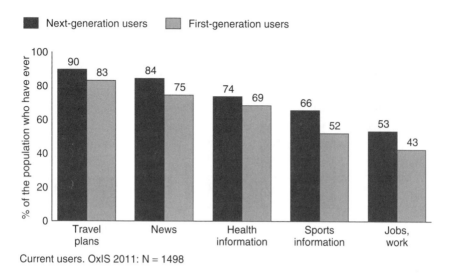

Current users. OxIS 2011: N = 1498

Figure 7.7   Next-generation vs. first-generation users by information-seeking.

For example, 84 percent of next-generation users go online for news, compared with 75 percent of first-generation users. The differences here are smaller than the differences observed above for content production and entertainment – only 7 to 14 percentage points – but they are statistically and substantively significant. The largest difference is looking for sports information. Since sport is an entertainment activity, the figures for sport have much in common with those for entertainment uses (Figure 7.4). Sport is the exception that proves the rule. Given that next-generation users can access the Internet from more locations on more devices at more times of the day, it might be surprising that their use of the Internet for information is not more extensive. One major reason is that information-seeking has become so common for all users.

Portability and Mobility

Do next-generation users access the Internet from more locations? Figure 7.8 shows that this is indeed the case. Next-generation users are no more likely than first-generation users to access the Internet from their homes but – importantly – they are also no less likely to do so. This underscores the continuing centrality of the household across the generations of users. However, next-generation users are far more likely to access the Internet on the move and from all other locations, including another person's home, work, school or university, a library, or an Internet café (Figure 7.8).

This finding might suggest the flaw in the technically rational argument that appliances undermine the generativity of the Internet (Zittrain 2008). Appliances

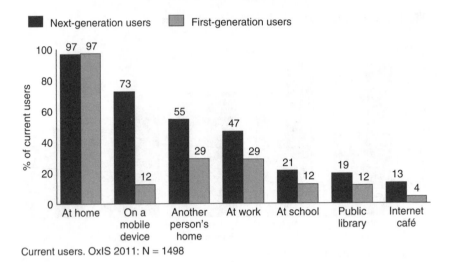

Figure 7.8   Next-generation vs. first-generation users by locations.

are generally not being substituted for personal computers and other more general-purpose devices but complementing these technologies, and extending them in time and place. Nearly everyone with a reader or tablet tends to use these technologies to augment rather than replace their other modes of accessing the Internet.

More generally, and in contrast to the technical argument and the domestication thesis, next-generation users appear to be empowered, relative to first-generation users, in creating content, enjoying entertainment online, and accessing information in ways and at times and locations that fit into their everyday lives and work in a more integrated way. Of course, those who want to create content and embed the Internet in more aspects of their everyday lives are more likely to adopt next-generation technologies, so in that sense a domestication process could be relevant. Through the social shaping of adoption and the empowerment of users, it is clear that the next-generation user has a more advantageous relationship with the Internet and the resources it can provide for accessing information, people, services, and other technologies.

This leads to the question of who the next-generation users are. Who is empowered by next-generation access, and who is not?

Who are the Next-Generation Users?

Are next-generation users simply the youth of the Internet age? Not really. Age and life stage are related to next-generation use, but primarily in the degree that people who are retired or of retirement age are much less likely to be next-generation users. Those who are unemployed are also somewhat less likely to be part of the next generation, while students and the employed are equally likely to be next-generation

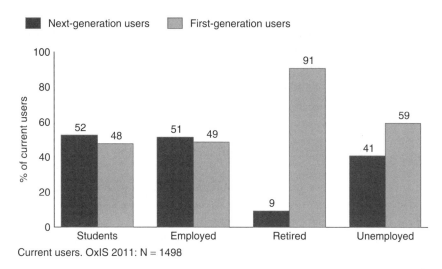

Current users. OxIS 2011: N = 1498

Figure 7.9   Next-generation vs. first-generation users by life stage.

users. This is not simply a function of youth or age cohorts. For example, only 52 percent of students are next-generation users (Figure 7.9). In short, domestication is not equal, as some people are more capable of bending new technologies to serve their needs and interests than are others. In this way, innovations are reconfiguring access by creating a new digital divide across people at different stages of life.

Another major factor related to next-generation users is household income. There are next-generation users at every income level, but there is clearly a greater proportion of next-generation users among the higher-income groups in Britain (Figure 7.10). It helps to have more money when buying a variety of devices, many of

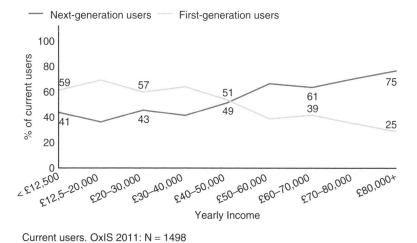

Current users. OxIS 2011: N = 1498

Figure 7.10   Next-generation vs. first-generation users by income.

which are expensive. The next-generation user is creating a new level of access to the Internet and the web that supports active patterns of information production and the integration of the Internet into everyday life and work. This pattern is creating a new cost for the Internet that is more accessible to the well-to-do, suggesting that there is a new digital divide developing in Britain, and probably other nations, between first- and next-generation users.

Multivariate Prediction of Next-Generation Users

These bivariate plots are informative but we can summarize the characteristics of next-generation users in a more concise fashion using a multivariate analysis, based on the seven independent demographic variables we used to describe the characteristics of respondents.[9] These are: age in years, household income, higher-education degree, gender, retired, use of the Internet at work, and married.[10] This model includes all of the demographic variables that we have available in the OxIS 2011 dataset.

In general, the results (Table 7.1) are not surprising; they are largely similar to, and reinforce, the bivariate results shown in the above figures. The results show that the strongest variable is probably retired respondents; only 9 percent of these are next-generation users compared to 49.3 percent of nonretired users (see also Figure 7.9).[11] The next strongest variables are having a higher-education degree and using the Internet at work. Activities specific to next-generations, such as content production and entertainment uses, require particular skills. For example, writing a successful blog requires the ability to write interestingly and persuasively. These sorts of skills are most common among people with more schooling. Using the Internet at work usually indicates a more complex job, possibly managerial or professional, and probably indicates more experience with the Internet (Dutton and Blank 2011)[12]. The concept of domestication suggests that we would find a more equivalent process across households but, clearly, some individuals and households are better placed to take advantage of technical innovations, and in that way they

Table 7.1 Logistic regression predicting next-generation users.

Variable	Odds ratio	P-value
Age	0.96	0.001
Income	1.21	0.001
Higher-education degree	1.49	0.016
Gender	0.75	0.041
Retired	0.33	0.006
Use of the Internet at work	1.47	0.019
Married	0.67	0.012

N = 1047. McFadden's pseudo R^2: 16.1 percent. Correctly classified: 70.2 percent.

are reconfiguring who has access to technologies that can support their needs and interests.

The multivariate analysis indicates that being married reduces the likelihood of being a next-generation user. This may reflect the fact that many next-generation user activities are time-consuming activities that often cannot be shared. Married people may have other priorities for their time and prefer to do things together. The coefficient for gender says that women are less likely to be next-generation users than men. The centrality of the Internet in the household has been associated with a narrowing of the digital divide. It might well be that the diffusion of more mobile devices that can be integrated into everyday life and work is reconfiguring gender divides to some degree.

Beyond Britain: The World Internet Project

Finally, while these detailed analyses are limited to Britain, our participation in the WIP enables us to compare our findings with those of over two dozen other nations.[13] From our work in this context, we have no evidence to question that these basic patterns are generally applicable in other nations. In less well-to-do nations, for example, there has been less focus on the household as the main site of access, with more importance placed on shared locations, such as Internet cafés. Likewise, some countries, such as Poland (World Internet Project 2011), have yet to see the rise in mobile- and appliance-based access to the Internet that Britain, the USA, and many other nations have experienced. But these are some of the few differences, and do not raise doubts concerning our analysis' general conclusions about the emergence of next-generation users over time and the ways in which these users have reconfigured their access to information, people, services, and technologies, such as by using appliances that complement other modes of access.

The Future

Clearly, more mobile phone users will be accessing the Internet in the coming years, but this forecast misses the broader picture: the twin trends of mobility and the use of multiple devices, and the synergy of these two trends, which creates next-generation use. As Figure 7.1 and Figure 7.2 suggest, these trends appear to be strong and likely to continue into the foreseeable future.

It is therefore important for research to begin to differentiate between Internet users in new ways. Speed remains one feature of new infrastructures that will shape patterns of access. But the days of a divide between narrowband dialup use and broadband are over (Dutton et al. 2004), as nearly all users in Britain have some level of broadband access. Wireless access will also grow as more households have multiple and portable devices. It is wireless broadband that enables portable devices to be used for accessing entertainment and information on the move. However, speed and wireless access are primarily enablers of new patterns of use and not the key factors discriminating among Internet users.

The central, new distinction – from the perspective of this study – is between first- and next-generation use. It will be important to track the growth of next-generation use in relation to nonusers, former users, and first-generation users. Research needs to look at the consequences of next-generation use on patterns of use and their societal implications. If, as we find, this next generation is truly empowering users in new ways, it will be equally important to address the new digital divides created by next-generation users.

The key theoretical contribution of this study is to expose some of the problems of both technologically and socially deterministic perspectives. Innovations that define the next-generation user are reconfiguring their access to information, people, and services in ways that are likely to empower them in relation to other users. And those in school or work and with more schooling and higher incomes are more likely to have the skills and wherewithal to exploit this potential. This contradicts expectations that the Internet may have become more technically dumbed-down compared to the PC-based Internet era, as quite the opposite appears to be the case. New devices are complementing and building on existing tools. In contradiction to the domestication perspective, some people are better able to domesticate these new technologies than others, and the technologies tend to have systematic implications for their users, such an enabling them to integrate them into their lives in ways that enhance their significance.

This study exposes a curious contradiction in domestication research. On the one hand this research claims to have its origins in an attempt to construct a theory that avoids technological determinism (Silverstone 2006) and focuses on how people actually integrate technological objects into their lives. On the other hand, most of the research focuses on individual objects, such as computers, mobile phones, and other ICTs. The complexity of the Internet shows the difficulty of this approach: on the Internet there is rarely a single "object." Next-generation users do not focus on objects. Their purposes include finding entertainment, finding information, finding a job, or publishing their creative work. To accomplish these ends, they combine and integrate an ensemble of objects: smartphones, tablets, readers, laptops, and desktops. For most people, the objects are not the point. Their goal is most often not to "use my tablet"; instead, they want to listen to music or watch a movie. A fascination with the technology per se might have typified early hobbyists, and still some users of the Internet, but is not the case with most users. This understanding of how ICTs are used in service of people's goals is consistent with domestication research's emphasis on how people appropriate and domesticate objects, but it moves research away from a focus on objects to concentrate on the purposes that human beings wish to achieve through those objects.

One of the most remarkable aspects of the Internet is that it is dynamic. It is never the same object from year to year; for example, the dramatic rise in the use of social networking sites since 2007 has introduced a whole new way for people to communicate in large numbers, and Apple's reinvention of the PDA as the iPad suddenly made the new "tablet" the next big thing. The Internet is a site for multiple ICTs and multiple innovations. A weakness of domestication theory is that it assumes a certain level of stability, specifically that there is an identifiable and stable object that is slowly adapted to fit into the life of the household. But the Internet is not stable: it is constantly being reinvented. Each new development has brought with it new challenges for people to incorporate into their routines. Continuing waves of innovation also challenge research. In the midst of continuing change, the challenge is to identify patterns of incorporation that have stabilized and will persist for an extended period of time. Next-generation users are the most recent of these patterns.

Other new research is also needed. Our survey data could well be complemented by more qualitative studies that would expand our understanding of next-generation users by investigating the meaning of these patterns of use to next-generation users, how next-generation users' identities are bound up in being a next-generation user, how use is negotiated within households, and other topics that are difficult for survey research to address.

Notes

1. Zittrain (2008) provides an overview of the emergence of such appliances and their potential implications for access to information and other services.
2. For a more complete overview of the OxIS methodology, see http://microsites.oii.ox.ac.uk /oxis/methodology.
3. Using response rate formula RR1, defined by the American Association of Public Opinion Researchers (AAPOR) (2011: 44).
4. For a more detailed description of the sample and methodology, see Blank and Dutton (2011).
5. The case for viewing Lessig's argument as technologically determinist is developed by Mayer-Schönberger (2008).
6. These correspond to common stages in the adoption of an innovation, from adoption to implementation to routinization, although Rogers (1962) and other innovation researchers assume a stronger ordering to these as more discrete stages than do domestication researchers.
7. For example, Wei's (2001) study of mobile phones.
8. The four applications are: browsing the Internet, using email, updating a social networking site, and finding directions.
9. This model includes all of the demographic variables that we have available in the OxIS 2011 dataset, with one exception: we also tried a variable measuring urban–rural residence but it was not statistically significant. For several variables in the model we tried numerous specifications. For marital status the full variable had five categories, but only the "married" category was statistically significant. Similarly, for education only the "higher-education degree" category was significant and for life stage only "retired" was significant.

10. The variables are defined as age, a continuous variable ranging from 14 to 92 years; income, an eight-category variable; higher-education degree, a dummy variable indicating whether or not a respondent has a higher-education degree; gender, a dummy variable using males as the comparison group; retired, a dummy variable indicating retired people; use of the Internet at work, a dummy variable indicating whether the respondent uses the Internet in their job; and married, a dummy variable indicating whether the respondent is married.

11. Strength is measured by the size of the odds ratio. With an odds ratio of only 0.33, retired respondents are the most important variable in the regression. Similarly, having a higher-education degree and using the Internet at work both have odds ratios near 1.50, making them the second most important variables in the regression.

12. Note, however, that when we substituted a direct measure of occupation in this model it was not statistically significant.

13. Information about the World Internet Project (WIP) and other national samples can be found online at www.worldinternetproject.net/#news.

References

American Association of Public Opinion Researchers (2011) *Standard Definitions: Final Dispositions of Case Codes and Outcome Rates for Surveys*, 7th edn. www.aapor.org /Standard_Definitions/3049.htm.

Blank, G. and Dutton, W.H. (2011) "Age and Trust in the Internet: The Centrality of Experience and Attitudes Toward Technology in Britain." *Social Science Computer Review*. http://ssc.sagepub.com/content/early/2011/02/21/0894439310396186.

Danziger, J.N., Dutton, W.H., Kling, R., and Kraemer, K.L. (1982) *Computers and Politics: High Technology in American Local Governments*. New York: Columbia University Press.

Dutton, W.H. (1999) *Society on the Line: Information Politics in the Digital Age*. Oxford and New York: Oxford University Press.

Dutton, W.H. (2005) "The Internet and Social Transformation: Reconfiguring Access" in W.H. Dutton, B. Kahin, R. O'Callaghan, and A.W. Wyckoff, eds., *Transforming Enterprise*. Cambridge, MA: MIT Press, pp. 375–397.

Dutton, W.H. and Blank, G. (2011) *Next Generation Users: The Internet in Britain. Oxford Internet Survey 2011*. Oxford: Oxford Internet Institute, University of Oxford.

Dutton, W. H., Gillett, S. E., McKnight, L. W., and Peltu, M. (2004) "Bridging Broadband Internet Divides: Reconfiguring Access to Enhance Communicative Power." *Journal of Information Technology*, 19(1), 28–38.

Haddon, L. (2006) "The Contribution of Domestication Research to In-Home Computing and Media Consumption." *Information Society*, 22, 195–205.

Haddon, L. (2007) "Roger Silverstone's Legacies: Domestication." *New Media & Society*, 9, 25–32.

Haddon, L. (2011) "Domestication Analysis, Objects of Study, and the Centrality of Technologies in Everyday Life." *Canadian Journal of Communication*, 36, 311–323.

Lessig, L. (1999) *Code and Other Laws of Cyberspace*. New York: Basic Books.

Livingstone, S. (1992) "The Meaning of Domestic Technologies: A Personal Construct Analysis of Familial Gender Relations" in R. Silverstone and E. Hirsch, eds., *Consuming Technologies: Media and Information in Domestic Spaces*. London: Routledge, pp. 113–130.

Mayer-Schönberger, V. (2008) "Demystifying Lessig." *Wisconsin Law Review*, 4, 713–746.

Punie, Y. (1997) "Rejections of ICT in Flemish Households: The Why-Not Question" in R. Silverstone and M. Hartmann, eds., *EMTEL Working Paper No. 3. Media and Information Technology: Regulating Markets & Everyday Life*. Brighton: University of Sussex, pp. 46–72.

Rogers, E.M. (1962) *Diffusion of Innovations*. New York: Free Press.

Silverstone, R. (1996) "Future Imperfect: Information and Communication Technologies in Everyday Life" in W.H. Dutton, ed., *Information and Communication Technologies – Visions and Realities*. Oxford: Oxford University Press, pp. 217–231.

Silverstone, R. (2005) "Introduction" in R. Silverstone, ed., *Media, Technology and Everyday Life in Europe*. Aldershot: Ashgate, pp. 1–18.

Silverstone, R. (2006) "Domesticating Domestication: Reflections on the Life of a Concept" in T. Berker, M. Hartmann, Y. Punie, and K.J. Ward, eds., *Domestication of Media and Technology*. Maidenhead: Open University Press. pp. 229–248.

Silverstone, R. Hirsch, E., and Morley, D. (1992) "Information and Communication Technologies and the Moral Economy of the Household" in R. Silverstone and E. Hirsch, eds., *Consuming Technologies: Media and Information in Domestic Spaces*. London: Routledge, pp 15–31.

Wei, R. (2001) "From Luxury to Utility: A Longitudinal Analysis of Cell Phone Laggards." *Journalism and Mass Communication Quarterly*, 78, 702–719.

World Internet Project (2011) *World Internet Project Poland 2011*. Warsaw, PL: Agora S.A. and T.P. Group.

Zittrain, J. (2008) *The Future of the Internet – And How to Stop It*. New Haven, CT: Yale University Press.

8

National Web Studies
The Case of Iran Online

Richard Rogers, Esther Weltevrede,
Erik Borra, and Sabine Niederer

Introduction: National Web Studies

In 2007, Ricardo Baeza-Yates and colleagues at Yahoo! Research in Barcelona published a review article on "characterizations of national web domains" in which they sketched an emerging field that we would like to call national web studies. Of particular interest in the article is the distinction the authors made between studies in the 1990s on the characteristics of *the web* and those a decade later on *national webs* (Kehoe et al. 1999; Baeza-Yates et al. 2007). The term "national web," we feel, is useful for capturing a historical shift in the study of the Internet, and especially how the web's location-awareness repositions the Internet as an object of study. A national web is one means of summing up the transition of the Internet from "cyberspace," which invokes a placeless space of email and packets, to the web of identifiable national domains (.de, .fr, .gr, and so on) as well as websites whose contents, advertisements, and language are matched to one's location. In other words, we are at once foregrounding a change to the object of study and asking how to study the new dynamics online. How should we approach the web after cyberspace? The notion of the national web, we argue, is also useful beyond the conceptual level. It enables the study of the current conditions of a web space demarcated along national lines, as Baeza-Yates and colleagues pointed out in comparing one national web with another. As we would like to pursue here, it also may be useful for the study of conditions not only of the online but also of the ground. That is to say, national web studies is another example of country profiling.

Here, building upon the web characterization work, we provide an approach to the study of national webs that both engages a series of methodological debates (how to study a national web) and provides an overall rationale for their study (why study a national web). Where the former is concerned, we put forward an approach that is cognizant of the multiplicity of user experiences of the web as well as the concomitant web data collection practices (that users may actively or

A Companion to New Media Dynamics, First Edition. Edited by John Hartley, Jean Burgess, and Axel Bruns.

passively participate in). Search engines and other web information companies such as Alexa routinely collect data from users who search and use their toolbars, for example. Platforms where "crowds share" by posting and by rating are also data-collection vessels and analysis machines. The outcomes of these data-gathering and data-counting exercises are often ranked lists of URLs, recommended to users. When location is added as a variable, the URL lists may be country- or region-specific. The same holds for language; namely, websites may be served that are wholly or in part in a particular language. Thus, in practice one is able to speak of country-specific and/or language-specific webs organized by the data collected and analyzed by engines, platforms, and other online devices. There is a caveat. Users of these devices draw upon their own data, and are recursively provided with a selection of considered URLs. Personalization may influence the country- and language-specific URLs served, however much to date the impact on search engine results appears to have been minimal (Feuz et al. 2011). Consequently, the effects of personalization are not treated here (Pariser 2011).

We give the term "device cultures" to the interaction between user and engine, the data that are collected, how they are analyzed, and ultimately the URL recommendations that result. In the case study in this chapter, we discuss a series of device cultures and the kinds of national webs they organize. We discuss a bloggers', an advertisers', a surfers', a searchers', and a crowd-sourced web, each formed by the online devices and platforms that collect their data and ultimately purport to represent or provide in one manner or another a country-specific and/or language-specific web. Put differently, we make use of web devices that "go local" – that is, devices that not only collect but serve web content territorially (usually nationally) or to a particular language group. We recognize that going local has those two distinct meanings, which in certain cases are reconcilable and in other cases are not. An engine may serve language-specific websites originating from inside the country as well as from outside the country in question. For example, in return for a query, the Bolivian "local domain Google" (Google.com.bo) may just as well serve results from Spain as from Bolivia or Colombia, with both being in Spanish. Thus, when discussing the demise of cyberspace, and the rise of a location-aware web, there is a tension between two new dominant ways of interpreting the object of study: national webs versus language webs. We are sensitive to the tension between the two new manners of approaching the web after cyberspace, and are aware that "the local," which as mentioned above is how Google terms its national domain engines, may refer to either a national web a language web or both.

We also discuss approaches to demarcating a national web, including sampling procedures. We are particularly interested in the fruitfulness of research outcomes from both keeping separate as well as triangulating the various parts of a national web – the bloggers', the advertisers', and so on. Are the URLs that are listed as "top blogs" by blog aggregators similar to the URLs that are listed as interesting by crowd-sourcing platforms? Does the list of URLs with high traffic and available advertising space for speakers of a particular language (e.g., Persian) resemble the list of the most visited websites in a related country in question (e.g., Iran)? We conclude that keeping the parts of the web and the lists of URLs separate may be beneficial, as a national blogosphere may have characteristics different from those of a national crowd-sourced web.[1]

The overall rationale for studying a national web not only implies a critique of the web as placeless space, and as universalized, but also is a means to develop further analyses of relationships between web metrics and ground indicators. That is, another focus of this study is the consideration of digital methods to understand the significance of national web space. By digital methods we mean algorithms and other counting techniques whose inputs are digital objects, such as links and website response codes, and whose application pertain to, but ultimately move beyond, the study of online culture alone (Rogers 2009). We discuss metrics for analyzing the health of a national web, such as its responsiveness, freshness, and accessibility. We have experimented with such analyses before, seeking to diagnose the condition of Iraq (in 2007, some four years into the Iraq War) by looking at "its web" (Digital Methods Initiative 2007). We found a broken web. Iraqi university websites were down or had their domains poached and parked. Iraqi governmental sites were suffering from neglect, with the exception of the Ministry of Oil (www.oil.gov.iq), which was bilingual and regularly updated. In our brief foray into the state of Iraq via the Iraqi web, we sought to develop a series of metrics for diagnosing the health of a web that were both conceptual and empirical.

Blocked yet Blogging: The Special Case of Iran

The case study we will consider in this chapter is Iran.[2] It is in many respects a special case, not least because the term "national web" itself may be interpreted to mean the separate Internet-like infrastructure that is being built there (Rhoads and Fassihi 2011). It is also a special case for the scale and scope of Internet censorship undertaken by the state, which is coupled with the repression and silencing of voices critical of the regime. In other words, the Iranian web is experienced differently inside Iran from outside Iran, which is of course the case for all countries where state Internet censorship occurs. It is also seemingly authored differently from outside than from inside Iran. As a consequence, many Iranians online, either site visitors or authors, whether inside or outside the country, need to cope with censorship. Inside the country, coping could mean being frustrated by it and waiting for a friend or relative to bring news about a virtual private network (VPN) or another means of getting around blockages. It could mean routinely circumventing censorship through VPNs, proxies, Google Reader, and other means. Both inside and outside the country, coping may mean actively learning about (and consciously not using) banned words, and perhaps employing code words and misspellings instead. It could mean self-censorship. Dealing with online thuggery is another matter. For example, one may be warned or pursued by the Iranian cyber army (Deibert and Rohozinski 2010). One copes, or protects oneself, through the careful selection of one piece of software or platform over another, based on which one provides safeguards and forms of anonymity. One may use wordpress.com for the ease with which one may choose a new email address as a login, or Friendfeed for the capacity to change usernames.

Having mentioned some of the reasons why it is a special case, we also would like to point out that certain general metrics such as site responsiveness and freshness may be put to good use when studying countries such as Iran. For example, if sites are blocked by the state yet still responding and updated, one may have indications of a reading audience, both outside and inside Iran. One may have indications of widespread censorship circumvention, as we have found. Here in particular the retention of the separate webs in our sampling procedure is beneficial. That is, the Iranian blogosphere, or the Iranian bloggers read through Google Reader and indexed by Likekhor, are roundly blocked by the state yet remain blogging. "Blocked yet blogging" may be the catchphrase for at least certain vital parts of the Iranian web.

Though perhaps not often recognized as such, national webs are nevertheless routinely created. It may be said that national webs come into being through the advent of geo-location technology, whereby national (or language) versions of web applications (such as Google) are served nationally (e.g., Google.gr for Greece) together with advertisements targeted to locals and information that complies with national laws (Goldsmith and Wu 2006; Schmidt 2009).

There is, of course, further literature to draw upon when studying national webs, from the pioneering ethnographic study of the national web of Trinidad and Tobago (where not global but rather Trini culture is performed) to well-known works on media as a means of organizing national sentiment and community more generally (Higson 1989; Anderson 1991; Miller and Slater 2000; Ginsburg et al. 2002). In policy studies, too, national webs, or portions of them, are increasingly "mapped" to inform debates about the extent to which the web, and especially the blogosphere, organizes voice (Kelly and Etling 2008; Etling et al. 2010). Of interest is the related work that seeks to build tools to circumvent censorship so that voice is still heard (Glanz and Markoff 2011; Roberts et al. 2011). In library science, national webs are routinely constructed by national libraries and other national archiving projects, which also have considered how to define such a web (Arvidson and Lettenström 1998; Arms et al. 2001; Abiteboul et al. 2002; Koerbin 2004). There are variously sized national web archives. Countries that have legal deposit legislation not only for books but also for web content (such as Denmark) tend to have notably larger web archives than the countries that do not (such as the Netherlands) (PADI n.d.; Lasfargues et al. 2008).

Defining National Websites, and the Implications for National Web Capture

Archivists' definitions of national webs and national websites are of special interest in our undertaking. How do national libraries define national webs and websites?

What may we learn from their definitional work? For example, the Royal Library of the Netherlands, following similar definitions of a national website from archiving projects in other European countries, defines a website as "Dutch" if it meets one or more of the following tests:

1. Dutch language, and registered in the Netherlands;
2. Any language, and registered in the Netherlands;
3. Dutch language, registered outside the Netherlands; or
4. Any language, registered outside the Netherlands, with subject matter related to the Netherlands. (Weltevrede 2009)

This scheme for what constitutes a national website, or at least one deemed relevant for a national archiving context, has consequences for their collection. Here in the first instance we would like to discuss how a definition affects the collection technique, whether automated or by hand. If one were to begin with sites from the national domain (.nl), those sites (whether in Dutch or other languages) could be automatically detected with software, and in the collection procedure one could remove from the list .be sites (from Belgium, where Dutch, or Flemish, is also spoken) unless they treated Dutch subject matters. (Dutch national web archive users likely would be surprised to come upon Belgian websites stored in it for whatever reason!) This approach by the Royal Library could be described, however, as an editorial approach; websites related to Dutch subject matters and websites in Dutch but registered outside the Netherlands (outside .nl) pose particular challenges to automation, especially when working on a large scale. As a research practice, one would not be able to automate the detection and capturing of these kinds of sites; one would more likely create a list of them before routinely capturing them over time. In the national web characterization studies reviewed by Baeza-Yates et al. (2007) and discussed at the outset, the national domain (known as the country code top-level domain, or ccTLD) is the organizing entity. In practice, however, many countries (or nationals) use URLs outside their national domains, such as .com, .net, and .org. As we note below, for Iran, sites with the .ir ccTLD in fact may not be the preferred starting points for demarcating a national Iranian web. As a case in point, in our data the percentage of .ir sites that is blocked is very low, compared to .coms, for example. Thus, .ir sites seem to have characteristics that differ from other sites authored and/or read by Iranians.

In order to describe the considerations an analyst may have when beginning to demarcate a national web, and at the same time to direct these thoughts specifically toward Iran, we first surveyed a selection of Iranian bloggers about the "Iranian web," and particularly the very ideas of an Iranian website and a national web.

We are particularly interested in contrasting definitions of a national web that are "principled" with those based on device cultures. By principled we mean a priori definitions of what constitutes a national web and a national website, such as that of the Royal Library above. By device cultures we mean the webs that are formed by collecting and analyzing user data, and outputting leading sites of a country and/or language. We mentioned above some of the consequences of demarcating a national web when national websites of interest to archiving are based on formalist properties of their content: it becomes difficult to make a collection at any scale.

In preliminary research about the notion of an Iranian web, a small survey, undertaken by a New Media MA student at the University of Amsterdam, was conducted of 141 Iranian bloggers using Google Reader (Gooder) in the student's Gooder network (Zarrinbakhsh 2011). A variety of definitions of a national web were put forward, and the respondents were asked to choose which definition was best suited (they could choose multiple answers). From the beginning, the question was met with suspicion, as the term itself was seen as a possible ruse by the Iranian government to create its own Internet, and further isolate the country and the people, as the student reported. In comments on the question, it was written that the Internet is a "free sphere" and ideas of a national web would "limit" such freedom.

The survey asked "What is an 'Iranian website'?" and gave the following possible options:

1. Only in the Persian language
2. In Persian and other languages (and dialects) spoken in Iran
3. Authored by Iranians
4. Related to Iranian issues
5. Accessed by Iranians
6. National domain (.ir)
7. Returned by Google

Note first the expansion of what could constitute a national web beyond what we have related so far, both in the national domain characterization studies and in the case of the constitution of the Dutch web by the Royal Library. In particular, the options "accessed by Iranians" and "returned by Google" are newly added candidate constructs of an Iranian web, where the former treats the Iranian web like a traditional media consumption survey about the sites most visited. The latter option, about Google's relationship with the Iranian web, is more ambiguous. Google could be equated with the web generally, as its entry point. Or, one could find the Iranian web with Google.

As a whole, 12 percent of respondents believed that only Persian websites could be considered national websites; 31 percent checked the box for Persian websites and other languages and dialects spoken in Iran; 45 percent thought that Iranian-produced the content could be counted as part of a national web; 29 percent were of the opinion that everything related to Iranian issues is in the area of the Iranian national web; and 19 percent indicated that websites accessed by Iranians should be considered their national web. It should be noted that some people were very much opposed to this fifth choice; they mentioned that every website can be accessed by anyone, so this item seems to be ill conceived. Only 4 percent of the total respondents chose websites with the Iranian domain (.ir), which implies that defining national web studies based on the domain only would prove unpopular, and 9 percent thought that websites that are shown in Google search results make up the (Iranian national) web.

Finally, in a follow-up question addressing the issue of any difference between writing from inside and outside the country, approximately one-third of the respondents seemed to agree with the following statement by the communications scholar Gholam Khiabany:

> If Iranian blogs are defined in terms of language, this means omission of a large number of Iranian bloggers who write in other languages, most notably English, while including a number of bloggers from Afghanistan or Tajikistan who write in Persian. Focusing on Iranian bloggers writing inside the country also leads to excluding a large number of Iranian bloggers writing in Persian outside Iran. (Khiabany and Sreberny 2007: 565)

On the basis of these survey findings, and extending Khiabany's argument, the analyst concluded that a national web could be defined as one that is authored by Iranians, no matter their location or language in which they write, and no matter the subject matter. In all, the definition of the national web appears to include sites with content authored by Iranians outside Iran in languages other than Persian, and on issues that may not be related to Iranian affairs. This definition makes it nearly impossible to demarcate an Iranian web! But, in any case, detecting sites authored by Iranians outside Iran in languages other than Persian would require manual work. It may be worth noting that the definition adhered to by the Royal Library of the Netherlands also requires manual work, but did not expand its definition of Dutch sites to sites authored by Dutch people abroad in languages other than Dutch, unless the subject matter was Dutch-related.

Having considered and discussed what we have termed principled approaches to defining national websites and webs, we instead chose to analyze the outputs of devices, which we will come to again in more detail shortly. That is, methodologically, we did not begin with a priori definitions of what constitutes an Iranian website, or the Iranian web, however fascinating such definitions may be in a formalistic and ontological sense. Rather, as we will explain and eventually defend, we relied upon the URL recommendations made by dominant web devices and platforms that, through various algorithms and logics, were deemed relevant for a specific country and/or language.

Our contribution to national web studies informs the literature on national web characterization, as discussed at the start of this chapter, as well as that on policy studies (and political science) about the organization of voice online. It also contributes to media theory and web studies by putting forward the national web as an object of study. The overall approach is not only conceptual but also empirical, in that we seek properties of national web spaces that are indicators of conditions on the ground. Such properties could relate to how responsive a national web is at any given time, and how accessible. Are responsive sites also fresh (recently updated)? Are sites that are blocked still responsive and fresh? We are also interested in more than the technical web data sets, and how they may be repurposed for social study. As alluded to already, for Iran in particular the content of websites is carefully monitored by the state; websites may be blocked and website authors may be pursued. In the following, we put forward an approach to demarcating a national web in order to study its current conditions.

Demarcating the Iranian Web: Studying the Outputs of Device Cultures

The purpose of the research is to demarcate a nominal Iranian web and analyze its condition, thereby providing indications of the situation on the ground. By "nominal web" we mean one that is predicated on the means by which it is organized by online devices and platforms as well as how it is retrieved, both by the user and by the analyst. Here we have chosen to demarcate an Iranian web through multiple, dominant online approaches for indexing and ordering that "go local," privileging language, location, and audience, broadly speaking. Working in July 2011, we found that the web given by three crowd-sourcing platforms aimed at an Iranian audience differed from the webs yielded by a marketing tool for Persian-language advertisers, a surfer pathway aggregator of users in Iran, and a search engine delivering .ir sites as well as other TLD sites (.coms, .nets, etc.) from the "region," even though each purported in some general or specific sense to provide the Iranian web. Ultimately, we have chosen to write about the Iranian webs in the multiple, and discuss each web's characteristics. We thereby addressed an issue faced by the analyst when deciding where to start collecting URLs, be it in terms of compiling seed URLs to crawl; stringing together keywords and operators to form a query; consulting lists of top blogs by inlink count, top URLs by rating, or top websites by hit count; and so on. For our analysis, we selected the outputs of the well-known aggregators of either Iranian or Persian-language websites, in a sense not choosing one starting point but retaining them all (or at least a number of significant ones).

We also took decisions with respect to dealing with the idea that a sample of the Iranian web would follow (only) from knowledge of its population. As we discuss, in the national web research area, one may expect that the population of a web is knowable (in terms of the number of websites, and some categorization of their types), and thus one would be able to make a sample from it and of its types. In thinking through such an undertaking, one may port scan the Iranian IP ranges and establish whether IP addresses respond to the standard http and https ports 80, 8080, or 443. The next step would be to count how many web servers are active within a specific IP range, and then roughly estimate the number of domains. Alternatively, one could consider approaching the Iranian Internet authority or Iranian ISPs for their data, or one could crawl a seed list of URLs (or multiple lists) using snowball techniques and subsequently sift the large catch using language-detection software and/or whois lookups. When one begins to rely on web services that have ceilings or have issues with spammers and scrapers (which is most if not all of them), the challenges of working with (relatively) large amounts of online data become apparent. One is unable to run batch queries without permission from corporate research labs, Internet administrative bodies, and others. Just when it is becoming interesting, the research focus turns to the administrative, legal, and social engineering arenas, bringing it all to a standstill. Simply gaining access and finishing a large collecting and sifting project becomes a great achievement in itself. While we have undertaken one medium-scale scraping and querying exercise for this research project, we have largely avoided the techno-administrative arena we refer to above, instead seeking to make use of what is available to web users. This was a conscious choice in favor of relatively small data.

Further, we would like to make a case for a method to demarcate a national web (or "webs") that is sensitive to the variety of ways in which one enters web space by belonging to particular device cultures, which we largely equate with engine and platform operations rather than in ethnographic sense (where an object may, for example, be equated with its less tangible qualities or "spirit"). Generally, we introduce national web demarcation methods that repurpose web devices that not only "go local" but also capture device cultures. In short, we are interested in capturing national device cultures. Repurposing web devices has two methodological advantages. First, popular devices may be viewed as mediating and quantifying specific usage. The devices do so by recursively soliciting user participation in content production and evaluation. They calculate the most relevant websites by aggregating links, clicks, views, and votes, thereby outputting collectively privileged sources. Second, the definition of an Iranian web is outsourced to the big data methodology used by devices to order content, which combines algorithmic techniques with large-scale user participation. Relatively small data sets are obtained from the output of these big data devices. Put differently, the repurposing of web devices is both a strategy for researchers of small data to sample from a big data set as well as a means to have samples that represent specific outlooks on how to organize and order web content, as we explain in our discussion of the privileging of hits, links, location, likes, and other measures by the platforms and devices under study.

In the analyses, we wish to chart language and other formal features that are in each Iranian web. More conceptually, in our particular approach to national web studies, we also would like to discuss which portions of the web are healthy, in the sense of (still) online and active, and which are broken, in the sense of unresponsive. Additionally, we are interested in the extent to which each is censored or filtered by the state, and whether there is a relationship between responsive (and fresh) websites and filtered websites. In order to pursue the question of whether censorship kills content, which we formulated in a previous (and preliminary) project on the Tunisian web (prior to the "Arab Spring" of 2011), we have developed means to chart changes in a special part of the Iranian web over time. We use time-series data from Balatarin (a leading crowd-sourced platform) that we scraped, comparing the significant URLs voted up around the presidential elections in 2009 with those of the same time period in 2010 and 2011. We run the hosts through proxies in Iran so as to check for indications of blocking. Generally we have found that Balatarin's collection of URLs is particularly susceptible to blocking. Prior to reporting on the longitudinal analyses, we will next describe the indexing and ordering mechanisms of the web platforms and devices relevant to the Iranian space. The data culled from these platforms and engines are employed to characterize the web types on offer.

Device Cultures: How Websites are Valued, and Ranked

The early web was organized by amateur as well as professional link-list makers, who took on the mantle of a librarian or specimen collector and made directories of websites, organized by category. Professional or "pro-am" website categorization by topic remains, in the larger-scale directories such as Yahoo! as well as in smaller-scale collections, though the practice has arguably declined in the face of other methods (described here) that have become more and more settled as dominant approaches for valuing websites (Deuze 2007; Bruns 2008). These approaches toward valuing websites we couch in technical as well as politico-economic terms – as "the hit economy," "the link economy," "the geoweb," "crowd-sourcing," and "the like economy" – that highlight what is counted, by whom, and/or where. Crowd-sourcing is a term coined by the Internet trade press (deriving from the practice of outsourcing but also described as the "worker-bee economy") for a situation in which both the so-called wisdom and also the labor of the crowd pollinates the beneficiary, often a Web 2.0 company or service (Howe 2006; Moulier-Boutang 2008). The other term we employ, geoweb (or "locative web"), has less of the connotation of a particular kind of economy yet embodies the means by which sites are sourced.

The hit economy, exemplified by the hit counter on early websites, ranks sites by the number of hits or impressions, where unique visitors count. For this view we chose DoubleClick Ad Planner by Google (referred to here as Google Ad Planner), which is a service that ranks sites by audience for the purposes of advertisers. While Iran is not among the countries listed (owing to the US economic sanctions against Iran that also account for the lack of an .ir local-domain Google), "Persian-speaking" is among the site-type categories in the available audience analytics. Thus, one Iranian web would comprise those sites that reach a Persian-speaking audience, as collected and ranked by Google Ad Planner. Using the options available, 1500 unique hosts for a Persian-speaking audience were collected from Google Ad Planner.

"Link economy" is a term that describes the rise of PageRank and other algorithms that value links (Rogers 2002). It also involves a shift in URL ranking logics away from an advertisers' model (counting hits) to a more bibliographic or scientometric manner of thinking (counting citations or links). The term is used to characterize

Google Web Search, though the other main component of Google's algorithm is user click-throughs. Searching Google for .ir sites (including .ir's second-level domains) as well as Iranian sites in generic TLDs in Google's regional search yielded some 3500 hosts.[3]

Alexa, like other companies offering browser toolbars, collects user location data (such as a postal code) upon registration and, once the toolbar is installed, tracks websites visited by the user (see Figure 8.1). It thereby keeps records of the sites most visited by user location, and a list the top 500 sites visited by users in Iran can be obtained from it.

Crowd-sourced sites such as the most well-known (Balatarin) and its emulators (Donbaleh and Sabzlink) require registration before the user may suggest a link, which is then voted upon by other registered users. Those URLs with the most votes rise to the top. For this exercise we collected approximately 1100 hosts from Balatarin, 2850 from Donbaleh, and 2750 from Sabzlink.[4] In the following analyses we grouped Donbaleh and Sabzlink together, for they share the device culture (crowd-sourcing). Together they resulted in 4579 unique hosts. We treated the other platform, Balatarin, separately because of its status as a highly significant Iranian website. Launched in 2006, Balatarin is considered to be the first Web 2.0 site in Persian, and was recognized as one of the most popular Persian websites in

Figure 8.1   Alexa toolbar installation and registration process, with a field for the user's postal code, August 2011. *Source*: © 2012, Alexa Internet (www.alexa.com).

2007 and 2008 (Wikipedia 2011). It was also pivotal for the Green Movement in the opposition before and after the Iranian presidential elections in 2009 (Sabeti 2010).

The introduction of the "like" button and other social counters in social media has brought with it what one may term the "like economy," which values content based on social button activity (Gerlitz and Helmond 2011). Likekhor, as the name suggests, ranks websites by likes; the likes are tallied from Google Reader users who have registered with Likekhor. Google Reader, or Gooder (as some Iranian users call it), is of particular interest because through it one is able to read the contents of websites that are otherwise filtered by the state. Google Reader thus effectively acts as a proxy to filtered websites. At Likekhor the focus is on blogs, pointing up a relationship between Google Reader users and bloggers, or blog readers. From Likekhor we extracted a list of 2600 hosts, collected from a page where all blogs on Likekhor were listed.

Thus, in July 2011 we collected over 10 000 hosts through platforms and devices significant to Iranian users (Google Reader, Google Web Search, and the crowd-sourcing platforms) and two that provide ranked lists of Iranian and Persian-speaking sites (Alexa and Google Ad Planner, respectively) on the basis of data collected from users located in Iran (Alexa) or from Persian-writing users (Google Ad Planner). We will characterize these Iranian webs individually as well as collectively. We have chosen not to triangulate them, for very few websites recur across the them.

Analyzing the Characteristics of the Iranian Webs: Language and Responsiveness

One area of research that we have built on is web characterization studies, in which one of the main difficulties repeatedly discussed is how to obtain a representative sample of a national web or other web types. According to Baeza-Yates and colleagues, the three common types of sampling techniques used in web characterization studies are "complete crawls of a single web site, random samples from the whole web, and large samples from specific communities" (2007: 1). For national webs, which the authors consider to be specific communities, the list comprises websites with the same ccTLD. For many national webs, however, such delimiting would be too partial, certainly for countries where generic TLD usage is prevalent. Our approach seeks to retain the .coms, .orgs, .nets, and so on when deemed relevant for Iranians and Persian-speakers by the devices and platforms upon which we rely.

To the sampling techniques described above, we thus would like to add a fourth type, which could be called "multiple aggregator site scraping" or, more concep-tually, device cultures. Google Ad Planner, Alexa, Google Web Search, Likekhor (Google Reader), and the crowd-sourcing platforms (Donbaleh, Sabzlink, and Balatarin) make available either through query results or (dynamically generated) listings of websites that are relevant for Iranians and Persian-speakers. In our case, with the exception of the searchers' web (gained through .ir and generic TLD queries

Table 8.1   Percentage of .ir sites in top websites collected from device cultures relevant to Iranians and Persian-speakers, July 2011.

Percentage	Iranian Web	Absolute Numbers
25	Alexa (geoweb)	126 of 496 hosts
24	Google Ad Planner (advertisers')	370 of 1525 hosts
16	Likekhor (bloggers')	397 of 2541 hosts
12	Donbaleh/Sabzlink (crowd-sourced)	535 of 4579 hosts
11	Balatarin (crowd-sourced)	116 of 1102 hosts

in Google's region search), the percentages of .ir sites among the significant hosts outputted by the devices are relatively low (see Table 8.1). The crowd-sourced web references the fewest .ir sites at just over 10 percent, while the advertisers' web and the geoweb, or web of surfers in Iran, reference the highest, at about 25 percent. As noted above, the .ir sites in our overall collection of URLs were much less likely to be blocked than the .com sites. Of the websites that were tested and found to be blocked from inside Iran, 80 percent were .com followed by 6 percent .net and 4 percent .org. The ccTLD .ir had 3 percent of all censored hosts.

Having reviewed how samples are generally made, Baeza-Yates and colleagues compared the 10 national web studies in order to arrive at a core set of measures that are shared across many of them (see Table 8.2). Our characterization of the Iranian web (or webs) has a particular point of departure that benefits from the metrics on offer. In reference to Table 8.2's metrics, in the category of "content" our project shares with Baeza-Yates and colleagues an interest in language, page age, and domain analysis (albeit top-level), and in the category of technology relies on http response codes. The codes yield what we refer to as "responsiveness," which we consider a basic health metric, together with page age (the freshness measure). There are other metrics that we have not employed, though we would like to mention how they could be employed. Whether or not a website is broken

Table 8.2   Metrics commonly used in national web characterization studies according to Baeza-Yates et al. (2007). **Bold** indicates metrics used in this study, but we analyzed the top-level domain over the second-level domain.

Content	Link	Technology
Language	Degree	URL length
Page size	Ranking	**Http response code**
Page age	Web structure	Media and document formats
Pages per site		Image formats
Sites and pages per domain		Sites that cannot be crawled correctly
Second-level domain		Web server software
		Programming languages for dynamic pages

could be gleaned from link validators, which would refer to broken links on a site. Additionally, establishing whether websites are "parked" or "hacked" may serve to measure abandonment by previous owners. Compared against proxy data, parked or abandoned site analysis may be used to make claims about the effectiveness of censorship, or suppression of voice. Fitness could refer to the "validity" of code, or its correct implementation; Baeza-Yates and colleagues refer to site structure and its "correctness" for a crawler. Other metric types that reside more in the realm of political economy may be of interest in terms of the available ways of expanding the undertaking. For example, media, document, and image formats could give us an indication of the extent to which a national web is proprietary, which from certain perspectives is a health issue.

The Iranian Web and Its Languages

One basic metric seeks to measure the composition of languages in the Iranian web (see Figure 8.2). Persian is of course the official language in Iran (the Unicode system incorporated Persian script in 2001) and it can be detected (Amir-Ebrahimi 2008). For language detection of websites we built a custom tool that makes use of AlchemyAPI and is able to detect Persian as well as the other languages, though not all languages spoken in Iran, as we relate below.[5] The results gleaned using this tool are manually checked.[6] Approximately two-thirds of sites in the Iranian web are in Persian, and English ranks second, making up approximately one in five. Of interest are the proportions of Persian used in the various webs. The results show that the bloggers' space, Likekhor, is on top with 91 percent of its sources in Persian, followed by Alexa's Iran-based surfer's web with 83 percent and the crowd-sourced web with 73 percent. At the bottom are the advertisers' web with 62 percent and Google Web Search with 52 percent. Balatarin, the special case, has

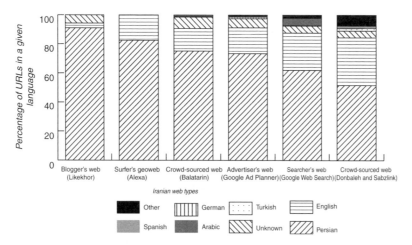

Figure 8.2 The distribution of languages on the Iranian web.

75 percent of its sites in Persian. Thus, there is a significant difference between the webs, including, notably, a Persian-dominant blogosphere (if the Likekhor list may serve as a short-hand reference to such).[7]

Here we can begin to discuss the kinds of webs that could be captured and analyzed if one were to formally define the Iranian web or an Iranian website a priori, as discussed earlier with respect to web archivists' conditions for a national website (in the Dutch example) and survey respondents' ideas concerning a national web (for Iran). The blogosphere and to a slightly lesser extent the geoweb (based on surfers in Iran) are the most closely related to the idea of an Iranian web as Persian-speaking only, though between them they still average over 10 percent non-Persian websites. The Iranian webs with larger percentages of non-Persian sites are the advertisers' and regional webs (from Google's advanced search region option). The advertisers' web is defined as that accessed by Persian speakers as detected by the signals Google compiles on its users and the content it indexes (Google Ad Planner). Both have far higher percentages of non-Persian sites, especially English, though we did not attempt to investigate whether these sites are authored by Iranians or concern Iranian affairs, however that may be defined. There is another, all-inclusive, web one could conceive of a priori that would have implications for the method by which one would construct the object of study. Being all-inclusive in terms of the languages spoken in Iran (Armenian, Assyrian Neo-Aramaic, Arabic, Azeri, Balochi, Gilaki, Kurdish, Lori, Mazandarani, and Turkmen) has consequences for the capturing techniques; of the secondary languages spoken in Iran, the language detection tool employed in this study detects only Arabic, Armenian, and Azeri and not Assyrian Neo-Aramaic, Balochi, Gilaki, Kurdish, Lori, Mazandarani, or Turkmen. To compile such sites one would rely on specialists' link lists, though we did not pursue the matter any further.

The Iranian Web and Responsiveness

To analyze the responsiveness of the Iranian webs, we retrieved the http response status codes with a custom-built tool. The inputs to the tool are the lists of hosts per web that were previously collected. Analyzing the results returned by the response code tool, we found that there are eight commonly returned codes in the Iranian web spaces (see Figure 8.3). The 400 class of status codes indicates that the client has erred in some way. "400 bad request" means that there was an error in the syntax, "403 forbidden" indicates that the server is refusing to respond, and "404 not found" means that the content is no longer available.[8] Commonly returned response codes besides the "200 OK" status are two redirecting response codes: "301 moved permanently" and "302 found." Redirecting is not necessarily an indication of unresponsiveness, and can have a range of reasons, including forwarding multiple domain names to the same location, redirecting short aliases to longer URLs, and moving a site to a new domain.[9] It also may be an indication of a parked website.

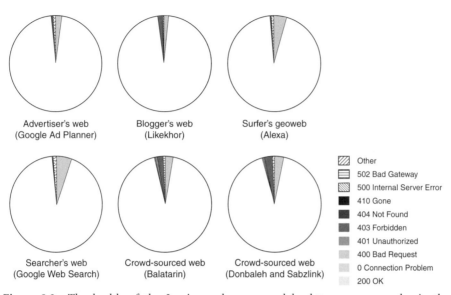

Figure 8.3 The health of the Iranian webs measured by http response codes in the Netherlands.

However, redirects also may be "soft 404" messages to hide broken links (Yossef et al. 2004). In our study, both 301 and 302 were followed if a location header was returned, which mostly resolved in 200 and 404 response codes. "0 connection problem" indicates that the tool was unable to connect to the server; the server may no longer exist, or it may mean that our tool timed out.

The findings of this portion of the study in the first instance indicate that the Iranian webs are relatively healthy overall. Concerning the crowd-sourcing webs (Donbaleh/Sabzlink and Balatarin), 92 and 94 percent of the sites resolved, respectively. The advertisers' space followed by the bloggers' space (delivered by Google Reader users) had the cleanest bills of health, with 96 and 95 percent. Thus, the (Persian-language) advertisers' space and the blogosphere can be considered to be vibrant and healthy.

The Iranian Web and Internet Censorship

Arguably, web devices are among the most well-informed censorship monitoring instruments. Search engines and platforms receive requests for deleting content – either specific URLs, specific queries, or more general instructions – thereby inviting the creation of an ongoing blacklist as well as a censorship index. For example, it has been reported that to adhere to Chinese government censorship instructions (prior to the redirect to .hk), Google engineers "set up a computer inside China and programmed it to try to access websites outside the country, one

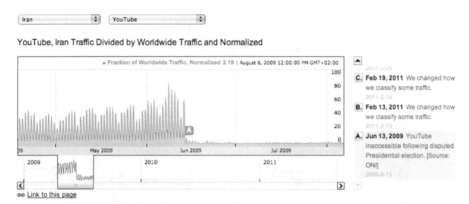

Figure 8.4   Iranian traffic to YouTube comes to a standstill after the 2009 presidential elections. *Source*: Google Transparency Report, August 25, 2011.

after another. If a site was blocked by the firewall, it meant the government regarded it as illicit – so it became part of Google's blacklist" (Thompson 2006). In the case of the Iranian web, which is among the most aggressively censored webs in the world, there are no reported requests from the government for removal (Open Net Initiative 2009; Google 2011). However, Figure 8.4 shows how Iranian traffic to YouTube increased in the run-up to the presidential elections in June 2009 before coming to an almost complete standstill one day after. The question of interest in this study is to what extent blocking important sites has had implications for the health of the Iranian webs. We therefore checked the collected Iranian webs for availability inside Iran by using proxies. Subsequently, as we will elaborate below, these findings were compared against the basic health measures, responsiveness and freshness. As mentioned above, one of the more remarkable findings is that a large portion of the Iranian blogs is blocked, yet continues to respond and is fresh.

The Censorship Explorer tool, which we have made available at http://tools .digitalmethods.net/beta/proxies, lists (fresh) proxies by country and may be used to check for censored websites. The tool returns website response codes or loads the actual websites in the browser as if you were in the chosen country in question. As a starting point in the censorship research procedure, one often checks website responsiveness in a country that is not known to censor (Iranian) websites (in this case, the Netherlands). Subsequently, one runs lists of hosts through proxies in the country under scrutiny and logs the response codes. Iranian servers typically return the 403 forbidden response code, which is a strong indication of a site being blocked (Noman 2008). Response code checks through proxies may give an indication of specific types of Internet censorship – for example, URL and IP blocking, which includes censorship techniques such as TCP/IP header filtering, TCP/IP content filtering, and http proxy filtering (Murdoch and Anderson 2008). (Other known filtering techniques, including DNS tampering and partial content filtering, are more accurately detected by other means.) Often multiple proxies are used, allowing the researcher to triangulate proxy results and increase the trustworthiness of the results. For example, "0 connection problem" may be a proxy problem but it may just as well be that the censors is returning an RST package, which resets the connection, effectively dropping it (Villeneuve 2006). Comparing multiple proxies can aid in confirming that it is not a proxy problem. We used 12 proxies, which are hosted in six different cities in Iran and operated by a variety of owners, including Sharif University of Technology and the popular Internet service provider Pars Online. Concern has been voiced that it is "false to consider Internet filtering as an homogeneous phenomenon across a country," considering that both the implementation and user experience of censorship may vary by city, Internet service provider, or even computer (Wright et al. 2011: 5). Taking note of this concern, we selected proxies from different cities and ISPs and subsequently considered the response code returned by the majority.

The results show that approximately 6 percent of the geoweb (29 out of 497) and 16 percent of the advertisers' web (241 out of 1525 hosts) are blocked. The crowd-sourced web has just over 50 percent of it blocked, with 2411 of 4579 hosts. Balatarin is the most aggressively censored Iranian web space with 58 percent blocked, or 639 of 1102 hosts, followed by the other two crowd-sourcing platforms (Donbaleh and Sabzlink) with more than half of the hosts blocked. Google Reader's web, which in the research work thus far has stood in for the Iranian blogosphere, had 1137 of 2541 sites returning the 403 forbidden code, or 45 percent (see Figure 8.5).

As discussed above, the bloggers' web is largely Persian language, and is one of the most responsive of all the webs under study, with 95 percent of the sites returning "200 OK" response codes. Moreover, it speaks for the Google Reader usage as a vibrant censorship circumvention culture. This study appears to render visible censorship circumvention at a large scale, or at least show that blocked websites are still online. Of the webs checked for filtering, the crowd-sourced sites as well as the Likekhor listing are the most blocked, raising the question not only of the substance of those spaces (we treat Balatarin's below) but also the convenience of the platforms as URL lists for monitoring. While many sites are blocked and still responsive, we are interested in examining those blocked sites for other signs of

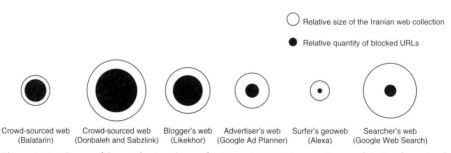

○ Relative size of the Iranian web collection

● Relative quantity of blocked URLs

| Crowd-sourced web (Balatarin) | Crowd-sourced web (Donbaleh and Sabzlink) | Blogger's web (Likekhor) | Advertiser's web (Google Ad Planner) | Surfer's geoweb (Alexa) | Searcher's web (Google Web Search) |

Figure 8.5 Censorship on the Iranian web, August 2011. *Source*: Censorship Explorer tool by the Digital Methods Initiative, Amsterdam.

health. Are they fresh? If the sites are blocked yet responsive and fresh, we have a strong indication of the ineffectiveness of censorship (to date).

The Iranian Web and Freshness

Having identified the spaces of particular interest to us (the crowd-sourced and bloggers' webs) and found that they were highly responsive as well as heavily blocked, we are interested in pursuing further the question of whether censorship kills content. Or, to put it another way, despite having their sites censored, do the bloggers keep on blogging and does the crowd keep posting and rating? Is there an expectation that the readers can routinely circumvent censorship and thus that content can continue to be recommended, commented on, and so on? Aside from the responsiveness test (which found nearly all of the websites to be online), we would like to know whether the websites were active. Is the content on the websites fresh? To do this we moved on to study a subset of the webs – the blocked sites in the crowd-sourced and the bloggers' webs. To determine how fresh these sites are, for each host (per list) we asked the Google feed API whether each site had a feed (e.g., RSS or atom). If it did, we parsed the feed with the Python Universal Feed Parser library and extracted the date of the latest post. Overall, 63 percent (5147 of the 8222) of the three webs had feeds. Of the blocked sites in these webs, 71 percent (2986 of the 4189) had a feed. Balatarin had 79 percent blocked sites with a feed (504 of 639 blocked hosts), Donbaleh/Sabzlink had 68 percent (1630 of 2413), and Likekhor had 75 percent (852 of 1137). These were the ones to be checked for freshness.

What constitutes a fresh site? We turned to blog search engines for advice about staleness. In an FAQ about blog quality guidelines, Technorati (2011) states that they "only index 30 days' content, so anything older than that will not appear on Technorati." Similarly, Blogpulse (a search engine and analytics system for blogs) takes 30 days as a measure of fresh content: "A blog's rank is based on a moving average of its citation counts over the past 30 days" (Blogpulse 2011). Thus, freshness is here considered as having at least one post published via a feed in the last month, counted from the moment we last checked for blockage. It is of interest to note that the well-known survey conducted by Technorati (2008) found that only about seven million of the 133 million blogs it followed had been updated in the past four months. *The New York Times* wrote that the finding implied that "95 percent of blogs [were] essentially abandoned, left to lie fallow on the web, where they become public remnants of a dream – or at least an ambition – unfulfilled" (Quenqua 2009). In stark contrast, we found that 65 percent of our list of sites were fresh. In the crowd-sourcing platform Balatarin, 78 percent of the blocked hosts that had a feed (395 of 504 hosts) were fresh, and in the crowd-sourcing web organized by Donbaleh and Sabzlink 56 percent of the blocked hosts with a feed (915 of 1630 hosts) were fresh. In the Likekhor list, 61 percent (525 hosts) had a latest post date of a month or less when they were tested and found to be blocked. The results confirm that there is no general indication that censorship kills content on the Iranian web under study. On the contrary, the most severely censored Iranian webs were both responsive and rather fresh.

Conclusion: National Web Health Index

In this study we sought to build upon national web characterization studies and put forward the emerging field of national web studies. First and foremost, we did this by making a methodological plea for capturing and analyzing the diversity of national web spaces, or webs. Rather than predefining national websites, and thereby national webs, according to a principled approach of formal properties (for instance, all websites with ccTLD .ir; all websites in Persian with Iran-related content; or all websites with authors inside Iran), we have concluded that such approaches are often not to be operationalized or automated. Instead, we propose the use of what we term "device cultures," and in particular the Iranian web spaces they provide – bloggers', advertisers', surfers', searchers', and crowd-sourced webs. Device cultures are defined as the interaction between user and engine, the data that are routinely collected, how they are analyzed, and ultimately the URL recommendations that result. We demarcated national webs through devices that "go local" – that have location or language added as a value that sifts URLs that are of relevance to Iranians and Persian-speakers. In an examination of the data sets, where we performed TLD analysis of the sample we found that the majority of the collected hosts from the various Iranian webs were .com websites, not .ir; this finding expanded the scope of national domain characterization studies and introduced a method of data collection for a broader national web studies.

Second, both building on and contributing to national web characterization studies, we proposed a rationale: a national web health index. It is conceptualized as a series of metrics, a limited number of which we have employed in this study, most readily responsiveness, page age, and filtering or blockage. (We also performed language detection and TLD analysis.) The contribution of this work to national web characterization studies is twofold. The first contribution is conceptual, in that we propose to repurpose metrics from national web characterization for national web health indices. Are websites responding? Are pages fresh? Are links broken? Is the code valid? Are file formats proprietary? A form of country profiling comes into view. The second is generalizable for countries that face state censorship, and applicable to our case study in question, Iran. We compared the results from the responsiveness tests to those from the filtering tests to investigate whether the blocked sites were still responsive. The approach led us to find a significant number of blogs that were blocked yet still responsive. The finding that there are so many sites that are blocked yet blogging also indicates an audience for the content, both outside Iran and inside, and we believe there to be widespread Internet circumvention in a particular space: the predominantly Persian-language blogosphere authored by Likekhor and Google Reader, which in tandem serve as important filters for Iranian blogs. Although heavily censored, the Iranian blogosphere as listed by Likekhor remains vibrant. This censored but active space is similar to the crowd-sourced web, organized by Balatarin. Blocked yet posting, Balatarin's recommended websites suggest similar findings to those for the blogosphere: an active audience for blocked websites. In additional, substantive analysis we found that the Balatarin web (as a collection of URLs highly rated and thus rising to the top of the platform) remains clamorous, perhaps even more so than after the presidential elections of June 2009 and the initial rise of the Green Movement. It is a web that neither appears to be widely practicing self-censorship nor one cowed and drained of spirit.

Third, we would like to mention certain implications of national web studies as a means for country profiling, as this affects both current and future policies with respect to the web (and its study) and the use of web indicators for social study more generally. As we alluded, regarding our early work on Iraq and the state of its web during the Iraq War in 2007, the study of national web health provides an additional set of measures regarding the current state of universities, ministries, and other institutions. Where is the activity, and where is the neglect? National web studies may also serve as a source of comparative study, and ultimately as a spur to addressing the ill health of one or more webs. Thus, it is an approach to the study of the web that for portions of it could have salutary consequences.

Acknowledgments

We would like to thank the Iran Media Program at the Annenberg School for Communication, University of Pennsylvania, for supporting this work, and Mahmood Enayat for his thoughtful commentary. We also would like to thank the Iranian web culture expert Ebby Sharifi, who gathered with us at the Annenberg School for the Mapping Online Culture workshop in May 2011, as well as Cameran Ashraf, Bronwen Robertson, Leva Zand, and Niaz Zarrinbakhsh, who participated in the 2011 Digital Methods Summer School at the University of Amsterdam.

Notes

1. The data for this study are online at the project website, http://mappingiranonline .digitalmethods.net.
2. According to the International Telecommunication Union, 13 percent of the Iranian population uses the Internet and 21 percent of Iranian households have Internet access (2011). The marketing research reports an urban concentration of users, with "the vast majority [being] young, mostly 15 to 40" years of age (NetBina 2010: 10). Figures on the Iranian diaspora are not available.
3. Google.com's web search was chosen for its dominance in Iran among users of search engines. Data from 2010 list search engine market shares in Iran as follows: Google 90.78 percent, Yahoo! 4.97 percent, Bing 3.64 percent, Ask Jeeves 0.46 percent, and AOL 0.07

percent (MVF Global, 2010). Another marketing research firm lists 2011 market shares in Iran as Google 87.15 percent, Yahoo! 7.27 percent, Bing 4.16 percent, Ask Jeeves 0.70 percent, AOL 0.12 percent, and Lycos 0.01 percent (Net Applications 2011). According to Alexa, in October 2011, Google.com was the most visited site in Iran, followed by Yahoo.com. We employed site queries in Google.com for the top-level (.ir) as well as the second-level (e.g., .co.ir) domains, and concatenated the results. The query technique did not allow for redirection to a local-domain Google. Because cookies had not been retained, it also did not allow for the personalization of the results.

4. In order to compare the different platforms, we chose to compare hosts instead of full URLs. That is, for Balatarin, we harvested all the URLs listed on the 150 pages of "hot" links, resulting in 1102 unique hosts.

5. The language auto-detection tool employed for this work is AlchemyAPI, which for academic researchers allows 30 000 queries per day. AlchemyAPI is at www.alchemyapi .com/api/lang.

6. We manually checked the results that returned sites as English or unknown, and corrected any errors. We have not explored further why dual-language sites are considered to be one particular language by AlchemyAPI. We also would consider using Google as a language detector. The "unknown" tags in the cloud indicate that neither the language detection tool nor the researcher was able to determine the language, for in most cases the site was no longer online.

7. Additionally, the Iranian webs show various degrees of language distribution, with Alexa being the least diverse (six languages) and Google Web Search the most (with 36 languages).

8. The http status codes are explained in the dedicated Wikipedia entry: http://en.wikipedia .org/wiki/List_of_HTTP_status_codes.

9. URL redirection is explained in the dedicated Wikipedia entry: http://en.wikipedia.org /wiki/URL_redirection.

References

Abiteboul, S., Cobena, G., Masanes, J., and Sedrati, G. (2002) "A First Experience in Archiving the French Web." Paper presented at the 6th European Conference on Research and Advanced Technology for Digital Libraries, Rome, Italy (September 16–18).

Amir-Ebrahimi, M. (2008) "Blogging from Qom, behind Walls and Veils." *Comparative Studies of South Asia, Africa and the Middle East*, 28(2), 235–249.

Anderson, B. (1991) *Imagined Communities*. London: Verso.

Arms, W.Y., Adkins, R., Ammen, C., and Hayes, A. (2001) "Collecting and Preserving the Web: The Minerva Prototype." *RLG DigiNews*. 5(2).

Arvidson, A. and Lettenström, F. (1998) "The Kulturarw Project – The Swedish Royal Web Archive." *Electronic Library*, 16(2), 105–108.

Baeza-Yates, R., Castillo, C., and Efthimiadis, E.N. (2007) "Characterization of National Web Domains." *ACM Transactions on Internet Technology*, 7(2), art. 9.

Blogpulse (2011) "FAQ: How do you Determine Blog Rankings?" http://web.archive.org/web /20110722023858/http://www.blogpulse.com/about.html.

Bruns, A. (2008) *Blogs, Wikipedia, Second Life, and Beyond: From Production to Produsage*. New York: Peter Lang.

Deibert, R. and Rohozinski, R. (2010) "Cyber Wars." *Index on Censorship*, 29(1), 79–90.

Deuze, M. (2007) *Media Work*. Cambridge: Polity.

Digital Methods Initiative (2007) "Diagnosing the Condition of Iraq: The Web View." https://wiki.digitalmethods.net/Dmi/DiagnosingTheConditionOfIraq:TheWebView.

Etling, B., Alexanyan, K., Kelly, J., et al. (2010) "Public Discourse in the Russian Blogosphere: Mapping RuNet Politics and Mobilization." Berkman Center Research Publication No. 2010–11. http://cyber.law.harvard.edu/sites/cyber.law.harvard.edu/files/Public_Discourse_in_the_Russian_Blogosphere_2010.pdf.

Feuz, M., Fuller, M., and Stalder, F. (2011) "Personal Web Searching in the Age of Semantic Capitalism: Diagnosing the Mechanisms of Personalization." *First Monday*, 16(2). http://firstmonday.org/htbin/cgiwrap/bin/ojs/index.php/fm/article/view/3344/2766.

Gerlitz, C. and Helmond, A. (2011) "The Like Economy: The Social Web in Transition." Paper presented at the MIT7 Unstable Platforms Conference, Cambridge, MA (May 13–15).

Ginsburg, F., Abu-Lughod, L., and Larkin, B. (2002) "Introduction" in F. Ginsburg, L. Abu-Lughod, and B. Larkin, eds., *Media Worlds: Anthropology on New Terrain*. Berkeley, CA: University of California Press.

Glanz, J. and Markoff, J. (2011) "U.S. Underwrites Internet Detour Around Censors." *New York Times* (June 12). https://www.nytimes.com/2011/06/12/world/12internet.html.

Goldsmith, J. and Wu, T. (2006) *Who Controls the Internet. Illusions of a Borderless World*. Oxford: Oxford University Press.

Google (2011) "Google Transparency Report." www.google.com/transparencyreport.

Higson, A. (1989) "The Concept of National Cinema." *Screen*, 30(4), 36–47.

Howe, J. (2006) "The Rise of Crowdsourcing," *Wired*, 14(6). www.wired.com/wired/archive/14.06/crowds.html.

International Telecommunication Union (2011) *Measuring the Information Society*. Geneva: International Telecommunication Union.

Kehoe, C., Pitkow, J., Sutton, K., et al. (1999) *GVU's Tenth World Wide Web User Survey*. Atlanta, GA: Graphics Visualization and Usability Center, College of Computing, Georgia Institute of Technology.

Kelly, J. and Etling, B. (2008) "Mapping Iran's Online Public: Politics and Culture in the Persian Blogosphere." Berkman Center Research Publication No. 2008–01. http://cyber.law.harvard.edu/sites/cyber.law.harvard.edu/files/Kelly&Etling_Mapping_Irans_Online_Public_2008.pdf.

Khiabany, G. and Sreberny, A. (2007) "The Politics of/in Blogging in Iran." *Comparative Studies of South Asia, Africa and the Middle East*, 27(3), 563–579.

Koerbin, P. (2004) "The Pandora Digital Archiving System (PANDAS) and Managing Web Archiving in Australia: A Case Study." Paper presented at the 4th International Web Archiving Workshop, Bath, UK (September 16).

Lasfargues, F., Oury, C., and Wendland, B. (2008) "Legal Deposit of the French Web: Harvesting Strategies for a National Domain." Paper presented at IWAW'08, Aarhus, Denmark (September 18–19). http://iwaw.europarchive.org/08/IWAW2008-Lasfargues.pdf.

Miller, D. and Slater, D. (2000) *The Internet: An Ethnographic Approach*. Oxford: Berg.

Moulier-Boutang, Y. (2008) "Worker Bee Economy." Paper presented at the Society of the Query Conference, Institute of Network Cultures, Amsterdam, The Netherlands (November 13–14).

Murdoch, S. and Anderson, R. (2008) "Tools and Technology of Internet Filtering" in R. Deibert, J. Palfrey, R. Rohozinski, and Zittrain, Z., eds., *Access Denied: The Practice and Policy of Global Internet Filtering*. Cambridge, MA: MIT Press.

MVF Global (2010) "Online Marketing in the top 50 Internet Economies: Lead Generation and Internet Marketing in Iran." www.mvfglobal.com/iran.

Net Applications (2011) "Search Engine Market Share: Iran, Islamic Republic of." https://marketshare.hitslink.com/search-engine-market-share.aspx?qprid=4&qpaf=-000%09101%09IR%0D&qptimeframe=Y.

NetBina (2010) "Online Marketing in Iran." http://new.netbina.com/resources/2/docs/Online_marketing_in_Iran_2010.pdf.

Noman, H. (2008) "Tunisian Journalist Sues Government Agency for Blocking Facebook, Claims Damage for the Use of 404 Error Message Instead of 403." *Open Net Initiative* (September 12). http://opennet.net/node/950.

Open Net Initiative (2009) *Internet Filtering in Iran, 2009*. Toronto, ON: University of Toronto. http://opennet.net/sites/opennet.net/files/ONI_Iran_2009.pdf.

PADI (n.d.) "Legal Deposit." *Preserving Access to Digital Information*. https://www.nla.gov.au/padi/topics/67.html.

Pariser, E. (2011) *The Filter Bubble*. New York: Penguin.

Quenqua, D. (2009) "Blogs Falling in an Empty Forest." *New York Times* (June 5). www.nytimes.com/2009/06/07/fashion/07blogs.html.

Rhoads, C. and Fassihi, F. (2011) "Iran Vows to Unplug Internet." *Wall Street Journal* (May 28). http://online.wsj.com/article/SB10001424052748704889404576277391449002016.html.

Roberts, H., Zuckerman, E., and Palfrey J. (2011) "2011 Circumvention Tool Evaluation." Berkman Center for Internet & Society. http://cyber.law.harvard.edu/sites/cyber.law.harvard.edu/files/2011_Circumvention_Tool_Evaluation_1.pdf.

Rogers, R. (2002) "Operating Issue Networks on the Web." *Science as Culture*, 11(2), 191–214.

Rogers, R. (2009) *The End of the Virtual: Digital Methods*. Amsterdam: Amsterdam University Press.

Sabeti (2010) "Balatarin: A Battleground for Defining Freedom of Expression." *Iran Media Program*. http://iranmediaresearch.org/en/blog/13/10/11/23/201.

Schmidt, E. (2009) "Prosperity or Peril? The Next Phase of Globalization." Princeton Colloquium on Public and International Affairs. www.youtube.com/watch?v=9nXmDxf7D_g.

Technorati (2008) "State of the Blogosphere 2008." *Technorati*. http://technorati.com/state-of-the-blogosphere.

Technorati (2011) "Blog Quality Guidelines." *Technorati*. http://technorati.com/blog-quality-guidelines-faq.

Thompson, C. (2006) "Google's China Problem (and China's Google Problem)." *New York Times* (April 23). www.nytimes.com/2006/04/23/magazine/23google.html.

Villeneuve, N. (2006) "Testing Through Proxies in China." *Nart Villeneuve* (April 10). www.nartv.org/2006/04/10/testing-through-proxies-in-china.

Weltevrede, E. (2009) *Thinking Nationally with the Web: A Medium-Specific Approach to the National Turn in Web Archiving*. Master's thesis. University of Amsterdam.

Wikipedia (2011) "Balatarin." http://en.wikipedia.org/wiki/Balatarin.

Wright, J., de Souza, T., and Brown, I. (2011) "Fine-Grained Censorship Mapping: Information Sources, Legality and Ethics." Paper presented at FOCI'11 (USENIX Security Symposium), San Francisco, CA (August 8). www.usenix.org/events/foci11/tech/final_files/Wright.pdf.

Yossef, Z.B., Broder, A.Z., Kumar, R., and Tomkins, A. (2004) "Sic Transit Gloria Telae: Towards an Understanding of the Web's Decay." *Proceedings of the 13th Conference on World Wide Web*. New York: ACM.

Zarrinbakhsh, N. (2011) "Living as a Criminal: An Ethnographic Study of the Iranian National Web and Internet Censorship." Master's thesis. University of Amsterdam.

Part 2
Issues and Identities

Agency

9

In the Habitus of the New
Structure, Agency, and the Social Media Habitus

Zizi Papacharissi and Emily Easton

Because things are the way they are, things will not stay the way they are.
(Bertolt Brecht, Poems 1913–1956)

Change requires processes of both interruption and continuity in order to advance newer modes of doing. Breaks from practices of the past enable switching over to practices of the present and future. At the same time, a measure of stability helps individuals to integrate these practices into their everyday routines and reassures all that change is here to stay. Thus, gradual change stabilizes only to be again rearranged by the same processes of interruption and continuity that brought it into being. The dynamics of new media are founded upon the premise and the promise of constant change and permanent evolution. This chapter examines how the dynamics of new media interrupt and sustain the sociality of everyday life. We use Bourdieu's construct of the habitus to understand what sorts of social places the media of permanent novelty present and the texture of social dispositions these places invite. We also examine the practices that habituated dispositions cultivate and how those are engaged by communities of practice. Ultimately, we employ the concept of the habitus to trace how structure and agency are evoked and reconciled via the practices of everyday (mediated) sociality.

The habitus is perhaps one of Bourdieu's most popular ideas, developed to overcome a number of binary divisions in the social sciences and, in particular, to address the duality of structure and agency. In explicating this relationship, Giddens underscored that "social structures are both constituted by human agency, and yet at the same time are the very medium of this constitution" (1979: 121). Broadly defined as a set of durable dispositions that enable structured improvisations of individuals, all guiding social life, the habitus invites both ambiguity and flexibility in terms of how it is interpreted, perhaps by design (Park 2009). Regardless, is it useful because it does not separate structure from agency, explaining how "embodied

A Companion to New Media Dynamics, First Edition. Edited by John Hartley, Jean Burgess, and Axel Bruns.
© 2013 John Wiley & Sons, Ltd. Published 2015 by John Wiley & Sons, Ltd.

dispositions . . . are generated by structural features of that same social world" and "agents' dispositions to act are themselves *formed* out of preexisting social contexts" (Couldry 2004: 358). In mediated architectures of everyday sociality, such as those presented by social network sites, social beings' behaviors emerge out of the social context they find themselves in. Claiming agency challenges pre-existing structure but is simultaneously reproduced by and reproductive of structure. In the context of technological convergence, the properties of online media afford the duality of structure and agency an accelerated reflexivity.

We argue that this accelerated reflexivity is both sustained and remediated via a habitus of the new – a set of dispositions invited and regenerated by and via a state of permanent novelty. This idea is applied to the context of sociality by what one might refer to as a social media habitus: a set of dispositions that emerge out of the social architecture of social media and frame but also constantly invite the remediation of agency. Although we refer to media platforms that differ, the term is defined broadly and intended to capture the ubiquity of a brand of sociality that popular social network sites have introduced. For greater specificity, one might refer to a Facebook habitus or speak of a Twitter or a Google+ habitus in reference to the predispositions that populate these social environments. All, however, are defined by the habitus of the new, the work of networked environments, actors, and convergent new technologies. We begin with an overview of the theory of the habitus, and examine how it connects with Bourdieu's communities of practice and generation of a variety of forms of capital. We then review the affordances of new(er) or convergent media, and discuss the social architectures they assemble, out of which a habitus of the new, and that of Facebook, is formed.

Habitus, Agency, and Structure

Bourdieu's concept of habitus provides a way of transcending the dualisms of theoretical paradigms and models (Park 2009; Abdelhay 2010). Through his theory of practice and the notions of habitus and field, Bourdieu makes it possible to problematize commonsense practices that are frequently taken for granted (Abdelhay 2010). Bourdieu suggests that "being the product of a particular class of objective regularities, the habitus tends to generate all the 'reasonable,' 'commonplace,' behaviours" (1990: 55), which provides a comforting homogeneity for the individual. The habitus is the product of long and ongoing processes of socialization that impart practices taken for granted, but is by no means merely a collection of embodied dispositions that are acted out mechanically. The reflexivity embedded in the habitus permits the cultivation of practices that connect to *fields*, or organized structures, dialectically and relationally. These practices do present habituated actions but are exercised through patterns that may be more organic and less codified or obedient to these structures. At the same time, these practices gain meaning as they are enacted within communities of practice, thus referencing structural context.

Habitus offers theoretical grounding that recognizes and incorporates both the internal and external construction of acquired and developing predispositions, schemata, and tastes, where the "habitus is not only a structuring structure, which organizes practices and the perception of practices, but also a structured structure" (Bourdieu 1984: 170). With roots in the writings of Aristotle and mentions in the works of many sociologists, the habitus has emerged as an optimal construct that reconciles structure and agency as mutually defined, in that structure "becomes something that is given meaning to the extent that it is embodied in individuals" (Park 2009: 4). In response to dichotomies that perceive agency and structure as separate and opposing processes, Bourdieu's description of habitus "depicts social practice as the outcome of a dialectic of incorporation and objectification" (Sallaz 2010: 296). For example, in discussing new entrants to the field of journalism, Benson notes how both the "objective structure" and the more personal habitus of each individual agent conflate to inform how the individual is able to structure their reality, so that the "complexity, capacities, and character of any particular agent is due not to his or her submission to or freedom from the effects of a field, but rather to the particularity of any life's trajectory within and through a series of fields" (Benson 1999: 467). All action and meaning are both personal and subjective while forming a mutual feedback loop with the more objective social structures outside the individual.

This process of navigation occurs organically and without conscious considera-tion, as the habitus resides so deeply in one's experience and expectation of social life as to be impossible to separate from the autopilot of almost every social action; we act reflexively within the boundaries of our social condition as the habitus "generates and orients an agent's practice, despite the fact that an agent would be hard-pressed to explain any 'rule' or 'purpose' behind their action" (Anderson 2004: 266). Since these mutually reinforcing exchanges occur so seamlessly, the theory affords a new way to explicate social relations and phenomena without assigning the burden of explanation to the objective or subjective. As such, it has been used to reconcile and explore issues where these ingrained practices might be problematic as personal history and expectation confront a new social structure – for example, cultural assimilation (Adkins et al. 2006; Kim 2007; Bangeni 2009; Sallaz 2010); translation (Inghilleri 2003; Ben-Ari, 2010; Meylaerts 2010); language rights and usage (Boussofara-Omar 2006; Brown and Crawford 2009; Abdelhay, 2010); or occupation of physical space (Parker et al. 2007; Centner 2008). The interplay of change, the old intersecting with the new, offers another dichotomy where habitus can help to explain how the individual navigates a shifting cultural structure while herself being an agent of that change.

Social actors navigate more specific social realms, or *fields*, that are shaped and shaping of a habitus, according to Bourdieu. These are broadly delineated as social, political, cultural, and economic and are differentiated based on the different forms of capital they afford and their relative autonomy from each other and dominant political-economic fields (Benson 1999). Each field operates as a distinct but interconnected and mutually influential cultural sphere of the larger social realm, made distinct by what types of capital offer the most value to the individual holders. Much (if not all) of this capital is not literal but symbolic, "accorded special meaning larger than itself by those exchanging the capital" (Centner 2008: 197). A vast collection of rare vintages or patchwork quilts may offer holders in the right field an advantage over their peers, but not because anyone is thirsty or chilly; the field and its members assign higher symbolic capital to certain objects and practices, regardless of the physical or actual benefits that might arise from possession. Unintentionally, every agent in the field will try to extract the maximum amount of profit (or, additional capital) from every symbolic exchange (Bourdieu 1991). As symbolic capital is exchanged and maximized, agents gain status in the field and adjust their dispositions, in relation to peers, field, and those outside, and revise their social standing. The value of capital thus shifts one's habitus, while the field adjusts to the individual changes as well, along with the value of the capital; fields, symbolic capital, and habitus are all interconnected and fluid.

Habitus has also become a popular theory for media culture scholars interested in how producers and consumers influence each other to create audience tastes and understandings (Jewkes 2002; O'Connor, 2004; Lewis 2006; Park 2009). While populists would assign taste to the personal and those in the Frankfurt School would fault the media producers, Bourdieu's theory takes a more comprehensive view of how taste is formed. As a product of the habitus, taste acquires a "double nature: on the one hand it is immediate and emotional, beyond strategic calculation; on the other, it is structured by and fundamentally linked to power and social position" (Scheuer 2003: 145). As a result, what we like is connected to who we are relative to our place in the larger structure, specifically which fields we associate and are associated with, so that

> the real locus of struggle over meaning lies not in the relation between any particular set of cultural producers and their audiences, but among fields of cultural production (both producers and homologous audiences) that vie among themselves over the power to produce legitimate knowledge about the social world. (Benson 1999: 487)

Meaning arises from the mutually constructed and agreed-upon values and mores of every field, leaving neither producer or consumer powerless or in control but subject to the same push and pull of structure versus agency that the theory of habitus helps to explain. In explaining our "cultural habitus," we must take into account both our own capabilities and also the surrounding field that helps to shape what is possible and what we come to value and prefer.

Structure and Agency in the Habitus of the New

As the media industry expands to increasingly digital territories, producers and audiences have come to occupy newly defined fields that act and react to modify their collective habituses. Analyses of the sociocultural and political impact of the Internet frequently evoke dualities of dystopia and utopia, promise and peril, constructionism and essentialism, determinism and free will and many other dichotomies that serve the purpose of organizing thought and theory around the net. While it is important to engage the perspectives implied in theoretical dichotomies, it is also necessary to realize that people live their everyday lives by constructing practices in the hope of reconciling and polarities, and so must a theory that explains human behaviors.

Naturally, the habitus is both structuring structure and is structured structure itself, reconciling fixity and change, while also allowing that change is defined by the parameters of structure that present its context (Abdelhay 2010). Thus, a habitus-based analysis examines not macro-level structures at work but rather how they connect to micro-level praxis. In the context of new media, a habitus-based analysis would acknowledge domination patterns in media ownership and convergence but would focus on connecting micro-level praxis that develops (Park 2009). It is the flexible structure of the habitus that provides a person and the family the ability to deal with the uncertainties in everyday life, even though that flexibility is framed by pre-existing structures (Bourdieu 1984).

The concept of the habitus is intended to describe the general tendency of people to reproduce certain patterns of action, including conformity but also divergence (Sela-Sheffy 2005). According to Bourdieu (1990), actions are not mechanical or rule-based but strategic. Actors employ conformity and divergence as specific strategies in relation to cultural, political, social, or economic fields of activity. Thus, the habitus is not static, although it is durable. The dynamics of new media invite and reward change, which can only be sustained at the micro level via a habitus of familiar predispositions that grant individuals some (promise of) agency in how changes impact their everyday spheres of sociality. In the context of change, agency means that individuals are able to maintain familiar practices despite change. And it also means that individuals maintain autonomy to define change, although within the habitus this autonomy is exercised mostly via habituated actions that develop gradually through communities of practice. The habitus of the new promises these forms of agency.

The affordances, or potentialities, of the structural environment form a social architecture that suggests a flexible set of choices for agency that both advances change in the habitus of the new and also sustains a comforting familiarity. The set of choices is flexible and affords autonomy in choosing, but is also specific via a social architecture that invites or encourages particular dispositions and actions. In the following section, we discuss the affordances of this social environment, the set of embodied dispositions they lend themselves to, and the practices that develop out of a habitus of the new. Alternatively, we may think of technologies as "crystallizations of socially organized action" and not "as exceptional or special phenomena" but rather as "other kinds of social practices that recur over time" (Sterne 2003: 367). In that sense, technology *is* habitus, and the habitus of the new *is* convergence.

Affordances and the Habitus

The dynamics of new media rest upon technologies of convergence, which collapse boundaries and combine the means through which individuals socialize (*convergence of technologies*) but also the physical and imagined architectures social individuals traverse (*convergence of spaces*) and the continuum of activities that shape and are shaped by a converged technological architecture (*convergence of practices*) (Papacharissi 2010). Like all fields, technologies are associated with habits and practices. They structure and are structured by practices, and embody the dispositions of the epoch that gives birth to them. Digital technologies shape and are shaped by users and producers, working within new fields where symbolic values shift with new means of communication. This impacts cultural consumptions and outputs from micro to macro levels, since "not only do the condition of the reader and the condition of the spectator overlap with more and more frequency; both are reinvented when, as Internet user, we download books, movies, and songs from the Web" (Canclini 2009: 142). Our tastes change as our ability *to* taste in the new structures shapes what we have come to consider possible in our cultural realms.

The set of embodied dispositions that form a habitus are turned into praxis through communities of practice, and in the context of convergent architectures these take the form of networked publics. boyd (2010) theorizes the following properties as the four structural affordances of networked publics: persistence, replicability, scalability, and searchability. *Persistence* refers to the automatic recording and archive of online expressions, *replicability* concerns the ease with which content made out of bits can be duplicated, *scalability* captures the potential of greater visibility of content in networked publics, and *searchability* permits content in networked publics to be accessed through search. Papacharissi and Yuan (2011) suggest a fifth structural affordance, pertaining to *shareability*, or the tendency of networked digital structures to encourage sharing over withholding information. What renders networks lively is the flow of information between individual network nodes. Without information flowing between individuals, the network becomes a static, asocial environment (Papacharissi 2009). Stutzman (2006) has referred to this attribute as the inherent sociality of social network communities and has explained that it accounts for the high level of disclosure of personal information online.

These affordances dispose networked publics toward particular behaviors. Together, they present a set of embodied dispositions that come to form a habitus of the new, characterized by persistence, replicability, scalability, searchability, and shareability. In this manner, the habitus of the new reflects the dynamics of convergent technologies but is also suggestive of a commonplace driving logic that blurs private and public boundaries in ways that run contrary to the dominant habitus of the field of sociality. The habitus produces practices, through the "durably instilled generative principle of regulated improvisations" (Bourdieu 1977: 78).

Thus, developing practices aim to reconcile these conflicts so as to adapt to the new but sustain the familiar.

For example, in the field defined by a social networking technology such as Facebook or Twitter, the theory of the habitus can be used to described how actors move through online spaces as new and crowded fields of meaning-making. While the premise of Facebook may appear to be to express one's unique and subjective personality, all users may only present themselves in the standard structure of the page template. Within these confines, however, individual agency and taste allow users to articulate and renegotiate the possibilities of the site and its meaning in the larger field, creating new meanings from familiar structures and commanding the newly valuable user attention with novelty. Freishtat and Sandlin (2010) understand Facebook as a cultural space wherein normative behaviors are established and policed via the premise of the habitus. They discuss how the habitus operates in digital and physical worlds similarly, leading users to adopt and adapt normative behaviors by performing online "in ways that are similar to the ways they perform in face-to-face interaction – policing the persona and actions of others within the social norms associated with those personas in particular cultural contexts" (2010: 517). In navigating these online spaces, individuals permit a hybrid set of established and newly formed predispositions to guide their behavior (Papacharissi 2009). Still, the premise of the habitus guides and explains how individuals reconcile new with old practices on territories digital and physical.

Individuals claim agency to reconcile the commonplace logic of the new into praxis. They do so by drawing from the affordances of the new to maintain/adapt dominant social practices and to define the shape of the habitus of the new, through means that are primarily linguistic (Anderson 2004; Bird 2007; Ostermann 2003). Markers of class, such as education and profession, inform the habitus of individuals, which in turn shapes digital tastes, creating and reproducing digital caste systems (Kvasny 2005; North et al. 2008). Locality and space are also further reflected in how systems of taste are digitally expressed, remixed, and reproduced (Parker et al. 2007; Centner 2008). The habitus of the new, as convergence, situates the user as social actor by inviting and producing certain practices that dominate online behavior. These are typically practices that revolve around *expression* of the self and *connection* with other social actors. We identify three dominant practices that are characteristic of the habitus of the new. These practices are richly afforded by the technology but are also a remediation of embedded predisposition.

(Authorship and) Disclosure

Bourdieu (1984) explains that the habitus is constituted via discursive practices. In this manner, structure is rhetorically created and affirmed, as language is a constituent dimension of the habitus (Abdelhay 2010). Agency is also discursively claimed. This renders social actors both creators and products of their habitus, as they use narrative practices for sensemaking and identity construction (Bird 2007). Bourdieu defined the linguistic habitus as

> a set of socially constituted dispositions that imply a propensity to speak in certain ways and to utter determinate things (an expressive interest), as well as a competence to speak defined inseparably as the linguistic ability to engender an infinite array of discourses that are grammatically conforming, and as the social ability to adequately utilize this competence in a given situation. (Bourdieu and Wacquant 1992: 145)

In the habitus of the new, technologies of convergence offer, emphasize, and reward authorship as a narrative strategy. The linguistic habitus is constructed via authorship practices afforded through blogs, microblogs, social network sites, and other platforms of expression and social awareness. Narrative practices such as blogging, tweets, and status updates sustain what Giddens (1991) termed the ongoing story or the reflexive project of the self. Textual events call networked publics into being. Language itself becomes mediated and remediated, and the discursive spaces afforded by convergence encourage persistence, scalability, searchability, replicability, and shareability. Individuals are invited to tell stories about themselves, and the stories told are made of words digitally traceable, remixable, and broadly accessible. The social architecture compels individuals, more than ever, to tell stories about themselves, and to make those stories public. This is frequently mistaken for excessive narcissism or excessively self-referential behavior, but may also be understood as an expression of agency that conforms to and seeks to relate the individual to the habitus. It is through the practice of authorship, afforded so richly through convergence, that individuals construct discourse, which serves as symbolic asset in Bourdieu's understanding of the habitus. In the context of the Facebook habitus, authorship takes on a particular form that supports specific tropes of connection and expression. In the context of the Twitter habitus, the form of authorship lends itself to different tropes of sociality, privacy, and publicity.

For example, the performativity and frequent dramatism of Facebook status updates and Twitter posts observe, but also provoke, the habitus of the new. They conform to it by giving in to its shareability; they dissent by sharing in ways that are distinctive from durable sets of social dispositions that the habitus of the new rests upon. As rhetorical claims of agency, they reference and remediate their structural context. The habitus of the new affords and rewards authorship, yielding social capital for those who share mini or lengthier narratives with their networks of contact. It compels individuals to author, to tell stories, and to share stories about themselves. The habitus predisposes in a way that is neither conscious nor intentional (Anderson 2004). Of course, individuals have always created narratives to sustain habitus, but the digital architecture enables and augments authorship in ways that promote particular forms of storytelling and invite others to listen in through specific practices. And, beyond sustaining authorship, it also rewards disclosure of narratives. As a result, whereas a personal narrative like that of a diary contains personal capital for the author, upon being disclosed within the habitus of the new as a blog entry it provides access to social, cultural, political, and possibly economic capital. Authorship is encouraged, and publicity becomes agency in the sense that it permits authors access to fields and forms of capital that were previously inaccessible. The habitus of the new, as sustained by convergent media, presents a structured structure and affords particular avenues for agency.

Listening

It is not uncommon for late modernity to create spaces to which individuals are invited as flaneurs or voyeurs. Pritchard (2000) argued that by removing personalized sales assistance supermarkets render consumers and commodities impersonal and voyeuristic. McCarthy has explained that ambient functions of television in public places serve to afford individuals a sense of privacy in public, rendering the individual "captive and mobile, both receptive and hostile" (2001: 100). Similarly, technologies such as the Walkman and more recently the iPod enable privacy in public spaces (du Gay et al. 1997). Apple commercials hail iPod-wearing individuals maneuvering upon neon-colored backdrops as displaced yet connected urban flaneurs (Papacharissi 2010). Communication technologies frequently create spaces that individuals must inhabit as complex container technologies (Adkins et al. 2006). The container technology embedded in social media frequently invites participants to engage either in voyeur or flaneur mode (boyd 2011).

Voyeurism and flaneuring present modes of observation that can also be understood as ways of listening in on one's peripheral environment. In the context of social network sites, the practice of surveying and traversing through friends' profiles permits "peripheral awareness and ambient community" (Erickson 2010: 1194). The practice of following opinion leaders on Twitter has been likened to emerging disciplines of listening in social media, characterized by background listening, reciprocal listening, and delegated listening (Crawford 2009). In this manner, the practice of listening may strengthen connectedness with others (Hennenburg et al. 2009), resemble the practices of conversation (Honeycutt and Herring 2009; Steiner 2009), and add elements of physicality to web design (Hohl 2009). Individuals maintain a social information habitus that helps them sustain social and peripheral awareness of their surrounding lifeworlds (Bock 2004). People claim agency via discursive practices of speaking (authorship) and listening (Scollon 2001). In the context of news aggregator sites, for example, the practice of reading and endorsing an article conveys agency, in the form of dissent, agreement, or interest in a particular viewpoint. The technologies invite individuals to survey and traverse, resting upon the habituated custom of social curiosity. In several cases involving organized structure, surveillance and flaneuring are commercially exploited.

In the context of the Facebook habitus, the practice of surveying and traversing through others' profiles is a remediation of listening; a reinterpretation of peripheral awareness with the means that the digital platform affords. Thus, predispositions that turn into practices of everyday sociality are sustained and reinvented in the habitus of the new. As a habitus of information, the habitus of the new sets a high price on attention, and listening is how we are socialized to communicate attention. In this manner, the structured practice of listening is reintegrated into the context of the new, as attention to or distraction from information. Like structure and agency, the old and the new modalities of listening exist in perpetual, dialectical shift, but to command attention in the online field the most valuable capital stands as the most novel.

Redaction

The practices of expression and connection on the habitus of the new involve both production of performances and simultaneous or subsequent editing of these per-formances. Redaction enables the bringing together and editing of identity traces, to form and frame coherent performances of sociality and self-expression (Hartley and Rennie 2009; Papacharissi and Yuan 2011). Thus, redactional figures are *pro-dused* as representational of the self – figures that present an edited mix of available meanings (Hartley 2003; Bruns 2008). Redactional processes are simultaneously simplified and compromised by the structural affordances of platforms at hand. Local and translocal performances of sociality are constantly edited, retweaked, and remixed to maintain the coherence (or purposeful incoherence) of the performance with varying audiences/publics. These redactional practices are developed so that individuals can manage the persistence, searchability, replicability, scaleability, and shareability convergent technologies afford.

Self-editing has always been a part of how we present the self to others, but online platforms frequently prompt self-sharing by default without easily permitting self-editing. Recent controversies around Facebook privacy settings present an example of how important self-editing is for individuals. By contrast, Google+ circles present a structural strategy for controlled disclosure and redaction, which are appealing to users who want to edit what gets shared and with whom. In the habitus mediated through social awareness systems, self-awareness and self-monitoring are heightened as individuals advance into a constant state of *redaction*, or editing and remixing of the self. Hartley refers to resulting performance as reflective of a "homo nuntius," or the "messaging human," a contemporary species that expresses identity *via* and *as* message and "*produces* individual *identity* out of social-network *interaction*" (Hartley 2010: 19).

In Hartley's words,

> Individuals in the species *homo nuntius* don't just 'send' messages as an action ('message' as verb), they *are* a system of messages ('message' as noun); they are both constituted by and productive through messages, which are the process by means of which reason emerges (it is the product of a process, not an input). (2010: 23)

We would in turn add that, in the habitus of the new, agency is claimed through authoring, listening, and redacting messages about the self and others. This practice becomes fluid and may present a strategic claim of capital across distinct, or combined, fields.

Digital Literacy as Agency

This theory of habitus offers insight into how actors are able to access and make sense of the resources in their field; some actors may not possess the proper disposition to appropriate the established meanings of the technological resources. In these cases, social actors may still claim agency but arrive at different understandings of how a technology can be and ultimately is used. These limitations form the boundaries of the field in which free play comes to constitute the social reality; within the "rules" of the game, each actress can be liberated to invoke her style, motivation, action, and reaction to contribute to the social world. Within the larger social structure, technology emerges as another field with its own structures, shaped by actors and the limitations of the social world, all while reacting to the capabilities and actions of its users; users drive technology as much as technology drives users.

We argue that individuals with redactional acumen may be able to manage the structural affordances of convergent environments fluently. Not only may they be able to optimally exploit the expressive and connective potential of online platforms but they are also able to capitalize on the embedded convergence to combine and accumulate capital that has value and translates across fields. In doing so, they may be able to edit performed actions in ways that remediate habits of the past into the habitus of the new, thus also availing themselves of a performative fluency that leads to enhanced agency. The ability to produce but also to edit rests upon heightened digital literacy, or fluency, that is essential for agency in the habitus of the new. Digital literacy permits dialogic negotiation of a complex set of texts that flow across a variety of fields and spaces (Bulfin and North 2007). Digital fluency in turn supports performative fluency online, across all fields of interaction, and permits that individuals cultivate *redaction acumen*.

The habitus of the new is a habitus of information, containing cultural and thus linguistic hybridity (Robinson 2009). Embedded into the premise of convergence, it collapses several publics and audiences that we must somehow reconcile, relying on practices that frequently borrow from translational norms and require skills that resemble a digital form of multilingualism (Inghilleri 2003). In navigating the spaces the habitus of the new affords, we are not just consumers but produsers of polysemic messages, some of which are central to crafting our sense of self. *Redactional acumen* is an editing sensibility essential to the storytelling of the self as that unfolds through the habitus of the new. Structured around the tendency to edit and integrate aspects of one's identity, redactional acumen enables individuals to present a coherent and polysemic performance of the self that makes sense to multiple publics, without compromising one's authentic, or rather intended, sense of self. In the habitus of the new, digital fluency paves the road to agency and redactional acumen presents the means for capital accumulation.

As recent findings on the digital divide indicate (e.g., boyd and Hargittai 2010; Hargittai 2010), it is not just access to technologies that blocks lower classes from using them – it is a fundamentally different disposition that does not enable the more acceptable (by certain standards) forms of action. Digital fluency, like the preference for smaller portions of haute cuisine or the ability to chat at a cocktail party, comes from the deeply ingrained worlds produced in class and education. While the rules of the habitus may have changed, the class connection remains firmly in place; those without fluency lose agency, and fluency is a product of class.

References

Abdelhay, A. (2010) "A Critical Commentary on the Discourse of Language Rights in the Naivasha Language Policy in Sudan Using Habitus as a Method." *International Journal of the Sociology of Language*, 206, 21–45.

Adkins, B.A., Smith, D.J., Barnett, K.R., and Grant, E.L. (2006) "Public Space as 'Context' in Assistive Information and Communication Technologies for People with Cognitive Impairment." *Information, Communication & Society*, 9(3), 355–372.

Anderson, D. (2004) "Questioning the Motives of Habituated Action: Burke and Bourdieu on *Practice*." *Philosophy and Rhetoric*, 37(3), 255–274.

Bangeni, B. (2009) "Negotiating between Past and Present Discourse Values in a Postgraduate Law Course: Implications for Writing." *Southern African Linguistics and Applied Language Studies*, 27(1), 65–76.

Ben-Ari, N. (2010) "Representations of Translators in Popular Culture." *Translational and Interpreting Studies*, 5(2), 220–242.

Benson, R. (1999) "Field Theory in Comparative Context: A New Paradigm for Media Studies." *Theory and Society*, 28, 462–498.

Bird, S. (2007) "Sensemaking and Identity: The Interconnection of Storytelling and Networking in a Women's Group of a Large Corporation." *Journal of Business Communication*, 44(4), 311–339.

Bock, M. (2004) "Family Snaps: Life-Worlds and Information Habitus." *Visual Communication*, 3, 281–293.

Bourdieu, P. (1977) [1972] *Outline of a Theory of Practice*, trans. R. Nice. Cambridge, MA: Cambridge University Press.

Bourdieu, P. (1984) [1979] *Distinction: A Social Critique of the Judgment of Taste*, trans. R. Nice. Cambridge, MA: Harvard University Press.

Bourdieu, P. (1990) *In Other Words: Essays Towards a Reflexive Sociology*, trans. M. Adamson. Cambridge: Polity.

Bourdieu, P. (1991) [1977–1984] *Language and Symbolic Power*, trans. G. Raymond and M. Adamson. Cambridge: Polity.

Bourdieu, P. and Wacquant, L.J.D. (1992) *An Invitation to Reflexive Sociology*. Cambridge: Polity.

Boussofara-Omar, N. (2006) "Learning the 'Linguistic Habitus' of a Politician: A Presidential Authoritative Voice in the Making." *Journal of Language and Politics*, 5(3), 325–358.

boyd, d. (2010) "Social Network Sites as Networked Publics: Affordances, Dynamics, and Implications" in Z. Papacharissi, ed., *Networked Self: Identity, Community, and Culture on Social Network Sites*. New York: Routledge, pp. 39–58.

boyd, d. (2011) "Dear Voyeur, Meet Flâneur ... Sincerely, Social Media." *Surveillance and Society*, 8(4), 505–507.

boyd, d. and Hargittai, E. (2010) "Facebook Privacy Settings: Who Cares?" *First Monday*, 15(8). http://firstmonday.org/htbin/cgiwrap/bin/ojs/index.php/fm/article/view/3086/2589.

Brown, B. and Crawford, P. (2009) "Politeness Strategies in Question Formulation in a UK Telephone Advisory Service." *Journal of Politeness Research*, 5, 73–91.

Bruns, A. (2008) *Blogs, Wikipedia, Second Life and Beyond: From Production to Produsage*. New York: Peter Lang.

Bulfin, S. and North, S. (2007) "Negotiating Digital Literacy Practices Across School and Home: Case Studies of Young People in Australia." *Language and Education*, 21(3), 247–263.

Canclini, N.C. (2009) "How Digital Convergence is Changing Cultural Theory." *Popular Communication*, 7, 140–146.

Centner, R. (2008) "Places of Privileged Consumption Practices – Spatial Capital, the Dot-Com Habitus and San Francisco's Internet Boom." *City & Community*, 7(3), 193–223.

Couldry, N. (2004) "Liveness, Reality and the Mediated Habitus from Television to the Mobile Phone." *Communication Review*, 7, 353–361.

Crawford, K. (2009) "Following You – Disciplines of Listening in Social Media." *Journal of Media and Cultural Studies*, 23(4), 525–535.

du Gay, P., Hall, S., James, L. et al. (1997) *Doing Cultural Studies: The Story of the Sony Walkman*. London: Sage.

Erickson, I. (2010) "Geography and Community – New Forms of Interaction among People and Places." *American Behavioral Scientist*, 53, 1194–1207.

Freishtat, R. and Sandlin, J. (2010) "Shaping Youth Discourse about Technology." *Educational Studies*, 46, 503–523.

Giddens, A. (1979) *Central Problems in Social Theory: Action, Structure, and Contradiction in Social Analysis*. Berkeley, CA: University of California Press.

Giddens, A. (1991) *Modernity and Self-Identity: Self and Society in the Late Modern Age*. Stanford, CA: Stanford University Press.

Hargittai, E. (2010) "Digital Na(t)ives Variation in Internet Skills and Uses Among Members of the 'Net Generation.'" *Sociological Inquiry*, 80(1), 92–113.

Hartley, J. (2003) *A Short History of Cultural Studies*. London: Sage.

Hartley, J. (2010) "*Homo nuntius* – Messaging Humanity." *Popular Communication*, 8(4), 293–311.

Hartley, J. and Rennie, E. (2009) "About a Girl: Fashion Photography as Photojournalism." *Journalism*, 5(4), 458–479.

Henneburg, S., Scammell, M., and O'Shaughnessy, N. (2009) "Political Marketing Management and Theories of Democracy." *Marketing Theory*, 9(2), 165–188.

Hohl, M. (2009) "Beyond the Screen: Visualizing Visits to a Website as an Experience in Physical Space." *Visual Communication*, 8(3), 273–284.

Honeycutt, C. and Herring, S.C. (2009) "Beyond Microblogging: Conversation and Collaboration Via Twitter." *Proceedings of the Forty-Second Hawai'i International Conference on System Sciences (HICSS-42)*. Los Alamitos: IEEE Press. http://ella.slis.indiana.edu/~herring/honeycutt.herring.2009.pdf.

Inghilleri, M. (2003) "Habitus, Field and Discourse – Interpreting as a Socially Situated Activity." *Target*, 15(2), 243–268.

Jewkes, Y. (2002) "The Use of Media in Constructing Identities in the Masculine Environment of Men's Prisons." *European Journal of Communication*, 17(2), 205–225.

Kim, T. (2007) "The Dynamics of Ethnic Name Maintenance and Change." *Journal of Multilingual and Multicultural Development*, 28(2), 117–133.

Kvasny, L. (2005) "The Role of the Habitus in Shaping Discourses about the Digital Divide." *Journal of Computer-Mediated Communication*, 10(2). http://jcmc.indiana.edu /vol10/issue2/kvasny.html.

Lewis, T. (2006) "Seeking Health Information on the Internet: Lifestyle Choice or Bad Attack of Cyberchondria?" *Media, Culture & Society*, 28(4), 521–539.

McCarthy, A. (2001) *Ambient Television*. Durham, NC: Duke University Press.

Meylaerts, R. (2010) "Habitus and Self-Image of Native Literary Author – Translators in Diglossic Societies." *Translation and Interpreting Studies*, 5(1), 1–19.

North, S., Snyder, I., and Bulfin, S. (2008) "Digital Tastes – Social Class and Young People's Technology Use." *Information, Communication & Society*, 11(7), 895–911.

O'Connor, A. (2004) "Punk and Globalization: Spain and Mexico." *International Journal of Cultural Studies*, 7(2), 175–195.

Ostermann, A.C. (2003) "Communities of Practice at Work – Gender, Facework and the Power of Habitus at an All-Female Police Station and a Feminist Crisis Intervention Center in Brazil." *Discourse & Society*, 14(4), 473–505.

Papacharissi, Z. (2009) "The Virtual Geographies of Social Networks: A Comparative Analysis of Facebook, LinkedIn and ASmallWorld." *New Media & Society*, 11(1–2), 199–220.

Papacharissi, Z. (2010) *A Private Sphere: Democracy in a Digital Age*. Cambridge: Polity.

Papacharissi, Z. and Yuan, E. (2011) "What if the Internet Did Not Speak English? New and Old Language for Studying Newer Media Technologies" in D. Park, N.J. Jankowski, and S. Jones, eds., *The Long History of New Media: Technology, Historiography, and Newness in Context*. New York: Peter Lang, pp. 89–108.

Park, D.W. (2009) "Pierre Bourdieu's Habitus and the Economy of the Media." *Democratic Communiqué*, 23(1), 1–21.

Parker, S., Uprichard, E., and Burrows, R. (2007) "Class Places and Place Classes: Geodemographics and the Spatialization of Class." *Information, Communication & Society*, 10(6), 902–921.

Pritchard, W.N. (2000) "Beyond the Modern Supermarket: Geographical Approaches to the Analysis of Contemporary Australian Retail Restructuring." *Australian Geographical Studies*, 38(2), 204–218.

Robinson, L. (2009) "A Taste for the Necessary: A Bourdieuian Approach to Digital Inequality." *Information, Communication & Society*, 12(4), 488–507.

Sallaz, J.T. (2010) "Talking Race, Marketing Culture: The Racial Habitus In and Out of Apartheid." *Social Problems*, 57(2), 294–314.

Scheuer, J. (2003) "Habitus as the Principle for Social Practice: A Proposal for Critical Discourse Analysis." *Language in Society*, 32(2), 143–175.

Scollon, S. (2001) "Habitus, Consciousness, Agency and the Problem of Intention: How We Carry and are Carried by Political Discourses." *Folia Linguistica*, 35(1&2), 97–129.

Sela-Sheffy, R. (2005) "How to be a (Recognized) Translator: Rethinking Habitus, Norms, and the Field of Translation." *Target*, 17(1), 1–26.

Steiner, H. (2009) "Reference Utility of Social Networking Sites: Options and Functionality." *Library Hi Tech News*, 26(5–6), 4–6.

Sterne, J. (2003) "Bourdieu, Technique and Technology." *Cultural Studies*, 17(3&4), 367–389.

Stutzman, F. (2006) "An Evaluation of Identity-Sharing Behavior in Social Network Communities." *Journal of the International Digital Media and Arts Association*, 3(1), 10–18.

10

Long Live Wikipedia?

Sustainable Volunteerism and the Future of Crowd-Sourced Knowledge

Andrew Lih

A favorite topic of debate among those who have watched two decades of dot-coms come and go has been: "Is Wikipedia dying?" It seems *The Wall Street Journal* (Angwin and Fowler 2009) and other news outlets try to find any narrative they can in the statistics about the online encyclopedia's health.

Consider how far Wikipedia has come to garner that much attention. It is considered such a fundamental resource on the Internet that users expect it to be constantly updated, mostly accurate, and always available. That's quite a change considering that in 2004 people were just hearing about it and wondering how an "encyclopedia anyone can edit" could ever find a place in the information eco-system. But, just as we are accepting Wikipedia as an essential part of our repertoire, it's useful to reflect on a decade of evolution, as it has gone from *emergence* to questions about *influence* and *permanence*. There is no doubt now that Wikipedia has succeeded, but we also have to note where it systemically suffers, and how long we can expect it to survive.

Wikipedia has changed how we negotiate knowledge, because it has compelled us to question what we considered "trustworthy" before it even existed. Inevitably, the rise of user-generated works has asked us to re-evaluate how good existing established "trustworthy" works (pre-Wikipedia) were in the first place. In a 2005 study by the journal *Nature*, articles in Wikipedia and Britannica were compared against each other, using experts in particular fields as evaluators. What was surprising was not that Wikipedia did relatively well but that Britannica did rather poorly, given its venerated status and long-standing reputation (Giles 2005). Britannica did yield better overall results than Wikipedia, as it averaged 2.92 mistakes per article compared to 3.86 for the encyclopedia anyone can edit. But, that the contest was even that close surprised many. We may be comparing Wikipedia and new

A Companion to New Media Dynamics, First Edition. Edited by John Hartley, Jean Burgess, and Axel Bruns.
© 2013 John Wiley & Sons, Ltd. Published 2015 by John Wiley & Sons, Ltd.

forms of knowledge against a hypothetical perfect and accurate source that we
have erroneously projected onto Britannica and others that have survived the test
of time.

Among the lessons we've learned are that the emergent phenomenon of encyclopedia writing and constructing knowledge has a complexity in signaling mechanisms,
both explicit and implicit. Biologist Pierre-Paul Grasse (1959) described how insects
signal each other implicitly using a stigmergic effect, by "stimulation of workers
by the performance they have achieved." Wikipedia's transparency and availability
of metadata such as edit histories, watchlists, and user contributions are an online
version of the stigmergic effect, by displaying artifacts and trails of people's work
to inspire (and incite) others. Grasse's observations were about termites that have
no way to communicate other than through stigmergy. Wikipedia editors, however, do benefit from explicit communication, from email lists to article discussion
pages and even live interaction through Internet relay chat. The combination of
these two modes accelerates the emergent behavior in Wikipedia, and has inspired
projects such as OpenStreetMap and Ushahidi, which apply these same principles
to mapping and geolocation, with the latter effort becoming a significant platform
for mobile crisis and disaster response.

As much as Wikipedia gets things right through the wisdom of the crowds, it is not
without substantial quality problems with respect to the project's prime directive:
write articles while maintaining a neutral point of view. Normally, there is a massive
imbalance in favor of the highly active and principled Wikipedia editors against
the undue influence of small numbers of non-neutral editors pushing toward a
particular viewpoint or conclusion. Whether the topic is political or religious (e.g.,
global warming, Israel and Palestine, etc.) more often than not, reason dominates
on Wikipedia because collusion by like-minded opinionated actors to influence an
article is low in amplitude and difficult to coordinate.

So, as much as Wikipedia is a positive example of an emergent phenomenon for
constructing knowledge – in which a few simple rules understood and acted upon by
independent individual editors can create larger, complex results – the same systems
can work against Wikipedia's process, in the form of systemic topical issues the
project now faces. Wikipedia has been able to repel engineered efforts to influence
and elide, from groups such as Scientologists (Singel 2009), global warming skeptics,
Holocaust deniers, and editors with earnest conspiracy and fringe theories. However,
consider the troublesome issue of entries about things as innocuous as universities
and colleges. With few exceptions, these articles start with the requisite history of
such institutions but quickly segue into glowing accolades, trumpeting selective
accomplishments in the opening paragraphs as the most significant, noteworthy
events, even if taken from obscure sources. Consider a paragraph of the Wikipedia
article about Wake Forest University:

> In the 2009 BusinessWeek Undergraduate Business Schools Rankings, the Calloway
> School of Business and Accountancy was ranked 14th overall, and #1 in terms of
> Academic Quality.

and another from the University of Leicester article:

> The university has established itself as a leading research-led university and has been
> named University of the Year of 2008 by the *Times Higher Education*. The university
> has consistently ranked amongst the top 15 universities in the United Kingdom by the
> *Times Good University Guide* and *The Guardian*.

These are hardly unique; a random sampling of articles about higher-education institutions will yield similar prose.

Successful participatory projects rely on certain qualities of the crowd – that there is independent action by editors and that there is a diversity of viewpoints (Powazek 2009). The situation with colleges and universities is perhaps the worst-case violation of the above principles, since alumni and current students are a passionate set of influencers of the article, who can easily number in the thousands to tens of thousands and engage in defense of their tribe. The power of emergent behavior becomes a battle between those applying the Wikipedia principles of neutral point of view and those loyal to their institution and alma mater. In these situations, the influence of school supporters is too great and a strong positive point of view pervades these types of pages. So it is now a given in Wikipedia – articles about colleges and universities are among the most highly problematic for balance and rigor and resemble marketing materials from the school itself. There is no solution in sight, and this is a problem endemic to Wikipedia.

This may be an ancillary concern, but there is a larger problem of long-term sustainability and permanence. After years of rapid and vigorous growth, Wikipedia editing saw a significant shift in 2007, when the number of editors registering each month decreased, and month-to-month growth slowed for the first time in the site's history. Since then, those studying Wikipedia's statistics have tried to determine what the "bend" in the curve means, since the growth in contributors and articles has remained flat ever since.

Perhaps the most probable explanation is that the initial rapid growth in 2001 that looked nearly exponential was the anomaly, and the current period of linear growth is not a malaise but in fact the normal and proper path. One theory from researchers is that Wikipedia's massive growth was a catch-up phase, filling an empty database with existing knowledge (Bongwon et al., 2009). It is not that we aren't discovering new things or adding to the global knowledge base in great leaps. However, the incremental increase in human knowledge today is not so massive as to rival the 2001–2006 growth spurt at Wikipedia's birth, which cataloged tens of thousands of years of human endeavors.

The challenge is that what got the community of volunteers energized in the first place (crafting community policies and creating articles) will be less appealing for new generations of editors. The heightened thrill of creating articles is gone. The bulk of contributors will have to find inspiration and excitement in maintaining, modifying, and reorganizing information within the virtual halls of millions of existing articles and established community norms.

Where Wikipedia still has high popularity is in serving as a current snapshot of the state of the world. News is often nicknamed "the first draft of history," but Wikipedia goes beyond that, becoming the instantly updated, participatory working draft of world history. But, even with a plethora of news sources to feed new content to Wikipedia, its growth trajectory is only a fraction of its early days. Recognition of Wikipedia's "news" mission gave rise to Wikinews as a project to further Wikipedia's principles. It would seem this would have provided a successful follow-on to Wikipedia's model, but sadly it has not. Volunteers found it was much harder to use the crowd-sourcing principles of Wikipedia for news production, for the reason that news has deadlines whereas Wikipedia depends on eventualism: the nickname for the concept that, given enough time, Wikipedia articles will get better with more eyeballs and edits from users – "eventually" being the key word. In that sense, an encyclopedia article is not deadline-oriented, as it can evolve on its own timeline.

News, conversely, loses value over time, and it is this decay that is inherently incompatible with eventualism. Wikis also depend on constraints in form (modular, structured writing) but not on temporal conditions (timelines) to do their best work. Mission-critical content is not what wikis are geared toward, making complete current news coverage hard, or impossible, given this constraint. Perhaps the best role the wiki method can facilitate is the creation of less-time-sensitive feature content, which could provide a new role for user participation in Wikipedia's mission.

Currently, it is not the health of the top 20 languages (English, French, German, etc.) in Wikipedia but the growth of the *next* 20 languages in the list (such as Arabic, Hindi, and Persian/Farsi) that is cause for concern. Especially for languages in India and Africa, finding a critical mass of contributors and online content is daunting. The "first-world" luxury of having large online repositories of news, books, documents, photos, and data sets as reference material has allowed for Anglo-European editions of Wikipedia to flourish. The high standard of verifiability and reliable sourcing in the top 20 languages by rank will be more problematic to enforce in the next 20. The efforts to bring digital source material online for these less popular languages still lags significantly behind those of developed countries.

Is there a way to accelerate this process? The crowd may be part of the solution. Wikipedia may find that its future is not just in sifting and summarizing what is already known and digitized in source texts. Rather, its future mission seems destined to coincide with that of the National Geographic Society and the documentary mission of public broadcasters around the world. Wikipedia started by reimagining the encyclopedia as a free-content project by "catching up" to human knowledge and cataloging the low-hanging fruit. That is, existing information that could be commonly obtained, referenced, and verified was what drove Wikipedia's early growth. With that task exhausted, it has the opportunity to turn its bounty of volunteers toward more ambitious and needed endeavors. Instead of settling for what is already known, imagine the crowd assisting in active exploration, discovery, and storytelling about the world. One such pilot project by Wikipedia editors (Prabhala 2011) seeks to document folk knowledge through audio and video interviews in India and Africa that can be used as reference material for Wikipedia entries. Since not all knowledge is written, this effort recognizes the role of oral history and folk knowledge in the human experience and seeks to document these through direct observation.

This is a dramatic shift in mission, as it is inherently an act of original journalistic research, something Wikipedia has shunned since its start. One can understand this stance, and the wisdom at the time, given the role of encyclopedias as a secondary-source references. However, with millions of articles in Wikipedia's English edition (an order of magnitude larger than any previous encyclopedic general reference), the easily obtainable "low-hanging fruit" of information is gone. It may be necessary to reach up and explore the higher branches of the tree of knowledge.

This is where Wikipedia sits: at a crossroads about what its identity should be. Now that it has seen several years of gradual slowdown in production, the community and the nonprofit that oversees it are facing serious questions about how it can sustain a community of productive volunteer users to further its vision to share in the "sum of all human knowledge."

There is a coming golden age of discovery and feature storytelling that will be facilitated by an Internet-connected, multimedia-capable crowd distributed around the globe. Unlike efforts in the past few centuries, it will not be driven by wealthy individuals seeking fortune in artifacts or explorers with patronage in service to a crown. The lessons of Wikipedia show us how crowds can do remarkably expert work if given the right collaborative incentives and emergent coordination systems. The sooner Wikipedia realizes it has already laid the ideological groundwork and the sociotechnical system to create this, the sooner it can energize its volunteer base and set them off creating feature content that will sustain the project and its community to create great works to extend human knowledge.

References

Angwin, J. and Fowler, G. (2009) "Volunteers Log Off as Wikipedia Ages." *Wall Street Journal*. http://online.wsj.com/article/SB125893981183759969.html.

Bongwon S., Convertino, G., Chi, E.H., and Pirolli, P. (2009) "The Singularity is Not Near: Slowing Growth of Wikipedia." Paper presented at the 5th International Symposium on Wikis and Open Collaboration (WikiSym), Orlando, FL (October 25–27).

Giles, J. (2005) "Internet Encyclopedias Go Head to Head." *Nature* 438(7070), 900–901.

Grasse, P.-P. (1959) La reconstruction du nid et les coordinations inter-individuelles chez *Bellicositermes natalensis* et *Cubitermes sp*. La theorie de la stigmergie: Essai d'interpretation du comportement des termites constructeurs [Reconstruction of the Nest and Coordination between Individuals in *Bellicositermes natalensis* and *Cubitermes sp*. The theory of Stigmergy: Test Interpretation of the Behavior of Termites Manufacturers]. *Insectes Sociaux*, 6, 41–81.

Powazek, D. (2009) "Design for the Wisdom of Crowds." South by Southwest 2009 presentation. www.slideshare.net/fraying/design-for-the-wisdom-of-crowds-by-derek-powazek-at-sxsw-2009.

Prabhala, A. (2011) "Grants:Fellowships/Oral Citations." *Wikimedia*. http://meta.wikimedia
    .org/wiki/Grants:Fellowships/Oral_Citations.
Singel, R. (2009) "Wikipedia Bans Church of Scientology." *Wired*. www.wired.com/epicenter
    /2009/05/wikipedia-bans-church-of-scientology.

Further Reading

Lih, A. (2009) *The Wikipedia Revolution: How a Bunch of Nobodies Created the World's
    Greatest Encyclopedia*. New York: Hyperion.
Reagle, J. (2011) *Good Faith Collaboration: The Culture of Wikipedia*. Cambridge, MA: MIT
    Press.

Mobility

11

Changing Media with Mobiles

Gerard Goggin

Introduction: The Emergence of Moving Media

Things and people have always moved (Braudel 1972–1973). A much noticed
feature of the modern world is that mobility has become prominent in how societies
are constituted – whether in the great, ceaseless global migration of people; the
new necessities and possibilities for travel; the patterns of settlements; the spatial
relations of cities, regions, and countries; the relationships between work and home
(indeed, all points in the life cycle and the institutions relevant to them, whether
of education, leisure, health, or ageing); the technologies of transportation and
communication; the distribution and portability of goods, services, and objects; or
the fluid nature of places themselves (Urry 2000; Sheller and Urry 2004; Canzler
et al., 2008). Media has been affected by these mobilities – and, in turn, has been a
condition of their possibility. Indeed, in the past three decades, mobility has been a
distinctive feature of new media and the dynamics of change that shape them. To
explore this mobility, this chapter focuses upon mobile phones, mobile media, and
the wireless technologies combining with them (often indistinguishably).

By "mobiles," I mean mobile phones and other devices that use SIM cards,
which mostly operate still on the cellular mobile telecommunications networks that
underpinned their commercial availability from the late 1970s onwards. Mobiles are
often called "wireless," especially in North America (for instance, by Murray 2001).
However, here I use "wireless" to refer especially to wireless Internet technologies
such as the popular Wi-Fi (Lemstra et al., 2011) – used in many public places as
well as through wireless routers in homes – and Wi-Max (the successor to Wi-Fi).
Since at least 2005, many mobile cellular phones have also included a wireless
chip, allowing automatic selection of the preferred connection. And smartphones
now ship with two forms of wireless network connectivity in addition to the
mobile network – namely Wi-Fi and Bluetooth (a short-range wireless connectivity
standard). With the development of fourth-generation and fifth-generation mobile

A Companion to New Media Dynamics, First Edition. Edited by John Hartley, Jean Burgess, and Axel Bruns.
© 2013 John Wiley & Sons, Ltd. Published 2015 by John Wiley & Sons, Ltd.

network standards; new wireless technologies such as Wi-Max; and other kinds of networks supporting location-based information, mapping, navigation, and sensing, mobiles are enmeshed in the creation of complex media ecologies (Goggin 2011a). Nonetheless, there are good reasons to retain the specific sense of mobiles as related to cellular networks, which will be my practice here.

During their first decade of business and consumer use in the 1980s, mobiles followed the trajectory set by their most closely related media form, the telephone. Developed in the late nineteenth century, the telephone had achieved universal coverage, access, and use in many countries by the close of the twentieth century – what was called, after the North American term, "universal service" (Mueller 1997). The telephone was widely regarded as an essential social and cultural technology, especially for interpersonal communication. Its diffusion had gone hand in hand with sociodemographic changes in both cities and rural areas in the twentieth century. Offering the capacity to communicate at a distance, the telephone was woven into changing patterns of mobility, represented by the rise of another mobile technology – the automobile (Fischer 1992).

Early on, the mobile's novelty lay in its ability to make the telephony portable. Providing coverage was available and the rules of the social situation permitted, the mobile allowed calls to be made wherever the two parties to the conversation wished. The freedom to range in the initial versions of mobile phones was greatly limited compared to what we expect now. Their bulky size meant they needed to be used in vehicles or carried around with briefcase-sized transmitting equipment. Nonetheless, mobiles become more and more widely used outside their initial industrial and business contexts. As the social innovations associated with them grew, mobiles became smaller in size and their cost dropped. With the availability of the phone came intensity and frequency of use across public and private spheres, captured in the evocative phrase "perpetual contact" (Katz and Aakhus 2002). The duration of calls also changed, with studies finding some tendency for more frequent calls of shorter duration, as Christian Licoppe suggested with his concept of "absent presence" (2004). As the mobile phone diffused more and more widely, its role in communication became strongly entrenched (Brown et al., 2001). Yet it took a little longer for the mobile phone to be recognized as a kind of media in its own right.

The Mobile Phone as a Medium

In considering whether mobile phones qualify as media it is worth briefing revisiting the history of their predecessor technology, the telephone. While the telephone was a widely used, highly significant technology of the twentieth century, its status as media was less well recognized – certainly compared to well-enshrined counterparts such as press and broadcasting. This marginality of the telephone as medium is ironic – not least because other media (in the second half of the twentieth century especially) depended upon it for their daily operations. The telephone emerged as a great tool for journalists in the business of reporting, gathering information, and interacting with their sources. In addition to these close links between the telephone and other media, there were early uses of the telephone that aligned more closely with mass media as they became defined by the middle of the twentieth century. In her fine history of electric communication in the nineteenth century, Carolyn Marvin (1988) notes the promotion of the telephone and the education of its potential users by public event and spectacle, as well as occasional uses of the telephone for information and entertainment. These were uses that formed part of media at the time, or that were closely attached to media – though, as Marvin notes, these "telephone occasions otherwise bear little resemblance to twentieth-century mass media programming" (1988: 222). A contrasting example identified by Marvin is the Hungarian Telefon Hírmondó service, which operated from 1893 until after the First World War, which "for almost a generation transmitted daily programming over telephone wires to supplement the regular telephone service" (1988: 223). Indeed, such services in Hungary and other countries, such as Italy, were instances of what Italian media historian Gabriele Balbi terms "radio before radio" (2010). It may be that there are further examples of such semiregular use of telephone networks for broadcasting that show that the telephone was far more deeply involved in broadcasting – and in what became regarded as central forms of twentieth-century media – than is widely accepted (Goggin 2011b).

When the mobile telephone became a portable technology, it became involved in the key trajectory of the *personalization* of media – something noted by Tomoyuki Okada in relation to the Japanese *ketai* (mobile phone). Okada observes that the *keitai* was "originally developed for official uses and for organizational purposes, as manifested by its birth as a shared telephone" (2005: 42). As mobiles were adopted during the 1990s, their uses became increasingly personal and individual (Katz 2003). Okada also points out that "the mid-1980s cordless and extension phones were commonly placed in bedrooms as the telephone found its way into the private room of each family member" (2005: 46). Thus, the personalization of the telephone in the domestic setting and the emergence of such dynamics with the new media of the mobile phones partake of "the individualization of television, radio, and other forms of mass media since the 1970s .... The popularity of the Walkman [for instance] illustrates this shift away from products used by the whole family to ones used by individuals" (Okada 2005: 46).

Placing the cell phone alongside other kinds of media is helpful in another way. Television, radio, and the press, not to mention (say) advertising and music, are all media widely recognized as having very wide consumption and use, and as constituting very large industries, with considerable economic and political implications. As the mobile phone developed in the 1990s especially, the sheer scale and scope of it diffusion and take-up matched and indeed exceeded this size and scope. The mobile phone, its industry, and its consumer and use base were inexorably placed on commercial, governmental, and popular agendas.

By the middle of the 1990s, a number of countries already had substantial take-up of mobiles, and this had been consolidated by the end of the decade. Finland, Sweden, and Norway were well-known early adopters. The UK had approximately

5.7 million subscribers in 1995, rising to 43 million in 2000, while the 33.8 million subscribers in the USA in 1995 grew to 109 million subscribers in 2000 (International Telecommunications Union 2000). In countries now regarded as the economic and cultural powerhouses of mobile innovation, the trajectories of diffusion were even more startling. For instance, mobile phone subscriptions in China numbered approximately 3.6 million in 1995. By 2000, subscriber numbers had exceeded 85 million and by 2010 they had reached 859 million. In the case of India, there were roughly 77 000 subscribers in 1995, quickly rising to some 3.5 million in 2000 and reaching 752 million by 2010. In the same period, Egypt, apex of the Arab Spring uprising of late 2010–early 2011, went from having 7400 mobile phones in 1995 to 1.3 million in 2000 and 71 million in 2010 (International Telecommunications Union 2000, 2010).

By the turn of the twenty-first century, mobiles were well established as a global technology. Before the first decade of the new century was out, mobiles were commonly recognized as a pillar of media and communications – and, allied with the Internet, a driving force in their transformations. Thus, mobiles feature prominently in Manuel Castells' comprehensive 2009 *Communication Power*. Castells writes:

> From the 1990s onward, another communication revolution took place worldwide: the explosion of wireless communication, with increasing capacity of connectivity and bandwidth in successive generations of mobile phones. This has been the fastest diffusing communications technology in history . . . [W]e can safely evaluate that over 60 percent of people on this planet have access to wireless communication in 2008, even if this is highly constrained by income. Indeed studies in China, Latin America, and Africa have shown that poor people give high priority to their communications needs and use a substantial proportion of their meagre budgets to fulfil them. (2009: 154)

Key to the world's mobile phones, networks, and applications establishing themselves as a specific media form were innovations in communicative and cultural practices accompanying the cell phone.

Perhaps the earliest innovation that marked out mobiles as distinctive media beyond portable voice communications was text messaging. Text messaging achieved a defining role in mobile phone culture by the end of the 1990s, credited with specific social functions. A classic Finnish study of teenagers located text messaging at the heart of mobile phone culture, productive of a new facet of friendship, relationships, and social networks (Kasesniemi 2003). Many studies that followed also documented the ways in which text messaging was involved in the making of youth cultures, new idea of intimacy, even new kinds of cultural expression (Harper et al., 2005) and language (Baron 2008) – especially with the much-invoked idea of a texting slang (Crystal 2008). Text messaging became more widespread, metamorphosing across different countries and setting. Its uses proliferated and text messaging was recognized as a significant kind of informal media in its own right, bridging interpersonal and group communication, social innovation and entrepreneurship, community development, and business (Donner 2009).

With the advent of text messaging, the cell phone took on some traditional functions of twentieth-century media. News, information, and views could now be relatively easily distributed by individual cell phone users, through the viral-like broadcasting function of text messaging. This function is distinct from the use of text messaging by commercial, nonprofit, and governmental organizations that use the facilities of phone companies or content service providers to broadcast messages to users. It is equally distinct from public authorities that establish national alert or emergency warnings that operate via text messaging. Here users themselves generate and snowball messages, as illustrated in the role text messaging has played in public assemblies, such as protest (the 2001 Manila "coup de text"), times of emergency or disaster (2004 Madrid and 2005 London bombings, 2008 Sichuan earthquakes), and riots (2005 Sydney race riots). Text messaging has become an important channel for alternative public communication, as in the case of China where it has moved from an interpersonal communication technology to a "quasi-mass communication channel" (Yu 2004; He 2008). Finally, text messaging has become a way that mobiles are integrated into broadcasting, forming an interactive channel for voting and comments in reality and participation television formats from the late 1990s onwards (Spurgeon and Goggin 2007; Goggin and Spurgeon 2008).

The rise of text messaging occurred at roughly the same time that the mobile phone was establishing itself as a vast medium (Oksman 2010). We can now turn to directly address the dynamics of new media specific to mobiles – and indeed something that mobiles contribute to the broader dynamics of change in post-broadcast, convergent new media. As well as the mobile phone itself – with distinctive endogenous practices such as text messaging – we can also point to the establishment of popular, widely used, socially significant, and lucrative forms of media in areas such as mobile music, mobile games, camera-phone photography, mobile advertising, and mobile-based magazines (particularly with the appearance of iPads and tablet computers). Increasingly, these different areas of mobiles are interwoven with each other, something that is a critical part of the new media dynamics of mobiles. To explore these dynamics further, I will briefly discuss three other areas of mobiles: mobile television; mobile Internet; and mobiles and place-making (especially through location, navigation, and mapping technologies).

From Personal to Social Television

Television remains a rich, important medium globally (Hartley 2008). Despite regular predictions of its demise, it remains alive and well – demonstrating its resilience as it is thoroughly reshaped. Much debate has focused upon the extraordinary way in which the Internet and television are finally having the epochal engagement long predicted (Owen 1999; Noam et al., 2004). Mobiles are also playing an important, if little-understood, role in this, as illustrated by the intriguing story of mobile television.

Mobile television was conceived and initially promoted by the mobile phone handset manufacturers, notably the Finnish company Nokia, in partnership with broadcasters and program and content providers (Christ and Pogrzeba 1999). From 2002 onwards, there were international trials and pilots of mobile television. From 2005 onwards, mobile television was offered in a number of countries and widely publicized, especially with the overdue concerted diffusion of 3G handsets and platforms (Balbi and Prario 2009). We can discern two broad kinds of approach to the mobile television programming that accompanied these roll-outs.

First, there were made-for-mobile genres and program formats, often the subject of publicity because of their novelty and the innovation in media use they represented. The second main kind of program offering in the early incarnations of mobile television was a marked contrast with the enthusiastic, if not utopian, promises of mobile television:

> The findings of a number of studies made on mobile TV confirm that the most popular mobile TV content is news.... Other popular mobile TV content types are: music videos, sports, cartoons, movies, soap operas and sitcoms.... (Oksman 2010: 15)

In Western countries, particularly, such as the USA, Australia, Britain, and European countries, much mobile television typically involved reworking, customizing, or abbreviating programs well known from other forms of television, especially free-to-air and subscription television. Brand played an important role as a bridge between the existing model of television (free-to-air and subscription television) and varieties of digital television (such as mobile) (Bria et al., 2007).

Thus much of the television delivered looked quite similar, if not identical to the brands that were already relatively well established in multichannel television environments, especially in subscription (cable) television. These kinds of familiar TV content seem to have been important in the development of mobile television in South Korea (Cui et al., 2007), where mobile television has attracted relatively strong uptake and use. Elsewhere there was certainly significant interest and some sustained take-up of mobile television, especially for watching events (sports, reality programming, major national or international events) and, even more so, for consuming short video or program excerpts. Yet in general take-up was disappointing – in Western countries at least. A 2011 review of mobile television has made the striking argument that the take-up of broadcast television to mobiles has been strong in China, Japan, Korea, and emerging markets such as Latin America because it has been "introduced as a handset feature – accessible for free, similar to the camera or FM radio, rather than a paid-for service" (de Renesse 2011: 10).

There have been various explanations offered for the failure of mobile television – as offered via the mobile network or direct broadcasting to handsets – to ignite the passion of the newly converged identities of television viewer and mobile phone consumer in the West (Curwen and Whalley 2008; Steen 2009; Goggin 2011a). There are also issues concerning the practice of watching mobile television – with viewers and users experimenting with what kind of television it actually is and where it fits into one's life and culture (not to mention one's repertoire of communications and media practices). Herein lies the most revealing part of the story of mobile television for the dynamics of new media. While mobile television as an "official" project has been uneven in its diffusion and take-up, mobiles have in other ways been vitally involved in the contemporary reinvention of television.

We could speak, for instance, of the popular mobile television that emerged from the combination of, on the one hand, the video camera and the increased screen capabilities of the cell phone and, on the other, new distributed broadcasting architectures such as YouTube, which has proved central to the new forms of participatory culture emerging via the Internet (Burgess and Green 2009). Rather than being used to create full-length motion pictures (as in the early visions of mobile movies), mobile phones are now well established as a quotidian video camera. The use of mobiles for recording video has underpinned many facets of the postbroadcasting world, as dramatized by the use of mobile video footage in nightly news broadcasting in circumstances where higher-quality video or broadcast television footage is not available (most recently, in the fall of Gaddafi's Libya and the uprisings of the Arab Spring, or, in another register, in the many scandals of celebrity culture). Video consumption, creating, and sharing are key to "unofficial" varieties of digital television, co-created by users with the available technologies. Mobiles are now also being used to record video for sharing via social media platforms, such as Facebook, via fixed or wireless Internet. However, with a sharp rise in the availability and use of mobile Internet, especially social media on mobiles, video can now be much more easily uploaded to Facebook using the mobile device itself.

Alongside the production and remix of video via mobiles sits the watching and consumption of all manner of video, including content that is recognizably from television (Lovink and Niederer 2008; Noam and Pupillo 2008). As portable devices, mobiles and tablets are handy for watching video when the user cares to do so – something underpinned by the reorganization of the economies of video, exemplified by peer-to-peer sharing, downloading, video-sharing sites such as YouTube, produsage (Bruns 2008), new models for monetizing video such as iTunes, and myriad other ways in which video is currently circulating. The mobile has been brought even more to the fore of the changing social landscape of video and television with the changes that have accompanied the rise of the smartphone and apps (discussed below). These developments in mobile media and Internet have further supported the new kinds of consumption of video and – I would argue – the informal reconfiguration of television. We need to be careful about making sweeping claims about mobiles' involvement in creating new social functions for television at such an early stage (Turner and Tay 2010); however, there are various reasons to indicate mobiles' critical role in the resurgence of informal economies central to the dynamics of media change around the world (Lobato 2010). Thus, while mobiles' entry into television may be associated with dynamics of personalization and customization, they are now caught up with the "social" turn of media, represented in rhetorics of social, connected television (Ducheneaut et al., 2008; Bulkeley 2010).

The Second Coming of Mobile Internet

As we have seen from the case of mobile television, a new set of dynamics is being created by the interactions – foreseen and unforeseen – between the system of classic cellular mobile networks and the system of the Internet. These connections between mobiles and the Internet are crucial for the future of both of these systems – as well as the future of media themselves. This is a complex and dynamic area, which I will sketch via three main themes: the role of mobile networks in Internet access, especially mobile broadband; the availability of the Internet on mobile devices; and the rise of smartphones.

In its mass diffusion phase in the 1990s and early 2000s, Internet access for most household users occurred through the telecommunications network (dial-up, then broadband) or subscription television networks (broadband access). Since 2006, there has been phenomenal growth worldwide in mobile broadband: access to high-speed Internet via modems that plug into the USB port of a computer and use cellular mobile networks. While it has been widely used in the global north, mobile broadband is especially important in countries of the global south (the majority of the world's population). Many developing countries lack the landline telecommunications or subscription television networks ubiquitous in wealthy countries. While satellite also provides a widespread technology for reasonable Internet access as well as entrenched television reception, the extensive coverage of mobile networks – which have famously leap-frogged the diffusion of traditional phone lines – means that a new form of Internet access is available. In one sense, mobile Internet is well on its way to leap-frogging fixed broadband globally. In 2010 there were 479 million fixed broadband subscriptions and 667 million mobile broadband (third-generation mobile) subscriptions worldwide (International Telecommunications Union 2010).

The relationship between mobile networks and fixed networks is further complicated, however, by two major developments in infrastructure. First, vast investment by governments and industry worldwide is going into next-generation networks. Underpinned by greater amounts of optical fiber, these networks promise substantial increase in capacity – as the example of Australia's $42 billion National Broadband Network illustrates. Further, the next-generation networks will mark a shift from traditional circuit-switched telecommunications networks to Internet-protocol networks. Second, there are various developments in both mobile networks and wireless networks that have the potential to offer serious increase in capacity. Often discussed under the imprecise rubric of 4G or 5G networks, such developments represent evolution from mobile 3G networks, on the one hand, and Wi-Fi networks (moving to Wi-Max), on the other. There is something of a disconnection between these two big areas of infrastructure development. Next-generation networks are forging ahead, ushering in an era of big, new public–private partnership funding. At the same time, mobile networks, handsets, and applications are building on their enormous user base, offering practical innovations in Internet access now.

The growth in mobile broadband underscores the fact that mobile Internet is now finally a mass media form. Internet on mobile devices was something first tried in the mid-to-late 1990s with the Wireless Access Protocol (WAP), and an adapted mark-up language for showing web pages on mobiles was developed at this time. However, it was not very successful, due to the relative slowness of networks as well as the limitations of handsets. The famous exception was the i-Mode mobile ecosystem developed in Japan, which proved very popular, pioneering mobile content such as ringtones, music, screensavers, and so on. From the late 1990s until 2006, concerted efforts were made in other countries to develop mobile Internet, especially with products and services such as music, games, and downloads, deploying a later version of WAP. However, the breakthrough in mobile Internet came with the advent of Apple's iPhone – and its galvanization of the previously sluggish smartphone market.

The Apple iPhone was launched in mid-2007 and quickly established itself in the mobiles market. The iPhone spurred many competitors to rework or develop their own smartphones. The Internet search titan Google launched its Google phone, based on the Android open-source operating system, and by mid-2011 claimed to have outstripped the iPhone. However, in 2010, Apple launched its iPad, which has resuscitated the tablet computer market. Smartphones and tablets, which switch easily between mobile and Wi-Fi networks, have become a central part of contemporary Internet experience for users able to afford the high cost of these devices – prompting previously successful predecessor technologies (such as the Canadian mobile email technology BlackBerry) to undergo drastic redesign.

The key to the success of smartphones and tablets lies in "apps" (short for "applications"), which have finally offered a viable structure for the potential market in mobile computing, applications, and data as well as creating affordances that make such software easy to use (Goggin 2011c). Apple launched its apps in July 2008, at the same time that the iPhone 3 went on sale. By January 2011, Apple was celebrating the 10 billionth download by the then estimated 160 million iPhone, iPod Touch, and iPad users worldwide – and the availability of some 350 000 apps on its store (Apple 2011). Competitor ventures such as Google's Android Market, BlackBerry App World, and Nokia's Ovi Store (now the apps of choice for Microsoft Phone) are gaining ground. There now exists a bewildering array of apps available, across a number of apps stores and handset types. These apps themselves have wrought a metamorphosis in our notion of mobile phones and media. With smartphones especially, the blurring of telecommunications and Internet is nigh complete, with VOIP (voice over Internet protocols) and video calling via the Internet often indistinguishable, in the user experience, from mobile calls. Most strikingly, social media such as the two leaders – Facebook and Twitter – are increasingly accessed via mobiles devices, making mobile social media the new face of the contemporary Internet. Such mobile social media, and other apps, are now playing an important role too in mobile technologies of place.

Placing Media with Mobiles

As much as space and time, place is a fundamental pillar of human identity (Casey 1983), and it has been a feature of recent theoretical work on media (Falkheimer and Jansson 2006). Place is also a key category of understanding the dynamics of new media. Commonly, new media have been thought to diminish or depreciate the role of place. For instance, in his influential 1985 book *No Sense of Place*, Joshua Meyrowitz raised concerns that electronic media were leading to a "nearly total dissociation of physical place and social 'place'" (Meyrowitz 1985: 115). With mobile media – even more so than the embedded, embodied contexts of watching television, consuming books or newspapers, listening to music or radio, or using the Internet – this sense of place has an odd ring (so to say). From their inception, mobile phones have been associated with a great solicitude for emplacement. Most obviously, users of mobile phones repeatedly speak of, text about, or make images of where they are – a theme of early mobile communication scholarship (Laurier 2001). As mobile media have developed, there has unfolded a profound two-way set of transactions between place and mobiles, whereby "place has been affected profoundly by the micro-scale of (largely localized) experiences of networked mobility" (Wilken and Goggin 2012), as well as other kinds of mobilities; and, for its part, place is woven into, and conditions, the dynamics of mobile media.

The cellular mobile industry has been keenly interested in location-based services for many years, especially since governments and regulators, such as the US Federal Communications Commission, stipulated that carriers were obliged to provide emergency services dispatchers with the telephone number of an emergency caller and the location of the cell site or base station transmitting the call (Goggin 2006). Such moves by policymakers provided additional impetus for cell phone operators to develop location technologies and capabilities for commercial purposes. Early mobile location-based services centered on providing information to users triggered by information regarding their location – but these were slow to develop. One class of services that drew upon location capabilities of mobiles and did achieve some greater success involved the use of Bluetooth – the short-range wireless protocol – for advertising, promotion, and user interaction with environments. Alongside the development of early mobile location-based services, another class of devices developed during the 2000s that would prove vastly influential. This was the satellite navigation (satnav) device, which used global positioning satellite (GPS) technology in conjunction with a database of information taken from street directory publishers to provide in-car navigation for drivers. Initially satnavs were built into cars, developed by leading companies such as Garmin and TomTom. But, within a few years, portable, personal navigation devices were replacing street directories, and potentially integrating with smartphones and PDAs.

Satnavs are a prosaic yet fascinating instance of the rise of mapping and location technologies. In the early 1990s there was strong interest in using the capabilities of GPS, a pervasive network of satellites first established by the military, for civilian, commercial, and noncommercial purposes. Mobile phones began to incorporate GPS technology, meaning that there was the possibility of triangulating location through both these satellite position technologies and also mobile telecommunications networks. Yet, it was the satnav that really gained the first solid acceptance. Once satnavs had become popular and relatively more affordable, establishing the profitability of the dedicated companies that specialized in them, mobile phone companies were quick to mount a competitive response. The obvious path for mobile phone companies to take, especially with the advent of multimedia and smartphones – as well as the fact that the mobile devices already had GPS built in – was to modify the software and supplant the satnav devices. Thus, a number of mobile phone manufacturers – Nokia most prominently, perhaps – made a concerted pitch to take a share of the domestic satnav market. However, moves by the mobile phone vendors to annex the satnav market via software extensions were nowhere near as successful as something rather unpredictable: the rise of Google Maps (and its companion program Google Earth), released during 2005. Google Maps for Mobile followed in 2006 (and a Maps Navigation app exclusively for Android phones in 2009), and Google's cartographic tour de force was quickly established as the first choice of many mobile users.

While there had been for some years experiments with new and different kinds of location technologies for mobiles – conceptualized as "locative media" – as well as the availability of prosaic applications such as enhanced emergency call services (such as E911 in the USA), the first mass uses of location technologies on mobiles were really represented by the wave of mapping, navigation, and wayfinding applications, such as satnav and Google Maps (the "geospatial web" appearing on mobiles), that appeared from 2005 onward. Soon after, location-aware and context-sensitive technologies became popular in a number of countries. One country where these have been emerging is the USA, where Pew Internet research undertaken in late 2010 found that 4 percent of online adults used a location-based service such as Foursquare or Gowalla. It was found that a higher proportion of users who accessed the Internet via mobile (7 percent) or wireless technologies (5 percent) used "geosocial" or location-based services, and the same was true of online adults aged 18–29 years (8 percent) (Pew Internet 2010). In research on location-based services released by Microsoft in early 2011, the countries that featured as early adopters were Japan and the USA. The top services used were overwhelmingly bound up with everyday place negotiation: GPS (70 percent), weather alerts (46 percent), traffic updates (38 percent), restaurant information and reviews (38 percent), and locating the nearest convenience stores (36 percent). Social networking (18 percent), gaming (10 percent), and geo-tagging photos (6 percent) lagged behind, alongside enhanced 911 (9 percent) (Microsoft 2011).

The emergence of everyday locative media has especially focused interest upon "geosocial" applications, such as Brightkite, Foursquare, Latitude, Loopt, and Whrrl, as well as the social networking capabilities being designed for other applications such as Facebook or Twitter. As is often the case with new media, these popular applications were preceded by early experiments that attracted much attention and debate – for example, the famous Dodgeball (USA) and Lovegety (Japan) mobile social software ("mososo") of the late 1990s and early 2000s. Another precursor to present locative media was the set of practices around camera phones: sharing, tagging, and annotating locations through photos. What has changed is the extent of access and use of such mobile locative media, especially with the steady diffusion of smartphones. Such "geomedia," especially as social media applications, are still in their relative infancy. Further, assumptions about their significance are often culturally specific, and propositions regarding their implications need to be approached carefully. For instance, this chapter was finished while travelling in Ecuador, South America. In Ecuador, there is widespread use of mobiles among most sectors of the population, burgeoning use of mobile Internet (a principal method for the country to achieve higher levels of Internet access in its national plan), and, among the middle- and upper-classes, a discourse concerning digital culture centering on Web 2.0. Yet use of smartphones and tablets in public places – a key theme of debates about location-based technology – is constrained by fairly obvious concerns regarding theft and personal security. Thus, Ecuador's capital city, Quito, has provided public Wi-Fi in many places, but take-up has been patchy – in part because multimedia mobile devices remain relatively expensive and a target for robbery. The uneven, culturally specific development of location technologies around the world is important to consider as debate takes off about topics such as the nature of place and space in such social, locative, mobile media (Gordon and de Souza e Silva, 2011; Wilken and Goggin 2012); the gathering of personal information by companies through locative media; the ethics of negotiation concerning sharing information about one's location when using geosocial media (such as Foursquare) in public places (de Souza e Silva and Frith 2012); interfaces and embodiment in locative media (Farman 2012); and the "encoding" of place-based information through location technologies – that is, what kinds of infrastructures and media ecologies are being created, and what rights publics, citizens, and users have to avail themselves of such information (Goggin 2012).

Conclusion

There is no doubt that mobility is a cardinal logic in new media dynamics, especially as represented by the kind of mobile media discussed in this chapter. The three-decade rise of mobiles from the late 1970s to the early 2010s has had far-reaching implications for how we understand media. The diffusion of cellular mobiles has seen concerns related to telecommunications and data networks move into center stage in media, whereas previously they were not regarded as mainstream media concerns. The mobile has quickly established itself as a global technology, but, more than this, has become a new medium in its own right.

Accordingly, mobiles are now a topic of equal importance alongside other long-established areas for those of us interested in the media. As new media, mobiles possess their own dynamics, drawing from the histories of telephony, telecommunications, and wireless technologies and the political and cultural economies of cellular mobiles, as well as the contemporary social innovations and cultural practices associated with the technology. Text messaging is a key example discussed in this chapter, but there are many aspects of mobile phone cultures (established especially through the period of mass take-up in the 1990s and early 2000s) where we see continuing evolution and adaptation in different contexts of use.

Especially as mobiles have become a fully fledged participators in media, their own dynamics have become much more complicated. Moreover, their interactions with other kinds of media – especially the Internet – have become richer and recursive. And the contribution of mobiles to the general dynamics of new media has gained greatly in significance. The interconnectedness between mobiles and other kinds of media can be observed across the various hybrid domains given much attention during the first decade of the twenty-first century, such as mobile television (discussed here). It turns out that the marriage between one media form, mobiles, and another, such as television, has been neither so smooth nor so felicitous as it was first hoped it would be. This comes as no surprise to the historian of new media – and much remains in development, in any case, with these varieties of mobile media. What is most striking, however, is the interaction between mobiles and the Internet, not only in terms of what the future of mobile media portends but in the general scene of media that is unfolding. There is a great fragmentation and proliferation of media devices, applications, and content, yet also strong logics that are reassembling these. Here smartphones have proved – for a few years at least – a powerful force in mobility, upon which much emotion, energy, connection, and capital is being concentrated. Yet mobile media, as media technology, are in a very dynamic stage of development, making them screens to watch, devices to touch and feel, and media by which to comprehend, produce, and, as in the watchword of the age, share for a very great number of the world's citizens.

References

Apple (2011) "Apple's App Store Downloads Top 10 Billion." www.apple.com/pr/library/2011/01/22appstore.html.

Balbi, G. (2010) "Radio before Radio: Araldo Telefonico and the Invention of Italian Broadcasting." *Technology and Culture*, 51, 786–808.

Balbi, G. and Prario, B. (2009) "Back to the Future: The Past and Present of Mobile TV" in G. Goggin and L. Hjorth, eds., *Mobile Technologies: From Telecommunications to Media.* New York: Routledge, pp. 161–173.

Baron, N.S. (2008) *Always On: Language in an Online and Mobile World.* Oxford and New York: Oxford University Press.

Braudel, F. (1972–1973) *The Mediterranean and the Mediterranean World in the Age of Philip II*, trans. S. Reynolds. London: Collins.

Bria, A., Kärrberg, P., and Andersson, P. (2007) "TV in the Mobile or TV for the Mobile: Challenges and Changing Value Chains." Paper presented at the 18th annual IEEE

International Symposium on Personal, Indoor and Mobile Radio Communications, Athens, Greece (September 3–7).

Brown, B., Green, N., and Harper, R., eds. (2001) *Wireless World: Social and Interactional Aspects of the Mobile Age*. London: Springer.

Bruns, A. (2008) *Blogs, Wikipedia,* Second Life, *and Beyond: From Production to Produsage*. New York: Peter Lang.

Bulkeley, W.M. (2010) "Social TV: Relying on Relationships to Rebuild TV Audiences." *MIT Technology Review* 10(May/June). www.technologyreview.com/communications/25084 /?a=f.

Burgess, J. and Green, J. (2009) *YouTube: Online Video and Participatory Culture*. Cambridge, UK, and Malden, MA: Polity.

Canzler, W., Kaufmann, V., and Kesselring, S., eds. (2008) *Tracing Mobilities: Towards a Cosmopolitan Perspective*. Aldershot and Burlington, VT: Ashgate.

Casey, E. (1983) *Getting Back into Place: Towards a Renewed Understanding of the Place-World*. Bloomington, IN: Indiana University Press.

Castells, M. (2009) *Communication Power*. Oxford and New York: Oxford University Press.

Christ, P. and Pogrzeba, P. (1999) "Introducing Mobile Multimedia Broadcasting Services" in H. Leopold and N.N. García, eds., *Proceedings of 4th European Conference on Multimedia Applications, Services and Techniques*. Berlin: Springer, pp. 564–572.

Crystal, D. (2008) *Txtng: The Gr8 Db8*. New York: Oxford University Press.

Cui, Y., Chipchase, J., and Jung, Y. (2007) "Personal TV: A Qualitative Study of Mobile TV users." Paper presented at EuroITV 2007, Amsterdam, The Netherlands (May 24–25).

Curwen, P. and Whalley, J. (2008) "Mobile Television: Technological and Regulatory Issues." *Info*, 10, 40–64.

De Souza e Silva, A. and Frith, J. (2012) *Mobile Interfaces in Public Spaces: Locational Privacy, Control, and Urban Sociability*. New York: Routledge.

de Renesse, R. (2011) "Mapping Digital Media: Mobile TV: Challenges and Opportunities Beyond 2011." *Open Society*. http://www.soros.org/reports/mapping-digital-media -mobile-tv-challenges-and-opportunities-beyond-2011.

Donner, J. (2009) "Mobile Media on Low-Cost Handsets: The Resiliency of Text Messaging Among Small Enterprises in India (and Beyond)" in G. Goggin and L. Hjorth, eds., *Mobile Technologies: From Telecommunications to Media*. New York: Routledge, pp. 93–104.

Ducheneaut, N.M., Oehlberg, L., Moore, R.J., et al. (2008) "Social TV: Designing for Distributed, Sociable Television Viewing." *International Journal of Human–Computer Interaction*, 24, 136–154.

Falkheimer, J. and Jansson, A., ed. (2006) *Geographies of Communication: The Spatial Turn in Media Studies*. Götenberg: Nordicom.

Farman, J. (2012) *Mobile Interface Theory: Embodied Space and Locative Media*. New York: Routledge.

Fischer, C. (1992) *America Calling: A Social History of the Telephone to 1940*. Berkeley, CA: University of California Press.

Goggin, G. (2006) *Cell Phone Culture: Mobile Technology in Everyday Life*. London and New York: Routledge.

Goggin, G. (2011a) *Global Mobile Media*. London and New York: Routledge.

Goggin, G. (2011b) "Telephone Media: An Old Story" in D.W. Park, N.W. Jankowski, and S. Jones, eds., *The Long History of New Media: Technology, Historiography, and Newness in Context*. New York: Peter Lang, pp. 231–252.

Goggin, G. (2011c) "Ubiquitous Apps: Politics of Openness in Global Mobile Cultures." *Digital Creativity*, 22, 147–157.

Goggin, G. (2012) "Encoding Place: The Politics of Mobile Location Technologies" in R. Wilken and G. Goggin, eds., *Mobile Technology and Place*. New York: Routledge, pp. 198–212.

Goggin, G. and Spurgeon, C. (2008) "Mobile Messaging and the Crisis in Participation Television" in M. Hartmann, P. Rössler, and J. Höflich, eds., *After the Mobile Phone? Social Changes and the Development of Mobile Communication*. Berlin: Frank and Timme, pp. 55–68.

Gordon, E. and de Souza e Silva, A. (2011) *Net Locality: Why Location Matters in a Networked World*. New York: John Wiley.

Harper, R., Palen, L., and Taylor, A., eds. (2005) *The Inside Text: Social, Cultural and Design Perspectives on SMS*. Dordrecht: Springer.

Hartley, J. (2008) *Television Truths*. Malden, MA: Blackwell.

He, Z. (2008) "SMS in China: A Major Carrier of the Nonofficial Discourse Universe." *Information Society*, 24, 182–190.

International Telecommunications Union (ITU) (2000) "Mobile Cellular Subscribers." www.itu.int/ITU-D/ICTEYE/Indicators/Indicators.aspx.

International Telecommunications Union (ITU) (2010) "Mobile Cellular Subscriptions." www.itu.int/ITU-D/ICTEYE/Indicators/Indicators.aspx.

Kasesniemi, E.-L. (2003) *Mobile Messages: Young People and a New Communication Culture*. Tampere: Tampere University Press.

Katz, J.E. (2003) *Machines That Become Us: The Social Context of Personal Communication Technology*. New Brunswick, NJ: Transaction.

Katz, J.E. and Aakhus, M., eds. (2002) *Perpetual Contact: Mobile Communication, Private Talk, Public Performance*. Cambridge: Cambridge University Press.

Laurier, E. (2001) "Why People Say Where They Are During Mobile Phone Calls." *Environment and Planning D: Society and Space*, 19, 485–504.

Lemstra, W., Hayes, V., and Groenewegen, J., eds. (2011) *The Innovation Journey of Wi-Fi: The Road to Global Success*. Cambridge and New York: Cambridge University Press.

Licoppe, C. (2004) "'Connected' Presence: The Emergence of a New Repertoire for Managing Social Relationships in a Changing Communication Technoscape." *Environment and Planning D: Society and Space*, 22, 135–156.

Lobato, R. (2010) "Creative Industries and Informal Economies: Lessons from Nollywood." *International Journal of Cultural Studies*, 13, 337–354.

Lovink, G. and Niederer, S., eds. (2008) *Video Vortex Reader: Responses to YouTube*. Amsterdam: Institute of Network Cultures. http://networkcultures.org/wpmu/portal/files/2008/10/vv_reader_small.pdf.

Marvin, C. (1988) *When Old Technologies Were New: Thinking about Electric Communication in the Late Nineteenth Century*. New York: Oxford University Press.

Meyrowitz, J. (1985) *No Sense of Place: The Impact of Media on Social Behavior*. New York: Oxford University Press.

Microsoft (2011) "Location-Based Services are Poised for Growth." www.microsoft.com/download/en/details.aspx?id=3250.

Mueller, M. (1997) *Universal Service: Competition, Interconnection and Monopoly in the Making of the American Telephone System*. Cambridge, MA: MIT Press.

Murray, J.B. Jr., (2001) *Wireless Nation: The Frenzied Launch of the Cellular Revolution in America*. Cambridge, MA: Perseus.

Noam, E. and Pupillo, L.M. (2008) *Peer-to-Peer Video: The Economics, Policy, and Culture of Today's New Mass Medium.* Dordrecht: Springer.

Noam, E., Groebel, J., and Gerbarg, D., eds. (2004) *Internet Television.* Mahwah, NJ: Lawrence Erlbaum.

Okada, T. (2005) "Youth Culture and the Shaping of Japanese Mobile Media: Personalization and the *Keitai* Internet as Multimedia" in M. Ito, D. Okabe, and M. Matsuda, eds., *Personal, Portable, Pedestrian: Mobile Phones in Japanese Life.* Cambridge, MA: MIT Press, pp. 41–60.

Oksman, V. (2010) *The Mobile Phone: A Medium in Itself.* Espoo: VTT Publications.

Owen, B.M. (1999) *The Internet Challenge to Television.* Cambridge, MA: Harvard University Press.

Pew Internet (2010) *4% of Online Americans Use Location-Based Services.* Washington, DC: Pew Internet. www.pewinternet.org/Reports/2010/Location-based-services.aspx.

Sheller, M. and Urry, J., eds. (2004) *Tourism Mobilities: Places to Play, Places in Play.* London: Routledge.

Spurgeon, C. and Goggin, G. (2007) "Mobiles into Media: Premium Rate SMS and the Adaptation of Television to Interactive Communication Cultures." *Continuum*, 21, 317–329.

Steen, H.U. (2009) "Technology Convergence, Market Divergence: Fragmentation of Standards in Mobile Digital Broadcasting Carriers." *Information Systems and e-Business Management*, 7, 319–345.

Turner, G. and Tay, J. (2010) "Not the Apocalypse: Television Futures in the Digital Age." *International Journal of Digital Television*, 1, 31–50.

Urry, J. (2000) *Sociology beyond Societies: Mobilities for the Twenty-First Century.* London: Routledge.

Wilken, R. and Goggin, G. (2012) "Mobilising Place: Conceptual Currents and Controversies" in R. Wilken and G. Goggin, eds., *Mobile Technology and Place.* New York: Routledge, pp. 3–25.

Yu, H. (2004) "The Power of Thumbs: The Politics of SMS in Urban China." *Journal of Asia-Pacific Studies*, 2, 31–44.

12

Make Room for the Wii

Game Consoles and the Construction of Space

Ben Aslinger

On April Fools' Day 2011, the popular gaming site IGN released a fake press release from PopCap Games profiling the upcoming UK and Ireland Christmas launch of the PlayWave, the first microwave game console (IGN 2011). With a touch screen in the door, the game Bejeweled preloaded into the device, and a "playtime" setting that cooked food according to a player's progress in the game, PopCap Games' fictional product satirized the growing proliferation of devices on which consumers can access and play games and the move of gaming away from the television-connected console into new spaces and new technologies. While humorous, the press release from the casual games developer highlighted an element of truth that lay beneath the April Fools' stunt – that so-called casual games signal profound changes in the gaming industry and that a multiplication of gaming platforms raises questions about how, where, and when we will play. By choosing to fictionally embed game technology into a kitchen appliance, PopCap Games also humorously highlighted a move away from highly masculinized game consoles to technologies associated with the kitchen, domesticity, and cultural constructions of femininity.

In January 2011, Sega began testing a new device called the Toylet in locations around Tokyo (Geere 2011; Parfitt 2011). Attached to urinals in men's restrooms, Toylets allow men to use the force and direction of urine to play mini-games that are broken up by advertising messages. Both Geere's and Parfitt's stories profile the movement of play into perhaps one of the most unlikely locations while reinforcing a kind of Orientalist fascination with patterns of Japanese technological usage. Sega's bathroom console is also an odd reintroduction into game hardware production for a firm that was once a major console manufacturer of the Genesis and Dreamcast systems but who restructured to become primarily a game publisher after the rise of the Sony PlayStation.

This chapter examines mobility through a consideration of how the game console has been defined and located and how industrial and cultural constructions of hardware, software, and distribution enable and disable forms of textual, player, and

A Companion to New Media Dynamics, First Edition. Edited by John Hartley, Jean Burgess, and Axel Bruns.
© 2013 John Wiley & Sons, Ltd. Published 2015 by John Wiley & Sons, Ltd.

device mobility. Michael Nitsche (2008: 15–16) analyzes five planes for analyzing space in video game cultures: mediated space (the game environment as rendered onscreen), fictional space (the player's imagined involvement with the narrative or game environment), play space (the physical environment and setting in which play is located and the location of game hardware), social space (interactions with other players and nonplayers), and rule-based space (the ways that game hardware, game engines, and algorithms construct sound, AI, levels, and so on). I am interested in extending Nitsche's taxonomy of game spaces by considering how the dynamics and problematics of location and mobility and the particularities of the gaming industry and gaming experiences add levels of complexity to the registers of space in game cultures. I am also interested in how digital media studies could benefit from further exploring the ludic, machinic, and imagined notions of space in what Alexander Galloway (2006) has called the "algorithmic culture" of games. Given that space is constructed in onscreen worlds and that players construct and navigate both physical and "virtual" worlds, the connections and disjunctures between different types of space in game design and game cultures deserve further exploration. I begin this chapter by examining the difficulties associated with locating the console in domestic spaces and how locating devices for play might add to or challenge definitions of domestic space that place television at the center. I then examine how a proliferation of play devices and debates over how consoles are distributed and what constitutes a console affect game mobilities in the transnational gaming industry.

Locating the Game Console

In her book *Make Room for Television*, Lynn Spigel (1992) argues that the introduction of the television dovetailed with changes in the architectural design and layout of houses in mid-century America. Raymond Williams (2003) argues that the introduction of the television enabled new forms of citizenship; the introduction of the television as a centerpiece of the living room in expanding postwar suburbs along with the rise of automobile culture helped to create mobile privatization. Both Spigel and Williams argue that the incorporation of television into everyday life and into domestic spaces changed the ways that television owners and viewers saw the world and their space in it.

Given that game consoles have been present in millions of homes since the success of the Atari 2600 in the 1970s, the question of how video game systems enter the home and how they affect the layout and design of space is an important one. Michael Nitsche writes,

> We are fairly familiar with our physical home environment: the television set, the favorite chair one sits on when playing games, the game controller, one's physical needs such as the ordered pizza, the preferred beverage, the level of lighting and sound to optimize the game experience. (2008: 42)

What is interesting to me is that Nitsche chooses his words carefully, arguing that "we are *fairly* familiar" (emphasis added) with our play spaces. As a gamer and a game scholar, Nitsche recognizes that games have the potential to render spaces unfamiliar and the remainder of his sentence highlights the intricate ways in which players set up their home environments and the kinds of planning and design activities that are conducted before intense play commences. Game players navigate where to locate game consoles; where to store game controllers, peripherals, and cartridges/discs; where to position televisions in relation to windows to avoid distracting glare from sunlight; and how to maintain optimal distance between the player's body and the screen so that game play is immersive without being too immersive. While gaming has been demonized as a cultural practice to blame for a lack of psychological development and physical mobility (i.e., the arguments that gaming leads young players to not move into new social circles and to retreat into the imaginary worlds of game space, leading them to become socially maladjusted – and potentially violent – adolescents, and that the "endless" hours of sedentary play are in part complicit in rising childhood obesity rates), scholars such as Melanie Swalwell (2011) argue that gaming has always been embodied – even if play has been embodied in nuanced ways visible only to those immersed in or familiar with game cultures. In addition to Swalwell's analysis of small-scale and micro forms of embodiment in game play, peripherals such as the Nintendo PowerPad illustrate that gaming was "active" and embraced a visible physicality long before motion-sensor technologies were incorporated into game peripherals. Thinking about movement or mobility as a new thing that is made possible by consoles such as the Nintendo Wii and peripherals such as the Sony Move and Microsoft Kinect ignores the complicated and circumscribed forms of movement and mobility that were part of gaming cultures and play practices when most game technologies (except the Nintendo Game Boy) depended on wired connections. We risk reinforcing the notion that physical mobility only became an identifiable part of game culture with the rise of wireless controllers, networked distribution, and/or the possibility of cloud-based gaming. In the process, we risk simplifying the history of video and computer games and dismissing the complicated ways that players have negotiated embodiment, physicality, and mobility in game cultures, play practices, and play spaces.

I encountered the challenge of balancing the domestic space of the living room with the physical space required for game play shortly after I purchased the Nintendo Wii console. Motion-controlled game systems require installation in spaces that allow a range of motion, thus privileging (or requiring) larger living rooms or play spaces. Excited about playing, I quickly hooked up the Wii in the living room of my one-bedroom apartment in the metro area of a major city on the eastern seaboard of the USA, where space is at a premium. Playing Wii tennis, I moved the Wii wand to return a forehand volley and rammed my hand into the wall of my apartment so hard it tore some skin off of my knuckles. The next day, I rearranged all of the furniture in my living room so that I could play without physical injury to my digits. I relate this anecdote because it illustrates the ways that players must redesign or customize play spaces in order to take advantage of game peripherals that rely on accelerometers or motion sensors.

While Lynn Spigel examines the ways that the introduction of the television helped to create the den or the living room by influencing architecture and home construction, the required dimensions of play space mean that users must sacrifice their own visions of domestic space to those required by the demands of the console and/or game hardware. In many cases, players must also rework living spaces designed with the physically passive activity of television spectatorship in mind into spaces in which more active modes of play are possible.

Game consoles are artifacts of modern industrial design, their clean lines and curves helping to make them technological fetishes not just because of the raw technical power inside but also because of the beauty of the devices themselves. In commercial and promotional campaigns, consoles become ornamental and decorative, their minimal modernism often paired with clean, modernist furniture. The Fall Inspiration 2011 catalog for the furniture retailer Crate & Barrel in the USA illustrated that game consoles such as the Xbox 360 could be integrated with the firm's modernist furniture. This articulation of gaming technologies with a sophisticated aesthetic sensibility was also illustrated by Sony's marketing campaigns, where avant-garde directors such as Chris Cunningham (2003) created ads for the PlayStation, and ads for the PS3 mixed elements of surrealism, horror, and science fiction/fantasy in ways that addressed a sophisticated consumer ("PS3 Baby Commercial" 2006; "PS3 Eggs" 2006; "PS3 Rubik's Cube Commercial" 2006).

When the Kinect launched in Japan, Kotaku's Brian Ashcraft (2010a, 2010b, 2010c) wrote that Microsoft had rulers available so that Japanese – especially Tokyo – consumers could measure their apartments. According to Ashcraft, the spatial dimensions indicated by the ruler appeared inadequate for the range of motion required by the Kinect. While some Kinect games need eight feet of space "to hit the sweetspot of certain games," the ruler Microsoft made available to Japanese consumers measured only 0.9 meters (2.9 feet). Ashcraft's piece, titled "How to Play Kinect in a Tiny Japanese Apartment," illustrates how game magazines, sites, and Microsoft as a corporation had to educate consumers on how to design/redesign living spaces to make room for the Kinect.

Microsoft was not the first manufacturer forced to educate players about how to set up or navigate play space. In fact, the Wii console always alerts players with both text and graphics to "allow adequate room around you during game play." Now-defunct sites such as Wiihaveaproblem.com (Zeller 2006) featured stories of game players who accidentally smashed windows or HD television screens when Wii wand straps broke and wands hurtled through the air, and tips from players such as how one grandfather crafted a museum-like Plexiglass cover so that his grandchildren wouldn't accidentally shatter his new plasma (citation unavailable).

Gizmodo's Matt Buchanan (2011) expressed the hope that the Nyko Zoom, a pair of lenses designed to clip on to the Kinect that reduces the footprint it requires by up to 40 percent, might make the device more attractive and useful to New York City denizens. While Microsoft's attempts to teach Japanese consumers how to construct and manage play space may be read as a desperate attempt for the American console manufacturer to achieve a greater install base on Sony and Nintendo's home turf, the Nyko Zoom illustrates how the design specifications and/or requirements of new game technologies open the door for third-party manufacturers of peripherals and ancillary gaming products to target consumers who want (or need) to work around specifications or limitations. In the case of the Nyko Zoom, it seems that motion-sensor gaming technologies have been made more practical for players living in settings that are less than ideal for the active modes of play preferred by manufacturers and designers. In the process, play has moved from the idealized embodied practice of play endorsed by the dominant players in the game industry to a practical, spatially contingent style of play enabled by an ancillary device installed and calibrated by players.

Limited Spatial Mobilities

Moving outside the domestic spaces where many hardware systems are located means interrogating the limited nature of mobilities in the transnational gaming industry. Mia Consalvo (2006), Hiro Izushi and Yuko Aoyama (2006), and Aphra Kerr (2006) discuss the limited nature of the "global" gaming industry, arguing that the distinct evolution of electronic media industries in national territories, national economic policies, distinct forms of game regulation, localized cultural tastes, different levels of consumer access to games and hardware, and issues of affordability mean that the industry is a transnational but not a truly global one. In her analysis of the Japanese firm Square Enix's business and design practices, Consalvo writes:

> As Square Enix and its competitors seek to enlarge their markets by bringing localized games to the USA and other places, or vice versa, they are at the same time attempting to ensure that this flow is properly controlled – by the interests of transnational corporations. (2006: 131)

Consalvo draws on Timothy Luke's (1995) concept of the technoregion, where corporate control and organization over production processes dominate localized forms of governance. She continues:

> The transnational video game industry is one such technoregion, but even within this region, further boundary markers must be found to help modulate and regulate flow. One such mechanism is localization, but this process only works with individual games – a larger system is needed to deal with consoles, game-related merchandise, and games on a larger scale. Within the technoregion, ironically, geography still matters, as the answer to problems of control (for now) is based on geographic region. (2006: 131)

Even in an age where distributed computing has altered our conceptions of mobility, travel, and access to information and goods, hegemonic players in the gaming industry – such as the big three console manufacturers and the major game publishers Activision, Electronic Arts, Konami, Namco, and Ubisoft – target global game players unevenly and approach national markets in different ways (if a national or regional market is acknowledged at all).

Inhabitants of the USA, the UK, and Japan are most frequently addressed as potential players. However, just because national markets are not addressed does not mean that games do not reach players in territories that are not considered part of the global games market. High piracy rates mean huge amounts of play and high levels of participation in gaming culture, but such forms of play and participation have proven difficult for firms to monetize through legal and commercial channels (Kline et al. 2003). Only recently did major Latin American nations such as Brazil and Mexico become visible as markets for the game industry. A cynical observer might think that the launch of alternative, locally manufactured consoles such as the Zeebo in Brazil and the iSec in China illustrate the potential presence of markets and that local firms serve as de facto research and development arms for major console makers and publishers. One might also wonder how effectively local development firms can compete with major publishers and developers in traditional console development; perhaps traditional console gaming is a niche market that will be dominated by firms in the technological capitals of North America, Europe, and Asia while mobile gaming becomes ever more diversified and localized as wireless networks expand faster than broadband networks and smaller development firms can more easily afford the costs of development for handsets. Will console game development retreat to an ever more finite range of locales while mobile gaming development expands internationally? Only time will tell.

The current development of the iSec (previously the Ebox) in China and the launch and failure of the Zeebo in Mexico and Brazil as an entertainment console illustrate issues involved in the flows of game consoles. While computer games such as *World of Warcraft* are extremely popular in China, console makers have had difficulty convincing Beijing to allow traditional consoles into the country (Reisinger 2010; Ashcraft 2011). Consoles such as the Xbox 360 are present in a highly visible gray market, and many game consoles are manufactured within the country. But, in order to legitimize gaming and perhaps capitalize on the Xbox 360 and Kinect's illegality, Lenovo created the local firm Beijing Eedoo Technology to craft a console that is basically a clone of the Kinect and the Xbox 360. The result, the iSec, raises the question of which consoles and devices will reach consumers and how the potential cloning of devices and products might work to create local game economies in territories that are either not targeted by transnational companies or that transnational capital has difficulty penetrating. Whether it succeeds or fails, the iSec can be seen as a call for game scholars to think about the future nature of the branded console and the tightly controlled development ecosystems that have been fundamental to the branded console's success.

Investment in game console production signals that there are financial and personal interests in constructing traditional consoles for local use – even if such consoles are technically inferior to the current-generation game hardware that dominates markets in industrialized nations. While entrepreneurs and venture capitalists in emerging economies such as Brazil and China seem to desire to participate in the console market (and the software and peripheral markets that traditional consoles create), the demise of the console or the death of console games seems a common refrain in the English-language game press and the game blogs that represent the "core" of the industry in the global north.

In my own analysis of the launch of the Zeebo console in 2009 in Brazil, I noted that, despite the console's development as a opportunity to reach the "next billion" gamers in the BRIC nations (Brazil, Russia, India, and China), the Zeebo was largely seen by dominant publishers and established developers as a way to port existing titles, not as a platform for creating new intellectual property (IP) (Aslinger 2010). Even though the console opened up new doors for Latin American developers to create and distribute content that would be regionally or culturally specific, the Zeebo was seen by established developers and publishers in industrialized countries as a way to make their titles more mobile in the "global" gaming industry.

Porting – the work of making games technologically mobile – need not be seen as a way to leverage old IPs. While some games and franchises are tied to particular platforms because games are developed in-house or studios are owned by a major hardware firm (e.g., the Mario franchise and Nintendo; *Halo* and Xbox), other games must be designed to work on various systems. In mobile game development, porting is considered critical work that is necessary to ensure that games work on devices or handsets from different hardware manufacturers and/or different operating systems. Part of the reason for Apple's success in the app and games market is that developers design for one device instead of designing for a range of devices that run the Android operating system. The idea that the closed platform that limits textual mobility and tethers the user to a particular device and to particular wireless providers stimulates innovation flies in the face of received tech wisdom that argues that open platforms stimulate innovation and diversity. In the case of the iPhone, developers need not port if they don't mind their games belonging to one wireless delivery ecosystem.

The rise of mobile and social gaming evidences a proliferation of devices on which consumers can play. Games proliferate on devices and platforms besides the traditional game console, and new forms of gaming such as alternate reality and pervasive gaming (Flanagan 2009; Montola et al. 2009) mean that games have moved out of the living room and into the hands of users on buses and city streets. Games use the materiality of physical spaces and infrastructures as play maps and spaces of play, and limitations of movement in real-life spaces influence level design and what winning conditions in games are possible. While the mobility of games is limited by technology, moving games beyond the television screen enables new populations to play and allows game design to take on real-world situations.

The shift to digital distribution may both accelerate and impede the global flow of games. Piracy will undoubtedly continue as a way of making games more mobile and, in that sense, the rise of networked digital distribution will likely create millions more game players who will be visible to scholars and net observers but largely faceless to transnational capital. However, the ways that geography and connectivity affect distribution may shrink game markets in odd ways. Scholars such as Lisa Parks (2005, 2007) point out that media distribution infrastructures such as undersea cables, cable television wires, cell towers, and broadband Internet infrastructures have physical limits. In her analysis of "where the cable ends" (2007), Parks analyzes how people access television in remote Californian communities. Game scholars must ask what happens to the digital distribution of AAA console titles (those titles that cost the most to produce) where the broadband ends. While big console manufacturers and AAA titles need broadband speeds to download, the rise of the mobile web as a major platform in the developing world has led to increased investments in casual games and mobile games. But such games come at a price that is on top of the cost of connectivity itself.

The move to digital distribution in consoles in the industrialized world ignores the ways that Internet infrastructures are being constructed in many parts of the developing world. Digital distribution involves layers of cost and account maintenance (not to mention the piracy issues sparked by the PlayStation network hack in summer 2011) that may limit game revenues under the regime of the digital in major markets. Consoles may be a gateway for networked digital distribution just like cell phone handsets, but how they construct the technical and economic requirements for participation and play will affect both the industrial and cultural footprints of game systems and game cultures. Finally, the rise of cloud-based gaming and online gaming also depend on server farms that must be built and operated. New forms of mobility, access, and play in game cultures depend on new ways of locating and administering central storage facilities.

Conclusion: Too Many Mobilities to Count?

While I have spent this chapter analyzing debates over locating the console and the limited physical and spatial mobility of games in a transnational framework, these are by no means the only issues connected to hardware and software flows. Assumptions about cultural taste made by executives at transnational firms, decisions by censorship and classification boards, the cost of games, and the costs of operating branch offices affect where games are made and where they are released. The release of Tecmo Koei's *Dead or Alive: Dimensions* was canceled in Sweden, Denmark, and Norway for fear that the game would be perceived as violating a Swedish law against child pornography (Brown 2011). Game spaces such as the environment of *L.A. Noire*, *Red Dead Redemption*'s western frontier, and *Fallout 3*'s postapocalyptic Washington, DC, are meticulously created for us to play in and through. Game costs limit the textual mobility of games, especially given the fact that games for most systems are cheapest within the USA. Local economic policies and tax cuts for gaming firms influence where firms go and where games are made, as municipal, county/state, and national governments fight to keep firms local or encourage firms to relocate for a "better" business climate.

In an age where iPods, iPhones, Android smartphones, the iPad and other tablets, handheld game devices, and the PC are all considered to be viable game platforms, why does the stand-alone game console attached to the television matter? What are the forces that enable how and where people can access games and how and where people can play? Gerard Goggin writes, "The place of the Internet in games has grown exponentially since the mid-1990s, with many gamers taking some form of networked game architecture and interaction as a natural thing" (2011: 99). With game consoles in millions of homes and new consoles in our hands, we have increasingly taken for granted how we access games and how we play. Taking new forms of interaction and play for granted blinds us to the fact that people may play differently or not at all.

References

Ashcraft, B. (2010a) "How to Play Kinect in a Tiny Japanese Apartment." *Kotaku*. http://kotaku.com/5716740/how-to-play-kinect-in-a-tiny-japanese-apartment.

Ashcraft, B. (2010b) "Kinect Clone Maker Understands Chinese Gamers 'Better.'" *Kotaku*. http://kotaku.com/#!5625193/kinect-clone-maker-understands-chinese-gamers-better.

Ashcraft, B. (2010c) "This Won't Help Kinect Work in Tiny Apartments." *Kotaku*. http://kotaku.com/5694010/this-wont-help-kinect-work-in-tiny-apartments.

Ashcraft, B. (2011) "Are China's Days of Cockblocking Console Makers Numbered?" *Kotaku*. http://kotaku.com/5818443/are-chinas-days-of-cockblocking-console-makers-numbered.

Aslinger, B. (2010) "Video Games for the 'Next Billion': The Launch of the Zeebo Console." *Velvet Light Trap*, 66, 15–25.

Brown, N. (2011) "*Nordic* Dead Or Alive *Release Cancelled.*" *Edge*. www.edge-online.com/news/nordic-dead-or-alive-release-cancelled.

Buchanan, M. (2011) "Nyko Zoom for Kinect Lets You Play in the Tiniest Apartments." *Gizmodo*. http://gizmodo.com/5809139/nyko-zoom-for-kinect-lets-you-play-in-even-the-most-cramped-quarters.

Consalvo, M. (2006) "Console Video Games and Global Corporations: Creating a Hybrid Culture." *New Media & Society*, 8(1), 117–137.

Cunningham, C. (2003) "Mental Wealth." *The Work of Director Chris Cunningham: A Collection of Music Videos, Short Films, Video Installations, and Commercials*. DVD: Palm Pictures.

Flanagan, M. (2009) *Critical Play: Radical Game Design*. Cambridge, MA: MIT Press.

Galloway, A. (2006) *Gaming: Essays on Algorithmic Culture*. Minneapolis, MN: University of Minnesota Press.

Geere, D. (2011) "Sega Installs 'Toylets' Game Consoles in Japanese Urinals." *Wired*. www.wired.co.uk/news/archive/2011-01/06/sega-toylets-japan.

Goggin, G. (2011) *Global Mobile Media*. New York: Routledge.

IGN. (2011) "April Fools: Microwave Game Console Allows Gamers to Play While They Cook." *IGN*. http://pc.ign.com/articles/115/1159051p1.html.

Izushi, H. and Aoyama, Y. (2006) "Industry Evolution and Cross-Sectoral Skill Transfers: A Comparative Analysis of the Video Game Industry in Japan, the United States, and the United Kingdom." *Environment and Planning A*, 38, 1843–1861.

Kerr, A. (2006) *The Business and Culture of Digital Games*. Thousand Oaks, CA: Sage.

Kline, S., Dyer-Witheford, N., and de Peuter, G. (2003) *Digital Play: The Interaction of Technology, Culture, and Marketing*. Montreal, QC: McGill-Queen's University Press.

Luke, T. (1995) "New World Order or Neo-world Orders: Power, Politics and Ideology in Informationalizing Glocalities," in M. Featherstone, S. Lash, and R. Robertson, eds., *Global Modernities*. London: Sage, pp. 91–107.

Montola, M., Stenros, J., and Waern, A., eds. (2009) *Pervasive Games: Theory and Design*. Burlington, MA: Morgan Kaufmann.

Nitsche, M. (2008) *Video Game Spaces: Image, Play, and Structure in 3D Game Worlds*. Cambridge, MA: MIT Press.

Parfitt, B. (2011) "Sega Launches Urinal Console." *MCV UK*. www.mcvuk.com/news/42413/Sega-launches-urinal-console.

Parks, L. (2005) *Cultures in Orbit: Satellites and the Televisual*. Durham, NC: Duke University Press.

Parks, L. (2007) "Where the Cable Ends: Television Beyond Fringe Areas" in S. Banet-Weiser, C. Chris, and A. Freitas, eds., *Cable Visions: Television Beyond Broadcasting*. New York: New York University Press, pp. 103–126.

"PS3 Baby Commercial." (2006) www.youtube.com/watch?v=gqkNPcUMffU.

"PS3 Eggs." (2006) www.youtube.com/watch?v=DyFrekxy7wg&feature=related.

"PS3 Rubix Cube Commercial." (2006) www.youtube.com/watch?v=7qamwVJaYW8.

Reisinger, D. (2010) "Report: Lenovo to Release Own Game Console." *CNET*. http://news.cnet.com/8301-13506_3-20014888-17.html.

Spigel, L. (1992) *Make Room for TV: Television and the Family Ideal in Post-war America*. Chicago, IL: University of Chicago Press.

Swalwell, M. (2011) "Movement and Kinaesthetic Responsiveness." Paper presented at Console-ing Passions, Adelaide, SA (July 22).

Williams, R. (2003 [1974]) *Television: Technology and Cultural Form*. New York: Routledge.

Zeller, Jr., T. (2006) "Wii Have a Problem." *New York Times*. http://thelede.blogs.nytimes.com/2006/12/08/wii-have-a-problem.

Further Reading

Hjorth, L. and Chan, D., eds. (2009) *Gaming Cultures and Place in Asia-Pacific*. New York: Routledge.

Enterprise

13

Improvers, Entertainers, Shockers, and Makers

Charles Leadbeater

Crudely put, there were three main ways someone could make their living from the culture business in the twentieth century. One route was to become an improver, someone who believed the point of culture was to elevate the downtrodden. Improvers were high-minded and well meaning but in danger of being a little patronizing. They headed for jobs at the BBC or one of the publicly funded national arts organizations. A second route was to become an entertainer, someone who believed the point of culture was to give people a good time, to charge them to dance, sing, clap, laugh, cry. Entertainers went into the commercial cultural industries that grew fast in the second half of the century, spurred by television, pop culture, advertising, and retail. Entertainers offered something like fast food: it looked filling but could leave you feeling empty soon after consuming it. The final route was to become a shocker, someone who believed the point of culture was to confront and shock people out of the complacency induced by life in late capitalism. The shockers headed for their garret, warehouse, or maybe just back bedroom to pursue their art and eke out a living as best they could. They wanted neither to lecture people nor to entertain and make money. They claimed they were only interested in their art but to many people the shockers seemed mainly obsessed by themselves.

To make your living in culture you needed to be an improver, an entertainer, or a shocker (or a mixture of two or more). The cultural significance of the web and digital culture, new and social media, is that these have brought back to life at mass scale another way to engage with culture, a new category: makers. Now, instead of experiencing culture as being improved, shocked, or entertained by other people, almost anyone can become, in some measure, a maker themselves. The emergence of this new route to be cultural – the mass making of culture together – has disrupted the old oligopolists and is creating a host of new possibilities that seem exciting and alarming in equal measure.

This chapter first introduces the old cast of cultural players – the improvers, entertainers, and shockers – in a little more detail. It then explains why the rise of

A Companion to New Media Dynamics, First Edition. Edited by John Hartley, Jean Burgess, and Axel Bruns.
© 2013 John Wiley & Sons, Ltd. Published 2015 by John Wiley & Sons, Ltd.

the makers is proving so disruptive to the old order. Finally it concludes by looking at where the more complex relationship between these four forces might be headed.

Improvers see culture as an educative, morally uplifting experience. Exposure to culture should raise people up, above the everyday, mainly material concerns of their lives to see deeper truths or wider possibilities. It should be good for us: a trip to the National Theatre, to a gallery, to a museum; a night with BBC Three; a learned lecture. The point is that culture is built on a giant asymmetry. The people who have culture done for and to them, the audience who are there to be improved, may not fully understand the significance of what is being offered to them. That is why they have to be encouraged to attend and educated to seek out the higher meaning in works of culture. That asymmetry, between those that provide and organize culture, because they know what is what, and those that consume it, who know what they like but little else, explains why leaving culture to the consumer market would be a disaster. Left to their own devices, consumers will not realise what treasures are available to them. They will tend to sink to the level of the lowest common denominator. Seeing the value of nonconsumerist, higher culture requires specialist knowledge. This kind of culture comes with its own ceremonials and mystique, institutions and rituals, high priests and sacred places. As a result and all too easily, this kind of culture can seem to be aloof, patronizing, and exclusionary.

Entertainers have a very different idea of culture: it is something to be enjoyed, activities that provide pleasure and entertainment, excitement and thrills – that mesmerize and amuse. The litmus test for good culture should be whether it is appealing rather than improving. At root it should be all about having fun together by being part of the audience for a great show that takes your breath away or to be moved by a great story, captivated by a line that stays with you. For the entertainers, culture should be accompanied by the antithesis of ceremonial: it should make itself easily available, at the supermarket if that is where the consumers want it. The entertainers, or at least their business backers, talk of culture in terms of assets, properties, auctions, brands, franchises. Cultural production is reduced to content that they develop, acquire, and then distribute to consumers. These industries have come to need blockbusters, stars, and celebrities to sustain themselves. At the end of the twentieth century, creative industries were widely seen as the great economic hope for former industrial cities in the developed world that had lost their economic rationale.

For the entertainers, popularity, reach, and profit – bums on seats – are the measures of success, rather than vague ideals about improving people. The apotheosis of this popular culture is commercial television, which is engaging without being too demanding. It offers people stimulation while they are at rest. As a result it is often wonderful but oddly hollow and disappointing. The entertainers would like us to believe they are no more than pleasure providers. Yet it is not so simple. They provide distractions from a world that seems full of injustice and correctable wrongs as if the chance for one person to get rich quick through a game show were an answer to the problems of social justice. That is where the third group, the shockers, come in.

For the shockers, the point of art and culture is to disturb; not to make everything seem pleasant but to point out how unsettling and unpleasant the world is. There are rarely happy endings in avant-garde art. For the shockers the purpose of art is not to reconcile us to the world but to pit us against it (or at least to show us that we are pitted against it even if we did not realise it). That does not mean, however, that the shockers side with the improvers, with their high-minded sense of moral purpose. On the contrary, the shockers revel in art that questions what is conventionally moral; they see their role as cultural whistle blowers, exposing double standards.

Improvers believe art and culture can help to make the world a better place. Entertainers hope art and culture will distract us, to laugh off whatever ails us. The shockers tend to be bleak: their role is to point out just out unremittingly painful and unjust life is. They offer little solace. To make art that takes people out of their everyday experiences that are shaped by advertising, brands, and the markets, the shockers have to live at the very edge of society themselves, in the moral and economic margins, outside conventional mores and lifestyles, courting the eccentric and idiosyncratic. The nature of their art depends on them being able to separate themselves from the rest of society to gain a brutally honest perspective. The avant-garde are like a guerrilla army of self-styled resistance fighters taking on the comfortable complacency of bourgeois society armed with little more than a paint brush. Many people find modern art remote and impenetrable, perplexing and disturbing. They are supposed to. Shocker art does not set out to give people what they want – pleasing chords and delightful pastoral scenes; it sets out to be dissonant and difficult, to make people think afresh.

Thomas Mann set the tone for this unforgiving kind of art and the apocalyptic artist who produces it in his 1904 story *At the Prophet's*, set in Vienna, then competing with Paris as the center for the avant-garde:

> At the edge of large cities, where street lamps are scarce and policemen walk by twos, are houses where you mount till you can mount no further, up and up into attics under the roof, where pale, young geniuses, criminals of the dream, sit with folded arms and brood; up into cheap studios with symbolic decorations, where solitary and rebellious artists, inwardly consumed, hungry and proud, wrestle in a fog of cigarette smoke with devastatingly ultimate ideals. Here is the end: ice, chastity, null. Here is valid no compromise, no concession. Here the air is so rarefied that the mirages of life no long exist. Here reign defiance and iron consistency, the ego supreme amid despair, here freedom, madness and death hold sway. (1936: 283)

Generations of artists in lofts, studios, warehouses, semi-derelict houses, ripped jeans, and second-hand clothes have been living out a version of Mann's archetype ever since. Artists could only do their job by adopting what Alex Ross describes in *The Rest is Noise* (2007) as a militant asceticism. Avant-garde art deliberately speaks not so much *to* people as often *at* them.

Culture in the developed world in the twentieth century was shaped by the intense relationships between the improvers, entertainers, and shockers, their different values and ideologies. This gave us the familiar distinctions between high and low, popular and elite, commercial and public culture that help to guide us to where we are going and for what: to the Shakespeare or *The Lion King*. The three tendencies compete for the same audiences and sometimes money: the entertainers, with their bawdy mass-market products, constantly threaten to marginalize the worthy improvers and the difficult shockers.

Yet there is as much mixing and blending as there is rivalry. The high-minded improvers are not averse to creating popular, commercially successful shows and products, to pull in the audiences they need to retain their claim to represent the public. The Tate Modern gallery hosts a large commercial operation – books, food, and merchandising – alongside its art. All of culture seems to involve some form of shopping. Some commercial industries, which operate largely without public subsidy, mix the improving and the entertaining, the pleasing and the unsettling, the blockbuster and the niche specialist. Book publishing is a prime example of this blend: many of its products are culturally distinctive and yet also have a commercial value. The book trade, at least large parts of it, has tried to make money, entertain, and improve all at the same time, holding an uneasy internal truce between these conflicting imperatives. Understanding how to make a commercially successful cultural product, something that enters the bloodstream of everyday life – *Harry Potter* – takes huge skill and creativity. Some cultural fields have prospered entirely without subsidy: for example, many museums in the USA and until relatively recently many newspapers. Some of the best television, *The Sporanos* to *The Wire*, has been produced by US commercial networks. For their part, the avant-garde shockers, especially the more successful, often fail to maintain their separation from mainstream commerce. Some of them seem only too willing to make money when the opportunity comes along, to cash in on their celebrity. As the competition among the entertainers has become more intense, so they constantly borrow from trendy subcultures to find the next trend. The shockers frequently find they are not set apart from mainstream culture but merely slightly ahead of it as their cool styles, sounds, and images become conquered by the mainstream faster than ever before.

The improvers, entertainers, and shockers are like sibling rivals: they compete and yet share a common cultural DNA. They see culture as something that should be separate from the rest of life, like money held in a bank. Art distinguishes itself by its account of how this cultural capital is withdrawn. For the entertainers it should be almost as easy as withdrawing cash from an ATM machine: as few barriers as possible should stand in the way of pleasure. For the improvers the important point is that the audience should be asked to do some work, to appreciate the deeper layers of meaning before they can make their withdrawal. For the shockers the point is to make the process difficult and even frustrating: like an ATM machine that only works with an ever-changing pin code.

These kinds of culture are delivered to us by specially skilled producers, working in special places using special skills, and when we enjoy this culture it often involves going to specialized places – galleries, cinemas, museums, concert halls, or just sitting in the sacred shared space of a sofa in front of the glow of a television. The work, whether a book, a film, or a television program, has a clear and separate existence, a start time and an end, a date when it was created and then published, a first and last page. In the twentieth century, cultural experience was mainly associated with watching, listening, and reading. Culture was something done for you and on occasion to you.

Then along came the web.

To make sense of the impact the web is having on culture, it might help to think in terms of the wine industry. The improvers are like the top end of the French industry, Bordeaux and Burgundy, fine products, clothed in mystique. The entertainers are disruptive innovators from the new world, Australia and New Zealand: they create experiences that are reliable and that can be unscrewed and enjoyed. The web means that all over the world, without seeking anyone's permission or knowing what they were doing, people have started to plant their own vines and harvest their own grapes to make their own wine. Sometimes people do this just for their own consumption. But quite a lot of them are creating informal cooperatives to share not just the grapes and the wine but also know-how and technology. They are aided and abetted by people selling new low-cost, high-powered wine-making kits (computers, programs, smartphones, and software) that make all cooperative wine-making possible at low cost. This mass of home-made wine is of highly variable quality. Often it is undrinkable. But some of it is very good indeed and it comes in varieties unimagined by the mainstream industry. Moreover, it comes with a special pleasure for consumers who like to drink wine that is made locally, by people they know. The commercial winners are the people making the kits for the winemakers. They are not at all concerned by what gets made so long as lots of people make wine, enjoy doing so, and want to make more.

The traditional alternative to the mass commercial culture of watching and listening was the more demanding, educational, and ascetic high culture of intellectual inspiration and challenge, the fare provided by the improvers and the shockers. But in the past decade, thanks to the web, an alternative has begun to emerge: a mass culture that is more participative and collaborative, that is about searching, doing, sharing, making, modifying. It is stimulating because through it people become makers, distributors, raters, and rankers and for them culture is something they do with other people: they pass it on rather than sit and watch.

Thanks to the web, culture has become a more complex four-way relationship between the patrician improvers, the lowbrow entertainers, the avant-garde shockers, and the growing rag-bag army of makers, who are an energetic, sometimes mutinous and unruly, force.

The makers are not part of the cozy culture oligopoly. Web culture threatens all the other three players, in different ways, at the same time. The improvers feel threatened because the highly permissive culture of the web seems to democratize taste and judgment, opening the floodgates to all sorts of cultural products and eroding the special position of the cultural elite to control what culture consists of. Their authority, which was their meal ticket, seems shot to shreds. The entertainers feel threatened because their markets are fragmenting and it is becoming well nigh impossible for them to control distribution when copying can be done for free. The entertainers need to reach mass markets but also to control who gets access to their products so that attention can be turned into money. That combination – control over distribution and reaching mass markets – is becoming increasingly difficult to pull off. Meanwhile, the iconoclastic, self-referential shockers suddenly find an alternative geek avant-garde is taking the limelight. This open-source avant-garde seems to espouse a collaborative ethic rather than seek to become superstars. The old cool was to be a lonely artist; the new cool is to be in the midst of a crowd of collaborators. Everyone seems to be losing out to maker culture.

Worse, not only do the improvers, entertainers, and shockers face more competition from the makers but they are also forced to compete with one another more intensely for their share of the cultural market, which suddenly seems a lot smaller than it did. The old, familiar tensions and rivalries have become less predictable as everyone is just a little more desperate and unsettled. Take the book trade as an example. The book trade used to be a civilized business, a place where English graduates could earn a living and pursue their passion for literature built on a coexistence between improvement and entertainment. It was both a commercial business and at the same time a contribution to civilization. As the publisher Jason Epstein put it in the *New York Review of Books*: "Far more than any other medium, books contain civilizations, the ongoing conversation between present and past. Without this conversation we are lost. But books are also a business" (Epstein 2011). But over the past two decades the book trade has become increasingly commercial, driven by the demands of mass-market, scale retailers who demand carefully prepackaged books they know how to sell. The book business was eating itself from within long before the web disrupted it. Once upon a time, book publishers relied on their back list – the fine books they had published in the past that kept on selling – to make money. Now they increasingly rely on celebrity blockbusters and promotable titles: book publishing has become more like a retail business than a high-minded contribution to civilization.

As their markets have fragmented, cultural entertainers have had to become more ruthlessly commercial, and shareholders more risk averse and less forgiving of failure. Popular formats that are guaranteed to hit the button have become more important. That is why Simon Cowell's influence has spread across commercial television in the UK with a series of talent shows that both seek audience involvement in live television – something that is difficult to copy – and create a sure-fire way to sell hit singles. Most of the West End in London now seems to be staging musicals based on famous films or books. The hot theater tickets are to shows that offer a chance to see film and television actors in the flesh. Popular franchises such as *Bridget Jones's Diary* are milked over and again for every last bit of commercial juice. Yet the growing fragility of the entertainment business, based as it is on fragmenting markets, means these commercial producers are more concerned than ever at the public subsidies given to the improvers to provide their high-minded art. The entertainers have started to complain loudly about markets being distorted by subsidies: witness News Corporation's attacks on the BBC.

Yet the improvers too find themselves caught on the horns of a painful dilemma. To maintain its claim to be the public service broadcaster, the BBC has to command a sizeable audience, which means BBC One has to fight toe to toe with the commercial channels ITV1 and Sky. Yet, as BBC One becomes more populist, so other parts of the corporation go in the opposite direction and become more high-minded, to protect the corporation's claims to high quality. Inside most large media organizations there is growing internal strife between those who want to respond to the competition from the web by adapting to new media and those who believe the future lies in sticking to their knitting. It is not just that there is more competition between different media producers but also that there is more tension within them. The job of running a cultural or media organization has become a lot more fraught. The chief dilemma is whether to invest in securing the traditional business – newspapers, books, television – or whether to invest in new media, which offers growth in numbers of clicks and page impressions but not necessarily in revenues. The risk of the first strategy is that it might be a cul-de-sac; the risk of the second is that at some point it will run straight into Apple and Google.

The same tensions run through other fields, such as history and literature. Take history as an example. We have more television-ready, attractive, and articulate young history dons than ever before. They stride across our screens explaining history with a series of passionate gestures and pithy soundbites. That is one response to a more accessible culture. Another response is to make academic history more abstruse, esoteric, and impenetrable. Meanwhile, amateur, do-it-yourself history mushrooms. The study of history is going in all three directions at the same time. Something similar is happening to literature. Literature has responded to the fragmentary culture of the web with publishers investing more in blockbuster and celebrity authors – Lee Child, Steig Larsson, Jamie Oliver. Yet there is also a more rearguard action: more highbrow literature, which seeks to clothe itself in reverential mystery. There are more literary festivals than ever before.

What this means is that old cultural coalitions and categories are further breaking down. Our cultural industries seem to be in the grip of what resembles a civil war in a failed state in which everyone seems to be fighting everyone else. A decade ago, Richard Florida presented the cultural and creative industries as the high road to success to cities, the least impregnable bit of the modern economy. Now the creative industries seem to be in a state of mayhem. Virtually every media business, other than Google or Apple, seems to be searching for a new business model.

Yet, as well as more conflict there are many more new potential alliances. Google is creating a new private–public cultural behemoth with an avaricious advertising machine funding huge public stores of arts, books, video, and text. Google, Apple, and Facebook may find themselves having to invest in public, open-source kinds of culture to forestall regulators inquiring into their monopoly power. Commercial entertainers, games companies, and television programs such as *The X Factor* are creating new ways for people to participate in a commercial version of maker culture. The improvers, the British Library chief among them, increasingly recognize that they need to marry their stores of content with communities of avid users. Even the shockers are learning to adapt to web culture by drawing on the lessons of the participative avant-garde of the 1960s. Allan Kaprow became one of the best-known practitioners of this philosophy, staging "happenings" that were forerunners of contemporary flashmobs, mass alternate reality games, and Facebook-inspired gatherings. Kaprow (1993) said he wanted to bring art to life; to break down the barriers between the artist and the audience, art and the everyday. He wanted an art that worked with people rather than seeking to do things to them. This avant-garde sees art as a conversation rather than as a shock to the system. The artist's role is not just to proclaim but to listen and interpret, to incorporate ideas and adjust. To achieve that, art cannot be sequestered in special zones. Kaprow argued that art should be grounded in the common experience of everyday life; it must be capable of expanding or dissipating to wherever the participants want to take it. Participatory art cannot be preplanned in every detail by the artist. It has to be free to emerge, adapt, and grow wherever the participants want to take it. Art becomes more powerful the more connections it makes – not by standing alone and unyielding, grand and imposing. A growing body of artists are exploring the potential of art done with people, from Ai Weiwei's web-based projects and Anthony Gormley's public sculptures to Ridley Scott's collaborative films.

So the relationships in cultural industries are becoming more complex, less pre-dictable, more collaborative, and more competitive all at the same time. Working in these industries will provide widely varying experiences. Some areas – newspapers, for example – are increasingly cast in dark shadow: keeping newspapers afloat is going to be a hard slog. Public cultural institutions may well continue to feel belea-guered. Many new areas of culture associated with the web will enjoy explosive growth and yet people working in them will often feel precarious and poor. A few people – blockbuster writers, celebrities, creators of crossplatform formats – will be immensely rich and successful. So, some parts of our culture will become increasingly defensive and others nostalgic. Commercial culture will become increas-ingly conservative as it seeks only sure-fire home runs. Web culture could become increasingly diverse but is unlikely to reward many with a decent income. Cultural industries used to provide professionals with a decent middle-class income. They still will but only for some.

The other possibility is a version of the future sketched by many people, among them Jonathan Zittrain in *The Future of the Internet – And How to Stop It* (2008), Tim Wu in *The Master Switch* (2010), and my own pamphlet *Cloud Culture* (2010). This is a future in which access to culture is increasingly controlled by technology companies who control the platforms, software, devices, and billing systems: Amazon, Apple, Facebook, and Google. Apple in particular is keen on creating a carefully managed version of open culture in which it keeps close tabs on how content is being used and distributed. Facebook promotes sharing but also wants to channel it. Google is making vast stores of culture available but in the process changing how we see it. Culture will increasingly be designed to show up well on search engines, to work well with algorithms. The promise a decentralized, diverse, and open culture might be short lived. Pretty fast we could find access to culture largely flowing through the hands of a few very powerful US high-technology companies. Their rise of course is not assured. Not only are they fighting one another to create different platforms and business models but they also face more assertive consumers, and regulators will eventually catch up with them and ask what public benefits flow from their market power. How these new media giants are held to account will be one of the big stories of the next decade.

So what we will get is a raucous mix of all of this, a culture that increasingly defies easy categorization and stable boundaries. That is because culture is not just driven by technology but by how technology allows people to see themselves. That is the real driving force. An irrepressible cultural change is afoot all around the world. People are no longer willing to be handcuffed to history, pinned down to where they come from. In millions of small ways all around the world, people are mutinying, refusing to accept a social order that consigns them to a particular place for life.

The way these mutinous, mainly young people see themselves is inseparable from the maker culture that the web is making possible. A new set of near-universal expectations is taking shape, carried not by overt political protest but spreading under the radar. The spread of Wi-Fi and smartphones is creating a universal expectation that people should be able to be connect to "the network" wherever they are. In the developing world, the acquisition of a mobile phone has become a vital rite of passage: once you have a mobile, you count. You have a place in society, a marker, even if you are very poor. Facebook and social media are creating the expectation that you will be able to link to people, to find friends and collaborators. Wikipedia and the open educational resources movement are creating the universal expectation that knowledge should be available to all. Google has created the expectation that if a piece of information exists it should be discoverable. YouTube and mobile phones with cameras are creating the expectation that if something has happened we should be able to see it. Twitter has created the expectation that if something is happening we should be able to hear about it first-hand, from people close to the real events. Blogging, feedback services, and collaborative rating have created an expectation that we should be able to give our assessment of virtually any experience. The web and social media are creating a kind of civic long tail, a mass of loosely connected, small-scale conversations around content that people expect to be able to enjoy, share, talk, and do. All systems, public and private, will have to contend with young people armed with these new expectations of how they should be treated. Our cultural industries are no exception. In the twentieth century, culture was a closed competition between an oligopoly: the improvers, entertainers, and shockers. Thanks to the arrival of millions of unruly, mutinous makers, the culture of the twenty-first century will be much more of a raucous, energetic free-for-all. Only a few will be able to stand apart or cut their way through this ruckus. The best advice is probably not to be too sniffy and to get stuck in.

References

Epstein, J. (2011) "Books: Onward to the Digital Revolution" [review of John B. Thompson's *Merchants of Culture*]. *New York Review of Books* (February 10). www.nybooks.com /articles/archives/2011/feb/10/books-onward-digital-revolution.

Kaprow, A. (1993) "Essays on the Blurring of Art and Life," ed. J. Kelley. Berkeley, CA: University of California Press.

Leadbeater, C. (2010) *Cloud Culture: The Promise and the Threat*. London: Counterpoint (British Council). www.edge.org/3rd_culture/leadbeater10/leadbeater10_index.html.

Mann, T. (1936) *Stories of Three Decades*. New York: Alfred Knopf.

Ross, A. (2007) *The Rest Is Noise: Listening to the Twentieth Century*. New York: Farrar, Straus and Giroux.

Wu, T. (2010) *The Master Switch: The Rise and Fall of Information Empires*. New York: Knopf.

Zittrain, J. (2008) *The Future of the Internet – And How to Stop It*. New Haven, CT: Yale University Press.

14

The Dynamics of Digital Multisided Media Markets

How Media Organizations Learn from the IT Industries How to Engage with an Active Audience

Patrik Wikström

Introduction

Digital technologies have equipped media audiences with tools that have dramatically increased their ability to comment on, create, remix, and distribute media content (e.g., Benkler 2006; Bruns 2008; Shirky 2008). This new kind of audience behavior has considerable implications for traditional media organizations such as newspapers, music companies, movie studios, and book publishers. During the past decade, many traditional media organizations have experienced significant problems when trying to cope with increasingly active audiences (e.g., Küng et al., 2008). Many organizations have perceived the new audience behavior as a threat to their traditional trade, and they have used means of law and technology in attempts to put a leash on the audiences' creative desires (Lessig 2004). Other organizations have made an effort to change and have launched various initiatives intended to adapt their businesses to the new conditions (e.g., Boczkowski 2005; Wikström 2009). This chapter offers a new perspective on these dynamics and explores how traditional media organizations develop new practices and strategies for coping with an active audience. The chapter argues that the information technology (IT) industries have served as a vital source of inspiration in this process and it shows how practices developed by organizations in these industries have been adopted by traditional media organizations. It uses theories on multisided markets (e.g., Rochet and Tirole 2003) as a theoretical lens and employs cases from the European media industry in order to support the argument.

Two-Sided Media Markets

Advertising-funded media outlets compete in a market with two distinct but tightly connected networks or "sides." One side of the market is turned toward the readers

A Companion to New Media Dynamics, First Edition. Edited by John Hartley, Jean Burgess, and Axel Bruns.
© 2013 John Wiley & Sons, Ltd. Published 2015 by John Wiley & Sons, Ltd.

and the other toward the advertisers. A newspaper, for instance, has to satisfy the needs of both these "stakeholder networks" in order to survive. What makes the dynamics of two-sided media markets especially intricate is that a media outlet's attractiveness, as perceived by a stakeholder in one of the networks, is immediately affected by the number and the character of the stakeholders in the other network. (e.g., Rochet and Tirole 2003; Evans and Schmalensee 2008)

This means that, from the advertisers' perspective, the attractiveness of a newspaper depends on the size of the readership. From the readers' point of view, the attractiveness of the newspaper is also shaped by the number and the character of the advertisers, even though the connection is not as straightforward as in the opposite direction (Figure 14.1). It is this interaction between the two networks that generates the fundamental dynamics of newspaper markets (Picard 2009). For instance, it is this interaction that underpins the theory known as the "circulation spiral" (Furhoff 1967), which posits that in a theoretical market with two newspapers the paper with the smaller circulation will always be disadvantaged and will inevitably dwindle and die.

The tight interdependence between the two networks means that decisions intended to affect one of the stakeholder networks often have unintended consequences for the other network. Coping with this interdependence is one of the most challenging tasks for newspaper business managers. Imagine for instance that the manager raises the price of the newspaper to increase the newspaper's revenues. The revenues from the readers may indeed increase but the number of readers will at the same time most likely drop since fewer readers will be willing to pay the higher price. The smaller readership will lower the attractiveness of the newspaper on the advertising side of the market and will thereby decrease the newspaper's revenues from ad sales. Consequently, as a result of the two-sided character of the market, the total effect of the manager's decision may be the opposite of what was intended (e.g., Picard 2009).

This simple thought experiment was intended to show that two-sided markets are difficult to manage and that they present considerable challenges for managers of media outlets operating in such markets. The next section will argue that digitization changes the structure of two-sided media markets and raises the complexity of the market dynamics even further.

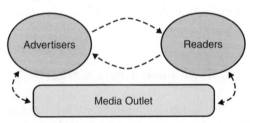

Figure 14.1   Advertising-based media outlets operate on a two-sided market with two distinct stakeholder networks consisting of advertisers and readers.

Digital Technologies Change the Dynamics
of Multisided Media Markets

This chapter was introduced by recognizing how digital technologies change the way information is produced, distributed, and used. Indeed, the Internet, personal computers, and a range of other digital innovations have affected the power structures in many media industries. Major media organizations may still control large parts of the production and distribution of media content, but user-generated content is rapidly becoming a force that has to be reckoned with. Digital media audiences are less inclined to passively consume media content and rather want to actively use – remix, comment on, share, mock – that content (e.g., Bruns 2008; Lessig 2008; Shirky 2008).

Many traditional media organizations have for different reasons perceived this development as a significant threat to their businesses. First of all, if the audience spend less time consuming corporate media content, the traditional media outlets will have a smaller audience to offer to their advertisers (Küng et al. 2008). Second, when amateurs act as substitutes for reporters or journalists, the position of the professionally trained journalists becomes threatened. As a consequence, some journalists argue, "high-quality" journalism may suffer, which in turn may harm the functioning of democratic societies (e.g., Jones 2009; McChesney and Nichols 2010). Third, the active audiences' use of media content often involves some kind of copyright infringement – again a major threat to the established ways of doing business in the traditional media industries (e.g., Lessig 2004; Wikström 2005).

Even though these and other reasons may make the active audience seem fairly off-putting to many media organizations, some of them have reluctantly accepted the development and have tried to embrace the new audience behavior (Wikström and Ellonen 2009). Today it is increasingly difficult to find corporate online media content that cannot be commented upon or shared among friends via social network services. The corporate media content is embedded in an elaborated system of blog posts, tweets, comments, and remixes that the media organizations cannot ignore. Even though studies show that only a small fraction of the audience actually contribute any kind of new material to this conversation, a much larger share of the audience perceive this user-generated content as an important and valuable part of their "total media experience" (e.g., Horowitz 2006; Olin-Scheller and Wikström 2009). From the media organizations' perspective, they no longer have the same control of this media experience as they had in the predigital days. In those days, the editor-in-chief or director (etc.) was still able to control what should be part of the finished media product, and it was this product that constituted the audience's total media experience. Indeed, media organizations have used freelancers and other contracted content contributors in the past, but they have always remained in control of the finished product. Today, that control is increasingly difficult to retain as the audience's media experience to such a large extent is determined by other content contributors that are beyond the control of the decision makers in traditional media organizations.

One way to understand this development is to apply the theoretical lens introduced in the previous section. The model (Figure 14.1) illustrated the interconnectedness of the two stakeholder networks, consisting of readers and advertisers respectively. It showed how the media outlet's attractiveness as perceived by one of the stakeholder networks was immediately linked to the number and character of the stakeholders in the other network. The emergence of the active audience disrupts this two-sided structure by adding yet another side to the market: the active, content-producing audience. However, the situation is actually even more complicated since the content-producing audience is quite heterogeneous and varies in the way they contribute to the conversation. For instance, in the case of newspapers, there are considerable differences between the behaviors of bloggers, commentators, and users who contribute to the discussion by sharing an article via Facebook, Twitter, and so on. The traditional two-sided structure of advertising-based media markets thereby has been transformed into a multisided structure (Figure 14.2). The multiple stakeholder networks all have their unique characteristics and collectively contribute to the value and attractiveness of the media outlet in the same way as when there only were two networks in the market.

So far in this chapter, advertising-funded media have been used as an illustrating example, but it is important to note that the market transformation described above is the same in those media industries that normally do not rely on advertising as their primary source of income, such as the book industry and the music industry. Even though the starting point is somewhat different for these industries, the increasingly active media audiences infuse a similar multisided logic into these markets.

In principle, a manager in a media organization operating in a multisided market has the same goal as during the predigital days, namely to ensure that the needs of the stakeholders in all the different networks are met. However, the complexity of the multisided market is significantly higher. Most traditional media organizations simply lack the capabilities and knowledge needed to manage such

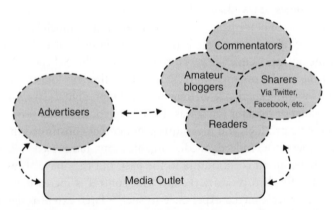

Figure 14.2   Digital technologies increase the complexity of multisided media markets.

complex dynamic systems, and many initiatives intended to cope with the new situation have consequently failed (e.g., Wikström and Ellonen 2009).

However, there are organizations in other industries that have been faced with similar challenges, and that have been able to manage the situation fairly well. The next section will look at how organizations in the IT industries have been able to develop practices and strategies for coping with a complex multisided market where their primary content producers reside outside their organizational boundaries and managerial control.

Amateur Developers in the IT Industries

The multisided market logic is not restricted to the media context; it can be observed in several other industries. In the IT industries, there are several examples of multisided markets. Computer operating systems such as Microsoft's Windows, Apple's iOS, and Google's Android are typical examples of IT products that compete in a two-sided market. Such products can be referred to as software *platforms*, which in this context are understood as software products that offer tools and resources that can be used by other software *applications* in order to fulfill some particular purpose. The value of a software platform, as perceived by a user, largely depends on how many different software applications are available on that particular platform. For example, Windows would be worthless to the average user without the thousands of software applications (e.g., Adobe Photoshop for graphic design and MS Word for word processing) that currently are available on the Windows platform. From the perspective of an organization or an individual developing such applications, deciding on which platform the applications should appear is strategically important. An application developer with limited resources often is unable to support more than one platform, since supporting a certain platform involves considerable investment in tools, training, and commitment to users who buy the application. Several factors are considered when such a decision is made, and one of the most important is the number of users already using a particular platform – simply since more users are likely to purchase more applications and generate more revenues for the developer (e.g., Evans et al. 2006; Evans and Schmalensee 2010; Gawer 2010).

In conclusion, platform operators in the IT industries face challenges very similar to the ones faced by traditional media organizations. In the same way as in two-sided media markets, the two stakeholder networks (users and developers) in the market for software platforms are tightly connected; and, in the same way as organizations in the media industries, organizations that create and operate software platforms (e.g., Apple, Microsoft, Google) have to satisfy the needs expressed by both networks in order to stay alive (Figure 14.3).

The impact of digitization on two-sided market structures is similar in the media and the IT industries. The IT industry equivalence to the active media audience essentially consists of creative individuals and entrepreneurs developing applications for a software platform. Increasingly accessible digital technologies and

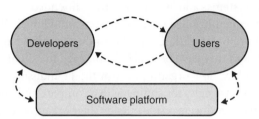

Figure 14.3   Markets for software platforms have the same logic and structure as two-sided media markets.

a growing IT competence among the general population enable more and more people to engage in application development. However, the emergence of such amateur and semipro application developers has quite a different history from that of the emergence of the active audience in the media industries. Computer hobbyists and digital enthusiasts have played crucial roles in the development of the IT industries since the mid-1970s, when computer technologies became accessible to the Western middle class (e.g., Levy 2010). Apple, Microsoft, and several other leading IT companies originated from computer hobbyist communities and a range of so-called open-source software projects, such as the Linux operating system, are still firmly rooted in these communities. Over the years, these amateur developers have continued to serve as a source of innovation and an ample supply of passionate, skilled, and not to mention cheap labor. It has been necessary for IT companies to learn how to engage with the developer networks in the multisided IT markets and involve skilled and creative amateurs in the development of corporate products (e.g., von Hippel 1988; Lakhani and von Hippel 2003; Chesbrough 2006).

In other words, contemporary markets for software platforms consist of stake-holder networks of different characters, ranging from large corporate application developers to enthusiastic amateurs without any intention of ever becoming IT entrepreneurs. Between these extremes, the networks consist of microenterprises and semiprofessionals, and they all develop applications for the platform, interact with each other, solve problems together, and collectively increase the general attractiveness and value of the platform (Figure 14.4). Multisided markets for software platforms are at least as complex and as difficult to manage as digital multisided media markets. However, while traditional media organizations struggle with the digital transformation of their market, software platform operators cope quite well since collaboration with developers beyond their organizational boundaries and managerial control has been their normal way of doing business for decades.

IT Industry Practices for Engaging with an Active Audience

The previous section established that organizations in the IT industries generally have more experience of engaging with independent content developers outside their

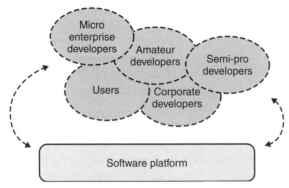

Figure 14.4   Multisided markets for software platforms are also affected by the development of digital technologies.

organizational boundaries than their colleagues in the traditional media industries. This section continues from that observation and examines specific practices used by software platform operators to interact and engage with independent application developer networks. While these platform practices were originally associated with computer operating systems and programming languages, they have over the decades also entered into other areas of the IT industry. For instance, one IT industry segment where such practices and strategies can be observed is the rapidly growing smartphone market. There are four platforms currently dominating the global smartphone market; namely, Android (by Google), BlackBerry OS (by Research in Motion), iOS (by Apple), and Windows (by Microsoft). The market where these platforms compete follows the logic presented in the previous section, with the addition that most of the platforms also have a stakeholder network consisting of advertisers as an important part of their business model. Other examples of sectors of the IT industry that also adhere to the platform logic are the online productivity service sector (e.g., Dropbox, Slideshare), the social network service sector (e.g., Facebook, LinkedIn, Twitter), and the videogame sector (e.g., gadgets such as Microsoft's Kinect, online games such as *Second Life*). Information about the sizes of these developer networks is not readily available. However, Twitter claims that in June 2011 there were 750 000 developers in its ecosystem and that as of March 2012 there had been more than 1 500 000 applications registered (Twitter 2011, 2012). The search engine Chomp, review site 148apps, and game publisher Chillingo jointly reported that there were 85 569 developers supporting the Apple iOS platform who had in May 2011 between them developed more than 500 000 applications (Chomp et al. 2011).

    Apple, Facebook, Google, and other operators use various practices and strategies to attract these hordes of independent application developers to their platforms. Most of the practices share a common purpose, namely to strengthen the loyalty between the application developer networks and the platform operator. Loyal (and creative) developers will add to the application portfolio, which in turn will attract users to the platform, which will make the platform even more attractive to developers – and so the snowball keeps on rolling. The platform operators' practices are implemented to ensure that both emotional and rational bonds are established between the platform operator and the developer networks as well as between the relevant developer networks. If the platform operator is successful, the application developers will feel that the platform is the superior place for fulfilling their needs and aspirations (e.g., Gawer and Cusumano 2002; Lakhani and Wolf 2005; Evans et al., 2006; Gawer 2010).

In order to achieve these goals, platform operators provide developers with various tools, resources, and rewards. Regardless of the part of the IT industries in which a platform operates, there are some specific practices that are more frequently used than others:

- *Tools, documentation, tutorials, and training*. Platform operators offer tools and resources that active and aspiring developers need for their application development. First and foremost, developers need so-called application programming interfaces (APIs), which provide access to the platform's various features. For instance, in the case of a photo-sharing platform such as Flickr, APIs enable applications to upload photos to the site and to access photos that have been uploaded. Developers also need tools for testing and assuring the quality of the applications they create and tools for monitoring how their applications are being used once they are available on the market. It is vital that these tools are easy to understand and easy to use so that as many developers as possible are encouraged to develop applications for the platform. Most operators therefore offer training sessions, tutorials, and documentation intended to make application development for the platform as easy and efficient as possible.
- *Online and offline conferencing*. Communication within and between the developer networks primarily takes place online (cf. Lakhani and von Hippel 2003), but platform operators also regularly arrange real-life events where the most passionate developers can meet, learn, and get new inspiration. Apple, as an example, hosts the annual Worldwide Developer Conference, where its CEO appears to the cheers of the attending developers. These events are important arenas for celebrating the growth of the platform and the community and rewarding those developers that the platform operators consider to be creative, successful, and inspirational.
- *Showcases and success stories*. Applications that have reached a certain degree of popularity among platform users are regularly highlighted and celebrated. The practice has several purposes: it teaches the developers what the platform operator considers to be a "success"; it allows less experienced developers to learn from these successes; and it strengthens hopeful developers' faith that by supporting the platform they will be able to fulfill their creative and commercial dreams.
- *Role models, evangelists, and advocates*. The major platform operators (e.g., Google and Facebook) have departments responsible for the platform's "developer relations." Evangelists and advocates serve as role models and sources of inspiration

and meet regularly with developers both online and at various real-life events. Developer Relations departments also manage communication campaigns to ensure that developers' needs are addressed and that the developers remain loyal to the platform. As an example, Figure 14.5 shows the logo of one such campaign – Facebook's "Operation Developer Love," which ran during parts of 2010 and 2011.

• *Revenue sharing.* While the emotional bonds between developers and platform operators are important, most platform operators create motivational mechanisms that are based on rationality and economy. For instance, application developers and platform operators generally split the revenues generated from advertisers and from users within the applications. Application developers normally keep more than 50 percent of the revenues with the platform developer keeping the rest.

This brief summary of common practices used by platform operators in the IT industries to engage with and motivate their active audiences does not make any claims of being exhaustive or complete. However, in spite of its deficiencies, the list shows how platform operators in the IT industries seek a very close relationship with their developer networks and how they encourage the developers' creativity, loyalty, and productivity. Platform operators spend considerable effort to facilitate interaction and collaboration between the multisided market's stakeholder networks. The goal of the practices is to stimulate the emergence of a self-reinforcing feedback loop where users and corporate, semiprofessional, and amateur developers contribute to the platform's value and attractiveness.

The practices presented above are not frequently used by organizations in the traditional media industries when they try to engage with their increasingly active audiences. As mentioned earlier in this chapter, media outlets do indeed invite their audiences to comment on their work and to relay links to their content via

Figure 14.5   "Operation Developer Love" is a marketing campaign aiming to improve the relationship between Facebook and the developers of applications for the Facebook platform.

the various social network services. However, such practices have limited potential to build a close relationship with an active audience, nor do they encourage the audience to use the corporate media content to create entirely new works and assemblages. While this behavior may be the norm for most organizations in the traditional media industries, some traditional media organizations have actually applied some of the practices used by platform operators in the IT industries. The next section will explore two such cases – one from the music industry and one from the news industry.

Media Organizations that Learn from the IT Industries

The process of convergence between media and technology industries that has been going on for decades is continuing with unrelenting force. It is increasingly difficult to identify the boundaries between industries and to determine whether an organization is (for instance) part of the media or the IT industries. Twitter and Facebook, which were used as examples of organizations in the IT industries in the previous section, are often referred to as media organizations rather than anything else, for instance. Another more significant consequence of these processes is that knowledge and practices travel much more easily between industries that previously were considered to be relatively disconnected. A very concrete way in which knowledge and practices are transferred between organizations and industries is through the movement of people. For instance, when people with education from technological universities and experience from the IT industries set up companies intended to solve a problem in the media industries, they tend to use practices they learned in their previous lives. One such example, which also will serve as the first case in this discussion, is an online music service by the name of Spotify.

Spotify is an on-demand music service with operations in 15 countries (as of June 2012) including major music markets such as the UK, Germany, and the USA. Spotify was established by a group of people trained at engineering and business schools with backgrounds in the IT industries and with a passion for business and technology rather than for music. Their goal was to create an advertising-funded music service that could offer music to consumers for free and thereby be able to compete with online piracy. In order to achieve this goal, they needed the rights-holders in the music industry to change a fundamental part of what since the early days of the music industry had become established music business practices. Traditionally, in the music industry money is mainly made when a song is performed to an audience or when a copy of a recorded version of the song is sold.[1] Regardless of whether the song is played by a broadcast radio station or sold as a data file from Apple's iTunes store, there are well-established international structures and regulations for how rights-holders should be compensated for the use of their music. A royalty is paid to rights-holders based on the number of times the song has been played by the radio station (and not by how much advertising sales the song will indirectly generate), and if the song is sold as a data file the online retailer pays a royalty that is based on the number of times the song has been sold (and not on how many times users actually listen to the songs they have purchased).

Spotify challenged this traditional structure and argued that a better method is to use the revenue-sharing scheme that is commonly used in the IT industries: namely, to share whatever revenues are generated by the retailer or media outlet. In principle, this means that, if the media outlet does not generate any revenues, no royalties are paid to the rights-holders for the use of their music. Spotify's negotiations took several years, and in the end they were to some degree required to abandon their original idea of an entirely free advertising-funded music service. However, without getting into the details of their business arrangements, Spotify created a music service where revenues from advertising at least to some extent serve as the basis for royalties paid to rights-holders. These revenues are then shared between rights-holders based on the number of times users have listened to the song and not on the number of times it has been downloaded.[2] This revenue-sharing model is very controversial and many rights-holders still refuse Spotify access to their music. However, slowly the industry is getting used to the model, and, since the launch of Spotify in 2007, other businesses that use a similar model have been set up in the music industry and attempts have been made to implement similar models for books and for films. While this revenue-sharing practice is not immediately linked to how Spotify engages with its active audiences, it is nevertheless a striking example of how a practice imported from the IT industry can instigate change in the traditional media industries.

Besides bringing in this radically new way of sharing revenues from the IT industries to a traditional media industry, Spotify has introduced a number of other novelties to the industry, intended to respond to the needs of their independent developers and active audiences. Like its peers in the IT industries, Spotify actively encourages independent developers to build applications based on the Spotify platform. For instance, Spotify has created a number of APIs that give applications access to some of Spotify's features. Spotify explains that it opened up its platform since its limited resources restrict the number of features that it can afford to implement. Using the Spotify API, independent developers can build applications that increase Spotify's attractiveness, relevance, and value without burdening Spotify's product development budget. Developers have, for example, created a service where playlist data from broadcast radio stations is combined with Spotify's music service features in order to allow users on-demand access to songs that have been played by the stations (www.radiofy.se). Another application created by independent developers is www.sharemyplaylists.com, which aims to enhance Spotify's music discovery features.

The Spotify case shows how a start-up launched by people with an IT background may instigate change in a traditional media industry. The next case does not concern a start-up at all but rather the second-largest newspaper in the UK, *The Guardian*, founded in 1821. Although *The Guardian* is one of the major traditional British newspapers, in 2009 it launched a platform strategy that actually is far more radical than what was presented in the Spotify case. *The Guardian* has for a number of years pursued a fairly aggressive strategy aiming to rapidly move the newspaper from paper format onto the web (*The Guardian* 2011). As part of this strategy, the newspaper launched what it calls the Guardian Open Platform in 2009, which in principle opens up the newspaper's entire article repository to independent developers. Stephen Dunn, head of Technology Strategy at *The Guardian* explains:

> The idea is that with the appropriate . . . approval you can essentially build a better version of the Guardian if you want to . . . so there's [sic] different tiers of access to it but essentially the idea is to completely lower or remove the barriers to business development with our content. (Rigsby 2011)

As a result of this initiative, a number of applications based on the Guardian platform have increased the newspaper's attractiveness and value without burdening its limited technology and business development resources. The business and technological risk associated with the application development is carried by the independent developer while the potential revenues created by the application are shared between the application developer and the platform operator – *The Guardian*. The Open Platform consists of a range of services that allow for different levels of interaction with the newspaper. The passionate political blogger, the amateur developer, and the corporate application developer gain different kinds of access to the platform, depending on the development projects that they intend to initiate. The newspaper's platform practices, which mimic IT industry practices regarding engaging with active audiences almost to the letter, also include other components such as online communities where developers are able to discuss issues related to application development for *The Guardian* and real-life events (so called "Hactivate" events) where developers can meet and develop applications together just for fun.

While the platform strategy involves the entire Guardian organization, it is nevertheless principally driven by the newspaper's IT department. This structure manifests a second way (next to the start-up route exemplified by the Spotify case) in which practices from the IT industry can be infused into traditional media organizations and industries. The power and influence of IT departments in traditional media organizations increase as digital technologies become ever more critical to the successful operation of a media outlet. In the early days of using digital technologies within newspaper organizations, the IT departments were often colonized by seasoned journalists who were looking for a career change and who had a passion for new technologies. However, the growing complexity of the IT field makes it difficult to continue that habit: it has become necessary to recruit people with a proper IT education or IT industry experience. When people with such backgrounds are put in charge of strategic development projects in a media organization, they tend to bring their previous experiences into the project. As a consequence, the IT industry practices eventually become naturalized parts of how things are done in the media organization.

The cases of Spotify and *The Guardian* are very different in their backgrounds and structures, but they both illustrate very well how IT industry practices are absorbed by the traditional media industries. It should also be noted these are far from the only media organizations that have followed this route; however, those cases will have to be presented and examined by other texts.

Discussion and Conclusions

This chapter has explored the dynamics of multisided media markets. It has argued that practices and strategies used by software platform operators in the IT industries for engaging with "active audiences" are being picked up by traditional media organizations, which do not have as efficient practices for engaging with active audiences as organizations in the IT industries, which have been able to refine their practices over several decades. The fundamental principles of these practices are to establish a close relationship with passionate and active audiences (and the independent application developers) and to provide developers with resources, recognition, and rewards that stimulate their creative work. The chapter has pointed at two media organizations that have incorporated these principles and practices into their operations. *The Guardian* and Spotify are two very different media organizations, but it seems that both have found practices that allow them to interact with their active audiences fairly successfully. They have applied "platform logic" to their businesses and have thereby been able to exploit their audiences' creative desires and to increase the attractiveness and value of their services.

There are several issues and questions that remain unanswered in relation to this development. If it continues, what will be the implications for media organizations, industries, and professions? How will the cultural output be affected if the motivational mechanisms that drive the creative work in the IT industries are implemented in the media industries? One development that does not seem entirely unlikely is that the number of staff writers at news organizations will continue to shrink and that eventually more or less all content contributors will be part of one of the stakeholder networks in the media market. As independent content contributors their payment will be based on the number of users who read their stories rather than on the length of those stories. This structure, which may be considered rather controversial, has actually been implemented to some extent already, for instance at the high-profile US-based news site *The Huffington Post*. The news site was acquired by AOL in February 2011 (AOL 2011), and it will be interesting to follow whether these principles will be allowed to extend to other parts of the AOL organization.

Another potential development concerns the use of APIs in the media industries. Several media outlets have already "opened up their platforms" and implemented rudimentary APIs to enable independent application developers access to news items, allow them to search for and add new metadata, and so on. This development may have significant implications for media organizations, for their relationships with other media outlets, for their audiences, and for their cultural output. As an example, in the spirit of open platforms and the so-called "semantic web" (e.g., Antoniou and van Harmelen 2008), even eBooks may be equipped with an API. The purpose would be to stimulate the development of applications that allow an active audience to enhance the narrative by adding data such as annotations, reflections, geographical information, and images to specific paragraphs or sentences in the book. The Golden Notebook Project (thegoldennotebook.org) and to some extent also BookGlutton (www.bookglutton.com) exemplify how these concepts can be implemented.

Developments such as those discussed above may be perceived as either promising or discouraging. Regardless of whether these particular developments will eventually be realized, it at least seems very likely that the increased complexity of multisided media markets is here to stay and that media organizations will need to develop practices and capabilities in order to cope with the new situation. Whether the importing of practices from the IT industry is the right way to go or whether media organizations will have to develop their own practices in order to cope with the specific conditions in their industries remains to be seen.

Notes

1. There exist other revenue structures in the music industry (e.g., synchronization), but for this particular argument these two (performance and mechanical royalties) are sufficient.
2. The fact that Spotify is essentially a streaming service does not change the reasoning.

References

Antoniou, G. and van Harmelen, F. (2008) *A Semantic Web Primer*, 2nd edn. Cambridge, MA: MIT Press.
AOL (2011) "AOL Agrees to Acquire the *Huffington Post*." http://corp.aol.com/2011/02/07/aol-agrees-to-acquire-the-huffington-post.
Benkler, Y. (2006) *The Wealth of Networks: How Social Production Transforms Markets and Freedom*. New Haven, CT: Yale University Press.
Boczkowski, P.J. (2005) *Digitizing the News: Innovation in Online Newspapers*. Cambridge, MA: MIT Press.
Bruns, A. (2008) *Blogs, Wikipedia, Second life, and Beyond: From Production to Produsage*. New York: Peter Lang.
Chesbrough, H.W. (2006) *Open Innovation: The New Imperative for Creating and Profiting from Technology*. Cambridge, MA: Harvard Business School Press.

Chomp, 148Apps, and Cillingo (2011) "Snapshot of Today's App Store Landscape." http://bit.ly/500kApps.

Evans, D.S. and Schmalensee, R. (2008) "Markets with Two-Sided Platforms" in W.D. Collins, J. Anglund, and American Bar Association, Section of Antitrust Law, eds., *Issues in Competition Law and Policy*, vol. 667. Chicago, IL: ABA Section of Antitrust Law, pp. 667–693.

Evans, D.S. and Schmalensee, R. (2010) "Failure to Launch: Critical Mass in Platform Businesses." *Review of Network Economics*, 9(4), 1.

Evans, D.S., Hagiu, A., and Schmalensee, R. (2006) *Invisible Engines: How Software Platforms Drive Innovation and Transform Industries.* Cambridge, MA: MIT Press.

Furhoff, L. (1967) *Upplagespiralen.* Stockholm: Esselte Studium.

Gawer, A. (2010) *Platforms, Markets and Innovation.* Cheltenham: Edward Elgar.

Gawer, A. and Cusumano, M.A. (2002) *Platform Leadership: How Intel, Microsoft, and Cisco Drive Industry Innovation.* Cambridge, MA: Harvard Business School Press.

The Guardian (2011) "Guardian News & Media to be a Digital-First Organisation" (June 16). www.guardian.co.uk/gnm-press-office/guardian-news-media-digital-first-organisation.

Horowitz, B. (2006) "Creators, Synthesizers, and Consumers." *Elatable* (February 17). www.elatable.com/blog/?b=5.

Jones, A.S. (2009) *Losing the News: The Future of the News that Feeds Democracy.* Oxford: Oxford University Press.

Küng, L., Picard, R.G., and Towse, R. (2008) *The Internet and the Mass Media.* London: Sage.

Lakhani, K.R. and von Hippel, E. (2003) "How Open Source Software Works: 'Free' User-to-User Assistance." *Research Policy*, 32, 923–943.

Lakhani, K.R. and Wolf, R.G. (2005) "Why Hackers Do What They Do: Understanding Motivation and Effort in Free/Open Source Software Projects" in J. Feller, B. Fitzgerald, S.A. Hissam, and K.R. Lakhani, eds., *Perspectives on Free and Open Source Software.* Cambridge, MA: MIT Press, pp. 3–22.

Lessig, L. (2004) *Free Culture: How Big Media Uses Technology and the Law to Lock Down Culture and Control Creativity.* New York: Penguin.

Lessig, L. (2008) *Remix: Making Art and Commerce Thrive in the Hybrid Economy.* New York: Penguin.

Levy, S. (2010) *Hackers: Heroes of the Computer Revolution.* Sevastopol: O'Reilly Media.

McChesney, R.W. and Nichols, J. (2010) *The Death and Life of American Journalism: The Media Revolution that will Begin the World Again.* New York: Nation Books.

Olin-Scheller, C. and Wikström, P. (2009) *Beyond the Boundaries of the Book – Young Peoples' Encounters with Web Based Fiction.* Paper presented at NordMedia09, the 19th Nordic Conference for Media and Communication Research, Karlstad, Sweden (August 13–15).

Picard, R.G. (2009) "The Economics of the Daily Newspaper Industry" in A. Alexander and J. Owers, eds., *Media Economics – Theory and Practice*, 3rd edn. Mahwah, NJ: Lawrence Erlbaum Associates, pp. 109–126.

Rigsby, J. (2011) "The Guardian's Open Platform Reinvents Open News with Apache Lucene." *CMS Wire* (June 7). www.cmswire.com/cms/information-management/the-guardians-open-platform-reinvents-open-news-with-apache-lucene-011497.php.

Rochet, J.-C. and Tirole, J. (2003) "Platform Competition in Two-Sided Markets." *Journal of the European Economic Association*, 1, 990–1029.

Shirky, C. (2008) *Here Comes Everybody: The Power of Organizing without Organizations.* New York: Penguin.

Twitter (2011) "One Million Registered Twitter Apps" (July 11). http://blog.twitter.com/2011/07/one-million-registered-twitter-apps.html.

Twitter (2012) "The Twitter Ecosystem Recently Hit more than 1.5 Million Registered Apps" (March 14). http://twitter.com/twitterapi/status/179611701195456512.

von Hippel, E. (1988) *The Sources of Innovation*. New York: Oxford University Press.

Wikström, P. (2005) "The Enemy of Music – Modelling the Behaviour of a Cultural Industry in Crisis." *International Journal on Media Management*, 7, 65–74.

Wikström, P. (2009) *The Music Industry: Music in the Cloud*. Cambridge: Polity.

Wikström, P. and Ellonen, H.-K. (2009) "The Implication of Social Media Investments on Print Media Business Models." Paper presented at the European Academy of Management Conference, Liverpool, UK (May 11–14).

Search

15

Search and Networked Attention

Alexander Halavais

In the early 1990s, when the Internet was on the verge of becoming enmeshed in the everyday lives of a significant part of the globe's population, it would have been difficult to predict just how important the search engine would become to this process. That a substantial industry would be built on indexing would have seemed as likely as telephone directories becoming the powerhouse of the telecommunications system. The ability to search was important, perhaps, but few anticipated how central it would become.

A keen observer, however, would have noticed that the rapid rise of the search engine marked an inflection point, not the starting point, of search becoming important to our social lives. The Internet and web, by making information available at our fingertips, fulfilled a future promise long dreamt of: the future, we all knew, would be marked by an abundance of easily accessed information. And, as Herbert Simon (1971) noted well before the rise of the networked society, attention becomes the scarce resource most in demand in an information-rich environment.

The term "search engine" obscures the role of these technologies. It suggests that they are agents of the user, sent to seek out particular answers to specific questions. While this represents one use of the search engine, they more broadly are technologies of attention. As Google reminds us each time we search, there is never just one page on the web that might suit our interests; it is a rare query that does not produce hundreds of thousands of results. Instead, search engines are designed to warp the information environment. They are a tool that allows us to blind ourselves to the distractions inherent to the web, and focus attention on a relatively small handful of pages that – the search engines assure us – are most applicable to the topic at hand.

To understand search engines it is first necessary to understand their role as a biasing technology; that is, the revelation search engines promise requires conceal-ment on a massive scale. By approaching search engines as technologies of attention, we can place them more easily in a long history of mediated communication. This

A Companion to New Media Dynamics, First Edition. Edited by John Hartley, Jean Burgess, and Axel Bruns.
© 2013 John Wiley & Sons, Ltd. Published 2015 by John Wiley & Sons, Ltd.

chapter begins with a pre-Internet history of communication media as technologies of attention. It then goes on to suggest ways in which the search engine has accelerated a long-term trend toward individualized attention setting, while at the same time creating a global gatekeeper. Finally, it suggests what this may mean for communication technologies yet to come.

Paying Attention

There is a long history of questioning the relationship between attention and communication media. A book like *The Shallows* (2010), in which Nicholas Carr decries the effect of the Internet on our ability to attend to long-form arguments and narratives, would require little rewriting to be applied to television, radio, or even the printing press itself when each of those technologies were new. Indeed, two millennia earlier, Seneca (n.d.) advised against collecting too many books to avoid becoming distracted by the many possible sources of knowledge. The concern that the way we think is changing goes hand in hand with the "moral panics" that are often produced by the adoption of new communication media. While Carr's book extends the critique to the Internet at large, a version of the argument appeared in his article in *The Atlantic* titled "Is Google Making Us Stupid?" (2008), to which Carr answered: yes.

The importance of attention to cognition has long been recognized. Attention is at the heart of consciousness and the ability to concentrate on a problem. William James described attention as

> the taking possession by the mind, in clear and vivid form, of one out of what seem several simultaneously possible objects or trains of thought. Focalization, concentration, of consciousness are of its essence. It implies withdrawal from some things in order to deal effectively with others, and is a condition which has a real opposite in the confused, dazed, scatterbrained state. (1890: vol. 1, 403–404).

We are only capable of reasoning to the degree to which we are able to reduce these distractions and selectively attend to particular stimuli. The natural environment represents a source of endless distraction, and humans have evolved to become adept at focusing our attention on a narrow subset of available sources, both natural and artificial.

The connection between cognition and attention has also long been related to communication and media. The ability to focus our attention is likely very closely linked to our ability to communicate ideas to one another – that is, humans are uniquely attentive animals. Ingar Brinck (2001) argues that our shift from attempting to affect the behavior of others to trying to affect their mental state requires new ways of attending to the environment and sharing those objects of attention with other people. Our ability to have some form of control over what we attend to is essential to how we come to think individually, and how we communicate those thoughts socially (Bruner 1975; Tomasello 1995).

Media of Attention

We might consider, then, communication media to be essentially media of attention. At the very least, it is a required element of communication – the reader or viewer or listener must attend to a message to have it be communicated. As a result, a great deal of the theory and research that has attempted to understand the role of media in society could easily be reframed as the study of media and attention.

This is most clearly the case in a set of theories often grouped under the label of "agenda setting," as well as "gatekeeping," "priming," and "framing" – all of which suggest ways in which the news media affect what we consider to be salient or important. But it runs through every form of media theorization, from structuration approaches to uses and gratifications. All require an understanding of how attention is related to communication.

While attention is clearly important to communication that is not technologically mediated, questions of crafting attention at a broader social level came to the fore as communication became mass mediated. As people began to attend to the same things, there was a certain degree of centralization of the structures, platforms, and values of thought and culture. Elizabeth Eisenstein (1979), for example, suggests that, once people began reading the same books across Europe, there were repercussions across culture, with national dress and music, for example, being replaced by pan-European fashion and opera standards. The rapid flood of books led people to attend to the same set of messages in mediated form, rather than to the variety of things they might notice in their localized physical and cultural environments.

The creation of mass newspapers likewise marked a leap forward in publishing technology, and with it the creation of national attention. James Carey (1969) suggests that this formation of new audiences happened at multiple scales. There was the creation of a new, national audience – something particularly important in the USA, given the geographic distribution of its populace. But the mass media also bound together subcultures that were geographically distributed but had never had a clear group identity in the past. Carey refers to these two tendencies as the "centripetal" and "centrifugal" forces introduced by mass publishing. Similar trends may be found in the media revolutions that followed.

Much of the early research on mass media was tied closely to the practice of propaganda. Early on, this meant seeking ways of better accomplishing such propaganda, as seen in Lippmann's *Public Opinion* (1922), among other works. After the Second World War, the word took on a negative tinge because of its use by totalitarian governments, and the question of how people learned about the world was addressed more critically. This led to, among other streams of research, Kurt Lewin's (1947) early observation that newspaper editors acted as "gatekeepers." The study of gatekeeping – and how those with editorial power decided which news was fit to print – has continued through to other mass media, both under that rubric and within studies of "agenda setting" and "priming" that might be considered an outgrowth of gatekeeping (McCombs and Shaw 1972).

The rise of electronic media heightened the potential for both centralizing and decentralizing attention. Especially with television, and with satellite connections, for the first time in human history a large portion of the species might be attending to exactly the same visual field. Of course, not all choose to expose themselves to television, and among those, not all will actively attend to the events represented (Chaffee and Schleuder 1986), but the visual nature of the medium provides the potential for concentrating large publics' attention on a relatively narrow set of topics.

Most people do not give over the entirety of their attention to the television. It is often one of many sources of distraction in their environment. Debates currently rage over whether and how people "multitask," or attend to several sources of attention at once, but that debate is not new. Walter Benjamin addresses the challenges of "new" media – predating television and the Internet – and recognizes that one of its hallmarks is the odd necessity to "master certain tasks in a state of distraction" (1968: 240). This, Benjamin suggests, has been the result of a retraining of the perceptual apparatus to make sense of the new media, and especially of film. In its simplest form, many of the critiques of these new media remind us of Carr's claim that our attention span is becoming ever shorter. The evidence of this is as weak today as it was when the claim was applied to earlier media (Newman 2010). Nonetheless, there is little question that these technologies are designed around the shaping of attention, that those who make use of them evolve new ways of managing that attention, and that this likely has profound effects on the way we make sense of the world as individuals and societies.

Networked Distraction

In societies dominated by publishing, the only way to put forward an idea contrary to those consuming the attention of the public is to acquire control of a printing press or other tools of reproducing text. The history of revolution and of resistance to propaganda is tied up in the production of pamphlets and samizdat literature. The emergence of broadcast television – particularly before the ubiquity of consumer videotaping – made it much more difficult for alternative ideas to be circulated, as the tools required to produce and distribute television were even more out of reach than printing presses. The absence of television would still provide room for propaganda (largely from the mouths of local authorities, as Raymond Williams (1974) argues), but the propaganda presented by broadcast media represents a more total, consistent, and centralized message.

The Internet inverted that balance of power. Samizdat became blogs, and the blogosphere often made its mark by responding to, and in some cases fighting against, mainstream media. The web provided a way of getting a message out relatively cheaply for those who had access and the ability to create websites. The emergence of blogging platforms accelerated this, making the technical knowledge needed to present a message to the world fairly trivial. When the Blogger service began, it used the tagline "Push-Button Publishing for the People."

The early days of the Internet were marked by the promise of open and distributed information, but the chances that what you were looking for online might actually be there was fairly low. As a result, the activity most people engaged in was "surfing" or browsing available content, both on the web and on precursors such as Gopher. Though people may have engaged in more purposive searching for specific information, particularly within limited domains of knowledge, this was so unlikely to bear fruit that the more common sorts of guides to information were those that plucked out new and notable resources that might be of interest to the surfer. Some of these kinds of peer guides went on to become what we now know as blogs.

As the number of resources increased exponentially, there became a greater need to categorize this material and make it more easily navigable. Yahoo's taxonomy of the web, for example, served an important role in making the transition from information scarcity to information abundance. Other efforts attempted to provide maps of the web based on a geographic metaphor, showing how different domains might be related to one another.

Such taxonomies were quickly overloaded by the hyperabundance of new material on the web. The amount of human effort required to make and use category sites was impossible to scale at a useful rate, and search engines – and their visual indicator, the search box – began to appear. Search engines were an indication that the web not only offered an answer to any question but several such answers. While a query at a library might yield no results at all, it was very difficult to create such a query for the web. (Indeed, creating search terms that might yield a single result – a "Googlewhack" – was for a short time a bit of a game on the web.)

Soon just about any query resulted in a number of pages containing the index word, and very soon these response from search engines became overwhelming and bewildering. A search that results in tens of thousands of undifferentiated results is not particularly useful. Google's ability to winnow these responses to the "best" ten sites to investigate put it well ahead of what had become a vibrant market of search providers.

The change in the way we expected information to be organized was both rapid and extreme. The Yahoo categorization was not that different from library taxonomies – not just the Dewey Decimal Classification but also ways of organizing physical libraries that reached back to the beginnings of libraries. Now, it was no longer necessary to know just where a particular document might be found or what its relationship was with other documents. By indexing the contents of the web, the search engines removed the necessity for overarching structures or narratives.

Or, more precisely, they removed such structures from the attention and perception of the person who was searching for information. As a whole, the library suggests a narrative, a collection of human knowledge that may no longer be comprehended by any individual but that is somehow held in the bureaucratic structure of the library itself. While no single librarian may know the relationship between the books in a given library, those relationships can to a certain degree be discerned through the records of information about the books. Likewise, the individual user of a search engine may not understand how any given document is related to billions of other documents on the web, but Google knows. Unlike the library, however, it is far less likely that a user of Google can easily or directly discover those relationships through the search engine.

The New Gatekeepers

The result is a paradoxical distribution and centralization of information on the web. A group of people sitting at lunch in a restaurant can, in a moment, access any piece of trivial information from any source around the world. This "anything, anywhere" capability is enabled by a small number of gateways. Search engines have become our interface to the vast, disconnected web, and therefore act as a significantly centralizing force.

The centralizing function of search engines may not readily be apparent. Some might think that they represent little more than a sort of conveyance of information, and, though they might be a guide, they certainly have little power over the content. But search engines are not merely a mirror of the web. Their chief function is, in fact, to distort the web. As the web became too large to effectively understand or manage, we turned to search engines to warp its offerings to suit our interests. Just as we asked journalists to filter the world and draw our attention to the things most important (both to us and presumed important to society by the journalists and editors), we ask search engines to reshape the web in our image (and again, the things the search engine thinks are socially important figure prominently). Because search engines do not merely reflect; they wield a tremendous amount of power, and do so largely invisibly.

Moreover, those sites that figure most prominently and attract the greatest amount of global attention tend to continue to grow in that position. Just as the rich get richer, the most viewed get more views. The mobility of content is generally rather constrained; without being pointed to by one of these centers of attention, it becomes difficult to be noticed. The web is wrongly seen as something countering the sort of fame and notoriety bestowed by large, mainstream media. One of the best ways to be noticed on the web is still to be interviewed by a large newspaper or appear on a television program, and one of the best ways of showing up in the mainstream media these days is to become a "meme" on the web. The two systems of attention attenuation support one another.

Scholars have attempted to adopt gatekeeping theories to the social web, under the terms "gatewatching" (Bruns 2005) or "network gatekeeping" (Barzilai-Nahon 2008). These attempts focus on the centrifugal effects on gatekeeping, as new gates are created and are kept by new constituencies. With rare exceptions (Meyer and Schroeder 2009), less attention has been paid to the most centralized gatekeeper: the search engine. The creators of search engines delegate to them the process of selecting and making salient certain pages over others. This algorithmic filtering is perhaps more obvious on Google News – where we can compare the selected stories with what a news editor might choose – than it is with the regular search results. Because we have very little to compare it to, search engines are seen as a natural part of the web ecology, and the ways in which they bias the web are seen as natural (Halavais 2008).

Has there been a response to this sort of search engine power? The blogosphere and social media have acted as a sort of counterweight to search centralization. Slashdot provides an interesting example here. The "Slashdot effect" refers to the phenomenon of "flash crowds," created when large numbers of people go to an otherwise unremarkable place. A number of sites encourage this sort of mass shift in attention, with millions of website hits being focused on a relatively unknown site due to a post on Digg, Fark, or any of a number of large social sites. This often results in a dead website, because the publisher had no way to expect so much attention so quickly and the server is unable to keep up with the burst of newfound fame. It also suggests that these sites lead to a kind of sudden shift in collective attention that is far rarer on search engines. This kind of sifting from the bottom of the results quickly to the top is encouraged by all sorts of social media, and, as social media become more popular, that churning is more pronounced (Halavais 2001).

In 1993, John Gilmore famously claimed that the Internet interpreted censorship as damage and routed around it (quoted in Elmer-Dewitt 1993). The design of the Internet is indeed intended to provide a venue for all sorts of information, and to make it difficult to set up roadblocks to that information. Active attempts to openly censor materials, however, are not necessary when people are unable to know what to look for. The most effective censorship is invisible.

Search Engine Thinking

This sort of paradoxical centralization and decentralization process imprints itself on our social organization and on our cognitive processes. Decades ago Lyotard (1984) suggested that postmodernity is marked by dissolving grand narratives in the face of smaller, more localized understanding. He was partially right. Even as these smaller narratives have gained ground, the centralizing force of the search engine has left its imprint behind in ways that are difficult to measure.

One of these ways is in the internalization of the search process. Even as search engines attempt to become better at understanding our natural writing and speech (see, for example, IBM's *Jeopardy*-playing computer, "Watson"), we strive to make our own world more comprehensible by machines. An entire industry has built up around the idea of search engine optimization and findability; that is, creating sites that better adhere to what search engines think is important. At its most extreme end, this leads to "content farms" that employ authors to create website content intended to please the algorithms of the major search engines (Shaver 2010;

Anderson 2011). But anyone who creates content in any medium must think about the degree to which search engines will value what they are producing, and change their work to better fit the demands of those search engines.

While we adjust socially to produce more "findable" texts, we also adjust our own search patterns to better match the requirements of the search engine. This sort of coevolution with our tools is common, and few see it as problematic. In fact, just the opposite is the case: those who are not fluent users of the search engine are seen to be even more at the mercy of its whim (Hargittai 2003). The only way to counter the influence of the search engine, even in some small way, is to become more proficient users of those same engines. In comparison with many other organisms, humans are particularly capable of learning within a single generation. We do not have to wait for generations of natural selection to see changes in how we think, work, and interact; our brains are plastic enough to rapidly adjust to changing environments. We coevolve with the tools we create, and so we begin to anticipate what we will need to remember in order to access knowledge.

It is difficult to know what the effects of such search engine thinking already are. No doubt, those who become sophisticated users of search engines see themselves thinking of knowledge in more atomized form, and attaching search terms to their questions about the world and the answers that they come up with. Even as Google and its competitors seek to learn more about the contexts and expectations of our search activities, those activities make use of search availability in novel ways. Particularly, those who have come to rely on the ubiquitous availability of search may become more reliant on "just-in-time" knowledge and form their thinking and learning strategies around that.

After Search Engines

The word "search engine" seems in some way a throwback to an industrial era. In a decade, these sites have come to dominate our relationship with networked information. Because these sites – and Google in particular – have become so central to the way we interact with information and with each other, it is natural to wonder what will come after the search engine. It seems almost an article of faith that the search engine is not a permanent part of our online lives.

Much of that question is tied up in definitions: what constitutes a search engine? If it is a system that merely indexes keywords, we might say that this has already faded away. If we say that it is something that helps us find documents, then it seems that search engines have a long life ahead of them. If it is computing that helps us answer questions, it seems we will be unlikely to ever see search engines disappear. To take a parallel example, despite some pretty drastic changes in what constitutes a newspaper over the past few centuries, newspapers remain, even when the "paper" does not.

Perhaps a better question is what central function search engines serve, and how that may continue to be served moving forward. That Facebook or Twitter could be a challenger to Google, for example, might have seemed a strange idea several years ago, but search has always been networked and social, and leveraging social connections to help people find what they are looking for becomes a natural extension of search engines. We have always used the people around us to discover information; the search engine merely extends that process and makes it easier to accomplish.

We should also expect the ways in which search functionality is presented to us to change. There can be little doubt that the front pages of search engines make up the entry to the web for many people, but search boxes now permeate every corner of the web, particularly for specialized search. It may be that the Googles of the world maintain their role as general search engines while more and more of our searching happens on narrower sites.

Search engines are attempting to draw more and more context into the search process. When you enter a query into a search box on Google, it knows more than just the query. In many cases, it weighs anything you have ever searched before, where you happen to be (geographically) at the moment, and who your friends are and what they have searched for. One could imagine a host of other information collected by Google that might also aid the search process: what your upcoming appointments are, what documents you have been writing lately, who you have been emailing or chatting with, who you have appeared in photographs with, or even your medical history or genetic makeup. All of this information is useful in generating search results that better meet the needs of the individual searcher.

It goes further than that. John Battelle (2006) has famously called Google a "database of intentions" because it can provide some indication of what individuals and groups are thinking about and desire at any moment. But that can be turned around. The listing above may seem invasive; as former Google CEO Eric Schmidt noted, "We don't need you to type at all. We know where you are. We know where you've been. We can more or less know what you're thinking about" (Thompson 2010). Of course, who we are and who we become is tied up in the kinds of questions we ask and the kinds of answers we receive. If Google is a database of intentions, it is far more than merely a passive record of those intentions. What we seek to learn is closely related to who we become, and search engines are increasingly in a position to determine a substantial part of how that happens.

This is particularly true when it comes to the relationship of advertising to search. Search engines generally take pains to separate the ads they run from the search engine results, and indicate that the two have no influence on one another. The reason for this is clear enough – as its pioneers suggested in an early paper about Google, a search engine that also hosted advertising would lack credibility. But the sort of contextualized search results that Google seeks to provide are not that different from the same kinds of contextualized advertising they serve. The ideal ad is presented to someone who is already primed and ready to become a customer, to someone who already has some form of intent. Google is not alone in this; any site that seeks to serve advertising to visitors is providing search functionality in this new form: things you didn't know you were looking for.

Here again we see the double effect of the search engine. By providing search results that are intimately tailored to a profile generated by modeling your behavior, you are receiving unique responses – a sort of individualized search engine that provides just what you want to learn, just when you are expecting to want to learn it. This is the result of search engines being designed in response to an overall social evolution toward "networked individualism" (Wellman et al. 2006), in which individuals shape and are shaped by the networks that form around them.

At the same time, this is a highly conservative structure. First, by knowing a vast amount about the trajectory of your life, and other lives like it, the dominant search companies are in an almost unassailable position of power. How can a rival even imagine competing with a company that knows that much about their own customers and can use it to provide personalized services? Second, any individual's perception will be dictated by a model that they know little or nothing about. As Jeremy Bentham suggested, it is very difficult to understand the impact of censorship because you can never know just how far it reaches (1840: vol. 2, 152). With personalization comes the peril of lost opportunity. People may be able to disable that personalization to some degree, but only if they know that it exists and understand that the blinders it imposes may limit their own opportunities. Personalization can lead paradoxically to a leveling of individuality.

This tension or paradox between personalization and the increasing power of global, mechanized gatekeepers results in the increased complexity of our media environment over time. This "glocalization" is not unique to the Internet or to mediated communication. It results in a continually more complex social system, in which our communication seems to become more individual even as it is handled through an increasingly global network with centralizing tendencies. The greatest danger we face is not this paradoxical process but a lack of attention to how these changes are happening, and what their social and cultural influences are. The ideal place to find this centrifugal/centripetal dynamic is in the technologies of attention that, for the moment, we call search engines. The engines themselves, and how they influence society, deserve our undivided attention.

References

Anderson, C.W. (2011) "Deliberative, Agonistic, and Algorithmic Audiences: Journalism's Vision of its Public in an Age of Audience Transparency." *International Journal of Communication*, 5, 529–547.

Barzilai-Nahon, K. (2008) "Toward a Theory of Network Gatekeeping: A Framework for Exploring Information Control." *Journal of the American Society for Information Science and Technology*, 59(9), 1493–1512.

Battelle, J. (2006) *The Search: How Google and Its Rivals Rewrote the Rules of Business and Transformed our Culture*. New York: Penguin.

Benjamin, W. (1968 [1955]) "The Work of Art in an Age of Mechanical Reproduction" in *Illuminations*, trans. H. Zohn. New York: Harcourt, Brace, Jovanovich, pp. 217–252.

Bentham, J. (1840 [1802]) *Theory of Legislation*, trans. R. Hildreth. Boston, MA: Weeks, Jordon, & Company.

Brinck, I. (2001) "Attention and the Evolution of Intentional Communication." *Pragmatics & Cognition*, 9(2), 259–277.

Bruner, J. (1975) "The Ontogenesis of Speech Acts." *Journal of Child Language*, 2(1), 1–19.

Bruns, A. (2005) *Gatewatching: Collaborative Online News Production*. New York: Peter Lang.

Carey, J. (1969) "The Communications Revolution and the Professional Communicator." *Sociological Review Monograph*, 13(1), 23–38.

Carr, N. (2008) "Is Google Making Us Stupid?" *The Atlantic*, 301(6), 56–63.

Carr, N. (2010) *The Shallows: What the Internet Is Doing to Our Brains*. New York: W.W. Norton.

Chaffee, S.H. and Schleuder, J. (1986) "Measurement and Effects of Attention to Media News." *Human Communication Research*, 13(1), 76–107.

Eisenstein, E. (1979) *The Printing Press as an Agent of Change: Communications and Cultural Transformations in Early Modern Europe*. Cambridge: Cambridge University Press.

Elmer-Dewitt, P. (1993) "First Nation in Cyberspace," *Time*, 49(December 6). www.time.com/time/magazine/article/0,9171,979768-3,00.html.

Halavais, A. (2001) *The Slashdot Effect: Analysis of a Large-Scale Public Conversation on the World Wide Web*. Doctoral dissertation, University of Washington.

Halavais, A. (2008) *Search Engine Society*. Cambridge: Polity.

Hargittai, E. (2003) "The Digital Divide and What to Do About It" in D.C. Jones, ed., *New Economy Handbook*. San Diego, CA: Academic Press, pp. 822–841.

James, W. (1890) *The Principles of Psychology*. New York: Henry Holt.

Lewin, K. (1947) "Frontiers in Group Dynamics; II. Channels of Group Life, Social Planning and Action Research." *Human Relations*, 1(2), 143–153.

Lippman, W. (1922) *Public Opinion*. New York: Harcourt, Brace.

Lyotard, J.-F. (1984 [1979]) *The Postmodern Condition: A Report on Knowledge*, trans. G. Bennington and B. Massumi. Minneapolis, MN: University of Minnesota Press.

McCombs, M. and Shaw, D. (1972) "The Agenda-Setting Function of the Mass Media." *Public Opinion Quarterly*, 36(2), 176–187.

Meyer, E.T. and Schroeder, R. (2009) "The World Wide Web of Research and Access to Knowledge." *Journal of Knowledge Management Research and Practice*, 7(3), 218–233.

Newman, M.Z. (2010) "New Media, Young Audiences and Discourses of Attention: From *Sesame Street* to 'Snack Culture.' " *Media, Culture & Society*, 32(4), 581–596.

Seneca, L.A. (1969 [n.d.]) *Letters from a Stoic*, trans. R. Campbell. London: Penguin.

Shaver, D. (2010) "Your Guide to Next Generation 'Content Farms.' " *MediaShift* (July 19). www.pbs.org/mediashift/2010/07/your-guide-to-next-generation-content-farms200.html.

Simon, H.A. (1971) "Designing Organizations for an Information-Rich World" in M. Greenberger, ed., *Computers, Communication, and the Public Interest*. Baltimore, MD: Johns Hopkins University Press.

Thompson, D. (2010) "Google's CEO: 'The Laws Are Written by Lobbyists.' " *The Atlantic* (October 1). www.theatlantic.com/technology/archive/2010/10/googles-ceo-the-laws-are-written-by-lobbyists/63908.

Tomasello, M. (1995) "Joint Attention as Social Cognition" in C. Moore and P.J. Dunham, eds., *Joint Attention: Its Origins and Role in Development*. Hillsdale, NJ: Lawrence Erlbaum Associates, pp. 103–130.

Wellman, B., Quan-Haase, A., Boase, J., et al. (2006) "The Social Affordances of the Internet for Networked Individualism." *Journal of Computer-Mediated Communication*, 8(3). http://jcmc.indiana.edu/vol8/issue3/wellman.html.
Williams, R. (1974) *Television: Technology and Cultural Form*. London: Fontana.

Further Reading

Spink, A. and Zimmer, M. (2008) *Web Search: Multidisciplinary Perspectives*. Berlin: Springer-Verlag.
Vaidhyanathan, S. (2011) *The Googlization of Everything*. Berkeley, CA: University of California Press.

16

Against Search

Toward A New Computational Logic of Media Accessibility

Pelle Snickars

Let's start off with one of the most compelling questions of our time: what does it mean to be human in the digital age? Well, one overwhelming challenge facing us all is having digital access to more information, data, and knowledge than any previous generation of humankind. A burden perhaps – at least for some. But, for the majority of us, this is a blessing. The often-invoked libertarian information-wants-to-be-free paradigm does not only require free flow of data. All these bits and bytes in the digital domain have to be organized and found, which, needless to say, is the underlying rationale for the most successful web behemoth of all. Suffice it to say, screens are ubiquitous and giving computers (and their mobile clones) textual and haptic commands has become normality. Access to whatever we want literally lies at our fingertips; information is there somewhere waiting, with the only question being where to look. So, you search.

Ever since Google introduced its clean, white search box interface in the late 1990s – the Internet Archive crawled the site for the first time in mid-November 1998 – the blank frame has been waiting for input.[1] During the past decade, this peculiar type of white box has become the new search default, especially within the information retrieval sector par excellence at archives, libraries, and museums. "Search the Collections," is the standard phrase awaiting every online user, implying a more or less vague notion that one already knows what one is looking for. Users are, of course, experienced since surfing the web basically means searching it. Subsequently, the notion of "search" is key for the digital domain in general, and the web in particular. Attempting to understand Google, Steven Levy notes, is like trying to "grasp our technological destiny" (Levy 2011: 7). From a more scholarly perspective, "Search Studies" is on the brink of developing into an academic field; search is, after all, *the* primary human–computer interaction mode. Mining search patterns and optimizing the engine is what Google and other search companies do on a daily basis, and can increasingly be anticipated through online "search" events in real life, such as the spread of flu. Search per se has in many ways somewhat paradoxically become the answer to questions asked.

The cultural logic of online search is, naturally, a vast topic – ranging from the omnipresent potential of Google analytics to the critique of the "Googlization of everything" and unfiltered initiatives such as Scroogle. Being coded and technical by nature, "search" remains highly complicated, with constantly upgraded algorithms exploiting the link structure of the web. Since studying tech infrastructures is a blind spot for media studies, the complexities are particularly striking from this perspective. Accessibility of a variety of media content in an age characterized by dynamics and volatility is, however, regulated by notions of search, and therefore it remains essential to analyze and grasp how and why "search" has become so important.

During the past decade, the notion of search has been challenged by new and alternative computational modes of accessibility, which is yet another argument in favor of taking "search" seriously (though, admittedly, few would argue otherwise). Tags, folksonomies, and social tagging are, for example, new transformative web-based practices and methods to annotate and categorize information and media content in an effort to collectively classify, tease out, and find data in other ways than simply through the mantra "search the collections." Online "browsing" is, of course, a widely used option, as well as simply "clicking." On YouTube – the quintessential new digital "archive" – one textual search is often enough, and then tags and linked videos lead the user into a streaming vortex of differentiated media. Context of content is often fleeting and arbitrary; odd juxtapositions are the norm rather than the exception, and material is regularly detached from its place of origin. Clicking rather than searching, thus, becomes an epistemic way of locating and perceiving media material, often in unintended ways. Usage resembles walking around in (weird) open library stacks, even if the much appraised digital "openness" on the net in general, and on Web 2.0 platforms in particular, always remains modulated on a protocological basis. A web browser is, after all, a translator of code and an interpreter of digital data that profoundly shapes user experiences. Then again, from a strict computer-science perspective, user-generated and participatory platforms such as YouTube are nothing but databases. Still, in any given cultural context, surfing onto a platform and watching a video at, say, YouTube obviously entails more than that. From a media studies perspective it is therefore debatable whether claims that we only "watch databases" (Lovink and Niederer 2008) – or claims that there is "no content, only data and other data" (Galloway and Thacker 2007) – have much relevance with regard to YouTube, or for that matter other cultural heritage and social media sites (for a discussion see Galloway and Thacker 2007; Lovink and Niederer 2008).

Nevertheless, given the sheer size of contemporary online media collections (from the vast information repositories of data at WikiLeaks or The Pirate Bay to the billions of items of user-generated content on YouTube and Flickr, or for that matter the 20 million digitized heritage objects at the Library of Congress), simply having a look what's inside the digital "archive" is no longer possible. However, the contemporary "flood of information" is by no means new. On the contrary, libraries and archives have during the past century repeatedly complained about there being too many books and documents. The major difference, today, is that in digitized form such material can be analyzed collectively as major cultural sets rather than on a singular basis only. Singularity works for analyzing the particular. But the general is arguably more interesting, and often of greater importance. Hence, massively linked data nowadays have the potential to reveal new human patterns that hitherto remained invisible. The notion of a particular "search," then, is not the answer to the more or less infinite digital archive.

New Modalities of Access

In this chapter – which borrows its title from a recent blog post by Lev Manovich (2011) – I will attempt to map out, explain and understand, and situate and critically examine new search modalities within a larger framework of information retrieval in general, and alternative forms of access to media archives in particular. In short, I will argue that new forms of different computational logics should increasingly be deployed in order to facilitate access to deep data as well as quantitative surface data in both web n.0 media collections and at more traditional digital archives and libraries currently being coded online. Archives and libraries are, however, conservative by nature; not even code changes that. Leaving aside the fact that memory institutions regularly use Web 2.0 services, at an institutional level archival material still needs to be *found* by way of a distinct, or even advanced, search (whatever that means). So, rather than taking advantage of the new properties of digital media – and in a sense "following the medium" – the notion of "search" is still embedded in traditional forms of archival access.

Open data, freely distributed application programming interfaces, and the increased sharing of networked data have, as is well known, led to new ways of distributing information (and knowledge). However, even though online access is surrounded by buzzwords such as "democracy," "free culture," and "networked society," accessibility is still regarded as a rudimentary and quite simplified question of search, not least within the cultural heritage sector. There are of course new ways of examining digital content through code and technological input rather than sheer human agency. New modes of content-based image retrieval or information visualization (for instance) are illustrative cases. An example of the former, related to Google's Similar Images, can be found at Europeana's ThoughtLab on heritage data, which presents an image search demo that scans 70 000 images from Europeana data providers and allows one to "perform image search based on a content-based retrieval technology using ... visual descriptors to decide on the similarity of images" (Europeana ThoughtLab n.d.). IBM's Many Eyes, which incorporates data visualization tools, is an example of an information visualization system in which users can upload data and then produce graphic representations for others to view and comment on. Data visualization is, often, understood as the mapping of digital data onto a visual image, and so-called "info vis" of large-scale collections of non-numerical information – as files or lines of code in software systems or bibliographic databases – has been a major contemporary trend during recent years. This is related to ways of scrutinizing "big social data" – that is, the ability to analyze data in scale within social networks, thus "enabling a range of intriguing and useful applications that can plug into social media networks and make use of the knowledge inside them," as *ZDNet* put it in May 2011 (Hinchcliffe 2011).

However, as Richard Rogers (2008, 2009) keeps reminding us, there remains an ontological distinction between the "natively digital" and the "digitized" – that is, between digital objects and content "born" in new media online, as opposed to, for example, scanned cultural heritage that has been migrated into the digital domain. The former, based on code, can be analyzed in myriad ways, whereas the latter often takes the form of a representational image file (to be searched for). In short, "digitized" material is not "digital." A new emerging computational logic of media accessibility, then – whether centered on haptic touch, information visualization, graphic similarities, or algorithmic search – needs to take this particular polarization of the "natively digital" and the "digitized" into account. Still, it goes without saying that various forms of "digital methods" ought to be used when approaching major social media collections or a heritage in bits online.[2]

From a "search" and media dynamics perspective, two current patterns are evident: on the one hand there are emerging new search patterns (especially in relation to the cultural heritage sector as well as models of algorithmic search); on the other, archives, libraries, and museums are currently working with new ways of (re)presenting their digitized collections, where rethinking design and archival interfaces is one way of altering and finding new modes (and nodes) of accessibility. In 2011, the British Library, for example, released an app for the iPad ("19th Century Historical Collection") that contains more than a thousand rare books with titles in fields such as travel writing, natural history, and philosophy. Users of the app have, of course, the ability to search the included books, but the individual items are predominantly viewed as high-resolution scans. Hence, one might argue that the iPad's touch screen per se functions as a kind of browse default to literally *handle* the included material. Perceiving these old books in digitized form, then, becomes not only a matter of "search" or reading but also (and more so) a means of haptic treatment and physical engagement – all smoothly executed with a gentle touch. According to a British Library press release, the app takes "advantage of the form and function of iPad, bringing a renewed sense of wonder to the discovery and enjoyment of antiquarian and historical books." As such, the app represents the latest landmark in the British Library's progress toward its "long-term vision of making more of its historic collections available to many more users through innovative technology" (British Library 2011). Another similar example of a sort of haptic archival immersion is the New York Public Library's "Biblion" app, centered around the official corporate records of the 1939–1940 New York World's Fair. The app contains some 700 documents, images, films, and audio material, and has been described as "one of the slickest media consumption experiences" that has yet been released for any tablet (Madrigal 2011). According to the New York Public Library, the app takes the user "literally into the Library's legendary stacks, opening up hidden parts of the collections and the myriad storylines they hold and preserve."[3]

Aspects of haptic immersion, then, make up one new fascinating computational logic of media accessibility within the heritage sector, mainly driven by new forms of tablet hardware and "the app revolution." Still, these apps also emphasize how technology always regulates access to the past, especially given that they are curated instances of selected entries into collections. It is essential to keep in mind when trying to map out new search modalities that underlying code regulates what can – and can't – be done. It should go without saying, but systems chosen for search and accessibility will always determine the output of information, as well as the research that can be performed. And again, needless to say, these are important epistemological issues. Searching the web is, as we know, critical to the ability to using the net, and whoever controls search engines has enormous influence. At present, Google shapes and regulates what "we read, who we listen to, and who gets heard. Whoever controls the search engines, perhaps, controls the Internet itself" (Grimmelmann 2009). Technology is not, and has never been, neutral. Nor can the way it arranges and systemizes knowledge. The suspicion that our writing tools are always working on "our thoughts" was, after all, voiced by Nietzsche as early as the 1880s. Hence, the massive efforts of arranging, cataloguing, and describing cultural heritage content made during the twentieth century in library systems, as Lev Manovich has stated, "made it difficult to browse a collection or navigate it in orders *not* supported by catalogs" (emphasis added). Walking from shelf to shelf one had to follow a classification system based on subjects, "with books organized by author names inside each category." Taken together, these distribution and classification "systems encouraged 20th century media researchers to decide before-hand what media items to see, hear, or read" (Manovich 2011). Today, however, the situation has changed and it is no longer impossible to imagine navigating – in one sense or another – through *all* collected material of a given topic, which, arguably, is an insight *in itself* that makes a difference.

More Data is Better Data

Under the heading "Humanities 2.0," *The New York Times* ran a series of articles during the winter of 2010–2011 on how digital tools are changing human scholarship. According to one of the pieces, members of a new generation of "digitally savvy humanists" no longer look for inspiration in the next "political or philosophical 'ism'" but rather want to explore how digital technology as an accelerating force is changing the overall understanding of the liberal arts. New methodologies, powerful technologies, and vast stores of digitized materials "that previous humanities scholars did not have" can potentially act as a revisionist model of what human research is all about (Cohen 2010).

Given the conservative culture of scholarship in general, and humanities research in particular, the basic arguments in these articles were striking, not least since they articulated the increasing role that computerized technology plays in humanities research (whether it wants it or not). If the computer, as some say, is the cultural machine of our age, the same goes for research. The field of digital humanities is rapidly picking up speed – often closely linked to the cultural heritage sector – and the discursive idea of the lone scholar, working in isolation with his or her own archiving solutions, will likely (at least in due time) fade away. As the report *Our Cultural Commonwealth* stated in 2006, humanistic researchers and users of

> massive aggregations of text, image, video, sound, and metadata will want tools that support and enable discovery, visualization, and analysis of patterns; tools that facilitate collaboration; an infrastructure for authorship that supports remixing, recontextualiza-tion, and commentary – in sum, tools that turn access into insight and interpretation. (Welshons 2006)

To be honest, we are not quite there yet. Still, there are many examples of a new media dynamics that involves upgraded modes of archival accessibility. One successful archival project, for example, is "Transcribe Bentham – A Participatory Initiative," under the auspices of the Bentham Project at University College London, which aims to produce new editions of the scholarship of Jeremy Bentham (see www.ucl.ac.uk/transcribe-bentham). "Transcribe Bentham" is, in short, an open-source and participatory online environment launched to aid users in transcribing 10 000 folios of Bentham's handwritten documents, and as such it has been invoked and discussed at length within the digital humanities. Speaking at a conference during the summer of 2010, Melissa Terras, for example, stated that crowd-sourcing and the harnessing of online activity

> to aid in large scale projects that require human cognition . . . [are] becoming of interest to those in the library, museum and cultural heritage industry, as institutions seek ways to publically engage their online communities, as well as aid in creating useful and usable digital resources. (Terras 2010)

If haptic entries and touch-screen interfaces on tablets constitute a minor current archival trend, then a major trend is heritage accessibility on a massive scale via large cultural data sets, as the example of Bentham's 10 000 handwritten documents show. Google has naturally paved the way for this overall change of perspective and scope, and has now digitized more than 15 million books – many of which belong to the public domain. According to a recent post on the *Inside Google Books* blog, 150 000 stem "from the 16th and 17th centuries, and another 450 000 from the 18th century" (Bloomberg and Groetsch 2011). Leaving aside the fact that Google Books has run into copyright problems, their digitization efforts have shown that massive scanning projects, on an hitherto unthinkable scale, can very well be undertaken. In addition, as Robert Darnton has pointed out,

> it is too early to do a postmortem on Google's attempt to digitize and sell millions of books, despite [current legal problems]. Google Book Search may rise from the ashes, reincarnated in some new settlement with the authors and publishers who had taken Google to court for alleged infringement of their copyrights. (2011)

Data from the scanned books are, in fact, already being widely distributed. With Google's Ngram Viewer, for example, it is possible to visualize the rise and fall of particular keywords across these scanned millions of hundred-year-old books. The respective terms "archive" and "database," for example, generated almost no interest before the late 1960s – then suddenly books started filling up with these very notions.

Mining textual archives and visualizing the results in various ways, is one contemporary strategy of moving beyond the white search box. "Text," however, largely remains the organizational mode of accessibility, and besides still makes up the bulk of content in "new" digital archives. Then again, the long-awaited celestial jukebox of all known media can no longer be discarded as a fanciful thought. On the contrary, it is already a reality through file-sharing and legal peer-to-peer sites such as Spotify, which as of 2011 boasted access to approximately 15 million songs and where social recommendations through "friends" increasingly point to alternative access modes for media. Everything that *can* be digitized *will* be digitized, the catch phrase once went during the 1990s, and a pertinent question is what such a claim actually implies. What practical consequences will it lead to on an institutional level, for instance? It is apparent that a new cultural logic of media accessibility has begun to emerge as a result of the sheer size of digital collections that is quite different from traditional and analogue search modalities.

Of course, browsing a library catalog has its particular media history. Ever since institutional heritage catalogs were transferred to digital formats during the 1970s and 1980s, similar search concepts and notions to those used today have been employed. These catalogs, once browsed manually by hand (often with the researcher leaning over giant stacks of index cards) in computerized form gave way to a new logic of access. Through input of textual commands on a computer screen, (re)searchers started to locate metadata – that is, information on and about the searched material, whether a book, an image, or a film – through highly subjective textual input. Today, with cultural heritage increasingly being digitized, transformed into, and represented as data, a similar mode of logic structures access, yet at the same time the potential is also there to navigate in completely new ways.

If user-generated content online has experimented with new classification systems during the past decade, institutionalized digitized heritage is still, basically accessible and found through ways of "searching" in online galleries. "See 30,000 items from our collection," as the British Library puts it (www.bl.uk). "Ideas and inspiration can be found within the more than 15 million items on Europeana," according to the major heritage portal Europeana.eu. Hence, searching a database of cultural items literally means executing a discrete set of commands: decide what to search for, browse the obtained metadata, and – if the object in question has been digitized – get access to an imagistic representation that can hopefully be downloaded for research or reuse. Europeana, for instance, boasts that it enables people to "explore the digital resources of Europe's museums, libraries, archives and audio-visual collections.

It promotes discovery and networking opportunities in a multilingual space where users can engage, share in and be inspired by the rich diversity of Europe's cultural and scientific heritage" (Europeana, n.d. a)

Then again, describing the above is merely stating the obvious. The bigger picture is how you actually search (or browse) 15 million cultural items – whether in a classical or Web n.0 fashion. Where do you start, and according to what principle do you try to make sense of *all* material potentially at your disposal? From a researcher's perspective, trying to relate to some scientific method, the task is (simply put) totally impossible. One just can't cope with so many items. No human user can do that – only a computer (or a network of them). There is no way of making analytical sense of 15 million cultural items. New digital dynamics of interlinkage, participatory tagging, and algorithmic search rather point toward the need for new mode(l)s of approach to such vast collections.

As a consequence, digital humanities scholars and researchers working with major cultural data sets have began to pose questions as to whether new digital archives, understood in a broad sense as massive collections of data, can be analyzed and searched *at all* in traditional ways. If humanities scholars previously worked by personally extracting data from archives, gleaning bits and pieces often found haphazardly, the millions of items in, for example, Europeana seem to call for (or at least imply) a new practice (as well as theory) of humanities research, involving the very machines that transformed heritage into data in the first place. "Digital archives can house so much data that it becomes impossible for scholars to evaluate the archive manually, and organizing such data becomes a paramount challenge," as a group of humanities–computer science researchers have stated (Simeone et al., 2011).

Accessing digital archives through algorithmic search has, for example, recently developed into a distinct way of moving beyond the search box. Broadly speaking, a search algorithm is an algorithm – that is, a set of procedures and instructions – for finding an item with specified properties within a collection, stored either individually as records in a database or as elements within a search space. The ability to share image data or major cultural data sets at full resolution, however, is crucial for all computational scientists and digital humanities scholars. But, with the right properties, algorithmic software can be applied and used in numerous graphical analyses as well as in advanced shape segmentation of digitized heritage. Interestingly, the same software can also be applied to different forms of material, be they illuminations in old paintings or geographical patterns in historical maps. With detailed replicas of objects to be analyzed, shape segmentation algorithms in one particular project (focusing on the study of historical maps) has been applied to the study of medieval manuscripts in another (Simeone et al., 2011).

The research initiative Digging into Data Challenge represents one way to tackle these issues. The idea behind the challenge, which hitherto has funded almost a hundred international research teams, is to address how "big data" has changed the research landscape for the humanities and social sciences. "Now that we have massive databases of materials used by scholars in the humanities and social sciences – ranging from digitized books, newspapers, and music to transactional data like web searches, sensor data or cell phone records," what forms of computationally based research methods can be applied? Since the world is becoming increasingly digital, what new techniques will actually be needed to "search, analyze, and understand these everyday materials." The projects undertaken within the Digging into Data Challenge have, as a consequence, devoted themselves to various forms of "big data" analyses, often grounded in a digitized cultural heritage. One project has, for example, mined data with "Criminal Intent" and developed tools and models for comparing, visualizing, and analyzing the history of crime using the Old Bailey Online and its extensive court records of almost 200 000 individual trials from 1674 to 1913. Another, "Digging into the Enlightenment," focuses on more than 50 000 digitized eighteenth-century letters and analyzes "the degree to which the effects of the Enlightenment can be observed in the letters of people of various occupations" (www.diggingintodata.org).[4]

A similar research initiative is "Cultural Analytics," proposed and undertaken by Lev Manovich at the University of California, San Diego. The project examines the use of digital image analysis and visualization for exploring massive visual data sets, and can be seen as a developing methodology within the digital humanities. "How do we analyze millions of digitized visual artifacts from the past?" the project's Facebook page asks. "How do we explore billions of digital photos and videos (both user-generated content and professional media)? How do we research interactive media processes and experiences (evolution of web design, playing a video game)?" To address such challenges, Cultural Analytics has developed methods, techniques, and software and applied these to progressively larger data sets. These techniques can be and have been used within various humanistic disciplines such as game studies and media studies, as well as in museum exhibitions.[5]

For Cultural Analytics – a term naturally linked to Google's similar offers – the notion of search, however, remains as puzzling as ever. In the aforementioned blog post, Manovich claimed that humanities and media studies researchers today have access to unprecedented amounts of media – "more than they can possibly study, let alone simply watch or even search." Nevertheless, the basic method that "worked fine when the number of media objects were [sic] small – see all images or video, notice patterns, and interpret them – no longer works." New research models and upgraded ways of seeing are needed since, according to Manovich, standard interfaces for massive digital media collections – such as lists, galleries, grids, or slides – do not allow one to see the "contents of a whole collection." Such interfaces regularly display only a few items at a time, which is an analogue access method that fails to allow a subtler and more sophisticated digital understanding of "the 'shape' of the overall collection" nor bring to the fore interesting patterns that might emerge (Manovich 2011).

If we take a critical stance, projects supported by the Digging into Data Challenge or undertaken within Cultural Analytics could be perceived as somewhat naïve in their technological optimism. Contemporary critiques of "info vis," for example, often ridicule a similar simple-minded tech positivism where the notion of "more data is better data" only leads to the paradoxical production of even more (visual) data. Quantitative methods do, after all, have their inherent problems, and even computers do not replace the need (sometimes) for human interpretation. Yet, what Cultural Analytics in particular has proposed is, actually, much more inclusive cultural histories and analyses of digitized heritage that ideally could take into account "all available cultural objects created in [a] particular cultural area and time period." A completely digitized history of *all* moving images would, for example, look radically different from today's canonical film history of artistic masterpieces and commercial blockbusters. Hence, the digitization of massive numbers of cultural artifacts and the progress in computational tools that can process huge amounts of data do in fact make possible a radically new approach to the humanities, not to mention a promise to move beyond simple "search." Mining data, in this respect, also means that humanist scholars no longer have to choose between "data size and data depth." Rather, they can potentially study "exact trajectories formed by billions of cultural expressions and conversations in space and time, zooming into particular cultural texts and zooming out to see larger patterns" (Manovich 2009).

Conclusion: The Politics of Data

"Think Culture," runs the subtitle on the heritage portal Europeana. Europeana is in many ways a pan-European political project with the overall purpose of boosting "Europeanness." The portal is, however, promising, even though a giant blank search page still awaits every visitor. "Search the collections" isn't explicitly stated, but inherently users are supposed to follow a standard logic. Then again, "Europeana always connects you to the original source of the material so you can be sure of its authenticity" (Europeana, n.d. a). After all, what is presented is "European heritage," not Web n.0 user-generated content.

At the same time, the notion of simple search has been called into question, and even been critically examined, as the guiding principle for access to cultural heritage material in general. Digital technology ought, of course, to be used to improve accessibility to Europe's cultural and scientific heritage in the future. Consequently, Europeana has launched a ThoughtLab where users can explore new initiatives, "participate and have your say, by viewing the demonstration models and sending feedback." Interestingly, one of the models (or projects) presented has the headline "New Ways of Searching and/or Browsing." A number of projects are listed, for example "A Semantic Search Engine for Europeana," which links data together for improved search, and "Europeana 4D," an interface that enables comparative visualization of multiple queries and supports data annotated with so-called time span data (see Europeana, n.d. b). The latter is also related to the project Europeana Connect, which aims to deliver core components (interfaces for mobile devices, rights licenses, user behaviors, and so on) essential for the development and enhancement of the portal.

If this chapter has tried to discuss the emergence of new search modalities, the experiments undertaken within Europeana ThoughtLab constitute but one example of how alternative forms of accessibility and novel interface design are trying to move beyond the white search box. Information visualization is, as has been stated, a growing field, and new forms of sophisticated data management are another. If Google Image Swirl organizes image search results based on visual and semantic similarities – by way of analyzing pixel values and presenting them in an "intuitive exploratory interface" – the Google Public Data Explorer makes large datasets easy to explore, visualize, and communicate. As charts and maps animate over time, changes are "easy to understand," as Google claims online. Simplicity is, then, key. "You don't have to be a data expert to navigate between different views, make your own comparisons, and share your findings" (www.google.com/publicdata/home).

Google has, of course, spearheaded such new forms of information retrieval, and tried to go beyond traditional text and hyperlink analysis to unlock information stored in, for example, image pixels. The same goes for the heritage sector – and the cooperation between various national libraries across Europe and Google is an illustrative case in point. Problems with funding digitization activities are, naturally, one reason for such partnerships, but more important for memory institutions is the transfer of know-how. "If our search algorithms can understand the content of images and organize search results accordingly, we can provide users with a more engaging and useful image-search experience" (Jing and Rowley 2009). In fact, "big data" approaches are currently being applied to a wide variety of "search problems" – all in an effort, perhaps, to move not against search but definitively toward a more dynamic mode of accessibility to media material and other forms of digital content. From books to maps to the structure of the web itself, "the world's information" is one "amazing dataset," as some Googlers recently stated in relation to the Google Books Ngram Viewer (Aiden and Michel 2011).

As Richard Wright reminds us, however, politics is always involved in any representation of data. More data might be better data, yet there are also implicit structures "in digital data, even when, and especially when, that expression takes us far from the realm of computer code." Then again, the greatest material distance between "human senses and computer code, when compared to the simplest material connections between them, delineates the imaginative possibilities of data visualization," as Wright puts it. According to him, this is an area where we currently can "explore the most extreme perspectives that software can create of itself" – its ability to put "cognitive and affective modes of perception into creative tension with data structures and with each other" (Wright 2008: 82). Such affective modes of perception are often as simple as they are convincing, and are regularly backed by one commercial interest or another. Then again, being human in the digital age constantly means deploying new perceptual functions and modalities, whether affective or not, in order to cope with the "information overload" paradigm. As this chapter has shown, one current trend (or strategy) is moving beyond mere "search," all in an effort to find (and with the expectation of finding) new interesting patterns that digital technology can offer.

Notes

1. For a snapshot of Google's earliest-retained search interface using Wayback Machine, see http://web.archive.org/web/19981111184551/http://google.com. For an intriguing as well as graphically mesmerizing presentation of the history of Google's search interface that makes use of all the available Google front pages in the Internet Archive, see Rogers (2008) and https://movies.digitalmethods.net/google.html.
2. For a general introduction to and discussion of "digital methods," see Rogers (2009) as well as the Digital Methods Initiative website: www.digitalmethods.net/Digitalmethods /WebHome.
3. For more information about the "Biblion" app, see http://exhibitions.nypl.org/biblion /worldsfair.
4. The Digging into Data Challenge website also contains information on a number of projects that have received grants.
5. For a description and introduction to Cultural Analytics, see Manovich (2009).

References

Aiden, E.L. and Michel, J.-B. (2011) "Culturomics, Ngrams and New Power Tools for Science." *Google Research* (August 10). http://googleresearch.blogspot.com/2011/08 /culturomics-ngrams-and-new-power-tools.html.

Bloomberg, D. and Groetsch, K. (2011) "Books from 16th and 17th Centuries Now in Full-Color View." *Google Books Search* (May 17). http://booksearch.blogspot.com/2011/05 /books-from-16th-and-17th-centuries-now.html.

British Library (2011) "BiblioLabs and the British Library Announce British Library 19th Century Historical Collection App for iPad" (June 7). http://pressandpolicy.bl.uk /Press-Releases/BiblioLabs-and-the-British-Library-Announce-British-Library-19th-Century-Historical-Collection-App-for-iPad-4f6.aspx.

Cohen, P. (2010) "Digital Keys for Unlocking the Humanities' Riches." *New York Times* (November 16). www.nytimes.com/2010/11/17/arts/17digital.html?pagewanted=all.

Darnton, R. (2011) "Google's Loss: The Public's Gain." *New York Review of Books* (April 28). www.nybooks.com/articles/archives/2011/apr/28/googles-loss-publics-gain /?pagination=false.

Europeana (n.d. a) "About Us." www.europeana.eu/portal/aboutus.html.

Europeana (n.d. b) "ThoughtLab: Think with Us." http://pro.europeana.eu/reuse /thoughtlab.

Europeana ThoughtLab (n.d.) "ThoughtLab: Think with Us: New Ways of Searching and/or Browsing." www.europeana.eu/portal/thoughtlab_semanticsearching.html.

Galloway, A.R. and Thacker, E. (2007) *The Exploit.* Minneapolis, MN: University of Minnesota Press.

Grimmelmann, J. (2009) "The Google Dilemma." *New York Law School Review*, 53, 939. http://works.bepress.com/james_grimmelmann/19.

Hinchcliffe, D. (2011) "How Social Media and Big Data will Unleash What We Know." *ZDNet* (May 12). www.zdnet.com/blog/hinchcliffe/how-social-media-and-big-data-will -unleash-what-we-know/1533.

Jing, Y. and Rowley, H. (2009) "Explore Images with Google Image Swirl." *Google Research* (November 23). http://googleresearch.blogspot.com/2009/11/explore-images-with-google-image-swirl.html.

Levy, S. (2011) *In the Plex*. New York: Simon & Schuster.

Lovink, G. and Niederer, S., eds. (2008) *Video Vortex Reader: Responses to YouTube*. Amsterdam: Institute of Network Cultures. http://networkcultures.org/wpmu/portal/files/2008/10/vv_reader_small.pdf.

Madrigal, A. (2011) "Did the New York Public Library Just Build the Magazine App of the Future?" *The Atlantic* (May 18). www.theatlantic.com/technology/archive/2011/05/did-the-new-york-public-library-just-build-the-magazine-app-of-the-future/239107.

Manovich, L. (2009) "Cultural Analytics." *Software Studies Initiative*. http://lab.softwarestudies.com/2008/09/cultural-analytics.html.

Manovich, L. (2011) "Against Search." *Manovich.net* (July 21). http://manovich.net/2011/07/22/against-search.

Rogers, R. (2009) "The End of the Virtual – Digital Methods." www.govcom.org/rogers_oratie.pdf.

Rogers, R. (2008) "The Demise of the Directory." *Digital Methods Initiative*. https://wiki.digitalmethods.net/Dmi/DemiseDirectory.

Simeone, M., Guilano, J., Kooper, R., and Bajcsy, P. (2011) "Digging into Data Using New Collaborative Infrastructures Supporting Humanities-Based Computer Science Research." *First Monday*, 16(5). http://firstmonday.org/htbin/cgiwrap/bin/ojs/index.php/fm/article/view/3372/2950.

Terras, M. (2010) "Present, Not Voting: Digital Humanities in the Panopticon" (July 10). http://melissaterras.blogspot.com/2010/07/dh2010-plenary-present-not-voting.html.

Welshons, M., ed. (2006) "Our Cultural Commonwealth." *American Council of Learned Societies*. www.acls.org/cyberinfrastructure/ourculturalcommonwealth.pdf.

Wright, R. (2008) "Data Visualization" in M. Fuller, ed., *Software Studies. A Lexicon*. Cambridge, MA: MIT Press.

Network

17

Evolutionary Dynamics
of the Mobile Web

Indrek Ibrus

Introduction

The conceptual presumption of this chapter is that, in relation to media change, both
the *media* and the process of *change* should be taken as organic phenomena. This
is effectively to conceptualize the media as an *ensemble* that consists of an infinite
number of representational forms and conventions; of practices of consumption
and production of these forms; of institutional forms of these practices; and of the
industrial organization of these institutions. When such an ensemble changes it does
so organically. Its components are in their evolution only semiautonomous; they
condition each other reciprocally and *coevolve*, affecting the evolution of the whole
of which they are parts. This chapter will investigate these kinds of interdependencies
in the evolution of mobile media as an ensemble. It will do this both conceptually
and empirically.

Traditionally, the component domains of the "media ensemble" and their specific dynamics have been studied in isolation, by disciplinarily distant academic
domains. For instance, semiotics or various forms of cultural studies have been
used for studying the evolution of media's textual forms; "media archaeology"
among others has focused on the changes in media technologies; political economy
approaches or media economics has investigated the changes in markets and in
forms of media production. To break out of these closed disciplinary perspectives,
I propose the use of an integrated set of varied disciplinary approaches that,
however, are all similarly distinct for conceptualizing the "evolutionary dynamics"
in their respective fields. These are: cultural semiotics (Yuri Lotman and others)
for interpreting the textual dynamics inherent in cultures; evolutionary economics
(Joseph Schumpeter and others) for understanding the market dynamics that
condition the formation of the modern media and communications industries;
and systems theoretical sociology (Niklas Luhmann and others) to understand the
broader dynamics of social organization in the contemporary period. Deploying

A Companion to New Media Dynamics, First Edition. Edited by John Hartley, Jean Burgess, and Axel Bruns.
© 2013 John Wiley & Sons, Ltd. Published 2015 by John Wiley & Sons, Ltd.

such a variety of disciplinary perspectives, I aim to conceptualize what Leydesdorff (1994) has called the emergence of theories of "relevant interactions" of subsystems. In this case those relevant interactions constitute the ground for a theory of media innovation.

The empirical focus of this chapter is on the early development of the mobile web, which according to many is about to evolve into one of the main, if not the most important, access platforms to the web and its resources. What is more, with this the web itself is about to evolve into a crossmedia phenomenon, providing as such a valuable case study to investigate how *networks* function as evolutionary "ensembles," how they converge and when they diverge. I will be looking for coevolving networks at different "levels" – not only the physical network infrastructures but also networks of people; "industrial networks"; and networks of meanings and discursive constellations. The study on which this chapter is based (including documentary research and interviews with three dozen industry executives; see Ibrus 2010) was conducted between 2006 and 2008. It investigated the evolution of the mobile-accessible web in a period that started with the launch of 3G networks in the Western world and ended with the arrival of Apple's iPhone, which represented a new phase in the evolution of the mobile web. However, I will demonstrate that some of the ongoing policy discussions, for instance the dilemma of web versus apps for content provision, originate from the historically contextual dynamics within the industry described in this chapter. To better understand the current alternatives for the further evolution of the networked media, we need to learn about how some of its historical path-dependencies were conditioned.

Conceptualization: Evolutionary Dynamics of Media

What are the "evolutionary dynamics" of media? With this term I refer to interactions between the different composites of the "media ensemble" as well as the interactions of this ensemble with its environment. In aggregate, all these dynamics could be seen to effect change in a particular ensemble or in a media system. I have found Yuri Lotman's concept of the "semiosphere" (Lotman 1990) useful in making sense of the relationships in such systems and subsystems. Lotman designed the concept of the semiosphere to analyze the positions and relationships of a culture's texts in a wider semiotic space. Within the semiosphere, one can analytically distinguish an endless variety of cultural subspaces that transect and intertwine with each other at different "levels." Some spaces, for example one single website, are small and parts of others – of the whole of the "web-sphere" of culture, for instance. Some could embrace numerous smaller ones. For instance, a national media system could consist of a variety of media types and genres (print media, TV, radio, Internet) or of several institutional systems such as competing publishing groups. At the same time, smaller spaces could also be perceived as parts of several bigger ones – a website could be seen as part of an internationally recognized webmedia genre, or as a component of a carefully designed crossmedia universe, or again be taken as an entity of a distinct national media system.

I also propose that such sub-semiospheres, for instance "mobile media" or "online journalism," should be understood as textual domains that have established certain social identities; they have started to function as "social subsystems," in Niklas Luhmann's (1995) terms. Luhmann argued that a social system comes together as a series of self-referential "communications" that describe the nature and purpose of the social domain. In Lotman's terms, we can establish that such communications can only materialize in "texts" of various kinds. Hence, a social system emerges as result of a "mesh of texts" that, as a specific whole, starts to work "autopoietically" (it is self-created). What this means is that there are texts that work meta-textually toward other texts of the same mesh or toward the whole of that mesh. For example, various normative guidelines or marketing texts describe the distinct specifics of the mesh, differentiate it from the rest of culture and society, and eventually codify it and set the norms and expectations for the future of the particular system.

In our context, in studying the evolution of media forms and the forms of social organization "around them," I suggest that the text-borne discourses that define the media forms in question also define the nature of practices of their production and, eventually, the forms and operations of the social organizations carrying out these practices. In other words, textual forms, "discourse communities," and institutional forms are interdependent in their evolution and, therefore, to understand the change in one we also need to investigate the others.

Among these texts, discourses, and institutions, what is the agent of *change*? Here we need to turn to Schumpeter's theory of economic evolution. In general economic theory, every system aims to minimize its inherent discontinuities and to achieve equilibrium. The mechanism of equilibration provides a resistance to change in the economic system. It is the self-defense mechanism of established business and institutional traditions; the creation of order and continuities that *subsume* the creation of novelties and discontinuities (Freeman and Louçã 2001). In that case, how does the system generate the innovative mutation and discontinuities that, according to the Schumpeterian argument, arise from the system itself? To explain this, we can return to Lotman's semiotics. In his terms, every cultural space has its self-defined boundaries in space and/or time. But a cultural system, while identifying itself, its boundaries, and the outside, also identifies the Other and its characteristics. It has to understand and translate those features for itself. Or, as Luhmann puts it, boundaries cannot be conceived without something "beyond," presupposing the reality of a beyond and thus the possibility of transcendence (Luhmann 1995: 28). When a "translation" through the boundary is conducted, a communicative act has taken place and, through this, new information has entered the cultural space. According to Sebeok (1991: 22), it is the act of communication that decreases entropy locally – that is, produces change within the system. Hence, it is *communication* between different societal subsystems or semiotic spaces (different disciplines, industries, professions, firms, countries, etc.) that facilitates production of new information and innovation. Defining cultural change broadly, we can establish that it is effected by dialogic acts between different social systems. New systems emerge from contacts between existing ones and the existing systems change following the dialogic acts between them.

Such evolution should not be understood as linear, in the way that biological evolution is. Once a living species is extinct, it stays that way. But, after reorganizing themselves, cultural systems do not simply leave previous selections behind to be forgotten. Instead, according to Lotman, communicational forms move constantly between the central societal focus and its periphery, according to the pace at which they "defamiliarize" themselves and/or acquire new innovative semantic potential. Hence, everything saved in the reservoirs of cultural memory is directly or indirectly part of culture's modern operations: it can be retrieved and reused. Therefore, cultural evolutionary change is not linear but a circular development, constituted by "remediations" from the periphery or memory of culture into its current mainstream, where they may appear as innovative disruptions.

Such necessary continuities, which link a culture's modern forms and applications with its histories, indicate also how the past or memory of culture may condition its futures. In evolutionary economics, such a function is recognized as one of "path-dependency" or historical "lock-in" of evolutionary processes. David (2000), one of the authors of the concept, argues that, in the case of technologies, where there is an advantage in sharing a common system (and most mass media technologies and communications platforms benefit from a shared standard), there is a point in the diffusion of a new technology where the spontaneous decisions of individual users lock in one technology and drive out the others. This understanding relates to the concept of "network externalities," where *agents* adopt a certain sort of behavior (or a media platform) simply because a considerable number of others have already adopted it.

In addition to positive network externalities on the end-user level, there are other sources of "positive feedback" that may lead a system to path-dependency; for example, *technological* interrelatedness, where the functioning of the parts is contingent on the functioning of the whole, which could deter revolutionary changes of the parts. Similarly, *industrial networks* may impede rapid development by sticking to established rules and regulations, routine transactions, relationship-specific investments, and so on. Finally, the process of *learning* itself, especially as a mass phenomenon, is unavoidably slow and thus hinders revolutionary changes in established systems. David points out that the configurations that result from such positive feedback processes could be understood as "self-sustaining equilibria" (2000: 26). That is, in the case of a path-dependent process, some particular historical event initiates a sequence of transitions, which selects the configuration that is going to be realized as the system's emergent property. In other words, a system's selections depend on and are limited by its autopoietic functioning, which in turn relies on its existing textual configuration.

In the light of the above, I propose that a *social subsystem* may be understood as a complex mesh of texts that reciprocally meta-communicate about each other and about the whole that they constitute in aggregate. If so, this process may be recognized as a cultural "lock in" that makes such systems, to an extent, path dependent. The different kinds of texts in this mesh – either the media forms as "object texts" or the different kinds of meta-texts that codify the object texts – cannot shake free from each other since they are simply made to model one another in various ways; they are contingent on the whole. Further, even if the textual systems and cultural codes happen to evolve, owing to the information exchanges between different systems, this cannot happen promptly, since it takes time for the variety of "speech communities" to learn the new codes so as to reach successful and adequate interpretations. Thus, the evolutionary *dynamics* of cultural systems could be argued to be constituted by the tension between, on the one hand, the drive for change effected by dialogic interactions between existing systems and, on the other, the autopoietic self-reinforcement of the those same systems.

In relation to the evolution of networks, I would like to bring forward the concept of "industrial networks," originally introduced and developed by several Swedish economists (see Lundgren 1991: 81–99). The emphasis of this concept is on the fundamental heterogeneity and discrepancy of markets in the economy, which is caused by the dynamics of innovation as described above. However, that process also conditions the plurality of institutional actors that operate the markets together with the plurality of interconnections between these institutions – interconnections across existing markets and across national or industrial borders. As the economy evolves in this way, industrial activities become increasingly interconnected, making up *complex networks*. However, there is a practical need to reduce complexities and manage uncertainties. So these interconnections, such as exchange relationships, need to be secured and coordinated. Eventually, the stabilization of interconnections brings about specific "industrial networks" of institutions, linked together by their interdependence in performing interconnected complementary or competitive industrial activities. This concept of the industrial network is seen to replace other formulations, such as single-market hierarchies and value chains. However, as Lundgren (1991: 98–99) proposes, such networks are also facilitated by the technological systems that are deployed in operations. For instance, shared technological standards or the installment of a new communications infrastructure could facilitate the settlement of an industrial network.

How is the concept of "industrial networks" relevant to the theoretical approach proposed above? I argue that, especially in the sphere of cultural and creative industries, the semiotic and discursive systems, intertextual connections, and other textual relationships have a similar facilitating role for the emergence and further coordination of an industrial network. And vice versa: the development of industry's specific institutional networks facilitates the development of textual and discursive systems "around them." Based on this I define "media evolution" as the emergence and further development of a certain organic textual, technical, and institutional system that is inherently heterogeneous but interconnected and self-reinforcing in real time.

Networks of the Mobile Web and Their Evolution

In this section, I will see what we can glean from the history of mobile media using the conceptual framework proposed above. It is important at the outset to recognize the dominant role that network operators have played in the history of mobile communications. Before the market liberalization of the 1980s and 1990s, telecommunications markets, in Europe at least, were usually dominated by state-controlled monopolies. These monopoly players had the power to control most of the related industrial activities downstream along the value chain, such as terminal design and related technology development. However, after the invention of the cellular principle, the initiative in developing mobile communications has been gradually shifting to the vendors of handsets and other technologies. For instance, 2G mobile standards (GSM) were initially developed by telecoms operators only, but soon afterwards the development work was shifted to a new European standards body (the European Telecommunications Standards Institute, or ETSI) that also included manufacturers. The manufacturers used this position, first, to capitalize on the intellectual property rights they acquired in the process and, then, to establish themselves as dominant players in a global marketplace that was facilitated by the spread of the GSM standard around the world. The development of both 2G and 3G standards had a similar effect on operators. Networks of operators of both European (Vodafone, T-Mobile) and Asian (Hutchison) origin were spreading around the world. The gradual evolution of an "international industrial network" of mobile communications can be observed in the subsequently global but ever-more-tightly-integrated roles of technology vendors and networks in service design and technology development.

At this point in the process of network convergence, the provision of media content and web services on mobile devices was still up for grabs. In this context it is important to note that, whereas GSM had been designed as a stand-alone system, 3G networks had to be integrated with fixed telecommunications networks. The planners of 3G services saw that the services available for fixed Internet users had to be made available to mobile users as well. Development toward an integrated personal communication environment was envisaged in which users would be able to access all services and content, irrespective of whether the means of access were fixed or mobile.

This convergence of fixed and mobile networks started to lead to the break-up of the operator-centric value chain (Wirtz 2001: 492; Yang et al. 2004). Content and "app" providers, aggregators and service houses, started to enter the fray. The bargaining power of these new stakeholders was on the rise (Sharma and Nakamura 2003: 67; Steinbock 2003: 12). However, this was a gradual process. As noted in a report by the Organisation for Economic Co-operation and Development in 2005, the year when most 3G services were launched in Europe, at that stage it was still the mobile operator who occupied the central position in the value chain for mobile content because of their direct, ongoing relationship with the customer (Kunin et al. 2005: 12). Most mobile users obtained mobile content through their operators' branded portals. These offered content only from providers with whom the mobile operator had established a relationship. These portals were, therefore, known as "walled gardens." The content offerings remained overwhelmingly proprietary, largely neglecting the experience of the Internet and the proliferation of SMS communication on mobiles. In the latter cases, innovation processes occurred in distributed, nonproprietary spaces and tended to be user-driven. Hence, as argued by Goggin and Spurgeon, the design of mobile content portals and premium-rate services could be criticized because design values and possibilities were guided mainly by the "power of capital" rather than by the "messy innovations of multitudes of users" (2007: 765). In addition, the operators' market power usually resulted in unilaterally established guidelines for the design of services and content, jeopardizing innovation in content provision (Pashtan 2005: 4; Noam 2007: 26–33).

However, change was about to be introduced to this state of affairs. In the previously separate fixed-line and wireless telecommunications networks, the service starting point for users was network access (Yang et al. 2004: 43–44). But, with the convergence of fixed and mobile networks, content became the new starting point. Customers demanded their content regardless of the type of network. Hence, the newly reconfigured value chain started to highlight the role of content providers, as they had the key role in bridging the gaps between different networks and value-chain components. They acted as the main drivers for the adoption of mobile content services. The emerging crossmedia narratives were about to give them more leverage in their negotiations with operators (Feldmann 2005: 181).

This was especially true after the launch of 3G networks. In the early stages, customers did not enroll in large numbers. That led to a growing realization among the operators that content creation was not their strength and thus there would be a role for brands associated with quality content. Network operators' "own-brand" news and sports content did not prove to be as compelling for customers as, say, BBC News and SkySports (to use UK examples). Hence, realizing this, the operators gradually retreated from creating content. At the same time, subscribers also appeared to be seeking "long-tail" content, evidenced by the rise in operators' revenues from Internet surfing. Open Internet browsing as an income source emerged as an increasingly appealing solution for operators, especially because this again allowed them to leave content creation and management to the media-centric vendors.

For all these reasons, by the mid-2000s the relationships between mobile operators and various content and service providers were cascading into dynamic change. Commentators at the time toyed with notions such as "co-opetition" and "value nets" that were understood to replace the competitive positioning in value chains (Feldmann 2005: 171–180; Schweizer 2006). Increasing convergence between mobile and Internet applications, and greater attention to network economics, caused "value nets" to emerge as a new paradigm for cooperation in the network industries, including wireless communications. Complex horizontal linkages between players in the value net, and inter-firm cooperation, were seen as important for the value-creation process and for building a new industry and a new attractive market (Srivastava and Finger 2006: 18). The formation of a new horizontal market was interdependent with industry convergence (Wirtz 2001: 495–496), resulting in a new form of industry organization – the converged "industrial network of mobile media."

However, despite these changes, in terms of the materiality of platforms, there still existed a clear divide between mobile and desktop devices, and their respective networked content environments – WAP (i-mode in Asia) and the web. Although structured somewhat similarly and utilizing Internet infrastructure, these two forms remained technically disconnected. It was not possible to lift content easily from one to the other. This was partly due to the technological limits of mobile devices, but there had also been the pursuit of mobile industries to develop WAP into a content domain that would constitute an alternative to the desktop web. Hence, also, the technological discontinuity.

But, with content providers trying increasingly to offer content for various mobile devices, this technical divide was addressed as a threshold. In addition, not only was WAP incompatible with the mainstream web but it was also itself internally fragmented with many semiproprietary islands. Therefore, it was not long before the content and service industry called for standardization of the mobile web, to enable content providers to create once and publish everywhere. With this purpose the industry was looking for a neutral platform for the standardization work. In the context of the regular web, the best track record in this regard belonged to W3C and it thus also gained mobile industry support. This marked the first step of the subsequent institutional convergence of mobile and web domains – that is, telecoms and handset vendors with W3C and major online service providers. In fact, the convergence agenda emerged as the common denominator of this camp. It should be emphasized that, despite what is claimed, the W3C was never a neutral site for consensus-seeking standardization of grassroots innovation. It had its own agenda, to protect the web from being broken up into device-specific subspaces. Instead, W3C's imperative has been the "One Web" idea – that the web should be indivisible, always the same on all possible access devices. Its vision was that the then uni-platform web should become crossplatform and spread out from the desktop devices to all other screen devices – mobiles, game consoles, and so on. This vision met a friendly response within the mobile industry. Companies and other institutions such as Vodafone, Deutsche Telekom, NTT DoCoMo, Google, Opera, dotMobi, and others agreed to sponsor or participate in W3C's new Mobile Web Initiative (MWI), and with that they effectively signed on to that imperative of the "One Web."

The actions of this group were first focused on overcoming fragmentation in terms of mark-up languages, both within the WAP platform and between the WAP and web platforms. The mobile industry facilitated dialogue between W3C and the mobile industry's own standardization body, Open Mobile Alliance (OMA). Not long afterwards, this cooperation gave rise to the formalization of XHTML Basic 1.1, a new universal standard for the mobile web, which was now also fully compatible with the "full XHTML." However, this development was only the beginning of an evolving effort to secure the convergence of the two platforms. Another step was undertaken via W3C's Mobile Web Best Practices guidelines (W3C 2006). With these, a different attempt to achieve the aim of "One Web" was made as compared to the earlier effort to make mark-up languages compatible. These were, in effect, design guidelines and were, in a rather accentuated way, independent of existing platforms. They offered guidelines on how to design a website in a way that did not presume the need for significant adaptation in order to be displayed on different access devices. With suggestions such as the need to avoid pop-ups, or not to use tables for layouts or graphics for spacing, the MWI hoped that it would be possible to achieve generic design – one that would be "good enough" on devices with very different capabilities. All this represented a design ideology that was expected to help to overcome a division into two webs that was unavoidably marked by the existence of two different form factors: "desktop" and "mobile."

The development of new codes for different levels and functionalities (programming languages, design guidelines), which would work to converge the two platforms, was also carried out by leading industry enterprises. For instance, the tier-1 network operator T-Mobile, when pioneering a "flat-fee and unlimited web access" offer in Europe, developed new automated transcoding technologies to enable users to view full websites on mobile screens. Then, at the level of meta-codes, first the price structure for browsing was matched to conventional pricing models for the desktop web and then, in advertising and other marketing, the sameness of the two platforms was industriously communicated – to convince users that there was continuity in the experience and that the dislocated medium would meet their "horizons of expectations" (Jauss 1982: 23). In other words, continuities were emerging in parallel at multiple levels, in a mixture of meta- and object-languages.

The convergence in meta-codes developed in parallel with the institutional convergence of those industry players who were motivated to work toward merging the two platforms. As a result, the emergence of a new industry subsystem – which I have termed "infrastructure enablers" – was identified. This new subsystem came together, first, from the former major telecommunications industry players (operators, handset manufacturers, and specialized software vendors); and, second, from the major online players (in particular search engines) and web-specific software vendors, including many of the major browser companies. The convergence was conditioned by the first of these groups being motivated to gain access to the web as a functional market (as opposed to WAP as dysfunctional). For the second group, the motivation was to extend their business to yet another platform, to gain new customers and to cement their position in the context of the newly ubiquitous and crossplatform web. The affiliates of this new subsystem or "industrial network" reciprocally conditioned each other's involvement and roles in the evolving network.

Once the new 3G networks were deployed, first T-Mobile and later other network operators launched business models that enabled unrestricted full web browsing on mobile devices, leading to the early take-up of this utility. This affected the activities of numerous software vendors – existing browser vendors and new transcoder vendors with their website re-rendering solutions – who saw their opportunity in improving the quality of such browsing. These browsers and transcoders were, in turn, deployed by operators as default solutions in their networks, or by Internet search engines to transcode their search results for mobile access. All of these stakeholders were in constant dialogue, working privately together on particular solutions and publicly on negotiating associated standards either in W3C, dotMobi, or OMA. In this way, their formation *as a system* was executed on many levels and in several "languages" – in discourses, institutional structures, and technologies that enabled their cooperation and formation as an industrial network.

However, I have also identified the historical emergence of a *competing social system*, favoring a different evolutionary trajectory for the mobile web. This second industry group was made up of various content and service providers. They were discursively cohesive in sharing similar interests and analogous perspectives on the further development of the mobile web that were different from those of the "infrastructure enablers." This opposition mounted most visibly once W3C started to regulate the presentational standards of the web. Content and service providers resisted the proposed "generic design" for all devices, because it would have meant leaving their content effectively "un-designed," ceding the power to determine the eventual design of their products to other parties such as browser and transcoder vendors. The content providers wanted to keep that power to themselves; to decide what content, in what form, to deliver in what circumstances to what platform. This meant nothing less than claiming the right to establish discontinuities between the various access platforms.

The technological solutions to how to create such discontinuities and to output content for different device classes or platforms differently – a technique now known as "content adaptation" – were developed by communities of independent mobile developers and by small content companies on the margins of the industry. Finding thereafter wide take-up among their colleagues, the content adaptation for different access devices evolved as another new technology, a code of conduct and a structuring principle for the web-media. It had the potential to develop into a new industry convention, one that would set the mobile web together with the general crossplatform web on a different evolutionary path. The institutions that developed these technologies shared similar discourses on the nature of the mobile web, and this made them collectively distinct as a "discourse community" and an "industry subsystem."

Power struggles and dialogue between the different parties has followed, on a variety of levels. At W3C the compromise that gradually emerged was that the "One Web" could mean continuities in the technological code, that content accessible from the same URL by different devices should stay "thematically the same" but that, when it came to the forms of the media (i.e., how content was to be presented), the discontinuities between access platforms were increasingly legitimated. In other words, the dialogical process between the different industry subsystems yielded standards that were to condition not the convergence but the divergence of media forms.

However, related power struggles were far from being over. W3C continued to promote its design guidelines for the device-agnostic web with its new MobileOK trustmark and automated checkers (these checked whether websites were compatible with the guidelines), all in order to make its favored design guidelines an industry standard. However, as these did not suit the interests of many of the web content and service developers, "local" codes of practice and design started to emerge. In parallel, being scared of the poor quality of automatically re-rendered websites, content providers were increasingly motivated to output mobile-optimized websites. This practice may be understood as a tacit counter-action to the conduct of the "infrastructure enablers" and as silent disapproval of the design the latter were favoring for the device-agnostic web of the future. Later the same trend was manifested in the momentous popularity of the apps format of mobile content developed and popularized by Apple. The app format was well received by the content providers since it enabled them to regain full control over what content was presented and how it was displayed on mobile devices. Overall, there was a whole *mesh* of power struggles taking place at different stages of the medium's evolution, at different sites of the industry and among different players, that had a bearing on the further evolution of the mobile web as a media platform.

Conclusion

Despite all the flux and ambiguity at the time, two major industry subsystems emerged with alternative agendas when it came to creating continuities or discontinuities between the two main access platforms to the web – the "infrastructure enablers" and the content industries. At the beginning of this chapter I discussed how it was during the WAP era that operator-centric value chains were disrupted by the influx of content and service providers, new players whose bargaining power was on the rise. The associated market horizontalization started to turn value chains into "value nets." This development was interdependent with the parallel process of industry convergence. My empirical study of the further development of the mobile or crossplatform web seems to confirm the continuation of these processes. Its findings reveal a flux in the roles of different stakeholders, in the boundaries separating and defining them, and in their social organization. There was a mesh of dialogic relationships, processes of "dialogic control" (Ibrus 2010:79) between an indefinite number of actors that in concert made up the evolutionary dynamics of the mobile web and conditioned its convergence with the regular web.

However, in parallel to flux and new discontinuities, path-dependencies were also partly reproduced. The "infrastructure enablers" were building on the legacies, roles, and positions of the online industries and the network operators, and were collectively working toward sustaining their position by developing technologies that enabled them to control the newly crossplatform web. The content providers, at the same time, were recursively building on their legacy of being in control of their contacts with users and of content delivery. With that aim they were developing related technologies of "content adaptation."

We may therefore conclude that the *evolutionary dynamic* of the crossplatform web was constituted by the *tension* between the dialogic activities effecting convergence and the autopoietic operations causing path-dependencies, which resulted in counter-movements toward the divergence of networks. We should, however, recognize how both forces and tendencies took place at different levels or modalities. The crossplatform web evolved not only via the convergence of technologies but also via converging institutions, discourses, and other meta-codes, as well as via the parallel divergence of media's textual forms. That being so, the evolution of the mobile web exemplifies the complexities inherent in the evolutionary dynamics of new media.

References

David, P.A. (2000) "Path Dependence, Its Critics and the Quest for 'Historical Economics'" in P. Garrouste and S. Ioannides, eds., *Evolution and Path Dependence in Economic Ideas: Past and Present*. Cheltenham: Edward Elgar, pp. 15–39.

Feldmann, V. (2005) *Leveraging Mobile Media: Cross-Media Strategy and Innovation Policy for Mobile Media Communication*. Heidelberg: Physica-Verlag.

Freeman, C. and Louçã, F. (2001) *As Time Goes by: From the Industrial Revolutions to the Information Revolution*. Oxford: Oxford University Press.

Goggin, G. and Spurgeon, C. (2007) "Premium Rate Culture: The New Business of Mobile Interactivity." *New Media & Society*, 9(5), 753–770.

Ibrus, I. (2010) "Evolutionary Dynamics of New Media Forms: The Case of the Open Mobile Web." Doctoral dissertation, London School of Economics and Political Science. http://etheses.lse.ac.uk/53.

Jauss, H. R. (1982) *Toward an Aesthetic of Reception*. Minneapolis, MN: University of Minnesota Press.

Kunin, C., Vickery G., and Wunch-Vincent, C. (2005) *Digital Broadband Content: Mobile Content. New Content for New Platforms*. Paris: Organisation for Economic Co-operation and Development.

Leydesdorff, L. (1994) "Epilogue" in L. Leydesdorff and P.V.D. Besselaar, eds., *Evolutionary Economics and Chaos Theory: New Directions in Technology Studies*. London: Pinter, pp. 180–192.

Lotman, Y. (1990) *Universe of the Mind: A Semiotic Theory of Culture*. Bloomington, IN: Indiana University Press.

Luhmann, N. (1995) *Social Systems*. Stanford, CA: Stanford University Press.

Lundgren, A. (1991) *Technological Innovation and Industrial Evolution – The Emergence of Industrial Networks*. Stockholm: Stockholm School of Economics.

Noam, E.M. (2007) "The Next Frontier for Openness: Wireless Communications" in D. Steinbock and E.M. Noam, eds., *Competition for the Mobile Internet*. New York: Springer-Verlag, pp. 21–38.

Pashtan, A. (2005) *Mobile Web Services*. Cambridge: Cambridge University Press.

Schweizer, L. (2006) "Convergence: A Challenge for Mobile Telecommunication Operators – the Case of the German T-Mobile." *International Journal of Mobile Communications*, 4(2), 143–162.

Sebeok, T.A. (1991) *A Sign is Just a Sign*. Bloomington, IN: Indiana University Press.

Sharma, C. and Nakamura, Y. (2003) *Wireless Data Services*. Cambridge: Cambridge University Press.

Srivastava, J.V. and Finger, M. (2006) *Fixed to Mobile Convergence: Technological Convergence and the Restructuring of the European Telecommunications Industry*. Paper presented at SPRU 40th Anniversary Conference, University of Sussex, UK (September 11–13).

Steinbock, D. (2003) *Wireless Horizon: Strategy and Competition in the Worldwide Mobile Marketplace.* New York: AMACOM.

W3C (2006) *Mobile Web Best Practices 1.0, Proposed Recommendation.* Mobile Web Initative, W3C. www.w3.org/TR/2006/PR-mobile-bp-20061102.

Wirtz, B.W. (2001) "Reconfiguring of Value Chains in Converging Media and Communications Markets." *Long Range Planning*, 34, 489–506.

Yang, D.-H., Kim, S., Nam, C., and Moon, J.-S. (2004) "Fixed and Mobile Service Convergence and Reconfiguration of Telecommunications Value Chains." *IEEE Wireless Communications* 1(5), 42–47

18

Pseudonyms and the Rise of the Real-Name Web

Bernie Hogan

Introduction

During her 2010 re-election campaign, Phyllis Morris, the mayor of Aurora, Ontario, Canada, was harshly criticized on the website Auroracitizen.ca. After Morris lost to a newcomer, she blamed the site, and three commenters in particular, for her loss. Furious that they could say things critical of a mayor, she took them to court. She sued the commenters, the moderators, and even Wordpress.com for hosting the content. Justice Carole Brown of the Ontario Superior Court oversaw and in the summer of 2011 ruled in favor of the commenters. In the ruling, the judge noted that "in the circumstances of this case … the public interest favoring disclosure clearly does not outweigh the legitimate interests in freedom of expression and the right to privacy of the persons sought to be identified" (Morris v Johnson 2011). Since the plaintiff could not point to any libelous content and it appeared that she simply did not like pointed, but legitimate, criticism, the defendants did not need to have their IP addresses or other identifying remarks revealed.

Now imagine instead that a site such as this only used Facebook connect. Next to each comment was an individual's face, their name, and a link to all manner of personally identifying information. Imagine the users of that site making similarly critical comments about a person of public standing. One might still be in a position to sue the site, or even Facebook itself; but one could now also choose to sue those people directly. Outside the legal system, one might even consider enacting a personal vendetta against the commenters, their friends, and their local networks. Under those circumstances, most importantly, would the commenters still feel comfortable making their claims? Facebook, Google, LinkedIn, and a host of related social media sites are presently pushing for the ubiquity of real names online. Their argument is that it minimizes inappropriate content and helps to create a more just society. However, their arguments are just as easily considered ones of technical convenience. In this chapter, I articulate the ideological underpinnings of the rise

A Companion to New Media Dynamics, First Edition. Edited by John Hartley, Jean Burgess, and Axel Bruns.
© 2013 John Wiley & Sons, Ltd. Published 2015 by John Wiley & Sons, Ltd.

of real names as a means of managing identity, and parallel it with the use of pseudonyms and anonymity online.

I contend that real names make a great deal of sense for many online contexts, but should not be considered as a totalizing regime. This is based on the tension between context-specific impression management and the brave new world of persistent content. We are not free if we are bound to all of our past content, regardless of context. Neither are we free if we can be subject to abuse by a cruel and faceless Internet mob. The Internet presents potential for both context-specific identities and a real-name identity. To hedge against those who would lobby exclusively for one or the other, this chapter reviews the logic of both, as well as the ideologies of some of their greatest contemporary proponents. Both ought to be considered legitimate choices for different purposes.

A Clash of Ideals

The real-name web is not a technology; it is a practice and a system of values. Moreover, it has been highly spectacular. Facebook has come to dominate social network sites and the real-name web. Hot on its heels, Google+ has been particularly explicit in its policy, stating "Use your full first and last name in a single language" and "Put nicknames or pseudonyms in the Other Names field" (Google 2011). The use of real names on Facebook was not an afterthought but a core part of the site from its very inception as a face book for Harvard University (Kirkpatrick 2010a). Recently, Facebook founder Mark Zuckerberg has been particularly adamant that a real-name web is an ideal space for communication: "Having two identities for yourself is an example of a lack of integrity" (in Kirkpatrick 2010a: 199).

Facebook is simultaneously a site for the management and consolidation of identity. Through its genesis at Harvard, and rapid Silicon Valley-based success, it evolved, added features, and retooled its interface. Yet underlying its many features is a notion that, with the right combination of technologies and culture, one can make sharing and socializing with one's personal network a sensible and desired online practice. As Zuckerberg states:

> When I got started in my dorm room at Harvard, the question a lot of people asked was "why would I want to put any information on the Internet at all? Why would I want to have a website?" . . . And then in the last 5 or 6 years, blogging has taken off in a huge way, and all these different services that have people sharing all this information. People have really gotten comfortable not only sharing more information and different kinds, but more openly and with more people. That social norm is just something that has evolved over time. (in Kirkpatrick 2010b)

As Zuckerberg notes, not only are people sharing but also they are also sharing *openly*. What he really means is that their sharing is tethered to a (typically) unique personally identifying moniker we typically call a real name. For Zuckerberg this is not simply an ideological principle but one that is supposed to guarantee Facebook's monetary success. People are not simply "liking" a product. A product is liked by someone whose age, gender, geographic location, network size, and personality are on display for better microtargeting and analyses. Zuckerberg's above argument helps to foster this sense that the individual is a singularly defined object that consumes. Facebook's role in fostering this sense of self is not active but merely incidental: Zuckerberg suggests that the continued use of real names is a norm that has simply "evolved over time."

In the wake of Facebook's success, one might ask: how far can this go? Will people continue to share more openly, or rather share with their real names? For Zuckerberg and many like-minded technologists, the answer to the first question seems to be "never far enough." Their answer is bolstered by a flawed conception of the unitary and decontextualized notion of identity. It is also based on a misconception that the negative space of one's real-name online presence is filled with demons and demagogues.

Alongside the rise of Zuckerberg as a defender of real names, a challenger has emerged. For almost 10 years, this challenger was only known as moot [sic]. Moot founded a site where people could opt to use their real names, pseudonyms, or simply no name at all. The site, 4chan.org, has been a source of Internet culture's most notable and notorious offerings. It spawned LOLcats, the earliest example of an explosive genre of photos where one uses white text with black outline over a funny picture. 4chan was the earliest stomping ground of "Anonymous," the Internet hacking group that has targeted corporations, governments, and child predators.

Moot may have continued to be known only by his moniker were it not for *Time* magazine's "World's most influential" poll of 2009. This Internet-based poll was gamed by members of 4chan to place moot at the top and further game the voting to arrange the next 20 individuals to form an acrostic – "Marble cake, also, the game" – a joke that was understood by 4chan's community. Subsequently, moot was revealed as Christopher Poole. Since then, Poole has become a staunch defender of the non-real-name Internet, where pseudonyms and anonymity reside.

Like Zuckerberg, Poole is an early-twenties white American with an upper-middle-class upbringing in New York. Also like Zuckerberg, he could barely anticipate that his site would come to dominate the press, albeit for very different reasons from Facebook. But, most importantly, like Zuckerberg, Poole has used the success of his site to lobby for a specific notion of identity, and a specific notion of authenticity.

As he stated at South By Southwest Interactive, a corporate conference discussing the state of technology and business, "Zuckerberg's totally wrong on anonymity being total cowardice. Anonymity is authenticity. It allows you to share in a completely unvarnished, raw way." For Poole this is a gateway toward creativity online. "The cost of failure is really high when you're contributing as yourself" (Poole 2011b).

Despite the fact that Facebook and 4chan appear to be on completely opposite ends of an identity spectrum, both Poole and Zuckerberg consider themselves to be champions of the authentic self. Zuckerberg believes that real names allow people to connect to their offline friends, and thus allow for a greater sense of connection than one might have otherwise. By contrast, Poole believes that the persistence of content and the tethering to real names is a burden. 4chan has no memory and all content can be posted anonymously.

It seems that both Zuckerberg and Poole cannot be right. Is social interaction with one's personal network more authentic than participation on anonymous message boards? Oddly, the social sciences have been rather indifferent to this question. Instead, much work has followed Goffman in inverting the question. That is to say, it is not a matter of whether a performance is authentic but a question of to what extent to people believe in the authenticity of the impressions they foster. In this vein, people can be cynical or sincere about either Facebook or 4chan. This leads to Goffman's extensive examination of performance as impression management (1959).

By focusing on authenticity, one is implicitly making normative claims about competing spaces as inauthentic. By focusing instead on impression management, one can ask what aspects of identity are excluded in real-name spaces and in pseudonymous spaces. The goal then is to articulate the dynamics of different social media based on naming conventions rather than lobby for one kind of space or another. In some senses, there are good reasons to believe real-name spaces are insufficient for free and unfiltered speech online, and these reasons give rise to the proliferation of pseudonyms. What may be more interesting than the rise of the real-name web are the limitations of the real-name web and the reasons for the persistence of pseudonyms.

A related question is why individuals post anonymously. 4chan allows, and tends to encourage, complete anonymity in posting. In simple terms, anonymity refers to the absence of personally identifying information. In technical terms, anonymity is remarkably difficult to define. When seeking to operationalize anonymity, new and clever forms of deanonymization constantly appear (cf. Narayanan and colleagues such as Narayanan and Shmatikov 2007).

I assert that pseudonyms and anonymity tend to work in tandem. We ought not to consider a scale moving from real names through pseudonyms to anonymity. Anonymity is a *state* implying the absence of personally identifying qualities. Pseudonyms are a *practice*, which is often meant to facilitate nonidentifiable content. Individuals can employ pseudonyms for one-time use or employ them as persistent alternate markers of identity. The graffiti artist Banksy has used this name to maintain his anonymity, whereas it is well known that Bob Dylan's real name is Robert Zimmerman, although it has not stopped him from maintaining the use of Bob Dylan. The arguments for real names tend to assume that both the practice of pseudonyms and states of anonymity are used for nefarious purposes that can be minimized by real names. I argue that this oversimplifies both the purpose of pseudonyms and the consequences of real-name policies.

Below, I give an overview of the use of pseudonyms both in history and in contemporary new media culture. In most cases, the rationales for the use of pseudonyms and the arguments against them are just as easily applied to anonymous content as well. Both occupy the negative space of new media that tends to foreground real names.

Pseudonyms in History

Pseudonyms have been a common tool for artists and public figures going back almost two hundred years. While the term has origins in Greek, it was not popularized in English until the 1850s. The Victorian women of this period took a great interest in writing, but feared dismissal based on their gender. Early publications by the Brontë sisters used the pen names of Currer, Ellis, and Acton Bell (Hargreaves 1970), and Mary Ann Evans received widespread acclaim for her work as George Eliot. The n-gram of pseudonyms shown in Figure 18.1 indicates that the term has steadily increased in usage since about this time.

Although pseudonyms have been in use for a variety of purposes, such as titles, religious conversions, and musical artists, it is this artistic use that may be most closely aligned with the contemporary uses of pseudonyms in social media. From the nineteenth century onwards, pseudonyms were used to mask features that authors and artists themselves believed would lead to unnecessary dismissal or outright rejection. This included not only gender but also ethnicity. At the turn of the twentieth century, many Jewish authors and artists adopted public names that appeared less Jewish, such as Phillip Guston (né Phillip Goldstein) and Mark Rothko (né Marcus Rothkowitz).

Pseudonyms are not simply used as a means to avoid discrimination. Others simply wanted to distinguish their artistic work from other aspects of their life and provide segmented personae. As examples, both Lewis Carroll (né Charles Dodgson) and Mark Twain (né Samuel Clemens) opted for playful names for their satirical work and kept their birth names for equally public serious work. In Clemens' case, this mainly concerned political essays, whereas for Dodgson it was publications in mathematics.

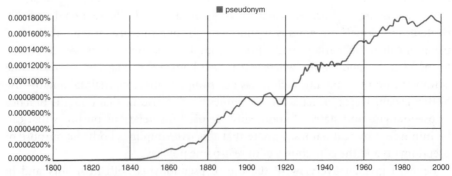

Figure 18.1 A Google N-gram search for pseudonym. Notice the sharp increase in occurrences after 1845. The occurrences are weighted by the number of books per year in Google's corpus of approximately 6 million books.

From these pen names we have two forces motivating pseudonyms. The first is an external pressure that motivates an individual to mask his/her real identity in order to be treated in a manner he/she desires. Because of these pressures, pseudonyms are considered useful for specific situations or contexts. People may behave as they would otherwise but simply want to do this without the baggage of personal identification. This was the case for the Brontë sisters. The second, internal motivation is a desire to adopt a different persona, as was the case with Carroll and Twain.

To these we may add a third functionalist motivation. This latter motivation can be seen in the naming of musical groups, papal and royal titles, and coping with individuals who have similar names. For example, handles on CB (citizens' band) radio are partially functional in that individuals need a phrase that is short, distinct, and audible.

All three of these uses emerge in the everyday usage of new media, and are in many senses amplified by new media. Below, all three are taken in turn. I begin with the functional pseudonym, as this is perhaps the most innocuous and also the most obvious given the historical trajectory of the web.

Functional Motivations

Functional pseudonyms make sense in a world where large numbers of people must all have a unique addressable name. Individuals trying to select a free email address (such as Gmail, Windows Live, or Yahoo!) for their child or their Internet-latecomer parents are now faced with the need to distinguish a name using all manner of permutations including middle names, birth years, spelling mistakes, and suffixes.

With free email services it is likely that many real names are in use. Other services might be sufficiently obscure to allow people to use their real names but make this process difficult through technical affordances and constraints: a very long full name would not be useful on Twitter. For example, Siva Vaidhyanathan tweets as @sivavaid since the site affords only 140 characters for both a name and a message. Other sites and media deliberately enforce names of a certain length or expect names to be in the Latin character set, rather than Chinese, Cyrillic, or some other language. For example, the original IRC (Internet relay chat) channels limited nicknames to nine characters (Stenberg 2011).

Functional pseudonyms may always be relevant when technical or cultural constraints inhibit individuals from considering their own name as a useful uniquely identifiable marker. Theoretically, people could always have used abbreviations or alterations of their own names. But most people would agree that "phe0nix" and "wizzard" are more memorable than john32 and dale4. Consider this quote from user Skyfaller on Wikipedia's username policy discussion: "if I use my real name, should I use my full name Nelson Pavlosky or just Nelson? I've been signing as Nelson, but then I realized it was kind of egotistical to think that I'm the only Nelson on Wikipedia. Although it may be true at the moment, I don't want to cause confusion in the future if another person with the first name 'Nelson' becomes an important contributor" (Wikipedia 2003).

Situational Motivations: Moving to Another Room

Even if one is given the opportunity to use their real name, there is a multitude of reasons to be reluctant to do so. Real names can become a key to link together disparate pieces of information. Granted, names are not the only tools for this. As Sweeney notes, it is possible to uniquely identify 87 percent of the US population using only gender, postcode, and date of birth (Sweeney 2002). More recently, browser configurations (Eckersley 2010) and simply behavioral traces can also do this (Pariser 2011). Although most people do not have access to the files needed for linking, they do have access to popular search engines. By posting things with one's real name, it is plausible that two completely different posts (from different mailing lists, blogs, or message boards) could be presented side by side in search results. Using a pseudonym for some topics and one's real name for others is a straightforward way to avoid such serendipitous linking.

Wikipedia has long understood this particular usage of pseudonyms. Only two years into the site's development, a page emerged for username policies. Among the ensuing discussions about regulating offensive names and how to cope with multiple languages and character sets, discussions about real names appear almost annually. The earliest discussions about real names centered on legitimacy. That is, would content made under a pseudonym be taken seriously?

Eight years later, the discussion intensified rather than attenuated. In addition to issues of legitimacy and attribution there arose real concerns for safety and the maintenance of personal boundaries. User CarolMooreDC noted that if one uses their real name then their content persists for others to use against them:

> The problem is the impression I have gotten from a recent WP:COIN [conflict of interest notification] User:Jehochman initiated and his comments above is [sic] that it is wiki-legal to track down everything relevant every professor, student, writer, etc. who is foolish enough to edit in their own name has written to use against them in POV [point of view] discussions. (Wikipedia 2011)

Carol is noting that real names make people findable. Therefore, people can find and drag up other ideologically tinged writing to suggest they are not capable of a neutral point of view, one of the central tenets of Wikipedia.[1] She later mentions regret about using her real name and others discuss personal safety amid stories of personal threats.

Carol is not looking for a pseudonym as a costume or a moniker that one puts on, but merely a way to segment her life. The persistence and searchability of content on Wikipedia make her a vulnerable target for saying things she believes are fair in this space. Pseudonyms create a new space in which content can be interpreted.

In the language of Goffman's (1959) dramaturgical approach, they provide a new "front stage," regardless of who is in the audience.

Personal Motivations: Putting on a Costume

If situational motivations make pseudonyms feel like different rooms that one walks into, personal motivations feel like different costumes that one wears regardless of where the event occurs. The use of pseudonyms as a masquerade is tied to the notion of the web as a "strange place." People can use text-based chats, gaming avatars, and niche websites as a way to creatively escape their everyday life.

Personal motivations for pseudonyms are the most maligned. There is a notion that in the absence of accountability individuals are likely to return to a Hobbesian state of nature where comments are nasty, brutish, and kinky. Kiesler and Siegel (1984) identified this nearly a decade before the web in a series of computer-mediated communication experiments. They observed many of the issues we now consider to define the Internet experience ("few status cues," "social inhibition," and "immature etiquette" among others) and painted a rather bleak future for behavior online. In the following decade, Turkle (1997) reported on some of the people who came to inhabit these strange text-based spaces with few status cues only to discover many who enjoyed playing with and deconstructing identity. She described how people would play with gender conventions, age, and all manner of personality.

Not all of this identity play is positive. In addition to personal exploration and discovery, people can use anonymity in order to display antisocial behaviors, such as "trolling" (distracting or misleading conversations) or "flaming" (overly aggressive or abuse comments). Donath (1999) notes how deception on UseNet through both anonymous remailers and pseudonyms fostered this behavior. Recently Lanier suggested that "user interface designs that arise from the ideology of the computing cloud make people – all of us – less kind. Trolling is not a string of isolated incidents, but the status quo in the online world" (2010: 61).

To justify the availability of pseudonyms, pundits and academics tend to talk about situational motivations – such as the whistleblower, the closeted teenager, or the inner-city youth trying to escape gangster life. For example, when boyd (2011) asserts that the real names policy on Google+ is an abuse of power, she simultaneously paints a sympathetic picture of those who have just reasons for segmenting their lives and also downplays Internet trolls. This makes sense, as personal motivations are a little more difficult to justify. For example, Randi Zuckerberg, sister of the Facebook founder and then-Marketing Director for Facebook, said, "I think anonymity online has to go away . . . . People behave a lot better when they have their real names down. . . . I think people hide behind anonymity and they feel like they can say whatever they want behind closed doors" (Galperin 2011). Here Zuckerberg creates an all-or-nothing dichotomy between real names and faceless anonymity, without considering persistent pseudonyms such as jmz, moot, or the denizens of social media communities such as Reddit, Digg, and Slashdot. In her talk and this quote, she assumes it is the social sanctions of being caught that provide discipline and good behavior. This is an ironic position in that she was trying to help with fighting cyberbullying, especially for gay and lesbian youth: these youth also depend on pseudonyms and anonymity, to sort out their sexualities before proclaiming them publicly. Moreover, gay youth tend to be bullied by known perpetrators on real-name Facebook pages.

Why So Many Names?

Considering the pre-Web 2.0 state of the Internet, the profusion of pseudonyms makes a great deal of sense. I offer three reasons.

The web was textual or "simplified." Before the widespread diffusion of digital cameras and webcams, a person was identified primarily by their texts. It is easier to pass for a different age, gender, weight, or ethnicity if you do not need to prove this through sound and video. Granted, recent machine learning work has indicated that it is possible to distinguish male and female authors with reasonably high accuracy (Liwicki et al. 2011) but this technology was not available 20 years ago. In this earlier era, an individual had to articulate every part of their persona, and was thus required to consider an appropriate persona. This also made the web ripe for postmodern analysis such as that of Turkle (1997), as all activity seemed to be self-articulated performance. Without the demand for an external referent, it fed into Derridean theories of deconstruction and poststructuralist notions of bricolage.

The web was sparsely connected. The first social network site did not arrive until 1998 (SixDegrees), and only with Friendster did the notion of publicly articulating networks appear culturally viable (boyd and Ellison 2007). In its absence, public discussions were focused on interests. Geocities pages and Yahoo Groups based on niche topics were a common way to locate content and find like-minded discussants. Similar people were found through a topic rather than through a personal connection. This sparsity probably also gave rise to the notion of the web as an "other" place, a notion that still haunts scholars trying to disentangle "online" versus "offline" spaces (Wellman 2004). If one is connecting to others based on an interest, a name that signals one's interest in that space makes more sense than a real name.

The web was strange. In the 1990s it was commonplace to hear about strange stories of people who met online and then got married, or cyberstalkers preying on children. The web was technically formidable because it was biased toward people with technical skills. The web exposed people to a great deal of information they might never have seen otherwise (such as the "Anarchist's cookbook" for making bombs and the deluge of niche pornography). Keeping one's real name off the web was seen as a reliable safety precaution since it was assumed that one never knew exactly who was on the other side of the screen.

The Real-Name Web

The real-name web is quite different from an old web that was sparse, strange, and simplified. Although it might be a deterministic stretch to suggest the World Wide Web was bound to end up at the real-name web, it is clear that the qualities that made the web sparse, strange, and simple were bound to recede.

The web is no longer simplified but detailed. In the past decade, digital cameras have dramatically dropped in price while webcams have steadily become a mainstay in computers. In 2005, Apple released their first iMac with a webcam built in. Six years later, even their iPods have cameras (alongside the cameras in the latest iPhones, iPads, and the entire line of laptops). Of course, Apple is not alone in this trend but it is nevertheless emblematic of it. As text gives way to photos, audio, and video, the chasm between a pseudonym and a persona becomes wider. Where Turkle's gender benders needed only to use a different name and maintain the facade during question and answering, creating an entire detailed persona online is a challenging task. With the continued advancement of face-recognition technology it might get even more challenging (to the likely dismay of many a rioter and amateur pornographer).

The web is now densely connected. In most developed nations, Internet users comprise a majority of the population, and developing nations are rapidly catching up (Kimura et al. 2011). With this sort of diffusion, it is plausible that people would be able to find their friends and family online rather than look to the web as a place "out there." In the absence of a phone book for email addresses and blogs, Facebook fills this role. Facebook's self-description is "A social utility that connects people, to keep up with friends, upload photos, share links and videos." A pseudonym does not make as much sense when one wants to be found by people who know one's real name. Google+ make this even more explicit in its terms of use: "Google+ makes connecting with people on the web more like connecting with people in the real world. Because of this, it's important to use your common name so that the people you want to connect with can find you" (Google 2011).

The web is no longer strange, but day-to-day. Online dating has reached critical mass and a sense of normalcy in most developed nations (Hogan et al. 2011). The web is being actively used as part of protest movements and insurgencies in the developing world. Profiles on many sites now suggest that people use a photo that personally identifies them alongside their real name. Consequently, people on the web can be seen as living, feeling others rather than avatars to be molded or blown up at will. Moreover, as more people join social network sites and link together friends of friends, the less strange the web gets. It moves from being a place out there (a "virtual" reality) toward being data about here (an "augmented" reality). As Hogan and Wellman (2012) suggest, it is less a transcendent Internet than an immanent one.

Life Off the Screen

Fifteen years ago, Turkle (1997) suggested the Internet was enabling a new form of identity that was decentered and mobile. It fit with the postmodernism of the day, and with a web that is strange, sparse, and simple. Yet in the past 15 years we have witnessed something else emerge entirely. People are not airing concerns over disassociated personalities from spending too much time in *Second Life* but over the hyperassociated personality that comes with the real-name web (Madden and Smith 2010). Even Turkle has changed her tune, from concern over disassociation to concern over too much performance of a specific identity (Turkle 2011). To explain this issue on the real-name web, I suggest that persistent content is primarily responsible. This content is sent to nonaddressed audiences rather than specific recipients, and is thus ripe for forwarding, redistribution, and curation. One potential consequence of this situation is that people assume any content associated with their name is likely to reach anyone who knows them by that name, leading in turn to a sense of pandering to the "lowest common denominator" of social media.

This idea draws upon the phenomenon of context collapse online (Hogan 2010a; Marwick and boyd 2011). Context collapse occurs because the use of real names does not inherently allow for the segmentation of social roles. Offline this segmentation occurs naturally through bounded contexts. By context, I refer to a place that is bounded in space and time with knowable roles and social norms. These contexts are also called behavior regions in environmental psychology (Barker 1968), stages in Goffman's (1959) dramaturgical approach, and focused constraints in social network analysis (Feld 1981). In a context, interaction tends to be evanescent rather than recorded by default. Thus, it does not matter whether one uses one's real name to discuss marital problems at the therapist, gambling at Gamblers Anonymous, or issues with one's boss at the pub; information is considered to be bounded to these spaces through social convention and the roles that people are expected to play.

That these contexts only partially overlap has been clear in sociology for at least a century. Georg Simmel described this situation as the partially overlapping social circles of modern life (1922). More recently, scholars have posited a connection between the arrangement of social ties in these social circles and one's ability to access important social resources, such as information about new jobs (Granovetter 1973) as well as one's capacity to gather cultural capital (Erickson 1996) and even to self-actualize (Coser 1975).

Google+ has directly internalized this notion of partially overlapping social circles. Yet, there are reasons to suspect that it is insufficient to allow segmentation by social circles, primarily because this metaphor is drawn from a world replete with contexts and evanescence rather than a world of curation and persistent content.

A great deal of online communication appears in nothing like a context. Where contexts are bounded in space and time, much online communication is available from anywhere at any time: it is persistent and searchable. Where people offline are understood as filling a role, online individuals are tethered to a name. The real-name web is thus a practice whereby people can post content that is linked to their offline identity and is available either publicly or to a publicly articulated list of individuals. The notion that this has led to collapse is due to the phenomenon whereby people from different offline social contexts are all equally considered "friends" or "fans" online. People have workmates, friends, family members, sports teams, past high school chums, and so forth all under the same roof (Hogan 2010b).

Undoubtedly, there are benefits to context collapse. It is now a simple process to send out regular updates about one's life, either in good times (as people post vacation photos) or in times of need (as when people are looking for work). Those who attend to this actively on Facebook do indeed report a greater sense of belonging and a greater capacity to accrue social resources than those who do not (Ellison et al. 2007).

Despite these benefits, the term "context collapse" almost inherently has negative connotations. This is on purpose. Context collapse means that individuals have to contend with competing roles at the same time, viewing photos from a friend's bachelor party next to communication with one's students (or teachers). People might want to discuss their politics, especially in the run-up to an election, but this might conflict with the politics of one's coworkers. Offline, one can easily avoid this by speaking in groups where such conversation is considered appropriate. If one uses a single real name as one's only voice online, this becomes difficult to do.

The prevailing solution, as suggested by Pariser, is algorithms that curate out the unwanted content (2011). He suggests this leads to a "filter bubble" where individuals train algorithms to give them only what they like, and in turn people consume only what pleases them. It is a vicious cycle in that it is never clear what is excluded.

The Nymwars

These issues came to a head in the summer of 2011 with the rise of the "nymwars." This term emerged to capture the dissatisfaction with Google+'s assertion that people who joined the service had to use their real name. This decision was widely derided as problematic by a host of scholars and policymakers. As mentioned above, in one such example boyd (2011) called this policy an abuse of power. The counter arguments, however, were just as strong, and based on two general claims (see comments on boyd's post for examples of this discussion). The first theme is "don't like it, don't use it; its Google's house, not yours." The second is "nothing to hide, nothing to fear." The third is "it doesn't matter since it is all going public anyway."

The first claim carries the most weight insofar as, indeed, Google is the architect of this system, and can make good claims to determining how it is run. However, Google's policy is nevertheless a presumptuous one. That is, it presumes its particular model for the distribution of content is sufficient for selective sharing, when there are good reasons to think otherwise. Google+ offers individuals the ability to place friends in lists (or "circles"). One can share content with these friends or any combination of lists. However, once the friends view this content, there is nothing except a polite pop-up preventing them from redistributing that content to whomever they choose.

The most concerning aspect about this claim is that Google's policy has the potential to become national or state policy as well. Eric Schmidt, former Google CEO, reinforced this with comments at the same *Marie Claire* panel where Randi Zuckerberg was quoted above. He believes that at some point all governments will demand real names.

The second claim is more easily discredited. In particular, Solove has made a strong case that "nothing to hide, nothing to fear" is a red herring. Even without the assertion of privacy as a fundamental right, Solove (2007) was able to demonstrate a convincing case for why individuals should have an interest in the sort of informational self-determination that is central to an interest in privacy. In particular, people self-incriminate in many unanticipated ways and lose control when they lose privacy. This claim dovetails with Nissenbaum's (2004) notion of "privacy as contextual integrity."

This article on privacy reframed the debate and crystallized the sentiments of many in both policy and academic circles. For example, if we are so close to our parents or spouses, why do we tell things to our doctor that we do not tell them? Nissenbaum argues that privacy is intimately bound up with the notion of contextual integrity. She explores not what privacy is from a positive point of view but what constitutes a *breach* of privacy. To breach privacy is to move information from one context where such information is understood or expected to reside and into another context where that information was neither intended nor appropriate given the existing social norms. For the hedonistic tourist, Las Vegas is a vacation, not just from another place but another context of norms. Consequently, the Las Vegas tourist board did well with the slogan "What happens in Vegas stays in Vegas."

This is privacy understood as informational self-determination. One has privacy when one can assume that information created by a person will be managed in the way that the person deems appropriate. A doctor who calls a patient's boss to tell them of a recent diagnosis is breaching privacy. It is unprofessional, but might happen if the doctor and the boss are friends. A website that reveals the IP address and email of someone who posts anonymously is breaching privacy. By linking all information to one's real name, one effectively transfers informational self-determination into information curation, and allows Google or Facebook to be the curator.

The third claim, typified by Marc Smith's notion of "the myth of selective sharing" (Smith 2011), draws upon Brand's earlier claim that "information wants to be free" (1987: 202). That is, it does not matter whether one uses a filter or not; information will end up unified and searchable in the end. This claim is a moderated version of the second claim as Smith is not saying people have nothing to fear but only that, if information is encoded in some form, it is both possible and plausible that it will first escape from the confines of the desired context and second make its way back to the producer. This makes the case a fortiori that labeling all information with one's real name will undermine informational self-determination. It remains to be seen whether a user interface will emerge that can allow selective sharing with audiences in a useable form, and in its absence we are again left with curation.

Human Flesh Search

To be clear, the rise of the real-name web is not simply the story of institutional powers coercing people into using their real names to make content more manageable. There are numerous incidents of crowd-sourced attempts to identify individuals based on some characteristics of their online content and, especially, photographs. The most notable of these is probably the example of "human flesh search." This practice involves massive numbers of people who all view a set of images, such as a hit and run, an example of corruption, or just a scandalous nude photo. Individuals can then contribute information based on features they recognize, such as which geographical area, hotel, or car is pictured in the photo. The practice has been widespread in China (Cheung 2009) and prevalent in other online forums (Shirky 2008). Recently, this practice has also been used to name and shame rioters from the 2011 Vancouver and London riots. Since the web is neither sparse nor strange, it is assumed that at least some people will be able to provide some information. Sometimes human flesh search leads to perpetrators being brought to justice and sometimes it leads to "outing" and tragedy.

Conclusion

I conclude by returning to the claim made at the beginning of the chapter: the real-name web is not a technology; it is a social practice. But, in light of this discussion, it is clear that there are both technical trajectories and historical antecedents that foster a trend toward real-name spaces as well as a persistent need for pseudonyms. In particular, the early days of the web were characterized by the paucity of social cues, the sparsity of one's social network, and the strangeness of people who might be quite different from what they say they are. Pseudonyms made sense both technically and contextually. The modern web, by contrast, is a rich multimedia experience where large corporations curate content on our behalf via cloud services. These corporations continually seek ways to assert their legitimacy, through technical interfaces (e.g., Google's social circles model) and politics (e.g., real-name policies). In essence, they are suggesting that they have figured out a solution to context collapse (their particular interface). To push people toward these solutions, it is conventional to publicly discourage the use pseudonyms, despite their efficacy.

The increasing use of real names does not, however, attenuate the motivations for pseudonyms. It only mitigates against the personal motivations of cranky and vulgar users and serves to make people and their content more findable. There still exist functional reasons for pseudonyms (such as a unique name or email address), situational motivations in response to context collapse, and personal motivations of identity play beyond trolling and flaming. Through pseudonyms people can express their competitive urges in gaming environments, their health concerns on specialist sites, their sexual urges on pornographic sites, and their political appetites on blogs without these getting in the way of each other or personal and professional obligations.

In light of this, there is much work to be done both academically and politically. Academic work ought to provide greater nuance to identity practices online – when do people adopt a different mask and "troll" or play with identity? Under what conditions, such as those of Wikipedia, do pseudonyms enable effective local collaboration? Are pseudonyms dying out or surging, especially in crosscultural contexts? Policy scholars ought to consider work such as the current Canadian legal trend of balancing privacy online and public interests for freedom of speech. Reidentification practices ought to be lifted out of discussions about vandals and terrorists and reframed in terms of free-speech practices in a new era of persistent content and collapsed contexts.

Finally, we ought to dispel myths that pseudonymous online interaction is a Hobbesian state. In its place we ought to consider such interaction as a *localized* social contract and response to the increasing array of technologies focused on identity consolidation for profit rather than for the social good. Sites such as the fleeting protest site http://my.nameis.me helped to focus the discussion to good effect. After a protracted public relations war, Google+ has dropped its real-name requirement and joined a growing number of sites that acknowledge the legitimacy, functions, and utility of pseudonyms as well as real names. This was announced at the 2011 Web 2.0 forum. At the same summit the day before, Poole (moot) made his most eloquent plea yet for rethinking identity: "Google and Facebook would have you believe that you're a mirror, but we're actually more like diamonds.... Look from a different angle, and you see something completely different.... Facebook is consolidating identity by making us more simple than we truly are" (Poole 2011a).

The web is not merely a highly connected place out there but a codification of the social relations that bind much of the developed and developing world. The real-name web helps to reinforce this sense of global connectivity. But it also runs against limits inherent in a system curated by third parties with persistent content. Pseudonyms are both an antecedent to this situation and also a partial solution. We may live in a global village but our huts still need curtains.

Acknowledgments

I would like to thank the editors as well as Marc Smith and Joshua Melville for helpful comments on an earlier draft of this chapter.

Notes

1. Whether a neutral point of view is even attainable is addressed in Lovink and Tkacz (2011).

References

Barker, R.G. (1968) *Ecological Psychology: Concepts and Methods for Studying the Environment of Human Behavior*. Stanford, CA: Stanford University Press.

boyd, d. (2011) "'Real Names' Policies are an Abuse of Power." *Social Media Collective* (August 4). http://socialmediacollective.org/2011/08/04/real-names-policies-are-an-abuse-of-power.

boyd, d. and Ellison, N. (2007) "Social Network Sites: Definition, History, and Scholarship." *Journal of Computer-Mediated Communication*, 13(1), 210–230.

Brand, S. (1987) *The Media Lab: Inventing the Future at MIT*. New York: Viking.

Cheung, A.S.Y. (2009) "China Internet Going Wild: Cyber-Hunting versus Privacy Protection." *Computer Law & Security Review*, 25(3), 275–279.

Coser, R.L. (1975) "The Complexity of Roles as a Seedbed of Individual Autonomy" in L.A. Coser, ed., *The Idea of Social Structure: Papers in Honor of Robert K. Merton*. New York: Harcourt Bruce Jovanovich, pp. 237–264.

Donath, J.S. (1999) "Identity and Deception in the Virtual Community" in M.A. Smith and P. Kollack, eds., *Communities in Cyberspace*. New York: Routledge, pp. 29–59.

Eckersley, P. (2010) "How Unique is Your Web Browser?" *Lecture Notes in Computer Science*, 6205, 1–18.

Ellison, N., Steinfeld, C., and Lampe, C. (2007) "The Benefits of Facebook 'Friends': Social Capital and College Students' Use of Online Social Network Sites." *Journal of Computer-Mediated Communication*, 12(4). http://jcmc.indiana.edu/vol12/issue4/ellison.html.

Erickson, B.H. (1996) "Culture, Class, and Connections." *American Journal of Sociology*, 102(1), 217–251.

Feld, S.L. (1981) "The Focused Organization of Social Ties." *American Journal of Sociology*, 86(5), 1015–1035.

Galperin, E. (2011) "Randi Zuckerberg Runs in the Wrong Direction on Pseudonymity Online." *Electronic Frontier Foundation Deeplinks* (August 2). www.eff.org/deeplinks/2011/08/randi-zuckerberg-runs-wrong-direction-pseudonymity.

Goffman, E. (1959) *The Presentation of Self in Everyday Life*. Garden City, NY: Doubleday.

Google (2011) "Your Name and Google+ Profiles." *The Google+ Project*. www.google.com/support/+/bin/answer.py?answer=1228271.

Granovetter, M. (1973) "The Strength of Weak Ties." *American Journal of Sociology*, 78, 1360–1380.

Hargreaves, G.D. (1970) "The Publishing of Poems by Currer, Ellis and Acton Bell." *Library Review*, 22(7), 353–356.

Hogan, B. (2010a) "The Presentation of Self in the Age of Social Media: Distinguishing Performances and Exhibitions Online." *Bulletin of Science, Technology & Society*, 30(6), 377–386.

Hogan, B. (2010b) "Visualizing and Interpreting Facebook Networks" in D. Hansen, M.A. Smith, and B. Shneiderman, eds., *Analyzing Social Media Networks with NodeXL*. Burlington, MA: Morgan Kaufmann, pp. 165–180.

Hogan, B. and Wellman, B. (2012). "The Immanent Internet Redux." in P.H. Cheong, P. Fischer-Nielsen, S. Gelfgren, and C. Ess., eds., *Digital Religion, Social Media and Culture: Perspectives, Practices and Futures*. Bern: Peter Lang, pp. 43–62.

Hogan, B., Li, N., and Dutton, W.H. (2011) *A Global Shift in the Social Relationships of Networked Individuals: Meeting and Dating Online Comes of Age*. Oxford: Oxford Internet Institute.

Kiesler, S. and Siegel, J. (1984) "Social Psychological Aspects of Computer-Mediated Communication." *American Psychologist*, 39(10), 1123–1134.

Kimura, K., Priftis, M., Zhenwei Q.C., and Yang, H. (2011) *The Little Data Book on Information and Communication Technology*. Washington, DC: World Bank.

Kirkpatrick, D. (2010a) *The Facebook Effect: The Inside Story of the Company that is Connecting the World*. New York: Simon & Schuster.

Kirkpatrick, M. (2010b) "Facebook's Zuckerberg Says the Age of Privacy is Over." *Read Write Web* (January 9). www.readwriteweb.com/archives/facebooks_zuckerberg_says_the_age_of_privacy_is_ov.php.

Lanier, J. (2010) *You Are Not a Gadget: A Manifesto*. New York: Vintage.

Liwicki, M., Schlapbach, A., and Bunke, H. (2011) "Automatic Gender Detection Using on-Line and Off-Line Information." *Pattern Analysis and Applications*, 14(1), 87–92.

Lovink, G. and Tkacz, N. (2011) *Critical Point of View: A Wikipedia Reader*. New York and Amsterdam: Institute of Network Cultures.

Madden, M. and Smith, A. (2010) *"Reputation Management and Social Media."* Washington, DC: Pew Internet & American Life Project.

Marwick, A. and boyd, d. (2011) "I Tweet Honestly, I Tweet Passionately: Twitter Users, Context Collapse, and the Imagined Audience." *New Media & Society*, 13(1), 114–133.

Morris v. Johnson (2011) ONSC 3996 (CanLII). http://canlii.ca/s/6kxmx.

Narayanan, A. and Shmatikov, V. (2007) "Robust De-anonymization of Large Sparse Datasets." www.cs.utexas.edu/~shmat/shmat_oak08netflix.pdf.

Nissenbaum, H. (2004) "Privacy as Contextual Integrity." *Washington Law Review*, 79, 119–157.

Pariser, E. (2011) *The Filter Bubble: What the Internet is Hiding from You*. New York: Penguin.

Poole, C. (2011a) "High Order Bit". Speech at the Web 2.0 Summit, San Fransisco, CA (October 17–19). www.youtube.com/watch?v=e3Zs74IH0mc.

Poole, C. (2011b) "Keynote: Christopher Poole." *SXSW Interactive* (March 13). http://schedule.sxsw.com/events/event_IAP000001.

Shirky, C. (2008) *Here Comes Everybody: The Power of Organizing without Organizations*. New York: Penguin.

Simmel, G. (1922) "The Web of Group Affiliations" in *Conflict and the Web of Group Affiliations*. New York: Free Press, pp. 125–195.

Smith, M.A. (2011) "The Myth of Selective Sharing: Why All Bits will Eventually Be Public (or Be Destroyed)." *Connected Action*. www.connectedaction.net/2011/07/25/the-myth-of-selective-sharing-why-all-bits-will-eventually-be-public-or-be-destroyed.

Solove, D.J. (2007) " 'I've Got Nothing to Hide' and Other Misunderstandings of Privacy." *San Diego Law Review*, May, 745–772.

Stenberg, D. (2011) "History of IRC (Internet Relay Chat)." *daniel.haxx*. http://daniel.haxx.se/irchistory.html.

Sweeney, L. (2002) "K-Anonymity: A Model for Protecting Privacy." *International Journal of Uncertainty Fuzziness and Knowledge-Based Systems*, 10(5), 557–570.

Turkle, S. (1997) *Life on the Screen: Identity in the Age of the Internet*. New York: Simon & Schuster.

Turkle, S. (2011) *Alone Together: Why We Expect More from Technology and Less from Each Other*. New York: Basic Books.

Wellman, B. (2004) "The Three Ages of Internet Studies: Ten, Five and Zero Years Ago." *New Media & Society*, 6(1), 123–129.

Wikipedia (2003) "Username or Real Name? Which Should I Use?" *Wikipedia Talk: User Account Policy/Archive 1*. http://en.wikipedia.org/wiki/Wikipedia_talk:Username_policy /Archive_1#Username_or_Real_Name.3F_Which_should_I_use.3F.

Wikipedia (2011) "Archive 18 of Wikipedia:Username Policy's Talk Page." http://en .wikipedia.org/w/index.php?title=Wikipedia_talk:Username_policy/Archive_18&oldid =419428764.

Surveillance

19

New Media and Changing Perceptions of Surveillance

Anders Albrechtslund

Introduction

The antagonist of George Orwell's *Nineteen Eighty-Four* (1949), the iconic Big Brother, sees all and knows all. He is at the center of a repressive regime that controls the population. Orwell's novel depicts a society without privacy and freedom, but with absolute state control: "Big Brother is watching you," as the famous posters say in the story's version of London. Since its publication in 1949, Orwell's novel has been the textbook example of a totalitarian society with all its fear, repression, and horror. According to the logic of the story, such a society is necessarily identical with a surveillance society, and this argument has been extremely influential, especially in public debates. In the novel, a society is described where power is based on a firm control of the mass media. Big Brother is the center of power and the image of his face is used aggressively on large "telescreens" as an intimidating presence everywhere. At the same time, historical records are rewritten into propaganda for the government – a job that is performed by the protagonist of the story, Winston Smith.

In this chapter, I explore how new media dynamics contribute to new surveillance practices. Orwell illustrated in his dystopian post-Second World War novel that media constitute a powerful apparatus for surveillance. In *Nineteen Eighty-Four*, the citizens are controlled through their own gaze, as they watch the incessantly appearing images of Big Brother. In a sense, the spectacle controls the spectator, even though surveillance technologies and practices permeate the society to the point of zero privacy for the people. My ambition is to introduce a radically different concept that more adequately reflects the surveillance practices associated with (especially) new media. When we share opinions, tastes, activities, and locations with a network, we proactively take part in our own surveillance. This "participatory surveillance" (Albrechtslund 2008a) is quite different from Orwellian and panoptic frameworks, as it points out the potentially empowering and social aspects of the surveillance practices that many of us engage in on a daily basis. In the following, my focus

A Companion to New Media Dynamics, First Edition. Edited by John Hartley, Jean Burgess, and Axel Bruns.

is on the experiences of the subjectivity involved in these different surveillance practices and, here, I am particularly interested in the mixing of and transition between broadcast media and social media. My approach is to explore and analyze the key concepts "privacy" and "transparency" to better understand how these are redefined according to the new media dynamics.

Media as a Surveillance Practice

The development from traditional broadcast media (e.g., television, radio, etc.) to social media is not simply a process of replacement. Broadcast media, obviously, still play a major role in today's culture and, thus, the proliferation of social media should be considered an addition to the general media landscape. If broadcast media can be described as "the many watching the few," then social media might be described as "the many performing for the few" in the sense that this latter type of media is characterized by mass participation and communication in egocentric networks (boyd and Ellison, 2007). Thus, I am suggesting that both broadcast and social media can serve as illustrative examples that point to the need for a pluralistic perspective on surveillance practices.

The Many Watching the Few

When we think of media as surveillance practices, an initial observation is that broadcast media connect equally well to democratic and totalitarian societies. Orwell's *Nineteen Eighty-Four* illustrates the "evil" conception of mass media in society in which the power of broadcasting is a one-sided propaganda tool for the totalitarian regime. The absolute power of media technology, specifically the camera, is a necessary assumption driving the entire story. The many are watching the few – or even just the one (the omnipresent image of Big Brother) – and this broadcasting of the figure of authority is part of the control apparatus. In democratic societies, broadcast media have been (and still are) something that significantly influences the political and cultural spheres, though in a very different way. Rather than forcing a certain perspective, such as in the model of the totalitarian society presented in *Nineteen Eighty-Four*, traditional mass media in democratic societies both facilitate and shape public understanding and discussions of political, cultural, and social issues by (for example) selecting certain types of content, using particular ways of portraying lifestyles, and including and excluding opinions and beliefs.

An example to illustrate this latter understanding of broadcast media as a surveillance practice is the Danish Broadcasting Corporation. This public-service organization, known in Denmark as "DR," was founded in 1925 and is the oldest and largest media enterprise in the country. It was the only national broadcaster for more than 50 years until the monopoly was broken in 1988 by the introduction of Danish TV2. During the many years of total broadcasting dominance, there was lively public discussion about how DR managed the monopoly: did they allow for a reasonably broad range of viewpoints to appear? Did the journalistic choices favor certain political opinions? One especially tenacious criticism characterized the debate during the 1970s and 1980s and has since reemerged from time to time in the era of postmonopoly broadcasting. This criticism by pundits from the right-wing political spectrum employs the infamous phrase "red henchmen" for DR's employees to reflect the latter's supposed promotion of socialist or even communist propaganda through their service at the broadcasting corporation.

Whether or not this criticism can be substantiated is part of ongoing discussions. It can be argued that to some extent only a few employees were in control of a media apparatus that was the de facto platform for public debate. At the same time, because of the way traditional broadcast media works, a very limited number of people had access to appear on the screen (and on the radio) to present opinions, beliefs, and perspectives on different issues. Thus, the many were watching the few, and the latter were in control of the media. However, a central characteristic of a democratic society like Denmark is the possibility of conducting such discussions in an open manner – including during debate programs on DR itself – and this openness underlines the insufficiency of an Orwellian understanding of mass media. In other words, monopolized broadcast media with only a few people having access to the screen is not necessarily totalitarian. To understand the complex historical relationship between mass media and audience we may begin by considering the way media are inextricably connected with home life.

The television set – a centerpiece in the traditional, Western world understanding of the home (Huston et al. 1992) – transmits images and sound from the "outside." This means that a power structure between broadcaster and receiver is established in a way that reaches into the privacy of the home. What is indicated here is that a home is traditionally considered to be a private place. This is in line with the idea of the home as the symbol of privacy, or even the home as the geographical place of privacy, an idea that is somewhat in contrast to the many current television series that focus on the home (those relating to buying/selling houses, displays of celebrities' houses, home make-overs, etc.). In these shows, the home becomes a public space with the television audience as voyeurs. Here, the home is a representation of everyday life as well as an indicator of social status often associated with a certain ideal of family living. However, the home has also, historically, been considered to be the cradle of the petite bourgeoisie, the suburban lifestyle dreaded by countercultural people and progressive artists. In this vision the home is a prison-like place with a respectable surface appearance – a place where privacy means isolation and ignorance, sustained by the reception of the one-way stream of information from broadcast media.

In recent years, the increase of more flexible work arrangements has meant that the home as a retreat from the world has changed to be a more transparent place. When we use mobile phones, computers with Internet connections, and other similar devices, we connect our home to the world in new ways. Especially, the Internet is opening the home to a two-way flow of information. However, the home remains a place for privacy and mundane living, becoming what could be described as a mixed zone with many openings to the world with the Internet as a "pulse" (Bell and Kaye 2002: 53) that can empower the inhabitants.

The Many Performing for the Few

The introduction of the Internet has obviously changed many people's media usage, as a range of new platforms for communication have appeared. Many of these new media platforms offer the possibility to customize or personalize the media experience, and they allow for new ways of engagement as well as extended social interactions. From a surveillance perspective, social media has brought about changes that call for a post-Orwellian understanding of practices.

Today, Facebook is the dominant online social network and, since its introduction in 2004, has grown to 901 million active users as of March 2012 according to Facebook's own numbers (Facebook n.d.). The communication structure of Facebook can be described as a collection of egocentric networks (boyd and Ellison, 2007), as the site is made up of individual users' specific ties to other users. These egocentric networks offer the users the possibility to share a wide variety of types of information about anything and everything. On Facebook, the users have two major ways of sharing: profile information and status updates. A user profile can be very minimalistic, only showing limited personal information, or it can be more elaborate, with details about political opinions, religious beliefs, and preferences in movies, music, and much more. Status updates can have a variety of forms: brief text; text in combination with a link, video, or picture(s); or simply a link, video, or picture(s) without text. Besides creating profiles and status updates, users can communicate with each other in a number of other ways, for example by creating or joining groups, participating in social gaming, and commenting on or "liking" pages or other users' status updates.

These manifold types of information are distributed in the Facebook "News feed," which is individual to all users based on their settings and personal networks of friends. The news feed is the interface in practice to the network, and this means that the users are presented with a stream of different types of information provided by their network. This ongoing personalized narrative is shaped simultaneously by the design of the social network website, the users' settings, and the ongoing social interactions between friends in the network.

Considering that online social networking practices involve sharing of personal information as a central activity, it becomes pertinent to think about surveillance in new ways. A panoptic or Orwellian interpretation of the surveillance practices of Facebook makes it difficult to adequately explain why so many users voluntarily engage in such social interactions. Why would users actively take part in a surveillance apparatus that exposes personal information that makes them vulnerable to privacy invasion and perhaps even corporate and governmental exploitation? To answer this question, it is necessary to reconsider the central aspects of Facebook use seen as a surveillance practice.

First, users are not only passive objects for others. Foucault famously described individuals in the panoptic apparatus as passive receivers of the gaze – that is, as objects of information, never subjects in communication (Foucault 1975: 234). Online social networks such as Facebook are not just personal panopticons, since applying such a perspective would clearly miss the point of the social interaction. This is of course not to say that panopticism is irrelevant to all aspects of online social networking; however, when it comes to the core activities of the egocentric social networks (i.e., users sharing information with each other), a more adequate description is needed. People use Facebook in many ways, but none of these reduce users to only being passive objects visible for others.[1] Rather, this particular surveillance practice involves users who actively take part in their own surveillance.

Second, when people voluntarily share personal information with a network, they should not be considered "victims" of surveillance. One of the most dominant understandings of surveillance practices is that they are constituted by power relations where the watched is controlled by the watcher, as in the panopticon. Orwell in *Nineteen Eighty-Four* of course brilliantly explores this scenario, though in its most dystopian and undesirable form. The idea of surveillance as a power relation is also central to the sociological tradition of surveillance studies (e.g., Rule 1973; Lyon 2001). In this power relation, the person under surveillance is controlled, disciplined (Foucault), or even brainwashed (Orwell). Considering social network sites such as Facebook, it is clear that we need alternative ways of describing how people take part in ongoing surveillance activities. Rather than being victims, people act as voluntary participants in the surveillance practice, and, given the nature of social interaction, it seems more appropriate to describe these users as potentially empowered.

Third, when people share personal information with their network, it should not be considered part of a trade-off. Interpreting this social interaction as a game of "I will give up my personal information if you also show me yours" would miss the point of that activity. Sharing information should not just be understood as a commodity that gives users access to a database of other users' personal information, even if curiosity about other people's lives is undoubtedly an important motivation for online social networking. Rather, sharing information is essential to the social interaction; in other words, surveillance practices actually facilitate online social networking. By sharing selected information, users can perform identities, for example by sharing thoughts, news, comments, interests, and so on. In this way, users have, at least partly, control over the personal information conveyed to the network. Thus, when people willingly share information with a network of other people, they are active participants in surveillance practices that even carry the promise of empowerment.

Obviously, social media are quite different from broadcast media, and this becomes even clearer when they are both considered as surveillance practices. These practices no longer involve only the many watching the few but also the many performing for the few. This is of course not to say that broadcast media necessarily only have large, passive audiences but that the design of egocentric social network sites not only encourages but also requires users to perform activities. The result is a collection of interconnected egocentric networks, each with few people, altogether creating a different kind of surveillance structure including new technologies, relations, and actors.

Privacy and Transparency

Online social networking makes it necessary to develop a new vocabulary to better understand and discuss the surveillance practices relating to it. I have elsewhere described this as "participatory surveillance" (Albrechtslund 2008a), drawing a reference to the notion of participatory culture, in which the consumer is actively participating in the production and circulation of media content (Jenkins 2006). In this section, I will explore how this post-Orwellian thinking, as it were, changes the perception of privacy and transparency, two central concepts for the understanding of surveillance.

From Being Left Alone to Being in Control

Traditionally, privacy has been understood as the ability to be left alone; the word's Latin root is "privatus," which designates being separated from other people, groups, and organizations. This definition of privacy is the basis for the Western understanding of classic dichotomies between citizens and states, consumers and corporations, workers and workplace, and so on. The introduction of databases in the second half of the twentieth century has intensified the general concerns about potential invasions of privacy, as in them familiar panoptic principles operate as a digitally enhanced and expanded "superpanopticon" (Poster 1990, 1996).

The advent of social media has increased public concerns about possible violations, because these media involve what is usually perceived as the most important aspect of privacy, namely personal information. The fact that people publish this information themselves has led some to consider online social networking to be a "snoop's dream" (Marks 2007) or, as the WikiLeaks founder Julian Assange once described it:

> Facebook in particular is the most appalling spy machine that has ever been invented. Here we have the world's most comprehensive database about people, their relationships, their names, their addresses, their location, their communication with each other, their relatives . . . all accessible to US intelligence. (in Chan 2011)

Over the years, privacy has been discussed fervently in the public debate, and Facebook has especially been accused in the wake of its numerous alterations to the service's interface and privacy settings. A result of these discussions, at least in the academic literature, is an awareness of the rather nuanced views and expectations of the users. In addition, the young audience, sometimes thought to be indifferent about others' and their own privacy, appears to be very careful and attentive concerning individual limits with regards to sharing personal information (boyd 2008; boyd and Hargittai 2010).

The many separate pieces of personal information available online – sometimes from different sources – can be put together like a puzzle, creating a coherent picture of a person. In this way, the collected information forms a whole that, in turn, constructs meaning for the individual pieces. David Lyon's concept of "leaky containers" (2001: 37–48) can be useful to describe this situation. In an information society in general, data flow more easily between sectors, groups, and organizations that have otherwise not been connected. The result is that information from (for example) people's private spheres, work lives, and shopping habits are being mixed rather than being contained separately. This is indeed the case in relation to online social networking, as different types of information are shared with people in a network consisting of contacts drawn from several different contexts, for example family, work, interests, school, and so on. Even though Facebook and other social network sites often offer the possibility to differentiate between groups of people in the network, it does not seem to be an option most people have embraced so far.

A way to address these challenges and to meet user expectations of privacy is to focus on awareness of the context in which people share information. In her book *Privacy in Context: Technology, Policy, and the Integrity of Social Life* (2010), Helen Nissenbaum elaborates on the reasonable expectations for and limitations of privacy in particular with regards to social media. She develops the concept of "contextual integrity" as a framework for evaluating the appropriateness of the flows of personal information. We need to rethink the widespread understanding of privacy as either the right to secrecy or complete individual control. Rather, the right to privacy is connected to the appropriate flows of information for the given situation – that is, what Nissenbaum labels "contextual integrity." Of course, this appropriateness varies from context to context, and a number of specific norms are important. Nissenbaum argues that these norms

> are a function of the types of information in question; the respective roles of the subject, the sender (who may be the subject), and the recipient of this information, and the principles under which the information is sent or transmitted from the sender to the recipient. (2010: 144)

Thus, it might be observed about online social networking that privacy is not about being anonymous. Rather, the discussion about privacy and social network sites indicates that users do not want to be secluded from other users – a wish that would be peculiar in combination with social interaction – but prefer to be in control of the stream of shared information. Of course, we cannot control every aspect of a context, as Nissenbaum argues, but social media users can expect to be in control of what they actively share with whom, and to know that these choices are violated neither by other people nor the social network site.

Visibility as Empowerment

A term central to this discussion is, of course, "visibility," inasmuch as the word "surveillance" is etymologically associated with the French word *surveiller*, which translates simply as "to watch over." The verb suggests the visual practice of a person looking carefully at someone or something from above. The visual metaphor implies a spatial hierarchy where the watcher is positioned *over* the watched, and this situation is favorable for the former as it makes it easier to keep an eye on the latter. This visual metaphor is at the root of the interpretation of surveillance as a power relation in which the watcher controls the watched. Consequently, transparency is a weakness, because those who are visible are at the same time vulnerable to a controlling gaze.

This conception of transparency as something that can be employed to break down, control, and eventually rebuild people is well known from novels (not least *Nineteen Eighty-Four*), cinema, and computer games (Albrechtslund and Dubbeld 2005; Albrechtslund 2008b). Moreover, surveillance is not only a frequently visited theme in fiction but can also be said to structure films' imagery and narration. Dietmar Kammerer (2004) has pointed to a trend in mainstream Hollywood cinema over the past decades to integrate the aesthetics of video surveillance as well as the imagery itself into films. Surveillance footage, often grainy images from a raised point of view, can be part of the imagery of the film and in that way influence the way films are structured. As Thomas Y. Levin put it: "surveillance has become the condition of the narration itself" (2002: 583). The post-9/11 TV series *24* (2001–2010), broadcast by Fox Network in the USA, illustrates both the thematic and structural role of surveillance. The fast-paced story and visual style of the series often depend on surveillance technologies, such as GPS tracking and knowledge obtained by computer hacking, and imagery from satellites and CCTV are integrated in all episodes. A characteristic mode of storytelling has Chloe O'Brien (Mary Lynn Rajscub), the computer expert, at her desktop and Jack Bauer (Kiefer Sutherland), the hero, somewhere in the field working on a mission. In this set-up, Chloe facilitates Jack's actions by providing him with information obtained by surveillance.

The cinematic gaze illustrates a paradox of surveillance, in that it allows us to be fascinated with our shame of watching and fear of being watched. The cinema facilitates a space where we, the audience, can explore and to a certain extent live out our issues with and feelings about surveillance. This pluralistic way of understanding visibility is equally appropriate for social media, since power relations are much more ambiguous than is suggested by the etymology of surveillance. As discussed in the previous section, surveillance does not necessarily imply a hierarchy, as the power relation can be "flattened." The flat surveillance relation has been described as peer-to-peer or "lateral surveillance" (Andrejevic 2005). Further, the traditional power relation has been challenged and even inverted, either negatively, as actively resisting the surveillance (Ball and Wilson 2000; McGrath 2004), or positively, as "exhibitionistic empowerment" (Koskela 2004).

When I use the label "participatory surveillance" to describe the active, sharing, and potentially empowered social media user, it is of course not to *replace* either flat or hierarchical understandings of surveillance. It is simply an attempt to broaden the concept of surveillance by emphasizing the potentially empowering characteristics that appear when surveillance is part of social practices. My ambition is to focus on subjectivity rather than system, and on participation rather than involuntary targeting. Thus, surveillance is intentional, as it most often involves a purpose, it is most often mediated by knowledge or technology, and – to introduce a new continuum – can be described as a practice that ranges from power exercise to sheer playfulness.

Conclusion

To share personal information with a network – which often includes more people than those whom we consider close friends – is a form of communication that should not be reduced to scary surveillance scenarios or simple trade-offs where users give up something private to gain knowledge about others. In this context, sharing (profile information, activities, links, opinions, location, etc.) is communication where questions and answers are unnecessary. Social surveillance – or, more precisely, the idea that surveillance is facilitating social interaction – underlines the need to approach this issue pluralistically. To adequately understand social media, we must equally embrace users' activities as surveillance practices. My ambition in this chapter is neither to replace other conceptions of surveillance nor insist that the understanding presented here offers an exhaustive account of all surveillance technologies and practices relating to online social networking. It is my aim to contribute to theoretical discussions within surveillance studies while also providing a new perspective on the historical development from broadcast to social media.

As mentioned above, social media are not replacing broadcast media; rather, it seems that these two types of media are increasingly interdependent. Social media is often a platform for sharing and discussing stories and other material that originates from broadcast media. Similarly, broadcast media are in different ways incorporating social media – or, at least, the participatory aspect of these – into parts of (especially) their live programming, either simply as text displayed on the screen (Twitter feeds, Facebook comments, etc.) or as the occasional reading aloud of ongoing discussions on social media relating to the show being broadcast. This coming together of different types of media will be exciting to follow over the coming years, and from a surveillance perspective this development is an opportunity to further rethink how we grasp these new flows of information. Understanding new practices is not only about finding answers; rather, it is about asking new questions, and a pluralistic approach to surveillance offers a framework to do this.

Notes

1. Critics might point out that on Facebook it is in fact possible to be a passive object visible to others; for example, if a user displays personal information in an open profile and then refrains from any interaction. In response to this argument it must be stressed that this is hardly in line with Foucault's description of what it means to be citizen in a discipline society. Moreover, the act of joining Facebook, sharing selected information, and choosing not to socially interact is in itself active, voluntary behavior.

References

Albrechtslund, A. (2008a) "Online Social Networking as Participatory Surveillance." *First Monday*, 13(3). http://firstmonday.org/article/view/2142/1949.

Albrechtslund, A. (2008b) "Surveillance and Ethics in Film: *Rear Window* and *The Conversation*." *Journal of Criminal Justice and Popular Culture*, 15(2). www.albany.edu/scj/jcjpc/vol15is2/Albrechtslund.pdf.

Albrechtslund, A. and Dubbeld, L. (2005) "The Plays and Arts of Surveillance: Studying Surveillance as Entertainment." *Surveillance & Society*, 3(2&3), 216–221.

Andrejevic, M. (2005) "The Work of Watching One Another: Lateral Surveillance, Risk, and Governance." *Surveillance & Society*, 2(4), 479–497.

Ball, K. and Wilson, D.C. (2000) "Power, Control and Computer-Based Performance Monitoring: Repertoires, Resistance, and Subjectivities." *Organization Studies*, 21(3), 539–565.

Bell, G. and Kaye, J. (2002) "Designing Technology for Domestic Spaces." *Gastronomica*, 2(2), 46–62.

boyd, d. (2008) "Facebook's Privacy Trainwreck: Exposure, Invasion, and Social Convergence." *Convergence: The International Journal of Research into New Media Technologies*, 14, 13–20.

boyd, d. and Ellison, N. (2007) "Social Network Sites: Definition, History, and Scholarship." *Journal of Computer-Mediated Communication*, 13(1). http://jcmc.indiana.edu/vol13/issue1/boyd.ellison.html.

boyd, d. and Hargittai, E. (2010) "Facebook Privacy Settings: Who Cares?" *First Monday*, 15(8). http://firstmonday.org/htbin/cgiwrap/bin/ojs/index.php/fm/article/view/3086/2589.

Chan, C. (2011) "Julian Assange Thinks Facebook Is the 'Most Appalling Spy Machine that has Ever Been Invented.'" *Gizmodo* (May 2). http://blog.gizmodo.com/5797923/julian-assange-thinks-facebook-is-the-most-appalling-spy-machine-that-has-ever-been-invented.

Facebook (n.d.) "Newsroom: Key Facts." http://newsroom.fb.com/content/default.aspx?NewsAreaId=22.

Foucault, M. (1975) *Surveiller et Punir: Naissance De La Prison* [Discipline and Punish: The Birth of the Prison]. Paris: Gallimard.

Huston, A.C., Donnerstein, E., and Fairchild, H. (1992) *Big World, Small Screen: The Role of Television in American Society*. Lincoln, NE: University of Nebraska Press.

Jenkins, H. (2006) *Convergence Culture: Where Old and New Media Collide.* New York: New York University Press.

Kammerer, D. (2004) "Video Surveillance in Hollywood Movies." *Surveillance & Society*, 2(2&3), 464–473.

Koskela, H. (2004) "Webcams, TV Shows and Mobile Phones: Empowering Exhibitionism." *Surveillance & Society*, 2(2/3), 199–215.

Levin, T.Y. (2002) "Rhetoric of the Temporal Index: Surveillant Narration and the Cinema of 'Real Time' " in T.Y. Levin, U. Frohne, and P. Weibel, eds., *CTRL [Space]. Rhetorics of Surveillance from Bentham to Big Brother*. Cambridge, MA: MIT Press, pp. 578–593.

Lyon, D. (2001) *Surveillance Society*. Buckingham: Open University Press.

Marks, P. (2007) "Pentagon Sets Its Sights on Social Networking Websites." *NewScientist.com* (July 14). www.newscientist.com/article/mg19025556.200.

McGrath, J.E. (2004) *Loving Big Brother: Performance, Privacy and Surveillance Space*. London and New York: Routledge.

Nissenbaum, H.F. (2010) *Privacy in Context: Technology, Policy, and the Integrity of Social Life*. Stanford, CA: Stanford University Press.

Orwell, G. (1949) *Nineteen Eighty-Four, a Novel*. London: Secker & Warburg.

Poster, M. (1990) *The Mode of Information: Poststructuralism and Social Context*. Chicago, IL: University of Chicago Press.

Poster, M. (1996) "Databases as Discourse; or, Electronic Interpellations." *Computers, Surveillance, and Privacy*. Minneapolis, MN: University of Minnesota Press, pp. 175–192.

Rule, J.B. (1973) *Private Lives and Public Surveillance*. London: Allen Lane.

20

Lessons of the Leak

WikiLeaks, Julian Assange, and the Changing Landscape of Media and Politics

Christoph Bieber

Journalism or Terrorism – What actually *is* WikiLeaks?

With hindsight, the distribution of the 17-minute video entitled "Collateral Murder" via www.wikileaks.org and www.collateralmurder.com on April 5, 2010 was merely the prelude of the events to come. Provided in two versions, the clip documented an airborne attack on a group of civilians by US military forces in New Baghdad back in July 2007. It generated enormous public attention, online as well as in traditional media environments (Benkler 2011: 8). WikiLeaks.org, then an obscure platform known only to a few well-informed online users, had begun to take center stage and immediately started to frame its activities as a new and necessary form of investigative journalism:

> WikiLeaks obtained this video as well as supporting documents from a number of military whistleblowers. WikiLeaks goes to great lengths to verify the authenticity of the information it receives. We have analyzed the information about this incident from a variety of source material. We have spoken to witnesses and journalists directly involved in the incident. WikiLeaks wants to ensure that all the leaked information it receives gets the attention it deserves. In this particular case, some of the people killed were journalists that were simply doing their jobs: putting their lives at risk in order to report on war. Iraq is a very dangerous place for journalists: from 2003–2009, 139 journalists were killed while doing their work. (www.collateralmurder.com)

The release of the video itself marked a step into new territory for WikiLeaks.org, as in earlier activities only text documents or raw material had been published. As of 2011, the "About" section of the website provided only brief information on the nature and mission of an only vaguely described organization:[1]

> WikiLeaks is a non-profit media organization dedicated to bringing important news and information to the public. We provide an innovative, secure and anonymous

A Companion to New Media Dynamics, First Edition. Edited by John Hartley, Jean Burgess, and Axel Bruns.
© 2013 John Wiley & Sons, Ltd. Published 2015 by John Wiley & Sons, Ltd.

way for independent sources around the world to leak information to our journalists. We publish material of ethical, political and historical significance while keeping the identity of our sources anonymous, thus providing a universal way for the revealing of suppressed and censored injustices. (WikiLeaks n.d.)

Although it went back to text-only material, the release of the so-called "Afghan War Logs" in July 2011 proved to be an even more innovative approach to an Internet-based model of collaborative publishing. No single website hosted the documents; the primary resources for information were provided by three partnering institutions: *The Guardian* (UK), *The New York Times* (USA), and *Der Spiegel* (Germany).[2] Having learned from the minor impact on public discussions of its earlier leaking activity, WikiLeaks.org (in the person of Julian Assange) established connections to globally known media actors in order to secure worldwide attention to the information to be distributed. Assange insisted, however, on the specific need for a new player like WikiLeaks within the media sphere, as the "digital nature" of the leaked materials would make it impossible for professional journalists to deal with the large amounts of raw data:

> So, it was my view early on that the whole of the existing Fourth Estate was not big enough for the task of making sense of information that hadn't previously been public. To take our most recent case as an example, all the journalists in the world would not be enough to make complete sense of the 400,000 documents we released about Iraq, and, of course, they have other things to write about as well. (Assange in Obrist 2011)

Although the multilateral cooperation became more and more complicated during the following disclosures of the "Iraq War Logs" (October) and, finally, the now-famous "Diplomatic Cables" (November), the multinational, collaborative mode of publishing became the key characteristic of WikiLeaks-related activity in late 2010.[3]

Because of this tight connection to the world of professional media, the self-confident statements on WikiLeaks' website, and of course the public perception of Julian Assange as an anchorperson, media activist, and successful "self-entrepreneur," WikiLeaks was quickly recognized as a new yet somehow undetermined form of media organization. According to Yochai Benkler (2011), WikiLeaks.org actively took this position during a "battle" with some media establishment and political actors who constantly criticized and even demonized WikiLeaks.org and/or Julian Assange as threats to American society:

> Throughout the events, Assange and Wikileaks emphasized their role as journalists. Inverting the practices of those who sought to analogize Wikileaks to terrorists, some commentators and reporters emphasized the basic argument that Wikileaks is a reporting organization, fulfilling a reporting function. (Benkler 2011: 30)

In an early post on his blog *Press Think*, Jay Rosen developed the phrase "world's first stateless news organization" to distinguish WikiLeaks from other media and nongovernment organizations because of the release of information without regard for national interest. In media history up to now, the press is free to report on what the powerful wish to keep secret because the laws of a given nation protect it. But Wikileaks is able to report on what the powerful wish to keep secret because the logic of the Internet permits it. This is new. (Rosen 2010)

Although WikiLeaks is in numerous aspects substantially different from established media outlets, it has to be treated equally and, as Benkler argues, the organization should be subject to "constitutional protection":

> The difference between the constituents of the networked fourth estate and the mass media cannot, then, be organizational size or complexity. Functionally, it is more important to provide robust constitutional protection to the weaker members of the fourth estate, who have less public visibility and wherewithal to withstand pressure from government officials, than it is to emphasize the rights of the organizationally and economically stronger members of the press. (Benkler 2011: 38)

The question of whether the practice of "leaking" is a current embodiment of investigative journalism has become the dominant framework for public debate about WikiLeaks. Nevertheless, there is a whole spectrum of different approaches representing specific "dynamics of change" triggered by WikiLeaks.[4] The following sections of this chapter can only explore a small selection: the upcoming changes in media communication related to the "economy of the leak" and the consequences of the "logic of the leak" for the relationship between citizens and members of the political system.

The Economy of the Leak

The dynamics of digitalization have continuously extended the opportunities for the creation, reproduction, and distribution of documents in a variety of formats – not only text but also pictures and videos can now easily be captured and edited in sophisticated ways, often equivalent to the products of media professionals. This "explosion" of digital data will be responsible for a future "economy of the leak," of which the WikiLeaks episode just is a harbinger. As it becomes easier to get hold of sensitive data, the probability of its circulation rises – a typical example is the digital compilation of "tax evaders": in the past few years, the bank account data of tax fugitives stored on compact discs have been exchanged between banks in Liechtenstein or Switzerland and German authorities. Under analog conditions, this process would have been much more complicated – in terms both of gathering the data and transmission and distribution.

Besides the technological aspect, the process of digitized leaking has also transformed the receiving end of the process. In the age of traditional mass media, typically members of the so-called "Fourth Estate" were provided with secret information, whereas now nongovernment organizations, watchdog groups, and even individual bloggers can act as relay stations for leaked data.[5] In many ways, the infrastructure of professional journalism is still needed to convert the unstructured mass of raw data into valuable information. The goal of generating global visibility for the various cases could only be achieved by the cooperation between WikiLeaks as the receiving end of the leaking process and professional media outlets such as *The Guardian*, *The New York Times*, and *Der Spiegel*. In this process, WikiLeaks claimed responsibility for the task of archiving and especially "cleaning" the digital data of any traces of the person who copied and transferred the material from military servers.

Substantial change becomes evident when assessing the aspects of the investigative "division of labor" among the participants in the event. WikiLeaks as a decentralized organization hiding in the empty spaces between different national legal systems (Benkler 2011: 48) obviously offers better protection for persons with "dangerous" information to leak, especially when providing the knowledge and the means to delete and suppress any links between the leaked data and the person transmitting it. Conversely, professional journalists can ensure the validation and authentification of raw material as well as adding narratives to the data that can guide readers (or users) through the sheer wealth of the material.

Although the publication of the documents was not limited to WikiLeaks.org as the platform for distribution, one could assume that Julian Assange and his organization were driving the process, if not controlling it. The search for the best mode of sharing this information to the largest possible audience made clear that the usage, the image, and the social position of the news media – and therewith the construction of the public sphere itself – is undergoing a radical transformation. Still, the political public to a large extent is constructed by the means of traditional mass media, but the series of publications "powered by WikiLeaks" is an indicator of the advent of a new breed of actors within the public sphere.

With WikiLeaks in a state of anesthesia, caused by Julian Assange being placed under house arrest, a couple of "offspring" organizations have tried to take the opportunity to enter the scene and present themselves as the next best address for accepting leaked data. Being itself a direct ancestor to WikiLeaks, the OpenLeaks initiative led by Daniel Domscheit-Berg, a former confidant of Julian Assange (see OpenLeaks n.d.), probably had the best perspectives to get into play – yet, as of mid-2012, with one and a half a years gone by since the public announcement of the project in early 2011, OpenLeaks.org has not leaked or transmitted any documents yet. But, despite the silence of the site, OpenLeaks has made some substantial contributions toward a better understanding of the leaking process in a digital age. Domscheit-Berg and his fellow activists propose a four-step model dividing the process into distinct phases and recommend a division of labor between submission-focused and publication-focused partnering institutions – each of which face intricate problems at their ends of the process:

> There are two major parts to the process of leaking: submission of material and publication of it. By concentrating on the submission part we attain two desirable goals: 1) increasing the security for all parties involved, 2) improving scalability by minimizing bottlenecks and reducing complexity in our organization. (OpenLeaks n.d.)[6]

The OpenLeaks community surely makes its point when comparing their security-driven model to the fast but often flawed projects developed by professional media outlets. Most prominently, the so-called "Safehouse" provided by the *Wall Street Journal* (https://www.wsjsafehouse.com) was not safe at all, according to reports of hackers and security analysts (though as of 2012 the bug has been fixed and the site remains open). Not only was the anonymization of submissions criticized but also the "terms of use" did not guarantee a full protection of sources (Adam 2011; Gillmor 2011).[7] While *The New York Times* and *The Guardian* are still hesitating to launch leaking portals on their own, in January 2011 Al Jazeera installed a so-called "Transparency Unit" (http://transparency.aljazeera.net) by publishing a trove of documents related to the Israeli–Palestinian conflict ("The Palestine Papers"). The initiative is framed as a new kind of "participative journalism," aiming to

> mobilize its audience – both in the Arab world and further afield – to submit all forms of content (documents, photos, audio and video clips, as well as "story tips") for editorial review and, if merited, online broadcast and transmission on our English and Arabic-language broadcasts. (Al Jazeera Transparency Unit n.d.)

With the success story of the WikiLeaks operations in mind, professional media outlets are obviously fostering the usage of leaked information from inside the media system. Still, there are concerns over whether their platforms provide sufficient security for submissions, and the juridical status of those ventures is sometimes kept unclear through carefully formulated "terms of services." In the end, professional observers are pessimistic about the "protective power" media outlets can offer individuals leaking controversial, secret, or even dangerous documents. Dan Gillmor expresses his mixed feelings with this kind of journalistic change triggered by WikiLeaks:

> While I tend to believe that every news organization should have a drop-off point for documents from whistleblowers, there's always going to be a question of how much a leaker should trust any private company on which a government can exert pressure, apart the [sic] issue of whether the company itself can always be trusted. (Gillmor 2011)

At that point, the close connection of the leaking process to the political system becomes clear. Although there is a rising number of leaking websites, encouraging and sometimes empowering single individuals to pass on critical documents to which they have access, media outlets may be subject to pressure by political actors. In addition to demonstrating an "economy of the leak," the case of WikiLeaks proves that there are ways to take action against the unwanted publication of official documents, such as "ex post" objections or exerting influence on partners and collaborators of leaking individuals and institutions.

Why Change? Politics Versus the "Transparency Movement"

Although the publication of classified documents provoked substantial reactions from political actors compromised by WikiLeaks, the general attitude and behavior related to secrecy, leaking, and transparency within the political process has not altered significantly – there is still a widespread consensus inside the political system about the need for *arcana imperii*.

Before taking the further effects of the "cablegate" episode into account, it is necessary to discuss why exactly these troves of documents can be described as a "tipping point" in the WikiLeaks saga. In light of their disturbing and classified content, the publication of military documents from Afghanistan and Iraq should have caused both more public attention and more anger, revealing "inconvenient truths" about contemporary yet ineffective warfare or violence against civilian populations in those territories. However, it was the diplomatic cables that caused a public outcry as well as a campaign against WikiLeaks, culminating in a virtual manhunt directed against Julian Assange. That is a remarkable development, which from a political scientist's perspective might shift the attention to the intra-disciplinary dimension of the different leaking strategies: while both the Afghan and the Iraqi War Logs can be assessed as *policy*-oriented leaks with the aim of discrediting the agendas in specific areas of US foreign politics, the unveiling of the diplomatic cables can be regarded as a form of *politics*-oriented leak. Insights into the networks, methods, and instruments of international political communication employed by members of the US government bureaucracy not only fuelled public interest but also critically challenged and embarrassed the targets of the leaking process – that is, even without bringing spectacular new information to light, "only" by revealing some mechanics of diplomatic communication in combination with gossip about international politicians.

In contrast to the war-related and often tragic stories displayed in the documents from Afghanistan and Iraq, the diplomatic cables feature some "celebrity effects" that make them compatible with more popular news cycles and audiences, thus improving the visibility of the leaked documents. In turn, the attention of the broader public was registered by the US political elite, provoking immediate answers to WikiLeaks' fourth publication in 2010. The popular label "Cablegate" evoked an unspecific but inconvenient connection to "Watergate" and urged politicians to take their stand in an intensifying public discourse (see Benkler 2011: 12–15; Fenster 2011: 8–11). As Benkler notes, "the response to the Wikileaks embassy cable release in the US was dramatic and sharp" (2011: 15). Yet, it has to be added, the response was carefully embedded into the hierarchy of the Obama administration – the president did not issue public statements, whereas Hillary Clinton had to react immediately. Acting in her role as Secretary of State, she had to claim responsibility for the branch of government under public scrutiny.

First, Clinton expressed her thoughts on leaking activities as a dangerous and potentially harmful act, joining a long line of critics: "The United States strongly condemns the illegal disclosure of classified information. It puts people's lives in danger, threatens our national security, and undermines our efforts to work with other countries to solve shared problems" (Clinton 2010). This positioning as "anti-WikiLeaks" (Sifry 2011) was followed by a short outline of a response strategy within the structures of the affected bureaucracy. Clinton made clear that, despite the revealed documents and the call for transparency orchestrated by WikiLeaks supporters and especially by Julian Assange, there is a genuine necessity for political actors to communicate in secrecy in order to serve their public duties:

> Every country, including the United States, must be able to have candid conversations about the people and nations with whom they deal. And every country, including the United States, must be able to have honest, private dialogue with other countries about issues of common concern. (Clinton 2010)

This call for a secure space of internal communication inside the realm of politics is based on the need for open and unshielded discussions in bi- or multilateral settings between politicians, interest groups, and other stakeholders while deliberating the best solution possible within the political decision system.[8] Following this normative statement, Clinton sketched the immediate practical reactions to be taken within the administration to counter the future challenges of leaking platforms:

> I have directed that specific actions be taken at the State Department, in addition to new security safeguards at the Department of Defense and elsewhere to protect State Department information so that this kind of breach cannot and does not ever happen again. Relations between governments aren't the only concern created by the publication of this material. U.S. diplomats meet with local human rights workers, journalists, religious leaders, and others outside of governments who offer their own candid insights. These conversations also depend on trust and confidence. (Clinton 2010)

The perspective that an external call for transparency has to be answered with a more rigid policy of secrets is not exclusive to Clinton as the head of the administrative branch in question. A series of commentators hold this position as well; Stancil voices a representative opinion: "There is a sensible middle ground somewhere between the culture of secrecy that dominates now and the kind of indiscriminate dumping that seems to be the goal of Julian Assange and WikiLeaks" (Stancil 2010).

The Memorandum of the Office of Management and Budget conceived in the White House echoes this strategy, far more openly demanding a strict and prohibitive internal communications policy:

> Each department or agency that handles classified information shall establish a security assessment team consisting of counterintelligence, security, and information assurance experts to review the agency's implementation of procedures for safeguarding classified information against improper disclosures. (Clinton 2010)

It remains unclear whether this "call to arms" inside the government bureaucracy will succeed. The perspectives prompted by consideration of a climate of fear, which might result from an internal communications regime enhancing the principles of secrecy and isolation, cannot be discussed here – but there are obvious indications of a consensus about the need for secure, confidential, nonpublic discourse spaces within the political process. And, more importantly, this idea is not limited to political actors but also a common view of professional observers and scientific experts on international diplomatic communication (see Fenster 2011). Presumably, there will be no substantial change in the future communications strategy and activity of US government authorities – confidential, secluded areas of internal discussion will persist, as will the strong political will to keep things secret.

Transparency, WikiLeaks, and Julian Assange

In his impressive attempt to collect and systematize the contributions to transparency and openness, Micah Sifry has laid out a first landscape of transparency activism throughout a huge spectrum of political systems (2011: 85–103, 167–188). He has also opened up the field for nonjournalistic, simply political ventures by noting that "it is people using the Internet who interpret secrecy as a democratic failure – as a reason not to trust government – and more and more we route around it until we get at the truth" (Sifry 2011: 83).[9] Among other things, Sifry refers to the Kenyan crisis mapping project Ushahidi (www.ushahidi.com), a crime-reporting service from Brazil (http://wikicrimes.org), and anticorruption websites in Croatia (http://pollitika.com) and India (http://ipaidabribe.com). Projects such as these do not need the entire ideological framework provided by Assange's concept of "government as conspiracy," and they also do not necessarily have to be too "radical." The technological structure of the Internet, the individual interest to collaborate on a specific issue one is affected by, and – of course – a variety of forms of misconduct within the political system may be sufficient to start digitally enhanced civic participation. Sifry concludes:

> The transparency movement is based on one core idea: that when information about what governments are doing and who is trying to influence them is made broadly available, we as individuals and as a society can better watch over our government, raise questions, root out corruption, highlight problems, elevate solutions, and, in so doing, foster real accountability. (Sifry 2011: 186)

Although in several of the cases hosted by WikiLeaks the process of "outsourcing" or "crowd-sourcing" investigative activity did not work out perfectly, the platform has functioned as a role model for a series of new journalistic models (as discussed) and has led the way for various watchdog organizations throughout the world. WikiLeaks itself appears to now be facing some substantial changes, perhaps relating to the personal future of Julian Assange as a leading character of the entire project.

At least in its early stages, WikiLeaks emphasized the participative aspects of enabling individual users to contribute to a process Assange described as "scientific journalism." After its first document leaks[10] did not lead to it gaining worldwide media attention, WikiLeaks redesigned its working process and turned to a collaboration with professional media outlets – with (at least) Assange being well aware of that this sacrificed the "Wiki" aspect of the project:

> So what we wanted to do was to take all that volunteer labor that is spent on writing about things that are not terribly important, and redirect it to material that we released, material that has a real potential for change if people assess it, analyze it, contextualize it, and push it back into local communities. I tried very hard to make that happen, but it didn't. (Assange in Obrist 2011)

WikiLeaks no longer uses its platform as an open, decentralized, hierarchy-free tool for collaboration, as insinuated by the "Wiki" prefix. This development has been noted (and criticized) by Wikipedia's founder, Jimmy Wales: "I would distance myself from WikiLeaks. I wish they wouldn't use the name. They are not a wiki" (Sheridan 2010). By acting in this way, WikiLeaks systematically seems to have decreased the potential for civic participation: by concentrating on cooperation with professional media partners, WikiLeaks is becoming a political actor in a more conventional mode. By cancelling the "wiki" mode of operation and by acting as a connector between important nodes within the "networked fourth estate" (Benkler 2011), WikiLeaks is transforming its gestalt from an open, collaborative leaking platform into an exclusive organization specializing in the brokerage of sensitive information.

At this point, the role and the importance of Julian Assange at the center of the WikiLeaks operations has to be taken into account. Since the core group started in 2010 to dissolve over internal differences, Assange seems to have controlled the organization single handedly. In a famous note to former WikiLeaks volunteer Herbert Snorason, Assange frankly explained his dominant position: "I am the heart and soul of this organization, its founder, philosopher, spokesperson, original coder, organizer, financier, and all the rest" (in Sifry 2011: 170). Felix Stalder has connected this overly powerful position of Julian Assange to the concept of "super-empowered individual," a term developed by military strategists to describe the damage potential of single terrorists. The concept

> highlights how individuals, or more likely, small groups, can affect these systems disproportionately if they manage to interfere with these critical nodes. Thus, individuals, supported by small, networked organisations, can now intervene in social dynamics at a systemic level, for better or worse. This picture fits WikiLeaks, organised around one charismatic individual, very well. (Stalder 2010)

Moreover, the series of publications by WikiLeaks (and the accompanying media coverage) have constructed some kind of political program or philosophy underlying the operational dimension of the WikiLeaks efforts, even if it only depicts the views of Julian Assange. His claims for "radical transparency" as an antagonistic position to "conspiracy as governance" (Assange 2006a) might be considered as the groundwork for a "transparency movement" or even the "age of transparency" (see Sifry 2011). The core of this philosophy is revealed in the first two sentences of Assange's essay "State and Terrorist Conspiracies" in an allusion to the challenge represented by technology to the static nature of political regimes:

To radically shift regime behavior we must think clearly and boldly for if we have learned anything, it is that regimes do not want to be changed. We must think beyond those who have gone before us, and discover technological changes that embolden us with ways to act in which our forebears could not. (Assange 2006b)

Based on his personal experiences,[11] Assange consecutively developed an abstract framework that led to the conceptualization of WikiLeaks as an antagonist to political elites and their increasingly sealed and protected processes of communication and decision-making.[12] From this perspective, Assange's role might be conceived not only as the founder and editor-in-chief of WikiLeaks.org but also as a public intellectual trying to "speak truth to power" (Wildavsky). Following the systematization of Theodore Lowi, Assange can be understood as a "movement intellectual" (MI): concentrating on a specific idea or concept, his work is familiar to a limited audience or community; within this, new ideas are spread and discussed, and a more coherent conceptualization is developed:

First of all, the MI lives a radical life but is not necessarily extremist and is certainly not violent. A "radical," following mathematics, is concerned with roots and getting at the roots. ... Consequently, the MI does not address the public at-large but instead concentrates on speaking to members and supporters already drawn in by the theory and ideology of the movement. (Lowi 2010: 676)

Certainly, Julian Assange is addressing the "public at large" – but he also acts as editor-in-chief of WikiLeaks and contributes to a "reformist agenda" aimed at modernizing the mainstream media (Fenster 2011: 19). But his more abstract writings and reflections on the ideas of "radical transparency" were received by a much smaller audience than the stories of the WikiLeaks publications and its journalistic narrative. For a better understanding of the idea of Assange as an intellectual, it has to be noted that his achievements not only consist of his more or less public writings.

In addition to his short outline of "conspiracy as governance," Assange has written a lot of "code" – which might well become an equivalent to the usual intellectual activity of contributing to public debates in textual form by conceiving articles, lectures, or speeches. Deeply rooted in 1990s "Cypherpunk" subculture, Assange discovered the transformative power of computing – and coding. During his Australian "career" as a hacker (see Dreyfus and Assange 1997), he not only gained advanced programming skills but also reflected on the potential for societal change within a transnational, subversive community:

The Cypherpunks were a combination of people from California, Europe, and Australia. We saw that we could change the nature of the relationship between the individual and the state using cryptography. I wouldn't say that we came from a libertarian political tradition as much as from a libertarian temperament, with particular individuals who were capable of thinking in abstractions, but wanting to make them real. ... Rather, our will came from a quite extraordinary notion of power, which was that with some clever mathematics you can, very simply – and this seems complex in abstraction but simple in terms of what computers are capable of – enable any individual to say no to the most powerful state. (Assange in Obrist 2011)

This aspect of Assange's idea and story within the WikiLeaks case explicates the changing circumstances of how individuals may intervene in and influence the political process on different levels. The ability to code has been taken into account when assessing the influence of public intellectuals; it has already started to supplement typical intellectual skills such as writing books, op-eds, or political punditry on television. Writing code and conceiving, testing, and publishing software can indeed bring individuals into the powerful position to "shift regime behavior," as Assange noted as early as 2006. Media critic Douglas Rushkoff hints at this process in his essay "Program, or be Programmed," carefully suggesting that coding is on the verge of becoming a new cultural technique:

> Finally, we have the tools to program. Yet we are content to seize only the capability of the last great media renaissance, that of writing. We feel proud to build a web page or finish our profile on a social networking site, as if this means we are now full-fledged participants in the cyber era. We remain unaware of the biases of the programs in which we are participating, as well as the ways they circumscribe our newfound authorship within their predetermined agendas. (2010: 139–140)

Actually, this would be Julian Assange's most prominent hack: speaking truth to power in "J'Accuse" style (Begley 2009) – but now in binary code.

Acknowledgments

Most of these perspectives were developed, tested, and discussed with students of the Haniel Master Course at the NRW School of Governance/University of Duisburg-Essen during the summer term of 2011. For supporting research and practical help while preparing this manuscript I would like to thank Markus Lewitzki.

Notes

1. For a better understanding and background information, see Khatchadourian (2010) and Sifry (2011). Also worth reading is the "memoir" of Daniel Domscheit-Berg (2011), a former member of the WikiLeaks group and close ally of Julian Assange – although he definitely does not write from a neutral point of view and mixes personal experiences with analytical passages.
2. Each of the three publishing houses provided "exclusive" background information on the editorial process; on *The Guardian* see Leigh et al. (2011); on *The New York Times* see Star and Keller (2011); and on *Der Spiegel* see Rosenbach and Stark (2011). Later in 2010, WikiLeaks.org expanded its publishing network to the newspapers *Le*

Monde (France) and *El Pais* (Spain). In June 2011, WikiLeaks began to cooperate with Pública, a not-for-profit media center in Brazil, which launched a "WikiLeaks Week" (http://publica.org/2011/06/semana-wikileaks).

3. There is no space here for further explication and analysis of the background developments during the series of publications. However, the publications mentioned in note 2 provide a deeper, yet biased, perspective on the working conditions "behind the curtain."

4. A more detailed analysis would also be able to find effects relating to scientific research (usage of data as source material, development and application of new research methods), media economy (new business models derived from the innovative mode of collaboratory publishing), and ethical questions related to the use and distribution of critical data and (personal) information.

5. The most prominent figures of this period of leaking were often cited during the WikiLeaks affair: Daniel Ellsberg, who copied the so-called "Pentagon Papers" and passed them on to *The New York Times*, and Bob Woodward and Carl Bernstein, reporters for the *Washington Post*, who were fed information by an anonymous source called "Deep Throat." Interestingly, the Pentagon Papers are often used as a blueprint for the legal discussion about the role of Julian Assange (Benkler 2011: 33; Bunz 2011).

6. Domscheit-Berg et al. (2011) describe four phases of leaking: submissions, rendering, content production, and publication. While the latter two are best provided by professional media outlets, the secure submission of information in digital form and extinguishing of the traces of its providers ("rendering") are key services in the concept – one could say that these skills and the requisite technological know-how resemble the "unique selling proposition" of the new generation of leaking platforms.

7. In Germany, a similar project was launched by the regional newspaper group WAZ (Westdeutsche Allgemeine Zeitung). Coordinated by the group's investigative branch, the website was to be able to provide secure online submissions of digital information by email (www.derwesten.de/recherche). No information is currently available as of mid-2012 on whether the system has been compromised. In a round-up of the first six months of activity, the system is described as a success, despite users mostly offering "story tips" and infrequently submitting documents (Schraven 2011).

8. The concept of open deliberation under the conditions of opacity cannot be discussed further within this article. However, reference should at least be made to a decision of the German Constitutional Court (Bundesverfassungsgericht) in support of Chancellor Gerhard Schröder's decision to dissolve the Bundestag (German parliament) in 2005. The court granted the existence of a "confidential space for politics" that could be withheld from political competitors as well as from the broader public unless it was serving the public good (www.bundesverfassungsgericht.de/entscheidungen /es20050825_2bve000405.html).

9. Sifry here is paraphrasing John Gilmore's statement on the unfiltered structure and uncontrollable nature of computer networks: "The Internet treats censorship as though it were a malfunction and routes around it" (in Barlow n.d.).

10. The early stages of WikiLeaks.org are described and analyzed by Benkler (2011: 4–8) and Fenster (2011: 6–7). See also the information and records provided at WikiLeaks (n.d.).

11. After his widely "successful" hacking career was discovered in the early 1990s, Assange was charged in multiple cases of computer-related crimes. For more details see his biographical page on Wikipedia: http://en.wikipedia.org/wiki/Julian_Assange.

12. This article cannot extensively discuss Assange's writings on his "theory" of "conspiracy as governance" as a forebear to the WikiLeaks project. Aaron Bady has contributed a very intricate interpretation, describing Assange's idea "that the most effective way to attack this kind of organization [governmental structures] would be to make 'leaks' a fundamental part of the conspiracy's information environment" (Bady 2010). Mark Fenster divides "WikiLeaks' Theories" in two sections: the more popular narrative of "liberal reform" referring to the journalistic approach and the idea of "radical resistance" rooted in Assange's "cypherpunk" past (Fenster 2011: 15–27). In the following, this article offers another conceptual connection by framing Assange's activities as those of an intellectual.

References

Adam, M. (2011) "Privacy Advocate Doesn't Trust the Wall Street Journal's Safehouse." *The Atlantic* (May 5). www.theatlanticwire.com/business/2011/05/privacy-advocate-doesnt -trust-wall-street-journal-safehouse/37410.

Al Jazeera Transparency Unit (n.d.) "About the Transparency Unit." www.ajtransparency .com/en/about-transparency-unit.

Assange, J. (2006a) "Conspiracy as Governance." *Cryptome.org*. http://cryptome.org/0002/ja -conspiracies.pdf.

Assange, J. (2006b) "State and Terrorist Conspiracies." *Cryptome.org*. http://cryptome.org /0002/ja-conspiracies.pdf.

Bady, A. (2010) "Julian Assange and the Computer Conspiracy." *Zunguzungu* (November 29). http://zunguzungu.wordpress.com/2010/11/29/julian-assange-and-the-computer -conspiracy-%E2%80%9Cto-destroy-this-invisible-government%E2%80%9D/#.

Barlow, J.P. (n.d.) "Censorship 2011." *On the Internet*. www.isoc.org/oti/articles/1000/barlow .html.

Begley, L. (2009) *Why the Dreyfus Affair Matters*. New Haven, CT: Yale University Press.

Benkler, Y. (2011) *A Free Irresponsible Press. WikiLeaks and the Battle over the Soul of the Net-worked Fourth Estate*. Working Paper. www.benkler.org/Benkler_Wikileaks_current.pdf.

Bunz, M. (2011) "Das offene Geheimnis: Zur Politik der Wahrheit im Datenjournalismus [The Open Secret: About the Politics of Truth in Data Journalism]" in *WikiLeaks und die Folgen. Die Hintergründe. Die Konsequenzen* [Wikileaks and its Aftermaths. The Backgrounds. The Consequences]. Berlin: Suhrkamp, pp. 134–151.

Clinton, H.R. (2010) "Remarks to the Press on Release of Purportedly Confidential Documents by Wikileaks." *US Department of State* (November 11). www.state.gov /secretary/rm/2010/11/152078.htm.

Domscheit-Berg, D. (2011) *Inside WikiLeaks: My Time with Julian Assange at the World's Most Dangerous Website*. London: Crown.

Domscheit-Berg, D. et al. (2011) *OpenLeaks 101*. http://vimeo.com/17850593.

Dreyfus, S. and Assange, J. (1997) *Underground. Hacking, Madness and Obsession on the Electronic Frontier*. Kew: Mandarin Australia.

Fenster, M. (2011) "Disclosure's Effects: WikiLeaks and Transparency." *ExpressO*. http:// works.bepress.com/mark_fenster/10.

Gillmor, D. (2011) "Wall Street Journal's (Fail) SafeHouse: Keep Trying." *Mediactive.com* (May 6). http://mediactive.com/2011/05/06/wall-street-journals-failsafehouse -keep-trying.

Khatchadourian, R. (2010) "No Secrets. Julian Assange's Mission for Total Transparency." *The New Yorker* (June 7). www.newyorker.com/reporting/2010/06/07/100607fa_fact _khatchadourian.

Leigh, D., Harding, L., and Pilkington, E. (2011) *Wikileaks: Inside Julian Assange's War on Secrecy*. London: Public Affairs.

Lowi, T. (2010) "Public Intellectuals and the Public Interest: Toward a Politics of Political Science as a Calling." *Political Science*, 43(4), 675–681.

Obrist, H.-U. (2011) "In Conversation with Julian Assange. Part I." *E-flux* (May). http:// openleaks.org/content/faq.shtml.

OpenLeaks (n.d.) "FAQ." http://openleaks.org/content/faq.shtml.

Rosen, J. (2010) "The Afghanistan War Logs Released by Wikileaks, the World's First Stateless News Organization." *PressThink. Ghost of Democracy in the Media Machine* (July 26). http://archive.pressthink.org/2010/07/26/wikileaks_afghan.html.

Rosenbach, M. and Stark, H. (2011) *Staatsfeind WikiLeaks: Wie eine Gruppe von Netzaktivisten die mächtigsten Nationen der Welt herausfordert* [Public Enemy Wikileaks: How a Group of Activists Challenges the Most Powerful Nations of the World]. Munich: DVA.

Rushkoff, D. (2010) *Program, or be Programmed. Ten Commands for a Digital Age*. New York: OR Books.

Schraven, D. (2011) "In eigener Sache: Nachrichten aus anonymen Quellen [Internal Affairs: News from Anonymous Sources]." *Der Westen* (June 29). www.derwesten -recherche.org/2011/07/in-eigener-sache-nachrichten-aus-anonymen-quellen.

Sheridan, M. (2010) "Wikipedia Co-founder Jimmy Wales slams Wikileaks: It's Not Even a 'Wiki.'" *New York Daily News* (September 28). http://articles.nydailynews.com/2010-09 -28/news/27076688_1_wikileaks-jimmy-wales-military-documents.

Sifry, M. (2011) *WikiLeaks and the Age of Transparency*. New York: Counterpoint.

Stalder, F. (2010) "Contain This! Leaks, Whistle-Blowers and the Networked News Ecology." *Metamute.com* (November 4). www.metamute.org/editorial/articles/contain -leaks-whistle-blowers-and-networked-news-ecology.

Stancil, J. (2010) "On WikiLeaks and Government Secrecy." *The Nation* (December 3). www.thenation.com/article/156835/wikileaks-and-government-secrecy.

Star, A. and Keller, B. (2011) *Open Secrets: Wikileaks, War, and American Diplomacy*. New York: New York Times.

Wikileaks (n.d.) "About." www.wikileaks.org/About.html.

Further Reading

Arendt, H. (1972) *Wahrheit und Lüge in der Politik. Zwei Essays* [Truth and Lies in Politics. Two Essays]. Munich: Piper.

Part 3

Forms, Platforms, and Practices

Culture and Identity

21

Cybersexuality and Online Culture

Feona Attwood

There is nothing new in the use of technologies for the purposes of sex, or in the concern that this use tends to arouse. Sex, media, and technological development have been closely associated with one another from the printing press onwards, through books, films, magazines, and video to today's mobile and digital media; an association always accompanied by anxious voices concerned with dangerous effects. However, online sexual activities seem to be particularly worrisome because of the way they appear to emblematize a range of concerns; the "accelerated intimacy" of online relationships (Ross 2005: 346), "a larger decentralizing trend in communications" (Coopersmith 2000: 34), the difficulty of regulating the Internet, and a broader uncoupling of sex from the material world and from familiar frameworks of kinship and romance. The sexual use of any technology continues to excite interest and grab headlines; a *Wired* report that claims "Internet pornography is the new crack cocaine, leading to addiction, misogyny, pedophilia, boob jobs and erectile dysfunction" (Singel 2004) typifies media coverage of the topic.

Sexual activities have become "a major variable in the technological and economic growth and development of the Internet" (O'Brien and Shapiro 2004: 115), where people now access porn, buy sex toys, seek sex advice, and connect and interact sexually in a wide variety of ways, commercial and otherwise. Nicola Döring notes the growth of research into this range of activities – the online use of pornography and sex shops, the provision of online sex education, the development of networking in sexual subcultures, and the myriad forms of interpersonal contact that stay online or draw online and offline sex lives together – yet she concludes that we know very little about most of these developments and that there are a "surprising number of gaps" in scholarship in the area (2009: 1089).

The processes of cultural change brought about by the Internet are exemplified by shifts in pornographic production, consumption, and distribution. Porn has become much more accessible, drawing in new and smaller, independent, and amateur producers and a variety of new audiences. Large mainstream companies now rub

A Companion to New Media Dynamics, First Edition. Edited by John Hartley, Jean Burgess, and Axel Bruns.
© 2013 John Wiley & Sons, Ltd. Published 2015 by John Wiley & Sons, Ltd.

shoulders with specialist and niche producers and "mainstream" representation itself incorporates a much broader range of kinks and subgenres than would have been thought possible only a few years ago (Paasonen 2007: 163). The migration of porn to the Internet not only complicates older models of cultural production and consumption but also makes it much harder to classify as a form of commercial sex. Although paysites continue to flourish, an enormous amount of pornographic material is now free to view, while the emergence of pornographic "tubes" as a platform for hosting and sharing material has challenged notions of porn ownership. Pornographers may operate independently of older industry models and some small groups of independent practitioners have become involved in experimenting with and reinterpreting what porn is (Jacobs 2007).

The new accessibility of porn is also one indication of the broader contemporary use of technologies for sexual purposes. As Ken Plummer notes, we have not yet come to terms with our "age of cyber-sex," which is paradoxically "a backdrop presence and taken for granted in sexual lives" yet is "profoundly shaking the ways in which human sexualities are taking place" and raising "many political and public arenas for heated debate" (2008: 19). As with pornography, other aspects of online sex have excited alarm: predatory pedophiles online, child pornography rings, the circulation of extreme sexual imagery, new forms of pseudo or virtual porn, cybersex addiction, and various forms of teenage "sexting" activities that have become the basis for bullying and even prosecution.

Cybersex generally refers to sexual encounters in real time, carried out in messenger systems and dedicated chat rooms, and undertaken, like other sexual activities, for the purposes of "desire, expression, intimacy, play, experimentation, arousal and/or orgasm" (Waskul 2006: 282). Its potential for anonymity and easy intimacy has made it a potent site for sexual expression and experimentation; a space where you can "be and do anything" (Odzer 1997: 43), better perhaps for "expressing and fulfilling desire than 'real' sex" (Ross 2005: 346) as well as providing "a kind of missing link between fantasies, desires for intimacy, the traditional role of text in expressing these, and sexuality" (Ross 2005: 344). As Dennis Waskul's work has shown, many people who practice cybersex "learn new sexual techniques, discover new sexual turn-ons, and vicariously experience sexual arousal in ways that they would not, or could not, experience in 'real' face-to-face sexual encounters," though paradoxically they often escape the limits of the physical body only to recreate themselves virtually "in highly predictable forms," especially in terms of accepted norms of attractiveness (2003: 21–25).

Cybersex has become more culturally visible as it has moved out of the older multiuser domains and away from text into animated platforms and the more familiar and widespread form of game playing (Lynn 2006), becoming part of multiplayer online sex games and virtual worlds such as *Second Life*, which allows participants to combine text or voice chat with avatar sex, to purchase genitalia and a range of sex-related products from in-world sex companies, and to engage in an astonishing variety of sexual practices (see Waskul and Martin 2010). The rapid growth in social networking technologies has also worked to extend the potential for sexual and romantic contact; Adult Friend Finder, a sex personals community, claims over 20 million members worldwide, while Gaydar has become a well-established part of gay culture. Combinations of different types of technology have made Internet-enabled sex toys available, and sites where toys can be integrated with instant messaging, phone, and webcams have emerged. Phone apps are being put to sexual uses too: Grindr allows gay men to pinpoint each other using GPS technology, showing how close other users are and what they look like. Predictions of what will become available in the future include "body augmentation," which will allow for "novel pleasure organs"; cybersex with "sensorama celebrity" avatars; new forms of sex tourism that will combine sex work, pornography, and entertainment to create an "immersive" experience (Barber 2004: 327–331); robot lovers providing "great sex on tap for everyone 24/7" (Levy 2008: 310); new combinations of sex and technology that will cause a shaking "of fundamental concepts like gender, fidelity, privacy and beauty" coupled with "more ways to share pleasure," and becoming "an outlet for personal expression and mutual connection unlike anything the world has ever seen" (Lynn 2005: 210).

The activities that I have described here are too varied and have too long and complicated a history to assess neatly in terms of their relation to new media; they encompass casual and committed sexual encounters, older forms of sex work and erotic performance, and auto-erotic practices that rely on technology for assistance and spice, as well as the various forms of sexual representation that we might struggle today to contain in the term "pornography." It is also difficult to gauge with precision how the businesses of sex have grown and developed, given that they must sometimes work in illicit ways (Maddison 2004). Of course, it has been claimed that sex – and particularly consumer demand for porn – has always shaped and driven change in the development of media technologies, working to impact on whether these are taken up and which variants survive (Johnson 1996; Perdue 2002; Coopersmith 2006). The growth of online sexual activities has been attributed to the interest of young men with disposable income, who are traditionally a key audience for pornography as well as a key group of consumers of commercial sex, and "classic early adopters of new technologies" (Coopersmith 2006: 4). From this viewpoint, demand for pornography is not only the "major economic success" of the World Wide Web (Lane 2001: 34) but has also driven the development of servers, e-commerce systems, DVD, mobile phones, and broadband (Maddison 2004), "accelerating the diffusion of new products and services" and pushing technological, legal, and social boundaries (Coopersmith 2006: 2).

Yet, while it has become accepted wisdom that pornographers are "lead users of any new communications technologies" (Jenkins 2007), some recent accounts have suggested that the more established producers have fallen behind because of their inability to confront "the centrality of community, interactivity and personalization" that underpins much new media use (Lynn 2007). Certainly, it seems that women, amateurs, and sexual subcultures have often been pioneers of new porn forms, while sex bloggers, erotica writers, and porn communities have created new spaces for engaging with sex media. Smart sex professionals have formed networks linking together artistic production, education, and political activism; amateur performers have negotiated the freedom and control of 2.0 technologies; previously isolated porn fans have congregated to discuss the conventions and pleasures of their collections; and amateur writers and readers have engaged in interactions that are both mutually arousing and culturally appreciative.

These developments can be understood as partly an effect of the broader trend toward user-generated media content and the creation of online community, while the array of sexual activities online may be seen as part of the "fusion of image and act" (Kibby and Costello 2001: 359) that has characterized recent technology use in the much wider context of a "striptease culture" of public intimacy (McNair 2002). Here, the shifting dynamics of sex media use make manifest broader economic and cultural transformations in which the relations of production and consumption, labor and leisure, public and private are being redrawn (Bernstein 2007) in particularly graphic form.

References

Barber, T. (2004) "A Pleasure Prophecy: Predictions for the Sex Tourist of the Future" in D.D. Waskul, ed., *Net.Sexxx: Readings on Sex, Pornography and the Internet*. New York: Peter Lang, pp. 323–336.

Bernstein, E. (2007) *Temporarily Yours: Sexual Commerce in Post-industrial Culture*. Chicago, IL: University of Chicago Press.

Coopersmith, J. (2000) "Pornography, Videotape, and the Internet." *IEEE Technology and Society Magazine* (Spring), 27–34.

Coopersmith, J. (2006) "Does Your Mother Know What You Really Do? The Changing Nature and Image of Computer-Based Pornography." *History and Technology*, 22(1), 1–25.

Döring, N. (2009) "The Internet's Impact on Sexuality: A Critical Review of 15 Years of Research." *Computers in Human Behavior*, 25, 1089–1101.

Jacobs, K. (2007) *Netporn: DIY Web Culture and Sexual Politics*. Lanham, MD: Rowman & Littlefield.

Jenkins, H. (2007) "Porn 2.0." *Confessions of an Aca-Fan* (October 15). http://henryjenkins.org/2007/10/porn_20.html.

Johnson, P. (1996) "Pornography Drives Technology: Why Not to Censor the Internet." *Federal Communications Law Journal*, 49(1). www.law.indiana.edu/fclj/pubs/v49/no1/johnson.html.

Kibby, M. and Costello, B. (2001) "Between the Image and the Act: Interactive Sex Entertainment on the Internet." *Sexualities*, 4(3), 353–369.

Lane, F.S. (2001) *Obscene Profits: The Entrepreneurs of Pornography in the Cyber Age*. New York: Routledge.

Levy, D. (2008) *Love and Sex with Robots*. London: Duckworth Overlook.

Lynn, R. (2005) *The Sexual Revolution 2.0*. Berkeley, CA: Ulysses Press.

Lynn, R. (2006) "Real Sex, Virtual Worlds." *Wired*. www.wired.com/culture/lifestyle/commentary/sexdrive/2006/06/71284?.

Lynn, R. (2007) "Web 2.0 Leaves Porn Behind." *Wired*. www.wired.com/culture/lifestyle/commentary/sexdrive/2007/08/sexdrive_0809?currentPage=all.

Maddison, S. (2004) "From Porno-topia to Total Information Awareness, or What Forces Really Govern Access to Porn?" *New Formations*, 52, 35–57.

McNair, B. (2002) *Striptease Culture: Sex, Media and the Democratisation of Desire*. London and New York: Routledge.

O'Brien, J. and Shapiro, E. (2004) "'Doing It' on the Web: Emerging Discourses on Internet Sex" in D. Gauntlett and R. Horsley, eds., *Web Studies*. London: Arnold, pp. 114–126.

Odzer, C. (1997) *Virtual Spaces: Sex and the Cyber Citizen*. New York: Berkley Books.

Paasonen, S. (2007) "Porn Futures" in S. Paasonen, K. Nikunen, and L. Saarenmaa, eds., *Pornification: Sex and Sexuality in Media Culture*. Oxford: Berg, pp. 161–170.

Perdue, L. (2002) *EroticaBiz: How Sex Shaped the Internet*. New York: Writers Club Press.

Plummer, K. (2008) "Studying Sexualities for a Better World? Ten Years of *Sexualities*." *Sexualities* 11(1–2), 7–22.

Ross, M. (2005) "Typing, Doing, and Being: Sexuality and the Internet." *Journal of Sex Research* 42(4), 342–352.

Singel, R. (2004) "Internet Porn. Worse Than Crack?" *Wired*. www.wired.com/science/discoveries/news/2004/11/65772.

Waskul, D.D. (2003) *Personhood in Online Chat and Cybersex*. New York: Peter Lang.

Waskul, D.D. (2006) "Internet Sex: The Seductive 'Freedom To'" in S. Seidman, N. Fischer, and C. Meeks, eds., *Introducing the New Sexuality Studies*. London: Routledge, pp. 281–289.

Waskul, D.D. and Martin, J. (2010) "Now the Orgy is Over." *Symbolic Interaction*, 33(2), 297–318.

Further Reading

Attwood, F. (2010) *Porn.com: Making Sense of Online Pornography*. New York: Peter Lang.

Paasonen, S. (2011) *Carnal Resonance: Affect and Online Pornography*. Cambridge, MA: MIT Press.

22

Microcelebrity and the Branded Self

Theresa M. Senft

Introduction: Identity Crisis

Kobena Mercer writes: "Identity only becomes an issue when it is in crisis, when something fixed, coherent and stable is displaced by the experience of doubt or uncertainty" (1990: 43). In this chapter, I'd like to consider a relatively new form of identity linked almost exclusively with the Internet and increasingly spoken about through the language of crisis: the notion of self as "microcelebrity." I coined that term in 2001 while researching a book on camgirls: young women who were broadcasting their lives over the Internet (Senft 2008). Back then I was trying to describe how camgirls utilized still images, video, blogging, and crosslinking strategies to present themselves as a coherent, branded packages to their online fans.

Since that time, the discourse of "brand me" has exploded into the public sphere: check the business section of any bookstore, and you will see at least half a dozen titles exhorting the importance of self-branding. In a similar vein, the practice of microcelebrity (which I define as the commitment to deploying and maintaining one's online identity as if it were a branded good, with the expectation that others do the same) has moved from the Internet's margins to its mainstream. When people request examples of microcelebrity practice, I respond by asking them to consider what they themselves do online. Have they ever agonized over whether something belongs on a work or home website? Deleted or untagged unflattering photos posted by others online? Worried about privacy settings on a social networking service? Read a website devoted to "praying for" or "in memory of" someone? All of these are part and parcel of microcelebrity.

Even for those who consider themselves off the grid with regard to social media use, some basic facts seem increasingly clear. First, there seems to be growing consensus that surveillance is the order of the day, especially when speaking about the time one spends on the Internet. Of course, employees have long understood how employers discipline their online behavior through instruments such as firewalls.

A Companion to New Media Dynamics, First Edition. Edited by John Hartley, Jean Burgess, and Axel Bruns.
© 2013 John Wiley & Sons, Ltd. Published 2015 by John Wiley & Sons, Ltd.

What's different today is that now they are also being subjected to surveillance from companies they use "for fun" where, increasingly, privacy is treated as something users opt into (rather than out of). What this means for users is that, unless they expressly state otherwise, their updates, interests, and "likes" are instantly publicized to others by way of architectural features such as tickers and feeds. Social media architecture also encourages users to monitor the activities of others, all in the name of social connection. As one media writer put it, these features "make it so you know your friends better than you ever thought you could" (Parr 2011). To act responsibly under these conditions, the logic goes, one must always behave on the Internet as one would if placed on a public stage, because, in a very real sense, one is.

Related to the belief that the Internet has become a stage is an argument that a successful person doesn't just maintain a place on that stage; she manages her online self with the sort of care and consistency normally exhibited by those who have historically believed themselves to be their own product: artists and entrepreneurs. Yet, at the same time that people are beginning to perceive a coherent online presence as a good and useful thing, they are also learning that negative publicity can be quite dangerous to one's employment, relationships, and self-image. This is the source of a growing cultural anxiety regarding "over-sharing" online, which takes many forms: stories of people fired from jobs for something they posted on Twitter; parents visited by authorities after a child posts a home video to YouTube; families angered when they learn about a daughter's pregnancy via her best friend's blog; lovers who learn their relationship is now "complicated" through Facebook – the list goes on.

Online Identity: Media, Naming, Doing

If microcelebrity is so fraught, why engage in it? When attempting to understand the "crisis" of microcelebrity, it can be helpful to recall that, online, identity functions in at least three ways. First, there is the identity of the Internet itself. As the recent rise of the prefix "social" makes clear, this identity has shifted over time: once originally conceived as a space for housing research and a tool for collaborating for scholarship, the Internet has morphed into a place fostering everyday congregation, communication, and "hanging out."

The second (and most common) notion of online identity has to do with the identities of the human beings who use Internet. Just as they do offline, users identify themselves, and are identified by others, through a range of overlapping categories such as gender, sexuality, race, age, religion, language, ability, nationality, and diaspora. This "naming" language is not accidental but rather inherited: most academics who write about online identity are trained in fields such as anthropology, sociology, race and gender studies, media studies, and cultural studies, where such language is common. Most began their careers doing identity-oriented work off the Internet and transferred that knowledge gained offline to online venues as the Internet grew in popularity.

With the rise of the "digital native" has come a third way of thinking about online identity: as framed by what people do while on the Internet. When identity is conceptualized in this way, language about performing, writing, reading, interacting, gaming, participating, lurking, and so forth comes up. Obviously, the second and third identity categories supplied above overlap: one can be a Farsi blogger who participates on one site and lurks on another; a deaf gay male Jewish gamer; a disabled camgirl; and so forth. This overlap between theories of "naming" and "doing" has been extremely valuable to the field of Internet research. Theories of "doing" – generally coming from scholars of Internet ethnography, games studies, and user experience – have provided observations about online identity that are full of thick description and longitudinal commitment. Conversely, "theories of naming" have been invaluable in staunching naïve (and often industry-driven) optimism that one can be "anything" online, regardless of psychological, sociological, and political realities offline.

The Internet as Marketplace; Users as Sellers, Buyers, Goods

Of all the identity changes the Internet has undergone over the past 40 years, perhaps the most contentious one has been its recent shift into a means for creating, buying, and selling goods, driven by online advertising and e-commerce. According to J.P. Morgan, over one-third of all shoppers now buy something online more than once per month. Globally, e-commerce figures were US$680 billion in 2011 and are expected to grow by another 20 percent by 2013 (Lao 2011). Ten years ago, it was possible to almost entirely avoid the increasingly commercialized aspects of the Internet. Today, ideologies of buying and selling are too deeply rooted online for that.

With changes in the Internet's identity as a medium have come changes in users' conceptions of themselves. It is not that older categories such as race, gender, or nationality have disappeared; rather, they have now been complicated by the fact that users are now also asked to think of themselves in categories such as smart shoppers, reputable vendors, trusted citizen journalists, popular fans, reliable information mavens, essential humor portals, and so forth. To complicate matters further, on the Internet, production, distribution, and consumption tend to be interlocking affairs. The very linguistic awkwardness of portmanteaus such as "prosumer" (Jenkins 2006) and "produser" (Bruns 2008) hint at the difficulty of describing Internet users' identities vis-à-vis what they create, pass on, consume, and remix online.

In addition to serving as a marketplace, the Internet contributes to a dynamic by which users frame *themselves* simultaneously as seller, buyer, and commodity. Each of us engage the notion of buying and selling the self online differently: some use their smart shopper skills to search for attractive online dating site prospects. Others worry over how the old adage of "looking good on paper" applies in a time of Google background checks. Some ask friends to critique their on-camera presence for an upcoming interview over Skype. Others attempt to delete cruel or unflattering comments (or worse – spam advertisements) from their blogs. Still others are busy calculating their popularity based on status update comments from high-school friends (this last example could apply both to those actually in high school and to those long graduated).

The Branded Self Online: The Paradox of Late Capitalism

To some extent, what appears as a relatively recent fixation with the branded self is actually the result of a long-blossoming growing paradox within late capitalism. On the one hand, many educated young people, prepared to enter an economy that cannot afford to hire them, are beginning to feel that the cultural promise of "making it" based solely upon capitalist principles (i.e., working within an economy based solely on supply and demand, largely free of interventions from the state) is suspicious at best and impossible at worst. Their suspicions are bolstered by market crashes around the world and increasing talk among experts that capitalism may have reached what some call a "zero growth" moment.

On the other hand, these same young people have noted that, whatever condition capitalism itself is in, opportunities to make and distribute media within capitalist markets exist as never before. Even more interesting, at the very same time that job markets appear to be shrinking and exclusionary, cultural notions about notoriety, celebrity, and fame appear to be expanding and inclusive, thanks in part to the rise in relatively recent media formats such as reality television, talent-search shows, and personalized broadcast "channels" on sites such as YouTube and MySpace.

The slowing down of certain segments of capitalism (labor, consumer spending power) and the speeding up of others (media creation and distribution) has not gone unnoticed by the world's largest corporations. Desperate to figure out new ways of profiting from the few products consumers will or can buy with their increasingly limited funds, companies are bankrolling media products they anticipate will be hits (e.g., films predicted as box office successes, heavily anticipated musical tours or videogame releases), routinely coordinating their efforts with experts in the publishing, fast food, and clothing markets to maximize profits. These exercises in crossplatform convergence are usually executed at the same time the original media material is scripted and shot, so as to minimize labor payouts to performers, writers, editors, costume directors, and so forth. On the Internet, it is common to see young people likewise curating, rearranging, and recirculating what they consider to be their best pictures, videos, and status updates in multiple venues online while dropping off their worst, carefully cultivating what in a professional venue would be a concerted audience-segmentation strategy.

From Subculture Stars to Microcelebrity Practices

To some readers, everything said above will appear to be trafficking in the logic of celebrity. In truth, Internet celebrity is not a new phenomenon: the net has long had its share of subculture "stars": Usenet's Doctress Neutopia; home page creator Justin Hall; pornographers such as Danni Ashe; webcam girls such as Jennifer Ringely; to name but a few. Similarly, the Internet has long been a place where people have gathered to discuss "real celebrities" (i.e., recognized film, television, and recording stars), beginning with fan newsgroups, moving to special sections of dialup bulletin boards and then on to tribute home pages, and winding up in locales such as MySpace. And not all those discussions have been entirely of an amateur nature: when the web arrived in the mid-1990s, entertainment companies such as Sony, Universal, and Barnes & Noble were not far behind, searching for ways to promote the newest album, film, or summer read. What marks today's Internet as different from yesterday's is not the presence of celebrity or corporations but their current pervasiveness and ubiquity.

Andy Warhol once argued that "In the future, everyone will be famous for fifteen minutes," which he later changed to "In the future, everyone will be famous *in* fifteen minutes." The concept of microcelebrity corrects to Warhol's notion of instant fame by adding musician-cum-blogger Momus' (1991) observation: "In the future, we will all be famous to fifteen *people*." As a social practice, microcelebrity changes the game of celebrity. Essentially, "fame to fifteen people" blends audiences and communities, two groups traditionally requiring different modes of address. Audiences desire someone to speak *at* them; communities desire someone to speak *with* them. Audiences and communities also require different social codes of participants. If an audience member draws attention to herself, she often draws censure (who is she to take focus off the star?). Not so in communities, where focus necessarily shifts between members.

Immaterial Labor and the "Attention" Economy

The act of code-switching between fans and friends, audiences and communities requires a fair amount of what Marx called "immaterial labor." Today, immaterial labor is often disguised with words such as participation, discussion, flirting, goofing off. When theorized through the so-called "attention economy," it is almost always cast in narratives of empowerment. For instance, Michael Goldhaber (2009) argues that, before the arrival of the Internet, media users were almost always passive consumers, purely on the receiving end of media markets. In new media, he argues, things are different: as we watch, link, click, and forward, we switch from being consumers to being producers of the most valuable resource of all: attention.

Although proponents of attention economy continue to (understandably) flourish in the business sectors of the web, there are many critics of the notion that we have entered a new sphere of economic production and consumption. In a recent debate with Goldhaber, Jonathan Beller argued that, rather than generating new forms of "attention property," users of commercially owned social network sites toil as largely unpaid laborers in what Trebor Schultz dubs "the Internet as playground/factory" (Goldhaber 2009).[1] In response to his critics, Goldhaber concedes that we haven't transcended a capitalist model – yet. Still, he points out, even in our transitional state, the "old kind of wealth flows easily to holders of the new." For instance, he argues, "We all know that these days stars generally have little trouble obtaining money in large amounts" (Goldhaber 1997).

Here, it seems important to stop and point out something Goldhaber misses: stars don't accumulate capital because they get attention; they accumulate capital because they have managed to *turn themselves from citizens to corporations*, vis-à-vis the proprietary organization of the attention of others.[2] This morphing from citizen to corporation is crucial when we consider the lure of celebrity for teens who feel themselves to be limited in their sense of agency. Even a cursory examination of the news displays that the only kids who count as people, rather than property, are those who have managed to somehow establish themselves as corporate entities: child celebrities, athletes, and so on. Why wouldn't a teen want to cast themselves online in an identity position that seems (on the surface at least) to generate not just capital but self-determination?

In truth, the lure of recreating the self as star/corporation isn't just for teens. As Alice Marwick notes in her recent work on Web 2.0 developers, these days, to frame one's labor in terms of self-development is to be seen by others in the workforce as a positive, entrepreneurial, and creative person. By contrast, to speak of work as labor is to be seen as boring, perhaps greedy, and, at base, a loser (Marwick 2010).

The Super-public and the Rise of Strange Familiarity

In addition to reframing labor issues, microcelebrity almost necessarily leads people to question distinctions between privacy and publicity. Sometimes, microcelebrity stories look like what we've seen before: the recent "discovery" of teen singer Justin Bieber on YouTube by recording executives doesn't differ much from the 1950s "discovery" of actress Lana Turner in a drugstore by Hollywood agents. Both tales feature a private individual who willfully "goes public" into stardom. But what are we to make of public figures who decide to "go publically private," as in the recent trend of already-famous performers who feel compelled to use social networking sites to speak "as themselves" to fans and friends (Marwick and boyd 2011a, 2011b)? How should we theorize "speaking as oneself" in light of the Twitter user who proposed marriage to his live-in girlfriend by having "Old Spice Guy" actor Isaiah Mustapha record a video on his behalf, which was then uploaded to YouTube for the world to watch? (By the way, she said "yes." Via Twitter.)

This erosion between private and public has spread beyond those who are famous and those who wish to be famous. Each day, "regular" people post their words and images to websites. Those websites may or may not be in existence in five, ten, fifty years. When we speak across time and space to audiences we cannot even conceptualize yet, we find ourselves faced with a self that danah boyd has dubbed "super-public" (2006). The super-public presents a necessarily challenging state of affairs, particularly as more young people find themselves recording and disseminating behaviors they may well "outgrow" later but that will surely outlive them on the Internet.

The rise of microcelebrity practice and super-public presence has led to a social condition that I have in the past dubbed "strange familiarity" (Senft 2008). The expression is a response to sociologist Stanley Milgram (1992), who uses the term "familiar strangers" to refer to people who know each other by sight but not by name (such as people from the same neighborhood who ride the train together at the same time each morning). According to Milgram, social convention dictates that familiar strangers acknowledge each other but, on the whole, keep a tacit agreement not to engage with one another beyond a quick nod and a smile. But does the same commitment *not to engage* exist when we find ourselves sitting on the train next to someone we watched for five hours last night via YouTube? What if, after reading the blog of a girl who talks about being sexually abused by her father, we suddenly and without warning find ourselves in a public space with the two of them? These scenarios move us from being familiar strangers to individuals bound in strange familiarity: the familiarity that arises from exchanging private information with people from whom we are otherwise remote.

It is hard to deny the disturbing quality of strange familiarity when participants are consenting adults. It is harder still when it happens without consent. There are growing numbers of videos on YouTube and elsewhere featuring individuals who never agreed to be filmed. There are still more cases where someone agreed to be filmed but did not agree to the film being distributed (this is a common scenario in "sexting" cases; see Lenhart 2009). And the practice spreads far beyond online video. These days, most newspapers with an online presence include a "guest book" in their obituaries section where readers are invited to leave notes for the family of the deceased. The guest book is part of the newspaper's standard online layout template, which means that any family who desires an obituary must also agree to an online space where veritable strangers are free to write anything about the deceased they wish. Even when they spring from the good intentions of others, exercises in strange familiarity can be unsettling and even traumatizing to those who did not ask for them. This is especially true in the case of online "tribute" sites devoted to the ill, mourning, or deceased.

In one of the most disturbing examples of well-intentioned Internet outreach gone wrong, an Iranian woman named Neda Soltani was mistakenly identified as someone else on Facebook. It was a mistake that eventually forced her to flee her country of birth. Here is what happened: in 2009, Iranian militia members killed a woman named Neda Agha Soltan on her way to a demonstration. The murder was captured on camera phone and uploaded to YouTube, where millions watched. The day the murder was first shown on YouTube, there was confusion over the name of the woman dying on camera, and a rush to locate information about her online. People searching Facebook turned up a page for Neda Soltani, an Iranian graduate student whose face bore an uncanny resemblance to the woman in the YouTube video. It was a case of mistaken identity, but the next morning Soltani's email account was full of letters from strangers saying she had not died in vain. Soon, the

Iranian police appeared at Soltani's door, asking her to appear on television and call the murder video a hoax. Fearing for her own safety, Soltani fled to Germany, where she now lives. She is no longer a graduate student, does not know how speak German, and barely makes enough money to live. All because people were so moved by the strange familiarity of watching a woman murdered on camera that they felt compelled to reach out to some one – anyone – via Facebook.[3]

It is not hard to hear the story just related as a case of undesired microcelebrity gone horribly wrong. Personally, I don't think that is a misreading. Yet, while Neda Soltani's story might inspire fear and pity – what happened to her could happen to anyone – it should also be taken as a call to a new sort of ethics. The reason microcelebrity is perceived in terms of crisis is because it reworks the old question "Who am I?" to read "Who do you think I am?" Identity, once believed to be the property of the bearer, now belongs to the perceiver. This flip, in some ways as old as the work of Immanuel Kant, is for many a new and challenging way to think about identity, but it is a way that most of the world has had to live with their entire lives. And, while it is admittedly disturbing that "perceivers" seem continually recast as "consumers" in the Western cultural imaginary, it is equally true that, on the Internet, those who perceive have historically unprecedented opportunities to establish whose identities, communities, and stories will matter to the rest of the world.

Microcelebrity means new threats and opportunities. It also means new responsibilities. In a time when we can intervene in the lives of others in so many ways remotely, we must explain why we've chosen to watch certain events transpire in front of our eyes, as if there were nothing to be done about them. We must also explain why we've chosen to take action, whether that action takes the form of sending money via PayPal, forwarding a video from an area of the world under police lockdown, or visiting an "in solidarity" site. Certainly, in a time of crowd-sourced information, we are responsible for getting facts straight about the people with whom we feel the need to build strange familiarity, particularly when those people live across the globe. Finally, we must begin to find ways to take responsibility for compensating what is sure to be a growing number of individuals harmed by our increasing need for instant and intimate news coverage. Because when everyone is truly famous to 15 people, nobody will be able to dismiss anyone else as obscure enough to be expendable.

Notes

1. "The Internet as Playground/Factory" was the title of a very successful conference devoted to the notion of "immaterial labor" on the web, held in November 2009 at the New School for Social Research, New York. For a link-filled wrap-up of the proceedings, see Sholz (2009).
2. For the phrase "vis-à-vis the proprietary organization of the attention of others" I am indebted to Jonathan Beller. His book *The Cinematic Mode of Production: Attention Economy and the Society of the Spectacle* (2006) is an extremely useful resource in debates on "attention economies."

3. I discuss the ethics of this case at length in my essay "Sex, Spectatorship, and the 'Neda' Video: A Biopsy" in the forthcoming anthology *New Visualities, New Technologies: The New Ecstasy of Communication* (Senft 2013).

References

Beller, J. (2006) *The Cinematic Mode of Production: Attention Economy and the Society of the Spectacle*. Dartmouth, NE: Dartmouth University Press.

boyd, D. (2006) "Super Publics." *Apophenia* (March 22). www.zephoria.org/thoughts /archives/2006/03/22/super_publics.html.

Bruns, A. (2008) "The Future is User-Led: The Path Toward Widespread Produsage." *Fibreculture Journal*, 11, FCJ066.

Goldhaber, M.H. (1997) "What's the Right Economics for Cyberspace?" *First Monday*, 2(7). http://firstmonday.org/htbin/cgiwrap/bin/ojs/index.php/fm/article/view/537/458.

Goldhaber, M.H. (2009) "A Primer on the Attention (Centered) Economy." *Institute for Distributed Creativity Mailing List* (October 22). https://lists.thing.net/pipermail/idc/2009 -October/004017.html.

Jenkins, H. (2006) *Convergence Culture: Where Old and New Media Collide*. New York: New York University Press.

Lao, R. (2011) "J.P. Morgan: Global E-Commerce to Grow by 19 Percent in 2011 to $680B." *Tech Crunch* (January 3). http://techcrunch.com/2011/01/03/j-p-morgan-global -e-commerce-revenue-to-grow-by-19-percent-in-2011-to-680b.

Lenhart, A. (2009) "Teens and Sexting." *Pew Internet Report* (December 15). http:// pewInternet.org/Reports/2009/Teens-and-Sexting.aspx.

Marwick, A. (2010) *Status Update: Celebrity, Publicity and Self-Branding in Web 2.0*. Doctoral dissertation. New York University.

Marwick, A. and boyd, d. (2011a) "I Tweet Honestly, I Tweet Passionately: Twitter Users, Context Collapse, and the Imagined Audience." *New Media & Society*, 13(1), 114–133.

Marwick, A. and boyd, d. (2011b) "To See and Be Seen: Celebrity Practice on Twitter." *Convergence*, 17(2), 139–158.

Mercer, K. (1990) "Welcome to the Jungle." In J. Rutherford (ed.), *Identity: Community, Culture, Difference*. London: Lawrence and Wishcart.

Milgram, S. (1992) *The Individual in a Social World: Essays and Experiments*, 2nd edn., J. Sabini and M. Silver, eds., New York: McGraw-Hill.

Momus. (1991) "Pop Stars? Nein Danke!" *Grimsby Fishmarket* (Swedish Fanzine). Reproduced at http://imomus.com/index499.html

Parr, B. (2011) "Prepare Yourselves: Facebook to be Profoundly Changed." *Mashable* (September 21). http://mashable.com/2011/09/21/prepare-for-the-new-facebook.

Senft, T.M. (2008) *Camgirls: Celebrity & Community in the Age of Social Networks*. New York: Peter Lang.

Senft, T.M. (2013) [forthcoming] "Sex, Spectatorship, and the 'Neda' Video: A Biopsy" in H. Koskela and J. Macgregor Wise, eds., *New Visualities, New Technologies: The New Ecstasy of Communication*. London: Ashgate.

Sholz, T. (2009) "Post-Mortem Conference Mashup: The Internet as Playground and Factory." *Institute for Distributed Creativity* (December 21). http://bit.ly/6rD5iu.

23

Online Identity

Alice E. Marwick

Introduction

What constitutes "identity"? If I am asked about my identity, I might describe myself
as a woman, a New Yorker, or a feminist. Other people may mention their ethnic or
racial background, politics, sexuality, or religion. Still other people would talk about
their personality traits, emphasizing who they "really are" or their "true selves."
Identity can mean subjectivity (how we think of ourselves), representation (how
different facets of identity are depicted in culture and media), or self-presentation
(how we present ourselves to others). It can refer to our personal identity as an
individual, or our social identity as a member of a group.

Online, most research on identity has focused on self-presentation (Wynn and
Katz 1997; Papacharissi 2002; Baym 2010; boyd 2010). Social media such as social
network sites, blogs, and online personals require users to self-consciously create
virtual depictions of themselves. One way of understanding such self-representation
is the information and materials people choose to show others on a Facebook
profile or Twitter stream. But identity is also expressed through interacting with
others, whether over instant messenger or email. Since there are fewer identity
cues available online than face to face, every piece of digital information a person
provides, from typing speed to nickname and email address, can and is used to
make inferences about them.

In this chapter, I discuss some basic theories of identity, apply them to new media
contexts, and look specifically at social network sites, blogs, and microblogging
services such as Twitter to examine some of the major issues surrounding identity
and new media today.

Theories of Identity

We typically think of identity as something that is singular, fixed, and unchanging
throughout a lifetime. This classic liberal humanist subject consists of what Sandy

A Companion to New Media Dynamics, First Edition. Edited by John Hartley, Jean Burgess, and Axel Bruns.
© 2013 John Wiley & Sons, Ltd. Published 2015 by John Wiley & Sons, Ltd.

Stone calls a "body unit grounded in a self" (1996: 85) – a single, essential personality tied to an earthly body, which remains constant. Thinking of identity as static makes it possible to group people based on characteristics such as race, class, and gender, whether for demographic or political purposes.

This model is not really how most people experience identity. The sociologist Erving Goffman (1959) concluded that people present themselves differently based on *context* (where they are) and *audience* (who they're with). Someone hanging out at a bar with friends will speak and act differently from how they would in a job interview. In fact, research in "symbolic interaction" shows that we present ourselves slightly differently to different people. Identity is flexible and changeable, and people are highly skilled in varying their self-presentation appropriately. Identity is thus socially constructed in tandem with the people around us. Cultural studies theorists such as Stuart Hall (1987) and Angela McRobbie (1994) proposed a *pluralist* subject that was not only socially constructed rather than biologically essential but also flexible and changeable over time. Terms such as "women of color" or "queer" were strategically constructed to encompass many different facets of modern identity for political action or affinity politics (Hall 1987; Lister et al. 2003). The concept of a multiple self explains why people vary identity performance based on context: multiplicity is an inherent property of identity rather than somehow dishonest or false (Baym 2010).

Another aspect of the social construction of identity was pioneered by queer theorist Judith Butler (1990), who maintains that popular understandings of gender and sexuality are constructed entirely through discourse and social processes. She argues that gender is *performative*, in that it is produced through millions of individual actions rather than being something that comes naturally to men and women. Similarly, anthropologists have long viewed race as a social construct rather than something rooted in the body. The implication of these theories is that the way that "race" or "gender" operates in society, both offline and online, is ideological – in other words, to maintain or further a particular balance of power (in this case, structural sexism or racism) (Omi and Winant 1993). Despite this, "race" and "gender" remain powerful concepts with very real effects on people's lives.

An alternative approach to identity construction comes from postmodern theorists, who theorized that people construct identities for themselves using mass media and consumer goods. Anthony Giddens (1991) famously referred to identity as a "project," something that can be actively worked on. According to this perspective, people construct their identities through the media they consume, the clothes they wear, how they adorn themselves, and even how they transform their bodies through exercise or plastic surgery. In other words, people differentiate themselves from their peers by buying and displaying goods that serve as symbolic markers that signal something about who they are (Woodward 1997). A Chanel bag, a Jay-Z sweatshirt, and a tweed jacket with elbow patches all mark personal identity. This concept of identity as project is exemplified by the makeover, a trope of popular culture in which people are actively transformed into "better" versions of themselves. Television shows such as *The Biggest Loser* and *What Not to Wear* are predicated upon the idea that people can improve aspects of their personality and appearance to correspond with prevailing social norms.

Social Media and Online Identity

When computer-mediated communication became common in the mid-1990s, it consisted primarily of textual conversation that took place through early social technologies such as Internet relay chat (IRC) and multiuser dungeons (MUDs): people met and talked without seeing photographs or videos of each other. As a result, some scholars theorized that this "disembodied" communication could free society from discrimination based on race, sex, gender, sexuality, or class. They speculated that communicating without traditional identity cues might enable people to experiment with different identities and personalities, making it obvious that categories such as gender were social constructions (Turkle 1995). More radical theorists posited that cyberspace would liberate people from their bodies, blur the lines between human and technology, and potentially evolve into a higher type of consciousness, becoming "post-human" (Stone 1996). Thus, new media would fundamentally change the way people thought about identity.

There are three primary reasons that the idea of the Internet as an "identity workshop" did not come to pass. First, most people did not create radically different selves, instead opting for relatively similar online personas (Baym 2010: 106). Second, forms of discrimination such as racism and sexism are not solely based on appearance. Oppression is structural, meaning it is fundamentally part of society, existing in everything from institutions to speech patterns. Early papers on textual chat frequently observed sexist speech or derogatory slang, as people communicating through chat rooms or IRC were still people (Herring 1999; Soukup 1999). Even if users couldn't see who they were talking to, their beliefs remained intact.

Third, the move to commercial social software such as social network sites, blogs, and media-sharing services has brought with it an impetus to adhere to a single, fixed identity. Rather than letting users choose nicknames such as "SoccerGuy91," Facebook asks users to provide a real name, such as "Jason Smith." Sites with similar policies claim that this design decision prevents deception and assures safety, but it also benefits their business model. Most commercial sites collect user data and aggregate it with information collected elsewhere, creating sophisticated personal dossiers (Nissenbaum 2010). Other technology companies sell advertising based on demographic information. If people maintain several different profiles on the same site or use obscure nicknames, they are difficult to track and there is no indication that the information they provide is accurate, making it less valuable for marketing purposes. The fantasy of the single, verifiable identity that follows a user from site to site is very appealing to advertisers and data-collection companies, and it is becoming possible with technologies such as Facebook Connect (Stone 2008).

Still, identity expression through media differs both across and within platforms based on several factors. First, the technological affordances of particular types of information and communication technologies constrain and enable different types of self-presentation. A telephone call allows for synchronous communication and tonality, but it is difficult to record or forward to another person and is missing gesture and facial expression. Second, groups of people hold different "idioms of practice" (Gershon 2010: 6). An idiom of practice is a set of norms around the use of technology. For instance, is it acceptable to call someone during dinner time? Should you share your sonogram pictures on Facebook? How someone's friends and family frame appropriate technology use will influence how they in turn use it. Third, different types of software invoke different social contexts. For example, in environments such as virtual worlds and gaming communities, anonymity, playfulness, and role-playing are typical, whereas it is normal on LinkedIn, a career-oriented social network, to post accurate and verifiable information. Finally, identity expression is influenced by the perception of audience. Posting to a community of close friends is different from the sprawling mass of contacts most people amass on Facebook, and will affect how people present themselves.

The term "online identity" implies that there is a distinction between how people present themselves online and how they do offline. But any split between "online" and "offline" identity is narrowing, for two reasons. In contrast to the Internet of the 1990s, people today use social media primarily to communicate with people they know in "real life" contexts such as home, work, and school (Ellison et al. 2007). Second, wireless networking and portable devices such as smartphones and tablets make it easy to access social media as part of day-to-day life, rather than having to formally "log on" to the Internet. People often use multiple social sites simultaneously, creating an ecosystem where they maintain the same username and basic information across social platforms, further complicating self-presentation on each site. Given all these complications, what can be said about how social media affect identity?

Identity Construction

Identity in social media sites is often expressed through customization. People who create blogs, homepages, and online profiles can use a variety of digital tokens such as pictures, avatars, icons, nicknames, fonts, music, and video to represent themselves. These items become symbolic markers of personal identity (Papacharissi 2002) that serve a function similar to clothing or bumper stickers: to establish and display one's identity. Just as postmodern identity theorists argue that people construct "face-to-face" identities through a bricolage of consumer goods, media, fashion, and styles, online profiles allow people to use the language of media to express themselves to others. The online presence becomes something to be "worked on" and perfected (Perkel 2008).

The first personal homepages were created before templates became widely available and, as a result, varied considerably. Despite the ability to represent themselves however they wanted, homepage owners defined themselves through a process of negotiation with others, establishing interpretive context for their online selves by linking to the homepages of friends, employers, and educational institutions (Wynn and Katz 1997). These personal homepages were gradually eclipsed by blogs and social network site profiles, which used HTML templates and standardization to facilitate web publishing. MySpace pages, for instance, required users to adhere to a template but allowed for a great deal of customization and personal expression through design. In contrast, Facebook profiles cannot be altered and thus all adhere to the look and feel of the site. As a result, user customization is restricted primarily to filling out predefined fields, such as favorite books, music, television, and films. These categories become "taste performances" (Liu 2007) in which items are chosen as symbolic markers based on how others will view them. For example, to appear artsy and sophisticated, a student might list obscure indie bands on his MySpace profile although he primarily listens to Top 40.

Judith Donath (2008) has applied signaling theory to social network sites to explain this phenomenon. Many people have been concerned about widespread intentional deception in social media, given the lack of face-to-face cues. Donath argues that social media such as Friendster and LinkedIn contextualize people within webs of social ties. If users significantly misrepresent themselves on these sites, their reputation and trustworthiness suffer and their social status drops accordingly. These social ties also provide clues on how to "read" a profile. Customizing and personalizing profiles signals status and cultural affiliation.

Identity and Difference

Another way to think about identity is to use categories such as ethnicity, gender, sexuality, class, and ability. Identifying oneself as a member of such a group can be individually empowering or used tactically for activism or politics. While some people argue that such identity politics are overly contentious, others maintain that they are necessary, as structural oppression still cleaves along lines of difference in most social contexts.

In day-to-day life, most people do not experience solely gender *or* class *or* sexuality but rather an identity that encompasses all of these things. For example, a working-class, older, white lesbian will experience gender discrimination differently from a straight, upper-class, Asian teenage girl. The concept of "intersectionality" is used to describe these multiple overlapping facets of identity and how they affect experiences of power and privilege (Crenshaw 1991). Intersectionality also demonstrates how forms of structural oppression such as sexism and racism are intertwined, making it impossible to separate one from the other. More recently, scholars in queer and feminist theory have advocated for a theory of assemblage rather than intersectionality (Puar 2007). Assemblage, a term borrowed from French theorists Deleuze and Guattari, indicates a grouping or network of interwoven pieces, in contrast to intersectionality, which (critics claim) implies that these lines of power can be disassembled. In other words, the experience of identity is less the intersection of stable, concrete categories such as "race," "age," or "religion" and more an unstable, incoherent set of feelings, emotions, and information that may be different for each person. While this is a sophisticated theoretical model, it makes it difficult to understand and resist the political and social frameworks that depend on conventional understandings of "race," "class," and "gender."

Social media can be a powerful tool for expressing solidarity, talking with like-minded people, and engaging in activism. Unfortunately, it can also be used to further oppression, such as white supremacy or sexism (Herring 2000; Daniels 2009). For example, Lisa Nakamura has extensively examined different representations of Asians and Asian-Americans online, including video game characters, website discourse, and instant messenger "buddies." She found that they adhered to stereotypical and racist stereotypes such as the geisha girl or martial artist. Nakamura argues that, online, the typical subject (or user) is assumed to be white, male, and straight unless "marked" otherwise. This means that what seems to be a context *unmarked* by race is actually strongly marked as heteronormative (straight) and normatively white. If a user indicates that he or she does not fit this profile, through a user picture or nickname, they may be criticized for bringing race into a conversation or inviting racist backlash (Nakamura 1999, 2008). While online interaction can be helpful for coalition-building, structural oppression still very much exists.

Context Collapse and Privacy

Maintaining a verifiable online identity brings with it a new set of problems and concerns. One of these is "context collapse," the theory that social technologies make it difficult to vary self-presentation based on environment or audience (Marwick and boyd 2011a). Large sites such as Facebook and Twitter group friends, family members, coworkers, and acquaintances together under the umbrella term "friends" (boyd 2006). While in real life it's possible to alter self-presentation depending on with whom one is interacting, in broad social sites one transmits information to many different types of people simultaneously. This creates conflict when the norms of these groups conflict. For instance, a joke between two teenagers could be misinterpreted negatively by one teen's mom, or a photo of a wild party could be used as evidence to fire an employee (as happened to a woman who lost her teaching credentials over a MySpace photo labeled "drunk pirate").

While some social media sites provide the ability to filter content to a specific subgroup of friends, these settings can be tricky to configure and often change without notice. As a result, people have developed a variety of techniques to handle context collapse. Some people maintain multiple accounts: one "safe for work" and one more personal. Others use nicknames that only their closest friends are familiar with. Still others use large sites such as Facebook for generic messages and save more personal interactions for text messaging, instant messenger, or niche communities. Some users create content appropriate for multiple groups simultaneously, or vary their messages to appeal to different audiences (Marwick and boyd 2011a). These creative strategies demonstrate both the significance of context collapse as a problem and the different ways in which users compensate for a lack of needed functionality in an application.

Because social media sites encourage people to share a great deal of social information, they bring up several issues around data privacy. People not only have to monitor the information they consciously and directly give to others but also the information that other people "give off" about them (Nissenbaum 2010). For example, Flickr and Facebook make it possible to tag photos with the names of people who appear in them. On Facebook, these photographs will show up on a user's profile unless the user specifically "untags" him or herself. On Twitter, @replies create affiliations between users even if one of them has no desire to be associated with the other. Because online interactions lack the rich feedback of face-to-face communication, any and all digital traces left by a person may be interpreted by curious viewers to augment their perceptions of the user.

Authenticity

A primary difference between mass media and new media is that new media allows for direct interaction between media producers and consumers. Sites such as YouTube and Facebook are full of videos, pictures, and text created primarily by "regular people." Some people have become very well-known as the result of a popular blog, YouTube channel, or Internet meme. These "microcelebrities" often use social media to strategically increase their popularity with their audience (Senft 2008). Unlike traditional celebrities, who remain sequestered from the public by a coterie of agents, managers, and bodyguards, people who use social media to stay in touch with their fans are expected to be accessible and "real" (Marwick and boyd 2011b).

The expectation of authenticity can be quite difficult to manage, as authenticity itself is never absolute and is always positioned in distinction to something else (e.g., a real jazz club rather than a corporate chain) (Grazian 2003). People practicing microcelebrity must uneasily navigate between revealing personal information to seem truthful and real to their fans and revealing something that could harm them personally and professionally.

Conclusion

Since the Internet became popular in the mid-1990s, people have asked whether new media changes identity or the way people express themselves. Certainly it has provided a new set of tools for self-expression, from blogs to tweets. Moreover, sites such as Friendster and MySpace have made the social construction of identity self-conscious and visible. People know that they must choose what facets of themselves they want to present online and – unlike in face-to-face environments, where it is possible to switch self-presentation strategies quickly – this must be determined in advance. While there are currently no tools to manage context collapse, people use a variety of creative strategies including obfuscation, multiple accounts, posting coded messages, and retreating to smaller sites for private conversations.

It is clear, however, that the Internet has not liberated people from the structural oppression of difference, and structural sexism, racism, heterosexism, and so forth are just as prevalent online as they are in face-to-face contexts. The fantasy of the Internet as disembodied playground is just that, a fantasy.

At the same time, social media's tendency to make identity construction explicit may have far-ranging effects that are yet to be determined. For instance, the Internet offers a plethora of tools for self-improvement, from exercise and diet trackers to study aids and educational materials. Sites such as RunKeeper, SparkPeople, OpenCourseWare, and Khan Academy combine a strong focus on one's own progress with support drawn from Internet-enabled interpersonal connections. These tools let people explicitly work toward desired identities in front of an interested audience, but they also further specific ideas of what it means to be an accomplished, modern individual – namely, fit and educated. Similarly, people draw from global networks to choose trends, fashions, and fads they want to follow, sometimes overshadowing local connections. For instance, fashion bloggers are often influenced more by other bloggers than the people around them, creating trends that spread via the Internet but play out in face-to-face display. Such interactions muddle the distinction between identity expression online and off, complicating our understanding of identity co-construction and performance. These changes suggest that multiplicity can be both encouraged and bound by social technologies.

Contemporary Internet users can find people to talk to about virtually any subject. It is easier to learn about punk rock, veganism, transgender issues, libertarianism, environmental activism, high fashion, bicycling, or any other pastime or identity position than ever before. The resources available to use to construct, perform, and mobilize identity make it possible to try out different lifestyles and subjectivities. However, sites such as Facebook that emphasize "verifiable" identity and the persistence of online content, facilitated by search engines such as Google, make it difficult for people to experiment with subject positions without leaving a permanent record. This back and forth between concepts of singularity and multiplicity is likely to remain in sharp focus, for Internet users, technology creators, and Internet scholars.

References

Baym, N.K. (2010) *Personal Connections in the Digital Age*. Malden, MA: Polity.

boyd, D. (2006) "Friends, Friendsters, and MySpace Top 8: Writing Community Into Being on Social Network Sites." *First Monday*, 11(12). http://firstmonday.org/htbin/cgiwrap /bin/ojs/index.php/fm/article/view/1418/1336.

boyd, D. (2010) "Social Network Sites as Networked Publics: Affordances, Dynamics, and Implications" in Z. Papacharissi, ed., *A Networked Self: Identity, Community, and Culture on Social Network Sites*. New York: Routledge.

Butler, J. (1990) *Gender Trouble: Feminism and the Subversion of Identity*. New York: Routledge.

Crenshaw, K. (1991) "Mapping the Margins: Intersectionality, Identity Politics, and Violence Against Women of Color." *Stanford Law Review*, 43(6), 1241–1299.

Daniels, J. (2009) *Cyber Racism: White Supremacy Online and the New Attack on Civil Rights*. Plymouth: Rowman & Littlefield.

Donath, J. (2008) "Signals in Social Supernets." *Journal of Computer-Mediated Communication*, 13(1), 231–251.

Ellison, N., Steinfield, C., and Lampe, C. (2007) "The Benefits of Facebook 'Friends': Social Capital and College Students' Use of Online Social Network Sites." *Journal of Computer-Mediated Communication*, 12(4), 1143.

Gershon, I. (2010) *The Breakup 2.0: Disconnecting Over New Media*. New York: Cornell University Press.

Giddens, A. (1991) *Modernity and Self-Identity: Self and Society in the Late Modern Age*. Cambridge: Polity.

Goffman, E. (1959) *The Presentation of Self in Everyday Life*. New York: Doubleday.

Grazian, D. (2003) *Blue Chicago: The Search for Authenticity in Urban Blues Clubs*. Chicago, IL: University of Chicago Press.

Hall, S. (1987) "Minimal Selves" in *Identity, the Real Me. ICA Documents*, 6, 44–46.

Herring, S.C. (1999) "The Rhetorical Dynamics of Gender Harassment On-Line." *Information Society*, 15(3), 151–167.

Herring, S.C. (2000) "Gender Differences in CMC: Findings and Implications." *CPSR*, 18(1).

Lister, M., Dovey, J., Giddings, S., et al. (2003) *New Media: A Critical Introduction*. New York: Routledge.

Liu, H. (2007) "Social Network Profiles as Taste Performances." *Journal of Computer-Mediated Communication*, 13(1), art. 13.

Marwick, A. and boyd, d. (2011a) "I Tweet Honestly, I Tweet Passionately: Twitter Users, Context Collapse, and the Imagined Audience." *New Media & Society*, 13(1), 114–133.

Marwick, A. and boyd, d. (2011b) "To See and Be Seen: Celebrity Practice on Twitter." *Convergence*, 17(2), 139–158.

McRobbie, A. (1994) *Postmodernism and Popular Culture*. London: Routledge.

Nakamura, L. (1999) "Race In/For Cyberspace: Identity Tourism and Racial Passing on the Internet" in V. Vitanza, ed., *Cyberreader*. Boston, MA: Allyn and Bacon.

Nakamura, L. (2008) *Digitizing Race: Visual Cultures of the Internet*. Minneapolis, MN: University of Minnesota Press.

Nissenbaum, H.F. (2010) *Privacy in Context: Technology, Policy, and the Integrity of Social Life*, Stanford, CA: Stanford University Press.

Omi, M. and Winant, H. (1993) "On the Theoretical Status of the Concept of Race" in C. McCarthy and W. Crichlow, eds., *Race, Identity, and Representation in Education*. New York: Routledge, pp. 3–10.

Papacharissi, Z. (2002) "The Presentation of Self in Virtual Life: Characteristics of Personal Home Pages." *Journalism and Mass Communication Quarterly*, 79(3), 643–660.

Perkel, D. (2008) "Copy and Paste Literacy? Literacy Practices in the Production of a MySpace profile" in K. Drotner, H.S. Jensen, and K. Schroeder, eds., *Informal Learning and Digital Media: Constructions, Contexts, Consequences*. Newcastle: Cambridge Scholars Publishing, pp. 203–224.

Puar, J. (2007) *Terrorist Assemblages: Homonationalism in Queer Times*. Durham, NC: Duke University Press.

Senft, T. (2008) *Camgirls: Celebrity and Community in the Age of Social Networks*. New York: Peter Lang.

Soukup, C. (1999) "The Gendered Interactional Patterns of Computer-Mediated Chatrooms: A Critical Ethnographic Study." *Information Society*, 15(3), 169–176.

Stone, A.R.[S.] (1996) *The War of Desire and Technology at the Close of the Mechanical Age*. Cambridge, MA: MIT Press.

Stone, B. (2008) "Facebook Aims to Extend Its Reach Across the Web." *New York Times*. www.nytimes.com/2008/12/01/technology/internet/01facebook.html&partner=rss&emc=rss.

Turkle, S. (1995) *Life on the Screen: Identity in the Age of the Internet*. New York: Simon & Schuster.

Woodward, K. (1997) *Identity and Difference*. Thousand Oaks, CA: Sage.

Wynn, E. and Katz, J.E. (1997) "Hyperbole Over Cyberspace: Self-Presentation and Social Boundaries in Internet Home Pages and Discourse." *Information Society*, 13(4), 297–327.

24

Practices of Networked Identity

Jan-Hinrik Schmidt

Introduction

One of the most-cited cartoons on online communication shows two dogs sitting in front of a computer screen, the one saying to the other "On the Internet, nobody knows you're a dog."[1] It expresses an important insight that has been observed, pondered, and discussed ever since computer-mediated, networked communication entered social life: when online, we have to explicitly construct and present aspects of ourselves in order to engage in communication. The particular practices – that is the nexus of individual routines, technological affordances, and cultural norms and expectations – of identity management through new networked media may vary widely.

This chapter discusses various aspects of networked identity, the very idea of which combines two ideas central to the argument developed here. First, identity always refers to the social context; identity without others is impossible. Second, identity is increasingly constructed and performed via networked media that include their own affordances and limitations. After briefly summarizing key ideas of classical theories of identity, some of the characteristics of networked identity will be discussed. Finally, a framework for analyzing practices of networked identity will be developed and discussed, with particular emphasis on the connection between self-disclosure and privacy.

Basic Concepts of Identity

The idea of identity as something unique to every person is inseparably connected to the development of modern societies, in particular to processes of individual-ization. These have, in conjunction with various other long-term trends of social

A Companion to New Media Dynamics, First Edition. Edited by John Hartley, Jean Burgess, and Axel Bruns.
© 2013 John Wiley & Sons, Ltd. Published 2015 by John Wiley & Sons, Ltd.

change (e.g., the Enlightenment and rationalization, industrialization, and democ-ratization) contributed to societies where individuals have both rights and options as well as the necessity to construct their own biographies (within certain historical and cultural contexts). In other words: developing your own identity and finding out who you are and who you want to be is one of the key developmental tasks in modern societies (Erikson 1959).

While a naïve assumption might hold that "identity" is an individual property determined and formed by oneself alone (identity as the sum of "what you are"), classical psychological and sociological scholarship has demonstrated that personal identity can only be developed through interaction and communication. In 1902 Charles H. Cooley (1964) coined the term "looking glass self" to describe how we recognize and reflect our own identity through other people's reactions, which are both observed and imagined by us. In 1934 George H. Mead (1967) distinguished two facets of the "self" – on the one hand the "I" that comprises inner feelings, thoughts, and impulses and on the other the "me" that consists of images, attributions, and expectations by other people.

The psychological insight that identity necessarily has both inner and outer subjective facets is expanded by sociological theory on the social aspects of identity. In 1908 Georg Simmel (1971) argued that these are realized within "social circles"; that is, within the various social ties and role sets people engage in over their lives: spouse, daughter, teacher, drummer in an amateur band, fan of a particular sports team, political activist, and so on. From this perspective, identity is the specific combination of roles, relationships, and positions that is unique to each individual. This structural argument on social aspects of identity is complemented by the work of Erving Goffman (1959) on the performance of identity in everyday situations. When interacting, people always engage in "impression management" and provide others with information or cues about their own identity. These include "cues given" (information that is deliberately or even strategically communicated) as well as "cues given off" (which are provided unconsciously – e.g., aspects of nonverbal communication).

These classical sociological arguments (and subsequent theories and empirical studies) show that identity is not fixed and stable but "something that is permanently 'under construction'.... Identity is something we *do* rather than simply something we *are*" (Buckingham 2008: 8). Depending on the context of the situation and the role relationship of the communication partner(s), people will highlight or hide certain facets of their identity in accordance with norms or expectations tied to their role and status position. However, this impression management is not always conscious and reflected but often habitualized and based on social scripts that include certain routines of behavior in specific situations.

Regarding the general concept of identity, a final argument is necessary: precisely because identity is fluid and depending on social contexts and contacts, and precisely because modern societies provide a variety of lifestyles, value systems, and role mod-els, constructing an identity is also a biographical challenge. This is particularly true during adolescence, when biological, cognitive, and emotional developments form the transition from childhood to adulthood. But also in later stages of life, people have to engage in identity work to adapt to the contingency, ambivalence, and dynamic of the social world (Erikson 1959). This includes dealing with smaller or larger "identity projects," which might refer to the realization of certain goals and dreams, coping with sudden changes in family relations or career, or planning and reacting to residential mobility. "Identity politics," conversely, refers to strategies to deal with marginalization of certain identity aspects within societies or cultures, for example with respect to race and ethnicity, sexual orientation, or disabilities. Constructing and performing one's identity against a cultural majority (and its often implicit idea of "normalness") can include individual as well as collective struggle and conflict.

Characteristics of Networked Identity

Media in general are an important part of identity construction and performance. They provide and convey not only identity resources such as role models or cultural values but also tools and channels for interpersonal communication as well as for self-reflection and introspection. Different media genres (e.g., the paper diary, the TV casting show, the fanzine) provide different affordances and settings for these processes of identity work. The following remarks concentrate on computer-mediated communication within networked media.

　　This is in itself a broad field, since networked media encompass the whole spectrum of communication modes that used to be tied to separate media technologies or channels. They afford interpersonal or one-to-one communication, for example in email or direct messages on a social network platform, as well as one-to-many communication through personal homepages or websites of mass media. Additionally, there are various "in-between" forms of few-to-few or many-to-many communication, for example in wikis, chat rooms, and topical discussion boards. While it seems rather futile to systematically allocate online-based platforms and services into these categories, recognizing the different modes of communication is nevertheless important for the discussion of networked identity because they each provide their own frames for self-disclosure and identity management.

　　Although computer-mediated communication might lack certain signals (such as nonverbal signals in the case of text-based exchange), people nevertheless rely on cues given and given off to make sense of the situation and to assess their communicative partner(s) (Walther and Tidwell 1995). These include not only the content of the communication as such but also paralanguage such as smilies, emoticons, and acronyms, as well as contextual factors such as the "place" of communication (e.g., a personal blog, a social network site, or an online newspaper?), the rhythm of conversation (e.g., synchronous or asynchronous?), and the quality of content (e.g., is a video of professional or of amateur quality?).

　　An important distinction in this respect concerns the difference between "personal identity cues" and "social identity cues" (Baym 2010: 108–119). The former are cues that are given (off) by me about myself, including personal information such as a username, date of birth, or profile picture on a platform, but also extended forms of communication such as postings and comments on blogs or in newsgroups as well as nonverbal information such as the particular design of an avatar in a virtual world. Not all of these personal identity cues have to be visible for everyone – in fact, as will be discussed below, selectively disclosing or withholding certain of these cues to particular audiences is an important mechanism of privacy management.

Social identity cues, which, in contrast, are given (off) by other people about me, might also be used by others to form an impression of my own identity. Again there is great variation in the nature, extent, and accuracy of these cues, which may include off-hand comments left on a video or picture of mine, crafted testimonials about my professional work used in a business-oriented networking site, or gossip and unfavorable pictures of me posted online without my knowledge. Social identity cues also include information about my position in a social network, which Donath and boyd (2004: 71) called "public displays of connection." Many social web platforms rely on the articulation of the social graph by making social ties explicit and visible, for example as "friends" or "contacts" on a social network site or as "followers" on Twitter. Attributes of these articulated social networks such as their size, their composition, or the set of mutual contacts can serve as additional identity cues (Tom Tong et al. 2008).

Taken together, both personal and social identity cues given (off) online contribute to networked identities as (at least somewhat) stable and recognizable representations of oneself. But, as there is variation in the identity cues, there is also variation in the networked identities as a whole, in three different dimensions:

- *Stability.* From the general remarks on identity, it follows that networked identities can (and have to) be more or less fluid. With regard to networked identities, this includes the fact that certain aspects of an online representation might be rather fixed and remain unchanged for a longer period of time, such as the username that is picked upon registration for a particular service, or the list of schools attended and occupations held that is entered into a profile on a networking site. Other identity markers, such as the profile picture or personal preferences, might be changed more often to reflect personal development, shifts in taste, or even spontaneous moods. Personal publishing tools such as blogs or Twitter, as well as status update functionalities on other platforms, introduce an additional kind of dynamics to self-representation online by suggesting continuous, even near-live updates and self-disclosure. Thus, they resemble chronicles or diaries and emphasize aspects of narrated identity rather than the discrete and segmented "database model of identity" (Sorapure 2003: 7).
- *Consistency.* While at least some stability of an online representation over time is a necessary condition of recognizability within a given online space, there is also variation in networked identities resulting precisely from their networked nature. As people engage in interaction and self-disclosure through various channels and in various "places" online, the degree to which these particular instances of self-representation overlap will vary. Networked identities thus can be characterized

by the (in)consistency of their different facets or manifestations, while keeping in mind that a separation of online identities is not necessarily an expression of dishonesty or even fragmented personality but more often a deliberate strategy to satisfy different needs and expectations connected to different roles one occupies. Technological features of networked communication – such as persistence or searchability of data, however – might counter these strategies since they facilitate the aggregation, linkage, and connection of cues and identities from different communicative contexts (see below for a more thorough discussion with respect to privacy).

- *Recognizability*. Networked identities can also be assessed or described by the degree to which they conform to aspects of one's "offline identity." Early analyses of computer-mediated communication emphasized practices of "identity play" (Turkle 1995) and argued that online spaces can provide opportunities to express identity facets that might have to be suppressed in other contexts such as school, work, or family. But, while it still holds true that the Internet provides spaces for interaction where online and offline identity are completely or mostly separate (e.g., virtual worlds such as *Second Life* or *World of Warcraft*), the notion of online media as a "virtual reality" that is separate from "real life" has mostly vanished. This is particularly due to the rise of social media where people extend and articulate social connections from their daily life, which requires at least some congruence between their online representation and offline identity.

Practices of Networked Identity

So far, this text has argued that identity is always performed and constructed with respect to and in relation to certain specific or generalized others. Identity relies on both personal and social cues, and as networked identity – which is formed and performed in different mediated communication spaces – it can display various degrees of temporal stability, consistency, and recognizability. In the remainder of this chapter the focus will be shifted to discuss networked identity practices, following a heuristic model (Schmidt 2007) that suggests networked identity is performed and (re)produced in individual episodes that are framed (but not determined) by the three contextual or structural factors of code, rules, and relations.

Code refers to the technological affordances of the Internet as media infrastructure as well as to the features of particular formats, platforms, and services. Networked identities rely on and are framed by complex constellations of hardware and software that make it possible to interact and communicate online in the first place. Code can be described on various levels. On a general level, boyd (2010) identified four characteristics of online-based communication spaces: persistence, replicability, scalability, and searchability of digital information online all influence how personal information and interaction can transcend time and space, since they directly impact temporal stability, consistency, and recognizability of networked identities.

A different way of describing code is on the level of functionalities that are common to various genres or formats. For example, the "profile page" as an interface to a database where certain personal information is entered, stored, and displayed is common to many services, even if the precise elements of the profile, let alone the information entered by the user, differ greatly between these services. Code can also be described on the level of particular features of a given platform, for example by looking at the options and default settings Facebook or LinkedIn provide to regulate visibility of profile information, pictures, or social connections.

But practices of networked identity are not only dependent on software features and the general architecture of the Internet. They are additionally framed by a similar complex set of social *rules*, consisting of shared routines and the corresponding norms or expectations about appropriate or inappropriate behavior – for example, about how to present oneself on a business-oriented network site in contrast to a discussion board devoted to a particular subculture. Rules of impression management are part of the implicit knowledge tied to a particular social role, and may serve as criteria for inclusion and exclusion into social groups, as has been shown by various studies on (sub)cultures online (e.g., Hodkinson 2006; Baker 2009).

Broader cultural values and norms such as honesty, authenticity, and creativity also influence self-presentation online. Other sets of rules are made explicit and laid down in laws, or the terms of service or community guidelines of a platform. They might, for example, ban (or encourage) anonymous or pseudonymous accounts, as well as prohibit certain forms of self-presentation, for example posting nude pictures or offensive comments.

A central aspect of rules of identity management online is the extent to which deception and inauthenticity are handled and sanctioned (see Chapter 18 in this volume, by Bernie Hogan). While impression management always includes (albeit often unconscious or habitualized) selecting and "staging" of certain identity facets over others, in many contexts inauthenticity is considered to be deviant behavior. For example, profiles in which a user creates a fictive identity might be a strategy to participate in communication while preserving anonymity and privacy. But these "fake profiles" can also be used to bully or harass other people, which is one of the main social problems associated with Internet use, especially of adolescents (Staksrud 2009). Other deceiving practices of identity management include "astroturfing" and "sock puppetry" – terms that originated in corporate and political communication. Here, identities are created to disguise these strategic interests and evoke impressions of genuine or noncommercial enthusiasm or interest (Howard 2003).

Like other social norms, rules of identity management also rely on sanctioning transgressions or breaches. Thus, rules are always tied to structures of power. While informal social norms are usually enforced through the interaction partners, more formal rules, provisions, and laws are usually sanctioned by the providers or even legal prosecutors, even if they often rely on other users to report inappropriate forms of self-presentation.

The final structural factor framing networked identity practices, *relations*, encompasses both software-based connections and social ties. Technological relations such as hyperlinks between web documents or relations within a network site database account for the networked nature of online-based identities, since they form and articulate the dense and multiple sets of personal data pieces – past and present comments, pictures, and texts – that are representations and expressions of a person's identity online. While these can be read as individual expressions, they usually also signify social ties, whether through regular comments and links to a friend's blog or through the formal connection that is written into a database when one accepts a friend request on Facebook.

Social ties, conversely, are not only a prerequisite and aspect of identity formation but also form particular audiences for impression management. Thus, they are an important reference for issues of privacy, which will be discussed next.

Drawing Boundaries: Self-disclosure and Privacy

The constellation of code, rules, and relations in which networked identity is practiced has a profound influence on self-disclosure and privacy (Trepte and Reinecke 2011). Similarly to identity, privacy should not be conceptualized as a fixed state. Rather, it is a constant and historically variant process of maintaining and exercising control over the extent of personal information that is communicated (Westin 1970) or over access to the self by others (Altman 1975). Privacy is always relational in the sense that certain personal information is held to be private in respect to other individuals, groups, or institutions, such as parents, colleagues, neighbors, strangers, the government, or corporations.

However, separating these audiences for self-disclosure is complicated online because of the aforementioned technological features (persistence, replicability, scalability, and searchability) that make it difficult to draw boundaries between distinctive social contexts. Social web platforms such as social network sites and (micro) blogs in particular contribute to new and peculiar "personal public spheres" (Schmidt 2009: 105–128) where the private and the public seemingly converge.

Personal public spheres are formed when and where users make available information that is personally relevant to them (instead of being selected according to journalistic news values); that is directed to an intended audience of strong and weak ties (instead of the dispersed, unconnected, and unknown audience of mass-mediated public spheres); and that is presented mainly to engage in conversation (in contrast to the one-way mode of publishing). But, rather than simply eroding privacy and fostering "digital exhibitionism," they reconfigure the context for networked identity in a more complex way. On the one hand, they contribute to the maintenance of "connected presence" (Licoppe and Smoreda 2005) by empowering users to share information that is relevant to them within an extended network of strong and weak ties. On the other, they demand certain routines and skills, for example the ability to "maintain equilibrium between a contextual social norm of personal authenticity that encourages information-sharing and phatic communication (the oft-cited 'what I had for breakfast') with the need to keep information private, or at least concealed from certain audiences" (Marwick and boyd 2011: 124).

An important point of reference for self-disclosure online is the intended audience; that is, the general, often vague impression of who might be reached via a blog, a platform, a chat service, and so on. Articulated social contacts or direct comments and feedback on previous interaction help to form an idea of the number and composition of these people, but often the audience remains invisible or unseen (Scheidt 2006). Thus, intended audience and empirical audience – those people who actually take notice of any given posting, tweet, or status update – do not necessarily correspond. In many cases, the latter will be only a subset of the former, since, for example, not all Facebook contacts will actually see a particular status update.

But the empirical audience might also be larger than the intended audience, and it is this potential audience that is of particular importance to privacy. Qualitative research suggests that, especially for teenagers, it is the "known, but inappropriate others" (Livingstone 2008: 405) who are problematic: parents or teachers who read a blog or discover a Twitter account that is not intended for them to read. The potential audience is highly dependent on technological features; under the conditions of persistence and searchability, it is hard to assess who might possibly have access to a blog posting or a tweet in the near or more distant future. But concerns and practices of corporate or state surveillance (see also Chapter 19 in this volume, by Anders Albrechtslund) can also be expressed as a divergence of intended and potential audiences.

Conclusion

In a way, identity in modern societies is always networked, since it can only be developed through interaction and communication in networks of social relationships where both personal and social cues are given (off) and connected to more or less stable conceptions of oneself. Digital media technologies, however, have added various new facets to these practices, and the consequences are far from uniform. As we have seen, networked identities may vary in their degrees of temporal stability, contextual consistency, and recognizability with respect to offline personae. How exactly identity is presented and performed online is not only up to the individual but rather framed by complex constellations of software code, formal and informal rules, and technological and social relations in which particular interactions take place. One consequence (among many) of this changing sociotechnological context for identity practices is the rising demand for privacy management that results from the possible incongruence of intended and addressed audiences of self-disclosure with the empirical and potential audiences afforded by digital media technology. This constantly reminds us how profound the changes of digital media are, even to something as basic to social life as "identity."

Notes

1. The cartoon even has its own Wikipedia page: http://en.wikipedia.org/wiki/On_the
   _Internet,_nobody_knows_you%27re_a_dog.

References

Altman, I. (1975) *The Environment and Social Behavior*. Monterey, CA: Brooks/Cole.

Baker, A. (2009) "Mick or Keith: Blended Identity of Online Rock Fans." *Identity in the Information Society*, 2(1), 7–21.

Baym, N.K. (2010) *Personal Connections in the Digital Age*. Cambridge: Polity.

boyd, d. (2010) "Social Network Sites as Networked Publics: Affordances, Dynamics, and Implications", in Z. Papacharissi, ed., *Networked Self: Identity, Community, and Culture on Social Network Sites*. New York: Routledge, pp. 39–58.

Buckingham, D. (2008) "Introducing Identity" in D. Buckingham, ed., *Youth, Identity, and Digital Media*. Boston, MA: MIT Press, pp. 1–22.

Cooley, C. (1964 [1902]) *Human Nature and the Social Order*. New York: Schocken.

Donath, J. and boyd, d. (2004) "Public Displays of Connection." *BT Technology Journal*, 22(4), 71–82.

Erikson, E. (1959) *Identity and the Life Cycle. Selected Papers*. New York: International University Press.

Goffmann, E. (1959) *The Presentation of Self in Everyday Life*. Garden City, NY: Doubleday.

Hodkinson, P. (2006) "Subcultural Blogging? Online Journals and Group Involvement among U.K. Goths" in A. Bruns and J. Jacobs, eds., *Uses of Blogs*. New York: Peter Lang, pp. 187–198.

Howard, P.N. (2003) "Digitizing the Social Contract: Producing American Political Culture in the Age of New Media." *Communication Review*, 6(3), 213–245.

Licoppe, C. and Smoreda, Z. (2005) "Are Social Networks Technologically Embedded? How Networks are Changing Today with Changes in Communication Technology." *Social Networks*, (27)4, 317–335.

Livingstone, S. (2008) "Taking Risky Opportunities in Youthful Content Creation: Teenagers' Use of Social Networking Sites for Intimacy, Privacy and Self-Expression." *New Media & Society*, 10(3), 393–411.

Marwick, A. and boyd, d. (2011) "I Tweet Honestly, I Tweet Passionately: Twitter Users, Context Collapse, and the Imagined Audience." *New Media & Society*, 13(1), 114–133.

Mead, G.H. (1967 [1934]) *Mind, Self, and Society*. Chicago, IL: University of Chicago Press.

Scheidt, L.A. (2006) "Adolescent Diary Weblogs and the Unseen Audience" in D. Buckingham and R. Willett, eds., *Digital Generations: Children, Young People, and New Media*. London: Lawrence Erlbaum, pp. 193–210.

Schmidt, J. (2007) "Blogging Practices: An Analytical Framework." *Journal of Computer-Mediated Communication*, 12(4), art. 13. http://jcmc.indiana.edu/vol12/issue4/schmidt.html.

Schmidt, J. (2009) *Das neue Netz. Merkmale, Praktiken und Folgen des Web 2.0* [The New Net. Characteristics, Practices and Consequences of Web 2.0]. Konstanz: UVK.

Simmel, G. (1971 [1908]) *On Individuality and Social Forms*, trans. D. Levine. Chicago, IL: University of Chicago Press.

Sorapure, M. (2003) "Screening Moments, Scrolling Lives: Diary Writing on the Web." *Biography*, 26(1), 1–23.

Staksrud, E. (2009) "Problematic Conduct: Juvenile Delinquency on the Internet" in S. Livingstone and L. Haddon, eds., *Kids Online. Opportunities and Risks for Children*. Bristol: Policy Press, pp. 147–157.

Tom Tong, S., Van Der Heide, B., Langwell, L., and Walther, J. (2008) "Too Much of a Good Thing? The Relationship Between Number of Friends and Interpersonal Impressions on Facebook." *Journal of Computer-Mediated Communication*, 13(3), 531–549.

Trepte, S. and Reinecke, L., eds. (2011) *Privacy Online. Perspectives on Privacy and Self-Disclosure in the Social Web*. Berlin and Heidelberg: Springer.

Turkle, S. (1995) *Life on the Screen: Identity in the Age of the Internet*. New York: Touchstone.

Walther, J.B. and Tidwell, L.C. (1995) "Nonverbal Cues in Computer-Mediated Communication, and the Effect of Chronemics on Relational Communication." *Journal of Organizational Computing*, 5, 355–378.

Westin, A. (1970) *Privacy and Freedom*. London: Bodley Head.

Further Reading

Ito, M., Baumer, S., Bittani, M., et al. (2010) *Hanging Out, Messing Around, Geeking Out: Living and Learning with New Media*. Cambridge: MIT Press. http://mitpress.mit.edu/books/full_pdfs/Hanging_Out.pdf.

Politics, Participation, and Citizenship

25

The Internet and the Opening Up of Political Space

Stephen Coleman

Opening Up and Closing Down

At the dawn of the twenty-first century, the spaces and practices of what we commonly refer to as "politics" were characterized by an intriguing tension. On the one hand, the enactment of politics seemed more than ever before to take the form of a performance: to be stage-managed and rehearsed for media consumption; to conform to standardized narrative tropes that seemed to turn each political episode into a segment of a quasi-soap opera; to reduce material reality to symbolic mediation; to close down space for public voice. On the other hand, a somewhat desperate rhetoric of participation was in the air: politicians were going to great lengths to show how "in touch" they were with public opinion; media interactivity (from phone-ins and live studio discussions to all manner of online, consultative projects) was exploited in order to galvanize the seemingly lethargic citizenry; and notions of coproductive governance were the subject of a range of government-driven experiments. Politics was opening up. Politics was closing down.

In fact, politics was – and still is – being redefined. Few any longer believe that the political can be confined to a narrow cluster of institutional activities in which voting is the high point of civic action and law-making the end point of governing. The political seems to be seeping out of all sorts of cultural corners and relationships, from claims and counter-claims about casual racism on reality TV to populist debates about what it means to be British, European, Western, or civilized; changes of national mood regarding healthy eating following a campaign by a TV chef; and public battles about the political implications of religious morality. This myriad conglomeration of contentions cannot be confined to old-fashioned partisan politics, resolved in museum-like chambers of parliamentary deliberation, or acted upon through traditional repertoires of collective action.

Just as new modes of political contention are emerging, however, public space seems to be contracting. In the face of an economic meltdown precipitated by the

A Companion to New Media Dynamics, First Edition. Edited by John Hartley, Jean Burgess, and Axel Bruns.
© 2013 John Wiley & Sons, Ltd. Published 2015 by John Wiley & Sons, Ltd.

unregulated behavior of conscienceless capitalists, the failure of governments and corporations to think beyond the constraints of commercial rationality, and intensified fear in response to accelerated global risks and deepening social complexities, official conceptions of democracy seem to be becoming ever more parsimonious, managerial, and disconnected from everyday culture. Spaces of unrestricted social interaction, such as public service broadcasting – once regarded as havens for civic communication – are everywhere under attack. For example, in the UK, the recent slashing of the BBC's license fee and Ofcom's proposal to top-slice the BBC's funding threaten the continuation of a form of publicly accountable media system that does not justify itself purely on the basis of market demand. Beyond the airwaves, public spaces, from local libraries to schools and universities, if they are to be sustainable, are under intensifying pressures to adapt to the uncivic language and priorities of the marketplace. For most people, official modes of public communication have come to be regarded as opaque, mystifying, dull, and irrelevant. The relentless monotone of political management-speak contrasts with the vibrancy of the informal public sphere. In these troubled times, scholars would do well to ask: what does it mean to be a citizen in an era of atrophying public space?

For, to be a democratic citizen is, at the very least, to be informed – not about everything but about enough to feel capable of contributing to the political conversation; to be encouraged to participate – not all the time, but at least some of the time; to feel engaged – at least to the point of not feeling like a permanent outsider; and to experience a sense of political confidence – a subjective belief that one has at least some chance to influence the world around one, and particularly its institutions of governance. Without public space and practices that nurture such basic elements of citizenship, what does it really mean to speak of politics as being democratic?

In the face of the complex and paradoxical forces that are opening up and closing down contemporary democratic space, it is important to look at emergent spaces of political communication. Much scholarly attention has been paid to the "vulnerable potential" of the Internet (Coleman and Blumler 2009) as a space for the reinvigoration of political talk. A transition seems to be taking place from the long period in which the broadcast model reigned supreme (roughly from the late 1920s to the late 1990s) to the global emergence in recent years of a model of public communication in which broadcasting is only one civic medium and the logic of interconnected online networks prevails.

In the era dominated by the broadcast model, the mediation of citizenship had four key characteristics. First, broadcasting operated within an environment of information scarcity. Dependence upon the industrial production and distribution of knowledge characterized by the press, radio, and television inevitably limited the scope for citizens to make or act upon their own sense of the world. The passing of information scarcity and emergence of information abundance lowers the entry barriers to collective sense-making. Wikipedia is but the most striking illustration of such a phenomenon. Second, the broadcast media model was state-centric. Public broadcasters were national broadcasters operating within politically bounded spaces. Globalization has destabilized communicative sovereignty, with hitherto tight boundaries becoming increasingly porous and political connections increasingly transnational. Third, the rhetoric of broadcasting's appeal was directed toward passive consumers and deferential citizens (even though audiences didn't actually behave that way). Western media audiences have become increasingly post-deferential, untrusting of authority, polysemic in their cultural interpretations, and unwilling to be mere receivers. Civic participation can no longer be promoted through spurious appeals to obligation or service, as it was in the heyday of the broadcast model. Fourth, broadcasting operated on the basis of relatively clear, though never absolute, distinctions between public and private issues. It was assumed that broadcasting would be consumed within private space, usually of the family, while prescribed acts of citizenship would be conducted within managed spaces of acknowledged publicness. These boundaries between public and private life have now become irrevocably blurred – and this in turn has led to a radical uncertainty about who the addressee of broadcast publicity might be. To speak of transition is not to suggest that we are now in a postbroadcast era; rather, we are in a period of flux, which is unsettling because of the vulnerability of public space to hostile encroachments but perhaps hopeful as well, because of the potential cracks in the edifice of officialdom opened up by new online spaces.

The Internet and Democratic Opportunities

In contrast to the press and broadcast media's approach to democratic citizenship, what can be expected from the Internet? First, unlike broadcasting, the Internet is a medium of predominantly active users who not only receive information about the world around them but also interact with it in ways that are often creative, challenging, subversive, and collaborative. By making it easier for individuals to find and follow what concerns them personally, and by lowering the cost of obtaining information, the influence of social status on political involvement is reduced. Citizens and groups with few resources can undertake acts of communication and monitoring that previously were the domain mainly of resource-rich organizations and individuals who were the most likely to be sufficiently motivated to participate (Bimber 2003). Lower costs of collective action and changed conceptions of efficacy (Coleman et al. 2011) stimulate real-world political effects. For example, while much online political communication starts out focused on a narrow or parochial issue, it often tends to develop into a more expansive network and broader agenda, involving both online and offline connections between a range of people who would not have otherwise met and discovered what they shared (Bennett 2005; Flanagin et al. 2006). What Bennett and Segerberg (2011) have called "the logic of connective action" suggests that, by creating often inadvertent linkages, publics are formed that could not have so gathered in the pre-Internet era.

Despite these high hopes, often accompanied by empirical findings indicating significant changes not only in patterns of media consumption but also in practices of broader social mediation, some scholars and policy-makers have expressed disappointment about the limited impact of the Internet upon long-established and deeply embedded political institutions and relationships. For, while there has been a great deal of e-experimentation by governments at various levels, examples of successful practice are still limited to relatively small numbers within a few countries. No structure exists to facilitate learning and exchange across the different pilot projects and experimental exercises. Governments have been slow to identify and institutionalize best practice. Despite the much-heralded deliberative potential of online discussion, there has been a serious failure to create substantial, trusted spaces for civic deliberation online. The Internet has proved to be good for letting people say what they would like to see happen and what they do not like, but has yet to develop constructive mechanisms for helping people to determine effective solutions in the face of scarce resources. In the absence of the kind of online public sphere in which citizens set agendas, bring their experience to issues, and coproduce policy, politicians have tended to regarded the Internet as a platform for their own disintermediated self-presentation. For all of their democratic limitations, mainstream press and broadcast journalism at least sometimes saw their role as being to hold power-wielders to account. Whose role is that online? In the face of these lingering questions and disappointments, there has been a growing sense that politics has somehow managed to insulate itself from the huge cultural changes that are associated with online communication in other areas, such as commerce, service delivery, socializing, and information-seeking. It is as if the structures and processes of politics remain frozen and resistant in a world where much else has moved on.

Fixing a Broken Relationship

Political communication revolves around a relationship between political elites and the citizens for whom they claim to speak. In political democracies, this relationship is expected to be based upon mutual respect, trust, and transparency. The elite–citizen relationship is mediated by journalists, whose principal role is to hold political power to account. As scope for change in the citizen–elite relationship is fundamental to any possibility that the democratic potential of the Internet might be realized, that is the central focus of this chapter. Three factors underlie the scope for a reconfigured relationship.

First, there is the indisputable fact that citizens are ahead of political elites (governments, elected representatives, political parties) in their communicative behavior. For much of the past century, citizens (conceived as audiences) were cast as outsiders, spectating upon a theater of politics that went on regardless of their critical commentary. Now, the buzz of not only public opinion but also public sentiment impose daily (sometimes hourly) steers and constraints upon the business of governing. Consider, for example, how the British political elite's response to Rupert Murdoch's media power changed from unqualified awe to collective condemnation and withdrawal from political association in the course of less than a week. What citizens feel, think, and say – not only to pollsters and politicians but also to one another via peer-to-peer communication – has come to matter politically.

Second, technologies of communication are now so inexpensive and accessible that citizens are able not only to create new kinds of linkage to one another but also to receive, modify, recirculate, and act upon political information in ways that are beyond the control of political institutions. Much of the political knowledge-sharing, debate, and organizing going on in the world takes place beyond the spaces of established state or media power. Only one part of the political narrative these days depends upon cozy relationships between politicians and journalists who went to the same universities, speak the same kind of language, and share similar values about public life. To be sure, that systemic entanglement still exists and is one of the reasons for public disengagement from politics, but alongside it are emergent narratives that inflect politics with a vernacular tone.

Third, everything that might happen in terms of reconfiguration of the elite–citizen relationship has to proceed from an acknowledgment of serious disrepair. Trust in political authority is low. Whether it is lower than before or simply stagnating, it would be hard for even the most sanguine of political scientists not to recognize the discrepancies between what most people understand by politics as usual (think of the film *In the Loop*) and what most people mean when they speak of living in a democracy (think of the Arab Spring). Without closing this normative chasm, it is hard to imagine the elite–citizen relationship providing the vigor needed to tackle some of the formidable policy challenges (climate change, global migration, terrorism, pandemics, market instability) that confront contemporary polities. Given these three factors, it is beginning to dawn upon political elites that strategies for embracing, or exploiting, or evading digital communication cannot be neglected. If 10 years ago it was possible for senior politicians to dismiss the Internet as an exotic space inhabited by those too young to vote, it is now clear that political communication cannot be effective without an online dimension.

Given the need to do something – anything – to demonstrate their digital credentials, many governments have adopted an *opportunist strategy*. The focus here is upon being seen to engage with the digital world, adopting all the language of interactive communication, while maintaining a strategy of monological self-display. There now exist thousands of politicians' blogs, Facebook pages, and YouTube videos, all characterized by a similar attempt to turn the Internet into television. Several quite awful things happen when politicians employ this strategy: what once seemed open and innovative feels staged, controlled, and depressingly obsolete; what once seemed to offer the promise of interactive dialogue degenerates into a form of spurious correspondence; what started out as a potential network of many-to-many is revealed as a call to attention by one-to-many (Coleman and Moss 2008; Coleman and Blumler 2011). The danger of the opportunist strategy is that citizens can see through it – especially when, in so many other contexts, their experiences of online communication feel authentic rather than managed. A consequence of failed digital opportunism is exacerbated public distrust in the political process.

An alternative to pretending to engage with the public online has been for political elites to see the Internet as a new space of governance. Increasingly, governments are adopting principles of governance that emphasize the need for distributed power, coproduced policy, and technocratic efficiency. Citizens are seen as "partners" who will take on aspects of social control hitherto reserved for elite centers. Despite their rhetorical commitment to such a transition, the culture of government is deeply encrusted and hard to shift. Nonetheless, some governments have adopted an *empowerment strategy*, intended to create a communication environment in which public information can be liberated from the official grip. As Tom Watson, a minister in the last British Labour government put it, "The future of government is to provide tools for empowerment" (speech delivered to the Tower 08 Conference, March 9, 2008). It remains to be seen just how far any government will go in making the mass of information it owns and has access to not only more transparent and accessible but usable in ways that might be disruptive to the settled routines of its own bureaucracy. Providing citizens with lots of unrefined data is not necessarily empowering, especially in the absence of three factors: a mechanism for making collective sense of the overwhelming volume of facts and figures surrounding any political problem; a means of debating the merits of competing interpretations of reality and proposed courses of action; and a likelihood that, once arrived at, public judgments will be politically consequential and not simply ignored, marginalized, or co-opted.

A third option facing political elites is to see digital communication as a way of moving away from the Machiavellian theater toward the deliberative forum. The *deliberative strategy* entails no less than governments moving from center stage in relation to policy formation and decision-making and adopting the role of social facilitator, enabling diverse social networks to be fully open and accountable to one another. A key function of government in this context would be to connect local experience, habits, knowledge, and common sense to official structures of political representation by promoting deliberative mechanisms that are sensitively responsive to asymmetries of social power between and within diverse networks. Coleman and Blumler's (2009) case for the establishment of an online civic commons, which would be run by an independent agency charged with the specific task of connecting the active and popular spaces of citizenship with the political processes of policy formation and decision-making, is an example of an attempt to place digital communication at the center of constitutional change within representative democracies.

Most political elites currently hover somewhere between the first and second strategy. Indeed, in many countries a combination of both strategies prevails, with some politicians and parties still trying to adapt the Internet to the ends of top-down message transmission while at the same time other sections of the political elite endeavor to implicate the online sphere within the project of distributed governance. Few within the political elite have paid any real attention to the democratic potential of online deliberation. Indeed, initiatives such as e-petitions to the British government conspicuously avoid any possibility for participants to compare, discuss, or revise their fixed opinions. In its elite-driven versions, online democracy replicates the normative deficits of discredited offline politics. Fortunately, however, much of what citizens say and do politically online is a world away from the well-spun messages and one-to-many modes of address that have thus far left parties, parliaments, and governments lurking in the digital shadows.

Forms of Digital Citizenship

There was a time when citizenship comprised a set of mainly dutiful and seldom joyful activities: voting silently; joining political parties that more than often ignored your input; following the news; and maintaining oneself in an obedient relationship toward the laws of the land. In the hyperpluralistic environment of online social connection and expression, there is a conspicuous sense in which civic political behavior is diverging, in both its communicative styles and substantive foci, from formal, institutional politics. This is not to say that there are two mutually insulated political agendas in play, one online and the other not, but that the ways in which citizens have tended in the past to imitate the repertoire of high politics have been destabilized by new forms of civic expression. Characterizing these new approaches to civic expression is difficult – and demonstrating that they are an "effect" of online communication would be impossible and foolish. It may be that these new civic dispositions would have emerged without the Internet, but we do not have the explanatory resources to address that counterfactual proposition; what we can observe are changes in the ways of enacting citizenship that correspond to ways of behaving online.

The first of these entails a rejection of what the philosopher Richard Rorty refers to as a "final vocabulary" that can fully describe reality. Instead, civic expression online is often characterized by what Rorty calls an ironic disposition: one that regards the reality, truth, and finality of big concepts such as citizenship or democracy to be elusive and even illusory. For ironists, epistemological foundationalism and the pursuit of closure are abandoned in favor of a pragmatic approach to the contingency of history. The aim of ironists is not to capture and finally define the terms of reality but to endlessly describe and redescribe them. So, applications such as YouTube abandon the media's traditional quest for the single objective depiction of reality in favor of a hyperpluralistic, polysemic montage of reality. Applications such as Wikipedia resist the ideal of the final word, seeing themselves instead as facilitating a perpetual process of redescription. The myriad discussions taking place in the blogosphere seem to be less geared to reaching correct conclusions than linking to dispersed sources of putative knowledge. Irony of this sort is not about the endless pursuit of paradox (as is so celebrated by certain postmodernists) but a democratic distaste for fundamentalist certainty.

A second dispositional feature of much online civic expression is a repudiation of institutional logic. That is to say, the domination of practice by established routines, regulations, and official memory is given no more automatic credence than the creative power of invention, local knowledge, shared feelings, and institutional parody. For example, online mashups, which recombine and modify official data with a view to making it usable to people outside the power loop, have allowed citizens to challenge and subvert political officialdom. New forms of citizenship can be seen as moving beyond the traditional notion of the informed citizen, dutifully absorbing appropriate forms of professionally produced knowledge, to the self-informing citizen, for whom the value of knowledge is enhanced by its distance from the custody of official gatekeepers.

Third, online civic expression tends not to be straitjacketed by distinctions between play and seriousness. What Bill Nichols has referred to as "discourses of sobriety" (1991: 8), such as news, voting, science, and documentary, are forced to share space with what has too easily been dismissed by political commentators as mundane, frivolous, and nonrational content. Through forms of playful self-representation, including jokes, videos, and songs, groups hitherto less likely to be seen or heard within the public sphere are making their civic mark.

In short, there is an opening up of politics taking place online, despite the continuing presence of dull government and party-managed websites that generally fail to relate to the new civic disposition. There are plenty of counterveiling tendencies related to proprietary software, corporate domination of online space, attempts to commercialize civic energies, and legal threats to freedom of expression. The Internet, like the rest of the social world, is replete with inequalities and frustrating injustices. Even so, there are opportunities in online communication that once seemed unimaginable within the mainstream political communication system. How such opportunities are used remains an ongoing empirical question.

References

Bennett, W.L. (2005) "Social Movements beyond Borders: Organization, Communication, and Political Capacity in Two Eras of Transnational Activism" in D. della Porta and S. Tarrow, eds., *Transnational Protest and Global Activism*. Boulder, CO: Rowman & Littlefield, pp. 203–226.

Bennett, W.L. and Segerberg, A. (2011) "The Logic of Connective Action: Digital Media and the Personalization of Contentious Politics." Paper presented at the 6th General Conference of the European Consortium for Political Research, Reykjavik, Iceland (August 25–27).

Bimber, B. (2003) *Information and American Democracy: Technology in the Evolution of Political Power*. Cambridge: Cambridge University Press.

Coleman, S. and Blumler, J.G. (2009) *The Internet and Democratic Citizenship: Theory, Practice and Policy*. Cambridge: Cambridge University Press.

Coleman, S. and Blumler, J.G. (2011) "The Wisdom of Which Crowd? On the Pathology of a Listening Government." *Political Quarterly*, 82(3), 355–364.

Coleman, S. and Moss, G. (2008) "Governing at a Distance – Politicians in the Blogosphere." *Information Polity*, 13(1&2), 7–20.

Coleman, S., Morrison, D.E., and Yates, S. (2011) "The Mediation of Political Disconnection" in K. Brants and K. Voltmer, eds., *Political Communication in Postmodern Democracy: Challenging the Primacy of Politics*. Basingstoke: Palgrave.

Flanagin, A., Stohl, C., and Bimber, B. (2006) "Modelling the Structure of Collective Action." *Communication Monographs*, 73(1), 29–54.

Nichols, B. (1991) *Representing Reality: Issues and Concepts in Documentary*. Bloomington, IN: Indiana University Press.

26

The Internet as a Platform for Civil Disobedience

Cherian George

A key affordance of digital media is their space-transcending capability, enabling messages to be sent from locations that are distant and even indeterminate. Therefore, it is not surprising that much of the research on new media and political contention has focused on how dissenting individuals and groups use these technologies to evade arrest. There are certainly enough case studies to support this line of enquiry, ranging from separatist movements such as the Zapatistas of Mexico and the Tamil Tigers of Sri Lanka to pro-democracy activists in Myanmar and Egypt and international terrorist organizations (see e.g. Knudson 1998; Ubayasiri 2004; Awan 2007; Shirky 2011). These practices fit within what we might call a "guerrilla" frame, drawing our attention to the use of digital media as a means of hit-and-run insurgency. Of course, every chosen frame excludes as well as includes. In this case, what is overlooked are other, quite distinct ways of using new media to challenge state power. This essay explores one strategy that could not be more different from the norm. Instead of using cyberspace as a hiding place, insurgents can treat the Internet as a stage on which to perform acts of peaceful rebellion, all the while remaining within physical reach of the authorities. Such seemingly irrational behavior is a textbook application of the well-established strategy of civil disobedience, in which nonviolent provocations are designed to draw out, expose, and delegitimize the repressive core of the state.

These dynamics are illustrated through a case study of Singapore. This small Southeast-Asian city-state has been an enthusiastic adopter of new information and communication technologies. Its authoritarian People's Action Party (PAP) government has maintained tight control of newspapers and broadcast media, but has refrained from blocking or filtering political content online. Since the arrival of the World Wide Web in the mid-1990s, critics and dissidents have used the Internet to spread their messages to the public (George 2006). The absence of prior censorship does not liberate online media from postpublication retribution. The laws of defamation and contempt of court, among others, have been used against

A Companion to New Media Dynamics, First Edition. Edited by John Hartley, Jean Burgess, and Axel Bruns.
© 2013 John Wiley & Sons, Ltd. Published 2015 by John Wiley & Sons, Ltd.

Internet dissent. As is to be expected, there have been cases of anti-PAP websites with
publishers and editors who opt for anonymity and are widely assumed to be based
overseas. Many critical posters on online forums also choose to remain anonymous.
However, several sociopolitical blogs operate openly and from within Singapore's
jurisdiction. Their writers exercise some self-censorship to avoid running afoul of
the country's strict laws on political expression, but they calculate that this cost
is outweighed by the increased credibility and influence they wield as a result of
their transparency. While most critics thus cope with the inhospitable regulatory
environment by either concealing themselves in cyberspace or carefully avoiding
obvious risks, there are also some who sally into the breach with targets painted on
their backs.

One such case occurred in 2008, when a lawyer and former opposition candidate,
Gopalan Nair, wrote in his blog that Singapore leaders Lee Kuan Yew and Lee Hsien
Loong were "nothing more than tin pot tyrants who remain in power by abusing
the courts to eliminate your political opponents" (Nair 2008a). He added:

> There is no doubt in the Singaporean sense, I have defamed [Lee Kuan Yew] and his
> Prime Minister son, not only in my last blog post but in almost all my blog posts since
> my blog's inception in December 2006.

Nair was by then an American citizen living in the San Francisco Bay Area.
Remarkably, however, he was now blogging from inside Singapore's borders. He
issued this challenge:

> Mr. Lee Kuan Yew, look here. I am now within your jurisdiction and that of your
> corrupt police and your corrupt judiciary who will do anything you want of them,
> however criminal and illegal. What are you going to do about it?

His blog carried his real name and his photograph. Indeed, he went to the extent
of providing the address and room number of his hotel and his local mobile
phone number (Nair 2008b). Nair was eventually arrested and served two months
in jail for the offence of insulting a judge. His arrest was criticized by Amnesty
International and Reporters Without Borders, and drew the attention of the US
State Department. Instead of exploiting the Internet's capacity to provide anonymity
and extra-territoriality, Nair had used the medium to magnify his physical presence
and, successfully, invite repression. To decipher this ostensibly irrational use of new
media requires a closer look at theories of power and censorship, as well as the
particular context of Singapore.

Hegemony and Censorship

In studies of online dissent, the guerrilla frame arises implicitly from a theory of
politics that associates power with violence. From this perspective, states enhance

their power by applying violence on their opponents, whose challenge, in turn, is either to evade that violence or to counter force with force. As intuitively appealing as it may be, this view overlooks important insights provided by at least a century's worth of political theory and practice. States based on violence are not known for their longevity. Hegemonic domination instead entails replacing overt coercion with seeming consent, even as state power continues to be underwritten by its capacity for violence (Anderson 1976). Hannah Arendt has noted that, while violence may emerge from centralized power, it also erodes power. "Single men without others to support them never have enough power to use violence successfully," she writes (1970: 50–51). Support is lost when violence is misapplied: "To substitute violence for power can bring victory, but the price is very high; for it is not only paid by the vanquished, it is also paid by the victor in terms of his own power" (1970: 54). Accordingly, every act of censorship – ultimately an act of violence against ideas – poses risks for the state. "Attempts to repress 'dangerous ideas' sometimes have the opposite effect: that is, they serve as catalysts for expanding the reach, resonance and receptivity of those ideas," write Sue Curry Jansen and Brian Martin (2003: 5).

A grasp of the inverse relationship between violence and power has been applied effectively by proponents of nonviolent resistance, notably in the celebrated cases of the Indian independence struggle under Mahatma Gandhi and the South African antiapartheid movement. Struggles against stronger opponents can exploit what Gene Sharp has called "political jiu-jitsu":

> The nonviolent resisters can use the asymmetry of nonviolent means versus violent action in order to apply to their opponents a political operation analogous to the Japanese martial art of jiu-jitsu. The contrast in types of action throws the opponents off balance politically, causing their repression to rebound against their position and weaken their power. (2003: 10–11)

Such techniques of nonviolence are not relevant or effective in all situations. They require a confluence of factors. First, the activist must be dealing with a hegemonic regime – that is, one whose dominance depends to a large degree on an ideological consensus that is based partly on the masking of coercion. Political jiu-jitsu would have no effect in societies where state terror is the routine means of preserving order: brutalization of the activists would simply be business as usual. Second, the acts of resistance or civil disobedience must succeed in provoking the state, which must then have the means and motivation to use its force. In societies where state capacity is extremely low, officials may lack the power to act decisively against disobedience – assuming that the state's surveillance mechanisms function well enough to register such acts. Third, the entire performance must be public, as nonviolent resistance requires an audience. When physically weak opposition confronts an overwhelmingly powerful state, it is publicity that levels the playing field. Singapore – as a soft-authoritarian hegemonic state where the unfettered Internet is available for publicity – satisfies all three of the above conditions.

The Singapore Context

Singapore is an advanced industrial economy with a hybrid political system. Although it holds regular elections, the country has been ruled by the PAP continuously since 1959. The republic is not constituted as a liberal democracy with strong civil liberties and checks against the abuse of government power. Instead, the executive dominates politics. Singapore has been described by Larry Diamond (2002) as an electoral autocracy – a state that has "elections without democracy." Diamond notes that, of the seven electoral autocracies in the 1960s and 1970s, Singapore is one of only two (the other being its closest neighbor, Malaysia) that have survived as such. The PAP has drawn upon the legitimating power of elections, which have remained contestable enough to attract the continued participation of all major opposition parties. It also banks on performance legitimacy, arising from the tangible results – rapid and equitable socioeconomic development – of effective government.

Coercion, however, remains central to PAP dominance. Anti-insurgency regulations inherited from the colonial era remain in the statutes, notably the Internal Security Act, which allows arrest without warrant and detention with trial. Press laws require newspapers to be licensed annually and publishing permits can be withdrawn at any time at the discretion of the government. Over the decades, however, the government has rendered such draconian laws less salient. It has engaged in more calibrated coercion in order to avoid the backlash associated with the spectacular use of force (George 2007a). For example, the Internal Security Act has not been used against political opponents since the mid-1980s; it has been reserved largely for antiterrorism and antiespionage operations. The last time that a newspaper was banned was 1971. Controls have been pushed behind the scenes. Economic sanctions are applied in lieu of those that violate the sanctity of the individual. For instance, the Newspaper and Printing Presses Act of 1974 empowered the government to appoint holders of management shares of newspaper companies without needing to take over ownership. Through the boards of directors, the government is able to ensure that newspaper editors are politically reliable. The result is an invisible system of self-censorship that replaces banning and arrest.

The strategy of calibrated coercion has also surfaced in Internet policy. Internet content regulations first surfaced in 1996, requiring Internet service providers (ISPs) to channel all traffic through proxy servers, enabling the filtering of content. ISPs have to accede to any instruction from the regulator to block content (George 2006). In practice, however, the government never engaged in the futile exercise of trying to censor all objectionable material. Instead, regulators promised a "light-touch" approach. They chose to ban only a "symbolic" list of a hundred sites, to signpost Singapore's societal values. The blocked sites purvey pornography and racial or religious extremism, not political content. The light-touch approach was not the result of any normative commitment to political liberalization, but rather pragmatic acceptance that Internet connectivity would be a major contributor to economic competitiveness. The Internet thus became the first medium for mass communication that was not subject to discretionary licensing.

Alternative Online Media

After the Internet became publicly available in Singapore, it rapidly emerged as the prime platform for counter-hegemonic alternative media. Several websites explicitly challenged mainstream media claims to reflect Singaporean public opinion and reporting independently on public affairs. They thus questioned the authenticity of the consensus that the PAP claimed (and claims) to legitimize its actions. While the Internet provided freedom from prior censorship, there was no amnesty from postpublication punishment. Further, since most online activism is just one link in a chain that includes offline activity, authorities could always crack down by restricting freedom of assembly, fund-raising, and so on. So, the online freedom paradoxically produced an increase in the number and range of prosecutions for expression-related offences. In the past, the authorized gatekeepers of establishment media could be counted on to practice self-censorship behind the scenes. Now, in the Internet age, the government finds itself provoked into using legislative weapons, that had been thought to be redundant, to discipline the insurgents. For example, in 2002 two activists were separately threatened with prosecution for criminal defamation, which carries a maximum penalty of two years in jail plus a fine. While Singapore leaders had regularly sued opponents in civil courts for attacks on their reputations published in printed periodicals and in political speeches, treating libel as a criminal action was unusual and harsh. Neither case was pursued very far by the authorities. One activist was allowed to leave the country while the other was given a reprieve on the grounds of being mentally ill.

In these and many other cases, the government showed a reluctance to punish online dissent to the full extent of the law. Most of the criticisms and jibes directed at it online were simply ignored. These included sustained attacks by individuals in Singapore who did not attempt to conceal their identities, such as the publishers of MrBrown.com, TalkingCock.com, TheOnlineCitizen.org, and YawningBread.org. The Internet's challenge for the Singapore authorities is not that it places opponents out of reach. Instead, it is that it allows highly visible intrusions into the public sphere that, if the government were to block or punish them, would give the lie to the construct of consensus-based rule. Licensed print and broadcast media are easier to regulate with a light touch. For example, mainstream news organizations are susceptible to commercial pressures that align their interests with a pro-business, pro-stability government. In contrast, Internet insurgents are mostly voluntary, not-for-profit projects that are immune to financial pressures. Independent bloggers already see themselves as marginalized and disqualified from the PAP's patronage. They face little disincentive against crossing the political boundaries.

Most bloggers nonetheless avoid direct and deliberate confrontation with the government if they can help it. A few, however, understood the value of the

Internet for exposing the government coercion that they provoked. The first to
use the Internet as a means of "political jiu-jitsu" was a political nongovernmental
organization, Think Centre. Its founder, James Gomez, recognized that government
obstruction and harassment could be exploited for counter-hegemonic advantage.
When the group organized public events, the complex process of applying for
permits was chronicled on its website. Any police investigations into Think Centre
activities were reported in detail on the Internet, usually in an irreverent tone. For
example, after being summoned for an interview at a police station, the activists took
a group photograph to commemorate the occasion (Think Centre 2000). Think
Centre also gave groundbreaking publicity to police surveillance. Gomez applied a
tactic of "watching the watchers" instead of suffering in silence like most victims,
who were "failing to acknowledge that they feel in some ways intimidated and
violated" (Gomez 2002: 77). His first "Internet counter-surveillance offensive" was
in mid-1999, when he posted on the web his observations of possible government
agents outside the venue of a meeting organized by two opposition politicians. "The
Internet has made surveillance interactive," Gomez said (2002: 76).

Political filmmaker and blogger Martyn See continued in this vein. The Films
Act prohibited any film "directed towards any political end in Singapore." But new,
low-cost technologies allowed media activists like See to produce and distribute
films with little commercial risk. In 2005 and 2006, two of his documentaries
on Singaporean dissidents were banned. The films surfaced on the World Wide
Web and remain freely available – since the government continued to refrain from
blocking any political content. In addition, See used his blog to publicize his dealings
with the police and regulators. "Under this climate of fear and self-censorship, the
only tool available to me by way of publicizing my story was the Internet," he said.
"So I posted updates of the police investigation on my blog, and immediately it
was picked up by news wire agencies based in Singapore" (See 2007). The case
thus attracted the attention of international human rights organizations. Statements
were issued by Amnesty International, Reporters Without Borders, the Committee
to Protect Journalists, and the Southeast Asian Press Alliance. Assessing the net
effect of the ban on See's film, *Singapore Rebel*, one scholar noted:

> Censorship has seriously backfired, having turned a mediocre film into an icon
> of freedom, a relatively unknown filmmaker into a martyr, and the perception of
> inconsistencies in the application of law into a sign of political hypocrisy. (Tan 2008: 268)

See himself acknowledged that the authorities had done him a favor:

> If the censors had cleared the film, it would have been screened to an audience of no
> more than 80 people, and not all of them would be interested or much less impressed
> with its content. It would have died a natural death not long afterwards. (See 2006)

From such experiments sprang a campaign of full-blown Internet-assisted civil
disobedience. The activists concerned sought nonviolent ways to break laws that

they considered unjust, drawing out the government's coercive might from behind the veil of consensus. The Internet was either the space within which the illegal acts were conducted – as in the case of Gopalan Nair's defamatory and scandalizing statements quoted above – or the medium through which offline acts were publicized. The prime exponent of this method was Chee Soon Juan, secretary general of the Singapore Democratic Party (SDP). In 2007, for example, SDP activists carried out a protest in support of democracy in Myanmar. After the junta's crackdown on demonstrators, the Singapore government expressed strong concern, but stopped short of reviewing its policy of engagement with the regime. The SDP were keen to use the Myanmar crisis to highlight Singapore's lack of respect for civil liberties both abroad and at home. The party used its website to announce that party officials would be outside Myanmar's embassy with petitions for members of the public to sign. A candlelight vigil would follow (SDP 2007a). These events were later reported in detail on the website.

In line with the strategy of nonviolent protest, these reports highlighted police actions at least as much as the substantive issues being ostensibly championed. The website featured photographs of plainclothes policemen videographing and approaching the protesters. The accompanying report said that the officers warned the activists they would be investigated as an illegal assembly (SDP 2007b). Another report contrasted the "dignified anger" of the protesters with "the pig-headedness of a government" that disallowed peaceful gatherings (SDP 2007c). A few days later, the party organized a protest march despite its application for a permit being rejected by the police (SDP 2007d). Their itinerary was advertised on the party website. They intended to hand a petition to the Myanmese ambassador at 11am and then proceed to the gates of the Prime Minister's Office to deliver a letter. They would then conduct a 24-hour protest against the Singapore government's "nefarious nexus" with the Myanmar regime. As expected, their plan was cut short by the police. Chee Soon Juan and three activists were escorted one by one to a police van. The only witnesses were members of the media. Brief news reports were filed by the Associated Press and the German Press Agency (DPA) and these were reproduced on the SDP website (SDP 2007e). Such activities by the SDP are examples of what Daniel Boorstin (1961) called "pseudo-events" – minor in themselves, their impact is largely contingent on their amplification by media. The activists hope that forceful state action will erode the state's hegemony. The strategy will only work if both their nonviolent action and the police reaction can reach a wide audience, for which the Internet provides an accessible publicity medium.

Despite the presence of committed activists and the availability of new media, however, the SDP's civil disobedience campaign had little impact. This is partly because its causes failed to seize the popular imagination. Disaffection with the Singapore government may not be deep enough for protests to gain traction. Another important reason is the notably muted response of the authorities. Civil disobedience is most effective when the state's response is disproportionately violent. Similar tactics used in neighboring Malaysia, for example, have yielded sensational images of policemen beating peaceful demonstrators. When bloggers circulated such photographs and videos, they succeeded in further fanning public outrage, which contributed to larger protests and electoral reversals for the government (George 2007b). The asymmetry in the use of force – between citizens waving flowers and flags, and armed men replying with batons and bullets – turns the state's monopoly of violence into a political liability.

In Singapore, however, the authorities dealing with protests on the ground have taken pains to err on the side of restraint. Demonstrations by the SDP were handled by small teams of police, usually including diminutive female officers, some in civilian attire, and none waving weapons. Officers did not raise their voices or use megaphones. At the protest outside the Myanmar embassy, for example, the YouTube video (SDP 2007f) shows nothing more explosive than an inspector walking amid the protestors informing them that they are committing an offence and that the police will be investigating the case. "We advise you all to leave," he is heard saying. One activist shouts "Don't let the police scare you; this is not Burma, although this is the Singapore police trying to act as if they belong to the Burmese junta." There is, however, no sign of Myanmar-style brutality. Police did not forcibly disperse the crowd, and the SDP's own report characterized the officers' response as "half-hearted and confused" (SDP 2007c). Other SDP civil disobedience events had similar dynamics, with activists and police trying to out-do each other in their displays of stoicism and civilized conduct. Even when activists provocatively hovered their cameras at arm's length from law enforcers' faces, the officers did not instinctively retaliate. The footage reveals a disciplined gritting of teeth by security forces, in stark contrast to countless videos of similar encounters from around the world.

The police were not turning a blind eye to such activity but instead choosing to deal with the perpetrators later, through the courts. As a result, activists have been fined or jailed for their peaceful demonstrations. But, by shifting the action away from the terrain picked by the protestors and into the controlled environment of the police station and court room, the authorities deny the activists the classic images of one-sided physical tussles. The judge's gavel may be no less powerful than the policeman's baton, but reports of a court jailing a protestor for a week or a month are not as effective as images of uniformed men using brute force to suppress a protest. Despite the authorities' calibrated response to civil disobedience, however, the government took steps to limit further the impact of such protests. In 2009, the Films Act was amended to make it illegal to film events that are themselves illegal, such as unlicensed demonstrations. Police can now stop or arrest videocam-wielding activists who are attempting to record civil disobedience efforts for a wider audience. Only licensed broadcast news media – such as CNN and the national broadcaster, Mediacorp – are exempted from this ban. Most foreign news organizations have not shown great interest in SDP's campaigns since they are too small and insignificant relative to other events in the region. Domestic news organizations have not been sympathetic to the protest actions either. Therefore, the government risks little by allowing factual coverage by licensed news organizations of illegal events. How the activists will respond to the restrictions was not yet clear at the time of writing. It is possible that the logic of civil disobedience will lead them to violate the ban on filming as well. Mobile Internet technologies would enable the "live" streaming of videos of police action against the filming of those videos, at least until the moment that the cameramen are physically stopped.

Thus, in Singapore, the Internet is being used by activists to circumvent the gatekeepers of mainstream media when engaging in public acts of defiance. The publicness of the Internet, rather than anonymity and distance, is what makes it an apt medium for activists whose strategy requires that they remain in harm's way. Coercion does not represent a failure of the medium but the intended reaction in a strategy of counter-hegemony. We can expect similar strategies to be deployed against other authoritarian regimes that are attempting to cloak their coercive core behind a veil of consensus. There have been signs of this in Malaysia, whose laws on public assembly and speech are similar to Singapore's (George 2007b). There, demonstrations are routinely documented by bloggers who come out to video-record anticipated police repression. While some of these citizen journalists work under-cover, others flaunt their contempt for undemocratic restrictions. Opposition and civil society have sustained a strong challenge to the dominant ruling alliance, and open defiance through the Internet has helped solidify and embolden the democratic movement. A few prominent individual bloggers have been able to leverage on their notoriety, with one, Jeff Ooi, even being elected to the federal parliament in 2008.

The rejection of anonymity and distance as weapons of offline dissent is more likely to be observed in "soft" authoritarian regimes such as Malaysia and Singapore, where the authorities' reaction, while intolerant, is rarely extreme. These countries have no record of politically motivated killings or disappearances. While there have been allegations of mistreatment while in custody and of confessions extracted under duress, these are not jurisdictions known for torture of political dissidents (US Department of State 2011). Sentencing norms for violations of restrictions on freedom of speech do not come close to the extremes seen in China or Iran, where bloggers have been imprisoned for years. Therefore, online activists in Malaysia and Singapore who challenge the state openly are generally taking a calculated risk that the worst that could befall them is a few days or weeks in jail, and perhaps thousands of dollars in fines. That calculation might be different in societies where state repression is less restrained, which is why the guerrilla mode of online dissent remains relevant throughout much of the world. However, authoritarian states are increasingly shifting away from spectacular repression toward less violent and visible modes of control that are less prone to backfire (Ligabo 2004; Simon 2008). As this happens, Singapore-style online dissent may spread.

Activists' tactics would depend not only on the anticipated reprisals but also on the expected audience. Government censorship only backfires when there is a bystander public that pays attention and feels moral indignation, and is then capable of being mobilized in ways that exact a political cost on the regime. For this reason, an active civil society and international public opinion are crucial factors; news organizations such as CNN, the BBC, and Al Jazeera play a key mediating role as well. In Egypt's 2011 revolution, for example, the case of Khaled Said – who was dragged out of a cybercafé and killed by police for blowing the whistle on corruption – stirred Egyptians into action. Wael Ghonim, a Google executive who set up a Facebook page in honor of Khaled, himself became a galvanizing figure when he was detained for 12 days by state security. News of his detention circulated rapidly within Egypt and was also widely reported in the international media. It came to symbolize the Mubarak government's futile attempts to stem the tide against it (Harb 2011; Hounshell 2011; Preston 2011).

Like Singapore's small protest movement, the full-scale revolutions in Tunisia and Egypt demand a rethink of the guerrilla model. It is possible that, with social media and mobile devices, protest organizers are able to accelerate the mobilization of the masses to such a degree that protestors can abandon anonymity, finding safety in huge numbers instead. The broader implication for Internet studies is that there is a dynamic, dialectical relationship between state power and Internet-assisted insurgency. This is in keeping with the literature on social movements, which shows that the powerful and the peripheral engaged in an iterative process of action and reaction, constantly and creatively seeking political advantage. New media studies needs to remain sensitive to such dynamics. The open-ended quality of new media platforms invites practices and processes that are not bound by convention.

References

Anderson, P. (1976) "The Antinomies of Antonio Gramsci." *New Left Review* I(100), 5–80.
Arendt, H. (1970) *On Violence.* Orlando, FL: Harcourt Brace Jovanovich.
Awan, A.N. (2007) "Virtual Jihadist Media." *European Journal of Cultural Studies*, 10(3), 389–408.
Boorstin, D.J. (1961) *The Image: A Guide to Pseudo-Events in America.* New York: Vintage.
Diamond, L. (2002) "Thinking about Hybrid Regimes." *Journal of Democracy*, 13(2), 21–35.
George, C. (2006) *Contentious Journalism and the Internet: Toward Democratic Discourse in Malaysia and Singapore.* Singapore: National University of Singapore Press and Seattle: University of Washington Press.
George, C. (2007a) "Consolidating Authoritarian Rule: Calibrated Coercion in Singapore." *Pacific Review*, 20(2), 127–145.
George, C. (2007b) "Media in Malaysia: Zone of Contention." *Democratization*, 14(5), 893–910.
Gomez, J. (2002) *Internet Politics: Surveillance & Intimidation in Singapore.* Singapore: Think Centre.
Harb, Z. (2011) "Arab Revolutions and the Social Media Effect." *M/C Journal*, 14(2). http://journal.media-culture.org.au/index.php/mcjournal/article/viewArticle/364.
Hounshell, B. (2011) "A New Leader for Egypt's Protestors?" *Foreign Policy* (February 7). www.foreignpolicy.com/articles/2011/02/07/a_new_leader_for_egypt_s_protesters.
Jansen. S.C. and Martin, B. (2003) "Making Censorship Backfire." *Counterpoise*, 7, 5–15.
Knudson, J.W. (1998) "Rebellion in Chiapas: Insurrection by Internet and Public Relations." *Media, Culture & Society*, 20(3), 507–518.
Ligabo, A. (2004) *Civil and Political Rights, Including the Question of Freedom of Expression. The Right to Freedom of Opinion and Expression. Report of the Special Rapporteur, Ambeyi Ligabo,* no. E/CN.4/2005/64. United Nations Economic and Social Council. www.ohchr.org.

Nair, G. (2008a) "Singapore. Judge Belinda Ang's Kangaroo Court." *Singapore Dissident*. http://singaporedissident.blogspot.com/2008/05/singapore-judge-belinda-angs-kangaroo .html.

Nair, G. (2008b) "Lee Kuan Yew: If Bloggers Who Defame Me Identify Themselves, I Will Sue them!" *Singapore Dissident*. http://singaporedissident.blogspot.com/2008/05 /lee-kuan-yew-if-bloggers-who-defame-me.html.

Preston, J. (2011) "Movement Began with Outrage and a Facebook Page that Gave it an Outlet." *New York Times* (February 5). www.nytimes.com/2011/02/06/world/middleeast /06face.html.

See, M. (2006) "'Singapore Rebel' Saga Ends after Police Issues 'Stern Warning.'" *Singapore Rebel*. http://singaporerebel.blogspot.com/2006/08/singapore-rebel-saga-ends-after -police.html.

See, M. (2007) "Martyn See Speaks out on Police Probe, Foreign 'Interference' and Burma." *Singapore Rebel*. http://singaporerebel.blogspot.com/2007/09/police-probe -almost-farcical-martyn-see.html.

Sharp, G. (2003) *There Are Realistic Alternatives*. Boston, MA: Albert Einstein Institute.

Shirky, C. (2011) "The Political Power of Social Media." *Foreign Policy* (January/February), 28–41.

Simon, J. (2008) "Attacks on the Press in 2007: Introduction." *Committee to Protect Journalists* (February 5). www.cpj.org/attacks07/pages07/intro07.html.

Singapore Democratic Party (2007a) "Sign Letter of Protest Outside Burmese Embassy" (September 29). http://singaporedemocrat.org/articleburmaprotest2.html.

Singapore Democratic Party (2007b) "Singapore Police Warns Dr Chee at Burma Embassy" (September 30). http://singaporedemocrat.org/articleburmaprotest5.html.

Singapore Democratic Party (2007c) "Steady Stream of Petitioners Despite Harassment by Singapore Police" (October 1). http://singaporedemocrat.org/articleburmaprotest6.html.

Singapore Democratic Party (2007d) "Police Rejects SDP's Application for Protest March" (October 5). http://singaporedemocrat.org/articleburmaprotest11.html.

Singapore Democratic Party (2007e) "Opposition Party Leaders Arrested During Burma Protest" (October 8). http://singaporedemocrat.org/articleburmaprotest19.html.

Singapore Democratic Party (2007f) "Petition-Signing at Burmese Embassy in Singapore" (September 30). *YouTube*. www.youtube.com/watch?v=P7Yg05RDcZ4.

Tan, K.P. (2008) *Cinema and Television in Singapore: Resistance in One Dimension*. Leiden: Brill.

Think Centre (2000) "Youths Let Off with 'Warning' for Organising Public Forum" (February 2). www.thinkcentre.org/article.cfm?ArticleID=5.

Ubayasiri, K. (2004) "A Virtual Eelam: Democracy, Internet and Sri Lanka's Tamil Struggle" in S. Gan, J. Gomez, and U. Johannen, eds., *Asian Cyberactivism: Freedom of Expression and Media Censorship*. Bangkok: Friedrich Naumann Stiftung, pp. 474–512.

US Department of State (2011) "2010 Country Reports on Human Rights Practices." www.state.gov/j/drl/rls/hrrpt/2010.

Further Reading

Downing, J.D.H. (2011) *Encyclopedia of Social Movement Media*. London: Sage.

Tarrow, S. (1998) *Power in Movement: Social Movements and Contentious Politics*. Cambridge: Cambridge University Press.

27

Parody, Performativity, and Play
The Reinvigoration of Citizenship through Political Satire

Jeffrey P. Jones

A nation's political culture is an ever-changing, amorphous thing, comprised and shaped at any given time by numerous forces and behaviors that are never quite stable. Yet for decades in most Western societies, television played an enormously powerful role in establishing and maintaining some of the most basic normative (and seemingly stable) assumptions comprising the communicative dimensions of its political culture. These include aspects such as what constitutes legitimate forms of representation, discussion, display, and participation in and through the medium; who can legitimately speak there; how such speech will be regulated; and the ways in which viewers are expected to engage with it. This role played by television broadcasting has, of course, been greatly challenged over the past few decades through changes brought on by new media dynamics. At first through increased competition in the US cable and commercial broadcasting system (as well as competition to state-run television monopolies elsewhere) and then through the digital revolution that swept through all media forms and platforms (Jenkins 2006; Lotz 2007), processes of disruption, challenge, and change have been occurring at a rapid pace. Within political culture, this has led to a measureable impact on the dominant conceptions and assumptions of what constitutes mediated political communication and participation and, at the broadest level, citizenship itself.

It is perhaps appropriate, then, that such disruptions have often been accompanied by (indeed, in some instances, *driven* by) speech acts and rhetorical techniques that are themselves intentionally "disruptive" – that is, political satire and parody. As has been well documented, especially in the USA (Gray et al. 2009; Baym 2010; Jones 2010; Day 2011) but also around the world (Mazzoleni and Sfardini 2009; Baym and Jones 2012), satirical and parodic entertainment talk shows and fake news shows have become not only increasingly popular forms of television programming but also important means for challenging static and restrictive norms of how politics is discussed, critiqued, and engaged with via television.

A Companion to New Media Dynamics, First Edition. Edited by John Hartley, Jean Burgess, and Axel Bruns.
© 2013 John Wiley & Sons, Ltd. Published 2015 by John Wiley & Sons, Ltd.

This chapter therefore examines the dynamics introduced by satirical forms of mediated political speech in the reconstitution of political engagement and citizenship practices in the early twenty-first century. In particular, through an analysis of satire and parody as performative speech acts and as play, we can see the impact satire is having on democratic citizenship and political participation. But first, it is perhaps helpful to discuss satire as a discourse situated within the fissures of a discontented political culture, and how formerly stable notions of citizenship are changing and why, especially in relation to new media dynamics.

Dynamics of Change in Mediated Citizenship

The story of satire's success as a reinvigorated form of popularized political speech, especially on television, must be seen within the broader dynamics of change occurring in the decade of the 1990s.[1] Appearing first and most prominently in the competitive landscape of cable television, such programming introduced a set of new actors and new voices onto the public stage – those who had previously been seen as political "outsiders" largely because of the artificial separation between the fields of entertainment and politics that had traditionally been maintained by the oligopolistic broadcast networks.[2] First through hybrid political entertainment talk shows (such as *Politically Incorrect with Bill Maher*) and then through fake newsmagazine shows (Michael Moore's *The Awful Truth*), fake news shows (*The Daily Show with Jon Stewart*), and fake political commentary shows (*The Colbert Report*), these new actors offered up brutal critiques of not only the world of politics but also the news media that routinely craft, construe, and convey the "realities" of political life. Through a series of crises events and failures in which the US news media (television in particular) could be implicated as a willing participant – a presidential sex scandal, a contested and controversial presidential election, a war waged on false premises, and the near economic meltdown of the US and global economy – satiric programming proved to be a source for the routine challenge, contestation, and rebuke of political and media power. In the process, such programming challenged the news media's "regime of truth" (as Foucault calls it) (Morris and Patton 1979: 46), the largely uncontested authority and license from which news media operate as the arbiters of truth and reality in regards to political life (Jones 2009a).

Such challenges, of course, are not attributable solely to the brilliance, wit, or courage of comedic writers, or to the political economy of media production that allowed upstart cable networks to offer and support such critical programming. Satiric and parodic programming found root within the broader dissatisfactions of civic culture. Whether we call it "civic malaise" or "postmodern" political conditions, the routine practices constituting citizenship were often found lacking by citizens. This includes the stultifying nature of a seemingly fabricated and managed public life and its presentation in news media, resulting in little more than political life as publicity culture (and the resulting dampening of belief in meaningful avenues for public political participation). As more populist outsider voices began to appear on talk shows and through new media discussion forums, traditional forms of media representation became increasingly questioned. Writing in those years, Jay Blumler and Michael Gurevitch (2000) succinctly identified these fissures within political culture, smartly connecting them to citizen dissatisfaction with old media and the resulting embrace of the new. Citizen angst with mediated politics, they argued, could be located in three areas:

> A widespread belief that democracy as conventionally interpreted is in trouble and that shortcomings of mainstream media coverage of politics are largely to blame for its "crisis;" the rising tide of populism in cultural, political, and media quarters, which upgrades the value of heeding the views and preferences of ordinary people; and an impression that certain qualities of the new media could be enlisted behind active forms of political participation. (2000: 167)

Citizen attraction to satirical fake news and entertaining political talk was part of this inherent criticism of the news media's control and regulation of political talk, as well as an embrace of the populist aspects of seeing and hearing and cheering on nontraditional political actors critiquing the system (Jones 2010: 207–234). These were important steps in the altered dynamics of mediated citizenship that were, of course, accompanied by perhaps more profound changes in citizens' ability to participate directly via digital technologies such as the Internet.

Connecting these insights to the digital era, Stephen Coleman has identified how new media dynamics have challenged the older democratic notion of indirect representation, built as it was on "some of the most enduring features of modernity: the intractability of distance, the bounded nature of place, the professionalization of mediation, and the spectacular nature of authority" (2005: 207). He contends that, in an interconnected world with "reconfigured patterns of interaction across space and time," such "justifications for indirect representation appear less credible." Instead he argues that political culture is undergoing change toward favoring "direct repre-sentation," using digital technologies that move us from "distance to co-presence," "place to networks," "transmission to dialogue," and "spectacle to play" (212).

John Hartley (2010) goes so far as to argue that this dynamic of change and discontent has led us to a new phase of citizenship that he dubs "DIY/DIWO citizenship." The term "do-it-yourself/do-it-with-others" emphasizes semiotic self-determination in how citizens formulate and live out their identities and actions *as citizens*, a position that is "increasingly reliant on *communication* and less on the *state*" (241; original emphasis). For Hartley, a component part of this is what he calls "silly citizenship," a recognition that, in the new media era, citizenship is as much constituted by play and performance (including the performance of deliberation and participation) as it is by Habermasian rationality in its "communicative action" (244). For, as he argues, "the *stage* for citizenship is literally that. It is as much dramatic and performative as it is deliberative" (241; original emphasis).

Lilie Chouliaraki echoes these arguments, recognizing that "publicness" is now constituted, in part, by "mediated self-representation." Direct representation is often textual in nature and composed of "performance, voice and claims to recognition" (2010: 227). And, in echoing performativity theory's contention that speech acts bring reality into being (the activity of *saying* is the business of *doing*; see Loxley 2007), Chouliaraki smartly notes that "such textualities [of self-mediation] do not simply represent pre-existing selves, individual or collective, but *constitute* such selves in the very process of representing them" (229, emphasis added). That is to say, citizenship is now very much constituted by textual behaviors. Traditional views of citizenship that focused on ends-oriented political behavior (voting, activism, and so forth) as central to good citizenship must also accommodate a performative view of publicness, one that recognizes that giving voice through textual and playful means is "a sovereign act of citizenship in itself" (228).

This brings us back to the notion of satire and parody as speech acts that constitute a revived form of engagement with the political world. As we will see in the discussion below, satire and parody have served not only as very popular alternative means for participating in the public realm but also as a constituent component of a playful and silly, yet all too serious, citizenship. We will discuss how and why that is so through the notions of "performativity" and "play."

Performativity and Play

One of the facts of contemporary political reality is that it may not adhere to the old Platonic ideal of truth's correspondence to fact – that is, that reality can or should be assessed in terms of its truth or falsity (Rorty 1999: xvi–xxxii). Much of journalism (not to mention logical positivism) has been built on the view that language produces true and false statements, and that journalists can discern reality by describing, reporting, finding, and discovering truth within public discourse. Theorists such as J.L. Austin and Jacques Derrida, however, would have us recognize that, rather than *representing* reality, language actually *creates* reality (Loxley 2007). Language, speech acts, or utterances not only describe reality but perform it – they are events or actions in and of themselves. Many politicians today fully realize this, and spend much of their time utilizing news media as conduits of such reality creation. Perhaps this was never more bluntly and boldly stated than when an adviser to President George W. Bush (widely believed to be Karl Rove) called journalists a "reality-based community," and said that a "judicious study of discernible reality" is "not the way the world really works anymore." The advisor continued:

> We're an empire now, and when we act, we create our own reality. And while you're studying that reality – judiciously, as you will – we'll act again, creating other new realities, which you can study too, and that's how things will sort out. We're history's actors . . . and you, all of you, will be left to just study what we do. (Rich 2006: 3–4)

Similarly, we can see the power of performative language in creating reality when former Alaska Governor and vice-presidential candidate Sarah Palin, in simply writing a post on Facebook, stated: "The America I know and love is not one in which my parents or my baby with Down Syndrome will have to stand in front of Obama's 'death panel' so his bureaucrats can decide ... whether they are worthy of health care." As two journalism scholars report, "The top 50 newspapers in the country [subsequently] published over 700 articles about the claim, while the nightly network news ran about 20 stories on the topic" (Shafer and Lawrence 2011). In that process, many journalists contested and debunked the claim. Nevertheless, one poll of citizens reported that 30 percent of respondents believed that the proposed legislation would "create death panels," and one month later (in a different study) 41 percent believed that this extreme rationing of health care was included in the legislation (Shafer and Lawrence 2011). In short, it really doesn't matter if what Palin said was true or untrue, or even how well journalists did in discrediting the claim. What matters is that Palin's utterance did, in many ways, *create* the reality she performed by speaking it.

It is into this political world that satire and parody are inserted, demonstrating how they can be powerful tools for rebuttal, challenge, and critique. Indeed, as the above example of journalism's supposed debunking efforts suggests, older forms of contestation may prove helpless in challenging such truthiness when people want to *believe* it. Satire and parody provide a different language – one that combines aggression and judgment with laughter and play (Test 1991). It is language well suited to the destabilization of meanings, although it can be used for deconstructive and constructive ends. Its deconstruction occurs through its critical frame. As Peter Childs argues,

> Critics must scrutinize the will to power inherent in texts. The critics' aim must include paying attention to that which the text has disallowed readers to think or conclude, to reveal the pattern of thought drawn by the text, and to lay bare what has been mapped out in advance. (2006: 8)

The satirist Jon Stewart, for instance, engaged in just such a critical deconstruction of dominant media and political discourses by crafting a brilliant eight-and-a-half-minute segment in which, through techniques of redaction, he spliced together news and stock advice segments from the financial news network CNBC (*The Daily Show* 2009a). In the process, he demonstrated how the channel was complicit in the financial bubble created by Wall Street, and, similarly to the politicians above, how the CNBC reporters, commentators, and stock analysts literally *performed* the reality they sought to create (Jones 2010: 115–119). But Stewart constructed his own performative speech act one week later when he brought one of the channel's personalities on for a very serious and aggressive interview (*The Daily Show* 2009b). Since few reporters or news media outlets had previously challenged the financial news network for its role in propagating the myths and inaccuracies that sustained the bubble, Stewart's performative acts – satirical *and* serious – became a significant contribution to the public reckoning with the reality of the financial crisis, as he became a public face of the outrage directed at Wall Street.

A similar performative speech act is seen in comedienne Tina Fey's parodic portrayal of vice-presidential candidate Sarah Palin on the sketch comedy program

Saturday Night Live. Responding to what was widely considered a disastrous television news interview by Palin just days prior, Fey served up a damning parody, in many instances simply repeating Palin's actual words (Jones 2009b: 177). A traditional journalistic frame for assessing Palin's performance did little to provide resources for "making sense" of the encounter (given the encounter's perplexing nature). The parodic performance as speech act, however, resituated the interview in a comedic frame, thus leading viewers away from the text's preferred patterns of interpretation (rational and deliberative) toward other patterns of thought and meaning – those invited by *play*. By shifting the interpretive frame, the ridiculousness of the original becomes much clearer. The parodic performance quickly went viral, but it also was circulated repeatedly by television news media. Fey had, in her performance, seemingly captured the best interpretation of Palin – that the governor was considerably unqualified to be vice president (or president) and was hoping to charm her way into office through obfuscation and preening. News media, embracing what they were seemingly impotent to do, gleefully yoked Fey's critique onto their reports and commentary of Palin and her original speech act.[3]

This, it seems, is where the performative power of parody and satire lies – not in rational or deliberative rebuttal, or even just in creative deconstruction, but in the creation of its own speech acts, ones that subvert by challenging the legitimacy of the first. As the performative political speech acts are iterated and reiterated across the digital mediascape, satire and parody exploit that space, inserting a second speech act dripping with the residue of the original.[4] The new performance becomes less a rebuttal than a parasite, sucking meaning from, living off, and limiting the prior event's full performative ability to create reality unchallenged. The original can no longer sit alone, at times competing with its doppelganger and at other times having to put up with its co-presence (as both can be and often are shown together).

Satire can also be used for constructive ends, often through play. Graham Meikle (2008) examines play at work in the use of tactical media – subversively creative and deliberate DIY/DIWO attacks on dominant discourses (video mashups and culture jamming are perhaps two easily identifiable examples; the work of the Yes Men is another). Meikle smartly asks whether our assessment of such efforts and undertakings should be changed from an instrumental and outcome-oriented question such as "does it work?" to "does it play?," which redirects the enquiry toward the creators or participants of tactical media or its users (i.e., toward the needs of citizens, not those of the state). It also calls attention to participatory culture itself and to opportunities for creative engagement within citizenship. Meikle contends that a focus on play directs our attention to the things that might contribute to a richer, fuller sense of being a citizen or *practicing* citizenship (see also van Zoonen 2005: 123), such as opportunities for learning and development, enjoyment, bonding and community forming, or resources for improvisation and imagination.

As Meikle suggests, play can easily be dismissed for its supposed lack of instrumentality or non-goal-directed activity, not to mention its connection to "child-like" behavior (Hartley 2010). Yet Theodore Glasser rightly argues that "play's creativity ... highlights nothing less than the nature of meaning and understanding.... Play illustrates how individuals *participate* in the meaning of what they encounter" (2000: 26). Thus, while satirists and parodists are often charged with being cynics whose work pushes people away from a commitment to politics and public life (Hart and Hartelius 2007), the concept of play suggests just the opposite – that citizens are invited into the speech act and asked to participate as more than simple consumers of pre-established meanings, positions, and opinions.

Perhaps what both Glasser and Meikle suggest can be seen in the playful engagements by comedians Jon Stewart and Stephen Colbert, who have demonstrated their willingness to move the rhetorical critiques outside the limited frame of entertainment television, inserting themselves – and their fans who play along – more directly into the public square. Both have crafted intentionally playful (and performative) political acts,[5] including their Rally to Restore Sanity and/or Fear. The rally was originally a sly wink to Fox News host Glenn Beck's Rally to Restore Honor (also held on the Washington Mall), but in the end it delivered the serious message that the divisive rhetoric and agon crafted and perpetuated by cable news networks (or what Stewart called the "24-hour politico-pundit-perpetual-conflictinator") was hurting America (Brown 2010).

Even more impressive was the fact that the rally attracted between a quarter and a half million people. Being held only a few days before the mid-term congressional elections, the tendency for journalists was to assess its "meaning" largely on instrumental terms – that is, whether it might affect voter turnout or vote choice (Jones et al. 2012). While it is difficult to ascertain the intentions or desires of so many people attending an event such as this, what is certain is that the event's indeterminacy in meaning (which is it – sanity or fear? Comedy or politics? Both?) invited a range of playful positions that people could assume by attending the event. Bodily showing up in the central location for political protest in the USA yet holding self-made signs that read proclamations such as "Stark Raving Reasonable," "Don't Believe Everything You Think," and "Hey Hitler! Give Me Back My Nuance!" (McGlynn 2010) provided opportunities for imagination, solidarity, and community-building, and sheer enjoyment in doing something that had never been done in quite such a fashion – that is, perform a different type of citizenship by demanding... "sanity." But sanity was not just *demanded* in an old style of political assertion. It was playfully performed, thereby creating that reality – at least for a day or weekend – in the absence of such from many traditional political actors.

Silly Citizenship within New Media Dynamics

Returning to pragmatist philosopher Richard Rorty and his discussion of the need for an abandonment of the traditional correspondence theory of truth, Rorty contends that the "Cartesian mind is an entity whose relations with the rest of the universe are representational rather than causal" and that "we need to stop thinking of words as representations... and to start thinking of them as nodes in the causal network which binds the organism together with its environment"

(1999: xxiii). It is precisely this conception of language, in conjunction with opportunities presented by new media dynamics, that can help us see the value of satire and parody as tools of modern citizenship. A previous good citizenship model (Schudson 1998) stressed that experts (such as journalists) would arrive at social and political truth and (re)present it as information to be consumed. The citizen's duty and obligation was to be attendant in those ways. Hartley's DIY/DIWO or silly citizenship, however, emphasizes the *agency* now available to citizens through their own creativity and construction of language, and the opportunities presented for inclusion and meaning-making through play.

Other new media dynamics that impact this discussion include *enterprise*, the ways in which satire and parody allow for creative deconstruction and construction. What is more, such enterprise can be seen in the ways that political activists employ satirical speech acts in their own efforts to establish truth and work for change through activist networks (Baym and Shah 2011). Indeed, one could argue that, as a rhetorical form, satire offers an encouragement for political participation through the distribution and circulation of such materials through social *networks*. Within Facebook, for instance, the circulation and sharing of political material of a serious nature is just that – seriously political, which is not typically an attractive option for those averse to a publicness that might be read as didactic, ideological, or polemical. Satirical play, conversely, invites and encourages laughter, typically a more socially acceptable form of exchange. As George Test notes, satire takes natural human emotions – "anger, shame, indignation, disgust, contempt" – and channels or domesticates them, transforming "a potentially divisive and chaotic impulse... into a useful and artistic expression" (Test 1991: 4).

Finally, contemporary manifestations of satire, such as *The Daily Show*, have demonstrated their enhancement to citizenship through their *surveillance* or monitoring function of public life. *The Daily Show* responds to the daily news cycle, bringing playful attention to those issues in politics and media that deserve comment and critique. It illuminates, educates, and perhaps in a Foucauldian sense even serves a disciplinary function for those people or organizations that typically see themselves as above scrutiny (e.g., Fox News). What is more, the show makes all of its materials available for replay and circulation. The show's entire archive (since 2000) is searchable, shareable, and embeddable in other media. In short, *The Daily Show* is satire that not only monitors political life but also invites users to engage with and embed such monitoring into their own behaviors as playful and attentive citizens. And again, as Rorty notes, the ultimate point about contingent language such as satire is not that it establishes an alternative truth but what use value it serves in the network that binds citizens together.

In sum, satire and parody's encouragement of performativity and play as tools of citizenship allows for, as the editors of this volume have articulated, means of disruptive renewal. If previous understandings of citizenship privileged "discourses of sobriety" (Nichols 1991) in the constitution of good citizenship, the language of poetry (in the broadest sense of the term) today enables a reinvigoration and reformulation of how citizens will constitute and perform their identity as citizens.

And, as readings of Foucault suggest, identity is formed through "negotiation and play," including our identity as citizens. For "identity is best seen as performative, something which we do and act out, something which we assemble from existing discursive practices, rather than something we possess" (Mills 2003: 92). The reappearance and revival of the ancient discursive forms of satire and parody could not, then, have arrived a moment too soon, as citizens respond to and embrace opportunities presented through new media dynamics to be, once again, identified as citizens not subjects.

Notes

1. Elsewhere I have discussed at length the economic, political, cultural, and technological forces that contributed to the rise of new forms of political television in the USA (Jones 2010: 5–13, 43–92).
2. The story in the US commercial broadcast system is similar to that in other parts of the world operating under state-run monopolies on broadcasting. Once broader competition was introduced through the availability of commercial alternatives, political program-ming expanded – through alternative forms of news but also political entertainment programming such as satire. See Baym and Jones (2012).
3. Even Fox News later mistakenly substituted a pictograph of Fey instead of Palin when reporting on the latter (who also happens to be a paid commentator for the network).
4. This yoking of parodic speech acts with original speech acts reiterates the interaction of parody itself – that is, the way in which the parodic utterance is a "double-voiced word," as theorists of parody describe it. See Morson (1989: 75).
5. Staying within his right-wing talk-show host persona, Stephen Colbert has testified before a US congressional committee on migrant labor issues, calling attention (ironically and playfully) to the lack of rights for migrant workers. He also has created his own SuperPAC, a political action committee (approved by the Federal Election Commission) that can raise unlimited amounts of cash to influence elections without having to reveal its contributors. This latter effort calls attention to and mocks the Supreme Court decision allowing the formation of such powerful entities under the premise of free speech rights for corporations (see Jones et al. 2012).

References

Baym, G. (2010) *From Cronkite to Colbert: The Evolution of Broadcast News.* Boulder, CO: Paradigm.
Baym, G. and Jones, J.P. (2012) "Not Necessarily the News? News Parody and Political Satire across the Globe," double special issue of *Popular Communication,* 10(1–2).
Baym, G. and Shah, C. (2011) "Circulating Struggle: The On-Line Flow of Environmental Advocacy Clips from *The Daily Show* and *The Colbert Report.*" *Information, Communication & Society,* 14(7). www.tandfonline.com/doi/abs/10.1080/1369118X.2011.554573.
Blumler, J. and Gurevitch, M. (2000) "Rethinking the Study of Political Communication" in J. Curran and M. Gurevitch, eds., *Mass Media and Society,* 3rd edn. New York: Oxford University Press.

Brown, L. (2010) "Rally to Restore Sanity – Jon Stewart's Closing Speech (Full Text)." *America Inspired* (October 30). www.examiner.com/article/rally-to-restore-sanity -jon-stewart-s-closing-speech-full-text.

Childs, P. (2006) *Texts: Contemporary Cultural Texts and Critical Approaches.* Edinburgh: Edinburgh University Press.

Chouliaraki, L. (2010) "Self-mediation: New Media and Citizenship." *Critical Discourse Studies*, 7(4), 227–232.

Coleman, S. (2005) "The Lonely Citizen: Indirect Representation in an Age of Networks." *Political Communication*, 22, 197–214.

Day, A. (2011) *Satire and Dissent: Interventions in Contemporary Political Debate.* Bloomington, IN: Indiana University Press.

Glasser, T. (2000) "Play and the Power of News." *Journalism*, 1(1), 23–29.

Gray, J., Jones, J.P., and Thompson, E. (2009) *Satire TV: Politics and Comedy in the Post-Network Era.* New York: New York University Press.

Hart, R.P. and Hartelius, J. (2007) "The Political Sins of Jon Stewart." *Critical Studies in Media Communication*, 24(3), 263–272.

Hartley, J. (2010) "Silly Citizenship." *Critical Discourse Studies*, 7(4), 233–248.

Jenkins, H. (2006) *Convergence Culture: Where Old and New Media Collide.* New York: New York University Press.

Jones, J.P. (2009a) "Believable Fictions: Redactional Culture and the Will to Truthiness" in B. Zelizer, ed., *The Changing Faces of Journalism: Tabloidization, Technology and Truthiness.* New York: Routledge, pp. 127–143.

Jones, J.P. (2009b) "Pop Goes the Campaign: The Repopularization of Politics in Election 2008" in R.E. Denton Jr., ed., *The 2008 Presidential Campaign: A Communication Perspective.* Lanham, MD: Rowman & Littlefield, pp. 170–190.

Jones, J.P. (2010) *Entertaining Politics: Satiric Television and Political Engagement*, 2nd edn. Lanham, MD: Rowman & Littlefield.

Jones, J.P., Baym, G., and Day, A. (2012) "Mr. Stewart and Mr. Colbert Go to Washington: Television Satirists Outside the Box." Special Issue: "Politics and Comedy." *Social Research*, 79(1), 33–60.

Lotz, A. (2007) *The Television Will Be Revolutionized.* New York: New York University Press.

Loxley, J. (2007) *Performativity.* London: Routledge.

Mazzoleni, G. and Sfardini, A. (2009) *Politica Pop: Da "Porta a Porta" a "L'Isola dei famosi"* [Pop Politics: From "Door to Door" to "Island of the Famous"]. Bologna: Il Mulino.

McGlynn, K. (2010) "The Funniest Signs From The Rally To Restore Sanity And/Or Fear! (PHOTOS)." *The Huffington Post* (October 30). www.huffingtonpost.com/2010/10 /30/the-funniest-signs-at-the_n_776490.html#s170117&title=Wheres_the_candy.

Meikle, G. (2008) "Whacking Bush: Tactical Media as Play" in M. Boler, ed., *Digital Media and Democracy.* Cambridge, MA: MIT Press, pp. 367–382.

Mills, S. (2003) *Michele Foucault.* London: Routledge.

Morris, M. and Patton, P., eds. (1979) *Michel Foucault: Power, Truth, Strategy.* Sydney: Feral Publications.

Morson, G.S. (1989) "Parody, History, and Metaparody" in G.S. Morson and C. Emerson, eds., *Rethinking Bakhtin: Extensions and Challenges.* Evanston, IL: Northwestern University Press.

Nichols, B. (1991) *Representing Reality.* Bloomington, IN: Indiana University Press.

Rich, F. (2006) *The Greatest Story Ever Sold: The Decline and Fall of Truth from 9/11 to Katrina.* New York: Penguin.

Rorty, R. (1999) *Philosophy and Social Hope*. New York: Penguin.

Schafer, M. and Lawrence, R. (2011) "Sarah Palin's 2009 'Death Panel' Claims: How the Media Handled Them, and Why That Matters." *Nieman Journalism Lab* (May 26). www.niemanlab.org/2011/05/sarah-palins-2009-death-panel-claims-how-the-media-handled-them-and-why-that-matters.

Schudson, M. (1998) *The Good Citizen: A History of American Civic Life*. New York: Free Press.

Test, G.A. (1991) *Satire: Spirit and Art*. Tampa, FL: University of South Florida Press.

The Daily Show (2009a) "CNBC Financial Advice" (March 4). www.thedailyshow.com/watch/wed-march-4-2009/cnbc-financial-advice.

The Daily Show (2009b) "Jim Cramer Pt. 1" (March 12). www.thedailyshow.com/watch/thu-march-12-2009/jim-cramer-pt--1.

van Zoonen, L. (2005) *Entertaining the Citizen: When Politics and Popular Culture Converge*. Lanham, MD: Rowman & Littlefield.

28

The Politics of "Platforms"

Tarleton Gillespie

Back in October 2006, Google purchased YouTube for US$1.65 billion. The press release announcing the purchase included quotes from the two proud fathers, trumpeting the potential symbiosis of their companies' partnership:

> "The YouTube team has built an exciting and powerful media platform that comple-ments Google's mission to organize the world's information and make it universally accessible and useful," said Eric Schmidt, Chief Executive Officer of Google....

> "By joining forces with Google, we can benefit from its global reach and technology leadership to deliver a more comprehensive entertainment experience for our users and to create new opportunities for our partners," said Chad Hurley, CEO and Co-Founder of YouTube. "I'm confident that with this partnership we'll have the flexibility and resources needed to pursue our goal of building the next-generation platform for serving media worldwide." (YouTube 2006a)

Around six months later, YouTube made a slight change to the paragraph it used to describe its service in all of its press releases. This "website," "company," "service," "forum," and "community" was now also a "distribution platform for original content creators and advertisers large and small" (YouTube 2007c).

Intermediaries such as YouTube – those companies that provide storage, nav-igation, and delivery of the digital content of others – are working to establish a viable, long-term position in a fluctuating economic and cultural terrain. Like publishers, television networks, and film studios before them, established companies are protecting their position in the market while, in their shadows, smaller firms are working to shore up their niche positions and anticipate trends in the business of information distribution.

YouTube's dominance in the world of online video makes it one of just a handful of video platforms, search engines, blogging tools, and interactive online spaces that are now the primary keepers of the cultural discussion as it moves to the Internet. As such, again like the television networks and trade publishers before them, they

A Companion to New Media Dynamics, First Edition. Edited by John Hartley, Jean Burgess, and Axel Bruns.
© 2013 John Wiley & Sons, Ltd. Published 2015 by John Wiley & Sons, Ltd.

are increasingly facing questions regarding their responsibilities: to their users, to key constituencies who depend on the content they host, and to broader notions of the public interest.

In the context of these financial, cultural, and regulatory demands, these firms are working not just politically but also discursively to frame their services and technologies (Sterne 2003; Gillespie 2007). They do so strategically, to position themselves to pursue both current and future profits, to find a regulatory sweet spot between legislative protections that benefit them and obligations that do not, and to lay out a cultural imaginary within which their service makes sense (Wyatt 2004).

In this chapter I will highlight the discursive work that prominent digital intermediaries, especially YouTube, are undertaking, by focusing on one particular term: "platform." The term "platform" has recently become increasingly familiar in the description of the online services of content intermediaries, both in their self-characterizations and in the broader public discourse of users, the press, and commentators. The point is not so much the word itself; examining these intermediaries' deployment of the term "platform" (or "Web 2.0," "community," "social media," "cloud") merely helps to reveal the characterization that they are constructing for themselves.

YouTube must present its service not only to its users but also to advertisers, to major media producers it hopes to have as partners, and to policymakers. The term "platform" helps to reveal how YouTube and others stage themselves for these constituencies, allowing them to make a broadly progressive sales pitch while also eliding the tensions inherent in their service: between user-generated and commercially produced content, between cultivating community and serving up advertising, between intervening in the delivery of content and remaining neutral.

As a term such as platform becomes a "discursive resting point" (Bazerman 1999), further innovations may be oriented toward that idea of what the technology is, and regulations may demand it act accordingly (Streeter 1996; Galperin 2004; Lyman 2004). Moreover, such terms "institute" a way of being: they "sanction and sanctify a particular state of things, an established order, in exactly the same way that a *constitution* does in the legal and political sense of the term" (Bourdieu 1991: 119). And, "platform" is a claim that arguably misrepresents the way YouTube and other intermediaries really shape public discourse online.

"Platform"

To call an online service a "platform" is not a meaningless claim, nor is it a simple one. Like other structural metaphors (think "network," "broadcast," or "channel") the term depends on a semantic richness that, though it may go unnoticed by the casual listener or even the speaker, gives the term discursive resonance. The *Oxford English Dictionary* notes fifteen different uses, in what I see as four broad categories:

- *Architectural*: "A raised level surface on which people or things can stand, usually a discrete structure intended for a particular activity or operation," such as a subway platform, Olympic diving platform, deep-sea oil rig platform, or platform shoes.

- *Figurative*: a more conceptual version, "the ground, foundation, or basis *of* an action, event, calculation, condition, etc. Now also: a position achieved or situation brought about which forms the basis for further achievement." We might describe our entry-level job as a "platform" for climbing the corporate ladder.
- *Political*: "the major policy or set of policies on which a political party (or later also an individual politician) proposes to stand"; this usage first emerged from the architectural sense – that is, the actual stage constructed for a candidate to address an audience.
- *Computational*: "A standard system architecture; a (type of) machine and/or operating system, regarded as the base on which software applications are run." That is, a computing infrastructure upon which tools are built – be it computer hardware, operating systems, mobile devices, or digital disc formats.

Drawing these meanings together, "platform" first suggests a functional shape, a "raised, level surface" designed to facilitate some activity that will subsequently take place. More than that, it implies a progressive and egalitarian arrangement, an implicit promise to support those who stand upon it. But the platform is defined not just by support but also by its level surface and its openness to those hoping to stand upon it. Even in its political context, where the platform by definition lifts someone above the rest (and is rarely used to describe the beliefs of ordinary citizens), it retains a populist ethos: a representative speaking plainly and forcefully to his constituents. In any of the senses of "platform," being raised, level, and accessible are ideological features as much as physical ones.

All four of these semantic areas are relevant to why "platform" has emerged in reference to online content-hosting intermediaries and, just as importantly, what value both its specificity and its flexibility offer them. Through the boom and bust waves of Internet investment (of both capital and enthusiasm), "platform" conveniently suggested a lot while saying very little. So, it should come as no surprise that the term again gained traction around user-generated content, streaming media, blogging, and social computing. There has been a proliferation of "platforms" just in online video: those visible to users (such as YouTube, Vimeo, and DailyMotion) and those known only to commercial producers looking to stream their content (such as Brightcove, Castfire, Real Media's "Helix Media Delivery Platform," and Comcast's thePlatform service). These join blogging platforms, photo sharing platforms, and social network platforms now jostling for attention on the web. Today, platforms are platforms not necessarily because they allow code to be written or run but because they afford an opportunity to communicate, interact, or sell.

Users, Advertisers, Clients

The business of the intermediary is a complex and fragile one, oriented as it is to at least three constituencies: end users, advertisers, and professional content producers. This is where the discursive work is most vital. Intermediaries such as YouTube must present themselves strategically to each of these audiences and carve out a set of expectations that is acceptable to each and also serves their own financial interests while resolving or at least eliding any contradictions between them. Curiously, tropes such as "platform" work across these discourses – in fact, the real value of this term may be that it brings these discourses into alignment without them unsettling each other.

It is the connotations – open, neutral, fair, egalitarian, progressive, facilitating – that make this term so compelling for intermediaries such as YouTube as a way to appeal to users. YouTube and its competitors claim to empower the individual to speak – lifting us all up, evenly. YouTube can assert that it is "committed to offering the best user experience and the best platform for people to share their videos around the world" (YouTube 2006c) and present its You Choose '08 project as a "platform for people to engage in dialogue with candidates and each other" (YouTube 2007a). This fits neatly with the long-standing rhetoric about the democratizing potential of the Internet, and with the more recent enthusiasm for user-generated content, amateur expertise, peer collaboration, and robust civic commentary (Benkler 2006; Jenkins 2006; Bruns 2008; Burgess and Green 2009). These activities, of course, pre-date YouTube. But YouTube has been particularly effective at positioning itself as the upstart champion of user-generated content. The "You" in YouTube is the most obvious signal, but the direct appeal to the amateur user is visible elsewhere. YouTube offers to help you "Broadcast Yourself"; or, as it suggests on its "Company History" page, "as more people capture special moments on video, YouTube is empowering them to become the broadcasters of tomorrow" (YouTube 2009a).

Of course, YouTube's aspirations are greater than being a repository for the world's funniest home videos – it is looking to profit from them. It is important to remember that YouTube is funded almost entirely by advertising (Allen 2008). This is certainly downplayed when speaking to regular users: commercial advertising is not a neat ideological fit with the ethos of the participatory web – not to mention that, for the most part, the users generating the content do not enjoy any revenue in return (Terranova 2000; Cammaerts 2008; Petersen 2008).[1]

Still, YouTube has historically failed to turn a profit. Google CEO Eric Schmidt has prophesied YouTube's profitability on several occasions, but, since Google does not split out YouTube's revenues and costs in its financial reports, market watchers can only guess (Miller 2010). But it has long been clear that instream ads and sponsored links would by themselves be insufficient.[2] YouTube has also aggressively sought strategic partnerships with commercial media, to include professional content alongside its user-generated submissions. Although it is still a minority of YouTube's total content, commercial content dominates the most popular and most viewed lists, particularly music videos from major-label artists.

Using the same terminology it employs to appeal to amateur users, YouTube pitches its service to advertisers:

> Marketers have embraced the YouTube marketing platform and [sic] as an innovative and engaging vehicle for connecting with their target audiences, and they are increasing

sales and exposure for their companies and brands in many different ways. (YouTube 2009c)

"Platform" in its more figurative sense also works as well for media partners:

> YouTube provides a great platform for independent filmmakers to build and grow a global audience for their short films and video projects. (YouTube 2007b)

and

> We look forward to partnering with [Warner Music Group] to offer this powerful distribution platform to our artists and their fans. (YouTube 2006b)

This is not the "means of expression" YouTube promises users. Rather, it is a "platform" of opportunity, and a distinctly commercial opportunity: when YouTube added "click-to-buy" links to retailers such as Amazon and iTunes alongside certain videos, the company blogged that "This is just the beginning of building a broad, viable eCommerce platform for users and partners on YouTube" (YouTube Team 2008b). YouTube is increasingly, perhaps always was, a platform from which to sell, not just to speak.

Intermediaries must speak in different registers to their relevant constituencies, positioning themselves so as to best suit their interests in each moment (Gieryn 1999). However, "platform" unproblematically moves across all three registers, linking them into a single agenda. For advertisers, YouTube can promise to support brand awareness, a public campaign, a product launch; for major media producers, content can be made visible and, even better, pushed to audiences. At the same time, the evocative rhetoric of "you" offers users the figurative and political connotations. The term seamlessly links the discursive registers in which YouTube must speak, even in the same breath:

> Ultimately, the online video experience is about empowerment. Consumers of online video are empowered to be their own content programmers, consuming the relevant mix of mass, niche and personal media they demand. Advertisers are empowered through data to better understand and engage with their audiences. And content owners are empowered, through sophisticated identification tools, to control their content and make smart business decisions with their content. (Hurley 2008)

This is where a term such as "platform," and the "empowerment" it implies, is so useful. YouTube can make a bid to be the new television, convincing media producers to provide their valuable content and advertisers to buy valuable consumer attention – on the back of user-generated content with all its democratic, egalitarian connotations, offered as television's antidote. Whatever tension there is between being a platform for empowering individual users *and* being a robust marketing platform *and* being a platform for major studio content is elided by the versatile term and the powerful meanings behind it.

Edges

That information intermediaries such as YouTube claim to be a "raised, level surface" open to all means that the interventions and choices these providers actually do make can be harder to see. But these platforms do have edges. Burgess and Green remind us that "YouTube, Inc. can be seen as the 'patron' of collective creativity, controlling at least some of the conditions under which creative content is produced, ordered, and re-presented" (2009: 60). These conditions are practical, technical, economic, and legal, and they stray far from the hands-off neutrality suggested by the platform rhetoric. YouTube has pursued a business model that, though not the traditional gatekeeper role of broadcasters and publishers, nevertheless does lead them to make curatorial choices about what they host and how they present it. These drive decisions about content, availability, organization, and participation (van Dijck 2009).

Whether these interventions are strategic or incidental, harmful or benign, they are deliberate. Take, for instance, YouTube's December 2008 announcement, in a blog entry blithely titled "A YouTube for All of Us" (YouTube 2008), of a stricter policy on profanity and sexually suggestive content: they promised to remove some videos entirely, cordon off others behind age barriers, and algorithmically demote others from their "most popular" lists, so that they would not automatically populate the site's front page. YouTube has long maintained rules against pornography, gratuitous violence, and unauthorized copyrighted material, and has revised these "Community Guidelines" over the years to restrict videos of drug use, underage drinking and smoking, and hate speech.

In some moments in which their posted content has been criticized, YouTube has positioned itself as a champion of freedom of expression, and "platform" suits this argument well. In response to a request from Senator Joe Lieberman to remove a number of videos he claimed were Islamist training propaganda (a request they partially honored), the YouTube team asserted,

> While we respect and understand his views, YouTube encourages free speech and defends everyone's right to express unpopular points of view. We believe that YouTube is a richer and more relevant platform for users precisely because it hosts a diverse range of views, and rather than stifle debate we allow our users to view all acceptable content and make up their own minds. (YouTube Team 2008a)

Yet, in other moments, calling its service a platform can be a way to downplay its role rather than trumpet it. Digital intermediaries have long sought to enjoy limited liability for the information they host. In a brief to the court in *Viacom v. YouTube*, YouTube's legal team praised the Digital Millennium Copyright Act (DMCA) for the safe harbor it provides:

> Congress understood that some of the material posted by the millions of people who use online services would infringe copyrights. But Congress recognized that requiring

service providers to engage in an arduous screening process for every user-posted text, picture, and video would inhibit free expression and stifle the growth of the Internet. The DMCA thus gives legitimate services "safe harbor" against potentially crushing infringement claims while providing copyright holders an expedient way to stop any misuse of their content.... The careful balance struck by the DMCA created the legal infrastructure for a free and open Internet. The safe harbors have allowed YouTube and services like it to flourish as platforms for creative, political, and social expression. (YouTube 2011: 1–3)

To shield themselves not only from legal charges but also from the cultural charge of being puerile, frivolous, debased, and so on, intermediaries such as YouTube need to position themselves as merely hosting – empowering all by choosing none.

Conclusion

A term such as "platform" does not drop from the sky, or emerge in some organic, unfettered way from public discussion. It is drawn from the available cultural vocabulary by stakeholders with specific aims, and carefully massaged so as to resonate for particular audiences. These are efforts not only to sell, convince, persuade, protect, triumph, or condemn but also to make claims about what these technologies are and are not, and what should and should not be expected of them. In other words, they attempt to establish the very criteria by which these technologies will be judged, built directly into the terms by which we know them. Whether these terms take root in the popular imagination, in the rhetoric of the industry, or in the vocabulary of the law is partly the result of this discursive work (Pfaffenberger 1992; Berland 2000).

However, these terms matter as much for what they hide as for what they reveal. Despite the promises made, "platforms" are more like traditional media than they care to admit. As they seek sustainable business models, as they run up against traditional regulations and spark discussions of new ones, and as they become prominent enough to draw the scrutiny not just of their users but also the public at large, the pressures mount to strike their own balance between safe and controversial, between socially and financially valuable, between niche and wide appeal. And, as with broadcasting and publishing, their choices about what makes it onto the platform, how it is organized, how it is monetized, what can be removed and why, and what is technically possible or prohibited, are all real and substantive interventions into the contours of public discourse.

Acknowledgments

This chapter is an abbreviated/updated version of a previously published article: Gillespie, T., "The politics of 'platforms,'" *New Media & Society*, May 1, 2010. Material reused by permission of SAGE Publications.

Notes

1. In 2007, YouTube began a revenue-sharing program with select "YouTube stars," then later opened it to any user applying to be a "partner" (YouTube 2009b). Approved partners get a cut of the Adsense revenue from ads paired with their videos. YouTube has not revealed exactly how much revenue they share, but a recent report suggests partners get 50 percent of ad revenue from their videos (della Cava 2010).

2. Most of YouTube's user-generated content cannot be paired with advertising. Many brands are wary of pairing ads with user-generated videos, despite their occasional "viral" circulation, out of fear of being associated with the wrong content. YouTube also does not want to undercut its defense against copyright complaints by inadvertently profiting from infringing material. Commentators have reported that YouTube only pairs ads with 9 percent of the content it streams to US users, which is less than a third of its total traffic (Learmonth 2009).

References

Allen, M. (2008) "Web 2.0: An Argument against Convergence." *First Monday*, 13(3). www.uic.edu/htbin/cgiwrap/bin/ojs/index.php/fm/article/viewArticle/2139/1946.

Bazerman, C. (1999) *The Languages of Edison's Light*. Cambridge, MA: MIT Press.

Benkler, Y. (2006) *The Wealth of Networks: How Social Production Transforms Markets and Freedom*. New Haven, CT: Yale University Press.

Berland, J. (2000) "Cultural Technologies and the 'Evolution' of Technological Cultures" in A. Herman and T. Swiss, eds., *The World Wide Web and Contemporary Cultural Theory*. New York: Routledge, pp. 235–258.

Bourdieu, P. (1991) *Language and Social Power*. Cambridge, MA: Harvard University Press.

Bruns, A. (2008) *Blogs, Wikipedia, Second Life, and Beyond: From Production to Produsage*. New York: Peter Lang.

Burgess, J. and Green, J. (2009) *YouTube: Online Video and Participatory Culture*. Cambridge: Polity.

Cammaerts, B. (2008) "Critiques on the Participatory Potentials of Web 2.0." *Communication, Culture & Critique*, 1(3), 358–377.

della Cava, M. (2010) "YouTube 2.0 Helping New Stars Redefine TV." *USA Today* (June 2). www.usatoday.com/tech/news/2011-06-03-YouTube-creators-camp-Michelle-Phan-Joel-Jutagir_n.htm.

Galperin, H. (2004) "Beyond Interests, Ideas, and Technology: An Institutional Approach to Communication and Information Policy." *Information Society*, 20(3), 159–168.

Gieryn, T. (1999) *Cultural Boundaries of Science: Credibility on the Line*. Chicago, IL: University of Chicago Press.

Gillespie, T. (2007) *Wired Shut: Copyright and the Shape of Digital Culture*. Cambridge, MA: MIT Press.

Hurley, C. (2008) "YouTube CEO Chad Hurley's MIPCOM Keynote Address" (October 15). www.youtube.com/watch?v=yXMPaQQ6y4A.

Jenkins, H. (2006) *Convergence Culture: Where Old and New Media Collide*. New York: New York University Press.

Learmonth, M. (2009) "Why Free-ride YouTube Is Finally Winning Ad Dollars." *Advertising Age* (April 13). http://adage.com/article/digital/free-ride-youtube-finally-winning-ad-dollars/135941.

Lyman, P. (2004) "Information Superhighways, Virtual Communities, and Digital Libraries: Information Society Metaphors as Political Rhetoric" in M. Sturken, D. Thomas, and S. Ball-Rokeach, eds., *Technological Visions: The Hopes and Fears that Shape New Technologies.* Philadelphia: Temple University Press, pp. 201–218.

Miller, C. (2010) "YouTube Ads Turn Videos into Revenue." *New York Times* (September 2). www.nytimes.com/2010/09/03/technology/03youtube.html.

Petersen, S.M. (2008) "Loser Generated Content: From Participation to Exploitation." *First Monday*, 13(3). www.uic.edu/htbin/cgiwrap/bin/ojs/index.php/fm/article/view/2141/1948.

Pfaffenberger, B. (1992) "Technological Dramas." *Science, Technology, & Human Values*, 17(3), 282–312.

Sterne, J. (2003) "Bourdieu, Technique, and Technology." *Cultural Studies*, 17(3&4), 367–389.

Streeter, T. (1996) *Selling the Air: A Critique of the Policy of Commercial Broadcasting in the United States.* Chicago, IL: University of Chicago Press.

Terranova, T. (2000) "Free Labor: Producing Culture for the Digital Economy." *Social Text*, 18(2), 33–58.

van Dijck, J. (2009) "Users Like You? Theorizing Agency in User-generated Content." *Media, Culture & Society*, 31(1), 41–58.

Wyatt, S. (2004) "Danger! Metaphors at Work in Economics, Geophysiology, and the Internet." *Science, Technology, & Human Values*, 29(2), 242–261.

YouTube (2006a) "Google To Acquire YouTube for $1.65 Billion in Stock." *News from Google* (October 9). www.google.com/press/pressrel/google_youtube.html.

YouTube (2006b) "Warner Music Group and YouTube Announce Landmark Video Distribution and Revenue Partnership." *RedOrbit* (September 18). www.redorbit.com/news/technology/660345/warner_music_group_and_youtube_announce_landmark_video_distribution_and/index.html.

YouTube (2006c) "YouTube Uploads $8M in Funding." *StockNews* (April 5). http://new.stocknews.ch/200604051950/Press-Releases-EN/Media-TV-of-the-future-share-for-free.html.

YouTube (2007a) "YouTube Ignites Online Campaigning with Its YouTube You Choose '08 Program." *RedOrbit* (March 1). www.redorbit.com/news/technology/856824/youtube_ignites_online_campaigning_with_its_youtube_you_choose_08/index.html.

YouTube (2007b) "YouTube Premieres First International Film Competition." *MarketWire* (October 1). www.marketwire.com/press-release/YouTube-Premieres-First-International-Film-Competition-775912.htm.

YouTube (2007c) "YouTube Seeks the Best Shorts on the Internet." *MarketWire* (May 21). www.marketwire.com/press-release/YouTube-Seeks-the-Best-Shorts-on-the-Internet-728034.htm.

YouTube (2008) "A YouTube for All of Us." *Broadcasting Ourselves: The YouTube Blog* (December 2). http://youtube-global.blogspot.com/2008/12/youtube-for-all-of-us.html.

YouTube (2009a) "Company History." www.youtube.com/t/about.

YouTube (2009b) "The YouTube Partner Program." www.youtube.com/partners.

YouTube (2009c) "YouTube Fact Sheet." [previously available at] www.youtube.com/t/fact_sheet.

YouTube (2011) "Brief, on Behalf of Appellee Google, Inc., Youtube, Inc. and Youtube, LLC." *Viacom International, Inc., et. al. v YouTube, Inc.* US Court of Appeals, Second Circuit, 10–3270 (March 31). https://www.eff.org/files/filenode/viacom_v_youtube/2011 -03-31_YouTube_Brief_3270.pdf.

YouTube Team (2008a) "Dialogue with Sen. Lieberman on Terrorism Videos." *Google Public Policy Blog* (May 19). http://googlepublicpolicy.blogspot.com/2008/05/dialogue -with-sen-lieberman-on.html.

YouTube Team (2008b) "Like What You See? Then Click-to-Buy on YouTube." *Broadcasting Ourselves: The YouTube Blog* (October 7). http://youtube-global.blogspot .com/2008/10/like-what-you-see-then-click-to-buy-on.html.

Further Reading

Hesmondhalgh, D. (2007) *The Cultural Industries*, 2nd edn. London: Sage.

Pariser, E. (2011) *The Filter Bubble: What the Internet is Hiding from You*. New York: Penguin.

Snickars, P. and Vonderau, P., eds. (2009) *The YouTube Reader*. Stockholm: National Library of Sweden. [See especially the essays by Andrejevic, Farchy, McDonald, and Wasko and Erikson.]

Vaidhyanathan, S. (2010) *The Googlization of Everything (and Why We Should Worry)*. Berkeley, CA: University of California Press.

Wu, T. (2010) *The Master Switch: The Rise and Fall of Information Empires*. New York: Alfred A. Knopf.

Zittrain, J. (2006) "A History of Online Gatekeeping." *Harvard Journal of Law and Technology*, 19(2), 253–29.

29

From Homepages to Network Profiles
Balancing Personal and Social Identity

Axel Bruns

The World Wide Web constitutes one of the most important inventions of the late twentieth century: it has changed culture, society, business, communication, politics, and many other fields of human endeavor, not least also by providing a more user-friendly pathway of access to its major underlying technology, the Internet itself. Key phases in its development can be charted, especially by how it has been used to present and share information – and here, the personal or professional, private or official homepage stands in as a useful representation of wider web trends overall. From hand-coded beginnings through several successive stages of experimentation and standardization to the shifting balance between personal sites and social networks, the homepage demonstrates how the web itself, and its place in our lives, has changed.

Phase 1: The First Homepages

To a significant extent, the history of the World Wide Web is also a history of the homepage. The first web pages, made available in 1990, necessarily *were* homepages – for the web itself, for the nuclear research center CERN where it was invented, and for key figures in its early history, including inventor Tim Berners-Lee (2000). Hand-crafted in rudimentary hypertext markup language (HTML), these early pages drew on their authors' experience with previous technologies – such as the online information retrieval protocol Gopher, which provided a menu- or directory-style access interface to stored documents rather than the more flexible structure of web pages. The first World Wide Web homepage, still preserved at CERN,[1] therefore provides little more than an ordered list of links to other documents.

As HTML gained further features, web browser capabilities developed alongside it; and, as a greater number of users learnt to "code" in HTML, organizational

A Companion to New Media Dynamics, First Edition. Edited by John Hartley, Jean Burgess, and Axel Bruns.
© 2013 John Wiley & Sons, Ltd. Published 2015 by John Wiley & Sons, Ltd.

and personal websites began to proliferate. Many early web users had at least some degree of access to personal storage spaces on institutional Internet servers, where they could now also store web-accessible HTML documents. Indeed, a shift from single home*page* to multipage web*site* began to occur: to link between web pages no longer meant only to link from one user's homepage to another's, but also to link between different pages in one's own website. Many personal homepages continued to maintain a logically ordered structure, however. This was by necessity as much as by choice: the significant manual effort involved in developing and maintaining a site's document structure and HTML code meant that different areas of personal interest were often collated on different pages, and then linked to from a central page. In spite of the significant changes to web technologies and web logics since the early 1990s, and despite the fact that later changes removed the need for such a hub-and-spokes organization, this logic still persists to substantial extent today.

One important element of hand-coded, multipage websites was the list of links to other sites; indeed, CERN's own homepage for the web ultimately constituted just such a list. Prior to the introduction of the first search engines, such lists and directories of other web resources provided the only means of discovering what content was available "on the web," other than through word of mouth. "Links lists" often served as an aide-mémoire for the users compiling them as much as a service to others: they were a means of publicly bookmarking other sites at a time when some web browsers had not yet begun to incorporate bookmarking functionality. They were also a way to share useful finds with other interested users; for some web authors, compiling an authoritative list of web resources in their field of interest even became the principal driver for maintaining their personal homepage.

Phase 2: Attempts at Organizing the Web

The wider popularization of the web as a means of many-to-many communication has been attributed to the introduction of Mosaic as one of the first graphical web browsers (Reid 1997), building in turn on the growing availability of personal computers with mouse-operated graphical user interfaces. Using such technology, it now became possible for a much wider range of users to begin to explore the World Wide Web. An immediate consequence of this influx of web "surfers" was the further proliferation of websites and homepages; in turn, the question of content discoverability became an ever more pressing issue for the new medium.

One attempt to address this issue lay in efforts to develop more comprehensive, searchable directories of web content: David and Jerry's Guide to the World Wide Web, renamed Yahoo! in 1995, became an early front-runner in this field. Such web directories took the idea of the "links list" and pursued it on an industrial scale. Later, such attempts to order the web into clearly defined areas of interest encountered the librarian's problem of developing a universal ontology for human interests, and a gradual shift from directory- to search-based access occurred (Halavais 2009).

Especially at this early stage, however, web directories necessarily lagged behind in their coverage of actual web content. They focused on the better-known, "official" sites on the web. An alternative to trying to have one's personal site listed in such directories, therefore, was to seek strength in numbers: to move to one of a handful of early homepage hosting solutions, which provided their own mechanisms of organizing, listing, and searching websites. If Howard Rheingold's romantic notion of "homesteading on the electronic frontier" (the subtitle of his 1993 book *The Virtual Community*) ever applied to the early web, then those isolated homesteads now began to give way to a first wave of urbanization – quite literally, in fact, as homepage provider GeoCities (launched in 1995) emerged as one of the first major web-native business successes.

The relevance of such metaphors to the day-to-day use of GeoCities and its hosted sites should not be overstated. However, GeoCities did deliberately organize its sites into a number of neighborhoods named for offline cities, including Hollywood and Silicon Valley, which were meant to signal the likely field of interest (entertainment, technology...) of each hosted site. Using GeoCities meant having access to a reliable, shared infrastructure, as well as a range of simple tools for building one's site; the pay-off for these benefits was having to subscribe to the rules of a commercial hosting provider (Fernback 2004). Nonetheless, this constituted an important step in mainstreaming the idea and practices of website design well beyond the initial in-group of technologists and hackers. GeoCities users created some 38 million pages before the site closed (Shechmeister 2009). A number of unofficial archival projects, such as ReoCities, now attempt to preserve this legacy of early web design.

The availability of standard hosting and development tools and the emergence of a common, interlinked space for homepages necessarily led to a certain degree of standardization in website design and features. GeoCities sites, in particular, often shared a certain style, caricatured as relying too much on animated graphics, flashing texts, and "page under construction" notices. Further, standard user interface features were imposed by the platform itself – such as a GeoCities watermark, displayed permanently in the browser window. This, in turn, spurred the next phase of homepage development, which emphasized a greater level of individualism in website design.

Overall, then, GeoCities can be seen as a precursor to social networking platforms such as Facebook. It provided a standardized and reliable platform for the development of personal homepages or profiles, even by users with comparatively limited technical skills; consequently, it had considerable success in attracting a large user base. Later platforms would add social networking and continuous update functionalities into the mix, but in the mid-1990s these features were still beyond the technical capabilities of the fledgling World Wide Web.

Phase 3: Dreamweaver and the Return to Individualism

The provision of standard website design tools, however rudimentary, by services such as GeoCities gave a first indication of future possibilities. New impulses for web design were provided with the launch of the first version of (offline) web authoring software Dreamweaver. Launched by Macromedia in late 1997, and acquired by Adobe a decade later, it would grow to become a comprehensive web authoring solution, but even in its early versions it provided basic WYSIWYG (what you see is what you get) editing functionality, enabling users without HTML skills to develop reasonably clean web pages.

The emergence of Dreamweaver as a content authoring tool coincided with another important shift. The second wave of search engines, led by Google, which first launched in 1996, now provided a considerably more comprehensive coverage of web content than the labor-intensive web directories of the mid-1990s (Halavais 2009). In turn, this meant that joining centralized hosting solutions such as GeoCities became less important; even sites hosted on comparatively obscure domains now became easily discoverable. During the second half of the 1990s, a growing number of individuals and groups registered their own domain names, rather than operating from a subdomain or directory on a web hoster's site. Hosting providers remained important, but stepped into the background and allowed their clients to redirect user-owned domain names to hosted web spaces (see also Chapter 17 in this volume, by Indrek Ibrus).

The combined result of these shifts was a return to a greater diversity of hand-crafted, Dreamweaver-authored websites across a broad range of individual domains, in a remote echo of the first phase of web-based homepages. However, link directories became less important as "Googling" emerged as a synonym for "finding" as and when required (see also Chapter 15 in this volume, by Alex Halavais). Owing to the greater flexibility afforded by later versions of Dreamweaver and similar graphical web authoring tools, the homepages of the late 1990s also contained a broader range of text, images, and basic audiovisual features than the hand-coded pages of web pioneers earlier in the decade. Dreamweaver, in turn, also introduced its own stylistic idiosyncrasies: an overreliance on the HTML "table" element for page formatting, for example, and a preponderance of link buttons and other "rollover" graphics.

Later versions of the software foreshadowed a major shift in web design and personal presence online, making the first steps toward interfacing with online databases to enable the delivery of dynamic web content. Even if supported by their web hosts, such functionality would have been well beyond the design abilities of most average Dreamweaver users. As dynamic and searchable web content became an increasingly desirable feature for websites, the balance from individual websites to standard site providers shifted once again.

Phase 4: Blogs and the Shift toward Web 2.0

Designing websites around a database backend that holds the core content enables the development of entirely different structural logics and user interfaces (Manovich 2001). Access to page content can be provided according to a range of ordering principles, for example by title, keywords, date, or author; content becomes easily searchable; and page design and content are decoupled from one another, so that the same material can be accessed in a variety of interface contexts. Further, if database backend and website interface are maintained by a third-party provider, users are able simply to concentrate on content authoring. This reduces the required level of technical skills even more, and thus broadens the potential number of users who can become active as content creators.

Emerging in the late 1990s and gaining popular recognition during the early years of the new millennium, blogs were the first type of mainstream website to be built around a database-driven backend (Gurak et al. 2004; Bruns and Jacobs 2006). Arguably, blogs took over from hand-crafted websites as the preferred form of personal homepage during these years. In doing so, they changed the underlying logic of homepages (Walker Rettberg 2008): earlier, static websites were comparatively simple repositories of personal and professional information, updated irregularly with considerable effort, and organized into a collection of interlinked pages. By contrast, the core defining feature of blogs is their reverse chronological organization: they are built around a stream of more or less regular activity updates by the blogger, and relegate background information to a number of secondary "about" pages, usually available from a sidebar on the main blog page. Using blog hosting solutions, such as LiveJournal or Blogger, to set up and operate a blog required little more of the author than to sign up, fill in their details, choose from a selection of basic design templates, and begin writing blog posts in a web-based or offline WYSIWYG editor. Consequently, a significant number of blogs were established (but often abandoned again) within a very short timeframe; in some cases they reacted immediately to breaking news events such as the September 11, 2001 attacks in New York and Washington DC, or the Hurricane Katrina disaster in New Orleans (Bruns 2006).

Importantly, blogs and other regularly updated websites popularized the concept of the update feed, provided for example in RSS (really simple syndication) format, containing titles, excerpts, and links to the latest updates posted to a blogger's website (Rothenberg 2003). Using aggregator tools such as Google Reader, readers were now able to be alerted to new updates on a large number of their favorite sites, without having to visit each of these sites regularly. RSS feeds also enabled general search engines and also specialized blog search and aggregation providers such as Technorati to track the latest content updates in the blogosphere in close to real time. New content discovery in previous phases depended on search engines returning to an existing site to reindex its latest contents, but now they could be actively informed about the new material they needed to add to their indices (Lasica 2003).

Earlier phases of development had been characterized by a comparative absence of reliable content indices. But now the very abundance of discoverable content meant that individual blogs could find it difficult to become known among their peers. As a result, the "links list" made a reappearance in the form of "blogrolls" and "webrings": respectively, individual lists of a blogger's favorite blog sites, or coordinated directories of thematically or otherwise related blogging communities. Such elements – usually placed in a sidebar or static page on the blog itself – constitute a further precursor to the social networking platforms that emerged during the late 2000s: they can be understood as simple, user-generated attempts to articulate the blogger's own network of friends and peers. Indeed, early and even some recent studies of national and international blogospheres explicitly attempted to map the social networks formed through blogroll interlinkages (see e.g., Adamic and Glance 2005; Park and Thelwall 2008; Highfield 2009).

Later developments reacted once again against the relatively limited scope for blog personalization provided by these standardized blog platforms. A greater range of design templates for hosting solutions was added, as were various open-source and commercial alternatives, which users were able to install on their own servers or on commercial content-hosting platforms. WordPress, for example, both operates the ready-to-use blog host WordPress.com and provides an open-source blogging package for installation on the user's own server via WordPress.org. Many more recent blogging solutions advance well beyond blogging itself (at its simplest, the reverse-chronological display of timestamped posts) and instead serve as fully featured content-management systems. As a result, they combine the ease of use and structural organization of blogging with the flexibility and diversity of applications found in more conventional, custom-designed websites (albeit only to users who have the design and development capabilities required to make full use of them).

Phase 5: Social Networking – You Are What You Tweet

Since the mid-2000s, development has continued to shift the balance further from personal presence to social networking online. Blogs and other forms of personal web 2.0 sites mainly continued to support the establishment of a homepage-style site containing personal information and updates, but social networking sites such as Facebook and Twitter embed this personal presence directly in a wide and complex network of peer-to-peer "friendships." In this transition from personal to social, the early social network MySpace, launched in 2003, can be placed at the mid-point. It provided scope for users to modify and customize their personal homepages within the MySpace system, to the extent that a very broad range of styles and designs was able to coexist on the platform. It also introduced significant functionality for individual users to connect with, befriend, and exchange messages with one another.

By contrast, the current global leader in social networking sites, Facebook, launched in 2004, offers a much more streamlined interface that provides far fewer opportunities for users to modify the look and feel of the site. Users can change their personal information and nominate affiliations and interests, as well as connect various on-site applications to their personal profile, but they have no control over fundamental design choices. However, Facebook's functionality for declaring and describing various forms of friendship and acquaintance between users, and for forming groups and communities around specific shared interests and concerns, far surpasses that of MySpace. This combination of social flexibility and streamlined, reliable user interface design can therefore be seen as an important factor in Facebook's unprecedented success.

Twitter, in turn, reduces the on-site personal profiles of its users to an even more rudimentary remnant. A profile image, a character-limited personal blurb, and a customizable page background and color scheme are all that remain available to them to express any permanent personal presence. Instead, on Twitter, users *are* what they tweet and who they connect to. The core indications of their personal identity are what they have posted recently, what other users they follow, and which users follow them. Indeed, even these connections are severely simplified, as "friendship" becomes a binary choice that cannot be qualified any further. Considered in isolation, then, Twitter is a social network between communicative entities who are defined almost entirely by their communicative acts alone (Bruns 2011).

Future Developments in the Personal/Social Dynamic

Having moved beyond the homepage, and in some cases having abandoned it altogether, individual personal presence is now spread across a range of homes, and exists in the interweavings between them. For example, although they are deprived of any detailed on-site profile, Twitter users can include a permanent link to their homepage, blog, or Facebook page. Blogs and other personal sites can embed the user's latest Twitter or Facebook updates, as well as the most recent materials posted to other social media spaces from del.icio.us to YouTube. The proliferation of social networking spaces has continued, as witnessed by the 2011 launch of Google's second attempt at social networking, Google+. Given the continued existence of a number of previous platforms, ranging from hand-coded homepage hold-outs to by now well-established personal and professional bloggers, it is clear that no one such website or platform can now be considered in isolation.

Such developments are directly encouraged by the providers of leading social media platforms, which offer embeddable Facebook "like" and Twitter "tweet this" buttons. Additionally, the developers of multiplatform client tools enable users to post the same or similar content to a wide variety of social networking platforms. Such functionality both enables and complicates the maintenance of different personas on different platforms, from (for example) the personal interest blog through the social network of friends on Facebook to a professional presence on Twitter: it allows users to direct specific forms of content only to selected groups of recipients, but at the same time it establishes an intricately interconnected media ecology in which a hermetic separation of one's public from one's private self is ever more difficult to uphold.

Considering the oscillation between customized, personalized sites and standardized, streamlined spaces that we have observed during the phases outlined above, we may next expect to see a renewed push toward greater diversity once again, beyond the "one size fits all" models exemplified by Facebook and Twitter. A range of boutique social networking platforms, such as Ning, has already emerged. They enable smaller communities of users to develop a shared space for personal profiles and social connection outside the leading generic social networks. At the same time, however, the embeddable functionality now offered by market leaders such as Facebook and Twitter may be seen as an attempt to fend off any potential exodus of users, or decline of participation in the generic networks, that may result from the emergence of off-site alternatives. Increasingly, the embeddable functionality that these generic sites are beginning to offer will enable them to reposition themselves as backend network providers to apparently independent sites, in much the same way that YouTube is a backend content host whose videos may be embedded into almost any other website.

The payoff to Facebook and Twitter of such developments would be that they remain central repositories of user-generated content, social network connections, and profiles. The benefit to users would be that participation need no longer take place only through the websites of these generic social networks (or through client software that connects to them). It would further complicate the maintenance of different professional and personal identities, however, and obscure the activity trails that participation on specific third-party websites may generate on these generic social networking platforms.

A fundamental criticism of such developments, in fact, is that they further enshrine the so far largely unpoliced capture of personal profiles and social networking activities by private enterprise. Facebook's fundamental business model is to monetize the "social graph" that its users have built. (The same is true of Twitter, to the extent that it has developed a business model at all.) But to do this necessarily conflicts with users' rights to privacy and their ownership of their personal information and content. By becoming a universal social networking backend layer for the World Wide Web, a service such as Facebook would cement its position even further, making even more difficult the development of alternatives or the policing and control of how personal data about users' actions and identities are used. This, of course, is not a problem limited to Facebook alone, but applies to any social networking platform with ambitions to take its place.

This brief overview of the historical trajectory from the early hand-coded homepages through a range of intermediate solutions to the large social networking platforms of today shows a number of contradictory forces at work, then. The desire for greater control over the design and structure of individual sites conflicts with the benefits of ease of use and standardized user interfaces that are available from mainstream platforms. Individual profiles, as central spaces for expressing and displaying personal identity, variously stand out from or are swamped by large-scale social networks for marking "friendship" and communicating with other users as nodes in the wider network. The need to maintain control and ownership of personal data and content clashes with the drive to share and exchange information in order to participate fully in social networking environments. Individual, fragmentary personae for specific communicative purposes and social contexts are difficult to maintain in an increasingly interconnected media ecology. These contradictions are unresolved; they are addressed mainly by developing technological platforms, communicative spaces, and personal strategies that position themselves a little closer to one or the other end of any one of these opposing values. Future evolution beyond the phases of development outlined here, then, is just as likely to return to the communicative models exemplified during those phases as it is to explore new combinations of these possible settings. The inherently irresolvable nature of the conflicts that lie at the heart of the challenge of balancing personal and social identity will also ensure that no one solution will remain uncontested for long. This remains a thoroughly dynamic, changeable space.

Notes

1. www.w3.org/History/19921103-hypertext/hypertext/WWW/TheProject.html.

References

Adamic, L. and Glance, N. (2005) "The Political Blogosphere and the 2004 U.S. Election: Divided They Blog." *Blogpulse* (March 4). http://nielsen-online.com/downloads/us/buzz/wp_PoliticalBlogosphere_Glance_2004.pdf.

Berners-Lee, T. (2000) *Weaving the Web: The Original Design and Ultimate Destiny of the World Wide Web*. New York: HarperCollins.

Bruns, A. (2006) "The Practice of News Blogging" in A. Bruns and J. Jacobs, eds., *Uses of Blogs*. New York: Peter Lang, pp. 11–22.

Bruns, A. (2011) "*Ad Hoc* Innovation by Users of Social Networks: The Case of Twitter." Paper presented at the Challenge Social Innovation Conference, Vienna, Austria (September 19–21). http://snurb.info/files/2011/Ad%20Hoc%20Innovation%20by%20Users%20of%20Social%20Networks.pdf.

Bruns, A. and Jacobs, J., eds. (2006) *Uses of Blogs*. New York: Peter Lang.

Fernback, J. (2004) "Community as Commodity: Empowerment and Consumerism on the Web" in M. Consalvo, N. Baym, J. Hunsinger, et al., eds., *Internet Research Annual: Selected Papers from the Association of Internet Researchers, 2000–2002, Volume 1*. New York: Peter Lang, pp. 224–230.

Gurak, L.J., Antonijevic, S., Johnson, L., et al., eds. (2004) *Into the Blogosphere: Rhetoric, Community, and Culture of Weblogs*. http://blog.lib.umn.edu/blogosphere/visual_blogs.html.

Halavais, A. (2009) *Search Engine Society*. Cambridge: Polity.

Highfield, T.J. (2009) "Which Way Up? Reading and Drawing Maps of the Blogosphere." *Ejournalist*, 9(1), 99–114.

Lasica, J.D. (2003) "News that Comes to You: RSS Feeds Offer Info-Warriors a Way to Take the Pulse of Hundreds of Sites." *Online Journalism Review* (January 23). www.ojr.org/ojr/lasica/1043362624.php.

Manovich, L. (2001) *The Language of New Media*. Cambridge, MA: MIT Press.

Park, H.W. and Thelwall, M. (2008) "Developing Network Indicators for Ideological Landscapes from the Political Blogosphere in South Korea." *Journal of Computer-Mediated Communication*, 10(4), 856–879.

Reid, R.H. (1997) *Architects of the Web: 1000 Days That Built the Future of Business*. New York: John Wiley & Sons.

Rheingold, H. (2000 [1993]) *The Virtual Community: Homesteading on the Electronic Frontier.* Cambridge, MA: MIT Press.

Rothenberg, M. (2003) "Weblogs, Metadata, and the Semantic Web." Paper presented at the Association of Internet Researchers Conference, Toronto, Canada (October 16).

Shechmeister, M. (2009) "Ghost Pages: A Wired.com Farewell to GeoCities." *Wired.com* (November 3). www.wired.com/rawfile/2009/11/geocities.

Walker Rettberg, J. (2008) *Blogging.* Cambridge: Polity.

Knowledge and New Generations

30

The New Media Toolkit

Mark Pesce

Introduction: The Age of Connection

Anthropologists have appropriated the word "toolkit" to describe the suite of technologies that accompanies a particular grouping of humans. Fifty thousand years ago, this toolkit would have encompassed stone implements of various sorts, together with items fashioned from bone and perhaps some early fabrics. By five thousand years ago, the toolkit had exploded with innovations in agriculture, urbanization, transport, and culture. Five hundred years ago, this toolkit began to look recognizably modern, with the printing press, gunpowder, steel, and massive warships. Fifty years ago we could find much of our common culture within that toolkit, with one notable exception, an innovation that didn't begin to appear in any numbers until just five years ago. Identified by the decidedly vague words "new media" (justifying McLuhan's (1964) observation that the first content of a new medium is the medium it obsolesces, down to its name), this newest toolkit promises to restructure human cultural relations as broadly as agriculturalization, urbanization, or industrialization.

The roots of the current transformation lie within the urban revolution, the gathering of humanity into cities, a process nearly ten thousand years old yet only halfway complete. The tribal model of human organization – coeval with the emergence of *Homo sapiens sapiens* – likely began to fracture under the stresses introduced by the emergence of agricultural practices. Agriculture leads toward sedentary populations with higher birth rates, and so produced greater concentrations of humanity than had theretofore been sustainable. These population centers rapidly transcended the human capability for modeling peer behavior as expressed in Dunbar's Number (Dunbar 1992), and in so doing drove innovations in the human toolkit intended to conserve stability and safety within an environment of strangers. Before the urban revolution, human culture was ruled by custom; afterward, it became ruled by law, and all that law implies: law-giving authorities, law-enforcing police, courts, jails,

A Companion to New Media Dynamics, First Edition. Edited by John Hartley, Jean Burgess, and Axel Bruns.
© 2013 John Wiley & Sons, Ltd. Published 2015 by John Wiley & Sons, Ltd.

and lawyers. This gap between custom and law is the most visible discontinuity between hunter-gatherer cultures and agricultural–urban civilization, forming a source of constant irritation between them.

Marshal McLuhan (1964) first noted the retribalizing effect of electric technologies; they collapse space to a point, effectively recreating the continuous, ambient (aural) awareness of the tribe. The tribe is completely connected. All of its members have direct access to one another; there is little hierarchy – instead, there is an intricate set of social relations. Everyone thoroughly understands their own place, and that position is constantly reinforced by the other members of the tribe. Tribal society is static, which is to say stable, over long stretches of time – at least tens of thousands of years.

Urban society is dynamic; the principal actor is the individual (often backed by an extended family unit), who works to build and extend a set of social relations that improve his own circumstances (in the language of sociobiology, selection fitness). As a consequence of the continuous actions of a dynamic network of actors, the history of the city is the history of crisis. Only a very few civilizations have maintained any sort of stability for a period of a more than a few hundred years. Egypt, China, India, Rome, Maya, and Inca each experienced dizzying climbs to power and terrifying collapses into ruin. The uncertainties of the postmodern period, with its underlying apocalyptic timbre, reflect several thousand years of inevitable, unavoidable rise and fall.

The Age of Connection now takes its place alongside these earlier epochs in humanity's story. We are being retribalized, in the midst of rising urbanization. The dynamic individuality of the city confronts the static conformity of the tribe. This basic tension forms the fuel of twenty-first-century culture, and will continue to generate both heat and light for at least the next generation. Human behavior, human beliefs, and human relations are all reorganizing themselves around connectivity. It is here, therefore, that we must begin our analysis of the toolkit.

Hyperconnectivity

How many people can any given person on Earth reach directly? Before the urban revolution, that value had a strict upper bound in Dunbar's Number. This number sets an functional limit on the troupe (tribe) size of *Homo sapiens sapiens*. Human units larger than this fragment and bifurcate along lines of relation and communication. One tribe grows from stability into instability, and fissions into two. In the transition to the city, humanity developed other mechanisms for communication to compensate for our lack of cognitive capacity; the birth of writing proceeded directly from the informational and connective pressure of dense communities.

The city is as much a network as a residence, perhaps even more so. It comprises neighborhoods – recapitulating the tribal within the urban – that, grouped together, form the larger conurbation of the metropolis. Each of these neighborhoods is tightly connected (the older the city, the older the neighborhood, the more likely this is to be true) and each maintains connectivity with near neighborhoods and the greater urban whole. Where one might have direct and immediate connectivity to 150 members of a tribe, one has some degree of mediated connectivity to thousands or tens of thousands within a city. It is possible to get a message to the other side of town through a chain of intermediaries, the "degrees of separation" explored by Stanley Milgram (1967).

Until the modern era, human connectivity stopped at the city's gates. Only a very few powerful individuals or institutions, able to afford their own messengers, could expect to have connectivity beyond the confines of a given urban area. Postal services extended this connectivity within the boundaries of then-emerging nation-states, at a price that made connectivity affordable to the new working classes. The telegraph gave connectivity global reach, and collapsed the time for message transmission from months to minutes. Yet the telegraph was highly centralized; until the widespread adoption of the telephone, about 50 years later, direct and instantaneous person-to-person communication remained impractical.

The landline telephone provided direct, instantaneous, global connectivity, but *to a place, not a person.* If you are not in range of a landline telephone, you gain no benefit from its connectivity. Even so, the lure of that connectivity was enough that it drew the landline into nearly a billion offices and dwellings throughout the twentieth century. The landline telephone colonized all of the Earth's surface where its infrastructure could be afforded. This created a situation (reflective of so many others) where there were connected "haves" and unconnected "have nots."

The mobile telephone spreads connectivity directly to the person. The mobile creates the phenomenon of *direct human addressability.* The mobile is an inherently personal device; each mobile and SIM are associated with a single person. With this single innovation, the gap is spanned between tribal and urban organizational forms. Everyone is directly connected, as in the tribe, but in unknowably vast numbers, as in the city.

The past decade has seen an accelerating deployment of direct human address-ability. There were predicted to be roughly six billion mobile subscribers as of June 2011 (Wireless Intelligence 2010). Roughly 10 percent of these individuals had more than one subscription, a phenomenon becoming commonplace in the richer corners of the planet. This meant that there were roughly 5.4 billion directly addressable individuals on the planet, individuals who could be reached with the correct series of numbers.

The level of direct human addressability of the species *in toto* can be calculated as the ratio of total number of subscribers to total world population: $5\,400\,000\,000 : 6\,900\,000\,000$, or 0.7826. As we move deeper into the twenty-first century, this figure will approach 1.0: all individuals, rich or poor, young or old, postgraduate or illiterate, will be directly connected through the network. This type of connectivity is not simply unprecedented, nor just a unique feature in human history. This is the kind of qualitative change that leads to a fundamental reorganization in human culture. This, the logical culmination in the growth in human connectivity from the aural tribe to the landline telephone, can be termed *hyperconnectivity*, because it represents the absolute amplification of all the pre-extant characteristics in human communication, extending them to ubiquity and speed-of-light instantaneity.

Every person now can connect directly with well over three-quarters of the human race. We may not choose to do so, but our networks of human connections overlap (as Milgram demonstrated), so we always have the option of jumping through our network of connections, short-circuiting the various degrees of separation, to make contact. Or we can simply wait as this connectivity, coursing through the networks, brings everyone in the world to us.

Hyperdistribution

What happens after we are all connected? For an answer to this, we must look back to the original human network, language. Our infinitely flexible linguistic capability allows us to put words and descriptions to anything real or imagined, transmitting experience from mind to mind. Language allows us to forge, maintain, and strengthen social bonds (Dunbar 1998) in a mechanism analogous to the "grooming behaviors" of other primates. The voices of others remind us that we belong to a cohesive social unit, that we are safe and protected.

Most mammals have a repertoire of vocal signals they use to signal danger. Humans can be incredibly precise, and, although this is important in moments of immediate peril, language serves principally as the vehicle of human cultural transmission: don't eat this plant; don't walk across this river; don't talk with your mouth full. This linguistic transmission gives human culture a depth unknown in other animals. Language is a distribution medium, a mechanism to replicate the experience of one person throughout a community.

This replication activity confers an enormous selection advantage: communities who share what they know will have increased their selection fitness versus communities that do not, so this behavioral tendency toward sharing becomes an epigenetic marker of the human species, persistent and conserved throughout its entirety. As a consequence, any culture that develops effective new mechanisms for knowledge-sharing will have greater selection fitness than others that do not, forcing those relatively less-fit cultures to either adopt the innovation, in order to preserve themselves, or find themselves pushed to the extreme margins of human existence.

As a result, two selection pressures push humans toward linguistic connectivity: the desire of individuals to connect for their own safety and the desire of the community to increase its group selection fitness,[1] for its own long-term viability. These twin selection pressures make humans extraordinarily social, the "social instinct" part of the essential human template. Humans do not need to be taught to share knowledge of the world around them. This comes freely and instinctively. Socialization places normative constraints around this sharing. Such constraints are both amplified and removed in the presence of hyperconnectivity.

Where humans are hyperconnected via mobile, a recapitulation of primate "grooming behaviors" appears almost immediately. Mizuko Ito, in *Personal,*

Portable, Pedestrian: Mobile Phones in Japanese Life (Ito et al. 2000), noted the behavior of Japanese teenagers sending hundreds of text messages a day to a close circle of friends, messages lacking significant extrinsic meaning and serving simply as a reassurance of presence, even at distance; Ito termed this phenomenon "co-presence." The behavior Ito observed among Japanese teenagers is now ubiquitous among teenagers within the developed world: American teenagers send well over 3000 text messages per month (Lenhart 2012).

Hyperconnected via mobile and perhaps via electronic mail, we repeatedly witness a familiar phenomenon: someone new to the medium begins to "over-share," sending along bad jokes, cute photographs of furry animals, and the occasional chain letter. This is the sharing instinct caught up and amplified by hyperconnectivity, producing the capability to send something everywhere, instantaneously: *hyperdistribution.*

Embarrassing photographs and treacherous text messages ("sexting" and damaging audio recordings) forwarded over and over through all the mechanisms of hyperconnectivity are examples of hyperdistribution. When any digital artifact encounters a hyperconnected human, that artifact is disseminated through their network, unless it is so objectionable that it is censored, or so pedestrian it provokes no response. The human instinct is to share that which piques our interest with those to whom we are connected, to reinforce our relations and to increase our credibility within our networks of relations (both recapitulations of the dual nature of the original human behaviors of sharing).

The instinctual sharing behavior of humans remains as strong as ever before, but has extended to encompass communities beyond those within range of our voices. We share without respect to distance. Our voices can be heard throughout the world, provided what we say provokes those we maintain relations with. Provocation carries with it the threat of ostracism; if a provocation proves unwarranted, relations will be damaged, and further provocations ignored. This functions as a selection pressure on hyperconnected sharing, which over time tends toward ever-greater salience.

Hyperintelligence

As far back as we can look into prehistory, concentrated acts of knowledge-sharing within a specific domain have been framed by ritual practices. Indigenous Australians continue the Paleolithic traditions of "women's business" and "men's business," which refer to ritually constrained bodies of knowledge, intended to be shared only within the context of a specific community of ritually purified (and thereby connected) individuals. These domains characteristically reflect gender-specific cultural practices: typically, women communicate knowledge of plants and gathering practices, while men invest themselves in the specifics of navigation and the hunt. These two knowledge domains are strongly defended by taboo; "secret women's business" is forbidden to men (and ritually impure women), and vice versa.

The association between domain knowledge and ritual has persisted through to the present day. From at least the Late Antique period, a system of guilds carefully guarded access to specific knowledge domains. Venetian glassblowers, Japanese bladesmiths, and Chinese silk weavers all protected their knowledge domains – and consequent monopolies – with a combination of legal and ritual practices, law, and custom. In preurban cultures, knowledge creates capability; in urban cultures, that capability is multiplied. Those who possess knowledge also hold power. The desire to conserve that power led the guilds to become increasingly zealous in the defense of their knowledge domains, their "secrets of the craft."

The advent of Gutenberg's moveable-type printing press made it effectively impossible to keep secrets in perpetuity. One individual could pen a single revealing text and within a few months all of Europe would learn what they knew. Secrets were no longer enough to preserve the sanctity of knowledge domains. Ritual cast a longer shadow, and in this guise, as the modern protector of the mysteries, the university became the companion to the professional association, indoctrinating then licensing candidates for entry into the professions. The professional associations of medicine, law, engineering, architecture, and so on emerged from this transition from the guilds into modernity. These professional associations exist for one reason: they assign place, either within the boundaries of the organization or outside it. An unlicensed doctor, a lawyer who has not "passed the bar," and an uncredentialed architect all represent modern instances of violations of ritual structures that have been with us for at least fifty thousand years.

Hyperconnectivity does not acknowledge the presence of these ritual structures; humans connect directly, immediately, and pervasively, without respect to any of the cultural barriers to contact. There is neither inside nor outside. The entire space of human connection collapses to a point, as everyone connects directly to everyone else, without mediation. This hyperconnectivity leads to hyperdistributed sharing, first at random, then with ever-increasing levels of salience.

This condition tends to produce a series of feedbacks: hyperdistribution of salient information increases the potential and actual effectiveness of any individual within the network of hyperdistribution, which increases their reliance on these networks. These networks of hyperdistributed knowledge-sharing tend to reify as a given network's constituents put these hyperdistributed materials to work. Both Kenyan farmers and Kerala fishermen (*The Economist* 2007) quickly became irrevocable devotees of the mobile handset, which provided them with accurate and timely information about competing market prices for their goods. Once hyperdistribution acquires a focal point, and becomes synonymous with a knowledge domain, it crosses over into *hyperintelligence*: the dedicated, hyperconnected hyperdistribution of domain-specific knowledge.

In a thoroughly hyperconnected environment, behaviors are pervasively observed. If these behaviors are successful, they will be copied by others, who are also pervasively observed. The behavior itself hyperdistributes throughout the network. This is a behavioral analog to hyperintelligence: *hypermimesis*. The development of "SMS language" is one example of hypermimesis; as terms are added to the language (which may be specific to a subculture), they are propagated pervasively, and are adopted almost immediately.

Hyperempowerment

A group of hyperconnected individuals choosing to hyperdistribute their knowledge around an identified domain can engender hyperintelligence. That hyperintelligence is not a static actor. To be in relation to a hyperintelligence necessarily means using the knowledge provided by that hyperintelligence where, when, and as needed. The more comprehensive the hyperintelligence, the greater the range of possible uses and potential effects.

Perhaps the outstanding example of a hyperintelligence, Wikipedia, provides only modest advantages in those developed parts of the world with ready access to knowledge. Yet in South Africa or India, where such knowledge resources did not exist, Wikipedia catapults individuals into a vastly expanded set of potential capabilities. Actions that would have been taken in ignorance are now wholly informed by the presence of hyperintelligence and are, as a consequence, different and likely more effective. This is a perfect echo of the introduction of mobile telephony: in the developed world the mobile remains nice but rarely essential; in the developing world it is the difference between thriving and subsistence. Hyperintelligence is a capability amplifier.

Individuals are not alone in their relationship to a hyperintelligence; it is the product of the hyperdistribution activities of a hyperconnected network of people. These activities tend to improve through time, as the network amplifies its own capabilities. These two levels of hyperintelligence, individual and collective, produce radical transformations in both individual power and the power of hyperconnected individuals as a network. This *hyperempowerment* is hyperintelligence in action, the directed application of the knowledge and capabilities provided via hyperintelligence.

Hyperempowered individuals and networks are asymmetrically empowered relative to any individual or group of individuals (whether as a collective, an organization, or an institution) not similarly hyperempowered. In any exchange, hyperempowered actors will always be more effective in achieving their aims, because in every situation they know more and know better how to act on what they know. The existence of hyperempowerment simultaneously creates a new class of selection pressure; as various social and cultural configurations interact with hyperempowered individuals and networks, they will be selected against unless they themselves use the techniques of hyperconnectivity, hyperdistribution, and hyperintelligence to engender their own hyperempowerment. *Once any one actor achieves hyperempowerment, all who interact with that actor must either hyperempower themselves or face extinction.* This leads to a cascading series of hyperempowerments, as hyperempowered networks interact with networks that are not hyperempowered, and force those networks toward hyperempowerment.

Dissecting Hyperempowerment

Two examples from 2011 illustrate the spontaneous emergence of hyperempowered polities from the necessary preconditions of hyperconnectivity, hyperdistribution, and hyperintelligence. In the wake of the June 15, 2011 riots in Vancouver, sparked by the loss of the Stanley Cup ice hockey championship, Vancouverites – shocked by the behavior of some of their civic brethren – began to pool their footage of the riots. This footage included still photography from newspapers, videography from television stations, and many thousands of images snapped by mobiles and uploaded to such sharing sites as Facebook and Flickr.

The embarrassment experienced by Vancouverites acted a catalyst, a salience filter around which a hyperintelligence grew, a directed form of sharing with the express goal of exposing the rioters. Those rioters presumed the anonymity of the mob would shield their activities. In a hyperconnected culture, such anonymity is nearly impossible to achieve. (In Canada's major cities, mobile subscription rates exceed 90 percent.) Images of these rioters, hyperdistributed throughout the community of embarrassed citizens, quickly led to the identification of many of them.

Once the rioters had been identified – and those identifications hyperdistributed – a hyperconnected community began to confront the rioters, demanding they turn themselves in to the police. Some of those identified have been harassed, others fired from their jobs. One prominent Vancouver family fled the city in fear after one family member was identified as a rioter (Ting 2011).

This situation perfectly frames a situation of asymmetric hyperempowerment. The embarrassed citizenry used the new toolkit to dramatically multiply their effectiveness in bringing vandals to account for their activities. The vandals had not themselves adapted to the opportunities afforded by the new toolkit, and therefore were completely overwhelmed. The future will see less asymmetry as both sides employ the new toolkit. Vandals could flood the channels of hyperdistribution with false or irrelevant data (as state actors sometimes do when threatened with leaks, or corporations when threatened with lawsuits). They could seek to disrupt any emergent hyperintelligence, snuffing these out before they can effectively self-organize. Finally, they could form a hyperempowered network of their own, dedicated to blunting advances from any competing hyperintelligence. *Bellum omnium contra omnes* (Hobbes 1983).

The second and converse counter-example comes from another civil disturbance, the London riots of March 26, 2011. Perhaps half a million participated in the protest march, with a smaller number engaging in direct actions, such as the vandalism of shops in the West End, Trafalgar Square, and Nelson's Column. The London Metropolitan Police, well-versed in protest management, have developed a technique known as "kettling," which corrals the protesters within bounds determined by the police. Kettling relies on informational asymmetry: the police must have a better situational awareness than the protesters, otherwise the protesters would effectively be able to evade the police.

The UK has a 122 percent mobile subscription rate – true hyperconnectivity. Before the protest march, a group of software engineers created a smartphone application, Sukey, designed to capture and hyperdistribute information about police activities and presence within a particular geographical region, providing broad situational awareness for those using the application (Stott 2011). The need to stay free from official interference acted as the catalyst for a temporary hyperintelligence (lasting only for the twelve hours of the protest) during which the protestors were consistently better informed about police movements than the police themselves, and thereby able to evade most kettling operations (Aron 2011).

In this example, asymmetric hyperempowerment gave protesters the upper hand against the authority of the state. The state, when sufficiently threatened, will shut down access to the mobile networks, in an attempt to disrupt any emergent hyperempowerment by attacking it at the root. This was a recurring feature in the Jasmine Revolutions in North Africa and the Middle East (Richtel 2011). Rather than adopting the new toolkit, the state seeks to deny access to that toolkit to any entity posing a threat to its existence. Such a reactive strategy is not effective: the opposing force uses its hyperintelligence, adapting quickly and then hyperdistributing those adaptations, repurposing media to meet the requirements of the toolkit (Kofman 2011). As of the time of writing, no state actor has adopted the toolkit in response to the existential threats of hyperempowered polities. Adopting the toolkit would of necessity transform the state beyond hierarchy and beyond recognition.

Conclusion

Hyperconnectivity, hyperdistribution, hyperintelligence, and hyperempowerment have propelled human culture to the midst of a psychosocial phase transition, similar to a crystallization phase in a supersaturated solution, a "revolution" that makes the agricultural, urban, and industrial revolutions seem, in comparison, lazy and incomplete. Twenty years ago, none of this toolkit existed nor was even intimated. Twenty years from now it will be pervasively and ubiquitously distributed, inextricably bound up in our self-definition as human beings. We have always been the product of our relationships, and now our relationships are redefining us.

Notes

1. The author is aware that group selection is a hotly debated topic within the field of sociobiology, but contends that it is impossible to understand highly social species such as *Homo sapiens sapiens* without the principle of group selection.

References

Aron, J. (2011) "Police Can't Keep Up with Tech-Savvy Protesters." *New Scientist* (February 9). www.newscientist.com/blogs/onepercent/2011/02/police-forces-in-the-uk.html.

Dunbar, R. (1992) "Neocortex Size as a Constraint on Group Size in Primates." *Journal of Human Evolution*, 22, 469–493.

Dunbar, R. (1998) *Gossip, Grooming and the Evolution of Language*. Cambridge, MA: Harvard University Press.

The Economist (2007) "To do with the Price of Fish" (May 10). www.economist.com/node /9149142?story_id=9149142.

Hobbes, T. (1983 [1642]) *De Cive*. Oxford: Clarendon.

Ito, M., Okabe, D., and Matsuda, M, eds. (2000) *Personal, Portable, Pedestrian: Mobile Phones in Japanese Life*. Cambridge, MA: MIT Press.

Kofman, J. (2011) "Libya's 'Love Revolution': Muslim Dating Site Seeds Protest." *ABC News* (February 24). http://abcnews.go.com/Technology/muslim-dating-site-madawi-seeds -libyan-revolution/story?id=12981938.

Lenhart, A. (2012) "Teens, Smartphones & Texting." Pew Research Center report. www.pewinternet.org/Reports/2012/Teens-and-smartphones.aspx.

McLuhan, M. (1964) *Understanding Media: The Extensions of Man*. New York: McGraw-Hill.

Milgram, S. (1967) "The Small World Problem." *Psychology Today*, May, 60–67.

Richtel, M. (2011) "Egypt Cuts Off Most Internet and Cell Service." *New York Times* (January 28). www.nytimes.com/2011/01/29/technology/internet/29cutoff.html.

Stott, P. (2011) "Sukey Takes the Kettle Off." *I Intend to Escape ... and Come Back* (February 18). http://paulstott.typepad.com/i_intend_to_escape_and_co/2011/02/sukey -takes-the-kettle-off.html.

Ting, I. (2011) "Vancouver's Cyber-Stazi." *Crikey.com.au* (June 29). www.crikey.com.au /2011/06/29/vancouvers-cyber-stasi-a-facebook-counter-revolution.

Wireless Intelligence (2010) "Snapshot: Global Connections Surpass 5 Billion Milestone" (July 8). https://www.wirelessintelligence.com/print/snapshot/100708.pdf.

31

Materiality, Description, and Comparison as Tools for Cultural Difference Analysis

Basile Zimmermann

Working in a Chinese studies department based in Europe, I am often confronted with the challenges not only of working with cultural difference but also of working with the concept of "culture" in itself – one of the most famously difficult concepts in the social sciences and humanities. Further, recent socioeconomic changes in China – and the new media dynamics of the "Chinese Internet" – have produced new situations requiring sociocultural analysis but lacking a clear theoretical or methodological framework. In this chapter I argue that an essential first step in dealing with these issues analytically is to provide an adequate description of them, which can only be achieved by focusing on the *materiality* of the things (websites, platforms, communities) one is considering or comparing. I build on this idea to propose a methodology and a theoretical framework to deal with cultural difference in the context of sociotechnical change, drawing on a single case study based on this approach.

The Circulation of Cultural Waves

Culture, as a scientific concept, is famous for the impossibility of its definition. A recent book (Baldwin et al. 2006) provided no less than 300 definitions, and the authors claimed that these are actually syntheses of an even larger corpus. I will not try to perform yet another authoritative synthesis here, for others have already done this well (see e.g. Kroeber and Kluckhohn 1952; Goody 1992; Borofsky et al. 2001; Baldwin et al. 2006; Triandis 2007), but I would like to quickly point out a few arguments, together with an illustration of where I believe the problem lies and where a solution can be found.

A shortcut through what could otherwise be a very long discussion is to say that "culture" concerns human beings and artifacts, and relates to the ways of life and of thinking of human populations. In common usage, the term's meaning

A Companion to New Media Dynamics, First Edition. Edited by John Hartley, Jean Burgess, and Axel Bruns.
© 2013 John Wiley & Sons, Ltd. Published 2015 by John Wiley & Sons, Ltd.

often has something to do with one of two domains: first, knowledge or art (e.g., when we speak about "a cultured person," "cultural goods," or "the industry of culture") and, second, that which is specific to a group of people and leads to the idea of cultural difference (e.g., "youth culture," or "Chinese culture" compared to "American culture"). Both aspects are of primary concern for the study of new media in a global context.

Drawing on the work of Baldwin et al., an interesting point can be made by considering definitions of culture that are difficult to use for obvious reasons, and then by using a metaphor to sketch a solution. Consider the following three examples:

- Definition 1:

  Culture consists of patterns, explicit and implicit, of and for behavior acquired and transmitted by symbols, constituting the distinctive achievements of human groups, including their embodiments in artifacts; the essential core of culture consists of traditional (i.e., historically derived and selected) ideas and especially their attached values; culture systems may, on the one hand, be considered as products of action, on the other as conditioning elements of further action. (Kroeber and Kluckhohn 1952: 181; see also Baldwin et al. 2006: 188)

- Definition 2:

  For our purposes, we define culture as "the deposit of knowledge, experience, beliefs, values, attitudes, meanings, hierarchies, religion, notions of time, roles, spatial relations, concepts of the universe, and material objects and possessions acquired by a group of people in the course of generations through individual and group striving." (Samovar and Porter 2003: 8; see also Baldwin et al. 2006: 208)

- Definition 3:

  Culture is the sum of stories we tell ourselves about who we are and want to be, individually and collectively. Culture works also as the staging ground of these identity narratives and of our daily routines. Culture comprises and constitutes the places where we live; it is the built environment and the peopled landscape. It also works in the memories that reside in the flesh, from the spark of recognition, an uncanny remembrance, to the dull reflex of forgetting and the dogged reminders inhabiting bone and muscle of a body once stretched in sport, childbirth, dance, labor, lovemaking. Culture works in the traditional sense as well, as sources of cultural wealth – the patrimony of state, nation, people – commissioned and collected through private and public patronage and stored in museums, galleries, film archives, corporate offices, or displayed in parks, plazas, and other public spaces. Finally, culture works in the ordinary sense of work taking place in the factories, studies, warehouses, schoolrooms, and other sites of cultural realization. Culture works where people work building the material fund, or hardware, from which we draw conceptual and narrative sustenance to understand the world. Every phone, computer, television, film stage, tapestry, celluloid strip, videotape, computer disk, semiconductor, printing press, cargo vehicle, or any other imaginable tool or bricks and mortar structure used in the culture industries embodies this culture work. (Maxwell 2001: 1–2; see also Baldwin et al. 2006: 194)

Here is the metaphor: imagine someone who had never heard about atoms and wants to write a definition of "matter." This person might come up with a definition such as

Matter is sometimes solid, sometimes liquid, sometimes in gaseous form, of homogenous or heterogeneous consistence, can be found in a living being but also in inanimate objects or artifacts, on earth or in outer space, and is usually in motion but can sometimes be immobile.

Does this look similar to the above three definitions of culture? I think it does.

One part of the problem we have with the multiple meanings of "culture" is that we miss something smaller – the "atoms" of culture – that can help us deal with the various forms "culture" takes in the real world. The fact that the word is heavily used both in scientific literature and common expression with such a wide range of meanings is an indication that everybody is referring to the same phenomenon but observing it from different angles and in different states. I argue that it is our inability to deal with culture at the micro level that prevents us from grasping it as an object of study. Instead, we end up working at the macro level with abstract entities such as "Chinese culture," "nationalism," "hybridity," and so on, which we then struggle to make sense of empirically. As a result, we often conclude (unsurprisingly) that things are more complicated than expected.

I have elsewhere defined the micro-level parts of culture as "cultural waves" (Zimmermann 2010, forthcoming), which I believe do not relate to matter itself but to the *shape* matter can take. In short, the idea is to use this concept to talk about the shape of matter in the same way we use atoms for its material structure (physicists have long gone beyond atoms but this is another story). The word "wave," inspired by previous research on music and "sound waves," is intended to bring the focus onto the shape of matter rather than matter itself, and to suggest the idea of the transmission of the shape from one material form to another. I use the related concept of "cultural element" (Zimmermann 2010) in order to speak about aggregates of "cultural waves" (e.g., as molecules are for atoms). In this perspective, a word, a picture, a sound, or even the shape of a tree are cultural elements, and as such they are constituted by cultural waves. The main idea is simply to go deeper in our handling of cultural issues, and get closer to their materialities.[1]

In order to study cultural differences, one needs to study the processes of formation, transformation, and dissipation cultural waves are going through. New media provide many illustrations of this argument with the flows of texts, sounds, and images they host and help circulate. As an example, think of a picture of a building, taken with a camera, sent by email to a friend who prints it on a sheet of paper and then gives it to his child to make a drawing based on the printed document. The building is still out in the street and the image is still in the camera, on the computer's hard disc, and on the sheets of paper (the printed one and the drawing); while the signals sent along the cables have already dissipated, what we observe is a shape that has circulated from the building to the child's drawing.

The task of analyzing these circulation processes is what interests me here. It can be achieved by staying close to the *materiality* of the observations one is making. Two key points are (1) *to use fewer abstractions* to express arguments and (2) *to stay as close as one can to a description* of what one has been doing. I aim to avoid abstract vocabulary and instead to focus on the words I have heard or read and the events I have witnessed or taken pictures of, describing them in the most precise way possible, taking as a motto this quote of Bruno Latour:

> The simple fact of recording anything on paper is already an immense transformation that requires as much skill and just as much artifice as painting a landscape or setting up some elaborate biochemical reaction. No scholar should find humiliating the task of sticking to description. This is, on the contrary, the highest and rarest achievement. . . . If a description remains in need of an explanation, it means that it is a bad description. (Latour 2005: 136–137)[2]

Here is an illustration of how one can move from explanations to descriptions. Consider the following two pairs of sentences:

> A. Information and communication technologies are a form of social empowerment for farmers in rural China.

> B. Author X argues that mobiles enable farmers in rural China to organize themselves in ways unseen before.

> A. In July 2008, a new social networking site was spreading among Mainland Chinese net surfers.

> B. In July 2008, while staying at a Chinese friend's place in Beijing, I noticed he was spending hours on a website I had never heard about before.

In each of these two examples, sentences A and B are both saying the same thing but, where the A sentences have a higher degree of abstraction, the B sentences are more concrete and descriptive. In the first pair, A is more difficult to grasp: we don't know what kinds of information and communication technologies and social empowerment the statement means; we only know that there is a correlation between the two. B is more concrete: it talks about a colleague's work on mobile phone technology that says that mobiles are changing the ways in which farmers organize themselves. In the second pair, A hides both the subject and the subjectivity behind the research. B, while it sounds more personal and less "scientific," is actually more precise in the sense that it gives more details about the process that produced the results.

What is needed to perform cultural difference analysis in the context of new media dynamics is a move from A to B sentences when reporting on research. By staying closer to the materiality of the circulation processes, we produce clearer research and avoid the macro-level trap. I will now give an example of a case study in which I apply the cultural waves theoretical framework. I use the methodology presented above, and provide a description written deliberately in the first person. I also discuss how comparison was used as a tool to improve the analysis.

Describing the Chinese Internet

In July 2008, while staying at a Chinese friend's place in Beijing, I noticed he was spending hours on a website I had never heard about before: "Happy Network" (开心网) (kaixin001.com). It was a new social networking site that had been launched a couple of months ago. I registered, and started to take screenshots and notes about what I saw on the web pages. This basic task of logging in and observing the changes in the design of the site and the contents provided by other users quickly became a daily routine.

At that time, a friend working in the advertising industry in Switzerland had told me about social networking sites being "advertisers' paradises" because users could be selected according to their age, gender, taste, habits, and so on, and targeted with appropriate advertisements. Economic incentives were also said to be the main engine behind the launch of social networking sites aimed at the general public (Mark Zuckerberg, the founder of Facebook, was known as the youngest billionaire in the world). Therefore, I chose as a research question: "How is advertising provided on Happy Network?"

This question made sense in that it was large enough for a research project that would probably last several years, and it also seemed to touch on a central aspect of the dynamics of the object chosen. If I could understand the way Happy Network dealt with the question of advertising, I hoped I would be able to understand better other aspects of its development as they would probably relate in one way or another to this first one. New media platforms often work hand in hand with venture capitalists so any question related to the way cash is brought in or out at some point of the development process is always worth asking.

Spending days on a social networking website waiting to see advertisements may be fun (at least it was for me), but one still needs a strategy to make sure the research is heading somewhere. In the context of new media studies, efficient tools to help the researcher figure out what the data (s)he is collecting is about and making something out of it can be borrowed from qualitative sociology. In particular, the "grounded theory" methodological approach as developed by Juliet Corbin and Anselm Strauss (1998) proves extremely useful,[3] with its focus on materiality, inductive research processes based on *asking questions* and *making comparisons*, and its emphasis on micro-level analysis.

During the first seven months of observation, I didn't see a single ad on Happy Network. This wasn't a problem for me because I knew that many web companies do not display advertisements when they start a new project. The search engine Google and the video-sharing website YouTube, for example, famously started to display advertisements only when they were sufficiently sure that people were using their services regularly and when they had developed knowledge about how to target their audience. So, in order to keep me focused on the data and to help me make sense of the documents I was collecting, I started to make comparisons. In 2008, Facebook – the USA's most successful social networking site at that time – provided me with an adequate source of comparison for Happy Network.

Figure 31.1 shows one of the first screenshots I took in July 2008. At that time, two main features of my Happy Network user page were radically different from Facebook. Where the latter used one page for my user information (a) and another for a news feed about my friends (b), Happy Network mixed the two functions on the user page. And, while Facebook stated explicitly that it would never tell my friends about whose profile or photos I viewed, Happy Network did exactly the opposite: a dedicated section called "Recent visitors" (最近来访) (upper right) displayed information about who had viewed my profile and when. If I found the avatar of an unknown visitor intriguing I could click on it in order to visit his or her user page, which would then display my avatar and time of visit in his or her respective "Recent visitors" section.[4]

In October 2008, I became interested in Happy Network's virtual gifts section. Figure 31.2 shows the fourth page of Facebook's virtual gifts window (upper left) and the first of Happy Network (upper right). One of the things that struck me while

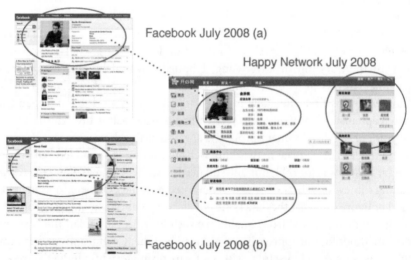

Figure 31.1   Comparison of screenshots on Facebook and Happy Network, July 2008 (users' names have been blurred to protect their privacy).

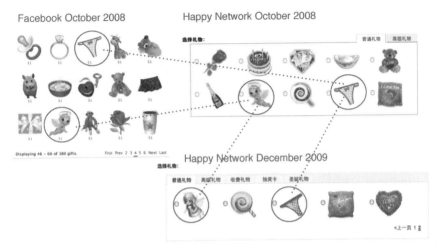

Figure 31.2   Screenshots of the virtual gifts sections on Facebook and Happy Network, October 2008–December 2009.

comparing the two websites was that some of the gifts were the same on the two platforms. Since Facebook had been launched four years before Happy Network, I wondered whether the latter had copied Facebook and then slightly modified the gifts (the underwear and the angel on Happy Network had additional glitter and heartbeat animation effects). This question progressed in December 2009, when I noticed the design of the gifts had changed on Happy Network (lower right): the underwear had become thicker and more colored, and the angel had now a new Tyrolean look (notice that the colors of the candy had changed as well). The cultural element "G-string" seemed to have circulated from Facebook to Happy Network and then within Happy Network, while its content of cultural waves had been first slightly altered and then heavily changed during its journey.

The comparison between the virtual gifts section of Facebook eventually caught up with my research question on advertisement. At the beginning of 2009, I noticed that various kinds of ads were starting to appear on Happy Network. Interestingly, whereas Facebook systematically displayed posters on my user page and on the news-feed page, Happy Network had none but seemed to rely mostly on in-game advertising (a technique sometimes also called "advergaming").[5] Ads were displayed inside the many games Happy Network provided, for example on a wall behind the cars within a "Parking Wars" game (see Zimmermann 2011).

At the end of 2009, I noticed that the gifts section featured advertisements too (I suspect it started several months earlier). It proposed virtual gifts such as a Kentucky Fried Chicken hot beverage for the winter, Nokia mobile phones, or a Smart car. Typically, "ad" gifts were placed at the beginning of the gifts section. They featured a short animation (something normally only available for higher-end gifts) and giving one of them three times during a single day allowed one to use a gift from the high-grade section for free. "Ad" gifts were often displayed in relation to a special moment such as Christmas or the Chinese New Year.

Figure 31.3 "Smart car" gift: screenshots from the gifts and the messages sections of Happy Network, February 2010 (users' names have been blurred to protect their privacy).

Figure 31.3 shows one of these gifts, a Smart car with a tiger skin, offered on the occasion of the Chinese Year of the Tiger. The screenshot shows the gift section (upper part), and then the gift displayed in my message section when I received it from someone and while I played the animation (lower part). The screenshot was taken at the end of the short animation, which lasted a few seconds. The animation first displayed the car in white and full of roses, then the roses popped out of the car and the color changed to yellow, and finally the tiger lines appeared while the petals slowly fell down and a message appeared above saying "Wish you love for the year of the Tiger." The second part of the sentence contains a double pun on the word "tiger," as its says literally "Love for the year of the tiger – Love the tiger's oil" (虎年有爱 爱老虎油). "Love the tiger's oil" (爱老虎油), *ai laohu you*, is a reference to a Tsui Hark movie in which a character uses this funny transcription for "I love you," but can also be understood as a way of saying "this car saves gas."

The Materiality of Culture

Since this chapter is not really about advertisements on social networking sites in China but about how to use case studies like this to analyze cultural differences, at this point it is worth making a short summary of these observations from a methodological point of view. What do we have? A Chinese social networking site that seems to recycle elements from other social networking sites in an ingenious way. Specific functions such as the news-feed and the virtual gifts feature both similarities and improvements when compared to Facebook.

While it is hard to tell the exact story of their development without pursuing more research, it seems pretty obvious that some cultural elements (i.e., aggregates of cultural waves) have been circulating from one platform to another and then been modified. The analysis of Happy Network that I began above is a description of how the observations and the comparisons took place, how the data were collected, and how a few cultural elements I selected (the news-feed section, the G-string and the angel, the car) seem to have circulated from one website to the other and how some other cultural elements (the advertisements) have circulated within the medium that hosts them.

It is worth noting that the chapter you are reading is part of the circulation process too, since the cultural elements (news-feed, G-string, etc.) have ended up on these pages – and this is why the accuracy of the description is so important, because we expect the cultural elements to be presented as similarly as possible to those actually observed. A good description is a description that makes the cultural elements it discusses circulate without modifying it too much and that is arranged in the clearest possible way for the reader.

Interestingly, as the respective developments of Happy Network and Facebook between 2008 and 2010 illustrate, differences in web design regarding virtual gifts did not seem to be small details but rather major strategic differences between the two social networking sites. Facebook finally suppressed its virtual gifts section in July 2010 while Happy Network made it a main tool of advertising, with users happily sending ads to each other on a daily basis. In other words, the observation and analysis of Happy Network has taught us something about "cultural differences" by showing us how design concepts evolved on its website.

Conclusion

Many of us, in speaking loosely of culture, point at ways of life and ways of thinking that lead to the general idea of differences between groups of people, groups of ideas, or groups of things. Then, when we need to use the concept in a scientific contribution, the idea of shared practices and shared meanings and the question of where to draw boundaries between "cultural entities" often becomes the center of our concern. In the examples above, one could be tempted to use macro-level categories such as "Chinese" or "Western," or a concept such as "hybridity." We could also be tempted to write more affirmatively by saying that the cultural elements "have circulated" rather than "seem to have circulated." But then how do we talk about the Smart car icon and its tiger skin, and how do we account for the uncertainty of the observations? Macro-level categories and affirmative statements would definitely be problematic, as none of the observations would fit them exactly.

My argument is that in order to study cultural differences we need to give up using macro-level categories and limit ourselves to the vocabulary used by people using the specific instances of media under study.[6] Researchers shouldn't rely on abstractions and explanations to discuss their observations but on their own personal story with the data. There is always someone behind the research – someone who read texts, observed things or people, used tools – and it is this very personal experience between the researcher, her data, and her tools that produces the result of any study. So don't speak about Chinese traditional culture or hybridity. Carefully select samples you consider representative of what you observed or of the arguments you want to put forward, as I did with the Smart car and its tiger skin,[7] tell about how you found them, what you understand about them, and, if you have room for more, as Howard Becker or Bruno Latour would argue, provide more details.

Acknowledgments

I would like to thank Jean Burgess, Axel Bruns, and John Hartley for asking me to write this paper and editing it; Nicki Hall for advising me on how to do it; Nicolas Nova for inviting me to Lift10 for a talk that became the first draft of this paper and for constructive feedback at various stages of the research (look out for our coauthored paper on design research, coming soon); and Nicolas Zufferey and Howard S. Becker for discussions, criticism, and friendship. The financial support of the Société Académique de Genève, Fonds Han Suyin, is gratefully acknowledged.

Notes

1. My focus on materiality is influenced by recent developments in science and technological studies, especially Trevor Pinch's work in sound studies. See for instance Pinch (2002).
2. My argument here is inspired by the work of Howard Becker, who shares Latour's view on description (see Becker 1998: 58). Becker's writing is the perfect illustration of the principles presented above. He has also published a book on the issue of writing that discusses at length the methodology he relies on (see Becker 2007).
3. Barney Glaser, who in 1967 coauthored with Anselm Strauss the famous book on grounded theory (Glaser and Strauss 1975) started a somewhat different approach from that of Corbin and Strauss. I rely here specifically on the latter's work.
4. I was told by a Swiss web designer that this feature, sometimes called "footprints," is standard on many social networking sites in Asia.
5. Facebook had other ways of displaying advertisements as well, but I do not discuss them because the comparison is only used here as a tool for analysis; the research is centered on Happy Network.
6. I borrow this argument from interactionism in sociology (Becker 1973), which suggests relying on how actors qualify themselves and others, and from science and technology studies' advice to "follow the actors" (Latour 1987). Generally speaking, Becker and Latour share the same procedures and put forward similar arguments (roughly speaking,

where the first discusses art and methodological issues in social sciences, the latter relies on science studies and philosophy).

7. I chose the few screenshots presented in this chapter from among a selection of over four thousand. The choice of the right example to illustrate one's point is a central part of the description work.

References

Baldwin, J.R., Faulkner, S.L., Hecht, M.L., and Lindsley, S.L., eds. (2006) *Redefining Culture: Perspectives Across the Disciplines*. Mahwah, NJ: Lawrence Erlbaum Associates.

Becker, H.S. (1973) *Outsiders: Studies in the Sociology of Deviance*. New York: Free Press.

Becker, H.S. (1998) *Tricks of the Trade: How to Think About Your Research While You're Doing It*. Chicago, IL: University of Chicago Press.

Becker, H.S. (2007 [1986]) *Writing for Social Scientists: How to Start and Finish Your Thesis, Book, Or Article*, 2nd edn. Chicago, IL: University of Chicago Press.

Borofsky, R., Barth, F., Shweder, R.A., et al. (2001) "A Conversation about Culture." *American Anthropologist*, 103(2), 432–446.

Corbin, J., and Strauss, A. (1998) *Basics of Qualitative Research: Techniques and Procedures for Developing Grounded Theory*. London: Sage.

Glaser, B.G. and Strauss, A.L. (1975 [1967]) *The Discovery of Grounded Theory: Strategies for Qualitative Research*. Chicago, IL: Aldine.

Goody, J. (1992) "Culture and Its Boundaries: A European View." *Social Anthropology*, 1(1a), 9–32.

Kroeber, A.L. and Kluckhohn, C. (1952) *Culture: A Critical View of Concepts and Definitions*. Cambridge, MA: Harvard University Press.

Latour, B. (1987) *Science in Action: How to Follow Scientists and Engineers through Society*. Cambridge, MA: Harvard University Press.

Latour, B. (2005) *Reassembling the Social: An Introduction to Actor-Network-Theory*. Oxford: Oxford University Press.

Maxwell, R. (2001) "Why Culture Works" in R. Maxwell, ed., *Culture Works: The Political Economy of Culture*. Minneapolis, MN: University of Minnesota Press.

Pinch, T. (2002) "Emulating Sound. What Synthesizers Can and Can't Do: Explorations in the Social Construction of Sound" in C. Zittel, ed., *Wissen und soziale Konstruktion*. Berlin: Akademie Verlag, pp. 109–127.

Samovar, L.A. and Porter, R.E. (2003) "Understanding Intercultural Communication: An Introduction and Overview" in L.A. Samovar and R.E. Porter, eds., *Intercultural Communication: A Reader*. Belmont, CA: Wadsworth, pp. 6–17.

Triandis, H. (2007) "Culture and Psychology: A History of the Study of Their Relationship" in S. Kitayama and D. Cohen, eds., *Handbook of Cultural Psychology*. New York: Guilford Press, pp. 59–76.

Zimmermann, B. (2010) "Redesigning Culture: Chinese Characters in Alphabet-Encoded Networks." *Design and Culture*, 2(1), 27–43.

Zimmermann, B. (2011) "Analyzing Social Networking Web Sites: The Design of Happy Network in China" in G. Adamson, G. Riello, and S. Teasley, eds., *Global Design History*. New York: Routledge, pp. 153–162.

Zimmerman, B. (forthcoming) *Technology and Cultural Difference: Electronic Music Devices, Social Networking Sites and Computer Encodings in China*.

32

Learning from Network Dysfunctionality

Accidents, Enterprise, and Small Worlds of Infection

Tony D. Sampson and Jussi Parikka

In February 2010, a characteristic outbreak of media panic spread through the British tabloid press concerning a new media marketing campaign developed by a company called DubitInsider (2010). In conjunction with affiliated brands – listed on DubitInsider's partner website as including Channel 4, Childline, Disney, Electronic Arts, Jetix, Ludorum, and Mattel – the DubitInsider concept presents a very simple marketing idea. It sought to recruit 13–24-year-olds who consider themselves to be "peer leader[s] with strong communication skills" to act as "Brand Ambassadors." In short, this required the clandestine *passing on* of online and offline product suggestions to these youths' peers via fly posting, posting on message boards and social networks, emails, instant messenger conversations, organizing small events, and hosting small parties. Significantly, the campaign ignited the moral indignation of *The Sun* (Hamilton 2010) and *The Daily Mail* (Poulter 2010) not simply because of the covert nature of the marketing strategy itself but also because these young Brand Ambassadors were apparently being paid to market "unhealthy" junk foods to minors.

Strategies based on tapping into the spreading of social influence are not particularly new. A reliance on seeking out influential individuals ("Influentials") has been the mainstay of word-of-mouth strategies and persists in so-called "word-of-mouse" variations on this theme. For example, another marketing firm, in4merz.com, endeavors to draw upon the anticipated infectious relations established between friends "on and offline" in order to promote music acts. As the company's website claims, "*In4merz* is about matching our artists to your friends who may like them" (in4merz n.d.). Young In4merz create posters, banners, and videos about acts, Twitter about them, and leave comments on Facebook or other social sites. For each level of promotion, In4merz earn points that are convertible into concert tickets, CDs, DVDs, and the occasional chance to meet their favorite act.

A Companion to New Media Dynamics, First Edition. Edited by John Hartley, Jean Burgess, and Axel Bruns.
© 2013 John Wiley & Sons, Ltd. Published 2015 by John Wiley & Sons, Ltd.

Beyond tabloid concerns regarding junk food and the exploitation of a potentially underage youth market, what interests us here is how the logic of these marketing strategies overlaps with the logic of distribution of spam and viruses. Indeed, in a different context, hiding unsolicited brand messages in social media and the potential for bulk sending of veiled product promotions for financial reward could arguably be called spamming. Further, designed as they are to spread Trojan-horse-like product suggestions through imitative social networks of friends, whether or not the strategies actually become contagious, their aim is to go viral.

More importantly perhaps, when these strategies become disconnected from the anomalous contexts of "bad" software and become attached to the legitimate remits of the business enterprise, they become part of a broader change, or at least a perception of change, concerning the way imitative social relations, contagious communication networks, vulnerable bodies, and unconscious moods can be harnessed. In continuance with our earlier work together (see Parikka and Sampson 2009: 1–18), we understand this process as part of the emergent spam logic and virality of network capitalism. In other words, once removed from a Nigerian cybercafé or Bulgarian virus writing scene, the logic adopted becomes a normalized online marketing activity, not only performed by corporations but also embedded in social relations of individuals as part of the strategies of business enterprise and brand design. All of this indicates that spamming and virality are no longer anomalies, but are fast becoming the standard, acceptable way of conducting social relations and doing business in the digital world. To be sure, if the peer-to-peer recommendations and thumbs-up buttons of "word-of-mouth 2.0" characterize the current paradigm of social media, these campaigns are indicative of a more aggressive and targeted Web 3.0 marketing of suggestion already on the horizon. Rather than simply looking to spread influence via networked software, Web 3.0 appeals directly to a user's emotional landscape and desire for intimacy (Ludovico 2005) and exploits the ready-made expediency and contagiousness of the networks that pass it on (Sampson 2010). It is not that networks are automatically the perfect platform for contagion but that the appropriation of certain forms of affective, intensive, and established high-contact network relations, such as friendship, are an emblematic way to think through the exercise of contagion-power across technical platforms: from human to software relations.

This chapter articulates the dynamics of spam, viruses, and other related "anomalies" as constituent parts of new epidemiological *worlds* "created" by the business enterprise. This refers to a change in focus from the objects that are contagious to environments – whether social media or urban space – that are designed to appropriate such contagiousness as a milieu feature. We focus here on the specific creative capacities of dysfunctionality in the production of network environments, and how "learning" from the irregularities of normalized communication adds new flesh to this world. We discuss how much of this new know-how concerning the productive powers of the anomalous is filtered through the cultural circuit of capitalism: "a feedback loop which is intended to keep capitalism surfing along the edge of its own contradictions" (Thrift 2005: 6). In this way, contradictory tensions, which underpin the seemingly "bad" processes of contagion, are appropriated by the expanding logic of profit-making and the social (re)production of capital. In short, this chapter articulates how new knowledge acquired from what seem to be the mostly accidental events of the network is seized upon by the business enterprise, leading to new consumer modeling intended to *make ready* environments so that the capricious spreading of social influence can be all the more effectively triggered and responded to.

The observation that the anomalous, accidental, and dysfunctional can be appropriated as part of what appears to be the norm is, again, nothing new. Our work has, as such, already questioned the political motivation of the nineteenth-century Durkheimian concept of anomie whereby the anomalous is grasped as a necessary evil that provokes the stabilizing (and law-abiding) tendencies of the collective social consciousness (Parikka and Sampson 2009: 11; Sampson 2010). In this chapter, we briefly draw on one of Emile Durkheim's contemporaries, Gabriel Tarde, who in sharp contrast linked the social milieu to accidental and mostly unconscious associations of imitation and influence. Recently, Tarde has enjoyed a new following through a variety of theorists trying to come up with alternative ways of grasping the social: Thrift, Maurizio Lazzarato, Bruno Latour, and Gilles Deleuze are among the more prominent developers of Tarde's ideas. Here we use Tarde to fleetingly point toward a growing understanding of how the accidents of contagion can indeed be steered toward specified commercial goals.

Our approach also complements, to some extent, more recent writings concerning the future of the Internet. For example, Jonathan Zittrain (2008) argues that viruses, spam, and worms are threats to the generative principle of the Internet. Similarly, we contend that such software-driven social actions are exploitative of the open principles of the Internet, but further acknowledge the extent to which these practices have enthused and inspired the commercial logic of the business enterprise. As already established in the field, viruses and spam can be thought of as "exploits" (Galloway and Thacker 2007), as well as examples of viral capitalism (Parikka 2007). They are shapers of network experiences (Parikka and Sampson 2009: 4) and symptomatic of imitative network cultures (Sampson 2010). "Bad" software is not necessarily "malicious" software. It becomes integral to an alternative generative logic of capture implicated in the production of *small worlds of infection* in which often-distracted consumers can be readily influenced and put to work in the reproduction of further influences. This chapter further relates, as such, to discourses concerning the appropriation of free labor in network culture (Terranova 2004). Our discussion nevertheless begins by charting how these epidemiological worlds were mapped by the computer sciences in the 1980s before they pervaded the burgeoning offshoots of the network security industry. We shall then go on to observe how epidemic worlds were also modeled by network science as early as the 1960s and are currently being exported, via the circuitry of capitalism, to the business enterprise.

Defining Dysfunctionality

Whether one approves or not, one cannot easily dismiss the significant impact the "evils" of software culture, such as spam and viruses, have on how we think about the Internet. Since the 1980s, it has been hard to ignore the effects of malicious software, which on the one hand threaten to destabilize digital utopias and on the other disturb the daily practices that make the Internet work. Despite many of the optimistic claims made in the 1990s concerning a drift toward a frictionless digital culture, the reality of how software guides our perception of digitality, and how software itself is continuously and meticulously governed, is far from friction free. Indeed, the balance of the discursive formations of the Net seems to have shifted from the digitopias of the late 1990s to the centrality of software *gone bad* – not just badly made operating systems and applications but software designed to *do* "bad" things. The dynamics of "bad" software such as viruses and spam have influenced the perception of software in general, and made software a central object in the governance of online social interactions.

Social relations are increasingly understood through software and software platforms, whether for instance this relates to the privacy issues surrounding Facebook's use of tracking and tagging formations (most recently the face recognition feature) or the "who-follows-who" logic that creates Twitter communities. All such social relations are at their core ever more algorithmically organized. It is this same algorithmic social relationality that is central to the functionality of "bad" software and that, as the dynamics of viruses and spam become part of network cultures, also begins to specify further practices and types of software that characterize new, wider processes emblematic of these cultures. Along these lines, we argue here that spamming and virality are implicated in a turn toward a new business enterprise that seeks to productively incorporate what was once considered "bad" into its very circuitry.

However, before grasping the significance of these emerging business models to social media and capitalism in general, we need to return to their origins in a much earlier biological turn. The two are, we propose, intimately intertwined in the biopolitical spaces that compose network cultures. The biological turn in computing has been well documented elsewhere by Terranova (2004), so here we wish to draw particular attention to the way in which the blending together of software technology and biological modeling plays a significant role in the production of security. Despite a distinct lack of proactive security measures effectively embedded into the infrastructure of the Internet, antiviral, immunological, and epidemiological models have become defining factors in the Internet age. Early on in computer science research, the link between programs with complex viral capabilities and network communication came to the fore. For example, Fred Cohen (1986) made important inroads into mapping the phenomenon of digital infection. Indeed, by the mid-1980s Cohen had expressed influential reservations concerning the limits of complete network security. He argued that open communication, realized through the sharing of information over a network, is commensurate to openness ripe for infection. In other words, complete security requires flow restrictions and closed subsets that become hierarchical elements, or bottlenecks, in network architectures that inhibit sharing (Cohen 1986: 85–86). Importantly, then, Cohen's epidemiological approach to network disruption demonstrates that information sharing and the computer virus problem are inseparable. *You can't have one without the other*.

Although this crucial realization in the approach to network architectures is not surprisingly glossed over in security industry rhetoric, the indivisibility of sharing and virality is increasingly recognized as a potential revenue stream for network business. As the Facebook model has demonstrated well, sharing is a crucial driver in the value creation of participatory media cultures. But virality is also imprinted in the fabric of software cultures, and its logic is engrained in the social habits, relationships, sharing of feelings, and mostly unconscious social actions exploited by emerging network business strategies.

The inseparability of sharing and virality introduces a very different network model from those commonly forwarded in communication studies. By definition, a network is not a frozen graph of representable nodes and edges geometrically connected to each other. The Internet is an open and dynamic time-space made up of eventful interactions and distributions. It is an assemblage of networks coming up against architectural vulnerabilities, in need of continuous governance and an ongoing maintenance project intended to filter out destabilizing network flows through incomplete security. In light of these fragilities, we again draw attention to how dysfunctionalities express a materiality, or logic, of action that has been (in our opinion) much neglected in the media and communication field. We see instead how dysfunctionality has figured writ large in engineering and science, and is now informing business attempts to tap into the potential of the Internet. This is a logical line in which automated *excessive multiple posting*, viral replication, and system hijacking are not necessarily indices of a dysfunctional relation with normalized patterns of sharing, communication, and informing but rather express the capacities of the symbiotic relation between anomalies and normality (Parikka and Sampson 2009: 1–18).

Key to these developments is an increasingly epidemiological understanding of network environments. But this is not an epidemiology solely dedicated to the eradication of malevolent computer viruses such as the infamous Melissa or Love Bug outbreaks. As Cohen noted, there is potential for a benevolent virus. Certainly, in the 1980s and early 1990s, it was not unusual to read about experimental software viruses used as part of new management, organizational, and security measures acting as "vaccines." Viral programs "able to travel through the computers on a network, collect information, spot glitches and report back to the network manager" ("Recombinant Virus Protects Network" 1994: 2) or organize information via "replicated database maintenance" (Demers et al. 1987) were considered as a "good idea" (Sampson 2005). It is perhaps not difficult to imagine how the potential for turning "bad" ideas into new effective inventions would soon grab the attention of the marketer. As Esther Dyson noted back in 1999, "most right-thinking people hear about Melissa the virus and shudder. But a few politically incorrect marketers are marveling at her ability to reach the masses overnight. Imagine attaching your marketing message to such a virus."

Modeling Dysfunctionality

The computer virus has played a decisive role in the generation of novel ideas in the science of networks. Research into human interaction with viruses feeds into models of social influence. The digital virus has, it seems, informed a decidedly universal understanding of epidemic spreading said to occur across a range of sociotechnical networks. Passing through the aforesaid cultural circuits of capitalism, these ideas (and associated practices) have persisted in research papers and popular science literature, linking together academic and business enthusiasts. However, the flow of these ideas has not gone uncontested. At their core has appeared a scientific dispute over the question of what sparks an epidemic. On the one hand, an established (and much cherished) epidemiological approach points to the predicable "stickiness" of so-called "Influentials": promiscuous elites that pass on trends to less significant others. On the other hand, new powerful computer simulations of contagion suggest a new paradigm of research in which accidental and unpredictable environmental factors are at play in the pass-on power of consumers.

Despite their differences, these two strands of epidemiology can be traced back to a distinctly social rather than medical research program. Both are inspired by Stanley Milgram's (1967) so-called Boston experiment from the 1960s. Milgram famously set out to better understand how people are connected to each other in the world by passing on letters addressed to a stock-broker friend of his living in Boston to randomly selected people in Omaha, Nebraska. Given the assumedly random set of social nodes that connect the wilderness of Nebraska to the urban sprawl of Boston, it was safe to suppose that the letters might never make it to their intended destination point. However, most of them did, remarkably passing through fewer connection points than had been previously anticipated. Although Milgram's early conception of what has become known as a small-world network or six-degree phenomenon does not directly infer epidemic-spreading, his model of social clustering has inspired others to consider how the spreading of things in general might pertain to a universal logic that is not exclusively random.

Most contemporary marketing circles have adopted their own take on the social epidemiological model dependent on the promiscuous role of the Influential. The concept of the Influential originally featured in this context in the bestseller *The Tipping Point* in 2000. The book's author, Malcolm Gladwell, a popular business, science, and medicine journalist, not only claims that marketing fads spread *like a virus* but also manages to blend together Milgram's Boston experiment with a crude rendition of epidemic threshold theory (Gladwell 2000: 34–36, 7–9) In short, an epidemic spreads via a few highly promiscuous and infected nodes whose influences can spill over into the network, eventually breaching a tipping or threshold point, wherein the number of infected nodes outlives the number of uninfected. Gladwell argues that tipping points can be breached when small-world clusters form around the social relations of a promiscuous few. He goes on to compare the spread of syphilis by promiscuous crack cocaine addicts in poor neighborhoods in Baltimore to a flourishing craze for hush puppies spread by influential trendsetters in New York. As one business magazine recently put it:

> In modern marketing, this idea – that a tiny cadre of connected people triggers trends – is enormously seductive. It is the very premise of viral and word-of-mouth campaigns: Reach those rare, all-powerful folks, and you'll reach everyone else through them, basically for free. (Thompson 2008)

Two of the more recent names frequently associated with this new paradigm of social influence (and exporting it to the business enterprise) are Duncan Watts and Albert-Laszlo Barabási. While also trying to get to grips with fad contagions by comparing them to biological and digital viral contagions, Barabási (2003: 123) ushered in a new approach by blending together Milgram's small-world phenomena and more recent scale-free epidemiological models. Based on studies of electronic networks, scale-free networks present a topological architecture in which order and randomness are in paradoxical mixture with each other. Using this idea, Barabási draws attention to how the epidemic persistence of the Love Bug computer virus undermines both the tenets of threshold theory and the predictability of the Influential (Barabási 2003: 131). Citing research published a year after it was first noted that the Love Bug presented a mystery to threshold theory, he points to a "new epidemiological framework" marked by the absence of a threshold and its associated critical behavior (Barabási 2003: 135). Simply put, in scale-free networks, any *promiscuous* computer in a hub is enough to create an epidemic, since it is likely to be unprotected and connected to so many other computers in a network that it will eventually spread a virus to another computer without the appropriate virus protection. The Internet is prone to the spreading and the persistence of infections, no matter how low their virulence (Patch 2001).

The potential for this new paradigm to be exported to the business enterprise becomes more visible in Duncan Watts' recent commercial work for Yahoo! (Thompson 2008). Following on from the success of his Milgram-influenced best-seller *Six Degrees: The Science of a Connected Age* (Watts 2003), Watts has been busy modeling consumer pass-on power by endeavoring to trigger contagious cascades in virtual simulations of a networked world. Unlike the predictabilities assumed in the theory of "Influentials," Watts' research seems to point more readily to the happenstance of events befalling a susceptible and (therefore) more infectable network of people. This means it is not solely Influentials who trigger contagion but anybody connected to the networked world dependent upon them who stumbles into a chance encounter. In fact, it is not so much the viral objects or the infected subjects that matter but rather the *infectability* of the networked world in which contagion spreads. *Infection becomes a characteristic of the environment.* As Watts puts it, "If society is ready to embrace a trend, almost anyone can start one – and if it isn't, then almost no one can" (in Thompson 2008: 3). This is a world of accidental influence that although decidedly capricious and unpredictable is not, it would seem, necessarily beyond the control of marketers. The research focus has in fact significantly shifted away from the Influential *subject* toward the production of infectable network *worlds*, which means that infectable spaces can be manufactured and designed.

Network Dysfunctionality as Biopolitical Theory

To conclude our discussion, we want to reflect on the potential role that network dysfunctionalities might play in a biopolitical theory of social influence and suggestion. In this way, we want to stress how the lessons learnt from dysfunctionality feed back into the new innovations of the business enterprise. Indeed, this new model of productivity is arguably part of an ongoing trend in capitalism already well identified by Lazzarato (2004). That is, unlike the old capitalist factory model, the capitalist business enterprise no longer creates commodity-objects or consumer-subject, but, as we see it, produces these infectious small worlds, or contagious "affective atmospheres," as Thrift (2008: 221–222) similarly describes them. Biopolitics refers in this case to the design of such milieux and environments that tap into the seemingly nonpolitical sphere of moods, affects, sensitivities, perceptions, and sociability.

   Of course, our intention here is not to engage in a business discourse that tries to harness consumer pass-on power for its own ends, as the hype surrounding Watts and others has sought to do. Nonetheless, it is worth noting what Thrift (2009) has to say about the import of the contagion models implicated in the creation of these worlds, and the ways in which they, in themselves, seem to infect the world they connect to. They do indeed have a "grip":

> Behind the hyperbole, a series of practical experiments continue to allow this kind of thinking to inch forward and to begin to produce prescriptions that work, not least, of course, because they begin to change how the world is thought to turn up – through a combination of rhetoric, new technologies and practical short-cuts – all against a background of a capitalism which is increasingly rooted in the exercise of biopower. (Thrift 2009: 21)

Two very important trends come into play in this exercise of biopolitical power. One concerns accidents, the other mood. First, there is a prominent trend toward a business enterprise that not only learns from network dysfunctionality but is also able to prime the accidental environments of the small world so as to make them more smooth and manageable, if not entirely predictable. We further recognize a second factor wherein the business enterprise is actively tapping into the collective mood of an "off-the-peg" contagious culture. By using methods of inattention, appeals to the gut, and emotional capture, there appears to be a parallel between the abstract diagrams at work here and those functioning in spamming and virus cultures. To put it another way, what we came to recognize as characteristic of software cultures in terms of contagion power is also characteristic of the design of affective social worlds in network culture.

With regard to the first trend, we note how the business enterprise is becoming more adept at steering the accident, or at least making certain events look as though they occurred by way of an accident. As one viral marketer puts it, pass-on power breaks away from the tyranny of being *advertised to* by making the very act of passing-on appear spontaneous (Godin 2000: 25–26). Yet, although such spontaneity appears to signal a rupture from mass marketing, we argue that it is not entirely disconnected from the tyrannical forces of old. Just because contagion appears to be accidental, this does not mean that it cannot be primed and "carefully steered" (Thrift 2009: 18). Building upon Milgram's initial modeling of small-world phenomena, Watts' work for Yahoo! is consummate in this respect, looking as it does at the potential to manipulate a connected world, regardless of its accidentalness. Watts' big idea is called "big seed" marketing, and in it he marries the "benefits of old-school mass marketing" with "clever six-degrees effects" (Thompson 2008), or what we might alternatively consider to be a blending of old-school tyranny with the new epidemic logic of small worlds.

With regard to the second trend, we agree with Thrift (2009: 13–14) that Tarde is an important figure to bring in to help us to better understand the role mood can play in the production of infectious worlds. Tarde is, after all, the forefather of a capricious contagion theory in which "the normal appears to originate from the accidental" (Tarde 1903: 7). As an early precursor to network thinking, Tarde was also interested in the micro level of social relation and tried to understand society as something "formed" around the chaotic flows of imitation and other microsocial events that he saw as more fundamental than the collective representations of social consciousness. Here, though, we need to bring in a somewhat resuscitated Tarde, for, as Thrift (2009: 18) argues, Tarde's nineteenth-century epidemiology tended to see these contagious overflows as mostly uncontrollable events. The contagion models of twenty-first-century network science seem to suggest otherwise. Yet, through Tarde, the unpredictable yet steerable pass-on power of the anomalous emerges in a new light. A closer look at Tarde suggests a fresh counterpoint to anomic thinking that considers the accidents of influence not as anomalies coming under the control of a Durkheimian collective consciousness but as affective contagions arising from mostly unconscious collective imitations that can be, as Thrift (2008: 245) argues, manipulated through appeals to mood.

Importantly, then, the infectiousness of influence is not necessarily, as Gladwell (2000: 89–132) argues, attributed to influential consumer-subjects, or indeed the "stickiness" of commodity-objects, but pertains instead to a strategy by which the spreading of feelings is coupled to the primed contagiousness of the worlds through which commodities and consumers pass. Early on, it was Tarde (1903: xxii) who in fact recognized that the social milieu is a "vital environment" that exercises "an influence . . . upon imitation[−suggestibility]." As Watts' research similarly sets out, in order to survive, a new product does not seek out someone or something to infect. It is more a case of "gauging the public's mood" for infection (Thompson 2008).

This notion of an infectable world composed of buoyed-up consumer mood should not, however, be confused with a biologically determined search for survival. Contrary to many viral marketers' beliefs in the network's vulnerability to an evolutionary meme (Godin 2000: 110), what spreads in a Tardean world of infection is not genetically programmed to survive regardless of the world it inhabits. What spreads is in fact a manifestation of the affective atmospheres in which the social encounter with products and brands, and the biological adaptation of consumer mood, come together. As spammers and virus writers have already well established, social engineering success depends on the visceral design of the viral encounter. The appeal to mood (via the gut) becomes crucial to infection. As the lessons from the LoveLetter virus outbreak clearly demonstrated: *tell someone you love them and your love bug will spread*.

To conclude, we acknowledge Cohen's (1986) prophetic notion of the network as the perfect environment for both the sharing of information and the dysfunctionality of viral spreading. Indeed, in the production of infectable worlds, in which consumer mood and the spreading of influence are writ large, it would seem to us that the indivisibility of sharing and viral dysfunctionality is of equal significance.

References

Barabási, A.L. (2003) *Linked: How Everything Is Connected to Everything Else and What It Means for Business, Science, and Everyday Life*. London: Plume.

Cohen, F.B. (1986) *Computer Viruses*. Doctoral dissertation, University of Southern California.

Demers, A., Greene, D., Hauser, C., et al. (1987) "Epidemic Algorithms for Replicated Database Maintenance." *Proceedings of the ACM SIGACT-SIGOPS 6th Annual Symposium on Principles of Distributed Computing*. New York: ACM, pp. 8–32.

DubitInsider (2010) www.dubitfamilypanel.co.uk.

Dyson, E. (1999) "Second Sight." *The Guardian* (April 8). www.guardian.co.uk/Archive /Article/0,4273,3850829,00.html.

Galloway, A.R. and Thacker, E. (2007) *The Exploit: A Theory of Networks*. Minneapolis, MN: University of Minnesota Press.

Gladwell, M. (2000) *The Tipping Point*. London: Abacus.

Godin, S. (2000) *Unleashing the Idea Virus*. London: The Free Press.

Hamilton, J. (2010) "It's a Fizzy Rascal." *The Sun* (February 15). www.thesun.co.uk/sol /homepage/news/2853471/Kids-are-being-groomed-online-as-mini-marketeers.html.

In4merz (n.d.) www.in4merz.com/in4merz.

Lazzarato, M. (2004) "From Capital-Labour to Capital-Life Theory of the Multitude." *Ephemera*, 4(3), 187–208.

Ludovico, A. (2005) "Spam, or the Economy of Desire." *Neural.it* (December 1). www.neural
.it/art/2005/12/spam_the_economy_of_desire.phtml.

Milgram, S. (1967) "The Small World Problem." *Psychology Today*, 1(1), 60–67.

Parikka, J. (2007) *Digital Contagions. A Media Archaeology of Computer Viruses.* New York:
Peter Lang.

Parikka, J. and Sampson T.D. (2009) *The Spam Book: On Viruses, Porn, and Other Anomalies
from the Dark Side of Digital Culture.* Cresskill, NJ: Hampton Press.

Patch, K. (2001) "Net Inherently Virus Prone." *Technology Research News* (March 21). www
.trnmag.com/Stories/032101/Net_inherently_virus_prone_032101.html.

Poulter, S. (2010) "Child 'Mini-Marketeers' Paid by Junk Food Firms to Secretly Push
Products among Their Friends." *Daily Mail* (February 15). www.dailymail.co.uk/news
/article-1250931/Child-mini-marketeers-paid-junk-food-firms-secretly-push-products-
friends.html.

"Recombinant Virus Protects Network" (1994) *Computer Fraud and Security Bulletin*, 4,
2–3.

Sampson, T.D. (2005) "Dr Aycock's Bad Idea: Is the Good Use of Computer Viruses Still
a Bad Idea?" *Media and Culture Journal*, 8(1). http://journal.media-culture.org.au/0502
/02-sampson.php.

Sampson, T.D. (2010) "Error-Contagion: Network Hypnosis and Collective Culpability" in
M. Nunes, ed., *Error: Glitch, Noise, and Jam in New Media Cultures.* New York: Continuum,
pp. 232–253.

Tarde, G. (1903) *The Laws of Imitation* trans. E.C. Parsons. New York: Henry Holt and
Company.

Terranova, T. (2004) *Network Culture. Politics for the Information Age.* London: Pluto.

Thompson, C. (2008) "Is the Tipping Point Toast?" *Fast Company Magazine* (February 1).
www.fastcompany.com/magazine/122/is-the-tipping-point-toast.html.

Thrift, N. (2005) *Knowing Capitalism.* London: Sage.

Thrift, N. (2008) *Non-representational Theory: Space/Politics/Affect.* London and New York:
Routledge.

Thrift, N. (2009) "Pass It On: Towards a Political Economy of Propensity." Paper delivered
at the Social Science and Innovation Conference, Royal Society of the Arts (RSA), London,
UK (February 11). www.aimresearch.org/uploads/File/Presentations/2009/FEB/NIGEL
%20THRIFT%20PAPER.pdf.

Watts, D. (2003) *Six Degrees: The Science of a Connected Age.* London: Vintage.

Zittrain, J. (2008) *The Future of the Internet – And How to Stop It.* London: Penguin.

33

Young People Online

Lelia Green and Danielle Brady

Introduction

"Teenagers," "older children," "young adults": Western society positions young-sters of high-school age on the cusp between childhood and adulthood, between dependency and responsibility. Like many subjects positioned on a culturally defined boundary, they embody the tension between "purity" and "danger" (Douglas 1966): between innocence, to be protected; and risk, to be curtailed and managed. The innocence is associated with the impressionability and vulnerability of the child, while the risk is inherent in the precocious individual with adult desires, passions, and strength but lacking the experience and wisdom to temper these in ways that conform to social expectations (Fionda 2001, 2005). In this context it is unsurprising that the foundational text for the extensive literature on moral panics (Cohen 1980) concerns itself with the analysis of a specific 1960s youth subculture, Mods and Rockers, and with the societal responses to this threat to British social values.

As well as embodying the transitional phase between child and adult, teenagers are often voracious communicators and many "everyday innovators" (Haddon et al. 2005; Green 2010: 10) are young people experimenting with ways of doing things differently. This was the case with the Finnish teenagers credited with popularizing texting in the late 1990s (Kasesneimi and Rautiainen 2002). Here the stated aim was not only to communicate with peers but also to communicate privately in ways that were beyond the ready surveillance of adults: "Messages often bear more resemblance to code than to standard language. A text filled with code language expressions is not necessarily accessible to an outsider," note Kasesneimi and Rautiainen (2002: 183), following on from a comment that some kinds of messaging are "a hidden aspect of teen text messaging culture. They are not meant for adults to see" (Kasesneimi and Rautiainen 2002: 180).

The public and private communications of young people, often incorporating the desire to do things differently from their parents' generation and to innovate

A Companion to New Media Dynamics, First Edition. Edited by John Hartley, Jean Burgess, and Axel Bruns.
© 2013 John Wiley & Sons, Ltd. Published 2015 by John Wiley & Sons, Ltd.

new ways of expressing themselves and their identity, make the teenage years a potent site for adult fears around dysfunction and subversion. This is particularly true when it comes to adolescents' uses of the Internet.

New Media and New Ways of Interacting

The first decade of the World Wide Web saw the construction of millions of websites to allow access to information, online chat, games, and email, among other applications. Participation was traditionally measured in "clicks" and click-throughs (Kane 2001), as people surfed the web and followed links to find more and more specific information. As the measurement of interactivity became more refined, designers prided themselves upon how long a web user would engage with a site: its relative "stickiness" and whether the user would return (Li et al. 2006). Also of professional interest was the attention paid to the information provided and the use of online tools to ask questions of, or send messages to, the teams monitoring communication. In some circumstances, sites were designed to allow the development of online communities where frequent interaction led to feelings of connectedness (Rheingold 2000).

By the start of the twenty-first century, "search" had become the dominant online activity, and Google had become the dominant new technology company. As well as eclipsing other search companies such as Yahoo! and Alta Vista, it was beginning to challenge the previous IT behemoth, Microsoft, whose power had been tied to the operating system and software for the pre-World Wide Web, stand-alone-computer days. Horrigan (2008), of the PEW Internet and American Life Project, has described the 1990s Internet as promising "one-to-many communication," often via office and work-based applications, followed in the late 1990s by "many-to-many communication," as Internet access became increasingly domesticated with people using dial-up modems to get online from home. By 2001 about 20 percent of online users in the USA were participating in online communities.

The development of what subsequently came to be known as "Web 2.0" was a game-changer. It marked the rise of a new kind of interactivity and the harnessing of "the hive" (Herz 2002) in purposeful collaborative engagement. With the growth of open-source software development and the advent of Wikipedia in 2001, the web increasingly became a site for people with shared skills and interests to work together on a project that was too big to be contemplated by an individual, or even an everyday organization or association. In Herz's term, harnessing the hive had led to "harvesting the honey" (2002: 9), and this level of multiple collaboration and extensive interaction often reflected participants' use of broadband services capable of supporting the downloading of complex files, documents, and graphics. Over the following years, a range of programs and applications emerged that relied upon the regular activity of millions of participants who used the sites to create innovative digital material and new forms of connection. MySpace (2003) and *Second Life* (2003) were followed by Flickr (2004), Facebook (2004), YouTube (2005), and Twitter (2006).

The innovations wrought by Web 2.0 increasingly enabled social applications, and connecting to others became a parallel motivation for web use alongside Internet search. A pivotal moment occurred in March 2010 when Facebook overtook Google as the most popular US site, with Facebook accounting for "7.07 per cent of website hits from the USA during the week ending 13 March [2010]" compared with 7.03 percent for Google (Clark 2010). At that point, Facebook hits were growing at 185 percent year on year in contrast with a 9 percent increase for Google. Arguably, the main reason for people going online was now to socialize rather than to seek out information.

Following on from the turn of the millennium, teenagers had increasingly been setting up their own accounts online. Many started the decade subscribing to livejournals, online games, and fanfiction sites and then added membership of social networking sites such as Beebo, MySpace, and Facebook. Given the hours young people sometimes spent on these sites, and the content of teenage interactions that in some cases became more visible to adult scrutiny, parents and regulators became concerned that young people's online activity was dysfunctional, subversive, or both.

Concerns around Children's Online Activities

Teenagers' private access to digital technologies has always raised concern in some quarters. Discussing computers and gaming consoles, P. David Marshall argued in 1997 that parents consider "computer literacy as the passage to a comfortable future [... but the] arcade game dimension of the computer shifts its value from information source to entertainment site" (1997: 71). Computer technology, and online skills and activities, became the locus of two differing visions of the child's future. One vision offered technological competence and a possible career as an IT professional, effectively "future-proofing" the young person as they moved through the workforce. The inverse possibility was that the child might become an indigent computer game player, or a hacker, lost to productive work. Parents feared the capacity of young people to wrest dysfunction and subversion from a technology that they'd provided for its educational and work-related potential.

In addition to regulating issues around education and work, or gaming and disruption, parents were primed to worry about whether their children would use the Internet to connect with dangerous strangers, and whether they would reveal personal information that would allow predators to search them out. "Do you know where your kids are – and who they're chatting with online?" asked the US Federal Trade Commission (2007), reminding parents to be vigilant about their children when they were at home as well as when they were out. A further risk was that children would access inappropriate, unsettling, or illegal material, or even create such material and post it themselves.

From the mid-2000s onwards, many of the world's more technological nations began to investigate children's and young people's uses of the Internet, sometimes specifically focusing on social networking sites. The aim was to minimize the risks of Internet use while maximizing the opportunities and benefits it offered. The hope was that research might provide a firm foundation for evidence-based policy development. In the USA the Internet Safety Technical Task Force (ISTTF) reported on appropriate policy responses to the risks that children might encounter as a result of their online activities. Reviewing the available literature, the ISTTF experts concluded that the situation was far from straightforward. Some children were at risk online, they said, but "depression, abuse and substances are all strongly correlated with various risky behaviors that lead to poor choices with respect to online activities. A poor home environment that includes conflict and poor parent–child relationships is correlated with a host of online risks (Wolak et al. 2003; Ybarra and Mitchell 2004)" (ISTTF 2008: 20). In other words, a dysfunctional environment was often in evidence well before the child's potentially dysfunctional use of the Internet became a factor.

In Australia, the Australian Communications and Media Authority (ACMA) commissioned research into "Media and Communications in Australian families" (ACMA 2007). The 369-page report analyzed a national survey of 751 families and of 1003 children's (aged 8–17) time-use diaries, alongside an extensive literature review. This survey, and other research carried out between 2008 and 2010, indicated that Australian parents generally trust their children's Internet use most of the time and adopt a range of strategies for educating them about risks online.

The most extensive and intensive research has been undertaken in Europe, however. Funded by the European Union's EC Safer Internet Plus Programme, the EU Kids Online project was designed to enhance "knowledge regarding European children's use, risk and safety online" (EU Kids Online 2012). Between 2005 and 2009, the project networked researchers from 21 European nations to establish what had already been discovered about European children's online activities and to identify any knowledge gaps that might be important for evidence-based policy development (Livingstone and Haddon 2009). One of the outcomes of EU Kids Online I was to identify that most online risks affecting children could be allocated to one of three categories: content risks, contact risks, and conduct risks. Hasebrink et al. (2009: 8) discussed these risk categories as follows:

1. Content risks describe what is found on the web, and address situations where the child is the recipient of mass communication, including children's exposure to "advertising, exploitation of personal information; violent web content; problematic sexual web content; biased information, racism, blasphemy, health 'advice.'"

2. Contact risks are where someone else makes contact with the child and the child is a participant in personal or peer communication. This risk category includes when the child encounters "more sophisticated exploitation, children being tracked by advertising; being harassed, stalked, bullied; being groomed, arranging for offline contacts; being supplied with misinformation."

3. Conduct risks are where the child is the actor, offering content or contacting someone else. These risky activities include "illegal downloads, sending offensive messages to peers; cyberbullying someone else, happy slapping; publishing porn; providing misinformation" and recognize that children themselves may be the perpetrators of risks that other children encounter.

On the basis of the outcomes from EU Kids Online I, a further €2.5 million was allocated for 2009–2011 to EU Kids Online II. This enabled the research network to commission new research across 25 European nations to investigate the online activities of 25 000 children (aged 9–16) who use the Internet – about a thousand families per country. Each child's data could be matched with data collected from the parent most involved in supervising the child's Internet use, so the project involved both a child and their relevant carer in each of the 25 000 families.

EU Kids Online II: Design

EU Kids Online II was designed to identify the opportunities offered to, and the risks faced by, children and young people as a result of their Internet use. The aim was to collect information that would provide a snapshot of children's online activity across a range of European countries to inform evidence-based policy development and support young people's positive Internet engagement. There was a specific emphasis placed on "key online risks: pornography, bullying, receiving sexual messages, contact with people not known face-to-face, offline meetings with online contacts, potentially harmful user-generated content and personal data misuse" (Livingstone et al. 2011: 5).

As well as young people's online interactions, EU Kids Online II addressed children's activities more broadly – at home, at school, and in the company of friends and peers. Similarly, the research focused not only on parental concerns about what children did online but also on parents' wider fears, including regarding school performance and worries over the child's safety in other circumstances, such as around alcohol use. Overall, the research explored the young person's risk-taking, vulnerability, and relative access to opportunity in a variety of situations. The design allowed fears relating to the subversive or dysfunctional aspects of children's lives to include emotional, sexual, educational, and legal risks separate from those posed by Internet activity, in addition to recognizing that some children are active risk-seekers and risk-takers both on- and offline.

Reflecting a desire to explore the likely positive benefits of parental intervention and support, the study examined parents' ways of keeping their children safe. Such strategies range from installing filters that limit access to online material to positioning computers in public areas within the home and monitoring the young person's Internet activity in terms of reviewing the sites visited after they finish browsing online. The research objective here was to investigate which strategies are associated with which child risk profiles, although it was accepted that parents might choose to be more interventionist in response to their child's established risk-taking behaviors.

The same market research company, or its international affiliates, was used across all the 25 European countries involved in the study. This helped to ensure consistency of approach, respondent recruitment, and comparable findings from the stratified random sample. Families were recruited according to a method known as "random walk." This protocol provides for the random selection of a geographical district in the country and the random selection of a starting address within the district. Families within the locale are approached and asked to participate according to a pattern of walking around the district of the starting address. The questionnaires used with the children (in two separate age categories: 9–10 and 11–16) and with their parents were made publicly available (LSE Survey 2010).

The project was preceded by cognitive testing to establish that the terms used conveyed the same meanings in different languages and cultures, and all the interviewing was carried out face to face, although sometimes the data were collected using paper and at other times they were entered directly into a computer. Parents and children were interviewed separately and the survey was designed so that the child would not have to verbalize accounts of distressing or troubling experiences but could instead write these down, knowing that neither the interviewer nor their parent would see what had been written, and also knowing that their name was not linked to their response. Although the research explored complex and challenging areas, it did so in a manner that allowed for valid comparisons to be drawn between different cohorts of children and across cultural boundaries.

EU Kids Online: Findings

The headline findings of the EU Kids Online II project, "Risks and Safety on the Internet" (Livingstone et al. 2011), were published within the year of the fieldwork. The findings, for 2010, established that 60 percent of European children aged 9–16 went online every day or almost every day, with 93 percent accessing the Internet at least once a week. In 2010, 59 percent of European children had a social networking profile, with percentages varying from 26 percent of 9–10-years-olds to 82 percent of 15–16-year-olds (Livingstone et al. 2011: 5).

The evidence indicates that, the more often children use the Internet, the more they develop digital literacy and the skills they need to stay safe online. These capacities reflect age as well as online experience, and younger children were less likely to be confident of their safety skills and more likely to be distressed if they encountered troubling content. The likelihood of a child encountering troubling material – such as pornography, bullying, or exposure to potentially harmful user-generated online content – increases with the age of the child and with the time spent online. While 14 percent of 9–10 year olds had been exposed to one or more of the risks investigated, this percentage rose to 63 percent for 15–16 year olds.

Most children, however, "do not report being bothered or upset by going online" (Livingstone et al. 2011: 6).

In general, parents were not aware of their child's online experiences and consistently underestimated the risks to which their child had been exposed. Where the child had seen pornography, for example, 40 percent of their parents said they had not. The percentage of parents who believed their child had not encountered troubling content or distressing communication rose to 52 percent in the case of sexting and 56 percent regarding online bullying and the receipt of nasty and hurtful messages. 61 percent of parents whose child had met offline a person that they had first got to know in an online context said that their child had not done this (Livingstone et al. 2011: 6–7).

While the EU Kids Online II research concentrated on opportunities as well as risks, the many positive benefits of Internet activity are less relevant to discussions around young people's dysfunction and subversion. Focusing on risks, the research established that what is constructed as risky behavior only sometimes results in what the child perceives as harm. In particular, the survey deliberately adopted a comparatively low threshold of disquiet in terms of whether the child had felt bothered by something, where "bothered" meant "for example, [something that] made you feel uncomfortable, upset, or feel that you shouldn't have seen it" (Livingstone et al. 2011: 45). The child was then asked separately about the intensity of the feeling and its duration. Most of the young people, most of the time, were either "a bit upset" or "not at all upset" about the things that bothered them, and the majority similarly were bothered "for a few days" or "got over it straight away" (Livingstone et al. 2011: 45–102). For almost all the children, almost all the time, exposure to risk did not equate to experience of harm.

The one exception to this generality was the case of online bullying. Here, almost one-third (31 percent) of those who said they had been bothered by being bullied online in the past 12 months judged themselves to be "very upset": this can be compared with 16 percent who had seen sexual images online and 15 percent who had been sent sexual messages (Livingstone et al. 2011: 69, 58, 81). In these cases, the bullies and the people sexting are often in the same age group as their victims and the two are commonly known to each other. This figure underlines the findings of previous research indicating that adults and children have different concerns about the online environment. Adults' worries concern pornography, stranger danger, and children accessing online information about self-harm, suicide, and anorexia (Livingstone and Haddon 2009: 27), while children worry about cyberbullying, identity theft, and spam (Livingstone and Haddon 2009: 51).

While boys and girls are both at risk of online bullying (Livingstone and Haddon 2009: 24), other risks are more likely to be related to age and gender. Boys are:

> more likely to seek out offensive or violent content, to access pornographic content or be sent links to pornographic websites, to meet somebody offline that they have met online and to give out personal information. Girls appear more likely to be upset by offensive, violent or pornographic material, to chat online with strangers, to receive

unwanted sexual comments and to be asked for personal information although they
are wary of providing it to strangers. (Livingstone and Haddon 2009: 23–24)

Although young people's Internet use provides some evidence of dysfunctional
and subversive activities, the "perpetrators" and "victims" of such reprehensible
behavior are generally young people who are known to each other in everyday life,
and the boundaries between aggressor and aggressed against may also be confused.
In particular, Wolak et al. (2007) report that "nearly all (99 percent) of Internet-
initiated sex crime arrests in the N-JOV study [a US national dataset] were aged
13–17" (cited in ISTTF 2008: 19). This implies that their peers are the people most
likely to be disturbing to 13- to 17-year-olds, and the Internet may simply be the
most contemporary conduit through which young adults communicate power and
intimidation.

At the start of the EU Kids Online I project, mobile Internet access was not
widely available to children. By 2010, one in three European children were accessing
the Internet via a handheld device (Livingstone et al. 2011: 22). Differences in
Internet access via mobile across countries suggest that these young people can
bypass infrastructure restrictions. While regulators argue about parental mediation
in the home environment, young people are taking the Internet, with both risks and
opportunities, out of the home. They are now almost as likely to go online using a
handheld device as to do so via a personal computer. The extension of mobile G3
networks, the launch of Apple's iPhone in 2007, and the proliferation of the various
Android smartphone competitors have altered the trajectory of Internet access.
Internet research will need to be open to new developments, such as location-based
Internet communications. In 2010 only some children in the EU Kids Online II
study were engaging in advanced and creative activities on the Internet such as file-
sharing (18 percent), blogging (11 percent), or spending time in a virtual world (16
percent) (Livingstone et al. 2011: 33). Young people's future participation in these
and unknown new activities may derive not only from new technical possibilities
but also from new conceptions of education and creativity generated by Internet
mobility. Devices such as the iPad (launched 2010), which is already being embraced
by educators, may provide young people with the means to escape the classroom
and set their own agenda.

Conclusions

Young people's online activities increasingly blur fixed access with Internet-enabled
cell phones and other handheld digital devices. The ability to access the Internet at
a distance from parental observation and comment leads to greater opportunities
to ignore, or subvert, family rules around online activity. Problems with direct
surveillance mean that older children will need to develop and refine personal
strategies for safe Internet use. The growing autonomy of children and teenagers in
this area complicates the already difficult challenge of agreeing upon a family-based

approach to keeping children safe online. The EU Kids Online I research established that children are likely to report fewer home-based restrictions in Internet use than their parents do, while parents believe their children have had less exposure to online risks than is reported by the children themselves (Livingstone and Haddon 2009: 28). Australian research also established that there "is a large and statistically significant difference in parents' and children's reporting of both rule-setting and parental supervision activity, with children reporting less supervision and rule-making" (ACMA 2007: 289). ACMA researchers note that such differences in opinion may represent "a tactic [by the child] to evade restrictions on access to pleasurable content and activities, particularly private communications with peers" (2007: 298)

The findings of a big study such as EU Kids Online II, with 25 142 children and their parents across 25 separate countries, are necessarily complex and nuanced. However, the indications are that over half of all children (55 percent) "consider that there are things on the Internet that will bother children about their own age [. . . but that, even so,] 90% think it true that there are lots of things on the Internet that are good for children of their age" (Livingstone et al. 2011: 47). Some research indicates that exposure to risk, and negotiating the resulting challenges, helps children to develop resilience (Livingstone and Haddon 2009: 34). Livingstone and Haddon comment that addressing "the risks faced by a vulnerable minority in a proportionate manner without extending undue surveillance and restrictions to the occasionally naïve, sometimes risk-taking majority is undoubtedly a difficult problem for public policy" (2009: 39).

In line with the perception of the dysfunctional and subversive young person, there is ample evidence that normal children and adolescents will sometimes do deliberately risky things. Indeed, Lobe et al. comment that "children may be expected to circumvent, evade or subvert adult expectations or norms for their behaviour" (2007: 17). For many young people, at this point in their lives, some dysfunctional and subversive behavior is to be expected, if not welcomed.

References

Australian Communications and Media Authority (2007) "Media and Communications in Australian Families 2007." www.acma.gov.au/webwr/_assets/main/lib101058/media_and _society_report_2007.pdf.

Clark, N. (2010) "Facebook Overtakes Google." *The Independent* (March 18). www .independent.co.uk/life-style/gadgets-and-tech/news/facebook-overtakes-google-1923102.html.

Cohen, S. (1980 [1972]) *Folk Devils and Moral Panics: The Creation of the Mods and Rockers,* 2nd edn. Oxford: Martin Robertson.

Douglas, M. (1966) *Purity and Danger: An Analysis of the Concepts of Taboo and Danger.* New York: Routledge.

EU Kids Online (2012) "EU Kids Online: Enhancing Knowledge Regarding European Children's Use, Risk and Safety Online." *London School of Economics.* www2.lse.ac.uk /media@lse/research/EUKidsOnline/Home.aspx.

Federal Trade Commission (2007) "Social Networking Sites: A Parent's Guide." www.ftc
.gov/bcp/edu/pubs/consumer/tech/tec13.shtm.

Fionda, J. (2001) *Legal Concepts of Childhood*. Oxford: Hart.

Fionda, J. (2005) *Devils and Angels: Youth Policy and Crime*. Oxford: Hart.

Green, L. (2010) *The Internet: An Introduction to New Media*. Oxford: Berg.

Haddon, L., Mante, E., Sapio, B., et al., eds. (2005) *Everyday Innovators: Researching the Role
of Users in Shaping ICTs*. Dordrecht: Springer.

Hasebrink, U., Livingstone, S., Haddon, L., and Òlafsson, K. (2009) "Comparing Children's
Online Opportunities and Risks Across Europe, 2nd edn." *London School of Economics*.
www2.lse.ac.uk/media@lse/research/EUKidsOnline/EU%20Kids%20I%20(2006–9)/EU
%20Kids%20Online%20I%20Reports/D32_SecondEdition.pdf.

Herz, J.C. (2002) "Harnessing the Hive: How Online Games Drive Networked Innovation."
Release 1.0 (October 18), 20(9), 1–22.

Horrigan, J. (2008) "Obama's Online Opportunities: What Our Research Suggests
About Where President-Elect Obama's Technology Policy May Lead." *Pew Internet &
American Life Project* (December 4). www.pewinternet.org/Reports/2008/Obamas-Online
-Opportunities.aspx.

ISTTF (2008) "Enhancing Child Safety and Online Technologies: Final Report of the Internet
Safety Technical Task Force to the Multi-State Working Group on Social Networking
of State Attorneys General of the United States." *Berkman*. http://cyber.law.harvard.edu
/pubrelease/isttf.

Kane, M. (2001) "Is the Click-Through History?" *CNET News* (July 13). http://news
.cnet.com/2100-1023-269865.html.

Kasesneimi, E. and Rautiainen, P. (2002) "Mobile Culture of Children and Teenagers in
Finland" in J.E. Katz and M. Aakhus, eds., *Perpetual Contact: Mobile Communication,
Private Talk, Public Performance*. Cambridge: Cambridge University Press, pp. 170–192.

Li, D., Browne, G., and Wetherbe, J. (2006) "Why Do Internet Users Stick with a Specific
Web Site? A Relationship Perspective." *International Journal of Electronic Commerce*, 10(4),
105–141.

Livingstone, S. and Haddon, L. (2009) "EU Kids Online: Final Report." *LSE Research Online*.
http://eprints.lse.ac.uk/24372.

Livingstone, S., Haddon, L., Görzig, A., and Òlafsson, K. (2011) "Risks and Safety on the
Internet: The Perspective of European Children. Full Findings and Policy Implications
from the EU Kids Online Survey of 9–16 Year Olds and Their Parents in 25 Countries." *London School of Economics*. www2.lse.ac.uk/media@lse/research/EUKidsOnline
/EUKidsII%20(2009–11)/EUKidsOnlineIIReports/D4FullFindings.pdf.

Lobe, B., Livingstone, S., and Haddon, L. (2007) "Researching Children's Experiences Online
Across Countries. Issues and Problems in Methodology." *London School of Economics*.
www2.lse.ac.uk/media@lse/research/EUKidsOnline/EU%20Kids%20I/Reports/D41
_ISBN.pdf.

LSE Survey (2010) "Data and Survey Methods: EU Kids Online [2010 Survey Question-
naires]." *London School of Economics*. www2.lse.ac.uk/media@lse/research/EUKidsOnline
/EU%20Kids%20II%20(2009–11)/Survey/Survey%20documents.aspx.

Marshall, P.D. (1997) "Technophobia: Video Games, Computer Hacks and Cybernetics."
Media International Australia, 85, 70–78.

Rheingold, H. (2000 [1993]) *The Virtual Community: Homesteading on the Electronic Frontier*.
Cambridge, MA: MIT Press.

Wolak, J., Mitchell, K., and Finkelhor, D. (2003) "Escaping or Connecting? Characteristics of Youth Who Form Close Online Relationships." *Journal of Adolescence*, 26, 105–119.

Wolak, J., Ybarra, M., Mitchell, K., and Finkelhor, D. (2007) "Current Research Knowledge About Adolescent Victimisation on the Internet." *Adolescent Medicine*, 18, 325–341.

Ybarra, M. and Mitchell, K. (2004) "Youth Engaging in Online Harassment: Associations with Caregiver–Child Relationships, Internet Use and Personal Characteristics." *Journal of Adolescence*, 27, 319–336.

34

Beyond Generations and New Media

Kate Crawford and Penelope Robinson

Historical generations are not born; they are made. They are a device by which people conceptualize society and seek to transform it.
(Wohl, The Generation of 1914, 1979: 5)

New media technologies – whether the microphone, radio, television, or the Internet – can become powerfully associated with a generation. Their initial magic, the heady feeling of new capacities and affordances, can create a marker for generational memory. Black-and-white televisions beaming out the moon landing, Orson Welles terrifying radio listeners with tales of alien invasion, or images of mass protest in Egypt ricocheting through Facebook and Twitter: the platform becomes an inextricable part of how an event is remembered and mythologized as a defining moment for a generation. But new media technologies can also emerge as part of a generationalizing strategy, where they are used to mark out a particular age group as different or problematic. This chapter will look at the recursive dynamics that surround new media technologies and generations: from the media histories of generational categories through to the emergence of the "digital natives" as part of a long line of "us and them" identity polarization around emerging media forms. We will then consider what other factors, aside from age, might give us a more nuanced understanding of new media use.

Old and New Media Generations

For the past hundred years, young people have been seen as particularly susceptible to the powers of media technologies. They have been targeted as a population

A Companion to New Media Dynamics, First Edition. Edited by John Hartley, Jean Burgess, and Axel Bruns.
© 2013 John Wiley & Sons, Ltd. Published 2015 by John Wiley & Sons, Ltd.

at risk of becoming addicted, antisocial, and dysfunctional. As one researcher described:

> The popularity of this new pastime among children has increased rapidly. This new invader of the privacy of the home has brought many a disturbing influence in its wake. Parents have become aware of a puzzling change in the behavior of their children. They are bewildered by a host of new problems; and find themselves unprepared, frightened, resentful, helpless. (Eisenberg 1936: 17–18)

The particular "new pastime" in question was listening to the radio: one of many technologies that became a terrain where anxieties about generations of young people were deployed. As communications scholars Ellen Wartella and Byron Reeves observe in a review of studies from 1900 to 1960 on the effects of media on children, the same arguments about media technologies keep recurring and "although the expression of concern highlights novel attributes of each medium, the bases of objections and promises have been similar" (1985: 120). Like a media déjà vù, the technologies may change but the typecasting remains.

Part of the problem with generational claims about media use is with the very idea of generations. As an organizing category for human behavior, it fails to capture difference and replaces it with false coherence. While demographic events – such as the baby boom or the Black Plague – may have distinct effects in terms of population, they do not reflect the vast diversity contained within an age group. The sociologist Karl Mannheim identified the concept of "generation" in 1928, and argued that the prevailing social and political discourses that individuals encounter in their youth have an impact on their perceptions of the world. Major events, if experienced at the same stage of the life-course, would have the effect of congealing a group of people into what he called a "generation as actuality" (1952: 304), whereby a group of people develop a generational consciousness – a sense that they collectively participate in effecting social change.

In developing the concept of "generation," Mannheim was seeking to move beyond the familial notions of generation toward an understanding of the role of the wider sociohistorical context (Pilcher 1994: 484–485). But the concept of generational cohorts is also very limited: it cannot account for stark divisions within an age group, nor for commonalities across age groups. The ethnic, cultural, and class differences even within a single nation are enough to shatter the idea of identity shared across a generation, let alone between nations. Nonetheless, generational identity became the basis for nebulous and inaccurate labels, where age groups were rounded into categories – such as "baby boomer," "Generation X," and "millennials" – that now routinely appear in popular debates about technology and social change (White and Wyn 2008: 10).

Networked technologies have triggered even broader attempts at categorization. June Edmunds and Bryan Turner have drawn on Mannheim's concept of generational consciousness to argue that communication technologies have allowed "global generations" to emerge: "Whereas print media and the radio shaped international and transnational generations, electronic technology has led to the globalization of trauma because new media mean that events can be experienced simultaneously, transcending time and space" (2005: 573). The concept of "global generation" effectively bleaches out all the variance and heterogeneity between an Internet user in Hyderabad and one in Beijing or London. There is, however, no such thing as a digital generation, as media scholar Siva Vaidhyanathan (2008) argues:

> Invoking "generations" demands an exclusive focus on people of wealth and means, because they get to express their preferences (for music, clothes, technology, etc.) in ways that are easy to count. It tends to exclude immigrants and non-English-speaking Americans, not to mention those who live beyond the borders of the United States. And it excludes anyone on the margins of mainstream consumer or cultural behavior.

As we will see, the term "digital native" substantively glosses over the uneven and gradual engagement with network technologies across age groups, cultures, and classes.

Inventing Digital Natives

Marc Prensky is considered to have coined the term "digital native" when he proposed that "students today are all 'native speakers' of the digital language of computers, video games and the Internet" (2001: 2). He makes a distinction between digital natives and "digital immigrants" who, because they have not grown up with the Internet, retain their "accent." Prensky applies his native/immigrant distinction to students and teachers in contemporary classrooms, suggesting that young people have different styles of learning that older "digital immigrant" teachers don't understand (2001: 4).

The term quickly gained popular currency, and was used to imply that anyone born after 1980 will be better at using technology and new media. Immersion in information and communication technology from an early age, the argument goes, ascribes young people with certain characteristics that set them apart from older generations (Bennett et al. 2008: 776). Prensky writes:

> Kids born into any new culture learn the new language easily, and forcefully resist using the old. Smart adult immigrants accept that they don't know about their new world and take advantage of their kids to help them learn and integrate. Not-so-smart (or not-so-flexible) immigrants spend most of their time grousing about how good things were in the "old country." (2001: 4)

The "digital natives" category cements the idea that young people should be considered as a separate category, asserting that, because they have grown up with the Internet, they have an inbuilt capacity for engaging with and understanding digital communication. Older people are relegated to the order of those who must struggle to understand. Many have convincingly argued that this is conceptually and empirically dubious. Critics of the digital native discourse have pointed out that it erects an artificial gap between younger and older users of technology (Tufts 2010); that focusing on age obscures other factors contributing to a digital divide, such as access and opportunity (Brown and Czerniewicz 2010); that claims about digital natives amount to a kind of moral panic (Bennett et al. 2008); and that such claims marginalize older people who are proficient in their use of communication technologies.

This determinist view that young people are automatically "fluent in the digital language of computers, video games and the Internet" (Prensky 2005: 8) runs counter to considerable international evidence that shows inconsistency in digital literacy, even within wealthy Western nations such as the USA and Australia. What several researchers have found is that, while the majority of young people have access to mobile phones and computers, the frequency and form of their engagement vary depending on factors including socioeconomic and cultural background, gender, and family dynamics (Livingstone and Bober 2004; Lenhart et al. 2005; Kennedy et al. 2006). In one of the most persuasive assessments of the claims about digital natives, Bennett et al. observe:

> The picture beginning to emerge from research on young people's relationships with technology is much more complex than the digital native characterisation suggests. While technology is embedded in their lives, young people's use and skills are not uniform. There is no evidence of widespread and universal disaffection, or of a distinctly different learning style the like of which has never been seen before. (2008: 783)

Arguments based on a distinction between young and old framed by generalizations and stereotypes of technology use are problematic already, but, when they include the language of "natives" and "immigrants," there is even more cause for concern. The young people talked about in these narratives are depicted as inherently foreign, inexplicable, and exotic.

For example, John Palfrey and Urs Gasser, authors of *Born Digital*, deploy the digital native concept even while acknowledging that there are vast differences in access to technology across the world and that the "majority of young people born in the world today are not growing up as Digital Natives" (2008: 14). After detailing some of the apparently puzzling behaviors of young people, such as a daughter who is always busy chatting online and a high-school student "putting up scary, violent messages on his Web page," they write: "There is one thing you know for sure: These kids are different. They study, work, write, and interact with each other in ways that are very different from the ways than you did growing up" (2008: 2).

With all the resonance of colonial descriptions of the natives and their strange customs, young people are classed as alien. In their critique of the concept, Cheryl Brown and Laura Czerniewicz explain that "in our South African context (and presumably previously colonized countries), 'native' is synonymous with colonialism, apartheid, and domination and does not connote images of superiority and the future" (2010: 359). This double meaning of native – as "primitive" and as belonging to one's character since birth – and Prensky's associations of immigration with inadequacy bring along some considerably uncomfortable baggage.

Finally, the rhetoric of digital natives assumes a kind of historical break: a moment in time when a wholly new form of social and technological identity emerged. In some ways, this is akin to any kind of generationalizing tactic – where each group emerges as something novel and distinct from the last. But the language around digital natives is even more hyberbolic:

> Today's students have not just changed incrementally from those of the past.... A really big discontinuity has taken place. One might even call it a "singularity" – an event which changes things so fundamentally that there is absolutely no going back. (Prensky 2001: 1)

Not only is there little empirical evidence for such a radical schism but also the language of "singularity" invokes the concept used by futurists such as Ray Kurzweil (2005) that there will be a moment of "superintelligence": when artificial and human intelligence expands in currently inconceivable ways. Thus, digital natives are located somewhere between the linguistic poles of high futurism and colonialism, something irretrievably of both the future and the past, without any continuity or association with the present. Dislocated from other age groups and forms of identity, the digital native appears more like a chimera: an imaginary creature devised to tell particular kinds of stories about social change.

From Generations to Networks of Association

If the idea of a generation has little concrete meaning, instead operating as a vague shorthand, why has it become so pervasive as a form of human categorization? In Mannheim's terms, generations are formed by a set of experiences shared by people in a similar cultural milieu at the same time. But, in a globalized world, cultural milieu are no longer strictly limited by geography or age, and are highly fractured and dispersed internationally. Significant events such as wars, recessions, mass protests, and so on may be shared by many or by a smaller subset within particular cultural, social, and economic niches. Rather than creating easily identifiable generations, digital media technologies create various networks of association and knowledge. These networks have varying levels of cohesion, power, and visibility. Some may be invisible, such as the network of friends listed in a "most called" list on a mobile phone. Others – brought together by politics, music, institutional or class association, a natural disaster, or a war – leave visible traces across social media sites such as Facebook and Twitter. Networks of association can be both voluntary and involuntary, and they have their own distinct patterns of technological engagement.

Australian researchers North, Snyder, and Bulfin suggest that social context and class are more influential determinants of young people's use of technology than age group:

> Young people's social background influences their relative exposure to ICT in their homes, their friends' homes and their leisure activities.... Young people make technologies their own – they use them according to what has a "sense of place," what fits their habitus. (2008: 897–899)

There is a more complex set of associations contributing to this sense of place, and multiple experiences of membership within a social milieu that go well beyond age. In a qualitative study of college students in the USA, McMillan and Morrison (2006) found that, while participants perceived there to be a difference between their use of the Internet and that of their parents and grandparents, more significant was that "within their age cohort vast differences and skill levels are evident . . . even within groups of siblings, media use differs" (2006: 89).

A study by communications researchers Eszter Hargittai and Amanda Hinnant (2008) in the USA similarly suggests gender, online experience, and education are significant influences on technological confidence. In their sample of 18–26-year-old American adults, women are less likely to claim knowledge about online terminology and features, and "those who use the Web infrequently also report lower levels of know-how about it" (2008: 617). They also found that, while self-reported online skill was not determined by educational background, it did influence the likelihood that people visited "capital-enhancing" sites: spaces that may increase human and financial capital (2008: 617). This study indicates that digital inequity exists even within populations that are already engaged in online environments and that the factors determining literacy are complex. Simply being connected is not enough.

Further, work done by social media researcher danah boyd has pointed to the influence of race and class on the use of social networking sites. "What distinguishes adoption of MySpace and Facebook among American teens is not cleanly about race or class, although both are implicated in the story at every level," she argues. "The division can be seen through the lens of taste and aesthetics, two value-laden elements that are deeply entwined with race and class" (boyd 2011: 204). When Facebook was first developed, it became a rite of passage for teenagers who saw it as "a marker of status and maturity": noticeable patterns emerged, with more white and Asian teens moving to Facebook while black and Latino teens remained on MySpace. Age was less powerful for determining online behavior than ethnicity, class, and cultural associations.

Conclusion

Studying networks of association, and the pervasive roles of race, class, and gender, can offer a more subtle account of new media and identity than generational categories. However, these complexities are not always welcome. As Vaidhyanathan (2008) writes, "We love thinking in generations because they keep us from examining uncomfortable ethnic, gender, and class distinctions too closely. Generations seem to explain everything." Generational terms have emerged as a shortcut for summarizing differences in technology use, but they do so at considerable cost. As an imprecise taxonomic tool, generational classifications have been used to bolster debates and policies that incorrectly seek to define age groups as monolithic and marginalize both the young and the old.

Researchers continue to provide evidence that digital participation is affected by multiple complex factors, yet problematic terms such as "digital native" still persist. Partly this is driven by a desire for simplicity, a simple line that can be drawn through the intricacies of social change. Partly it is due to the power that such a simple frame can give: it has been used within arguments to reshape the kinds of media used in classrooms, to influence pedagogical method, to affirm the feelings of educators and parents who feel left behind or alienated (Siemens 2007; Bennett et al. 2008). It seems unavoidable that, over a long historical trajectory, the term – or terms like it – will recur, operationalized to mark out particular groups from others and problematize (or glorify) their patterns of technology use. But using blunt tools such as the "digital native" terminology cannot bring us closer to developing a granular, differentiated understanding of how different groups are using online technologies. Instead, we need to take a fuller account of the rich miscellany of associations that more powerfully shape the relationships between humans and networks.

References

Bennett, S., Maton, K., and Kervin, L. (2008) "The 'Digital Natives' Debate: A Critical Review of the Evidence." *British Journal of Educational Technology*, 39(5), 775–786.

boyd, d. (2011) "White Flight in Networked Publics? How Race and Class Shaped American Teen Engagement with Myspace and Facebook" in L. Nakamura and P. Chow-White, eds., *Race After the Internet*. New York: Routledge, pp. 203–223.

Brown, C. and Czerniewicz, L. (2010) "Debunking the 'Digital Native': Beyond Digital Apartheid, Towards Digital Democracy." *Journal of Computer Assisted Learning*, 26(5), 357–369.

Edmunds, J. and Turner, B.S. (2005) "Global Generations: Social Change in the Twentieth Century." *British Journal of Sociology*, 56(4), 559–577.

Eisenberg, A.L. (1936) *Children and Radio Programs*. New York: Columbia University Press.

Hargittai, E. and Hinnant, A. (2008) "Digital Inequality: Differences in Young Adults' Use of the Internet." *Communication Research*, 35(5), 602–621.

Kennedy, G., Krause, K., Judd, T., et al. (2006) *First Year Students' Experiences with Technology: Are They Really Digital Natives?* Melbourne: University of Melbourne.

Kurzweil, R. (2005) *The Singularity is Near: When Humans Transcend Biology*. New York: Viking Press.

Lenhart, A., Madden, M., and Hitlin, P. (2005) *Teens and Technology: Youth are Leading the Transition to a Fully Wired and Mobile Nation*. Washington, DC: Pew Internet & American Life Project.

Livingstone, S. and Bober, M. (2004) "Taking Up Online Opportunities? Children's Use of the Internet for Education, Communication and Participation." *E-Learning*, 1(3), 395–419.

Mannheim, K. (1952 [1923]) "The Problem of Generations," trans. P. Kecskemeti, in P. Kecskemeti, ed., *Essays on the Sociology of Knowledge*. London: Routledge & Kegan Paul, pp. 276–322.

McMillan, S.J. and Morrison, M. (2006) "Coming of Age with the Internet: A Qualitative Exploration of How the Internet has Become an Integral Part of Young People's Lives." *New Media & Society*, 8(1), 73–95.

North, S., Snyder, I., and Bulfin, S. (2008) "Digital Tastes: Social Class and Young People's Technology Use." *Information, Communication and Society*, 11(7), 895–911.

Palfrey, J. and Gasser, U. (2008) *Born Digital: Understanding the First Generation of Digital Natives*. New York: Basic Books.

Pilcher, J. (1994) "Mannheim's Sociology of Generations: An Undervalued Legacy." *British Journal of Sociology*, 45(3), 481–495.

Prensky, M. (2001) "Digital Natives, Digital Immigrants Part 1." *On the Horizon: The Strategic Planning Resource for Education Professionals*, 9(5), 1–6.

Prensky, M. (2005) "Listen to the Natives." *Educational Leadership*, 63(4), 8–13.

Siemens, G. (2007) "Digital Natives and Immigrants: A Concept Beyond Its Best Before Date." *Connectivism* (April 16). www.connectivism.ca/?p=97.

Tufts, D.R. (2010) *Digital Adults: Beyond the Myth of the Digital Native Generation Gap*. Doctoral dissertation, Fielding Graduate University.

Vaidhyanathan, S. (2008) "Generational Myth." *Chronicle of Higher Education* (September 19). http://chronicle.com/article/Generational-Myth/32491.

Wartella, E. and Reeves, B. (1985) "Historical Trends in Research on Children and the Media: 1900–1960." *Journal of Communication*, 35(2), 118–133.

Wohl, R. (1979) *The Generation of 1914*. Cambridge, MA: Harvard University Press.

White, R. and Wyn, J. (2008) *Youth and Society: Exploring the Social Dynamics of Youth Experience*, 2nd edn. Melbourne: Oxford University Press.

Further Reading

Bennett, S. and Maton, K. (2010) "Beyond the 'Digital Natives' Debate: Towards a More Nuanced Understanding of Students' Technology Experiences." *Journal of Computer Assisted Learning*, 26(5), 321–331.

Crawford, K. (2006) *Adult Themes: Rewriting the Rules of Adulthood*. Sydney: Pan Macmillan.

Helsper, E.J. and Eynon, R. (2010) "Digital Natives: Where is the Evidence?" *British Educational Research Journal*, 36(3), 503–520.

Turner, B.S. (1997) "Ageing and Generational Conflict: A Reply to Sarah Irwin." *British Journal of Sociology*, 49(2), 299–304.

Index